Flying Officers *of the* USN

Schiffer Military History
Atglen, PA

Cover Design by Robert Biondi.

Library of Congress Catalog Number: 96-70853.

Printed in the United States of America.
ISBN: 0-7643-0219-1

We are interested in hearing from authors with book ideas on related topics.

Published by Schiffer Publishing Ltd.
77 Lower Valley Road
Atglen, PA 19310
Phone: (610) 593-1777
FAX: (610) 593-2002
Please write for a free catalog.
This book may be purchased from the publisher.
Please include $2.95 postage.
Try your bookstore first.

OUR HOPE IS THAT THIS BOOK MAY SERVE AS A HUMBLE TRIBUTE TO OUR BROTHER AVIATORS WHO SO WILLINGLY GAVE THEIR LIVES THAT DEMOCRACY SHOULD LIVE. TO THEM WE RESPECTFULLY DEDICATE THIS WORK.

(C) Harris & Ewing

HON. JOSEPHUS DANIELS,
Secretary of the Navy.

PREFACE

IN producing this book the aim has been two-fold: to provide as a permanent record of the great war a pictorial muster-roll of all the officers and student-officers of the Naval Air Service, and to present in narrative form the history and achievements of the Naval Aviation Corps. To the former end every effort has been exerted to obtain as many photographs of individual members of the officer-personnel as was possible under the many difficulties encountered. Every trick of the printers' art has been employed to reproduce these pictures to the best advantage, it being borne in mind that most of them were snapshots and totally unsuited for reproduction. Because of the large number of men in the corps and the many photographs collected, the data relating to each member of the personnel must necessarily be brief.

A brief history of the corps, together with articles pertaining to a few of its branches and activities, and a comprehensive collection of pictures illustrating its salient features comprise the remainder of the book. Primary consideration has been given to the personnel section of the volume, and the text matter has consequently been made secondary in some instances. To have done full justice to the excellent work which was performed at the air stations and to have treated all the various branches and activities would have required more space than was available.

Especial thanks are due, and are hereby acknowledged, to the following men for their hearty cooperation and assistance in producing this book:

Commander L. H. Maxfield.
Lieut. Comdr. A. C. Read.
Lieutenant F. M. Smith.
Lieutenant J. H. Cummings.
Lieutenant A. M. Baldwin.
Lt. (j.g.) D. B. Alvord.
Lt. (j.g.) T. H. Chapman.
Lt. (j.g.) A. J. Ditman.
Lt. (j.g.) R. Emerson.
Lt. (j.g.) J. W. Lancto.
Lt. (j.g.) J. J. MacAttee.
Lt. (j.g.) J. C. Menzies.
Ensign R. L. Banks.
Ensign D. L. Brown.
Ensign W. W. Coile.
Ensign L. K. Dickey.
Ensign A. H. Edward.
Ensign C. F. Harper.
Ensign J. M. Graffis.
Ensign T. H. McClure.
Ensign H. C. Mitchell.
Ensign DeLos Thomas.
Ensign E. H. Wales.

(C) Harris & Ewing

FRANKLIN D. ROOSEVELT,
Assistant Secretary of the Navy.

THE ASSISTANT SECRETARY OF THE NAVY,
WASHINGTON.

August 28, 1919.

N. A. WAR BOOK COMMITTEE,
WASHINGTON, D. C.

To the Naval Aviators:

WHEN in August, 1918, I found on visiting France a complete chain of Naval Aviation Stations engaged in a systematic patrol of the waters of that "neck of the bottle" through which our troops and supplies had to pass, I had but to examine the weekly charts of German submarine operations to realize how much our aviators were doing to make these waters safe. To the men engaged in these duties, whether on land or actually flying, there came few of the thrills of actual war, but they will always have the deep satisfaction of knowing that their work, though silent, counted much in the winning of the war. I venture to predict that when the records of the German naval activities become available, we will find that the enemy also recognized the importance of the American Navy in the air as well as on the sea.

There is one outstanding feature of American Naval Aviation in the great war—it conducted actual and active operations against the enemy for many months, and conducted them with credit and success. When the United States entered the war, our Naval Aviation was almost less than a nucleus in both matériel and personnel. In the summer of the following year, our Naval Aviators were doing patrol work in American-built planes, not only in our home waters but also on the coasts of England, Ireland, France and Belgium. In addition, we were conducting operations on a large scale with lighter-than-air craft in France and were taking an important part in the work of the Northern Bombing Group near the Belgian border.

Taking the work as a whole from the conception and working out of the broad operating plans in the very beginning down to the training of the personnel, the creation of the matériel and the final operations against the enemy, the enterprise must be stamped with the approval of the country as a whole.

Franklin D Roosevelt

U. S. Naval Aviation in the War

Operations and Achievements of the Naval Air Force

By John R. Cox

WHEN America entered the war, the United States Navy possessed but one aircraft station and twenty-two training seaplanes with none fit for service use, and a lighter-than-air equipment that was negligible. There were thirty-eight naval aviators. When the armistice was signed, there were in operation twenty-eight United States naval air stations overseas, thirteen in the United States and insular possessions, two in Canada, and twelve land squadrons for special offensive operations against submarines at their bases, not to mention the numerous schools, storehouses, assembly plants, repair depots, and the naval aircraft factories which were required to furnish the necessary personnel and facilities for the operation of those air stations.

The aviation personnel at the close of hostilities had reached a total of 42,000—more than two-thirds the entire naval personnel prior to our entry into the war.

EXPERIMENTAL PERIOD

The first scientific demonstrations of aeronautic principles were made by Professor Langley at Quantico, or Widewater on the Potomac, Va., in 1896. Langley was subjected to so much ridicule that he broke down under the attack and his death occurred before he was able to complete his experiments. In 1903 the Wright Brothers made their first successful flight with a "heavier-than-air" craft carrying the pilot. Then followed numerous experiments, both in this country and in Europe, extending over the ensuing seven years. In November, 1910, Eugene Ely made the first flight from the deck of a naval vessel, when he flew from the U. S. S. *Birmingham*, a scout cruiser, at Hampton Roads, out over the waters of the Roads and Chesapeake Bay. This marked the beginning of naval aviation. A few months later, in the spring of 1911, flights were made by Curtiss in a hydroaeroplane to and from the armored cruiser *Pennsylvania* (now the *Pittsburgh*) in the harbor of San Diego, Cal. To conduct these experiments, on both vessels were built false decks forward. From that time until the winter of 1917, the time was occupied in experimentation, and the formation of the nucleus of a naval aviation section. The first naval aviator to qualify for flying was Lieut. T. G. Ellyson, who, it should be said, was also the first to use the catapult as a launching apparatus, from which he made an ascent at the Naval Academy. Other pioneers in 1911–12 and 1913 were Lieuts. John Rodgers, John H. Towers, P. N. L. Bellinger, C. K. Bronson, Chevalier, Billingsly, Stolz, Saufley and Whiting; Lieut. Comdr. H. C. Mustin; Lieuts. B. L. Smith and A. A. Cunningham, U. S. Marine Corps; Naval Constructor H. C. Richards, Civil Engineer J. V. Rockwell, Ensign V. D. Herbster, and perhaps half a dozen more of the regular Navy and Marine Corps. The toll was heavy among these adventurous young pioneers, for the machines were frail and crude, and the hazards were great. Lieut. Billingsly was killed in a crash in 1913, and in the following two or three years, Stolz, Rockwell, Saufley and Bronson sacrificed their

Official, U. S. N. A. S.

LIEUT. R. C. SAUFLEY.

lives to the development of naval aeronautics.

The first aviation camp to be established by the Navy was located at Annapolis in 1913; prior to which naval flyers and students trained at the Curtiss school at San Diego, Cal. At about the same time a camp was started at Guantanamo, Cuba, and operated while the fleet was in Caribbean waters. In December, the Annapolis camp was transferred to Pensacola, Fla., where the battleship *Mississippi* (later sold to the Greek Government) was assigned as station ship. Shortly afterwards, an air station was constructed ashore at Pensacola, which was destined to be the first fixed aviation station in America. During the following summer the *Mississippi* was sold and the armored cruiser *North Carolina* became the aviation and station ship. She was the only vessel, and Pensacola the sole station, engaged in naval flying at the time we entered the war with Germany in April, 1917. At that time the Navy had thirty-eight qualified aviators, and all of 163 enlisted men detailed to aviation duty; while the assortment of twenty-two seaplanes were fit for training purposes only; the equipment comprised five kite planes, two free balloons and no dirigibles.

ADMINISTRATION OF THE AIR SERVICE

Back of the marvelous expansion of naval aviation was a superb administrative organization, without which the service would have proven a failure no matter how much zeal, inventive genius and patriotic enthusiasm had been mustered in the cause. As has been pointed out, production at once jumped to enormous proportions, and the necessity for establishing stations in remote parts of the world called for rapid construction, equipment of all kinds in quantities and transportation facilities. These problems required administrative ability of a high order, and the success of the operations is largely due to the officials who administered the affairs of the naval air service. Captain Noble E. Irwin, U. S. N., was early in the war detailed as Director of Naval Aviation, and Supervisor of the Naval Reserve Flying Corps, under the Chief of Operations at the Navy Department. Both Secretary Daniels and Assistant Secretary Roosevelt gave their heartiest support to the air service, and allowed the director practically a free hand to carry out his campaign. Associated with Captain Irwin were the pioneers of naval aviation: Capt. H. C.

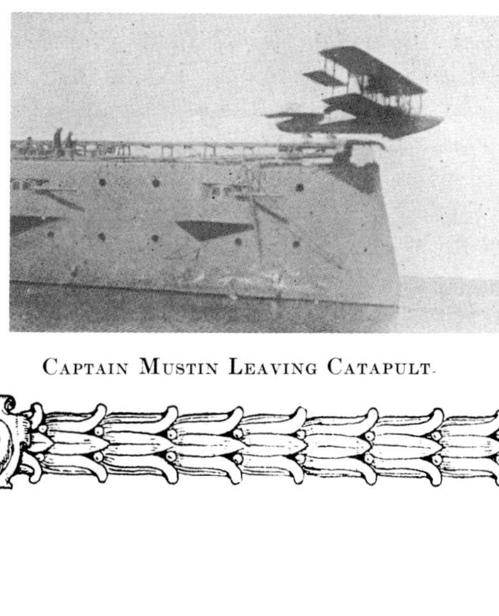

CAPTAIN MUSTIN LEAVING CATAPULT.

BURGESS-DUNN SEAPLANE.

Mustin; Comdrs. Kenneth Whiting, J. H. Towers, W. G. Childs; Lieut. Comdrs. P. N. L. Bellinger, G. deC. Chevalier, A. C. Read, and E. O. McDonnell; Maj. B. L. Smith of the Marine Corps, and other young enthusiasts who had demonstrated their ability in the profession of flying. The naval aviation forces in Europe were under the command of Capt. T. T. Craven, who after the demobilization succeeded Captain Irwin as Director of Naval Aviation at the department. The air service afloat was under Capt. Hutch I. Cone, aide for aviation on Vice-Admiral Sims' staff. Captain Cone was seriously injured when the British steamer *Leinster* was torpedoed on October 10, 1918, while returning from an inspection trip of the naval air stations in Ireland, but later resumed active duty.

At the Navy Department, the work of the aviation service was divided among a number of bureaus, all of which cooperated to the fullest extent. The activities of the service were under the Office of Operations; the personnel, officers and men, was supplied in sufficient number by the recruiting division of the Bureau of Navigation; the Bureau of Steam Engineering furnished motors and radio equipment; the Bureau of Construction and Repair the hulls and wings of the planes; the Bureau of Ordnance the machines, guns, bombs and other armament; the Bureau of Yards and Docks conducted the building operations at the many stations throughout the world and furnished the motor transportation; the Bureau of Medicine and Surgery supplied trained personnel of the medical and hospital corps, conducted the special examinations required for aviators and looked after the physical welfare of the air forces at home and abroad; the Bureau of Supplies and Accounts brought to bear its magnificent purchasing and supply organizations in keeping a constant stream of material, provisions and equipment, besides paying and feeding the men wherever they were serving. The headquarters of the Marine Corps supplied both marine personnel and material for the operations in which both services participated.

Naval Air Station, Pensacola,
Before the War.

DEVELOPMENT BEGAN WITH THE WAR

From this review of pre-war conditions, it will be seen that the naval aviation corps was almost wholly developed after America began hostilities. Despite the lack of preparedness for war, however, it is a source of pride to all members of the corps that the first organized American fighting force to land in France was a detail of naval aviators. This advance guard, under Commander Kenneth Whiting, arrived at Bordeaux on June 6, 1917, just two months to the day after war was declared, and consisted of trained and student aviators selected at the request of the French Navy to assist in combating the Hun submarines which were working havoc along the French coast.

At the very outset a board of officers was sent abroad to study foreign types of machines, and returned with some startling facts concerning the submarine menace, which had assumed proportions much uglier than was at that time fully appreciated in this country. It became apparent at once that not only must America send over aircraft of a far superior type to any which the Navy had, but they must be shipped across in quantities that astounded the authorities. After a conference in which theories and preconceived plans were ruthlessly trampled down, a definite program of types was agreed upon, which when once adopted, was scrupulously followed throughout the war, regardless of all doubts and criticism. As a consequence of the faithful adherence to the program, an uninterrupted production was accomplished with no loss of material which had to be scrapped, and what was still more vital, with no loss of time. The performance of the aircraft in actual service amply vindicated the selection of the types. In a marvelously short time the Navy had embarked upon an aviation program, on both sides of the Atlantic, on a scale which astonished all who were cognizant of its development.

No less remarkable was the growth of the personnel. From the handful of aviators who had conducted the experi-

NAVAL AIR STATION, PENSACOLA.
In August, 1918.

mental work at Pensacola, there grew almost overnight a corps of officers and men and a system of training that soon met the demands which were made upon it. Men from every walk of life were gathered into the aviation service, and there was no lack of recruit-material from the outset; on the contrary, the difficulty lay in taking care of the large force and in providing adequate training facilities. These were soon forthcoming, and within a few months a series of schools had been established and commissioned, where special instruction was imparted. Trade schools were opened all over the country, and new aerial ratings were improvised to provide for the diversified mechanical duties which were required. No time could be spent in obtaining new legislation; and despite the arbitrary table of seagoing ratings which had been rigidly fixed for the Navy years before by law, the aviation corps soon built up a large force of aerial machinists skilled in gas engines, quartermasters who were expert pigeon keepers, coppersmiths who could do acetylene welding, boatswain's mates who were aerial photographers, carpenter's mates who could build and repair wings, and gunner's mates who could operate a machine gun from aircraft. All these men were given an intensive course, the best qualified sent to finishing schools, and then distributed to the various stations at home and abroad for actual experience. Officers were specially trained not only in flying, but in bombing, navigation, gunnery, radio, aerography, internal combustion engines and for executive duties. Many technical and manufacturing experts were enrolled as officers and immediately sent abroad to install and operate machinery and equipment at assembly and repair bases.

MASS. INSTITUTE OF TECHNOLOGY

Principal among the schools conducted in the United States was that at the Massachusetts Institute of Technology, officially designated as the U. S. Naval Aviation Detachment. This school

PARADE GROUNDS, MASSACHUSETTS INSTITUTE OF TECHNOLOGY.
U. S. Naval Aviation Detachment.

was opened in July, 1917, with forty-three students, all possessing a technical education. The first commanding officer was Lieut. E. H. McKittrick of the regular navy. The plan of instruction called for a highly intensive course of eight weeks, with a class graduating every two weeks. Later two weeks were added to the course. Instruction was imparted by the faculty of the Institute, which also turned over the necessary buildings and equipment for the school. Later, Walker Memorial Building was assigned to the naval detachment for use as quarters and a cafeteria. On December 21, 1917, Lieut. Comdr. R. W. Cabaniss, U. S. Navy, relieved Lieutenant McKittrick in command, and in the following March the building at 84 Massachusetts Avenue was acquired for use as a receiving ship, with Lieut. (j.g.) S. W. Sargent, USNRF, in command. At the receiving ship all men who reported from other stations for training were held for from two to six weeks before assignment to the main school, serving meanwhile under instruction. It was there that the weeding-out process was conducted, no men being sent to the school who were not fully qualified, mentally, morally and physically.

CALISTHENICS, 6 A.M.

The discipline of the school was kept at all times at a high standard, and the secret of the success of the detachment was the development of the greatest degree of energy within the least possible time. Many young men who could not stand the tension dropped out, which only stimulated the remainder to greater effort. There was no let-up in the drills or the discipline from the date the school opened until hostilities ceased.

The Pump, Camp Saufley, Pensacola.
Clear, cold, spring water!

Commander Cabaniss served as commanding officer until July 3, 1918, when he was relieved by Lieut. Comdr. H. C. Van Valzah. Great credit is due Commander Cabaniss for the success of the school; and the pace which he set, as well as the standard of discipline he insisted upon at all times, was maintained under his successor.

Over 200 colleges were represented in the student body, the greatest number of men being from Cornell, Yale, Massachusetts Institute of Technology, Harvard, University of Pennsylvania, Princeton, Dartmouth, University of California, University of Michigan and Columbia, in the order named. Most of them were members of the Naval Reserve Force, although not a few came from the regular Navy, the Marine Corps and the National Naval Volunteers (afterwards made a part of the Naval Reserve). Just before the armistice, in November, sixty flight cadets of the Canadian Royal Naval Air Service entered the school, but before they were able to complete their ground course they were demobilized.

After the school had been in commission a short time the civilian instructors of the Massachusetts Institute of Technology were supplemented by ground officers who were retained after graduation for instructors. The school reached its maximum strength in September, 1918, when about 1,600 men were under training, with approximately 115 instructors.

The curriculum in the ground school embraced aerial gunnery, photography, navigation, observation and aerography; bombing, aeronautical engines, electricity, seamanship, signals, flight theory and the Naval Regulations. Student flight officers received special instruction in meteorology, balloons and studies particularly prepared for flyers.

OTHER SCHOOLS

Students were also sent to the school at Cambridge after they had qualified at some other school or training station. These stations were located all over the country, wherever a course of instruction could be given. At Bluehill Observatory, Mass., was maintained an aerography class composed largely of men drawn from the Weather Bureau. At Pelham Bay Training Camp, there was a school for winchmen, and for instruction in kites. There was a class for carpenter's mates at the works of the Aeromarine Plane and Motor Co., Keyport, N. J. At Bay Shore there was an air station and school for aviation mechanics, and at Rockaway Beach there was a school for hydrogen engineers. Men who had some experience in photography were sent to the works of the Eastman Kodak Company, Rochester, N. Y., to learn camera construction and repair, and the art of photography. A bombing school was located at Ardmore, Pa., where a factory was turning out bombs. At Hampton Roads there was a school for quartermasters at the operating base and a kite and balloon school at the Naval Air Station. An aviation photographic school was maintained at Miami, Fla., while at the old air station at Pensacola were schools for instrument mechanics, quartermasters, carpenters, machinists, aerial gunners, bombers, radio operators, etc.

At the training station, Great Lakes, a number of classes were conducted during the war, and shortly after the armistice all the training service for the aviation force was rounded up there under one department.

At Dunwoody Institute, Minneapolis, there was a ground school of the same general character as at Cambridge and in addition the school had the benefit of the mechanical facilities of Dunwoody Institute for instruction in a number of artificer branches, particularly carpenters, machinists, coppersmiths, etc.

A school for the training of men in the operation of the Liberty motor was conducted at the works of the Packard Motor Co., Detroit. At the Curtiss works in Buffalo was a school for carpenter's mates, coppersmiths, blacksmiths and aviation quartermasters.

On the Pacific coast were two schools, one at the Naval Air Station, San Diego, Cal., where machinists and quartermasters were trained, and at Seattle, where there was a ground school for the instruction of technically trained young men, similar to that we have described at the Massachusetts Institute of Technology.

STATIONS ABROAD

From the beginning it was realized that the primary function of the naval aviation service was to protect allied shipping and to "get" the Hun submarine. This necessitated the establishment of stations all the way from northern Ireland to the southern toe of Italy, in the Azores, and on our own coast from Nova Scotia to the Canal Zone. Locations were selected because of their strategic value, regardless of communications or conveniences. For example, eight stations were located on islands off shore, requiring special water transportation; very few were in or near settled communities, hence they must needs be altogether self-supporting.

The work abroad was divided into three general classes: overseas patrol of a routine nature; emergency patrols or

HS-1 Patrol Plane Taxying.

responding to S. O. S. calls, and bombing enemy bases.

Seaplanes of large cruising radius and airships were used for routine patrol, each station being assigned a zone which was covered as thoroughly as possible from dawn until dark. The patrol routes were so laid out that the greatest area was covered with the least mileage, each seaplane traversing courses definitely set forth in the pilot's flight instructions. They were armed with bombs of 230 or 500 pounds and with machine guns for use against a submarine on the surface or against hostile aircraft. The planes could cruise from four to nine hours, depending on the nature of the patrol, while the airships could remain out for forty hours or more. To give an idea of the operations of a single air station, a flying squadron or patrol frequently covered from 10,000 to 15,000 nautical miles in the course of a week. In one day the patrol squadron attached to one station put in fifty-four hours and twenty-six minutes flying time, covering a distance of 2,827 nautical miles, and by establishing re-fuelling depots this station was able to send out patrols each covering 400 miles, and extending 112 miles north, 125 miles south and 115 miles out to sea from the station.

That these seaplanes were built for durability is illustrated by the experience of an H. S. type in October, 1918, which sustained itself for twenty-four hours after an enforced landing on the water, in spite of a 50-knot gale and seas mounting over 20 feet high.

THE EMERGENCY PATROL

The emergency or S. O. S. patrol was made only when an enemy submarine was reported within the zone covered by the station, a limited number of seaplanes being held in reserve for that contingency. Success depended upon the rapidity with which planes, fully equipped, could be gotten away, with complete instructions as to the supposed location of the submarine. On a surprise inspection, the longest time required to get out orders, launch two planes completely equipped and manned, in the air with full instruc-

Naval Aviation Cadets in Training at Lake Bolsena, Italy.

Pilots of Field "B," Northern Bombing Group, Campagne, France.

tions, was seven minutes, an illustration of the rapidity with which seaplanes can be operated as compared with surface craft. As a result of the vigilance of these patrols, the German submarines late in the winter of 1918 began to avoid the areas embraced in aircraft patrol, and extended their operations much farther out to sea, which greatly diminished their chances of destroying ships, but with the advantage that if they located an unescorted ship, the greater distance from protection rendered it more probable that the submarines would accomplish their work of destruction before destroyers or other vessels from allied bases could render assistance.

BOMBING ENEMY BASES

This development led to the campaign against the enemy's submarine bases. Six squadrons of land bombing airplanes for daylight, and six similar squadrons for night bombing were organized under the name of the Naval Northern Bombing Group. The personnel of the organization was part naval and part marine, and was combined with the air forces of the British to bomb the German submarine bases at Zeebrugge, Bruges and Ostend. The day bombing squadrons were generally composed of marines and the night squadrons of naval aviators. Army land machines were used because they were speedier and could carry more bombs than the seaplanes; and for the further reason that the German bases and submarine docks were along the Belgian canals, where seaplanes could not be operated as advantageously as land machines. At first the field was located at Calais, but the Germans soon found it and bombarded it both from the air and from their long range guns, and it was decided in the summer of 1918 to split the squadrons up into several stations which were located at Antingues, St. Ingleverte, Oye, Campagne, and Calais, all incorporated with the big station at

Submarine Photographed from a Seaplane.

Dunkerque. The Germans bombed the stations 750 times from the air, and with the long range guns 500 times. Dunkerque itself was under almost continuous bombardment for a year immediately preceding the armistice. The dugouts at Dunkerque were exceedingly popular during the enemy raids, which were of almost nightly occurrence. During one night the Huns dropped 320 bombs, varying from 600 pounders to 20-pound pit-squeaks, on the Dunkerque station and its immediate vicinity. The dugouts were 15 feet underground and protected with corrugated sheet iron, sand, cement and cobblestones. The personnel was so distributed that a direct hit on a dugout would not have killed more than fifty men. Nevertheless, the constant bombardment got on their nerves at times.

Although the Northern Bombing Group had only gotten into full operation when hostilities ceased, nevertheless the group accomplished much effective work, and was in position to do the enemy a great deal of damage if the war had continued.

Bombing operations were also conducted extensively by the American naval aviators in Italy, of which more will be said later.

These were the primary functions performed by naval aviators—overseas patrol, response to emergency calls, and bombing enemy bases. Secondary duties consisted of the escort of convoys, which was of no mean importance, and, particularly in the latter part of the war, spotting and reconnaisance duty with the battle fleet. To this end several of the American battleships were equipped with fast planes for this work. Had the German fleet come out and given battle there is no doubt that these aviators would have rendered a good account of themselves and proven an invaluable part of the fleet not only in scouting but in actual engagement with the enemy. They were not permitted, however, to demonstrate their usefulness in this field of endeavor.

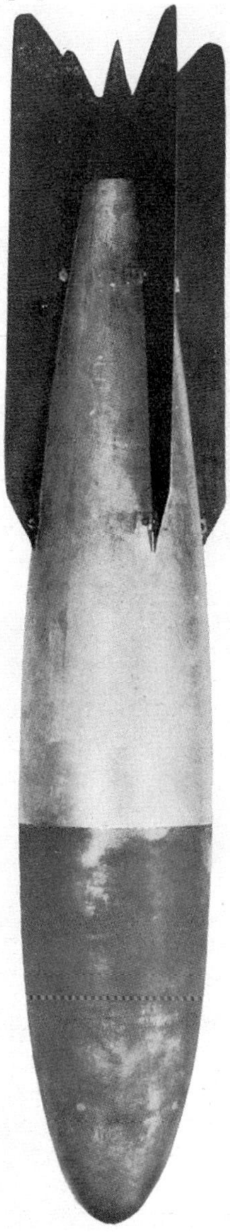

NAVAL AIR STATIONS IN ENGLAND

Principal among the stations in England was that at Killingholme, a small town located on the east coast. This inconspicuous little place had nothing to recommend it as a residential center, and before the war was known only by the fact that oil tanks had been constructed on the beach, and oil-burning coastwise vessels stopped there occasionally to replenish their supply of fuel oil. Killingholme, however, possessed a strategic value as an air station, and was early utilized by the Royal Air Force which stationed a squadron there, later so greatly augmented that by the summer of 1917 it had become one of the leading air stations in Great Britain. When a British and American joint board decided that the United States would cooperate in patrolling the North Sea, Killingholme was made an all-American station. In December, 1917, Commander Whiting, who was then in Europe, was ordered home for the purpose of organizing the necessary personnel and to obtain the equipment to operate it by the Navy. Men and material were dispatched from time to time, but it was not until May, 1918, that the big collier *Jason* left New York with a large force of men, a cargo of supplies, and the first American sea-

Air Station, Killingholme, England, Being Taken over by U. S. Forces, July 20, 1918.

Expansion of the station as it was turned over by the British was conducted by the Public Works Department of the United States Force, and the additional buildings were constructed at a rate which astonished the British, twenty-eight buildings being built in thirty days with green crews, lacking only plumbing and wiring. By this time, the complement had reached 1,500 men, and the Naval Air Station was ready for business. From July 20 until the fateful 11th of November, there was constant work at Killingholme. Some of the activities reduced to figures were:

planes to be sent to Europe. She arrived on June 1, when the necessary additional buildings to house the men and accommodate the planes were promptly erected, and steps were taken to relieve the British forces at the station. The work progressed so rapidly that on July 20, Commander Whiting relieved Wing Commander Bowhill, RNAS, who had served with great distinction in the war, especially in command of the Royal Air Force in Mesopotamia, where he supplied food by airplane to General Townshend's besieged army.

Killingholme had meanwhile become the center of great shipping activities; convoys were constantly passing up and down the coast; it was within striking distance of the lines of submarine travel; and, moreover, it was in the path usually taken by Zeppelins in their raids on the English coast. By pushing the patrols out on somewhat extended flights, great assistance could be rendered to fleet maneuvers and observations from this base.

Over 6,000 ships were convoyed; the distance covered in war patrols was nearly 60,000 miles, not including test flights or experiments. For several weeks when German subs were believed to come to the surface under cover of dark-

DH-4

Used by N.A.'s with British for day bombing.

Patrol Plane Being Picked up at Sea by Submarine Chaser.

ness to recharge their storage batteries, nightly patrols were conducted of seven and eight hours' duration. Notwithstanding the almost constant fog, often attended by high winds and rainstorms, the weather was not permitted to interfere with the daily patrols and convoys.

Despite the exigencies of the war,

Hanriot Hydravion de Chasse.
One-man scout plane.

recreation and welfare work were not overlooked. Baseball, football and track athletics were encouraged, and many spirited games were played between the station teams and teams from nearby stations. The first American game of baseball ever played in Hull was between a Killingholme team and another American team from the aviation construction camp at Driffield. The welfare activities were under the supervision of the Y. M. C. A., the Red Cross and the British Ministry of Information.

Some of the exploits of the Killingholme flyers will be mentioned briefly. Pilots Schieffelin and Cutler in a large seaplane on July 19 sighted a submarine cruising on the surface 25 miles from Whitby. They dropped a bomb, which fell 20 feet from the center of the submarine. After the explosion the submarine's screws were seen to rise and almost break the surface, then the submarine disappeared. No further movement was discerned, and the plane returned to the station. The submarine was not put out of business, however, for she later in the day attempted to attack a convoy, but was repulsed by a motor launch which dropped depth charges, forcing the submarine to the surface. In the fight which ensued, a destroyer rammed the submarine, which was unable to submerge, and after being again rammed, she capsized and sank.

On June 13 a seaplane, with Lieutenant Cleeve of the Royal Air Force as first pilot and Ensign Allen, USNRF, second pilot, sighted a submarine's wake. They immediately dropped two bombs in the line of the wake, whereupon oil and wreckage came to the surface, but the submarine continued its course. Destroyers were signalled, and depth bombs brought more oil and wreckage to view. The submarine was not again sighted.

On July 9 Ensigns Schieffelin and Staub, first and second pilots, both USNRF, with Wireless Operator Rollhause and Machinist's Mate Bernstein, sighted an oil patch while flying at 2,000 feet altitude, and new oil was constantly appearing, indicating the presence of a submarine nearby. Two bombs were dropped, one scoring a direct hit, and the other very close. Destroyers were signalled, and upon their arrival dropped several depth charges, when bubbles rose to the surface, and the oil patch widened to more than twice its former size. According to the records of the British Admiralty this submarine is classified as "seriously damaged."

On June 8, while the station was still under joint control, pilots Captain Munday of the British air service and Ensign Rumill, USN, sighted a periscope 15 miles east of Spurn. The periscope disappeared immediately and the plane upon arriving at the position noticed a disturbance of the water, as if the submarine were lying on the bottom, and bubbles were seen to rise. Two bombs were dropped, whereupon more bubbles as well as oil came to the surface. No further results were observed, but owing to lack of fuel the seaplane was compelled to put back to the base.

On the occasion of a distressing accident when two flyers were killed and a third seriously injured as a result of their seaplane crashing into Humber River, a gallant attempt was made to save the victims. Seaplane 4067 was starting for Dundee on October 28, 1918, with Ensigns Benjamin Lee and J. Garrison, both NRF., as pilots, and R. G.

Camp Borden, Canada.
For a short time Naval Aviators were trained here.

Fisher, machinist's mate, 2d class, when the seaplane crashed into the Humber River. Lieut. R. H. McCann and Ensign G. S. Hodges dove overboard from a rescue launch, under the burning wreckage in their endeavor to save the lives of the flyers. Hodges brought Garrison unconscious through the burning wreckage to the rescue boat, keeping him under water intermittently and with his own person protecting the unconscious officer from the flames. In his rescue Hodges himself was severely burned, and it was solely due to the heroic rescue work that Garrison was not lost. Both Lee and Fisher were drowned.

Other naval air stations in the British Isles were maintained at Felixstowe, Wexford, Queenstown, Lough Foyle, Whiddy Island, besides the assembly and repair base at Eastleigh, 70 miles southwest of London, which was established for the purpose of serving the entire Northern Bombing Group, acting in conjunction with the delivery and distribution at St. Ingleverte, France, which was located inland four or five miles from Calais.

Watch Tower, Pensacola.

Copyright by Underwood & Underwood, N. Y.

Rescue by British Destroyer.

In the early summer of 1918, the Huns were very active in this western front and grave alarm was felt that the enemy might break through to the channel ports and overrun the country adjacent to Calais, in which section the original plans were to establish the repair and assembly base. It was deemed urgently necessary to seek another location more protected from bombardment and possible capture, and where mechanics could turn out the planes and assemble parts without interference, yet accessible to the patrols and air stations of France and England. The British had partly completed an "acceptance base" at Eastleigh, which the Air Ministry offered to the U. S. Navy. The offer was accepted, and the station was taken over in July, 1918, completed in record time, and for the remaining months of the war this base rendered efficient service to the American naval air service in supplying equipment as needed.

The first naval air station to be established in France was Dunkerque, near the Belgian line on the Strait of Dover, and close to the front. Construction was undertaken by the French authorities, which was expected to be completed by September, 1917. October came, and it was still but 30 per cent done, when a detachment of fifty Americans was detailed to push the work. In November, 100 more bluejackets were sent to Dunkerque and every effort was made to expedite the construction. Shortly thereafter the station was ready for occupancy, and in January trained personnel began to arrive. Patrols, however, could not be carried out for lack of ordnance and flying equipment.

At first the operations consisted of anti-submarine patrols over the English Channel, and by arrangement with the French Seaplane Station almost constant daylight patrol was maintained. Due to the inferior types of planes it was not possible to patrol the nearby Belgian coast, but an occasional offensive patrol was made with the Hanriot single seaters, the usual plan being to send out two or three DD flying boats equipped with two 130-pound bombs, accompanied by a flight of five Hanriots as protection from enemy craft. The DD's carried a gunner forward and aft, but still were not considered self-protecting and were, moreover, slow and unwieldy. Great trouble was experienced with equipment, especially the flying boats' power plants, which caused a large percentage of patrols to be abandoned because of motor failure. Notwithstanding, numerous "alerts" were answered and on many occasions submarines were bombed. The station was credited with one submarine. At critical periods the entire station force was turned over to the British, and every assistance was lent them and the French, particularly during the enemy drives in that area. American pilots frequently joined French and British squadrons operating with land machines. Observers were loaned and

HANRIOT SCOUTS AT DUNKERQUE.

the station personnel assisted the allies in the erection of airdromes and in other essential work.

Lieutenant Chevalier, who was in command from the fall of 1917, was relieved in July, 1918, to take charge of the aviation repair base at Eastleigh, being relieved by Lieutenant Gates, NRF, who distinguished himself as a daring flyer and who was later brought down inside the enemy lines while flying with a French spad squadron and was captured, but possibly due to the approaching break in the enemy's resistance, he was saved, and after the armistice obtained his release.

During the entire occupancy of the station, Dunkerque was subjected to enemy bombing raids, many of them severe, and resulting in much damage to the station, but fortunately without casualties. The almost continuous night bombing as well as bombardment by long-range guns made living conditions very difficult, despite which the behavior of the men was at all times most admirable.

At one time a British night bombing squadron was driven from its airdrome and the airdrome completely wrecked by an enemy night raid. To permit the British to continue their night bombing operations, the repairs must be made immediately, and with the assistance of the American force the airdrome was put in shape, and by evening the British were again able to operate.

At another time the British were driven from their airdrome, and the American contingent erected new barracks and hangars for them on another field, so that the British operations might be continuous.

One day a German seaplane was reported operating off Ostend. Five American Hanriots were dispatched on offensive patrol into the area, where they remained for an hour or more without locating the Boche. Meanwhile a fog came up, and the flight became scattered. One machine landed in Dieppe, 150 miles from its station. Another pilot found himself well inland on coming out

Awaiting Secretary Roosevelt's Inspection, Dunkerque, France.

of the fog; seeing troops below, he descended to see whether they were Huns or allies. He found them to be Belgians and he landed safely on a convenient marsh. To his surprise he learned that he was directly back of Dixmude, and by skillful maneuvering he managed to get out of the marsh and proceeded safely over the treetops back to Dunkerque.

No American seaplanes were ever used at this station. The reasons were that the harbor was extremely narrow, and all the American seaplanes which were provided were too large for use at Dunkerque. Furthermore, there were no American seaplanes suitable for operations in direct contact with the enemy such as were required at Dunkerque.

During the summer this station was exceedingly active, and rendered notable service in practically eliminating the submarine menace along the French coast. On August 12, a squadron sighted a Hun submarine and released eight bombs, one of which scored a direct hit. The submarine rolled slowly to starboard, lying bottom upwards for five minutes, when she gradually sank. The other seven bombs exploded close alongside the hull. After dropping the bombs the seaplanes circled around, firing 500 rounds of ammunition into the hull until she sank bodily.

Three days later an airplane squadron sighted a submarine off Ostend, which submerged before the patrol arrived, and no trace could be found. Three bombs were dropped, two of which exploded 20 yards astern of the suspected position. but no further trace of the submarine was found than the appearance of two oil patches.

During the summer and fall the enemy works at Ostend, Zeebrugge, Brugeoise, Bruges docks and canal and airdomes at Ghisbelles and Marialter were frequently bombed by airmen from Dunkerque, inflicting serious damage.

LE CROISIC

One seaplane was assembled in the old French hangar at Le Croisic in October, 1917, and in a few weeks three others were ready for flight, the first

U. S. Naval Air Station, Queenstown, Ireland.

Running before a Storm.

flight being made on November 13. Henceforth, both patrol and convoy flights were made regularly. Communication was poor, and the time and position of passing convoys were uncertain, so with no adjoining air stations to cooperate in convoy work, long flights were necessary.

After the station began to operate, Le Croisic was used as an assembly base for Tellier, DD and Le Peu seaplanes. As more machines, equipment and spare parts were received and hangar space provided, more extensive work was undertaken. The installation of radio ashore and in planes enabled the intelligence officer to keep better informed of the positions of planes on patrol, and with the addition of a machine shop and a carpenter shop, damaged planes and worn engines were quickly put back in commission.

Not long after the station was in commission, four submarines were sighted off Belle Isle, and two planes sent on patrol. They did not get the submarines, and one plane failed to return on time. This plane, which was piloted by Ensign K. R. Smith, NRF, with N. Wilkinson, Elect., and Brady, Mach. Mate, as members of the crew, had an experience, thrilling in itself, which illustrates the variety of hazards of aerial warfare.

Upon leaving Le Croisic, the clouds were very low and quite a sea running. Search was made for mines and submarines, but none were found. After cruising several hours, their motor went dead and about 3 p. m. they were forced to make a tail-to-wind landing on the surface with a big sea running. A pigeon was dispatched for help. They were not certain of their location, and the sea became very rough. As night came on they stood watches, one bailing while the other two slept. The next morning they sent out another pigeon, urgently calling for help. They had no food and all hands were seasick. It developed that the motor trouble was due to failure of the gas tank to feed. About 11 o'clock the second day, Wilkinson got the motor started, and tried to put back to Ile

D'You, but they made little headway because of the rough sea. Then their left pontoon filled with water. In making a desperate attempt to get the machine off the water, they broke their left wing, and in the words of the report of the pilot, they "got themselves into a hell of a scrape." Things then began to look pretty black, but the men were game. Night again came, and they again took watches, first lying on the wing, then bailing, then sleeping. They had many anxious moments when it was feared the craft would roll over. They passed a mighty uncomfortable night and were growing very weak from lack of food or water. The morning of the third day found them in a still more precarious condition, with the wing getting near the boat as it crumpled. They had to bail constantly and stay out on the wing tip. As the waves came over they felt they were going steadily lower. They finally decided to cast off the wing and tried to get the other wing off, but they were too weak to loosen the nuts. They were gradually sinking on the starboard side and all staying to the portside to keep her righted. They saw their only hope was to cast off the wing, and were about to give up hope, when Wilkinson gave a yell that he had sighted something. At first they thought it was a submarine, and their only hope was that it would blow them up and end it all. It proved, however, to be a French destroyer which was one of the many vessels and aircraft that were searching for the missing plane. The men were in bad condition from the trying ordeal, but they soon recovered after getting back to station. Their plane sank a few minutes after they had been taken off.

COOPERATION WITH FRENCH

Throughout the American activities, there was hearty cooperation with the French Air Service, although for the first few months the French were sorely handicapped, due to their own pressing needs, in supplying motors and accessories. This cordial teamwork dates

U. S. NAVAL AIR STATION, PAUILLAC, FRANCE.
Supply base.

from the memorable visit of Marshal Joffre and his mission to Washington in April, 1917. Among the requests made upon the American authorities was the dispatch of seaplane pilots to France to assist in an aerial submarine patrol. The French admiral of the mission was informed that American aviators were not available, as the output of American planes had already been sent to Europe, leaving but a small number at home for training purposes, but that while we were sorely lacking in trained aviators we had a plentiful supply of student aviators. Accordingly, it was agreed that the first detachment of student aviators and student mechanics should be sent over immediately, the French admiral explaining that there were many schools and abundant facilities for training. U. S. Naval Aeronautic Detachment No. 1 was quickly organized, comprising fifty student aviators, fifty student mechanics and twenty-two men of the ratings of yeomen, cooks, bakers, hospital corpsmen, messmen, etc. In the detachment were seven officers of whom four were naval pilots, two supply officers and a doctor.

With this force went about 50 tons of stores, provisions, clothing, canteen supplies, aviators' necessities, galley and mess gear, tents, lumber, tools, hardware and whatever was required to make a camp habitable. The detachment and material were sent via two colliers, the *Jupiter*, which landed at Bordeaux June 6, and the *Neptune*, which arrived at St. Nazaire on June 8. Upon arrival it developed that the French authorities were quite unaware of their coming, or of the purpose for which they had been sent, and hence no arrangements had been made for their accommodation or training. After several conferences with the French ministry and the U. S. Naval attaché in Paris, it was decided to send the student aviators to Tours, and the student mechanics to St. Raphael for training. It was further agreed that the detachment should work under American officers commanded by Americans, and manned entirely by American personnel,

Official U. S. N. A. S.

U. S. Naval Air Station, Ile Tudy, France.

rather than to try to infiltrate American personnel into French stations. The detachment furnished a basis for operation of three stations, 500 additional Americans being needed to man them, performing such duties as boatmen, truck drivers, chauffeurs, waders, yeomen, hospital corpsmen, cooks, bakers, stewards, messmen, etc., based upon the French organization plan of about 200 men to a station of sixteen flying boats.

The French undertook to erect the three stations at points to be mutually agreed upon, to be reimbursed by the U. S. Navy. It developed, however, that while the ground training and preliminary instruction in flying at land stations were to be handled by the French, the subsequent training in flying boats, bombing and aerial gunnery could not well be undertaken by the French, because of crowded conditions at their schools. The French thereupon proposed that the U. S. Navy establish a school for the finishing training of student aviators in French flying boats, as well as in bombing and in aerial gunnery. This plan, together with the proposal of the French to establish three seaplane stations and one school, was submitted to Washington for approval; and on June 21, 1917, the training was actually started at Tours and at St. Raphael. Dunkerque was selected as the first American station, because of its proximity to the German lines, and because of its great importance in preventing the coming and going of submarines from the German bases in Belgium. It was especially desired that the United States should actively engage in offensive operations with the Allies as soon as possible. Dunkerque offered this opportunity, and the only suitable location for a seaplane base, where it was hoped our aerial patrols would come in contact with the aircraft of the enemy.

In the Harbor of Brest, France.

The French were quick to see the efficacy as well as the sentimental value of having the other two bases located adjacent to the principal points of entry for American troops landing in France, and

U. S. Naval Air Station, Le Trinité, France.

material. Consequently, a policy was adopted covering developments of naval aviation in France that the United States Navy would look to the French Navy for seaplanes, motors, instruments, armament, bombs and accessories; while the preliminary training of pilots would be conducted in the United States, with the finishing training at French schools until such time as the American schools should be in operation, and that the U. S. Navy would bring to Europe the required quota of motors, automobiles, trucks, and boats, bringing over as soon as practicable its own construction material, machine tools and camp equipage.

suggested points on the Loire and Gironde Rivers, and after a survey was made of the coast Le Croisic was chosen as the site for the station, as aerial patrols could operate for the protection of convoys entering the Loire River, and St. Trojan as the base near the Gironde River. Moutchic was chosen as the site for the school.

In the course of subsequent conferences with the French Ministry of Marine, it was developed that the French had shortcomings in both personnel and material. These were candidly admitted, since, due to the mobilization by the army of every able-bodied Frenchman and the transfer to the army early in the war of all naval pilots, the French navy was seriously embarrassed in obtaining the young men who were mentally, physically and temperamentally qualified for successful aviators; but the French flying boats were superior to anything that could be found at that time in the United States. On the other side of the account, America had an abundance of excellent aviator material, as well as an ample supply of trucks, autos, boats and construction

In August it was agreed in conference that the production of the English type of Curtiss bi-motored flying boat, an American development, should be pushed in the United States. Accordingly, the French asked that the Navy undertake the maintenance of a station at Brest from which to operate this seaplane,

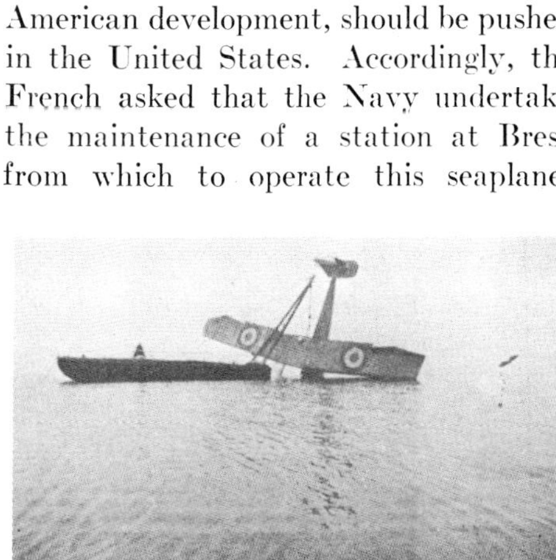

Nose-In, Lake Bolsena.

Panorama of "Goat Island City."

which was larger, of greater radius, and of more seaworthy qualities than any French flying boats.

At the request of the French, the U. S. Naval Air Service constructed and operated a station at Ile Tudy to augment the French station near Cape Pen March, where the Huns were sinking a large number of vessels. The Navy Department then proposed to construct seven additional stations if the French could outfit them with flying boats. The French replied they could equip one station a month, beginning with October and ending with February, 1918, when it was expected that American production would be available in Europe.

The sending over of set-up seaplanes would make too great a demand on the tonnage, and consequently the policy was adopted of setting up, assembling and testing the planes in France. A base for this work was required and it was determined to make it a supply base as well. A plot of ground at Pauillac had been assigned as a base for patrol vessels of the U. S. Navy in the Gironde River, and this site was used for the new station.

By September the training of our pilots and mechanics at Tours and St. Raphael was completed, and the detachment was consolidated at Moutchic, small parties being sent thence to the French seaplane schools at Hourtin, to the school of aerial fire at Cazeau and to the bombing school at St. Raphael.

Kite Down at Sea.

French railroads at that time were sorely overtaxed and could not be relied upon for the movement of freight along the coast. It was taking three weeks to make a shipment from Brest to Bordeaux, less than 500 miles. Being plainly evident that with the advent of the American troops this situation would become worse, water transportation was provided when the French requisitioned the *Mecknes*, a steamer of 300 tons net capacity, and the *Bella* of 750 tons capacity was requisitioned by the U. S. Shipping Board. Sailing vessels were later chartered, and the problem of the transportation and distribution of stores between Brest and Pauillac and intermediate stations was solved.

By October 1st, additional men began to arrive from the States. Pilots were trained and they awaited only the completion of the stations and the delivery of seaplanes to begin operations. Le Croisic was first to be finished, the work being principally done by German prisoners under the supervision of Commandant Vaschalde of the French service. Dunkerque, as we have stated, was retarded, due to shortage of French labor, and was eventually taken over and completed by the Americans. St. Trojan, similarly, was badly delayed by labor

U. S. Naval Air Station, Porto Corsini, Italy.

shortage, abortive strikes and the contractors' inability to get material. Similar conditions prevailed at Moutchic, which was completed with the aid of our own men. After many discouraging delays the stations were finally commissioned and their influence was soon felt in the rapid diminution of sinkings along the French coast. Prior to the coming of the Americans, the destruction of allied ships averaged one a day; within ten months after our patrols became active only three ships were lost in the patrol area between Pen Marche and Ile D'You, a 99 per cent reduction!

The harmony which in general prevailed between the Americans and the French was demonstrated by the friendships built up between our men and the natives, as well as by the cooperation existing between the air forces of the two countries. The personnel at the American stations was much larger than at the French stations, due, of course, to the depleted man power of France. This larger complement of men accounted for the better humor, higher morale, and consequently greater efficiency at the American air stations, which was noticeable to the French officials themselves.

In the matter of food, our men fared as well as might be expected under conditions which then existed in France. Practically all non-perishable foodstuffs, were brought from the United States. Fresh meats, eggs and vegetables were obtainable in the vicinity of the stations, at very high prices it is true, but not more than the French themselves paid. In many instances these supplies were obtained on French commissary contracts.

OPERATIONS IN ITALY

The part played by the United States naval aviators in Italy differed in several important respects from the operations already described in England and France. In Italy there was much more bombing and less patrol work, due, of course, to the different methods of warfare employed. Their special objectives were the enemy bases of Pola and Trieste.

First of American naval aviators to operate in Italy was Lieutenant Commander McDonnell, who in January and February, 1918, made test flights in Caproni planes while on inspection duty. As a result of these tests, Caproni bombing planes were extensively used in the Northern Bombing Group. McDonnell, while visiting the Italian front at Padua, was the first American officer to make a flight over the Italian-Austrian front. The objective was a German airdrome behind the Austrian lines. McDonnell acted as gunner on this raid, which was successful, it was afterwards learned, in

"Ferrying" over the Alps.

Porto Corsini Station from Air.
The station of worried landings.

setting fire to a German hangar and destroying three or four German machines. The raid was particularly thrilling from the start. The machine got away during an Austrian attack on the Italian airdrome, and had to pass through the Italian barrage and under the bombfire from the Austrians. His was the only machine of the squadron which left the airdrome. Return was made with great difficulty, the Austrians having meanwhile destroyed one of the hangars and fourteen planes. Landing was made with greatest hazard, but without accident. For this exploit McDonnell was cited for a silver medal by the Italian government.

Subsequently, an American bombing station was established at Porto Corsini, a village on the Adriatic, at the mouth of the canal leading to Ravenna, about 70 miles south of Venice. The principal objective of the American squadron was Pola, Austria's main naval base. During the Italian retreat, a temporary air station had been hastily established near Ravenna, and when the new line was formed at the Piave, the Italian authorities proceeded to erect a permanent camp at Porto Corsini, which the Americans took over, supplementing its equipment with about thirty-five Italian flying boats, which the American pilots had learned to operate at the U. S. Air Station, Lake Bolsena, Italy. While the station at Porto Corsini was still under construction, the first contingent, or thirty-five officers and about 300 men, arrived. Additional pilots were added to the complement, and more men sent from the station at Pauillac, so that by the latter part of August, 1918, Porto Corsini had become a thriving American city, known to the natives and the newcomers alike as Goat Island City.

Many of the pilots had formerly been in the American ambulance corps and had later been trained in the ground school at Moutchic, with a flying course at Lake Bolsena. The station rendered most effective service in cooperation with the Italians, who were frequently in contact with both land and sea machines. Night bombing expeditions were continuous, and frequently daylight expeditions were conducted for the purpose of distributing propaganda and taking photographs. The type of planes used for bombing were the Italian FBA's, L-3's and Macchi 8's, and for the chasse the Macchi 5's.

Porto Corsini itself was subject to frequent bombing attacks. On the night of August 21–22, 1918, an attack was made by about ten enemy planes which dropped forty-nine bombs, ten falling on the station, the others across the canal. In retaliation, two M-8's, with pilots Ensign R. B. Read and Quartermaster George W. Knowles, left the station the same night and bombed Pola, dropping several bombs in the arsenal and hangars. This was the first night-flight from the American station, and the results were excellent. Pola was easily located, likewise Porto Corsini on the return trip.

After that, attacks and counter-attacks were continuous. An aerial combat occurred in August over Pola, in which the Americans gave a good account of themselves. A patrol of two bombing planes and five chasse planes left the station to distribute propaganda on Pola. Two machines had motor trouble and put back before the engagement. After dumping the reading matter over Pola, the fight began. The Austrians used their anti-aircraft guns, but with poor results, when five land chasse planes and two hydroplanes assembled to attack them. Ensign Ludlow, leading pilot of the chasse machines, gave the signal to attack three Austrians, and dived at them with Pilots Parker and Hammann following. Voorhees, a fourth pilot, was unable to enter the combat because his machine guns jammed. The fight started with Ludlow attacking the center machine, Parker one to the left, and Hammann engaged two others. Ludlow's engine was damaged by bullets, and Parker's right gun jammed. Ludlow started home, fighting off two machines, when his motor broke down due to the damage it had earlier received, and his plane caught fire. He entered a spin and

Liberty Loan Parade, U. S. N. A. S., Porto Corsini.

threw off one of the enemy, at the same time putting out the fire. The other enemy plane followed him down to 500 meters. Ludlow landed a short distance from Pola, and the enemy plane returned to its base. Hammann saw Ludlow land, and after throwing off the two machines with which he was engaged, landed near Ludlow and after destroying the damaged machine, Ludlow returned in Hammann's machine, sitting on the boat directly under the engine. They did not leave, however, until they had made certain that the abandoned machine had sunk, firing 100 rounds at it from the air to complete the destruction. The men were badly bruised and cut up, but otherwise no injury was inflicted. All pilots returned to base.

On September 15, an unfortunate accident occurred in which two flyers gave up their lives. Ensign Louis J. Bergen, pilot, with Gunner Thomas L. Murphy, observer, left the station in a Macchi. They followed the course of the canal toward the sea. When the machine was about over the naval base, it started to turn to the right, went into a right spiral and crashed to the ground, landing in a corn patch. At the time of the descent the machine was flying at an altitude of 250 meters. Both Bergen and Murphy died from the injuries they received.

In accordance with instructions from the Italian authorities, Porto Corsini worked in conjunction with the Venice squadron in offenses against the enemy bases, and in carrying out these instructions joint raids were made by the two squadrons on Pola and the Austrian hangars. Pola was bombed on July 17 by American planes, destroying four hangars belonging to the Austrians, and one of the Germans. The battleship *Babenburg* was hit, sending her to dock for repairs.

In August, 1918, four seaplanes, under the direction of Lieut. R. B. Read, made a flight in which the pilot of one, Smith, was forced to land, owing to engine trouble. Because of darkness and rough sea, his

Copyright by Underwood & Underwood, N. Y.

Transport Picking up U. S. Patrol Plane in Mediterranean Sea.

left wing was badly damaged, and after remaining in the water five hours his machine was sighted by an Italian patrol boat which towed him within 5 miles of the Italian coast. Another, Pilot Stuart, lost his direction owing to heavy mist and darkness. When he sighted the Austrian coast, thinking he was south of Pola, he changed his course due north and flew up the coast, sighting a town which was probably Cittanuova. He flew over the town and dropped several bombs and after flying over the Piave lines he landed at Venice for refuelling, when he returned to the station. The other machines continued northeast and headed for the Austrian coast, near which was sighted a line of Italian destroyers, which aided them in their course by their flashes. Near the Austrian coast they encountered a heavy strata of clouds at a height of 2,000 meters. They arose to an altitude of 3,400 meters, which was kept while flying over Pola. They released four bombs, all of which were seen to explode, and although a heavy barrage was put up, no damage was done to the machines, and they returned safely to their station.

These activities were continued almost daily through August, September and October.

(C) Harris & Ewing

ADMIRAL SIMS

A PERSONNEL OF HIGH GRADE

A gallant and adventurous lot of men were attracted to the naval air service; young men to whom danger was but an incentive to greater effort. Of all the fine, up-standing, clear-eyed young Americans who entered wholeheartedly into the war for the liberties of mankind, none were of a higher class than those who were attracted to the naval flying corps. Its hazards, as well as the boundless opportunities it offered for individual endeavor, appealed to them. Vice-Admiral Sims at the close of hostilities, in a message couched in the conservatism of an official dispatch, asked the Navy Department to, "Please express to the naval aviators of America my most sincere appreciation of their courageous and loyal performance of duty at home and abroad throughout the war. Their brilliant exploits, their determination to win will ever remain one of the highest tributes to American manhood. The performance of duty of these young naval aviators under my command has not only been in keeping with the very best traditions of our naval service, but has in addition won for America the enthusiastic praise of her allies."

Admirals are not wont to "slop over" in their official correspondence; in fact there is some regulation against effusiveness, so we may infer that Admiral Sims would, in an informal expression, be still more enthusiastic over the gallant exploits and the chivalry of these young knights of the air. And well he may, for the record is replete with acts of heroism and daring. To mention all of them would far exceed the limits of this narrative, and to speak of a few would be showing an unfair discrimination. Yet our story would be incomplete if we failed to call attention to some achievements, for they were inextricably woven into the

HS-2 Patrol Plane Equipped with Davis Non-Recoil Aircraft Gun.

history of the naval air service in the war.

Take, for example, Lieut. A. L. Gates, whom we have mentioned. Gates was serving at Dunkerque when a signal was received that a British plane had been brought down by the Germans up along the Belgian coast, and had fallen in the sea within range of the German guns ashore. Gates immediately jumped into a seaplane and without waiting for assistance or for an observer or a machine gunner, "shoved off" at a 90-mile clip. Reaching the place where the British aviators were clinging to the wreck of their plane, still being the target of the guns on shore, Gates swooped down beside them, and reckless of the wicked Hun fire, made a skillful landing, pulled the three wrecked aviators into his plane, soon rose and beat it back to Dunkerque, meeting on the way the other rescuers who were hurrying to the scene in planes and coast water craft, motioning them to go back to avoid the enemy gunfire, which by this time had gotten very angry. For this service Gates was awarded the distinguished flying cross by the King of England.

On October 4, Gates was one of the pilots in a squadron of seven Spads which left St. Pol airdrome with orders to patrol the Ypres salient over territory around Courtrai, Roulers, Dixmude and Foret d'Houthoulet—a lively part of the western battle front at that time. After being out forty minutes they encountered about fifteen enemy aircraft, consisting of Fokker scouts, biplanes and a few triplanes. The Spads quickly dived to a point within the allied lines, and the enemy craft did not pursue them; whereupon, the Spads climbed and returned to enemy territory. Two of the Americans had engine trouble and returned to base, but the other five machines kept on. While flying over Courtrai at an elevation of 4,000 meters, a superior enemy air squadron was sighted—probably the same Fokker squadron—and the signal was given to dive and return to base. At the moment of the last dive several Huns were directly above them and Gates' machine was seen to be making a right

Funeral of Two Naval Aviators at Porto Corsini.

vertical virage. This was the last seen of him, and he was given up as lost. He was captured and after the armistice, a little over a month later, was safely returned. Doubtless he owes his life to the fact that the enemy resistance had begun to crumble, and the Huns saw the wisdom of treating him with humane consideration.

Then there was Lieut. D. S. Ingalls, to whom the British Air Ministry awarded the distinguished flying cross, with the comment that "His keenness, courage and utter disregard of danger are exceptional and are an example to all. He is one of the finest men this squadron ever had." The feats which brought forth this eulogy covered an active period of several months bombing and fighting. In August he flew over the Hun airdrome at Varsenaere, firing 650 rounds with his machine guns into it, besides dropping four bombs and, although flying very low, the Huns were unsuccessful in getting him. On September 15, he made the Huns another call, this time at the Uytecirke airdrome on a low-bombing raid, obtaining a direct hit. On his way home, assisted by another Camel he shot down a 2-seater enemy plane in flames. He was a glutton for low bomb raids, for the citation mentioned two other trips in which he did good work with bombs and machine guns, besides helping destroy two enemy airplanes, and once, single handed, he attacked six enemy machines, driving one down damaged. Ingalls also shot down an enemy kite balloon in flames near Ostend.

For thrilling experiences, we cite the case of Ensign E. A. Stone, a young American reservist, who, with Sub-Lieut. Eric Moore of the Royal Air Service, was on patrol in March, 1918, when the engine stopped dead, forcing a landing in a rough sea. The craft was without radio or kite to call for assistance. Two carrier-pigeons were released, one of whom refused to budge from the machine until Moore threw the clock at him. One pigeon, with the one word "sinking," reached home, but as they had lost their course their location was unknown. The men were continuously soaked and lashed by the March seas, for eighty hours, without food or water, until finally picked up by a trawler. Reports meanwhile had been sent to headquarters that they were lost.

Comdr. L. H. Maxfield, of the regular Navy, was recommended for a gold lifesaving medal for an exploit as unusual as it was heroic. The dirigible "Capitaine Caussin" under his command was patroling a convoy north of Quiberon, when the pressure began to fall, and after making every effort to keep the dirigible in the air, she came down. Upon striking the water, two of the crew, Allely and Elliott, were thrown into the sea. They were having considerable difficulty swimming, because of their combinations, or "teddy bears," which greatly impeded their movements, and Allely called out for help. By this time the ship had drifted 75 yards, but Mr. Maxfield, shouting to Allely to hold out, jumped into the sea. He swam to them, but by this time the dirigible was three-quarters of a mile away. A small motor boat appeared and picked them up, afterward coming to the dirigible and removed several members of the crew. The remaining men were left in the ship, which rapidly drifted ashore. Had Maxfield not gone so promptly to the rescue of the two men, Allely certainly, and Elliott probably, would have drowned.

For their gallantry in action near Ile Tudy, two American pilots, R. H. Harrell and K. R. Smith, were recommended by the French commandant for the Croix de Guerre. A southbound coastal convoy was off Pen Marche when two avions were seen dropping bombs 2 miles to seaward. The destroyer *Stewart* left the escort and proceeded at full speed to the scene, and a French destroyer approached from the northward. With the aid of planes which dropped smoke bombs at the spot where the submarine was seen from the air, the destroyer headed for the position, dropping charges as it encircled the submarine. The avions continued to drop bombs until they brought up clear water. Between the destroyers and the planes the Hun had no chance of escape. O. E. Williams and H. W. Studor were the observers in the two planes, and rendered very efficient service in placing the bombs and guiding the destroyers.

And so we could go on almost indefinitely, recounting exploits such as these, which would be recalled by the readers of this book as merely a part of their daily routine in the adventurous days of comradeship and unselfish service in the United States Naval Flying Corps.

Great credit is due the enlisted personnel of the naval air service. No finer class of men was ever brought into a military force than the members of the crews of the air stations abroad. Many of these men won commissions, and still others rendered equally praise worthy service in the enlisted grades. All the radio operators and a great many observers were enlisted men, and not a few gave a good account of themselves as pilots. All honor to the bluejackets and marines of the naval aviation service!

The Liberty Motor

COMPILED FROM OFFICIAL SOURCES

DURING the time that the production of airplane engines for training was getting under way, careful thought was being given to the possibilities of producing combat engines quickly in the United States.

Engines of increasing horsepower were being demanded at the front, this indicating the early abandonment of sizes and types of engines previously in favor. In fact, up to May, 1917, there was not among the Allies any well-proved engine (with the possible exception of the Rolls-Royce) of a horsepower sufficiently large to insure its popularity and suitability for two years. American experience with large-scale production of automobile engines had shown that two years would be required to tool up for and to obtain a year's output of a given engine.

At that time England was manufacturing or experimenting with thirty-seven different kinds of engines and France with forty-six. It seemed wise, if possible, for the United States to avoid a similar situation, with its exacting requirements for innumerable repair parts —a situation which would be complicated still further by long distance from the scene of war.

There were in the United States extensive facilities for the production of the simpler forms of internal-combustion engine, such as those used in automobiles. American engineers and manufacturers had had wide experience in designing such engines and in producing them in quantity. American engineering talent, ingenuity and knowledge of design was at least equal to that abroad.

It was apparent that prompt action was necessary to meet the enormous requirements for engines and spares demanded by the contemplated program. It was also clear that these requirements could not be met unless the automobile-engine industry could be mobilized for that purpose; furthermore, even with the talented organizations and experience of this industry, there was little chance of completing the task unless their efforts could be concentrated on one type of standardized engine designed especially to suit American quantity-production methods.

After many preliminary investigations, Col. Edward A. Deeds came to the conclusion that it was essential for the United States to concentrate its energies upon the smallest possible number of types of engines and to give special attention to equipment which could be manufactured in quantity, and which would be least affected by the rapid advances in the art.

He considered it entirely possible to design and build an engine suitable for war purposes and adapted to American ideas of quantity production in less time than the Bolling Commission could complete its investigations and negotiations and send us drawings and models of European types that in all probability would be wholly unsuited to our production methods. He believed that the United States should concentrate its greatest effort on a type of aircraft engine which could be made in powers sufficiently high to assure continued usefulness for a term of years and which would possess the maximum degree of interchangeability between similar parts. Colonel Deeds proposed this plan immediately to his associate, Col. S. D. Waldon, who, after giving it careful consideration, agreed entirely with the plan. A few days later J. G. Vincent, of the Packard Motor Car Company, arrived in Washington and proposed substantially the same idea, which had been developed as the result of his experience with aircraft engines, and which had been crystallized by conferences held in Detroit with the French and English commissions then touring the United States.

As subsequent investigation proceeded this conclusion received the unanimous support of both the American and European authorities and its wisdom has been absolutely demonstrated by the results which have been attained. Colonel Deeds, Colonel Waldon, and Messrs. E. J. Hall and J. G. Vincent met at Colonel Deeds' apartment in the New Willard Hotel in Washington and considered in a general way the requirements which the engines must meet. It was determined that they should be built around a 5 by 7 inch individual steel cylinder with aluminum piston, forked rods, and direct-drive propeller, and that nothing experimental or untried should be used.

Messrs. Vincent and Hall set to work on May 29 to combine their knowledge and information, and within two or three days they had outlined the important characteristics of design of the Liberty engine. These preliminary layouts were submitted to the Aircraft Production Board and the Joint Army and Navy Technical Board, who approved the design and on June 4 authorized the construction of five each of the 8 and 12 cylinder sizes. Every feature in the design of these engines was based on thoroughly proven internal-combustion engine practice.

Parts for ten engines were at once started through the tool rooms and experimental shops of various motor car companies. This work centered in the plant of the Packard Motor Car Company, which most cheerfully and patriotically gave to this work its entire energies and wonderful facilities.

Meanwhile the plans of the engine had been submitted to H. M. Crane, engineer of the Simplex Motor Car Company, and of the Wright Martin Aircraft Corporation, who had made a special study of

PROGRESSIVE ASSEMBLING OF LIBERTY MOTORS.

aviation engines in Europe and who for upward of a year had been working on the production of the Hispano-Suiza 150-horsepower engine; also to David Fergusson, chief engineer of the Pierce-Arrow Motor Car Company, and to many of the best experts in the country on the production of motors. Representatives of many other companies, including plane and engine makers, machine tool builders, etc., were called in; these men went over the drawings thoroughly and were consulted on many production features of the engine.

From the foregoing statements it is clear that the Liberty engine was not developed by any species of magic nor by any single individual or company, but was a well-considered and carefully prepared design based on much practical aviation engine experience. The promptness with which the design was completed and the samples built was the result of complete cooperation among all interested parties.

Fundamentals of the design of the Liberty engine have not been altered from the date of its original layout, with the single exception of the scupper feed system for lubricating the crank pins, which was abandoned in favor of the full pressure feed system of lubrication. Numerous manufacturing changes in materials, limits, clearances, etc., have been made to facilitate production, exactly as such changes are made in production of any piece of machinery. As time went on it became necessary to increase the horsepower of the 12-cylinder engine from 330 to 375 and later from 375 to 440. These increases made it necessary to increase the size and strength of certain parts of the engine.

By the method outlined above the first 8-cylinder engine was delivered in Washington and set up at the Bureau of Standards on July 4, 1917, and the first 12-cylinder engine was built and successfully passed a 50-hour endurance test by August 25, 1917.

At first it was believed that both 8 and 12-cylinder engines would be required and negotiations were started looking to the production of both sizes. The Ford Motor

Two Liberty Twelves Constitute the Power Plant of the H-16.

Company agreed to produce 10,000 of the 8 cylinder engines, but before the contract had been made information from abroad indicated that efforts should be concentrated on the 12-cylinder engine. Contracts were therefore let for 22,500 Liberty 12-cylinder engines to six concerns.

This number was sufficient to take care of the requirements of both the Navy and the Army. The first of these contracts was signed in August, 1917, and production work started immediately. It was at once apparent that, to avoid delay and confusion, the engineering and standardization required for developing and manufacturing the engine must necessarily be done in close proximity to the production plants. A district office was therefore established in Detroit, and James G. Heaslet, formerly vice president and general manager of the Studebaker corporation, an engineer and manufacturer of wide experience, was appointed district manager. At the request of the Chief of the Engine Production Department an order was issued in October, 1917, which placed all engineering, inspection and production of the Liberty engine in charge of a committee of engineers and manufacturers composed of Lieut. Col. E. J. Hall, Maj. James G. Heaslet, Henry M. Leland, C. Harold Wills of the Ford Motor Company, and Messrs. Beall and Roberts of the Packard Motor Car Company. With them were associated D. McCall White, engineer of the Cadillac Motor Company, and Walter Chrysler, general manager of the Buick Company. Presided over by Major Heaslet, these men in their respective plants and in joint meetings pushed forward the development and production of Liberty engines. Each without reservation revealed all the trade secrets and processes which they had developed in their plants during the preceding years. The Packard Motor Car Company gave to this developmental work all of its equipment and personnel. The wonderful organization of the Ford Motor Company was devoted to solving the problems presented by the production of this engine. The unique method of making a rough cylinder from a piece of steel tubing, also a new method of making durable and satisfactory bearings, were among the extraordinary results of the work of the Ford Motor Company, and its highly skilled organization.

Difficulties which ordinarily would have been well-nigh insuperable, or which at least would have prevented rapid progress, were immediately encountered; for example:

The existing motor-building plants had practically no machinery of sufficient size to handle the parts of the Liberty engine; it was therefore necessary to build and frequently to design the machine tools for this purpose.

Between 2,500 and 3,000 small jigs, tools, and fixtures are required to produce all the parts of a Liberty engine. For large outputs much of this equipment must be duplicated many times. This made it necessary to requisition practically the total capacity of all the tool shops east of the Mississippi.

It soon developed that men who were able to make the comparatively simple automobile motors did not have the skill required to machine the parts of a Liberty engine; it therefore became necessary to educate thousands of men and women to do this work.

A large amount of unfriendly influence was encountered, a considerable portion of which was doubtless pro-German. This was manifested in the tool shops, where many of the tools made for this work were found to be incorrect and had to be remade before they could be used in the engine-building plants. In the engine-building plants tools mysteriously disappeared or became injured, cans of powder were found in the coal, fire-extinguishing apparatus was plugged up, and numerous other treasonable acts were committed.

As rapidly as skilled men were developed they were requisitioned by nearly every department of the Government. The draft took a great many men, and their return was either impossible or was secured only after great delay.

The materials required for the engines were frequently of a much higher grade than the corresponding materials in automobile motors and much patient work was required to secure their production.

The procurement of necessary transportation and fuel during the winter of 1917-18 presented difficulties which at times were almost insurmountable. Notwithstanding the difficulties encountered, production actually started with the delivery of twenty-two engines during December, 1917.

The Liberty engine as originally manufactured was of approximately 330 horsepower. Information received from overseas led to the conclusion that a higher horsepower would be desirable. Therefore, after about 300 of these engines were in production, the engineers stepped up the horsepower to 375. Under the additional stresses induced, certain parts of the engine, particularly the crank shaft, required strengthening. This was done and several hundred engines were delivered at this horsepower. Then final and definite information arrived from abroad to the effect that if an engine of 400 horsepower or more could be produced, the United States would lead the combatant nations in size and power of engine during 1918 and 1919. The engine was therefore stepped up by the engineers to 440 horsepower. This enormous increase in power necessarily required an increase in strength of practically all the working parts of the engine. This required changes in a very large percentage of the jigs, tools, and equipment used in manufacture. It also required certain metallurgical changes in some of the parts, which in turn involved the development of new and better methods of producing steel for them. These changes in equipment were required in the engine plants, the parts plants, and the forging shops; in like manner they affected all manufacturers throughout the production line, including the producers of the raw metal.

These changes were made with such speed and energy that by May 29, 1918, one year from the date when the design of the engine was begun 1,243 Liberty engines had been produced and delivered for service.

The magnitude of this accomplishment may be realized when it is compared with the development of automobile motors. Practically no automobile motor of any size or importance has ever been put into production and into service without at least one year being devoted to its design and development. This time was not required for the Liberty engine, because its original design required substantially no change and also because the best ability in the country was devoted without stint to its development and production.

During six months, from May 29 to November 29, 1918, the production of Liberty engines increased by leaps and bounds; during October, just preceding the armistice, 150 12-cylinder engines were being produced and delivered into service on each working day.

The record of monthly deliveries of these engines is as follows:

December, 1917	22
January, 1918	39
February	70
March	122
April	415
May	620
June	1,102
July	1,589
August	2,297
September	2,362
October	3,878
November	3,056
Total	15,572

These engines were distributed as follows:

American Navy	3,742
Plants manufacturing airplanes	5,233
Aviation fields for training purposes	907
American Expeditionary Forces in France in addition to those which went over installed in planes	4,511
Allies—England, France and Italy	1,089
Total	15,572

In January, 1918, three of these engines were shipped to the American Expeditionary Forces. In March, ten engines were shipped to the British, six to the French, and five to the Italians. By June 7 tests abroad had proceeded so far that the British Air Minister cabled to Lord Reading that the excellent results obtained from the Liberty engine had placed it in the first class of high-powered engines, and that they were convinced that it would be a most valuable contribution to the allied aviation program. On September 26, the British Air Ministry reported that the Liberty performed at least as well as the Rolls-Royce, in identical airplanes, and that their opinion of June was fully confirmed.

Birkight, the designer of the Hispano-Suiza engine in France, advised Count Poinatowski that the Liberty engine was superior to any high-powered engine then developed on the Continent.

The British placed an order for 1,000 Liberty 12-cylinder engines and subsequently stated their desire to increase this to 5,500, to be delivered by December 31, 1918. The French made inquiry as to the possibility of their securing 20 per cent of all of these engines produced. The Italians also indicated their desire to purchase a large number for immediate delivery.

The vision of Colonel Deeds and the decision to develop an American aviation engine has been fully and completely justified by the results obtained. The engine which approaches nearest to the Liberty in power and efficiency is the English Rolls-Royce. However, this weighs approximately 100 pounds more and delivers approximately 100 horsepower less than the Liberty. The maximum production of the Rolls-Royce engine in England has never exceeded 70 per week; the average production has ranged from 40 to 45 per week.

There can be no doubt that, had the war continued, the Liberty engine in planes piloted by American, British and French aviators would soon have dominated the air on every front. America, and America alone, had the facilities and the vision to produce airplane engines with the necessary power and in the necessary quantities to carry the war in the air into Germany's own territory.

The Liberty engine was a development made necessary by war, but it has already proved that it will show its value in time of peace. This past May four Liberty's successfully drove the NC-4 from America to Europe on the first trans-Atlantic flight.

"Uh, uh! Not Me!

Co'se Ah ain't saying Ah won't do
Jes whut ma country want me to,
But dey's one job Ah fo'see
Ain't gwine to teach itself to me—
Uh, uh! Not me!

Dat's dis heah aihrplane stuff—No, Boss,
Ah'll bah some othah kind ob cross
Lak drive a mule, er tote a gun,
But Ah ain't flirtin wif de sun—
Uh, uh! Not me!

If ah mus' do a loop-de-loop
Let mine be 'round some chicken coop;
It ain't gwine be up whah de crows,
Kin say Ah's trompin on deer toes—
Uh, uh! Not me!

It sho' look sweet, Ah don't deny,
To be a-oozin' 'round de sky,
But dat's fo' folks dat's in de mood,
Not fo' me tho' cose Ah's shrewd—
Uh, uh! Not me!

Down heah Ah firs' saw light ob day
Down heah am whah Ah's gwine to stay;
Folks, Ah don't keer to hab ma feet
Git too blamed proud to walk de street—
Uh, uh! Not me!

Copyright by International Film Service.

Operations with the Fleet

AVIATION played a part in the long vigil kept by the Grand Fleet. In this respect the British Navy had made great advances, by the development of the seaplane carriers, a vessel with a flush deck from stem to stern, enabling the returning planes to land on board without difficulty. Nothing appears above the deck of these vessels, except a small deck house, which disappears when the planes are about to return. The British had some four or five of these carriers, strange looking craft, with their stacks protruding from the sides. Of our own battleship force, the *Texas* alone was equipped with airplanes, and that only a short time before the armistice.

It was not until the winter months following the armistice that the American Navy utilized effectively the planes for control of great gun fire. Lieut. Commander E. O. McDonnell, who made a brilliant record on both the western and the Italian fronts, particularly in bombing and night raiding, conducted experiments in fire control at Guantanamo, Cuba, which demonstrated the great value of aircraft in battle practice. Here also the *Texas* was used in making the experiments. She was equipped with a small two-seater and two single-seaters, and a false deck was constructed on the turret, with removable planking over the guns themselves, which was taken away when the large guns were fired. The single seater was intended for short range scouting and fighting, the two-seaters being used for reconnaisance, fire control and spotting. While the fleet was at Guantanamo, the *Mississippi* was

Scout Plane on U. S. S. Texas.

Copyright by Underwood & Underwood, N. Y.

A Floating Aerodrome.
H. M. S. "Furious" on a Zeppelin strafing expedition.

similarly equipped, and flights were made from both of these dreadnaughts. Land planes, however, were used during the tests of fire control of the *Texas,* when ten 14-inch guns fired salvos on a range of 20,000 yards, the maximum elevation of the guns. Lieutenant Commander McDonnell controlled the fire by means of both radio telephone and telegraph, using the telephone first, immediately followed by the telegraph signals. Every spot received from the ship was immediately acknowledged from the plane. The firing was done in the open sea under weather conditions that were favorable, but with a great deal of interference from smoke from the stacks of the ship, which at one time was so bad that the targets were lost to view from the tops. Indeed, after the third salvo the targets were totally obscured, and reliance was made entirely upon the control from the planes. The average time for the transmission of the message was five seconds from the seaplane to the plotting officer, which period could with practice, have been reduced it was believed, to two seconds. As this was the first occasion when any naval vessel had depended entirely upon telephone communication from a seaplane or airplane for target-practice spotting, the results were most gratifying to the gunnery officers who watched the tests with the keenest interest. Of special importance was the fact that communications were accurate both ways, in both receiving and sending. The flight was not made from off the *Texas* because of the uncertainty as to the required amount of wind, and the low-powered airplane used, although it later developed that there was sufficient wind to have made the flight from the turret with safety, and without delaying the target practice.

Return landings were made on the beach during these tests. Three methods of return were possible; to the beach, on the water near the ship, or on board the ship. When landings were made on the surface of the water, the wheels were released by the tripping gear of the planes, the air bags were immediately filled, and the craft would float safely for twelve hours if necessary.

Both types of machines were equipped with radio sets, but only the two-seater had the apparatus necessary for both sending and receiving. The single-seater could send but could not receive.

KITE BALLOONS

During the operations of the battleship force in the North Sea, one vessel in each division of the U. S. battle squadron was equipped with kite balloons. They were used to some extent for fire control, but their principal duty was to look for submarines, torpedoes and mines. They were also used by the ships of the convoys while traversing the submarine zone, and to some extent by our destroyers. Trawlers operating in the submarine zone were also supplied with kite balloons. It is planned to equip at least one ship in every four of the battle fleet with them.

THE FLEET AIR DETACHMENT

Another development which has come since the war ended is the organization of a fleet air detachment, with the U. S. S. *Shawmut* as parent ship and carrier. This vessel rendered valuable service during the war as a mine-layer, being part of the force operating in the North Sea in laying the celebrated mine barrage which did so much to break the submarine menace, and destroy the morale of the Hun undersea pirates. After her return from this duty, she was equipped as the mother-ship of the fleet air detachment, consisting of a squadron of large seaplanes, which may be used for reconnoisance, for scouting, for bombing submarines and mines, and for attack by bombing on any enemy position where anti-aircraft guns are not used. Their principal duty, however, is scouting and spotting. The squadron consists of five of these seaplanes. The *Shawmut* carries gasoline and spare parts, and acts as a tender to the air squadron. She will operate with the fleet in the battle manoeuvers, in which the air detachment will doubtless, in the future, play an important part.

During the cruise to the West Indies the *Shawmut* and the fleet air detachment accompanied the fleet, making many flights en route.

Bomb Explosion Photographed from Seaplane.

"Lighter-Than-Air"

By Commander L. H. Maxfield, U. S. N.

LIGHTER-THAN-AIR, while being the youngest branch of the Naval profession, has had the greatest rate of progress. Two years ago we had practically nothing; now we have some of the best non-rigids in existence, and our pilots, though far from numerous, are equal to any in the world. While it is, of course, a fact that war has been the great incentive, we may still hope to keep up a good rate of progress, and in time equal, in quality at least, the lighter-than-air craft of Germany and England.

What has been done by the Navy in the past two years may be summarized in a few brief paragraphs. The ship built by the Connecticut Aircraft Company made but a few short flights, then went out of commission forever, so had very little good effect upon personnel or material. The kite balloons tested out on the U. S. S. *Oklahoma* and *Nevada* in the fall and winter of 1916-1917, proved that good spotting could be done from this type of aircraft, but little interest, unfortunately, was aroused in the department, so that they were soon ordered off the ships. Next, in the spring of 1917 came the orders for the first small blimps, modeled after the lines of the British. The Goodyear Tire and Rubber Company built the first envelopes, and Curtiss the Nacelles. About the time the first ship was to be delivered, a class of students was started in Akron. This was in June, 1917, and during that summer the students took their free balloon course, their aerostatics, their meteorology, as well as their regular naval studies. The dirigibles were flown, but the envelopes were constructed of such poor material that they could not be kept inflated more than a week. Hence to get the maximum benefit out of the ships during their short lives, they were used twenty-four hours a day.

In the early fall of 1917, the first contingent of naval lighter-than-air officers and men was sent to France, and in November and December regular war patrolling was done in the French ships at Rochefort and Paimboeuf. In January, 1918, all hands were assembled at Paimboeuf and a start was made in cleaning, rebuilding and enlarging that station, which was later completely taken over by us and operated under our flag.

R-34, the First Lighter-than-Air Craft to Cross the Atlantic.

Students in Training at Akron.

Meanwhile, students were sent from the United States to England for training, and some of these were later given important billets under the British and performed valuable and efficient war service. Paimboeuf continued to grow and improve until the signing of the armistice. Active patrols were carried out and engagements with enemy submarines were reported.

Guipavas, the American dirigible station near Brest, was practically completed when the armistice was signed. This station did, however, do active flying and, at the time of the President's first arrival at Brest, the station sent out two ships to escort the *George Washington* into port. Kite balloon stations had been established all along the coast of France, and good work was being done by the pilots.

In the United States active work had been carried on at Chatham, Montauk, Rockaway, Cape May, Hampton Roads, Key West, Pensacola and Akron. Officers had been given Ground School training at Tech, and flying training at Akron and Pensacola. Important patrols and experimental flights were made both by kite balloons and dirigibles. The Technical Bureaus of the Navy Department had pushed rapidly ahead, had conducted valuable research work and had turned out the "C"-type ship; so it can be seen that abroad and at home interest was growing in lighter-than-air craft, and much good work was done.

The necessity for lighter-than-aircraft for the Navy is now fully realized by strategists, and work to provide our Navy with lighter-than-air craft is being pushed by those in authority. The General Board has for many years realized the importance of this sort of craft, and has recommended their construction time and again. The work done by the German Zeppelins in patroling and scouting over the North Sea, and the effect of the British lack of rigids, has brought this necessity home. To the popular mind the Zeppelin did not make good in the war. This opinion is based wholly upon the results of the raids over England, in which many ships were lost. Admitting that these raids were on the whole unsuccessful, although they most certainly did keep a great number of British heavier-than-air craft in England that were sorely needed at the front, and most certainly did at one period keep the people of London, to say the least, under a nervous strain, we do know that a constant and efficient patrol was kept over the North Sea which could not have been kept by any other type of water or air craft.

Hangars at Akron

It is proposed from now on to have the following types of lighter-than-air craft. These may never be placed in quantity production, but certainly will be used and experimented with:

Free Balloon.—There is nothing new about this. It has been used since 1783, and its use will be continued. There is nothing better in which to train kite or dirigible students, and, by some, free ballooning is looked upon as the greatest sport in the world.

Kite Balloon.—This will be used by the Navy for search, and possibly for spotting. The Army will certainly continue to use it for the control of fire, and other uses will most surely be forthcoming. Two distinct types are now recognized—the French Cacquot and the Italian Avorio-Prassone.

Non-Rigid.—This type, in various sizes, will always have its use in the Navy for patrols, search, and convoy duty, and will continue to prove a most useful unit of the Naval forces. It is doubtful whether land forces will be able to derive much benefit from it. However, that remains to be seen.

Rigid.—This will be the greatest of all aircraft, and will revolutionize all naval strategy and tactics.

No one realizes the limitations of lighter-than-air craft better than those who work constantly with them. They are not the ones who see small rigids

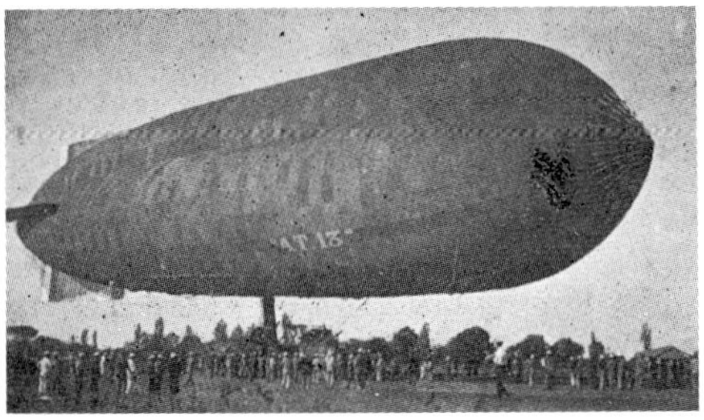

AT-13 at Paimboeuf.

Rescue at Sea.

taking the place of yachts, nor do they see daily scheduled trips for passenger and freight being carried out this year. They leave that sort of propaganda to the stock sellers and to the editors of popular aviation magazines. What they do see, however, as the scout of the future, is a rigid of somewhere between five and ten million cubic feet capacity, filled with some inert gas, driven by reliable gasoline, steam, or electric motors, capable of staying out two or three weeks, with guns sufficient to fight off any fighting plane, and bombs sufficient to wreck a battleship. It is quite useless to attempt to make the real surface craft man believe that some day the slow moving battleships and cruisers will be of little use, but most certainly the day is fast approaching when such will be the case.

Production of Spruce for the Navy

By F. M. SMITH, Lieutenant, U. S. N.

(In Charge of Spruce Production for the Navy)

Few of us have given more than a passing thought to the many problems of forced production which had to be successfully met before any aggressive aviation policy could be even seriously considered. But for the initiative and ability of the men who silently shouldered these responsibilities in the background of the war, American aviation could not have been the potent factor for victory which it proved to be.

The story of the production of spruce lumber for the construction of the Navy's aircraft tells of a difficult task undertaken in the face of many discouraging obstacles and of hard work carried on throughout a season of severe New England weather. Experience had shown that spruce of a very high grade was the only material perfectly suited to the manufacture of many airplane parts. Substitution of other woods in the place of spruce had never been successfully accomplished, and when tried was usually accompanied by failure of the plane in action. The pre-war construction of aircraft had been very small and spruce of sufficient quality and quantity had been easily obtained. This normal supply, however, was totally inadequate to meet the demands of war-time construction and for many months constantly jeopardized our entire aviation program.—Editor.

. . . .

IN DECEMBER, 1917, it was apparent that on account of the enormous demands for airplanes both at home and abroad the Spruce Production Section of the Army, which had absolute control of spruce production in the west and south would be unable to produce sufficient material to meet the demands. It was, therefore, considered extremely doubtful if the Navy, which was forced to purchase airplane spruce through the Army, could obtain the requisite material for the proper maintenance of its building program. As an insurance against the non-receipt of sufficient airplane stock from the Army to carry out the building program, steps were immediately taken to develop the as yet unexploited resources of New England and New York State for production of white spruce.

While it was recognized that material of the size of that obtained in the west could not be secured from New England, very good quality material of small size could be manufactured and the material was considered at least the equal in both size and quality of that obtained in the south by the Army and by the British Government.

A representative of the Bureau of Construction and Repair who had formerly been on duty in New England as Timber Inspector and who was thoroughly familiar with lumber conditions in that district, was sent to New England on December 20, 1917, to investigate the situation, ascertain the possibilities of the district as a source of supply, and make arrangements for issue of contracts, preparation of specifications and methods of inspection and shipment.

Lumbering conditions in New England differ radically from those in other sections of the country as there are no lumber associations and no standard grading rules, and it was therefore necessary to interview all the different operators and arrange for individual contracts.

The highest grade of lumber produced in New England for commercial purposes was a grade called "Clear and No. 1," and only 20 per cent of this top grade was found suitable for aircraft construction purposes.

A great deal of patriotic enthusiasm was aroused among the New England operators. In spite of the immense distances to be traveled to interview the different manufacturers, and the difficulty of traveling in New England during the winter months in order to visit the different mills, practically every large operator was personally interviewed and satisfactory agreements as to specifications and contracts drawn up, such contracts issued by the Bureau of Supplies and Accounts to cover 100 concerns. Inspection and shipment of material commenced by January 19, 1918. Contracts were made to allow for the purchase of all the material which could be produced in accordance with the specifications for a period of six months, inspection to be made at the mill by a representative of the Navy Department as the material left the saw.

The Office of Spruce Production for the Navy was established with headquarters at Boston to handle all matters connected with the production and shipment of spruce, and at the time of the signing of the armistice 121 contracts were in force covering operations at 375 mills. Contracts were so drawn that cancellation was effected immediately upon the signing of the armistice without the necessity of reimbursement for cancellation in advance of completion. The amicable cancellation of contracts on November 11, 1918, was estimated to have saved the Government $473,628.03, the value of 4,572,845 feet of lumber which would have been produced had the contracts been allowed to run to expiration.

The obtaining of sufficient competent inspectors was a difficult job, as the mills operate ten hours per day necessitating working by artificial light for four hours per day on an open platform with the temperature often 40° below zero, and the material often covered with snow and ice. No ordinary inspector from an aircraft factory could or would perform such duty, and inspectors had to be recruited from the mills. This necessitated detailed instruction regarding quality of material desired and in the finer points of wood inspection.

The entire territory, including Maine, New Hampshire, Vermont, New York and the Canadian Provinces of Ottawa, Ontario, New Brunswick, Quebec and Nova Scotia, were divided into districts, each district being numbered and embracing several mills, between which facilities for travel were fairly well established. An inspector was detailed to each district with an official stamp bearing the district number. In this way objectionable shipments could be easily traced.

The first shipments were naturally not up to standard, but inspection rapidly improved until during the latter part of 1918 better material was being produced than was being received from the west. Out of the entire British order of over 3,000,000 feet, unfavorable report was made on only nine cars after its receipt in England, and only 5 per cent of the contents of the nine cars was rejected. All nine carloads were traced to an inspector who had been released for incompetency.

Special operations were undertaken during 1918 for production of airplane stock from especially fine stands of spruce by culling all the choice logs from the river drives of the big pulp and paper companies and having them specially sawn.

Early in the spring of 1918 the British War Mission sent a representative to New England to determine if the quality of spruce being produced was suitable for their purposes, and as a result of a favorable report, contract was entered into for shipment of 1,000,000 feet. The quality of the stock was found so satisfactory that an additional contract was entered into for 3,000,000 feet of the same material. The Imperial Munition Board immediately attempted to develop the Canadian Provinces along the lines adopted by the Navy in New England, but without success.

A representative of the British War Mission and a representative of the Imperial Munition Board then thoroughly investigated the activities of the Navy in New England and reported to the Imperial Board that it would be an extremely difficult, if not impossible matter, to establish an organization of the efficiency of that of the Navy in New England. Consequently they decided to turn over to the United States Navy the development of the Canadian Provinces with the understanding that a fair percentage of the material would be supplied the British Government at cost price.

In addition to the development in New England for the production of spruce, the Office of Spruce Production for the Navy located and developed sources of supply of tough northern-grown bending ash, which was found absolutely necessary for airplane construction. Over 560,000 feet of this material were inspected and shipped to various naval establishments during the fall of 1918.

In September, 1918, the labor situation as regards lumber operations was very acute in New England, and it was apparent that unless relief was obtained, lumber operations would practically cease. New England operators failing to obtain assistance from the Labor Board, requested help from the Office of Spruce Production. Special employment agencies were established and operated under their supervision for the proper allocation of the men, and as this source of supply was not found sufficient, negotiations were opened with the Army for the assignment of limited service men for this duty. Arrangements were finally made for the allocation of 2,000 men from camps in the middle west to the New England mills. The entire transaction of obtaining these men and transporting them from camp to the mills and their return to camp upon the signing of the armistice, was handled by the Office of Spruce Production for the Navy. Every man so allocated was returned to camp or satisfactorily accounted for.

The economy effected by this work was considerable; grade "A" spruce, for example, costing the Navy $125 per 1,000 feet to produce, while the same grade previously purchased from the Army cost $667 per 1,000 feet. The magnitude of production reached may be seen from the following summary of shipments from January to November, 1918:

To the British	3,807,000
Overseas for Caproni Machines	230,000
To the French	200,000
Army	708,382
Navy	2,265,120

Developments of Aerial Photography

As a result of experiments extending over a period of several years, the United States naval air service developed what is believed to be the best aerial hand-held camera constructed in America or by the Allies during the war; a camera which embodies all the good qualities of several other designs which were manufactured here and abroad to meet the requirements of the aerial photographers of all allied countries.

Aerial photography in the U. S. Navy dates from June, 1915, when a second class machinist's mate was detailed for photographic duty at the naval air station, Pensacola, for the purpose of obtaining record photographs of yard, construction, aircraft experimental work, etc. In the following March, aerial photographs taken of a dummy fort at Fort Morgan were used in connection with the long range firing by the U. S. S. *New York* and the U. S. S. *Arkansas*. Upon his return from this detail, the photographer recommended to Capt. Mark L. Bristol, USN, then director of aviation, that a long-range aerial camera be developed for use in great gun target practice, in order that more detail might be secured in photographs taken from high altitudes than was possible with the cameras they had at that time.

Accordingly several camera manufacturers were interested in the project, and by the following December a camera had been constructed for the Navy, which

H-16 at 6,000 Feet.

Shot with a Camera Gun, Low.

stood a satisfactory test at an altitude of 6,100 feet over Pensacola, although the lenses were not all that was desired. Tests of aerial cameras of several types were continued during the ensuing months, with varying results, until the development of the naval camera, which is recognized to be the most complete among all the machines that were used by the allied air services. At the time of the armistice, the naval air service had about perfected plans whereby photographic negatives made of the enemy's battle craft, harbors and fortifications could be developed by the naval photographer in the seaplane while in flight en route from the scene, and a print dispatched by a pigeon within ten minutes after the photograph was taken! A great deal more in the nature of advanced photographic experimental work was in contemplation for the furtherance of naval aerial warfare, but which cannot be disclosed now.

Training of aerial photographers began with the detail of a naval photographer to the army school of aerial photography at Langley Field, Hampton, Va., in November, 1917, for a course of instruction. Upon graduation he passed an examination for commission and was appointed ensign in the reserve force, whereupon he was sent to Miami, Florida, for the purpose of establishing a similar school for naval photographers. This school was put in commission in April, 1918, and in June the first group of naval photographers, consisting of nine trained men, went abroad for duty at the various United States naval air stations. At the same time several trained photographers were sent from the school to stations in this country.

The course at the school of aerial photography covered a larger field than that of the army school; instead of confining the instruction to aerial photography alone, several phases of the profession were taught, and upon completing the course, the graduates were competent to perform whatever record photographic work might be required at a Naval air station, or on board a warship carrying aircraft, in addition to aerial photographic map-making.

By the time hostilities ceased, the trained personnel of aerial photography in the naval service comprised nine photographic officers (all ensigns, Naval Reserve Force), seventy-seven printers and ten machinist's mates, the latter being camera repair men; of this force, forty-two were abroad, or were en route to France. The first class of twenty photographers was formed from among candidates who had passed a competitive examination among reservists at New York. The second class came from Great Lakes training station, and the remainder were recruited from civil life or through individual examinations at the various stations. The instruction of camera repair men was conducted at the factory in Rochester, where the machinists were taught the construction of cameras, their repairs and general mechanism.

Parachutes

BY LIEUT. R. EMERSON, U. S. N. R. F.

HOW CAN the many dangers encountered by aviators be minimized to the greatest degree of safety?

Upon this problem has been centered the inventive genius and talent of many intrepid pioneers of aerial navigation not only in the United States but in every country in which the development of aeronautics has made any appreciable progress. After the war cloud had descended upon the earth and aerial warfare became a reality instead of a thrilling chapter by Jules Verne, the problem of lessening the dangers of aerial combat became acute, resulting in a coordination of effort which advanced safety devices and appliances for aircraft to a degree that leaves one speechless with wonder and admiration at the patience, scientific skill and acumen of those responsible for making the lanes of the air almost as safe as the macadamized road for the automobile.

Returning to earth without mishap is contingent upon the aviator's skill as a pilot, upon the proper functioning of engine and the correct operation of the component parts of the craft. Every stage in the manufacture of an airplane is the equivalent stage of making the plane safe for flight. Safety is the primary consideration; but when the throb of the motor is silenced by a bullet from an enemy machine gun, or likewise if the gas bag of a dirigible is badly torn, the navigator of the air is compelled, as Julius Caesar says in his commentary, "to seek safety in flight." It is then that the parachute comes into its own.

The operation of the parachute is familiar to almost everyone. Ask a child to describe a parachute and he will mentally picture a pygmy-like figure high in the clouds clinging to a slowly descending opened umbrella. Devotees of county fairs have long been familiar with the parachute descent from the old fire-balloon as the thrilling and breath-taking event of the day.

A PERFECT DESCENT.

The parachute is really the only practical aerial life-saver. It appeared a century ago coincidentally with the appearance of the first successful fire-balloon. The evolution of the parachute has been a series of improvements upon the basic ideas conceived at that time. Descents by parachute in the earlier days of its development were resorted to only in cases of the greatest emergency, for so uncertain was the possibility of making a safe landing that it was deemed almost as safe to take one's chances with the burning balloon. As a consequence no appreciable progress in the development of the parachute as a practical aerial life-saving device was made until a generation or so ago.

It may be said without fear of contradiction that to America is due the credit for developing parachuting to the point where it is now a science and indeed a practical life-saving device for the pilot of lighter-than-air craft. Since the war, experiments by both the Navy and the Army have indicated that the time is not far distant when the utility of the parachute for heavier than air machines will be manifest.

In the days when parachuting was regarded as a particularly hazardous stunt, that intrepid pioneer, Maj. Thomas S. Baldwin, popularly known as Tom Baldwin, set out to develop a safe parachute. For many years he gave demonstrations throughout the United States and Europe, demonstrating the practicability of the parachute. Major Baldwin's efforts did much toward arousing a popular interest in free ballooning and parachuting.

Then as suddenly as a bolt of thunder from a clear sky the great war came upon a surprised world, and it was very soon realized that aircraft of all kinds would play an all-important rôle in the great conflict. It was many months, however, before any of the belligerents equipped their aircraft with parachutes, while in the meantime hundreds of men in the air service were lost as their machines and balloons fell in flames or were shot down. Allied and enemy war lords then fully realized that the mastery of the air would achieve the ultimate victory. How could this great advantage be gained if there was no insurance against the loss of the only men skilled and equipped to carry on this work after months of arduous training? A parachute must be developed which will cut down the heavy casualties of the air, was the decision of those in charge of the aerial program. We can better afford to lose planes and balloons than we can to sacrifice the lives of the men whose skill alone gives the command of the air its potential value.

With these outstanding facts forming the basis for concerted action no time was lost in devising and manufacturing in large quantities a type of parachute at once efficient and safe. A degree of development in parachuting was attained in time to bear an important influence on the value of aircraft in the war.

The type of parachute developed for war purposes was an improvement on the older one-man type, used to permit men in the basket to descend in case the

A Drop from a Blimp.

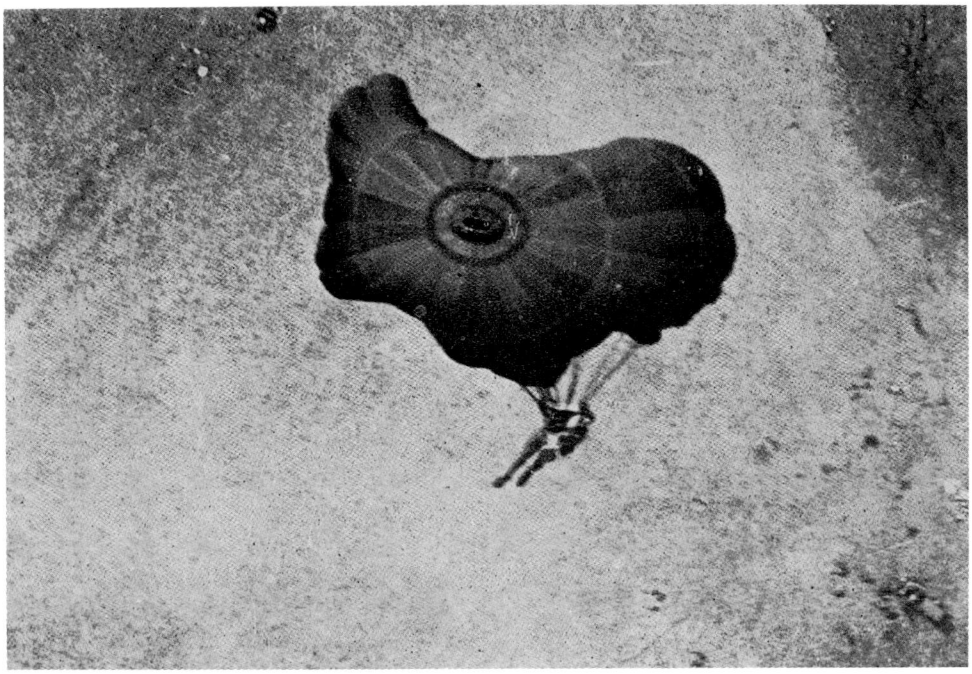

Copyright Underwood & Underwood.

PLUCKY 19-YEAR-OLD ENGLISH GIRL STARTING 2,000-FOOT DROP.

balloon caught fire, in that the balloonists were enabled to remain in the basket, which, cut away from the burning balloon, descended safely to earth bearing its load of human freight. This is known as the basket parachute, and made possible the saving of maps, records and instruments of great value and of potential danger should the basket fall into the hands of the enemy. The basket parachute is considerably larger in diameter than the one-man or individual type, and those who have made descents by means of both declare that the only sensation caused by the basket drop is merely the pleasurable thrill of slow and gradual descent, very similar to an elevator ride, while with the individual type one must jump out of the basket and undergo the hair-raising sensation of a suspense of from three to six seconds, which seems like an eternity, the period elapsing from the moment the pilot jumps over the edge of the basket until the parachute, umbrella-like, opens up.

It is a remarkable fact, which in itself is significant, that during the entire time in which American forces operated on European soil during the recent war, only one death resulted as the direct result of a parachute drop. In that particular instance the burning balloon fell directly upon the opening parachute, setting it on fire and causing the observer to fall to earth. That the parachute proved its value in lessening the number of air fatalities is demonstrated by the fact that one observer jumped to safety four times in one day, while another made three safe descents in four hours. During the historic Argonne drive thirty parachute jumps were made by allied aviators. Without these safety devices, not only would the lives of many brave and valuable airmen have been lost, but valuable data, maps, records, etc., would have fallen into the enemy's possession, making it necessary for allied leaders to reshape long thought out plans.

Naturally more than one type of parachute resulted from the concentration of effort upon this important problem, which caused still another problem, choice of the most desirable type. There were the Baldwin, the Stevens and a few other American types; at least a half-dozen French makes; the Spencer and "Guardian Angel," both of British make. The United States Navy has experimented with all these and a number of others.

To Lieut. J. Keily, USN, is due the credit of making the first parachute jump in the American navy. This test was made in England, in October, 1917. Later jumps were made in the United States from balloons, dirigibles and planes. During the period of war naval experimental pilots also worked with the Army in the effort to develop a parachute which would be as nearly perfect as scientific and inventive genius could devise.

On March 30, 1918, the basket parachute was tested in the Navy for the first time. An observer descended from a balloon in the basket, together with maps, instruments, etc. The very next day the French army, hundreds of miles away, made its first successful experiment with the same type parachute. The American parachute was designed by Bankston, who made the first test, while J. R. Gammeter, of the B. F. Goodrich Company, designed the release mechanism, which was a lever by means of which the basket with all its contents could be released from the burning balloon.

Among the many foreign models purchased by the American Navy and experimented with in this country while army and navy experts were actively studying the parachute question in Europe are the Usuelli and mobile Italian types. In Italy an American naval aviator jumped from a huge Italian dirigible, using an Usuelli parachute, into the Mediterranean Sea 1,400 feet below, carrying with him a small pneumatic life-boat (designed by Major Leone) which he successfully used upon landing in the water.

In June, 1918, the navy began experimental work with parachutes as applied to seaplanes. On August 4, 1918, Maj. T. Orde Lees, AFC, RAF, successfully demonstrated the popular British parachute, "The Guardian Angel," by droping from a swiftly moving HS-2 flying boat, piloted by Lieutenant Barron. Almost a year before this the Germans had made successful tests of the parachute as a life-saving device for airplanes. This spurred the British to greater effort.

The war not only served as a medium for advancing the development of all types of aircraft to a degree which in pre-war days could not have been foreseen by even the most hopeful air enthusiasts, but at the same time carried forward with an equal rapidity of advancement the development of the parachute as a life saving device for airplanes as well as balloons.

The Navy Department is now experimenting with a type of parachute designed by Airplane Inspector Coughlin, of the Bureau of Construction and Repair, which is said by experts to hold great promise as a still further degree of parachute development. The Coughlin parachute is designed for use on balloons and dirigibles. The most efficient parachute for heavier-than-air craft, according to expert opinion based upon more than 200 successful tests, is the British "Guardian Angel." Experimental work on all types is being pushed rapidly, and important improvements in design and application are now in process of development.

Among the new phases contemplated is a reduction in size of parachutes used over water because of the need of one that is small, light and more easily stowed on heavier-than-air craft. This is declared to be practicable, as a plunge can safely be made into water with far greater velocity than a drop to land. Still another contemplated improvement is a parachute which is independent of any connection with the aircraft to facilitate its opening. Test after test has proven that most of the accidents occurring result from failure of the parachute to open in sufficient time to check the fall of the flier before he hits the earth. There are two main causes which, in the case of the ordinary parachute, account for a delay or an entire failure to open.

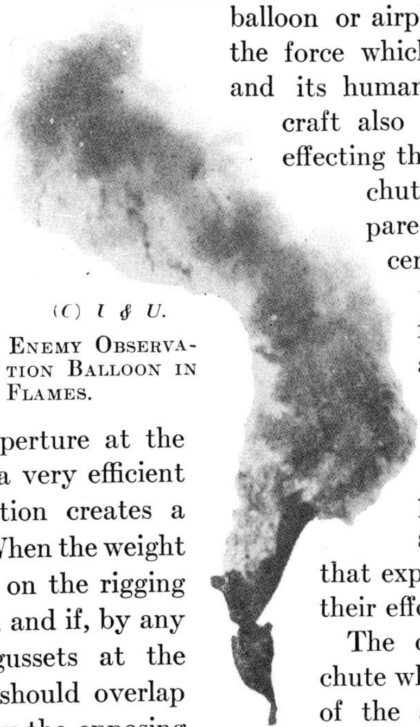

(C) U & U.
ENEMY OBSERVATION BALLOON IN FLAMES.

The first is that the aperture at the apex of the body acts as a very efficient air ejector, and the suction creates a partial vacuum within. When the weight of the airman first comes on the rigging it pulls the cords together, and if, by any fatal chance, the silk gussets at the mouth of the parachute should overlap and be pressed together by the opposing current of air, the vacuum extends to the mouth, sucks the silk gussets together and seals up all entrance of the external air. A parachute in such cases never opens, and the aviator falls to certain death.

The second main cause accounting for the failure of the parachute to open is entanglement of the rigging, which is composed of fine coiled cordage. A large number of coiled cords are in contact and they have a strong tendency to become entangled. When the weight of the descending aviator makes a snatch at this cordage, all bunched together, the least air current will whip these cords round each other, with the imminent risk of their loops taking a grip and binding themselves in knots. A partial entanglement of rigging means a lopsided parachute body, and a dangerous increase in the speed of descent. A badly knotted entanglement means constriction of the mouth of the parachute, and a high speed fatal fall.

In the past a type of parachute was used which was connected with the balloon or airplane in such a way that the force which breaks the parachute and its human load away from the craft also serves the purpose of effecting the opening of the parachute. It soon became apparent, however, that under certain conditions, particularly in modern warfare, it would be preferable to have a type entirely independent of any such connection between aircraft and parachute. It is upon such types among others that experts are now centering their efforts.

The development of a parachute which reduces the hazards of the air to an absolute minimum is now being sought. In Great Britain the Air Ministry has created a special Parachute Committee. The important work done by the United States Air Service at the experimental field, Choisy Le-Roi, in cooperation with the French Section Technique at St. Cyr, Chalais-Meudon and Villacoublay, will be carried on in the United States. The navy, which has made many successful tests, is preparing to carry on the good work along definitely laid-out and well-conceived plans. The present policy of the navy in regard to parachutes can be summarized thus.

One parachute for each member of the crew of dirigibles because of fire danger; for observation balloons, in case of enemy attack; for heavier-than-air planes when subject to attack, or when special circumstances warrant.

That the work done by the pioneers in this dangerous and thrilling field formed one of the most exciting chapters in the war and constitutes one of the most important phases in the development of aeronautics is conceded by all who have a first-hand knowledge of the many elements of personal danger involved.

Official, Naval Air Service.

NC-4 At Ponta Delgada.

© Underwood & Underwood, N.Y.

NC-4 and NC-1 at Rockaway, (May 8.)

The First Trans-Atlantic Flight

By Lieut. Commander A. C. Read, U.S.N.

THE expedition which resulted in the NC-4 crossing the Atlantic was planned and engineered by the Navy Department; all of the personnel were acting under orders. There was doubtless hardly a single naval aviator that would not have given most anything he possessed for the privilege of going. The eligibles, however, were not as numerous as is generally thought, for the flyers for this trip were selected from those unfortunate ones who had seen no overseas duty during the war.

The original plan was to send all four NC's over, but when NC-1 was partially wrecked by dragging her moorings in a gale, and going ashore, it was at once seen that all four could not be prepared at the time scheduled for the start. The hull of Number 1 was then assembled with the upper works of Number 2 and the combination designated NC-1.

The ships detailed to assist the flight were of three classes: "base ships," five in number, carrying supplies and aviation personnel, sent to the ports where stops were scheduled; "Meteorological ships," five battleships, stationed at points about 400 miles off the courses, to obtain meteorological data; and "Patrol" or "Station ships" consisting of sixty-eight destroyers placed at 50 mile intervals wherever the line of flight led over the open sea. Later five other destroyers were placed by the Commander Destroyer Force on a line tween Lisbon and Cape Finisterre, so that the total number was seventy-three. Besides these there were several other

© *Naval Air Service.*

Showing Shattered Wing of NC-3.

ships necessary to fuel the destroyers. In short, the Trans-Atlantic Flight was distinctly an "All Navy" project.

All three planes started together from Rockaway on May 8th. NC-4 was forced down 80 miles off Cape Cod by motor trouble, while en route to Halifax, and finally taxied into the Naval Air Station, Chatham, the following morning, NC-3 and NC-1 meanwhile reaching Halifax and later going on to Trepassey Bay, Newfoundland. NC-4, after making repairs at Chatham, was held up six days by a "northeaster," but finally the weather moderated in time to fly to Halifax and then to Trepassey before the others started.

The day following her arrival the three planes started together in the late afternoon for the Azores. At dark, finding that it was impossible to maintain formation, they separated, each making the best of its way along the course.

The next morning when still about 250 miles from the Azores, a dense fog was encountered which nearly proved the undoing of all three planes. Both NC-3 and NC-1 eventually landed, hoping to locate themselves. They found the sea so rough that all hope of getting up again was abandoned; in fact, the crews had considerable difficulty in staying afloat. The crew of NC-1 was picked up by a tramp steamer, six hours after landing, the plane later sinking. NC-3 sailed stern-first for about 200 miles until off Ponta Delgada, then started up her engines and taxied into port, after weathering nearly sixty hours of gale and waves as high as 30 to 40 feet. Nobody

© *Naval Air Service.*

NC-3 at Ponta Delgada.

© *Underwood & Underwood, N. Y.*

LIEUT. COMDR. READ LEAVING NC-4 AT PLYMOUTH, ENGLAND.

except those who went through the experience will ever realize how they did it. No one previously had thought it possible.

NC-4 was fortunate enough to sight land and reached Horta, Fayal, the morning after leaving Trepassey; then a few days later, as soon as the weather permitted, ran the 150 miles to Ponta Delgada in order to fuel up for the 800-mile run to Lisbon.

NC-3 was too badly battered to continue the flight and was consequently dismantled and sent back to the States; she is now being thoroughly overhauled and will fly again.

© *U. & U, N. Y.*

NC-1 AT ROCKAWAY.

NC-4 left after a week of waiting for sea and weather conditions to moderate. The run to Lisbon was made without particular incident. Later she continued on her way to Plymouth, England, stopping in the Mondego River for minor repairs and again at Ferrol, Spain, to spend the night; this was necessary, due to the delay experienced at the Mondego River.

All of the European cities visited were most enthusiastic about the flight and everywhere the crews were treated as distinguished guests. The Portuguese awarded them their highest decoration, that of the "Tower and Sword"; the British awarded them the Royal Air Force Cross; banquets, receptions and "what-not" were in order. It was a continuous ovation. And later the same was true in this country.

It seemed very strange that the success of a naval expedition should create such excitement, but the whole world seemed to regard this flight as a feat of individual daring rather than a carefully thought out government project. The object of the flight was attained; that of gaining information concerning the seaplanes and their operation over long distances at sea and that of adding to the prestige of naval aviation and the Navy at large. And although we were disappointed that all three of the seaplanes did not reach Lisbon, more valuable information concerning the seaplanes themselves was obtained by the failure of NC-3 and NC-1 than by the success of NC-4.

(Times are Greenwich Mean Civil)

		Time	*Distance sea miles*	*Elapsed time in air*
Left	Rockaway	2.02 p.m.— 8 May		
Arrived	At sea—off Chatham	6.53 p.m.— 8 May	284	4 hrs. 51 min.
Left	Chatham	1.07 p.m.—14 May		
Arrived	Halifax	5.10 p.m.—14 May	355	4 hrs. 03 min.
Left	Halifax	12.53 p.m.—15 May		
Arrived	Newfoundland	9.39 p.m.—15 May	474	6 hrs. 23 min.
Left	Newfoundland	10.05 p.m.—16 May		
Arrived	Horta Fayal	1.23 p.m.—17 May	1,206	15 hrs. 13 min.
Left	Horta Fayal	12.39 p.m.—20 May	153	
Arrived	Ponta Delgada, San Miguel	2.24 p.m.—20 May	153	1 hr. 45 min.
Left	Ponta Delgada	10.18 a.m.—27 May		
Arrived	Lisbon	8.01 p.m.—27 May	786	9 hrs. 43 min.
Left	Lisbon	5.29 a.m.—30 May		
Arrived	Mondego River, Portugal	7.21 a.m.—30 May	134	1 hr. 52 min.
Left	Mondego River, Portugal	1.38 p.m.—30 May		
Arrived	Ferrol, Spain	4.47 p.m.—30 May	237	3 hrs. 09 min.
Left	Ferrol, Spain	6.27 a.m.—31 May		
Arrived	Plymouth, England	1.26 p.m.—31 May	487	6 hrs, 29 min.
		Total............	4,116	53 hrs. 58 min.

NOTE: On water 2 hours and 23 minutes not included in elapsed time.

CREWS

NC-3

Comdr. J. H. Towers, USN, Commanding
Comdr. Holden C. Richardson, C. C., USN.
Lieut. Comdr. Robert A. Lavender, USN.
Lieut. David McCulloch, USNRF.
Boatswain Lloyd R. Moore, USN.

NC-4

Lieut. Comdr. Albert C. Read, USN, Commanding
1st Lieut. Elmer E. Stone, USCG.
Lieut. James L. Breese, USNRF.
Lieut. Walter Hinton, USN.
Ensign Herbert C. Rodd, USNRF.
CMM Eugene S. Rhoads, USN.

NC-1

Lieut. Comdr. P. N. L. Bellinger, USN, Commanding.
Lieut. Comdr. Marc. A. Mitscher, USN.
Lieut. Louis T. Barin, USNRF.
Lieut. (j.g.) Harry Sadenwater, USNRF.
Machinist Rasmus Christensen, USN.
CMM (A) C. I. Kesler, USN.
Lieut. Comdr. R. E. Byrd, USN., and Lieut. J. B. Rhodes, USNRF., went as far as Newfoundland.

The Homing Pigeon

A Fearless Messenger in Time of War

By Lieut. (j.g.) J. J. McAtee, R. F.

ALTHOUGH a descendant of that feathered family which has furnished the whole world with a commonly accepted emblem of peace, the homing pigeon of today has proven itself to be really a bird of war, as the part it has played recently on land and water, has been of great military value to the governments it served.

The pigeon has established itself not only as a carrier that can be trusted to faithfully and fearlessly perform its mission but it delivers its messages with a speed almost equal to that of the wireless.

The heliograph, telephone, telegraph and wireless—the principal means of communication used during the recent war—all have one great weakness. Messages so transmitted are as clear to a watchful enemy as they are to the friends for whom the message is intended. Special corps of experts for the interception and interpretation of enemy messages were maintained by all of the belligerents and much important data was secured by both sides concerning location and intentions of enemy units. Carrier pigeons alone carried messages silently, swiftly and directly to the parties for whom they were intended, and enemy bullets dispatched to interrupt their flight seldom stopped these faithful couriers.

In the Navy the pigeon did important scout duty along the sea coast and proved a sure means of communication between air pilots and their stations. They were also carried by practically every patrol boat operated in European waters, and in many instances were instrumental in bringing aid that saved the lives of crews after their ships had been torpedoed by submarines.

The establishing of pigeon lofts at the various naval air stations was not seriously considered until February, 1918. Since that time fourteen lofts at the following stations have been completed and equipped with pigeons: Chatham, Rockaway Beach, Bay Shore, Cape May, Anacostia, D. C.; Hampton Roads, Morehead City, Miami, Key West, Pensacola, San Diego, Coco Solo, and Great Lakes.

Upwards of 600 pigeons were trained at the above mentioned stations and previous to the signing of the armistice there were more than 2,500 trained pigeons in the U. S. Naval Air Service abroad. These birds performed admirably when it is considered that they were all in their first year of training.

An idea of their efficiency might be gained from the records of the work done by the birds at Pauillac, where a complement of seventy-eight birds delivered 698 messages in one month—219 of these messages being of an urgent nature, sent by seaplanes down at sea.

Since the historic occasion on which a dove carried to Noah unmistakable evidence that the flood was subsiding and land and a safe harbor were not far distant, the pigeon has been proving its utility and versatility and its unquestioned ability to serve man in many extremities. There is a case on record of a navy air pilot doing patrol duty on the coast of France who completely lost his bearings when his compass failed him. After aimlessly wandering around for some time, this pilot thought of the two pigeons he carried. He quickly liberated the birds and followed them in their flight. They guided him safely back to his station.

Messages to be carried by pigeons are written on small blocks of onion skin paper. The message is then rolled into a small pellet and inserted in a light aluminum container which is strapped to the bird's leg. As the pigeon needs light to guide his flight it is not possible to use them at night nor in heavy, foggy weather. The distance a bird will accomplish depends largely upon its individual training and capability. In the second year of training, however, a bird should be able to travel up to 500 miles with accuracy, and 200 miles has been accomplished by birds in their first year of training.

The very nature and importance of the work entrusted to these winged messengers has given them numerous opportunities to distinguish themselves in the military and naval service. Hundreds of stories of their accomplishments have been recorded and many of the birds have won world wide fame. A few examples of the nature and value of the work may be determined by the following extracts from records on file in the Navy Department.

One instance is that ensuing when a British patrol boat was attacked early one morning by a German submarine. The vessel was torpedoed and rapidly began to sink. The skipper, however, had time to write a brief message, roll up the scrap of paper and attach it to the leg of a pigeon before the shattered craft sank under his feet. Just in time he threw the bird into the air and within the next minute he was struggling in the water clinging to a bit of wreckage. By this time the U-boat had risen to the surface the crew quickly discovered the pigeon and opened fire on it with rifles. The skipper, struggling in the water saw that the bird had been hit and gave up all hope of rescue.

However, he failed to consider the plucky nature of the bird and the tremendous power of its homing instincts. Some 20 miles away the pigeon alighted on the deck of a patrolling destroyer, its silvery gray plumage speckled with blood, one of its wings crippled and the tail feathers completely shot away. The bird was quickly carried to the commander of the destroyer who took the message from its leg and three minutes later the destroyer was speeding to the rescue, with her wireless filling the air with news of the enemy's location. In less than an hour the survivors of the sunken vessel were safe on board the rescuing ship. A game little bird had saved their lives. The pigeon later recovered from its wounds and resumed its place on the "active" list.

A seaplane of the Royal Naval Air Service got into trouble at sea and tossed its pigeons into the air at 7.24 a. m. The pigeon reached its loft at 8.00 a. m. with this message: "Am down off North Goodwin; light vessel; very rough sea." At 8.04 a patrol boat was on its way to the rescue.

On another occasion a pigeon reached its loft carrying the following message: "Down at Nieuport; compression tap blown off; radiator empty; filling up with salt water and will return as soon as possible." Another seaplane was sent to the rescue but was unable to discover the disabled machine. Five days later the seaplane's second pigeon homed with a message written in German, dispatched from the German seaplane station at Zeebrugge. It read: "English machine and pilot Cooke are prisoners. Observer Crothers dead."

At a certain seaplane station in Flanders early one morning a pigeon was seen to dive from the clouds and enter its loft hurriedly. The thin piece of tissue paper carried in the small cylinder on its leg read: "Potvin, shot down 10 miles N. N. E. Nieuport; one Hun down; my tanks shot; French destroyer on its way; send fighters. Graham."

At the seaplane station this meant

that Flight Lieut. R. Graham, who had left that morning on special patrol duty, had encountered enemy aircraft, that a seaplane had been shot down whose pilot was, he thought, Flight Lieutenant Potvin, that a German machine had also been shot down; that shots had pierced his own tanks; that a French torpedo-boat destroyer was approaching, and that more combat seaplanes were needed at once.

Five minutes later another pigeon homed with this message: "Shot landed O. K.; down 10 N. N. E. Nieuport Potvin. I shot one down but he did not crash. My tanks are no good, can't climb. French T. B. D. on its way, send more fighters quick. Graham."

Eighteen minutes later a third pigeon homed with a message from another member of the patrol. "Am shot down, hit in tank and radiator. Rogers dead. I am unhurt. Please send help at once. Paine."

This was from Flight Lieut. L. I. Paine whose observer was Lieut. Rogers.

Seven minutes later a fourth pigeon reached the air station with this message: "Machine turning over to port. Have jettisoned everything; am on wing tip; sea calm; machine has seemingly steadied. Nothing in sight. I think the machine will float for a long time. Land bus just made one circuit, but I don't think he saw me. If machine sinks I will swim to buoy close by. Rogers was killed instantly, wound in head. Paine."

Two seaplanes were sent to guide a French torpedo boat destroyer to the scene. They located the damaged plane 8 miles from Nieuport. They had just reached it when a German submarine and four German torpedo boat destroyers arrived and shortly after a French motor lighter and a small craft, zigzagging madly to avoid the courtesies of the German submarine.

Lieutenant Graham reached home safely with his machine, which was taken in tow by one of the patrol vessels.

That ends the story. It all happened in one-half hour and a few feathered friends of the human flyers had carried the messages that made the rescue possible.

"THE EYES OF THE NAVY"

Oh, it's up thru the clouds,
And away from the crowds,
We go flying on the wings of the morn,
And the sun, he's just risin'
O'er the eastern horizon,
And we feel we are glad we were born.

With the engine a-roarin;
Away we go soarin'
And the exhaust sparks go flying by.
The wires all a-singin'
Up we go swingin'
Just to say how-de-do to the sky.

The earth like a picture,
A beautiful mixture,
Of yellow and purple and gold.
As pure and clean,
As an idealist's dream
Or the heart of a prophet of old.

Hidden the squalor,
The filth and the wallor,
Of man-made cities and towns.
It's good to be there,
In the rarified air,
Far from such sights and sounds.

And all that's betwixt us,
And a fall that will fix us,
Is spruce and some doped cotton cloth.
But it's the game, it's the game,
And honor and fame,
That attract like the flame to the moth.

We came from the hills,
The cities and mills,
And we put on Uncle Sam's green.
We're the Eyes of the Navy,
And if we don't go to Davy,
We'll tell of the sights we have seen.

—Ensign Alfred Curtis Wilson.

In Memoriam

HE died as he had willed to die,
A warrior of the embattled sky,
Who deemed his life's work hardly done
Had he not struck the godless Hun;
Struck with the ardent strength of youth
For Peace, for Liberty, for Truth,
For every gift that makes life dear,
That men might live devoid of fear,
That Mothers, with their babes in arms
Secure, may dwell, from wars' alarms.
That the young wife with eager care
Her spouse's evening hour prepare,
That children at their school or play
Be no more blood-mad German prey.

IN sweetest youth full well he died
Fighting to stem the Huns' red tide,
Offering as sacrifice to Heaven
The dearest gifts to mankind given—
His love's young dream, his school girl wife,
His boyhood's home; Oh! cruel strife
Calling the boy at manhood's brink
The fiery cup of War to drink.
Dauntless he grasped the fatal cup
Nor faltered to its deepest sup;
Hurling defiance at the foe,
The German beast, the World's worst woe.
Brave boy, he willed no better end,
Than home, than friends, than wife, defend.
To heed the call of Lafayette,
Of Noble France's bloody sweat
His fair young face upraised to Heaven
For these, resigned his life, God given.
Glad was his life, and great his death,
Nor faltered to his dying breath
Oh! gentle boy but light we weighed
The greater part your death portrayed
To our dull minds; while now we mourn
All that was you, unduly borne
To mysteries unfathomed deep
Where sleep our heroes—where you sleep,
Midst France's sons, in France's breast,
So doubly honored, doubly blest.

TO the far eons while the sun
His burning cycles daily run
Your name shall live in France's name,
America's undying fame,
In Belgium's dauntless few who stood
Checking the hell-loosed German brood;
Where Britain's sleepless bulwarks ride
Sweeping the Huns from every tide,
Where Italy, true to her fame,
Withstood the hordes of sin and shame,
Graved is your name—'mongst heroes all,
Who sprang like falcons to the call,
Of Country, Liberty, of Right
At the high dawn of Freedom's fight.
Sleep, gentle boy, where heroes sleep,
In France's earth—nor shall we weep,
Knowing the glory of your end
For France, for Lafayette our friend,
Bearing aloft the blazing brand
Of freedom from our Western Land.
Teaching the World with proud last breath,
America was true to death.

—SAMUEL W. B. HOSFORD.

Name	*Rank*	*Killed*	*Place*
Adams, Harry E.	Lieut. (j.g.)	Oct. 5, 1918	Pauillac
Adams, Hugh Jacobs	Ensign	May 5, 1919	Rockaway
Alden, Spencer T.	Ensign	May 4, 1918	Bay Shore
Anderson, Walfred A.	Electrician	Oct. 22, 1918	Abroad
Anderson, Wallace C.	Seaman	Oct. 30, 1918	
Andrews, J. F.	Ensign	July 13, 1918	Chatham
Ashley, J. Wm.	Lieut. (j.g.)	May 19, 1919.	
Baker, Claude A.	Seaman	Dec. 5, 1917	Moutchic
Barnett, Lester A.	Quartermaster	Aug. 22, 1918	Abroad
Barr, Chapin C.	Lieutenant	Sept. 29, 1918	Dunkirk
Barrett, T. W.	Quartermaster	July 1, 1917	France
Barron, Harold C.	Ensign	April 29, 1919	Cape May
Barry, E. B.	Ensign	August, 1918	St. Trojan
Behan, Wm. J.	Student Officer	July 12, 1918	Bay Shore
Bell, A. M.	Ensign	Feb. 28, 1919	Hampton Rds.
Bell, C. A.		Feb. 23, 1918	Fishermans Island
Bennett, J. W.	Boatswain	March 2, 1918	Cape May
Bennett, Thos. Henry	Quartermaster	Oct. 20, 1918	Rockaway
Berger, Frederick G. B.	Lieut. (j.g.)	April 29, 1918	Cape May
Bergin, Louis J.	Ensign	Sept. 15, 1918	Ravenna, Italy
Bishop, Donald G.	Student Officer	Feb. 16, 1919	Miami
Blair, A. B. Jr.	Ensign	June 18, 1918	Pensacola
Boorse, A. L.	Ensign	Aug. 21, 1918	Brest
Bose, Herman	Quartermaster	Nov. 23, 1917	Pensacola
Bournique, Joy C.	Ensign	Sept. 24, 1918	Pensacola
Brice, Milton D.	Ensign	Jan. 22, 1919	Pensacola
Buchanan, J. S.		April 27, 1919	
Burnes, John Irving	Quartermaster	Oct. 24, 1918	Liverpool
Butler, Thos. J.	Lieutenant	Aug. 21, 1918	
Campbell, Dale Vern	Ensign	Aug. 22, 1918	Abroad
Canfield, Herbert F.	Student Officer	Aug. 26, 1918	Miami, Fla.
Catchpole, Harry G.	Ensign	Sept. 14, 1918	Cape May
Cate, Lawrence H.	Ensign	Oct. 9, 1918	Pensacola
Chapin, M. J.	Quartermaiter	April, 4, 1918	Dunkirk, France
Childs, Wm. McKinley	Machinist	....	
Churchill, James L.	Student Officer	Aug. 29, 1918	Pensacola
Clark, James	Ensign	Jan. 28	Hampton Rds.
Clark, Robert F.	Ensign	Aug. 21, 1918	Brest, France
Clemens,t J. r.	Ensign	Oct. 8 1918	Paris
Coggins, Lawrence	Quartermaster	Aug. 11, 1918	Porto Corsini
Corey, Harold Bedford		May 5, 1919	Rockaway
Crailie, Charles C.	Ensign	May 27, 1918	
Crosscup, W. F.	Ensign	July 7, 1918	Moutchic
Crowe, Edmund J.	Seaman	Dec. 26, 1917	Pensacola
Davidson, Delozier	Ensign	Aug. 22, 1918	
Delahanty, Michael		Feb. 23	Fishermans Island.
Douthitt, Raymond Edwin	Gunner	Sept. 21, 1918	Gallup's Island
Draper, W. M. Thos.	Ensign	Mar. 25, 1918	Pensacola
Dyer, Jay N.	Ensign	May 17, 1919	Pensacola
Easterwood, J. L.	Lieut. (j.g.)	May 20, 1919	Coco Solo
Eaton, Thos. Windell	Student Officer	April 5, 1918	Key West
Ehrke, A. E.	Machinist	July 15, 1919	League Is., Phila.
Eichelberger, Ed. C.	Quartermaster	Feb. 27, 1918	
Ellis, Albert E. K.	Lieut. (j.g.)	July 25, 1919	Coco Solo
Elwood, Samuel W.	Student Officer	Sept. 10, 1918	Mass. Inst. of Tech.
Evans, G. B.	Ensign	May 31, 1918	Miami, Fla.
Fazio, Chas. J.	Machinist	Mar. 16, 1918	Pensacola
Fisher, Raymond R.	Machinist	....	Dundee, Scotland
Fenton, Jos. J.		Aug. 13, 1918	Pensacola
Fisher, Lorm H.	Student Officer	Sept. 21, 1918	Chelsea
Flieshman, Charles	Electrician	Aug. 2, 1917	Bay Shore
Fowler, Francis M.	Ensign	May 17, 1919	Pensacola
Fraley, Guy B.	Student Officer	Aug. 12, 1918	Pensacola
Frothingham, Philip B.	Ensign	Sept. 14, 1918	St. Inglevert
Ganster, J.	Quartermaster	May 18, 1918	Dunkirk
Gendran, B. Lamcon	Gunner	Mar. 29, 1918	Miami, Fla.
Gerhardy, Theo. W.	Student Officer	Nov. 23, 1918	Key West
Gibbs, John F.	Lieutenant	Oct. 27, 1918	Schoondijk
Goggins, James L.	Quartermaster	Aug. 11, 1918	Porto Corsini
Goldman, P.	Quartermaster	August, 1918	Flanders Coast
Goodspeed, Pearson, Jr.	Student Officer	Oct. 7, 1918	Chelsea
Grassel, A. G.	Gunner	May 20, 1919	
Gray, James J.	Student Officer	Jan. 18, 1919	Pensacola

Name	*Rank*	*Killed*	*Place*
Gustav	Machinist	May 19, 1919	
Halstead, R. H.	Quartermaster	July 31, 1917	France
Hammann, Charles H.	Ensign	June 14, 1919	Hampton Roads
Hammond, Kensey J., Jr.	Student Officer	Mar. 21, 1919	Pensacola
Hartel, Orrin Francis	Machinist	Aug. 21, 1918	Turino, Italy
Harvie, L. S.	Boatswain	Feb. 28, 1918	Ile Tudy
Herr, Hugo Julius	Quartermaster	Oct. 13, 1918	Calais
Hobby, Roy Law	Machinist	Feb. 28, 1919	Norfolk
Hogan, John Lee	Quartermaster	....	Whiddy Island
Holley, Miles Henry	Quartermaster	Aug. 22, 1918	St. Trojan
Homer, Joseph W.	Ensign	Nov. 9, 1918	London
Honeywell, A. D.	Ensign	Jan. 18, 1919	Pensacola
Hosken, Wm. Stanley	Machinist	Oct. 27, 1918	Rockaway
Hough, F. W.	Quartermaster	Mar. 13, 1918	Ayr, Scotland
Howard, John G.		April 27, 1919	Pensacola
Hynson, Henry P.		Feb. 25, 1919	
Johnson, Claude Raymond	Quartermaster	Oct. 22, 1918	Killingholme
Jones, Merwyn Clynder	Student Officer	Aug. 1, 1919	Key West
Jilian, Wm. H.	Student Officer	Oct. 28, 1918	Calais
Jaegle, Wm. C., Jr.	Machinist	Aug. 25, 1918	Rockaway
Jones, Thos. Owen	Ensign	Sept. 24, 1918	Pensacola
Keadass, C. S.	Ensign	Feb. 27, 1918	Dunkerque,
Kneeland, Leonard L.	Quartermaster	Aug. 20, 1918	St. Trojan
Kemp, Edward C.	Machinist	July 1, 1918	France
Krueger, Chas. Edward	Electrician	July 31, 1918	Moutchic
Lamport, Nathan H.	Seaman	Sept. 3, 1918	France
Lee, Benjamin	Ensign	Oct. 12, 1918	Dundee, Scotland
Lenderman, W. B., Jr	Lieutenant	Oct. 16, 1918	Calais
Lingard, Eric	Ensign	Oct. 29, 1918	Coco Solo
Lohges, Robert J.	Ensign	Oct. 12, 1918	Pensacola
McCalla, R. C.	Student Officer	May 10, 1918	Pensacola
McCarthy, Thos. Carroll	Ensign	Sept. 25, 1918	Pensacola
McCormack, Ralph R.	Ensign	Feb. 7, 1919	Pensacola Bay
McCormick, A. A.	Lieutenant	Sept. 29	Calais
McKinney, Dooley O.	Machinist	Oct. 4, 1918	Pensacola
McKinnon, Thos. Neil	Ensign	Aug. 20, 1918	Dunkerque, France
McLean, James Thos.		Oct. 5, 1918	Phila., Pa.
MacLeisch, Kenneth	Lieutenant	Oct. 14, 1918	Abroad
McMahon, Ambrose B.	Student Officer	Oct. 28, 1918	Calais
McMeekin, James W.	Machinist	Oct. 10, 1918	Paris
MacNaughton, L. M.	Ensign	Mar. 13, 1918	Hampton Roads.
McVeigh, John J.	Quartermaster	Aug. 23, 1918	St. Trojan
Mandville, Garrett T.	Student Officer	August 12, 1918	Pensacola
Manley, G. E.	Machinist	Aug. 22, 1917	Tours, France
Marshborn, D.	Quartermaster	May 18	Dunkirk
Martin, Van M.	Student Officer	Oct. 21, 1918	Seattle
Mayo, Henry Carl	Machinist	Oct. 31, 1918	Paris
Miller, Samuel, Jr.	Quartermaster	Oct. 21, 1918	Bay Shore
Mingle, D. B., Jr.	Ensign	Feb. 7, 1919	Pensacola
Monteith, R. Howard	Lieutenant	Aug. 25, 1919	Sea Girt, N. J.
Mutty, Louis L.	Student Officer	July 9, 1918	Miami, Fla.
Murphy, J. G.	Ensign	Oct. 18, 1918	
Murphy, Thos. L.	Ensign	Sept. 15, 1918	Ravenna, Italy
Nelms, Frank, Jr.	Lieutenant	Oct. 27, 1918	Schoondijk
Nelson, Clarence A.	Machinist	Mar. 20, 1918	Abroad
Newman, Frederick A.	Machinist	Aug. 24, 1918	New York
Nichols, A. L.	Ensign	Aug. 21, 1918	Turino, Italy
Norman, Harvey C.	Lieutenant	Oct. 22, 1918	Bruges, Ghent
O'Day, Daniel H.		May 19, 1919	
O'Gorman, Matthew E.	Quartermaster	Aug. 20, 1918	Dunkirk
Ostridge, C. L.	Lieut. (j.g.)	May 19, 1919	
Page, P. W.	Ensign	Dec. 17, 1917	Felixstowe
Palmer, Clyde N.	Ensign	Sept. 14, 1918	St. Inglevert
Parker, Bradstreet	Student Officer	Sept. 21, 1918	Mass. Inst. of Tech.
Percival, Charles Edward	Student Officer	July 17, 1918	Miami, Fla.
Perkins, Reger Conant	Seaman	Mar. 14, 1918	Key West
Pero, Donald C.	Machinist	Aug. 25, 1918	Rockaway
Perry, L. A.	Ensign	April 13, 1918	Moutchic
Petersen, Heter Andreas	Lieut. (j.g.)	Dec. 4, 1918	At Sea
Peterson, Carl C.	Ensign	Oct. 4, 1918	Pensacola
Poland, Clarence J.		July 12, 1918	
Potter, Stephen	Ensign	April 25, 1918	Felixstowe
Pou, Edwin S.	Ensign	Oct. 28, 1918	Abroad

Name	*Rank*	*Killed*	*Place*
Pulliam, Harold A.	Ensign	April 4, 1919	
Read, C. S.	Ensign	Feb. 26, 1918	Dunkirk
Ritchie, David		May 7, 1919	Charleston, S. C.
Redman, Wm. Frederick	Machinist	Aug. 21, 1918	Brest
Reed, Curtis S.	Ensign	Feb. 27, 1918	Dunkirk
Reed, Chas. E.	Ensign	Aug. 16, 1918	Castletown-Berehaven
Reid, Geoffrey L.			
Rice, Charles B.	Student Officer	Sept. 27, 1918	Dunwoodie, Minn.
Richardson, Jesse	Machinist	Aug. 22, 1918	St. Trojan
Richter, George	Quartermaster	Dec. 7, 1917	Hampton Roads
Richardson, Robert E.	Electrician	Oct. 11, 1918	Killingholme
Ries, Fred E.	Ensign	Nov. 16, 1918	Calais
Riley, Frank William	Ensign	Oct. 12, 1918	Miami, Fla.
Ritchie, Davie		May 17, 1919	Charleston
Roben, D. B.	Captain	Oct. 27, 1918	Calais
Robinson, H. A.	Ensign	Mar. 31, 1919	Pensacola
Roehrig, Harold L.	Ensign	July 15, 1919	League Is., Phila.
Rutledge, Daune Horton	Ensign	Feb. 7, 1919	Pensacola
Saufly, R. C.	Lieutenant	June 9, 1916	Pensacola
Saunders, Stewart Benton	Ensign	Sept. 24, 1918	Pensacola
Schneider, Anthony	Student Officer	Sept. 22, 1918	Chelsea, Mass.
Scherding, Walter Tips	Student Officer	Oct. 20, 1918	Seattle
Scott, W. R.	Quartermaster	Mar. 17, 1918	Chelsea, Mass.
Sergai, Bennett	Machinist	Oct. 11, 1918	Abroad
Skaggs, A. D.	Quartermaster	Feb. 28, 1918	Ile Tudy
Smith, Edward A., Jr.	Student Officer	April 30, 1918	France
Smith, Winthrop F.	Ensign	Oct. 10, 1918	Bay Shore
Soulder, H. G.	Boatswain.	July 15, 1919	League Is., Phila.
Souther, A. F.	Lieutenant	July 19, 1918	Narragansett Bay
Sparkes, James A.	Student Officer	Oct. 30, 1918	Seattle, Wash.
Sprague, Wm. Griffith	Ensign	Oct. 26, 1918	Ile Tudy, France
Stoker, Ellsworth W.	Machinist	Aug. 20, 1918	
Stoltz, M. L.	Lieutenant	June, 1915	Pensacola
Sturtevant, A. D.	Ensign	Feb. 18, 1918	Weymouth, Eng.
Sturtevant, Eldred	Midshipman	Oct. 9, 1918	North Sea
Sylvester, Byrl E.	Student Officer	June 19, 1918	Pensacola
Talaska, Walter Paul	Student Officer	September 2, 1918	
Tate, James Alexander	Student Officer	Mar. 21, 1919	Pensacola
Taylor, C. W.	Lieutenant	Oct. 22, 1918	Bruges Ghent
Taylor, Ermond Albert	Student Officer	Feb. 19, 1919	Miami, Fla.
Taylor, Harvey John	Quartermaster	Oct. 18, 1918	Hartford, Conn.
Taylor, Roderick P.	Machinist	Oct. 10, 1918	Abroad
Terres, Hugh	Ensign	Aug. 21, 1918	Turino, Italy
Terrier, Stewart McD.	Ensign	Feb. 23,	Fishermans Island
Thomas, R. H.	Machinist	July 25, 1919	Coco Solo
Tibbetts, Russell D.	Ensign	Oct. 8, 1918	Cape May
Timkham, Edward I.	Ensign	Mar. 30, 1919	Ravenna, Italy
Tolnas, Trygva J.	Ensign	Dec. 31, 1918	Pensacola
Topp, Augustus	Student Officer	Aug. 12, 1918	Pensacola
Tornes, Bernhard		April 27, 1919	
Treble, Hector Wm.	Student Officer	Oct. 1, 1918	Chelsea, Mass.
Truex, Eldone H.	Ensign	Mar. 31, 1919	Pensacola
Tucker, L. F.	Quartermaster	Aug. 1918	St. Trojan
Tyson, C. McC.	Lieut. (j.g.)	Oct. 11, 1918	Killingholme
Van Kirk, Dean R.	Ensign	May 1, 1917	Pensacola
Vath, Earl J.	Electrician	Aug. 20, 1918	St. Trojan
Velie, H. G.	Quartermaster	May 7, 1918	Scotland
Vornauer, Glenwyn A.	Student Officer	Nov. 2, 1918	
Walker, Donald	Ensign	April 7, 1919	Key West
Walker, Guy Adler	Ensign	Oct. 19, 1918	Bay Shore
Wats, Earl Joseph	Electrician	Aug. 22, 1918	St. Trojan
Weddell, T. M.	Quartermaster	Mar. 7, 1918	Le Croisic, Fr.
Weed, Walker	Ensign		
Weigel, Carl Herrmann	Ensign	Mar. 31, 1919	
Wells, Harry M.	Seaman	Aug. 6, 1917	Huntington, L. I.
Wigmore, John	Student Officer	Jan. 18, 1911	Pensacola
Willmoth, George T.	Seaman	Oct. 30, 1918	
Wilcox, DeWitt G.	Student Officer	Aug. 29, 1918	Pensacola
Wissman, Frederick A.	Quartermaster	Oct. 28, 1918	Abroad
Zeller, George J.	Machinist	June 28, 1918	

NOBLE E. IRWIN,
CAPTAIN, U. S. N.
Supervisor of the Naval Reserve Flying Carps and Director of Naval Aviation from May 1917 to April 1919.

THOMAS T. CRAVEN,
CAPTAIN, U. S. N.
Supervisor of the Naval Reserve Flying Corps and Director of Naval Aviation from Apil 1919.

ALLEN, FRED S.

Lieutenant

Pelham Manor, N. Y. Marblehead, Boston, RFC, Canada; Washington, Pensacola. USNRF. N. A. No. 143. HTA.

ARNOLD, DAVID B.

Lieutenant

1559 Beacon St., Brookline, Mass. Key West. USNRF. N. A. No. 448. HTA.

BAKER, CHAS. S.

Lieutenant

4925 Conduit Road, Washington, D. C. Pensacola, Great Lakes, Bureau of Operations, Wash., D. C. USNRF. N. A. No. 191. HTA.

BARIN, LOUIS T.

Lieutenant

802 E. Ash St., Portland, Oregon. Pensacola, Miami, Hampton Roads. USNRF. N. A. No. 56. HTA.

BELL, COLLEY W.

Lieutenant

Colorado Bldg., Wash., D. C. Rockaway Beach, Aviation Aide, Third Naval District. USNRF. N. A. No. 106. LTA.

BLAIR, WILLIAM M.

Lieutenant

4830 Drexel Blvd., Chicago, Ill. Great Lakes, Hampton Roads, Pensacola, N. Bomb. Gr. USNRF. N. A. No. 436. HTA.

BLASIAR, ARTHUR F.

Lieutenant

Guilford, N. Y. Pensacola, Columbia University, Great Lakes. LTA and HTA.

(F)
BRISCOE, BENJ.

Commander

709 W. Main St., Jackson, Mich. Naval Aide to Capt. H. I. Cone, Foreign Waters. USN.

BRUSH, GRAHAM M

Lieutenant

Greenwich, Conn. West Palm Beach, Huntington, L. I. USNRF. N. A. No. 79. HTA.

CHENEY, CHARLES C.
Lieutenant
241 Walden Drive, Glencoe, Ill. Pensacola, Fla. N. A. No. 1756. LTA.

CONEY, A. C.
Lieutenant
262 Berkeley St., Rochester, N. Y. Mass. Inst. of Tech., Pensacola. USNRF. HTA.

COOMBE, R. G.
Lieutenant
116 East 63rd St., New York City. Palm Beach, Huntington, Moutchic, Le Croisic, Milan, Calais, Eastleigh. USNRF. N. A. No. 92. HTA.

CORBETT, M. Q.
Lieutenant
Carnegie, Pa. Pensacola, Akron, Hampton Roads, Washington, Paimboeuf, USNRF. N. A. No. 549. LTA.

CORBIN, HORACE W.
Lieutenant
Grand Isle, Vt. Philadelphia, Brooklyn, Boston. USNRF. N. A. No. 621. HTA.

CUMMINGS, JAMES H.
Lieutenant
Care of John B. Stetson Co., 5th & Montgomery Ave., Philadelphia, Pa. Bay Shore, L. I., Miami, USNRF. N. A. No. 377. HTA.

CURTIS, LAURENCE
Lieutenant
464 Beacon St., Boston, Mass. Newport News, Pensacola. HTA.

DICKERSON, JOHN S.
Lieutenant
Red Bank, N. J. Bureau C. & R., Naval Operations, Wash., Brunswick, Ga. USNRF.

DITMAN, ALBERT J.
Lieutenant
Englewood, N. J. Bay Shore, Experimental pilot, Bu. of Ordnance. Wash. USNRF. N. A. No. 103. HTA.

DOLE, PARR HORATIO
Lieutenant
Garrison, N. Y. Bu. St. Eng., Wash., D. C. London, Paris, Brest, Balloon Sect., A.E.F. at Paris, Fr. USNRF.

DONNELLEY, THORNE
Lieutenant
Thornehurst, Lake Forest, Ill. Bay Shore, Miami, Buffalo. USNRF. N. A. No. 109. HTA.

FALLON, NUGENT
Lieutenant Commander
67 William St., NYC. Newport News, Norfolk, Paris, Moutchic, Felixstowe, Washington, Pensacola, Boston. USNRF. N. A. No. 113. HTA.

FRY, SHERIDAN B.
Lieutenant
Columbia Club, 4 West 43rd St., New York City. Bay Shore, L. I.; Miami, Bureau Operations, Wash.; USNRF. N. A. No. 1092. HTA.

FULLER, PERCIVAL S.
Lieutenant
826 Main St., Racine, Wis. Buffalo, Pensacola, Coco Solo, C. Z. USNRF. N. A. No. 131. HTA.

GARTZ, RICHARD C.
Lieutenant
Pasadena, Cal. Akron, Cape May, Rockaway, Paimboeuf, Paris. N. A. No. 83½. LTA.

GOULD, ERL C. B.
Lieutenant
Woodland Road, Pittsburgh, Pa. West Palm Beach, Huntington. Bay Shore, Key West. USNRF. N. A. No. 68. HTA.

GREENE, PAUL A.
Lieutenant
Rogers, Texas. Pensacola, Akron, Hampton Roads, Washington, D. C., Rockaway Beach, New York. USNRF. N. A. No. 612. LTA.

GUGGENHEIM, H. F.
Lieutenant Commander
870 Madison Ave., New York City. H. Q. in Paris, London, Rome; Northern Bombing Gr., R.A.F.; duty at most foreign N. A. Stations. USNRF. HTA.

HAMLEN, W. L.
Lieutenant
1563 Mission St., San Francisco, Cal. Akron, Rochefort, Paris, Paimboeuf, Washington. N. A. No. 101. LTA.

HOLMES, EARLE F.
Lieutenant
U. S. Naval Air Station, Anacostia, D. C.

HOOD, DONALD T.
Lieutenant
77 Warren St., Brookline, Mass. Akron, USNRF. LTA.

IVES, PAUL F.
Lieutenant
167 Court St., Dedham, Mass. Pensacola, Calchot, Portland, Felixstowe, Killingholme, Eng. N. A. No. 195. HTA.

IVEY, JULIAN D.
Lieutenant
Boston, Ga. Mass. Inst. of Tech., Key West, Miami, N. A. No. 521. USNRF. HTA.

LEE, WILLIAM JUSTICE
Lieutenant
Box 378, Jacksonville, Fla. Construction & Inspection Officer, Buffalo, Wash., D. C., Philadelphia, Garden City, Rockaway. USNRF. HTA.

(*H*)
LOWREY, ALAN J.
Lieutenant
Harvard Club, 27 W. 44th St., New York City. Mass. Inst. of Tech., Pensacola, Washington. USNRF. N. A. No. 282. LTA.

(*O*)
McCANN, RICHARD H.
Lieutenant
E. Washington Lane, Germantown, Pa. R. F. C. Toronto, Can., Hampton Roads,Ft. Worth, Washington, Killingholme, Eng. USNRF. N. A. No. 147. HTA.

MASEK, WILLIAM
Lieutenant
4866 Winthrop Ave., Chicago, Ill. Pensacola, Bay Shore, Hampton Roads, Le Croisic, Fr. U.S.N. N. A. No. 58. LTA. HTA.

MAXFIELD, L. H.

Commander

627 Goodrich Ave.,* St. Paul, Minn. Pensacola, Akron, Paimboeuf, Fr., Washington. U. S. N. N. A. No. 17. LTA. HTA.

MOLONEY, JOHN F.

Lieutenant

316 W. 93rd St., New York City. C. O. at Guipavas and Whiddy Island. U.S.N.

NAYLOR, HENRY R.

Lieutenant

42 East 78th St., New York City. Bay Shore, Miami, Wash., D. C. USNRF. N. A. No. 242. HTA.

(K)
OTIS, J. S.

Lieutenant

1709 Prairie Ave., Chicago, Ill. Yale Unit No. 2, Buffalo, N. Y., Pensacola; Sq. 1. Northern Bombing Gr. USNRF. N. A. No. 127. HTA.

PIERCE, THOMAS J. H.

Lieutenant

1086 Narragansett Blvd., Cranston, R. I. Squantum, Mass., Pensacola, Hampton Roads, Coco Solo, C. Z. USNRF. N. A. No. 169. HTA.

PULZ, JOHN LEGGETT

Lieutenant

88 Broad St., Boston, Mass. Mass. Inst. of Tech., Pensacola, Fla.

READ, A. C.

Lieutenant Commander

Comdr. NC-4 Trans-Atlantic Flight. USN. N. A. No. 24. HTA.

(H)
REEMELIN, C. B.

Lieutenant

3061 Cleinview Ave., East Hill, Cincinnati, Ohio. Mass. Inst. of Tech., Pensacola, Bureau Navig. (Training Section). HTA.

RICHARDSON, A. B.

Lieutenant

2023 Collingwood Ave., Toledo, O. Mass. Inst. of Tech., Hampton Roads, Pensacola. USNRF. N. A. No. 1886. HTA.

SARGENT, SAMUEL W.
Lieutenant
360 Penn Rd., Wynnwood, Pa. Mass. Inst. of Tech. In charge of Receiving Ship. USNRF.

SHUMWAY, CARL E.
Lieutenant
25 Bellevue Ave., Melrose, Mass. Akron, Rockaway Beach, Queenstown, Ire., Castletown, Ire., RAF. Balloon Base No. 16, Merifield, Cornwall, Eng. N. A. No. 319. LTA.

SMITH, CLINTON M.
Lieutenant
Box 14, Dighton, Mass. Miami, Pensacola, Montauk, Anacostia. HTA.

SMITH, F. M.
Lieutenant
Kittery, Maine. Bu. of C. & R., Wash., Officer in charge of Spruce Production for the Navy, Superintending Construction of Aircraft, Boston, Mass. USN.

SQUIRES, J. G. F.
Lieutenant
1125 Lexington Ave., New York City. Bu. Construction & Repair, Wash., D. C. Sup. Con. Aircraft, New York. USNRF.

STARK, EDWIN M.
Lieutenant Commander
365 Park Ave., Mansfield, O. Ass't to the Manager Naval Aircraft Factory, Navy Yard, Philadelphia. USNRF.

STONE, A. J.
Lieutenant Commander
℅ General Ordnance Co., 2 W. 43rd St., New York City. Washington, D. C., USNRF.

STRONG, ALEXANDER
Lieutenant
39 Court St., Dedham, Mass. Mass. Inst. of Tech., Pensacola, Hampton Roads, USNRF. N. A. No. 374. HTA.

TAYLOR, MOSELEY
Lieutenant
225 South St., Brookline, Mass. Newport News, Norfolk, Moutchic, Dunkirk, USNRF. N. A. No. 118. HTA.

TOWNSEND, R. S.
Lieutenant
6 Otis Place, Boston, Mass. Newport News, Hampton Roads, New London. USNRF. N. A. No. 119. LTA.

VORYS, JOHN M.
Lieutenant
441 East Town St., Columbus, Ohio. Palm Beach, Huntington, L. I., Moutchic, Hourtin, St. Raphael, Felixstowe, Hampton Rds., USNRF. N. A. No. 73. HTA.

WALKER, SAMUEL S.
Lieutenant
Garrison, New York. Le Croisic, Fr., Milan, It., St. Inglevert, Fr. USNRF. N. A. No. 86. HTA.

WALSH, J. HENRY
Lieutenant
166 Washington Ave., Prov., R. I. Squantum, Mass., Hampton Roads, Anacostia, D. C. USNRF. N. A. No. 525. HTA.

WALTON, MARK W.
Lieutenant
5737 Woodlawn Ave., Chicago, Ill. Hampton Roads, Moutchic, Fr., Bolsena, It. USNRF. N. A. No. 120. HTA.

WATKINS, R. A., Jr.
Lieutenant
307 East State St., Marshalltown, Iowa. Pensacola; USS L-4, Phila.; Instructor Columbia Univ.; Detroit, Packard; Bu. St. Eng. USNRF.

WHITEHOUSE, W. P., Jr.
Lieutenant
108 Vaughan St., Portland, Me. Paimboeuf, Brest, Paris, London. USNRF. N. A. No. 99. LTA.

WOLCOTT, ROBERT W.
Lieutenant
1819 West Washington Ave., Bethlehem, Pa. Mass. Inst. of Tech., Drill & Discipline Officer. USNRF.

ZUNINO, FRANK A., Jr.

495 8th Ave., Brooklyn, N. Y. RFC. Toronto, Can., Bay Shore, Mass. Inst. of Tech., Seattle, San Diego. N. A. No. 152. HTA.

ALLEN, F. H., Lieutenant, Kenilworth, Ill.

AMES, ALLAN W. Lieutenant, Care of James C. Sawyer, Andover, Mass. Palm Beach, Huntington, Bay Shore, Ft. Worth, Hampton Roads, Dayton, Washington, Paris, London, Tex. N. A. No. 67. R. F. HTA.

AMORY, FRANCIS I., JR., Lieutenant, 413 Commonwealth Ave., Boston, Mass. Toronto, Can., Marblehead, Boston Navy Yard, Op. Nav.. Hampton Roads, Pensacola, Bay Shore, Mass. Inst. of Tech. N. A. No. 144. HTA.

BABBITT, LEMAN L., Lieutenant, Houghton, N. Y. Pensacola, U. S. S. *Seattle*, San Diego, Rockefort, Paimboeuf, Gujon. N. A. No. 283. U. S. N. HTA.

BALCH, GORDON H., Lieutenant Commander, 120 Broadway, New York City. Washington, D. C., Bureau of Operations. R. F. N. A. No. 495. HTA.

BALDWIN, AUGUSTUS M., Lieutenant, 73 Remsen St., Brooklyn, N. Y. Treguier, Fr., Cotes du Nord (C. O.). R. F. N. A. No. 699. HTA.

BARNABY, R. S., Lieutenant, 257 Hamilton Ave., New Brighton, N. Y.

BARRY, EDWARD H., Lieutenant, 1412 Massachusetts Ave., Washington, D. C.

BARTLETT, H. T., Lieutenant. N. A. No. 21.

BATTLE, C. E., Lieutenant.

BEACH, CHARLES FREDERIC, Lieutenant, West Hartford, Conn. Huntington, Moutchic, Dunkirk, Escadrille de St. Pol. N. A. No. 75. HTA.

BIGGERS, ROBERT L., Lieutenant, Care of W. O. Biggers, Book Bldg., Detroit, Mich. Pensacola, Miami. R. F. N. A. No. 215. HTA.

BOETTCHER, ARTHUR H., Lieutenant, 1645 Jarvis Ave., Chicago, Ill. Bu. of Ordnance, Washington, D. C. R. F.

BRACKENRIDGE, GAVIN, Lieutenant, Church St., Richmond Hill, New York City. R. F. C. Canada, Bay Shore, Pensacola, Miami, Operations, Washington, D. C., Foreign Service. R. F. N. A. No. 155. HTA.

BREWER, A. DOUGLAS, Lieutenant. N. A. No. 103.

BRANSOME, E. D., Lieutenant, Engineers Club, Philadelphia, Pa. Pensacola. R. F. N. A. No. 286. HTA.

BRYANT, ROUTT A., Lieutenant, 735 Clarkson St., Denver, Colo. Mass. Inst. of Tech., Pensacola, Coco Solo, C. Z. N. A. No. 339, R. F. HTA.

BULMER, BAYARD T., Commander.

BUSH, RUFUS H., Lieutenant. N. A. No. 1774.

BYRD, R. E., Lieutenant Commander, Powhatan Hotel, Washington, D. C. N. A. No. 608.

CABOT, GODFREY LOWELL, Lieutenant, 16 Highland St., Cambridge, Mass. Marblehead, Hampton Roads. R. F. N. A. No. 1339. HTA.

CALLAN, J. L., Lieutenant Commander, 46 N. Pearl St., Albany, N. Y. N. A. No. 1442.

CAPEHART, WADLEIGH, Lieutenant Commander, N. A. No. 19.

CARTER, W. L., Lieutenant, 28 Concord Ave., Nashua, N. H.

CATHCART WM. L., Lieut. Commander.

CECIL, H. R., Lieut. Commander. N. A. No. 42

CHAMPLIN, F. M., Lieutenant, 2720 13th St., N. W., Washington, D. C.

CHASE, N. B., Lieutenant Commander, Brunswick. N. A. No. 37.

CHENEVERT, C. T., Lieutenant, 301 Grosse Points, Detroit, Mich.

CHILDS, W. G., Commander. N. A. No. 29.

CLAUSSEN, H. P., Lieutenant, 491 Commonwealth Ave., Boston, Mass.

CORRY, W. M., Jr., Lieut. Commander, New York City. N. A. No. 23.

COX, H. B., Lieutenant, 2035 Walnut St., Philadelphia, Pa.

CRAIG, DONALD B., Lieutenant, 20 Anderson Place, Buffalo, N. Y.

CRAIG, JOHN F., Lieutenant.

CULBERT, F. P., Lieutenant. U. S. N. N. A. No. 94.

CUTLER, ROGER, Lieutenant, Charles River, Mass. The Ledges. N. A. No. 371.

DAVIS, JOHN A., Lieutenant, 19 Hamilton Road, Brookline, Mass.

DAVISON, H. P., JR., Lieutenant, Huntington, L. I., N. Y.

DELANO, M. P., Lieutenant, 308 Prince St., West Newton, Mass. N. A. No. 104.

DEPEW, GANSON G., Lieutenant, 165 Summer St., Buffalo, N. Y. N. A. No. 121.

DEXSEY, WALTER SMITH, Lieutenant.

DICMAN, G. C., Lieut. Commander. N. A. No. 30.

DOHERTY, WM. E., 72 Pleasant St., Marblehead, Mass. N. A. No. 430.

DOMINICK, GAYER G., Lieutenant, Stamford, Conn. Akron, New London, Montauk, Rockaway. N. A. No. 982. LTA.

DOUBLEDAY, NELSON, Lieutenant, Oyster Bay, N. Y.

DOUGLAS, A. H., Lieut. Commander, Pensacola. N. A. No. 753.

DUCRAY, JULIAN A., Lieutenant.

EDDY, M. F., Lieutenant, 916 Jule St., St. Joseph, Mo. Mass. Inst. of Tech., Pensacola, Hampton, Roads. N. A. No. 1768. R. F. HTA.

EEKHOUT, BERNARD V., Lieutenant. N. A. No. 2447.

ELLYSON, T. G., Lieutenant Commander. N. A. No. 1.

EVANS, FRANK T. J., Commander. N. A. No. 26.

FARRELL, STEPHEN A., Lieutenant.

FEARING, G. R., JR., Lieut. Commander, 168 Beacon St., Boston, Mass.

FELLERS, W. M., Lieutenant. N. A. No. 2474.

FINCH, CARL E., Lieutenant, 2101 Alameda Ave., St. Louis, Mo. N. A. No. 472.

FISHER, R. A., Lieutenant, Markeen Hotel, Buffalo, N. Y.

FITZGERALD, J. P., Lieutenant.

FLOWER, H. C., JR., Lieutenant, Fidelity Nat'l Bank, Kansas City, Mo. Key West, Washington, Miami, Pensacola, Bay Shore, Squantum, San Diego. N. A. No. 1278. HTA.

FORRESTAL, J. V., Lieutenant, 28 Nassau St., New York City. R. F. C., Toronto, Bay Shore, Hampton Roads, Washington. N. A. No. 154. HTA.

FROST, H. H., Lieut. Commander.

FULLER, CHAS. F., Lieut., A. D. Club, Cambridge, Mass.

GATES, A. L., Lieut. Commander, Oakhurst, Clinton, Iowa. Palm Beach, Huntington, Northern Bomb. Group. N. A. No. 65. HTA.

GEARY, JOHN W., JR., Lieutenant, Chestnut Hill, Pa. N. A. No. 134.

GIBB, EDWIN D., Lieutenant, 6 Mascot St., Boston, Mass. Key West, U. S. N. N. A. No. 2494.

GILLESPIE, G. S., Lieut. Commander. N. A. No. 32.

GOLDTHWAITE, DUVAL R., Lieutenant. N. A. No. 146.

GORDON, HARRY B., Lieutenant, Bronxville, N. Y. N. A. No. 151.

GRIFFIN, V. C., Lieut. Commander. N. A. No. 41.

GRIFFIN, WALTER B., Lieut. Commander, 243 Saratoga St., E. Boston, Mass. N. A. No. 544.

GROW, HAROLD B., Lieutenant. N. A. No. 2354.

HAMMOND, EDWARD L., Lieutenant.

HART, HOWARD P., Lieutenant, 50 Buckingham St., Waterbury, Conn. Hampton Roads., Pensacola. U. S. N. N. A. No. 1997. HTA.

HAVENS, BECKWITH, Lieutenant, Aero Club of America, New York City. N. A. No. 524.

HAVILAND, WILLIS BRADLEY, Lieutenant. N. A. No. 577.

HERBSTER, V. D., Lieut. Commander. N. A. No. 4.

HINKAMP, CLARENCE N., Lieutenant.

HINTON, WALTER, Lieutenant. N. A. No. 135.

HOOPER, WM. E., Lieutenant, Tufts College, Medford Hillside, Mass.

HOYT, H. W., Lieutenant, Clearwater, Fla. Pensacola, Huntington, Hampton Roads, Akron. U. S. N. N. A. No. 545. LTA. HTA.

HUNT, JAMES STONE, Lieutenant.

HUTCHINS, HURD, Lieutenant, 131 Beacon St., Boston, Mass. N. A. No. 123.

IRELAND, ROBERT L., JR., Lieutenant, 11719 Lake Shore Blvd., Cleveland, O. N. A. No. 84.

JAMES, O. B., Lieutenant, 7 E. 70th St., New York City. Huntington, Operations, Washington, Bu. Navigations, Washington, U. S. N. Mission to Brazil. N. A. No. 80. R. F. HTA.

JAMESON, WILLIAM B., Lieutenant.

JOHNSON, C. Y., Lieut. Commander.

JOHNSON, E. F., Commander. N. A. No. 25.

KELLEY, MARTIN F., Lieutenant, 615 Lexington Ave., New York City.

KIELY, RALPH, Lieutenant., 116 East 54th St., New York City. N. A. No. 1076.

KIRKPATRICK, R. D., Lieutenant. N. A. No. 48.

KNOWLES, ROBERT W., Lieutenant, 5 Longfellow Park, Cambridge, Mass. Pensacola, Operations, Washington, D. C., R. F. N. A. No. 915. HTA.

LAMAR, L. V., Lieutenant, 514 N. Baylen St., Pensacola, Fla. N. A. No. 248.

LANDON, H. H., JR., Lieutenant, 19 E. 53rd St., New York City.

LANZSDOWN, Lieut. Commander, New York City. N. A. No. 105.

LEFTIN, EDW. H., Lieutenant.

LEIGHTON, BRUCE GARDNER, Lieut. Commander, Tunkhannock, Pa. Pensacola, Hampton Roads, Killingholme. U. S. N. N. A. No. 40. HTA.

LITTLE, CHARLES G., Lieutenant, 227 High St., Newburyport, Mass. Goodyear Tire & Rubber Co., Akron, Rochefort, Paimboeuf, St. Cyr. Guipavas, Fr., Cape May. N. A. No. 102. LTA

LOFTIN, EDW. H., Lieutenant.

LOFTIN, FRANK., Lieut. Commander.

LOHMANN, ALFRED P., Commander, Perkins Hill, Akron, Ohio. Naval Aircraft Factory, Navy Yard, Philadelphia. R. F. HTA.

LOVETT, ROBERT A., Lieut. Commander, Locust Valley, L. I., N. Y. West Palm Beach, Huntington, France. R. F. HTA.

LYNCH, FRANK R., Lieutenant, 25 Logan St., Lawrence, Kan.

MCADIE, ALEXANDER G., Lieut. Commander, Readville, Mass.

MCCOID, PAUL H., Lieutenant, 612 E. Monroe St., Mt. Pleasant, Iowa. N. A. No. 159.

MCCRARY, F. R., Commander.

MCCULLOCH, DAVID H., Lieutenant, 280 Madison Ave., New York City.

MCILWAINE, ARCHIBALD, Lieutenant, 682 Prospect Ave., Hartford, Conn.

MCNAMARA, J. F., Lieutenant, 32 Everett St., Arlington, Mass. N. A. No. 199.

MACDONALD, KENNETH B., Lieut. Commander, 69 Fordham Drive, Buffalo, N. Y.

MADDEN, WILSON E., Lieut. Commander.

MALE, A. E. J., Lieutenant, Stoneleigh Court, Philadelphia, Pa. Naval Aircraft Factory, Navy Yard, Philadelphia. R. F.

MASON, C. P., Lieutenant. N. A. No. 52.

MILLER, ROMAN J., Lieutenant.

MIMS, HARVEY B., Captain. N. A. No. 576.

MITCHELL, JOHN R., Lieutenant, 251 Fourth Ave., 14th Floor, New York City. Cape May, Northern Bomb. Group, Queenstown, Ire. R. F.

MITSCHER, M., Lieut. Commander. N. A. No. 33.

MOLONEY, JOHN F., Lieutenant, 316 W. 93rd St., New York City. Commanding, Guipavas, Fr., Whiddy Island, Ire.

MONFORT, J. C., Lieut. Commander, Mason, Ohio. Pensacola, Navy Dept., Washington, Great Lakes, Seattle, Rockaway. U. S. N. N. A. No. 35. HTA.

MOULTHROP, BURR, Lieutenant, 1270 11th Ave., San Francisco, Cal. Pensacola, Akron, Paimboeuf, Fr. R. F. N. A. No. 646. LTA.

MOUNT, DAVID A., Lieutenant, Bayhead, N. J. Annapolis, Key West, Rockaway, Aviation Aide Third District. R. F. N. A. No. 2065. LTA.

MURRAY, CECIL D., Lieutenant, 38 W. 51st St., New York City. Hampton Roads, Moutchic, Paris, St. Inglevert, London, U. S. S. *Texas*. R. F. HTA.

MUSTIN, H. C., Captain. N. A. No. 11.

NORFLEET, Lieut. Commander. N. A. No. 555.

O'CONNELL, WM. J., Lieutenant, 5712 Sixth Ave., Brooklyn, N. Y.

PALMER, EDWARD G., Lieutenant, 1619 Pearl St., Sioux City, Iowa.

PARIS, IRVING, Lieutenant, 124 E. 72nd St., New York City. Mass. Inst. of Tech., Hampton Roads, Pensacola. N. A. No. 317. HTA.

PARSONS, ROBERT D., Lieutenant, Care of The B. F. Goodrich Rubber Co., Akron, Ohio. Bu. of Construction & Repair, Washington, D. C. R. F.

PAUNACK, R. R., Lieut. Commander. N. A. No. 27.

PENNOYER, RALPH G., Lieutenant. N. A. No. 100½.

PETERSON, LOUIS A., Lieutenant, 152 Bird Ave., Buffalo, N. Y. Pauillac, France. USNRF.

PIKE, C. M., Lieutenant, Lubee, Maine. Squantum, Mass., Hampton Roads. N. A. No. 293. HTA.

POOR, ROGER M., Lieutenant, 777 Madison Ave., New York City. Bay Shore, Bu. Operations, Washington; London, Northern Bomb. Gr. N. A. No. 558. R. F. HTA.

PUMPELLY, H. A., Lieutenant, Owego Tioga Co., N. Y. Pensacola, Naval Aircraft Factory, Philadelphia. R. F N. A. No. 214. HTA.

RANDOLPH, R. D., Lieutenant, 20 Courtland Place, Houston, Texas. R F. C., Canada, New York, Boston, Washington, D. C., Hampton Roads, Pensacola, Foreign Waters, London, Eng. N. A. No. 161. HTA.

RECKFORD, JOHN KING, Lieutenant, 220 Fifth Ave., New York City. Naval Aircraft Factory. R. F.

REED, WM. F., JR., Lieutenant, 1238 N. 12th Ave., Pensacola. R. F.

REID, M. E., Lieutenant, Racquet Club, Philadelphia, Pa. N. A. No. 1825.

RICHARDSON, H. C., Commander. N. A. No. 13.

ROBERTS, CHARLES H. J., Lieutenant, 10 Franklin Place, Flushing, L. I. N. A. No. 240.

ROBERTS, WM. E., Lieutenant, Canton, N. C. Naval Aircraft Factory, Navy Yard, Philadelphia, Pa. R. F.

RODMAN, T. C., Lieut., care of Wm. A. Read & Co., Cor. Cedar and Nassau Sts., New York City. Volunteer Aerial Coast Patrol, Buffalo, New York, Pensacola. R. F. N. A. No. 1763.

RUTTAN, CHARLES E., Lieutenant. N. A. No. 64.

SCHIEFFELIN, JOHN JAY, Lieutenant, 5 E. 66th St., New York City. Buffalo, Moutchic, Fr., Felixstowe, Eng., Killingholme, Eng. R. F. N. A. No. 124. HTA.

SCOFIELD, H. W., Lieut. Commander, Morenci, Michigan. Buffalo, N. Y., Montauk, L. I. N. A. No. 28. U. S. N. HTA.

SHAMEL, FREDERICK R., Lieutenant.

SHEPPARD, H. B., Lieutenant, East Derry, N. H.

SIMPSON, FRANK, JR., Lieutenant, 670 Wilshire Place, Los Angeles, Cal. Pensacola, San Diego, Key West. R. F. N. A. No. 51. HTA.

SLATER, H. N., Lieutenant, Port Washington, L. I. N. Y. N. A. No. 329.

SMITH, G. W., JR., Lieutenant, 309 Hillside Ave., Jenkintown, Pa. Naval Aircraft Factory, Philadelphia, Pa. R. F.

SMITH, GORDON A., Lieutenant, 27 W. 44th St., New York City.

SMITH, K. R., Lieutenant, Patchogue, L. I., N. Y. Palm Beach, Huntington, Le Croisic, Moutchic, Ile Tudy, Paris, St. Inglevert, Fr. N. A. No. 87.

SPENCER, E. W., JR., Lieut. Commander, 109 Wade St. Highland Park, Ill. Pensacola, Squantum, San Diego. U. S. N. N. A. No. 20. HTA.

STAHL, RUDOLPHE, Lieutenant, Jackson, Mich.

STARR, F. C., Commander.

STIMSON, H. C., Lieutenant, Hollywood, King Co., Wash.

STONE, E. A., Lieutenant, Red Gate Apt., Norfolk, Va. Newport News, Hampton Roads, Calshot, Bembridge, Felixstowe, Eng., Anacostia. N. A. No. 138. HTA.

STONE, GEORGE LEWIS, Lieutenant, Care of Stone-Hoult Furniture Co., Grand Rapids, Mich. Pensacola.

STRADER, RALPH M., Lieutenant, 7057 No. Ashland Blvd., Chicago, Ill. Akron, Paris, Paimboeuf, Guipavas, Fr., Pensacola. N. A. No. 97. LTA.

STRICKLAND, G. B., Lieut., N. A. No. 34.

SWIFT, HENRY, Lieutenant, 4 Liberty Sq., Boston, Mass. Squantum, Toronto, Hampton Roads, Pensacola, Great Lakes. R. F. N. A. No. 149. HTA.

TAYLOR, CHARLES F., Lieutenant, 31 Clinton Ave., Montclair, N. J. In charge Aeronautical Engine Laboratory, Washington, D. C. USNRF.

THOMAS, WALLACE S., Lieutenant, 721 E. High St., Springfield, Ohio. Mass. Inst. of Tech., Seattle, Great Lakes, Pensacola. R. F. N. A. No. 2093. HTA.

TOD, R. E., Lieutenant.

TOWERS, J. H., Commander. U. S. N. N. A. No. 3.

TOWNSEND, JULIUS C., Lieut. Commander.

VAN DER VEER, N. R., Lieut. Commander. U. S. N.

VAN VALZAH, H. C., Lieut. Commander. Mass. Inst. of Tech., Miami, U. S. N. N. A. No. 665B.

VERNON, VICTOR, Lieutenant, Huntsville, Ala. N. A. No. 606.

WESSON, H., Lieutenant, 220 Maple St., Springfield, Mass.

WEYERBACKER, R. D., Lieut. Commander, U. S. N. N. A. No. 2126.

WHITE, NEWTON H., JR., Lieut. Commander, U. S. N. N. A. No. 2281.

WHITE, ROBERT W., Lieut., 17th Floor, 30 E. 42nd St., New York City. Rockaway, Pensacola, Washington, Abroad. LTA.

WHITEHOUSE, WM. PENN, JR., Lieutenant, 108 Vaughan St., Portland, Maine. Paimboeuf, Paris, Brest, Fr., London, Eng. R. F. N. A. No. 99. LTA.

WHITING, K., Commander, Washington, U. S. N. N. A. No. 16.

WILLCOX, WESTMORE, JR., Lieutenant, 516 Warren Crescent, Norfolk, Va. Newport News, Hampton Roads, Pensacola, Naval Operations, Washington, D. C. R. F. N. A. No. 136. HTA.

WILLIAMS, J. F., Lieutenant, Darien, Conn. Naval Aircraft Factory, Ass't Chief Engineer, Philadelphia Navy Yard.

WITMER, C. C., Lieut. Commander.

WORTHINGTON, J. P., Lieutenant, 3924 Morrison St. N. W., Washington, D. C. Mass. Inst. of Tech., Pensacola, Hampton Roads, Chatham, Bay Shore, Brunswick, Washington. HTA.

WRIGLEY, P. K., Lieutenant, 2466 Lake View Ave., Chicago, Ill. Great Lakes, R. F.

YOUNG, S. D., Lieutenant.

HS OVER MIAMI, FLORIDA.

THE preceding section and the one following comprise a grand muster of the commissioned personnel of the Corps. The Senior Division includes officers of the rank of Lieutenant or above, while the following embraces those of the rank of Lieutenant (junior grade) or below, and includes also student officers who were training as pilots or for commissions but who had not completed their course upon the signing of the armistice.

Of necessity the amount of data concerning each man has had to be brief, consequently only those facts have been given which would aid in recognition and enable the reader to communicate with other members of the Corps. No attempt could be made to include citations or other honors, or the particular capacities in which each man served. The order of this data is: name, rank, home address, stations served at, and whether he was in the heavier-than-air or lighter-than-air branch. Naval Aviator designation numbers have sometimes been given as they usually indicate the comparative length of a man's service.

To avoid confusion all addresses which were found to be incorrect have been omitted. This accounts for some apparent oversights in this respect.—EDITOR.

ABBOTT, BOYD R.
Ensign
224 Park St., Lancaster Ohio. Mass. Inst. Tech. Miami, Pensacola. HTA

ABBOTT, MAURICE J.
War Machinist
60 Howe St., Lewiston, Me. Pelham Bay, Columbia Univ., Rockaway, Wash., Key West. HTA.

ADAIR, EARLE T.
Student Officer
233 Marshall Ave., N. S., Pittsburgh, Pa. Mass. Inst. Tech., Akron, Ohio. LTA.

ADAMS, CHARLES H., Jr.
Lieut. (j.g.)
1365 Belle Ave., Lakewood, Cleveland, Ohio. Mass. Inst. Tech., Key West, Fla., Cape May, N. J. N. A. No. 457. HTA.

(*H*)
ADAMS, EUSTACE L.
Ensign
% H. D. Cabot, Newtonville, Mass. M. I. T., Bay Shore, Squantum, Key West, Cape May, Montauk, Wash. N. A. No. 447. HTA.

ADAMS, J. DUDLEY
Student Officer
614 Rector Ave., Little Rock, Ark. Mass. Inst. of Tech., Key West, Miami, Pensacola. HTA.

ADSIT, HAROLD C.
Student Officer
302 West Penn Street, Hoopeston, Illinois, Seattle, Wash. HTA.

AFFLECK, W. RUSSELL
Ensign
674 North Broadway, Yonkers, N. Y. Mass. Inst. of Tech., Pensacola, Miami, Moutchic (Fr.). N. A. No. 705. HTA.

AICHER, FRED, Jr.
Ensign
2501 Ridge Road, Berkeley, Cal. Mass. Inst. Tech., Key West, Miami, Pensacola. N. A. No. 1771. HTA.

AICHER, JOHN W. H.
Student Officer
Hollywood, California. Dunwoody Inst., Minn.; Miami. HTA.

ALBERTSON, R. D.
Lieut. (j.g.)
125 Main St., Geneva, N. Y. Mass. Inst. Tech., Bay Shore, Key West, Cape May, Montauk. N. A. No. 461. HTA.

ALBRITTON, PAUL C.
Ensign
Bee Ridge, Fla. Mass. Inst. Tech., Akron, Pensacola. LTA.

ALDEN, M. A.
Ensign
475 5th Ave., New York City. Dunwoody Inst., Miami, Key West, Pensacola.

ALEXANDER, W. H.
Lieut. (j.g.)
Houlton, Maine. Mass. Inst. Tech., Pensacola, Atlantic Fleet Air Detachment. N. A. No. 175½. HTA.

ALLEN, PHILIP, Jr.
Lieut. (j.g.)
35 Charles Field St., Providence, R. I. Mass. Inst. Tech., Pensacola, Anacostia. N. A. No. 721. HTA.

ALLEN, ROBERT B.
Student Officer
Denver, Colorado. Mass. Inst. Tech., Cambridge. LTA.

ALLEN, WM. ROWLAND
Ensign
149 Newbury St., Boston, Mass. Mass. Inst. Tech., Miami, Pensacola. N. A. No. 1991. HTA.

ALLISON, FRANK F.
Student Officer
Spring Mills, Center Co., Pa. Mass. Inst. of Tech., Bay Shore. HTA.

ALLISON, T. LYLE
Student Officer
822 Concord St., Bremerton, Wash. Seattle, Wash. HTA.

ALVORD, DONALD B.
Lieut. (j.g.)
Clearwater, Fla. M. I. T., Pensacola, Yarmouth, Felixstowe, Lough Foyle, Queenstown, Bolsena, N. A. No. 225. HTA.

ALWARD, EDWARD E.
Ensign
Pataskala, Ohio. Mass. Inst. of Tech., Great Lakes. Pensacola. Aerographer, N. A. No. 2249.

AMSLER, HERVEY M.
Ensign
Farmers Nat'l Bank, Hempstead, Texas. Mass. Inst of Tech., Miami, Pensacola. N. A. No. 2230. HTA.

ANDERLE, EMIL J.
Ensign
132 Hudson Ave., Dayton, Ohio. Mass. Inst. of Tech.. Key West, Pensacola. N A. No. 1571. HTA.

ANDERSEN, CARL J.
Ensign
17 South Kilby St., Gloucester, Mass. Mass. Inst. of Tech., Pensacola, Hampton Roads, Va. N. A. No 267. HTA.

ANDERSEN, FRANK A.
Student Officer
21 St. Luke's Rd., Brighton, Mass. Mass., Inst. of Tech., Bay Shore, Long Island. No. 1933. HTA.

ANDERSEN, SIDNEY W.
Student Officer
South Shore Country Club, Chicago, Ill. Dunwoody Inst., Minneapolis. HTA.

ANDERSON, A., Jr.
Ensign
St. Augustine, Fla. Mass. Inst. of Tech., Miami, Pensacola. N. A. No. 1206. HTA.

ANDERSON, CHAS. C.
Student Officer
Boswell, Indiana. Mass. Inst. of Tech., Cambridge. HTA.

ANDERSON, C. W.
Ensign
983 Sonoma Ave., Santa Rosa, California. Mass. Inst. of Tech., Miami, Pensacola. N. A. No. 1353. HTA.

ANDERSON, GEO. H.
Student Officer
Box 285, Lake Forest, Illinois. Dunwoody, Miami, Key West. HTA.

ANDERSON, GORDON B.
Lieut. (j.g.)
267 Logan Hall, U. of P., Philadelphia, Pa. Mass. Inst. of Tech., Chatham, Miami, Pensacola, Phila. N. A. No. 1826. HTA.

ANDERSON, MERRILL
Student Officer
Center St., Exeter, N. H. Mass. Inst. of Tech., Miami. HTA.

(C) Com. Pub. Inf.

A Fitting Finish.

ANDERSON, OSCAR F.
Ensign
P. O. Box 31, Forestville, Conn. Mass. Inst. of Tech., Miami, Pensacola, N. A. No. 2140. HTA.

ANDERSON, S. W.
Student Officer
208 So. 15th St., La Crosse, Wis. Dunwoody Inst., Minn., Miami. HTA.

ANDERSON, W. C.
Ensign
131 Lincoln Road, Brooklyn. Mass. Inst. of Tech., Miami, Pensacola, Coco Solo, C. Z. N. A. No. 1133. HTA.

ANDRETTA, S. A.
Student Officer
462 Farmington Ave., Hartford, Conn. Mass. Inst. of Tech. HTA.

ANDREWS, GEO. L.
Ensign
333 Front St., Owego, N. Y. Mass. Inst. of Tech., Bay Shore, Brunswick, Ga., Miami. N. A. No. 2047. HTA.

ANDREWS, LEROY L.
Ensign
3305 Windsor Mill Road, Baltimore, Md. Mass. Inst. of Tech., Miami, Pensacola. N. A. No. 1609. HTA.

ANDROUS, PAUL A.
Ensign
1040 W. Onondaga St. Syracuse, N. Y. Mass. Inst. of Tech., Bay Shore, Pensacola, Hampton Rds.

ANEWALT, HENRY P
Ensign
2518 17th St., Fulford, Apt. 6, Washington, D. C. Mass. Inst. of Tech., Miami, Pensacola. N. A. No. 1356. HTA.

ANSLEY, JOHN S.
Ensign
La Porte, Texas. Univ. of Wash., Seattle, San Diego, Pensacola. N. A. No. 2182 HTA.

ANTHONY, W. B. E.
Ensign
1931 Fairview St., So. Berkeley, Cal. Seattle, Miami, Pensacola. N. A. No. 2234. HTA.

APPEL, RONALD B.
Ensign
82 Hale Ave., White Plains, N. Y. Mass. Inst. of Tech., Key West, Pensacola. N. A. No. 2241. HTA.

APPLEGATE, RAY P
Ensign
4637 No. Paulina St., Chicago, Ill. M. I. T., Key West, Miami, Pensacola, Great Lakes. N. A. No. 1204. HTA.

ARCHER, LUTHER B.
Student Officer
Holland, Texas, Seattle, Washington. HTA.

ARMSTRONG, H. C.
Ensign
215 Lexington Ave., Ft. Smith, Arkansas. Seattle, San Diego, Pensacola. N. A. No. 2413. HTA.

ARMSTRONG, L. F.
Ensign
335 W. Francisco Ave., Chicago, Ill. Mass. Inst. of Tech., Great Lakes, Akron, Pensacola. N. A. No. 1974. LTA.

ARMSTRONG, OWEN
Student Officer
635 So. Willett St., Memphis, Tenn. Mass. Inst. of Tech., Akron, Rockaway Beach. LTA.

ARNOLD, R. S.
Student Officer
Paint Lick, Ky. Dunwoody Inst., Minn., Miami. HTA.

ARNSPIGER, RODES A.
Ensign
Lexington, Ky. Mass. Inst. of Tech., Pensacola.

ARP, LOUIS C.
Ensign
718 5th Ave., Moline, Illinois. N. A. No. 1725.

ARROWSMITH, J. E.
Ensign
526 Park Ave., East Orange, N. J. Mass. Inst. of Tech., Bay Shore, Pensacola. N. A. No. 1741. HTA.

ASKEW, MILES A.
Ensign
Dayton, Alabama. Mass. Inst. of Tech., Great Lakes, Pensacola, Washington, D. C., Miami. HTA.

ASTRY, PERRY D.
Lieut. (j.g.)
Lincoln Rd., Salem, Ohio. Mass. Inst. of Tech., Pensacola, Coco Solo. N. A. No. 641. HTA.

ATHA, KIMBALL
Ensign
24 Waverly Ave., Newark, N. J. Mass. Inst. of Tech., Key West, Miami, Pensacola, N. A. No. 1375. HTA.

ATHA, STUART K.
Lieut. (j.g.)
24 Waverly Ave., Newark, N. J. Mass. Inst. of Tech., Miami, Pensacola. N. A No. 1028. HTA.

COMING ABOARD!

ATHERTON, HAROLD G.
Ensign
22 W. 5th St., Anderson, Indiana. M. I. T., Key West, Miami, Pensacola, Killingholme. N. A. No. 1266. HTA.

ATKINS, WARNER L.
Ensign
4008 Rose Hill Ave., Cincinnati, Ohio. Mass. Inst. of Tech., Bay Shore, Hampton Rds., Pensacola. N. A. No. 1748. HTA.

ATWOOD, ALLEN A.
Ensign
Security State Bank Bldg., St. Cloud, Minn. Dunwoody, M. I. T., Pensacola, Key West, Miami. N. A. No. 640. HTA.

AUSTIN, RAYMOND M.
Ensign
Mountain Ave., Caldwell, N. J. Mass. Inst. of Tech., Pensacola, Miami, St. Inglevert, Moutchic. HTA.

AVERILL, L. B.
Lieut. (j.g.)
Bancroft Hotel, Worcester, Mass. Mass. Inst. of Tech., Pensacola, Charleston, S. C., Operations, Washington. HTA.

AVERY, NATHAN C.
Ensign
293 S., M. Ave. New Britain. Conn. Bureau of Operations, Pauillac, Bay Shore, Key West. HTA.

AVERY, WALTER H.
Lieut (j.g.)
7803 St. Martin's Lane, Chestnut Hill, Phila., Pa. Mass. Inst. of Tech., Pensacola, N. A. No. 890. HTA.

AYLING, F. C.
Lieut. (j.g.)
601 University Ave., Syracuse, N. Y. Mass. Inst. of Tech., Boston, Pensacola. N. A. No. 674. HTA.

◈ ◈ ◈ ◈ ◈ ◈

ABBOTT, G. M., Student Officer, 110 Edgemore Lane, Ithaca, N. Y.

ABBOTT, RANSFORD J., Student Officer, Port Republic, Atlantic Co., N. J. Pelham Bay, Cape May, Mass. Inst. of Tech. HTA.

ABBOTT, ROBERT D., Student Officer, 48 Rhodes Ave., Akron, Ohio.

ABELES, FRANCIS, Ensign, 4140 Washington Blvd., St. Louis, Mo. N. A. No. 1711.

ACHOR, LEONARD B., Student Officer, Martinsville, Ohio. Mass. Inst. of Tech. HTA.

ACHORN, ALBERT H., Student Officer, Sigma Nu House, South Bethlehem, Pa.

ACKER, STEADHAM, Ensign, 315 S. 80th St., Birmingham, Ala. Miami, Pensacola. N. A. No. 2541. HTA.

ACKERMAN, M. S., Ensign, 131 Crescent Ave., Plainfield, N. J. Mass. Inst. of Tech., Bay Shore, N. Y., Pensacola, Fla. N. A. No. 1203. HTA.

ACOFF, I. Z., Student Officer, Foxoboro, Mass. Mass. Inst. of Tech., Miami, Fla. HTA.

ACTON, FRANCIS NEWLIN, Student Officer, Salem, N. J. Dunwoody Institute.

ADAMS, ARTHUR J., Student Officer, Summit Hill, Carbon Co., Pa. Mass. Inst. of Tech.

ADAMS, HENRY H., Student Officer, 50 Church St., New York City.

ADAMS, IRVING E., Student Officer, 412 23d Ave., South Seattle, Wash. Univ. of Washington, Seattle.

ADAMS, PHILIP C., Student Officer, Cluster Springs, Va.

ADAMS, ROBERT D., Student Officer, 169 E. First St., New London, Conn.

ADAMS, SCHUYLER R., Student Officer, 605 S. Buron St., Cheboygan, Mich.

ADAMS, STANLEY B., Student Officer, 17 Parkview Ave., Bangor, Maine. Mass. Inst. of Tech. HTA.

ADAMSON, G. F., Ensign, 37 Kempton St., Boston, Mass. N. A. No. 1046.

ADKINS, F. B., Ensign, 824 Park Ave., Richmond, Va. Mass. Inst. of Tech., Pensacola, Miami. N. A. No. 2043. HTA.

AGAR, HERBERT S., Student Officer, 56 Bayard Lane, Princeton, N. J. Mass. Inst. of Tech. HTA.

AGRAMONTE, JULES, Student Officer, 11 E. 68th St., New York, N. Y. Mass. Inst. of Tech., Key West, Fla. HTA.

AHERN, WILLIAM J., Ensign, South Whithouse St., New York, N. Y.

AINSWORTH, ERIC, Student Officer, 223 Kenyon Ave., Swarthmore, Pa. Seattle, Wash., San Diego, Cal. HTA.

ALCORN, J. W., Ensign.

ALDEN, H. S., Lieut. (j.g.).

ALDEN, SIDNEY, C., Student Officer, 50 Meigs St., Rochester, N. Y.

ALESHIRE, MERLIN C., Lieut. (j.g.), 2151 E. 70th St., Chicago, Ill. Great Lakes, Ill., Eastleigh, Eng.

ALEXANDER, HOWARD B., Student Officer, 255 Farrington St., Wollaston, Mass.

ALEXANDER, JOHN, JR., Student Officer, 3817 N. Park Ave., Philadelphia, Pa. Mass. Inst. of Tech., Key West.

ALEXANDER, KENNETH D., Student Officer, Spring Station, Ky.

ALLBRIGHT, N. J., Ensign, 4937 Dorchester Ave., Chicago, Ill. Mass. Inst. of Tech., Akron, Rockaway Beach, Long Island, N. Y. LTA.

ALLEN, C. L., Lieut. (j.g.), 625 Front St., S. Weymouth, Mass. Pensacola, Bay Shore, Brunswick, Miami. N. A. No. 110½. HTA.

ALLEN, DOLPH C., Ensign, 206 No. St. Andrews Place, Los Angeles, Cal. Mass. Inst. of Tech., Miami, Pensacola, Key West. N. A. No. 1639. HTA.

ALLEN, FRANCIS G., Lieut. (j.g.), Kenilworth, Ill. N. A. No. 190.

ALLEN, FUDEM WOLCOTT, Student Officer, 265 Waterman St., Providence, R. I. Mass. Inst. of Tech. HTA.

ALLEN, I. J., Student Officer, 300 Oil Operations Bldg., Ft. Worth, Tex. Mass. Inst. of Tech., Miami. HTA.

ALLEN, THEO. F., Student Officer, Care of J. F. Allen, Meriden, Conn. Mass. Inst. of Tech., Key West, Fla. HTA.

ALLER, C. E., Ensign.

ALLIOTT, ERIC, Lieut. (j.g.), 30 High Street, Newport, R. I. N. A. No. 513.

ALLISON, CHARLES C., Student Officer, 410 S. 39th St., Omaha, Nebr.

ALLISON, GEORGE H., Ensign, 17 Beaver St., Worcester, Mass. N. A. No. 1205.

ALLISON, JOHN S., Ensign, 179 Crafts St., Newtonville, Mass. Mass. Inst. of Tech., Hampton Roads, Pensacola, Miami, Marine Field, Moutchic, Fromentine. N. A. No. 539. HTA.

ALLISON, STANTON T., Student Officer, Bryn Mawr, Pa., also Williams College, Williamstown, Mass. Mass. Inst. of Tech. LTA.

ALMY, FREDERICK, JR., Student Officer, 19 W. 54th St., New York, N. Y.

ALMY, WILLIAM F., JR., Student Officer, 367 Winter St., Fall River, Mass. Mass. Inst. of Tech. HTA.

ALSTON, GEORGE J., JR., Student Officer, 1322 23d Ave., Tuskaloosa, Ala.

ALSTON, SAMUEL W., Machinist.

AMBERG, THEODORE WM., Ensign, Griffin Wheel Co., Packers Station, Kansas City, Kans.

AMES, CHARLES BURTON, Ensign, 300 High St., West Newton, Mass. Pensacola, San Diego. N. A. No. 193. HTA.

AMES, WALTER M., Student Officer, 58 Linden Ave., Dayton, Ohio.

ANDERSON, ARTHUR V., Student Officer, 544 Eighth St., Brooklyn, N. Y.

ANDERSON, FRANCIS J., Student Officer, 102 W. Pleasant Ave., Syracuse, N. Y.

ANDERSON, GEORGE D., Lieut. (j.g.), N. A. No. 666.

ANDERSON, J. B., Lieut. (j.g.), 48 Forge St., Akron, Ohio.

ANDERSON, JOHN P., Student Officer, Georgetown College, Washington, D. C.

ANDERSON, PAUL A., Student Officer, 112 Broadway Ave., Wilmette, Ill. Mass. Inst. of Tech., Key West, Fla. HTA.

ANDERSON, ROBERT C., Student Officer, Upper Montclair, N. J.

ANDERSON, ROWLAND, War. Gun.

ANDERSON, SIDNEY W., Student Officer, 5332 Hyde Park Blvd., Chicago, Ill.

ANDERSON, WILTON H., Student Officer, David City, Nebr. Mass. Inst. of Tech., Key West, Fla. HTA.

ANDREWS, AARON R., Student Officer.

ANDREWS, CHESTER W., Student Officer, East Lansing, Mich.

ANDREWS, H. V., Ensign, Pensacola. N. A. No. 1194.

ANDREWS, HERBERT J., Student Officer, Napoleon, Mich.

ANDREWS, JAMES B., Student Officer, 1210 Springfield Ave., Urbana, Ill.

ANGELL, NORMAN H., Student Officer, 2501 Ridge Road, Berkeley, Cal.

ANKENY, DEWALT HOSMER, Student Officer, 920 Chamber of Commerce, Minneapolis, Minn.

ANTHONY, H. M., Ensign, 113 Commonwealth Ave., Boston, Mass.

ANTONIDES, H. R., Student Officer, 360 Humbolt St., Denver, Colo. Mass. Inst. of Tech., Key West, Fla. HTA.

APGAR, HENRY H., Student Officer.

APPLEBY, JOHN L., Ensign, Glen Cove, Long Island, N. Y. Mass. Inst. of Tech., Pensacola, Pauillac, Moutchic, Arcachon. N. A. No. 720. HTA.

ARCHIBALD, F. X., Student Officer, 750 E. 175th St., New York City. Mass. Inst. of Tech., New Haven Pensacola. HTA.

ARCHIBALD, WALTER D., Student Officer, 538 W. 142d St., New York City. Mass. Inst. of Tech. LTA.

ARMOUR, LESTER, Ensign, 8 E. 69th St., New York City. Mass. Inst. of Tech., Bayshore, Pensacola, Fla. N. A. No. 2207. HTA.

ARMOR, ROBERT J., Student Officer, 4622 Polk Ave., Houston, Tex.

ARMS, LOUIS L., Student Officer, New York Tribune, New York City.

ARMSTRONG, H. K., Student Officer, 1775 Hennipin Ave., Minneapolis, Minn. Dunwoody Inst., Miami. HTA.

ARMSTRONG, PAUL L., Ens.

ARMSTRONG, ROBERT E., JR., Ensign, 915 Oakland Ave., Ann Arbor, Mich. N. A. No. 2405.

ARMSTRONG, W. L., Ensign, Goodyear Tire & Rubber Co. N. A. No. 2380.

ARMSTRONG, WESLEY A., Student Officer, 409 W. Delavan Ave., Buffalo, N. Y.

ARNOLD, GEORGE C., JR., Student Officer, 238 Adelaide Ave., Providence, R. I. Mass. Inst. of Tech. HTA.

ARNOLD, JUNIUS H., Student Officer.

ARONSON, ISRAEL I., Ensign, 122 Bellingham St Chelsea, Mass. N. A. No. 912.

ARTHUR, JOHN W., Student Officer, 52 Magee Ave., Rochester, N. Y.

ARTHUR, REGINALD W., Ensign, Maryland State College, College Park, Md. N. A. No. 1501

ASHBY, JOHN S., Student Officer, Fairmont, Fillmore Co., Nebr. Seattle, Wash.; San Diego, Cal. HTA.

ASHLEY, JOHN W., Lieut. (j.g.), 315 Main St., Amesbury, Mass. Mass. Inst. of Tech., Pensacola, Moutchic, Brest, Fr.; Chatham. N. A. No. 281. HTA.

ASHTON, C. E., Lieut. (j.g.), 7702 Frankstown Ave., Pittsburgh, Pa.

ASHTON, OLIVER, Student Officer.

ASTLETT, HUGH G., Student Officer, 387 Upper Mountain Ave., Montclair, N. J.

ATKINS, FRANK EDWARD, JR., Student Officer, 30 E Walnut St., Merchantville, N. J. Mass. Inst. of Tech. HTA.

ATKINS, JOHN B., JR., Student Officer, 1524 Fairfield Ave., Shreveport, La.

ATKINSON, LEON G., Student Officer, 35 Victoria Circle, Newton Center, Mass.

ATWATER, W. B., Lieut. (j.g.), Central Valley, N. Y. Newport News, N. Y. Navy Yard, Hampton Rds.; Moutchic, Fr., Paris; Bolsena, It.; Charleston. N. A. No. 112. HTA.

ATWOOD, CLARENCE C., Ensign, Gardner, Kansas.

ATWOOD, RAYMOND LORING, Lieut. (j.g.), Paris, Maine. Mass. Inst. of Tech., Pensacola, Fleet Air Detach., Killingholme, Hampton Roads, Forth Worth. N. A. No. 292. HTA.

AUCHINCLOSS, REGINALD LA. G., Ensign, 134 E. 71st St., New York City.

AUERSWALD, RICHARD R., Ensign, 441 Lafayette Ave., Brooklyn, N. Y. N. A. No. 1202.

AUGUSTINE, IRVING D., Student Officer, 1616 W. 2d St., Grand Island, Nebr.

AUKERMAN, LEWIS C., Student Officer.

AUSTILL, JERE, Ensign, Spring Hill, Mobile Co., Ala. Mass. Inst. of Tech., Key West, Pensacola. N. A. No. 1879. LTA.

AUSTIN, D. F., Student Officer, 92 Montclair Ave., Caldwell, N. J. Mass. Inst. of Tech., Newport, R. I., New London, Conn. HTA.

AUSTIN, JAMES MASON, Student Officer, Middletown, Conn.

AVERILL, HAROLD G., Student Officer, 206 West St., Worcester, Mass.

AVERY, LYMAN C., Lieut. (j.g.), Brockport, N. Y. N. A. No. 864.

AVERY, THEODORE STRONG, Ensign, 174 Washington Ave., Albany, N. Y. N. A. No. 1749.

AUSTRIAN LIGHT BOMBER.

Photo taken from Austrian Files al Polo.

BACHMAN, R. H.
Ensign
40 East 40th St., New York City. M. I. T., Bay Shore, Pensacola, Montauk, Hampton Rds. N. A. No. 1412. HTA.

BAEHR, MAX J.
Lieut. (j.g.)
923 Locust Ave., Long Beach, Cal. M. I. T., Cranwell, E. Fortune, Paimboeuf, H. Q. London. N. No. 1085. LTA.

BAHR, M. CASTLE
Ensign
R. F. D. No. 3. Helena, Mo. Mass. Inst. of Tech., Miami, Key West, Pensacola. N. A. No. 2376. HTA.

BAILHACHE, P. L.
Student Officer
2901 Scott St., San Francisco, Cal. M. I. T., Akron, San Pedro. U. S. S. *Madrono*, U. S. S. *Goliah* (Foreign Waters). LTA.

BAKER, CHARLES W.
Student Officer
76 Hardenbrook Ave., Jamaica, N. Y. Mass. Inst. of Tech. HTA.

BAKER, EDMUND F.
Ensign
431 Shady Ave., Pittsburgh, Pa. Aviation Beach, Great Lakes, Hampton Roads, Norfolk. HTA.

BAKER, GEORGE F.
Ensign
Wellesley, Mass. Mass. Inst. of Tech., Pensacola, Moutchic, Guipavas. N. A. No. 352. HTA.

BAKER, S. SAMUEL
Student Officer
19 Amory St., Cambridge, Mass. Mass. Inst. of Tech. HTA.

BAKER, WILLIAM C.
Student Officer
Middlebrook Pike, Knoxville, Tenn. Great Lakes, Ill. HTA.

BALL, TOM LEE
Student Officer
R. F. D. No. 2, Care of Wenonah Mines, Bessemer, Ala. Mass. Inst. of Tech. HTA.

BALLORD, HAROLD B.
Ensign
144 Brunswick Ave., Gardiner, Maine. Mass. Inst. of Tech., Key West, Miami, Pensacola, Hampton Roads. N. A. No. 974. LTA.

BANIK, ADOLF T.
Ensign
East Grand Forks, Minn Mass. Inst.of Tech.,Miami, Pensacola. N. A. No. 2495. HTA.

BARNES, A. S., Jr.
Student Officer
Glenwood, Raleigh, N. C. Mass. Inst. of Tech. HTA.

BARNES, DANA A.
Ensign
161 Bay State Rd., Boston, Mass. Mass. Inst. of Tech., Miami, Pensacola. N. A. No. 1670. HTA.

BARNES, EARL C.
Ensign
450 W. Eldorado St., Decatur, Ill. M. I. T., Great Lakes, Pensa., Miami, Moutchic, Campagne, Malpensa. N. A. No. 675.

BARNUM, WM. N.
Ensign
78 Front St., New York City. Mass. Inst. of Tech. Miami. HTA.

BARON, FREDERICK J.
Ensign
51 Lawn St., Roxbury, Mass. Bolsena, Italy; Hdqts. Paris, Tours, Bolsena, Italy; Chatham. N. A. No. 1511. HTA.

BARR, HARRY C.
War. Machinist
20 East 3rd St., Waynesboro, Pa. Pensacola, Hampton Roads, Miami. HTA.

BARR, J. S.
Ensign
101 Pleasant St., Ithaca, N. Y. Mass. Inst. of Tech., Bay Shore, Pensacola, Hampton Roads. N. A. No. 745. A. HT

BARRINGER, EUG. E.
Student Officer
1745 9th Ave., Huntington, W. Va. Mass. Inst. of Tech. HTA.

(C) *International Film Service*

PATROLLING WITH THE FLEET

BARRY, ELMER L. W.
Student Officer
Concord St., Holliston, Mass. Mass. Inst. of Tech. HTA.

BARRY, THOMAS D.
Ensign
1930 Girard Ave., South Minn., Minn., Dunwoody, Inst., Minn., Miami, Pensacola. N. A. No. 2229. HTA.

BARRY, WALTER A.
Ensign
5045 N. Robey St., Chicago. Ill. Seattle, San Diego. Pensacola. N. A. No. 2412. HTA.

BARSE, HORACE N.
Ensign
28 West 23rd St., New York City. Mass. Inst. of Tech., HTA.

BARTEMEIER, CARL M.
Ensign
6804 Brookville Road. Chevy Chase, Md. Dunwoody Inst., Minn.; Miami, Pensacola. N. A. No. 2286. HTA.

BARTLETT, FRANK L.
Student Officer
Exchange Nat'l Bk. Bldg., Tulsa, Oklahoma. Mass. Inst. of Tech. HTA.

BASCHE, J. V.
Student Officer
518 Columbia Ave., Los Angeles, Cal. Univ. of Wash., Seattle, San Diego, North Island. HTA.

BATCHELDER, R. B.
Lieut. (j.g.)
7 Cedar St., Salem, Mass. Mass. Inst. of Tech., Pensacola, Hampton Roads, Washington, D. C.

BATCHELLER, H. C. C.
Ensign
1214 Magnolia Ave., Los Angeles, Cal. Mass. Inst. of Tech., Miami, Pensacola. N. A. No. 1856. HTA.

BATES, DONALD N.
Ensign
807 Ashbury St., San Francisco, Cal. Mass. Inst. of Tech., San Diego, Pensacola. N. A. No. 1236. HTA.

BATES, JEFFERSON B.
Student Officer
Wateree, South Carolina. Mass. Inst. of Tech., Miami. HTA.

BAUCH, CHAS. E.
Ensign
Ashmont, Mass. Mass. Inst. of Tech., Akron, Rockaway, Bureau Construction and Repair. LTA.

BEACH, CHAS. T.
Student Officer
15 Liberty St., Catskill, N. Y. Mass. Inst. of Tech., Miami. HTA.

BEALL, WM. R.
Student Officer
691 Highland Ave., Takoma Park, Washington, D. C. Mass. Inst. of Tech., Navy Yard, Washington, D. C. HTA

BECKER, CHARLES W.
Student Officer
5207 Ingleside Ave., Chicago, Ill. Mass. Inst. of Tech., Bay Shore. HTA.

BECKER, FREDRICK H.
Lieut. (j.g.)
Hutchinson, Minnesota. Mass Inst. of Tech., Pensacola, Moutchic, Le Croisic, Hampton Roads. N. A. No. 309. HTA.

BEEMAN, OTIS
Lieut (j.g.)
11061 Esmond St., Morgan Park, Ill. M. I. T., Pensa., Moutchic, R. A. F., N. B. G., Calais, Avord-Cher. N. A. No. 354. HTA.

BEGGS, ALAN H.
Lieut. (j.g.)
289 Ridgewood Ave., Glen Ridge, N. J. Mass. Inst. of Tech., Hampt. Rds., Pensa., Bay Shore, Miami, Anacostia. N. A. No. 514.

BEHNER, HERBERT C.
Ensign
125 Stubing Place, Seaside. Rockaway Beach, N. Y., Hampton Roads. HTA.

BELL, BYRON E.
Student Officer
735 Main St., Reynoldsville, Pa. Mass. Inst. of Tech. HTA.

BENDER, E. S.
Ensign
Reno, Nevada. Mass. Inst. of Tech., Miami, Pensacola. N. A. No. 1982. HTA.

BENEDICT, PAUL A.
Machinist
206 Park Place, Bridgeport, Conn. Columbia University, New York.

BENNER, P. K.
Ensign
Tuscarawas, Ohio. Dunwoody Inst., Minn. Miami, Key West, Pensacola. N. A. No. 2383. HTA.

BENSON, HUGH E.
Ensign
720 West 9th St., Erie, Penn. Mass. Inst. of Tech., Bay Shore, Brunswick, Key West, Pensacola. N. A. No. 2369. HTA.

Starting after a Crash

BENZ, HERBERT G.
Student Officer
668 Cable Ave., St. Paul, Minn. Dunwoody Inst., Minn. HTA.

BERCAW, CORLISS A.
Ensign
426 No. Newlin Ave., Whittier, California. Seattle, San Diego, Pensacola. N. A. No. 2384. HTA.

BERGHORN, W. H.
Ensign
25 Reservoir Ave., Jersey City, N. J. Mass. Inst. of Tech., Miami, Pensacola. N. A. No. 1398. HTA.

BESWICK, HOWARD A
Ensign
Ludlow, Vt. Mass. Inst. of Tech., Pensacola, Bay Shore, Wexford, Ire., Hampton Roads. N. A. No. 963. HTA.

BETTS, CLAUDE S.
Ensign
1430 Perry St., South Richmond, Va. Mass. Inst. of Tech., Miami, Key West, Pensacola. N. A. No. 2547. HTA.

BEVENS, MAXSON I.
Student Officer
611 No. Chaparral St., Corpus Christi, Texas. Mass. Inst. of Tech. HTA.

BEYRLE, THOS. T.
Ensign
1402 Malvern Ave., Los Angeles, Cal. Mass. Inst. of Tech., Bay Shore, Pensacola. N. A. No. 1570. HTA.

BIGELOW, E. S.
Ensign
25 Pine St., New York City. Mass. Inst. of Tech., Key West, Miami, Pensacola. N. A. No. 1574. HTA.

BILLINGS, ARTHUR S.
Boatswain
9 West St., W. Somerville, Mass. San Diego, Cal., Pensacola, Squantum, Mass. HTA.

BISCHOF, JACOB H.
Student Officer
5100 Ellis Ave., Chicago, Ill. Dunwoody Inst., Minn., Mass. Inst. of Tech. HTA.

BISKAMP, ERNEST J.
Student Officer
1806 W. Matamoros St., Laredo, Texas. Seattle, Washington.

BIXBY, H. M.
Student Officer
4943 Pershing Ave., St. Louis, Mo. Mass. Inst. of Tech., Cambridge, Akron. LTA.

BIZZELL, CAREY K.
Ensign
1810 Calvert St., N. W. Washington, D. C. Mass. Inst. of Tech., Pensacola, Hampton Roads. N. A. No. 956. HTA.

BLAGDEN, B. D. S.
Lieut. (j.g.)
Upper Saranac, N. Y. Mass. Inst. of Tech., Pensacola. N.A. No. 742. HTA.

BLAIR, GEORGE
Lieut. (j.g.)
Wynnewood, Penn. Bureau of Ordnance, Washington, D. C., Anacostia, D. C.

BLEAKLEY, PAUL L.
Student Officer
536 North Broadway, Yonkers, N. Y. Mass. Inst. of Tech. HTA.

BLETHEN, MELVIN S.
Ensign
1 Winter St., Foxcroft, Maine. Mass. Inst. of Tech., Miami, Key West, Pensacola, Hingham. N. A. No. 2626. HTA.

BLOCK, HERMAN
Student Officer
17 Battery Place, New York City. Mass. Inst. of Tech., Key West. HTA.

BLODGETT, LEO S.
Ensign
31 Winter St., Portland, Maine. Mass. Inst. of Tech., Buffalo, N. Y.

BLOSSER, HERMAN G.
Student Officer
7129 Schoyer Ave., Swissvale, Pa. Seattle, Washington. Dunwoody Inst., Minn.

BLOUNT, H. FLOYD
Ensign
Oswego Co., Lacona, N. Y. Mass. Inst. of Tech., Miami, Pensacola. N. A, No. 1239. HTA.

BLOUNT, JOHN G., Jr.
Ensign
590 Seventh St., Memphis, Tenn. Mass. Inst. of Tech., Miami, Pensacola. N. A. No. 1787. HTA.

BOEDEFELD, B. S.
Ensign
Colusa, Cal. Mass. Inst. of Tech., Miami, Pensacola. N. A. No. 1858. HTA.

BOLANZ, HENRY L.
Ensign
2924 Holmes St., Dallas, Texas. Mass. Inst. of Tech., Cambridge; Miami, Pensacola. N. A. No. 2271. HTA.

F Boat Crash at Miami

BOLIN, ERICK E.
Student Officer
2686 Hennepin Ave., Minn., Minn. Miami, Chatham, Hampton Roads, Le Croisic, Fr. HTA.

BOLTON, FREDK. R.
Student Officer
531 E. Grand Boulevard, Detroit, Mich. Dunwoody Inst., Minn: Miami, Key West. HTA.

BOND, NELSON A.
Ensign
Jefferson, Missouri. Bay Shore, Pensacola. N. A. No. 1345. HTA.

BONNER, WALTER D.
Boatswain
Mason, Nevada. Pensacola, U. S. S. *Huntington*, Rockaway Beach. N. A. No. 50. HTA.

BOONE, A. D.
Ensign
539 12th St., San Pedro, Cal. Mass. Inst. of Tech., Miami, Pensacola, Hampton Roads. N. A. No. 1681. HTA.

BOOT, HARRY EARL
Ensign
1717 Race St., Denver, Colo. Mass. Inst. of Tech., Pensacola, Rockaway Beach, Moutchic, L'Aber Vrach. N. A. No. 639. HTA.

BOOTH, E. W., Jr.
Lieut. (j.g.)
230 Fountain St., Grand Rapids, Mich. Mass. Inst. of Tech., Pensacola, N. A. No. 1021. HTA.

BOSTICK, E. ELLIS
Ensign
Memphis Coal Co., Memphis, Tenn. Mass. Inst. of Tech., Pensacola, Paris, Moutchic, Pauillac, Bay Shore. N. A. No. 288.

BOTTA, RICO
Lieut. (j.g.)
Johnson Curtiss Aeroplane Co., Montgomery, Ala. Mass. Inst. of Tech., Pensacola. N. A. No. 2641. HTA.

BOTTOMS, R. R.
Ensign
Athens, Alabama. Pensacola, Akron, Rockaway Beach, Key West. N. A. No. 2676. LTA.

BOURQUIN, MARION M.
Ensign
Butte, Montana. Mass. Inst. of Tech., Bay Shore, Hampton Roads, Pensacola, English Stations. N. A. No. 1257. HTA.

BOWERS, ANDERSON
Ensign
313 N. McKean St., Kittanning, Pa. M. I. T., Key West, Miami, Pensacola, Brest, Moutchic. N. A. No. 1257. HTA.

BOWKER, W. K., Jr.
Student Officer
2660 Menlo Ave., Los Angeles, Cal. Seattle, Washington. HTA.

BOWSER, ARDA C.
Student Officer
11th St., Ford City, Penn. Mass. Inst. of Tech. HTA.

BOYD, ROBERT M.
Student Officer
1617 S. Washington Ave., Saginaw. Mich. Mass. Inst. of Tech., Miami. HTA.

BOYD, SAMUEL N.
Ensign
320 E. Capitol St., Washington, D. C. Mass. Inst. of Tech., Pensacola.

BOYD, THEODORE P.
Lieut. (j.g.)
77 Union Ave., Framingham, Mass. Bay Shore, Key West, Brunswick, Ga. N. A. No. 175. HTA.

BRACKEN, D. F.
Ensign
321 E. Chestnut St., Bloomington, Illinois. Mass. Inst. of Tech., Miami, Pensacola. N. A. No. 2233. HTA.

BRACKEN, GORDON R.
Ensign
465 W. 152nd St., New York City. Mass. Inst. of Tech., Key West, Pensacola. N. A. No. 2341. HTA.

BRACKEN, L. M.
Ensign
713 West First St., Oil City, Penn. Mass. Inst of Tech., Key West, Miami, Pensacola. N.A. No. 1797. HTA.

BRADLEY, LOYD M.
Ensign
Suite 112, New Hamilton Bldg., Carbondale, Ill. Mass. Inst. of Tech., Cambridge· Akron, Rockaway Beach. LTA.

BRADY, H. WILLIAMS
Ensign
916 S. Michigan Ave., Saginaw, Mich. M. I. T., Akron, Pensacola, Montauk, Cape May. N. A. No. 728. LTA.

(B)
BRANDT, RODNEY LEE
Student Officer
Albion Hotel, Baltimore, Md. Seattle, Washington. HTA.

BRANN, MAURICE R
Ensign
201 4th Ave., Warren, Pa. Mass. Inst. of Tech., Akron, Pensacola. N. A. No. 1726. LTA.

SCOUT PLANE ON BOARD U. S. S. TEXAS

BRANT, ROBERT A.
Ensign
3131 So. Figueroa St., Los Angeles, Cal. Univ. Wash., Seattle, San Diego, Pensacola. N. A. No. 2113. HTA.

BRENHAM, CHARLES J.
Ensign
698 Bush St., San Francisco, Cal. Mass. Inst. of Tech., Miami, Pensacola. N. A. No. 2301. HTA.

BRENNAN, J. C.
Student Officer
214 Taylor St., E. Savannah, Ga. Seattle, Wash. HTA.

BRES, HAROLD A.
Ensign
Box 865, Hammond, La. Mass. Inst. of Tech., Pensacola, Queenstown, Ire.; Bay Shore. N. A. No. 944. HTA.

BRESNAHAN, M. E.
Ensign
128 Chestnut St., Lynn, Mass. Mass. Inst. of Tech., Miami, Pensacola. N. A. No. 1929. HTA.

BRESNAHAN, WM. H.
Student Officer
128 Chestnut St., Lynn, Mass. Mass. Inst. of Tech. HTA.

BREWER, FRED L., Jr.
Lieut. (j.g.)
224 Burr Oak Ave., Blue Island, Ill. Columbia Univ., Philadelphia, Hampton Roads.

BRIDGMAN, DON. S.
Ensign
H. F. Bar Ranch, Buffalo, Wyoming. Mass. Inst. of Tech., Pensacola, Washington, Miami. N. A. No. 2449. HTA.

BRIGGS, LANDRUM O.
Ensign
100 Grace St., Suffolk, Va. Mass. Inst. of Tech., Key West, Miami, Pensacola. N. A. No. 1808.

BRIGGS, M. G.
Ensign
858 East 21st St., Brooklyn, N. Y. Mass. Inst. of Tech., Bay Shore, Pensacola, Hampton Roads. N. A. No. 1640. HTA.

BRIGGS, WM. WRIGHT
Ensign
Cassville, N. Y. Mass. Inst. of Tech., Miami, Pensacola, Hampton Roads. N. A. No. 2280. HTA.

BRIGHAM, WM. W.
Ensign
41 Wheatland Ave., Dorchester, Mass. Mass. Inst. of Tech. Miami. HTA.

BRIMER, F. C.
Ensign
Stockton, Md. Mass. Inst. of Tech., Bay Shore, Pensacola. N. A. No. 1770. HTA.

BRIMER, WALLACE E.
Ensign
Snow Hill, Md. Mass. Inst. of Tech., Akron, Pensacola. N. A. No. 2293. LTA.

BRINKERHOFF, R. J.
Student Officer
408 Union St., West Springfield, Mass. Mass. Inst. of Tech., Bay Shore. HTA.

BRISTOL, L. HASTINGS
Ensign
282 Washington Ave., Brooklyn, N. Y. Mass. Inst. of Tech., Pensacola. N. A. No. 1714. HTA.

BRITT, GEORGE H.
Ensign
622 Scranton Life Bldg., Scranton, Pa. Pauillac, Fr., Eastleigh, Eng. HTA.

BRITTINGHAM, EDW. G.
Ensign
Care of British Vice Consulate, Gomez Palacio, Durango, Mexico. Mass. Inst. of Tech., Pensacola, Miami. N. A. No. 2053. HTA.

BRITTON, J. W.
Student Officer
1314 11th St., Wichita Falls, Texas, Seattle, Wash., San Diego. HTA.

BRITZ, EVERETT F.
Ensign
126 West 129th St., New York City. Mass. Inst. of Tech., Bay Shore, Pensacola, Rockaway. N. A. No. 1704.

BRIX, EARL B.

Ensign

Monroe, Wash. Pensacola, San Diego. N. A. No. 2621. HTA.

BROMLEY, INNIS M.

Ensign

439 Washington St.,Sonora, Toulumne Co., California. Seattle, Wash., San Diego, Pensacola. N. A. No. 2242. HTA.

BRONK, DETLEV W.

Ensign

Stoneham, Boston, Mass. Mass. Inst. of Tech., Key West, Miami, Pensacola. N. A. No. 1898. HTA.

BROOKER, F. DONALD

Student Officer

10,603 Miles Ave., Cleveland, Ohio. Mass. Inst. of Tech. HTA.

Aerial of Town of Bolsena, Italy

BROOKS, EVERETT L.

Ensign

6306 Waterman Ave., St. Louis, Mo. Mass. Inst. of Tech., Key West, Miami, Pensacola. N. A. No. 1608. HTA.

BRORSEN, WILLARD A.

Ensign

280 Lee St., Oakland, Cal. Mass. Inst. of Tech., Langley Field, Miami, Pensacola, Washington, D. C.

BROW, HAROLD J.

Lieut. (j.g.)

95 Peace St., Providence, R. I. Mass. Inst. of Tech., Pensacola, Miami. N. A. No. 571. HTA.

BROWN, ALBERT L.

Ensign

28 Presidio Terrace, San Francisco, Cal. Seattle, San Diego, Pensacola. N. A. No. 2331. HTA.

BROWN, C. Y.
Ensign
Chapman Bldg., Spartanburg, S. C. Mass. Inst. of Tech., Miami, Pensacola. N. A. No. 1385. HTA.

BROWN, CARROLL G.W.
Student Officer
20 Fenelon St., Dorchester, Mass. Miami, Brest, Finistere, Fr. LTA.

BROWN, H. E.
Ensign
Stratford, Conn. Mass. Inst. of Tech., Newport, Akron, Rockaway Beach, Key West. LTA.

BROWN, J. W. A.
Ensign
407 New Rochelle St., Pittsburgh, Penna. M. I. T. Blue Hill Observatory, Operations, Wash., Montauk, New London. HTA.

BROWN, KENNETH G.
Student Officer
St. Albans, Vermont. Mass. Inst. of Tech., Cambridge. HTA.

BROWN, RAYMOND R.
Ensign
30 Park Ave., Detroit, Mich. Mass. Inst. of Tech., Akron, Pensacola. N. A. No. 2657 LTA.

BROWN, VINCENT S.
Ensign
533 Clayton St., San Francisco, Cal. Mass. Inst. of Tech., Akron, Pensacola. N. A. No. 1866. LTA.

BRUCE, FRANK P.
Student Officer
2519 11th Ave. So., Minn., Minn. Dunwoody Institute, Minn. Miami. LTA.

BRUCE, LYSCOM A., Jr.
Ensign
61 Rockwell St., Dorchester, Mass. Mass. Inst. of Tech., Akron, Pensacola. N. A. No. 1566. LTA.

BRUCE, WALTER T.
Ensign
518 Hampton Place, Portsmouth, Va. Mass. Inst. of Tech., Pensacola, Hampton Roads. N. A. No. 978. HTA.

BRUNER, JAMES D.
Student Officer
1216 22nd St., Rock Island, Ill. Dunwoody Inst., Minn., Miami. HTA.

BRUSH, M. W.
Lieut. (j.g.)
Route No. 2, Germantown, N. Y. Mass. Inst. of Tech., Key West. N. A. No. 2112.

BRYAN, JOHN B.
Ensign
1207 Avenue V., Sheepshead Bay, L. I., N. Y. Columbia Univ., Packard Factory, Hampton Roads, Pauilliac, Fr. HTA.

BRYAN, WALTER C.
Ensign
473 Franklin Ave., Brooklyn, N. Y. Mass. Inst. of Tech., Bay Shore, Pensacola. N. A. No. 1567. HTA.

BRYAN, WALTER D.
Student Officer
Y. M. C. A., Beaumont, Texas. Seattle, Washington. HTA.

BUCHANAN, W. G.
Ensign
21 Roosevelt Ave., Chicopee, Mass. Mass. Inst. of Tech., Miami, Pensacola. N. A. No. 1980. HTA.

BUCHANNAN, D. H.
Ensign
603 North 9th St., Temple, Texas. Seattle, San Diego, Pensacola. N. A. No. 2228. HTA.

BUCKLEY, EMMETT W.
Student Officer
602 American Nat'l Bank Bldg., San Francisco, Cal. Dunwoody Inst., Minn. HTA.

BULKLEY, CHARLES S.
Ensign
Jefferson Rd., Short Hills, N. J. Great Lakes, Pensacola. HTA.

BUMANN, ALBERT T.
Ensign
614 Madison St., Litchfield, Ill. Mass. Inst. of Tech., Bay Shore, Pensacola. N. A. No. 1208. HTA.

AND THIS AT 3,000 FEET

BUNNELL, RALPH D.
Ensign
Scranton, Pa. Mass. Inst. of Tech.

BURBANK, PAUL E.
Ensign
28 Francis Ave., Pittsfield, Mass. Mass. Inst. of Tech., Miami, Pensacola. N. A. No. 1903. HTA.

BURGESS, GEORGE P.
Ensign
303 Richards St., Joliet, Ill. Mass. Inst. of Tech., Key West, Miami, Pensacola. N. A. No. 1237. HTA.

BURGESS, LEWIS H.
Student Officer
L.c.o. M. E. Smith and Co., Omaha, Nebraska. Mass. Inst. of Tech., Miami. HTA.

BURGESS, SÙLLIVAN
Ensign
2501 Ridge Rd., Berkeley, Cal. Mass. Inst. Tech., Akron, Rockaway, Hampton Roads, Key West. N. .A. No. 2679. LTA.

BURGESS, W. EARL
Ensign
Wayne, W. Va. Mass. Inst. of Tech., Pensacola, Miami, Northern Bomb. Sq., Fr., Moutchic, Fr. N. A. No. 900. HTA.

BURGUNDER, B. J.
Student Officer
Esplanade Apts., Baltimore, Md. Mass. Inst. of Tech., Miami. HTA.

BURKE, C. B., Jr.
Lieut. (j.g.)
1635 Laurel Ave., Knoxville, Tenn. Mass. Inst. of Tech., Cambridge, Pensacola, Hampton Roads. HTA.

BURLEIGH, L. A., Jr.
Ensign
9 Western Ave., Augusta, Maine. Mass. Inst. of Tech., Bay Shore, Pensacola, Queenstown, Ire. N. A. No. 1267. HTA.

BURNETT, C. E.
Ensign
3612 Wyandot, K. C., Mo. Mass. Inst. of Tech., Key West, Miami. N. A. No. 1532. HTA.

BURNETT, T. J.
Student Officer
Fischer Store, Texas. Mass. Inst. of Tech., Key West. HTA.

BURNHAM, H. C.
Ensign
4 Middle St., Old Town, Maine. Mass. Inst. of Tech., Miami, Pensacola, Rockaway Beach. N. A. No. 1317. HTA.

BURNS, E. R.
Lieut. (j.g.)
15 Pleasant St., Meriden, Conn. Rockaway Beach, Hampton Roads. Bu. Steam Engineering, Wash. LTA.

BURNS, JOSEPH A.
Ensign
419 Denniston Ave., Pittsburgh, Pa. Mass. Inst. of Tech., Miami, Pensacola. N. A. No. 1919. HTA.

BURRAGE, CHAS. W.
Ensign
20 South 15th St., Flushing, N. Y. Columbia University, Pensacola, Detroit, Great Lakes. HTA.

BURRAGE, WALTER S
Ensign
42 Eliot St., Jamaica Plain, Mass. Mass. Inst. of Tech., Bay Shore, Pensacola, Moutchic, Fr. N. A. No. 1248. HTA.

(*U*)

BURROWS, JULIAN S.
Lieut. (j.g.)
Saginaw, Mich., Mass. Inst. of Tech., Pensa. Moutchic, Pauillac, Ile Tudy, L'Aber Vrach., Fr. N. A. No. 308. HTA.

BURRY, WILLIAM, Jr.,
Ensign
1432 Astor St., Chicago, Ill. Mass. Inst. of Tech., Bay Shore, Pensacola. N. A. No. 1905. HTA.

BURT, HENRY R.
Lieut. (j.g.)
Bronxville, New York Eastleigh, England.

BURTON, J. GILBERT
Ensign
1529 Henry Clay Ave., New Orleans, La. Mass. Inst. of Tech., Miami. HTA.

BURTON, J. H., Jr.
Lieut. (j.g.)
31 Archer Ave., Mt.Vernon. Bay Shore, Miami. N. A. No. 1531.

BURTON, JOHN F.
Ensign
Boston, Mass. Mass. Inst. of Tech., Pensacola.

BUSHNELL, J. H.
Ensign
1829 Vine Place, Minneapolis, Minn. Dunwoody, Key West, Miami, Pensacola. N. A. No. 957. HTA.

BUTLER, STUART M.
Lieut. (j.g.)
5534 Bartmer Ave., St. Louis, Mo. R. F. C. Toronto, Canada; Pensacola, Calais, Fr., North Bomb. Gr. N. A. No. 150. HTA.

ANOTHER JOB FOR THE WRECKING CREW

BUTT, DALE J.
Ensign
Newberg, Oregon. Seattle, Wash., Miami, Pensacola. N. A. No. 2240.

BUTTOLPH, ALBERT C.
Student Officer
1200 New York Ave., Pasadena, Cal. Seattle, Washington; San Diego. HTA.

BUTTS, JOHN R.
Student Officer
1508 Cherry St., Vicksburg, Miss. Seattle, Washington. HTA.

BYNON, JOHN F.
Student Officer
Care of Great Western Sugar Co., Sterling, Colorado. Seattle, Washington; San Diego. HTA.

Baber, Malcolm J., Ensign.

Backus, Clinton D., Lieut. (j.g.).

Bade, William H., Student Officer, 546 Third St., Brooklyn, N. Y.

Badger, Jack Moore, Ensign, 963 E. South Temple, Salt Lake City, Utah. N. A. No. 1650.

Baer, E. B., Student Officer, 4 Crocus Hill, St. Paul, Minn. Seattle, Wash.; Miami, Fla. HTA.

Bailey, Albert A., Lieut. (j.g.), Hampton, Va. Mass. Inst. of Tech., R. N. A. S. Roehampton, Cranwell, Pembroke, Paimboeuf, Guipaver. N. A. No. 1086. HTA.

Bailey, D. C., Jr., Student Officer, 829 Park Ave., New York City.

Bailey, Morris H., Ensign, 45 Davidson Road, Worcester, Mass. N. A. No. 313.

Bailey, Roscoe S., Ensign, Care of Western Colorado Power Co., Montrose, Colo.

Baily, Livingston B., Student Officer, Lancaster Ave., Ardmore, Pa. Mass. Inst. of Tech. HTA.

Baird, Benjamin H., Lieut. (j.g.), Fairmont Hotel, San Francisco, Cal. Moutchic; French Foreign Legion, Ile Tudy; Bolsena, Italy; Brest. N. A. No. 554. HTA.

Baker, C. F., Ensign, 16 Welen Head, Wellesley, Mass.

Baker, Chas. W., Ensign, 628 Empire St., Ishpeming, Mich.

Baker, Frederick, Student Officer, 215 Market St., Rockland, Mass. Mass. Inst. of Tech., Miami, Key West, Fla. HTA.

Baker, J. L., Lieut. (j. g.), 140 W. 105th St., New York City.

Baker, H. E., Student Officer, 363 Main St., Plymouth, Mich.

Baker, Loyal S., Student Officer.

Baker, Martin R., Student Officer, Hurston, R. F. D. No. 7, Knoxville, Tenn.

Baker, Myers E., Lieut. (j. g.), Great Neck, L. I., N. Y. N. A. No. 524.

Baker, Philip D., Ensign, 2231 E. 3d St., Duluth, Minn.

Baker, Virgil P., Lieut. (j.g.), 2137 W. 21st St., Los Angeles, Cal.

Baker, W. C., Jr., Student Officer, 1863 Victor St., Bronx, New York City.

Baker, William, Ensign, 1807 Madison Ave., Toledo, Ohio. Mass. Inst. of Tech., Key West, Fla. N. A. No. 1467.

Bakewell, Benjamin P., Ensign, 5529 Fifth Ave., Pittsburgh, Pa. Mass. Inst. of Tech., Pensacola.

Baldwin, G. O., Gunner.

Baldwin, Leo A., Ensign, 493 Classon Ave., Brooklyn, N. Y. N. A. No. 1572.

Baldwin, M. A., Lieut. (j.g.), 504 11th St., South Fargo, N. Dak. Mass. Inst. of Tech., Akron, Ohio; Pensacola, Fla.; Montant, L. I., N. Y. LTA.

Baldwin, Walter S., Jr., Ensign, 19 Woodruff Ave., Brooklyn, N. Y. Mass. Inst. of Tech., Akron, Ohio; Rockaway Beach. LTA.

Baldwin, W. Lester, Ensign, 1101 Fidelity Bldg., Baltimore, Md. Mass. Inst. of Tech., Bayshore, Pensacola, London, Eng. N. A. No. 1328. HTA.

Ball, Frank R., Student Officer, 300 N. Summer Ave., Creston, Iowa.

Ballantine, Herbert W., Ensign, 550 Park Ave., New York City.

Ballantine, John H., Student Officer, Cedarhurst, L. I., N. Y.

Ballard, Harry D., Student Officer, Winona, Miss. Mass. Inst. of Tech., Pensacola, Fla.; New Orleans, La.

Ballew, A. D., Ensign, Tuckerman, Ark. Mass. Inst. of Tech., Miami, Pensacola. N. A. No. 2134. HTA.

Ballou, Howard M., Student Officer.

Bamrick, Edward Joseph, Ensign, 9616 Indiana Ave., Chicago, Ill.

Banker, William J., Student Officer, Ukiah, Cal.

Bankhead, Clarence A., Machinist, 1915 Woodward Ave., Detroit, Mich.

Banks, Robert L., Ensign, 2017 Ogden Ave., Superior, Wis. Mass. Inst. of Tech., Key West, Pensacola. N. A. No. 2406. HTA.

Bannan, Francis E., Student Officer.

Bannister, John E., Student Officer, 100 Conduit St., Annapolis, Md.

Barbee, Harry, Ensign, 619 N. Blount St., Raleigh, N. C.

Barber, Albert C., Ensign.

Bard, William H., Ensign, 27 S. Ninth St., Reading, Pa. N. A. No. 704.

Barchi, Joseph P., Ensign, 474 West St., West Hoboken, N. J.

Barbot, H. V., Student Officer, 414 N. 2d St., Camden, Pa.

Barger, James A., Student Officer, 144 Green Ave., Detroit, Mich.

Barie, William L., Ensign, 490 Bewick Ave., Detroit, Mich. Key West, Miami, Pensacola. HTA.

Bark, Earle B., 732 West Ave., Elyria, Ohio. N. A. No. 707.

Barkclew, Elwood H., Ensign, 140 W. 37th St., Los Angeles, Cal. N. A. No. 2416.

Barker, Francis M., Student Officer, Care of Wadsworth Noyes, 120 Exchange St., Portland, Maine. Mass. Inst. of Tech. HTA.

Barker, G. S., Ensign, 1851 E. 97th St., Cleveland, Ohio. Mass. Inst. of Tech., Akron, Hampton Roads, U. S. S. *Nevada*; Bantry Bay, Ireland. LTA.

Barker, Raymond, Student Officer, 409 W. 71st St., Chicago. Mass. Inst. of Tech. HTA.

Barkley, Lacy E., Student Officer, Enfield, N. C.

Barlow, Harry N., Student Officer, Bethany, Mo. Seattle, Wash. HTA.

Barnaby, Conrad, Ensign.

Barnes, A. K., Ensign, Dublin, Texas. Mass. Inst. of Tech., Miami, Pensacola, Key West. N. A. No. 1807. LTA.

Barnes, Baron S., Ensign, 1140 Wood Ave., Colo. Springs, Colo. N. A. No. 1207.

Barnes, Donald D., Ensign, New York Mills, Oneeda Co., New York State. Mass. Inst. of Tech., Norfolk, Pensacola; Wash., D. C.; Chicago. N. A. No. 562.

Barnes, Harry P., Student Officer, Ambler, Pa.

Barnes, J. P., Carpenter, N. A. No. 670.

Barnes, Philip J., Lieut. (j.g.), Williamstown, Mass.

Barnes, Walter G., Student Officer, 2639 Aldrich Ave., South Minneapolis, Minn.

Barnett, Daniel W., Ensign, 210 E. Ninth St., Rome, Ga. Mass. Inst. of Tech., Bay Shore, N. Y.; Pensacola, Fla. N. A. No. 1935. HTA.

Barnett, Marshall D., Student Officer, 5456 Vickery Blvd., Dallas, Texas Mass. Inst. of Tech., Pensacola, Fla.; New Orleans, La.

Barnett, Robert F., Ensign, Latrobe, Pa. Mass. Inst. of Tech., Bayshore, L. I.; Pensacola, Fla. N. A. No. 2032. HTA.

Barnum, D. S., Ensign, 312 Highland Ave., Syracuse, N. Y. N. A. No. 677.

Barr, C. C., Student Officer, 169 Park Place, Brooklyn, N. Y.

Barr, Samuel D., Ensign.

Barr, Thomas Turner, Jr., Ensign, Metuchen, N. J. Mass. Inst. of Tech., Pensacola, Miami, Pauillac, Moutchic, Trojan. HTA.

Barr, W. M., Lieut. (j.g.), 14 Wall St., New York City. Mass. Inst. of Tech., Bay Shore, Key West, Moutchic, St. Trojan, France. N. A. No. 381. HTA.

Barratt, Roswell F., Lieut. (j.g.), 133 Harrison St., East Orange, N. J. Mass. Inst. of Tech.; Blue Hill, Washington, Paimboeuf, Paris, London, U. S. S. *Aroostook* (Transatlantic Flight Duty).

Barrett, Joseph D., Student Officer.

Barrett, William S., Student Officer, 20 Babcock St., Providence, R. I.

Barrie, O. S., Boatswain, 1442 Temple Place, St. Louis, Mo. Great Lakes, Ill.

Barrie, Robert, Jr., Student Officer, Rose Lane, Haverford, Pa. Mass. Inst. of Tech. HTA.

Bartholomew, Herbert, Student Officer, 410 John St., Champaigne, Ill.

Bartholomew, O. A., Ensign, 2809 Irving Ave., South Minneapolis, Minn.

Barthleson, August C., Ensign, 811 Gibson St., Muskegon, Okla. N. A. No. 2355.

Bartlett, William E. A. S., Student Officer.

Barton, Charles W., Student Officer, 126 23d St., Elmhurst, L. I., N. Y.

Barton, Fred B., Ensign, 835 W. Market St., Akron, Ohio. Mass. Inst. of Tech., Rockaway, Akron. LTA.

Baruch, Walter B., Machinist.

Barus, Maxwell, Student Officer, 5 Nassau St., New York City.

Basham, A. B., Student Officer, 438 W. 11th St., Shawnee, Okla. Mass. Inst. of Tech., Key West, Fla. HTA.

Bass, Walter H., Student Officer, 82 Metlin Ave., Akron, Ohio. N. A. No. 1993.

Bassett, C. C., Jr., Lieut. (j.g.), Harvard Club, New York City. Lafayette F. C., Moutchic, Dunkerque, Northern Bomb. Gr., R. A. F., Miami. N. A. No. 1316. HTA.

Bassett, Norman Douglas, Student Officer, Demonat Printing Co., Moeliser, Wis. Dunwoody Inst. HTA.

Baskette, Geo. Lemoyne, 143 Bloor St. West, Toronto, Ontario.

Batchelor, Henry A., Lieut. (j.g.), N. A. No. 755.

Bateman, J. W., Student Officer, Dividing Creek, Cumberland Co., N. J. Seattle, Wash. HTA.

Bateman, Roland, Student Officer, 349 Mt. Vernon St., Lawrence, Mass. Mass. Inst. of Tech., Bay Shore.

Bates, Bennett, Ensign, 471 Park Ave., New York City. Mass. Inst. of Tech., Miami, Pensacola. N. A. No. 2382. HTA.

Bates, Chester A., Ensign, 78 Ridge Ave., Pawtucket, R. I. N. A. No. 1510.

Bates, Harold Q., Lieut. (j.g.), 481 Seyburn Ave., Detroit, Mich. Buffalo, New York City.

Bates, Harold, Ensign, 481 Seyburn Ave., Detroit, Mich.

Bates, Harrison, Ensign, 314 C St., N. W., Wash., D. C. N. A. No. 2219.

Battle, C. E., Lieut.

Battle, G. K., Student Officer, 13 Washington Terrace, St. Louis, Mo. Seattle, Wash. HTA.

Batts, Walter H.

Baum, James E., Jr., Lieut. (j.g.), Daniel, Lincoln Co., Wyoming. Mass. Inst. of Tech., Pensacola, Washington, Killingholme, Eng.; Dundee, Scotland. N. A. No. 226. HTA.

Bauman, Walter M., Student Officer, 1810 Calvert St., N. W., Washington, D. C.

Baur, Raymond A., Ensign.

Baur, William R., Student Officer, Phi Kappa Psi House, Easton, Pa.

Bayless, Alec C., Student Officer, The News-Journal, Dallas, Texas.

Beadleston, C. P., Lieut. (j.g.), 500 Madison Ave., New York City. N. A. No. 501.

Beales, D. T., Ensign, Inter-State Nat'l Bank, Kansas City, Mo.

Beattie, James S., Ensign, 1359 Vermont Ave., Detroit, Mich. N. A. No. 2154.

Beatty, John L., Student Officer, 691 Highland Ave., Washington, D. C.

Beauchamp, Richard A., Ensign, San Pedro, Cal. N. A., No. 1691.

Beaver, Jacob Julius, Student Officer, 24 Baker Ave., Dover, N. J.

Beazley, R. J., Student Officer, Upper Zion, Va. Seattle, Wash. HTA.

Beck, John E., Ensign, 540 Powell St., San Francisco, Cal. Mass. Inst. of Tech., San Diego, Pensacola. N. A. No. 1238. HTA.

Becker, Charles B., Ensign, Irvington-the-Hudson, New York City.

Beckhart, Benj. H., Student Officer, 433 Pearl St., Denver, Colo.

Beckwith, Alfred A., Ensign, 728 Stanley St., New Britain, Conn.

Beckwith, Paul S., Ensign, Siller, Nebr.

Beede, F. R., Ensign, Antioch, Cal. N. A. No. 1649.

Beeker, Samuel T., Student Officer.

Beer, Ethan A., Student Officer, 400 Charles River Rd., Cambridge, Mass.

Beers, Henry Samuel, Student Officer, 63 Fair St., Guilford, Conn. Mass. Inst. of Tech. HTA.

Beggs, Eugene W., Student Officer, 289 Ridgewood Ave., Glen Ridge, N. J.

Begley, John S., Ensign, 214 Lymen St., Holyoke, Mass. Mass. Inst. of Tech., Pensacola. LTA.

Beirne, Milton J., Student Officer, 3731 2d St., Richmond, Va.

Bell, Harold W., Ensign, Lakeview, Oregon. N. A. No. 1565.

Bell, Leland M., Ensign, 2729 Forest Ave., Berkeley, Cal. Seattle, San Diego, Pensacola, Fla. N. A. No. 2377. HTA.

Bell, William W., Lieut. (j.g.), Palisade Ave., Englewood, N. J. Pensacola, Huntington; Moutchic, St. Trojan (Fr.); Bay Shore, Hampton Roads. N. A. No. 287.

Bellen, Dalton M., Student Officer, 316 Huntington Ave., Boston, Mass.

Bellman, Russell S., Ensign, 1931 S. First St., Louisville, Ky. Mass. Inst. of Tech., Miami, Pensacola. N. A. No. 1689.

Belmer, Charles W., Student Officer, 163 W. 12th St., New York City.

Benedict, H. G., Ensign, 149 Fifth Ave., Roselle, N. J. Mass. Inst. of Tech., Bay Shore, Pensacola, Moutchic, Arcachon (Fr.). N. A. No. 919. HTA.

Benedict, Thomas H., Ensign, 149 W. 5th Ave., Roselle, N. J. Mass. Inst. of Tech., Key West, Miami, Moutchic, Malpensa (Italy). N. A. No. 1452. HTA.

Benjamin, Baret O., Student Officer, 340 W. 86th St., New York City. Mass. Inst. of Tech., Miami. HTA.

Benjamin, Henry R., Lieut. (j.g.), 2 E. 87th St., New York City. Bay Shore, Miami, Moutchic, Cusuha, Malpensa, Italy; St. Inglevert, France. British Squadron 214, France; Brouge, Belgium. N. A. No. 238.

Benner, Charles V., Ensign, Englewood, N. J. N. A. No 2466.

Benner, Robert L., Student Officer, 921 Belmont Ave., Grand Forks, N. Dak.

Bennet, Augustus W., Student Officer, 415 Ft. Washington Ave., New York City. Mass. Inst. of Tech. HTA.

Bennet, J. W., Boatswain.

Bennett, Frederick M., Student Officer, 823 Lincoln Ave., Cincinnati, Ohio.

Bennett, Harry W.

Bennett, Hubert D., Ensign, 3232 Collingwood Ave., Toledo, Ohio. Mass. Inst. of Tech., Miami, Pensacola, Killingholme, Eng. N. A. No. 1269. HTA.

Bensing, Geo. W., Gunner.

Berg, Einar A., Student Officer, 468 State St., St. Paul, Minn.

Berger, F. C. B., Lieut. (j.g.). N. A. No. 174.

Bergin, Thomas M., Lieut. (j.g.), 81 Columbia Road, Boston, Mass. N. A. No. 232.

Bergman, Ralph W., Student Officer, Newton, Iowa. Dunwoody Inst., Miami, Fla. HTA.

Bering, Robert E., Jr., Ensign, 1500 Page St., San Francisco, Cal. N. A. No. 2002.

Berkey, Russell S., Lieut. (j.g.).

Berns, Julius I., Student Officer, 11 Blackstone St., Boston, Mass.

Berschaback, Clarence F., Student Officer.

Bertine, Edwin K., Ensign, 57 S. Second Ave., Mt. Vernon, N. Y. N. A. No. 2115.

Bertolett, Edwin A., Student Officer, 569 Lancaster Ave., Bryn Mawr, Pa.

Bertoneire, G. W., Ensign.

Best, Herbert W., Ensign, 493 Commonwealth Ave., Boston, Mass. Mass. Inst. of Tech., Bayshore, Pensacola, North Sydney, Miami. N. A. No. 1137. HTA.

Bethel, E. Turner, Student Officer, 910 W. Grace St., Richmond, Va. Mass. Inst. of Tech., Key West. HTA.

Bettridge, John Clarence, Ensign, 1210 Logan Ave. Minneapolis, Minn.

Betz, Geo., Jr., Student Officer, Ashersville, Ky. Mass. Inst. of Tech., Bay Shore, Brunswick, Key West.

Bevier, R. B., Ensign, 212 Berkeley Place, Brooklyn, N. Y.

Bidwell, Clyde C., Student Officer, 175 Beacon St., Hartford, Conn.

Bidwell, G. H., Ensign, Kinsley, Kans. Mass. Inst. of Tech., Bay Shore, Pensacola. N. A. No. 2222.

Bigelow, Loyal A., Student Officer, 10 S. LaSalle St., Chicago, Ill.

Bigelow, Robert B., Ensign, 1520 Hill St., Ann Arbor, Mich. Mass. Inst. of Tech., Bay Shore, Pensacola. N. A. No. 2250. LTA.

Biggers, Clyde E., Ensign, Stephenville, Texas.

Biggs, Carl H., Ensign, 1 Central Ave., Ithaca, N. Y N. A. No. 1273.

Biggs, James R., Ensign, N. A. No. 708.

Bigler, Frederick A., Machinist, 501 Superior Ave. Chippewa Falls, Wis.

Bigler, Paul G., Galveston, Ind. N. A. No. 2381.

Bilderback, Gordon B., Student Officer, Church St., Champaign, Ill.

Billings, Dwight B., Lieut. (j.g.), 9 West St., North Somerville, Mass. N. A. No. 2473.

Bingham, Robert Worth, Jr., Student Officer, Cherokee Park, Louisville, Ky.

Bingham, R. W., Jr., Student Officer, Glenview, Ky. Mass. Inst. of Tech., Bay Shore. LTA.

Bingham, Roy R., Ensign. N. A. No. 2435.

Bishop, Carey W., Ensign, 5203 S. Jay St., Takoma, Wash. N. A. No. 2358.

Bitter, Herbert C. Student Officer, 3700 N. Hermitage Ave., Chicago, Ill.

Black, Hulon W., Student Officer, 1906 Guadalupe St., Austin, Texas.

Blackburn, James D., Ensign. N. A. No. 2428.

Blackstock, B. T., Machinist, 13524 Earlwild Rd., Cleveland, Ohio.

Blackwell, W. E., Ensign, 2326 Webster St., Berkeley, Cal. Mass. Inst. of Tech., San Diego, Pensacola, Rockaway Beach. N. A. No. 1428. HTA.

Blackwell, William M., Ensign, Marion, S. C. Mass. Inst. of Tech., Miami, Key West, Pensacola. N. A. No. 2633. HTA.

Blade, Estle J., Gunner.

Bladsworth, Timothy P., Machinist.

Blagden, Francis Meredith, Student Officer, 176 E. 70th St., New York City. Mass. Inst. of Tech., Bay Shore, Pensacola.

Blair, Francis King, Ensign, 653 Waveland Ave., Chicago, Ill. N. A. No. 1112.

Blair, Geo. B., Student Officer, 209 Beall Ave., Wooster, Ohio.

Blair, Lawrence D., Lieut. (j.g.), 808 Devonshire St., Pittsburgh, Pa. Mass. Inst. of Tech., Operations, Wash., D. C., Key West. N. A. No. 2111. HTA.

Blair, Octave, Ensign, 995 Madison Ave., New York City.

Blair, Roy R., Student Officer, 758 Stout Ave., Wyoming, Cincinnati, Ohio. Mass. Inst. of Tech., Miami, Fla. HTA.

Blair, Thomas S., Lieut. (j.g.), 745 N. Michigan Ave., Chicago, Ill. Mass. Inst. of Tech., Key West. N. A. No. 1491. HTA.

Blakeslee, Marshall E., Student Officer, North Chelmsford, Mass.

Blakey, R. K., Lieut. (j.g.)

Blalock, John W., Student Officer, Southern Bank & Trust Co., Valdosta, Ga.

Blanchard, Donald D., Ensign, 1818 Topping Ave., Bronx, N. Y.

Blanchard, Harold F., Lieut. (j.g.), 12 W. 103d St., New York City.

Blanchard, Isaac M., Student Officer, Williamstown Mass.

Blanchard, M. B. N. A. No. 284.

Blandford, John B., Jr., Student Officer, 174 Terrace Ave., Hasbrouck Heights, N. J. Mass. Inst. of Tech. HTA.

Bleecker, T. B., Ensign, 12 S. Portland Ave., Brooklyn, N. Y. N. A. No. 716.

Bleistein, C. W., Lieut. (j.g.), 743 Main Street, Buffalo, N. Y.

Blewitt, Bertram J., Student Officer.

Bliss, Wyllys King, Student Officer, 4929 Lotus Ave., St. Louis, Mo. Seattle, Wash.; San Diego. HTA.

Bloch, Bernard, Ensign, Mallyn Road, Merion, Pa.

Bloch, Harold S., Ensign, Wheeling, W. Va.

Blodgett, Frank C. P., Lieut. (j.g.), 825 Court St., Janesville, Wis.

Blomfeldt, Allen A., Student Officer, 108 W. Jefferson St., Chicago, Ill.

Blood, Geo. Whitefield, Ensign.

Bloomfield, H. E., Machinist, 170 E. 75th St., New York City.

Blossom, F. M., Ensign, 1630 Glen Oak St., Peoria, Ill. N. A. No. 1798.

Blossom, H. M., Ensign, 41 Kudder St., Detroit, Mich. N. A. No. 2129.

Blotner, Felix M., Ensign, N. A. No. 920.

Bludworth, T. F., Machinist, Fanwood, N. J.

Blue, Edward B., Ensign. N. A. No. 1509.

Bluemanthan, A., Ensign.

Bockius, G. H., Lieut. (j.g.), 1512 N. Cleveland Ave., Canton, Ohio. N. A. No. 1087.

Bodine, Richard H., Student Officer, 1323 Carr Avenue, Memphis, Tenn., Mass. Inst. of Tech., Key West, Fla. HTA.

Boedicker, Earl O., Ensign, 161 N. Portage Drive, Akron, Ohio.

Boehmer, Frank C., Student Officer, 1220 S. 20th St., Lincoln, Nebr. Mass. Inst. of Tech. LTA.

Boehnlein, Charles, Student Officer, 2004 Grand Ave. S., Minneapolis, Minn. Mass. Inst. of Tech. HTA.

Boeing, W. E., Lieut. (j.g.), Care of Boeing Aeroplane Co., Seattle, Wash.

Bogart, Gilbert D., Student Officer, 142 Ascension St., Passaic, N. J. Mass. Inst. of Tech. LTA.

Boger, Frederick, Jr., Ensign, 64 St. Marks Place, New Brighton, N. Y. Bay Shore, Mass. Inst. of Tech., Pensacola, Moutchic (France), Killingholme, Bay Shore, Long Island. N. A. No. 290.

Boggs, E. C., Ensign.

Bohacket, Lawrence A., Ensign, 579 Cross Ave., Detroit, Mich.

Bohmfalk, J. F., Student Officer, 851 Lexington Ave., New York City.

Bokien, Ernest A., Machinist, 938 W. 61st St., Seattle, Wash. Columbia Univ., Seattle, Wash; San Diego, Cal.; Detroit, Mich.; Philadelphia.

Bolinger, John C., Ensign, Methow, Okanogan Co., Wash. N. A. No. 1669.

Bolton, Raymond E., Student Officer, National Press Club, Washington, D. C.

Bomgardner, H., Lieut. (j.g.), La Junta, Colo. Mass. Inst. of Tech., Bay Shore, L. I.; Pensacola, Fla. N. A. No. 948. HTA.

Bonaparte, Anthony, Gunner.

Bond, George H., Student Officer, 742 Highland Ave., Atlanta, Ga. Seattle, Wash.

Bone, Lewis Bernard, Student Officer, 3615 Noble Ave., Dallas, Texas.

Bonehill, James Henry, Ensign.

Bonin, Pierre E., Student Officer, 256 Aspinwall Ave., Brookline, Mass. Mass. Inst. of Tech., Miami, Fla. HTA.

Bonnefond, Raymond E., Student Officer, Hancock, Delaware Co., New York.

Bonnor, Charles A., Student Officer, 6750 Merrill Ave. Chicago, Ill.

Borchers, William C., Student Officer, 755 Irving St., Portland, Oregon.

Boreman, Robert W., Student Officer, Middlebourne, W. Va. Mass. Inst. of Tech. HTA.

Boren, Norman A., Student Officer, Pamona, N. C.

Borland, R. M., Ensign, Martinez, Cal. Mass. Inst. of Tech., Akron, Rockaway Beach. LTA.

Bosak, M. J., Jr., Ensign, 452 Riverside Drive, New York City. Mass. Inst. of Tech., Bay Shore, Key West, Miami. N. A., No. 1533. HTA.

Boswell, Roland R., Student Officer, 1625 York St., Quincy, Ill.

Botzum, Charles A., Ensign, 1512 Oxford St., Berkeley Cal. N. A. No. 1607.

Bouldin, William, Ensign, 107 Mt. Pleasant Ave., West Orange, N. J.

Bourne, Bradley W., Student Officer, Lancaster, Ky. Mass. Inst. of Tech. HTA.

Bourquin, C. R., Student Officer, 223 N. Excelsior St., Butte, Mont.

Bowen, John B., Ensign.

Bower, D. V., Student Officer, Campbell, Va. N. A No. 2454.

Bowers, Charles E., Student Officer, 35 Park St. Canton, N. Y.

Bowes, Harvey R., Ensign, 6105 Woodland Ave., Phila., Pa.

Bowlin, Emil R., Student Officer, Hedrick, Iowa Mass. Inst. of Tech.

Bowman, B. W., Student Officer, 92 Oakland Ave. Akron, O. Seattle, Wash. HTA.

Bowman, Marquis, Student Officer, Psi Upsilon House, Williamstown, Mass.

Bowman, Riley, Ensign, Parkersburg, W. Va.

Bowman, Ripley, Ensign, 17 Rock Creek Church Rd., Washington, D. C.

Bowman, W. H., Ensign, Bridgeport, Conn. Pelham Bay, Columbia Univ., Calais, Pauillac. HTA.

Bowser, Alan W., Student Officer, 108 W. 3d St., Oklahoma City, Okla. Seattle, Wash.; San Diego.

Bowyer, Frank P., Student Officer, Care of Tampa Casket Co., Tampa, Fla.

Boyd, J. C., Lieut. (j.g.), 314 Upper Mt. Ave., Montlair, N. J.

Boyd, Thomas F., Ensign, Care of Union Oil Co. of Cal., Oleum, Cal. Mass. Inst. of Tech., Pensacola, Key West, Miami, Anacostia, Washington, D. C. N. A. No. 1302.

Boydler, Einar, Machinist, Monroe Place, Larchmont, Norfolk, Va. Annapolis, Md., Pensacola, Hampton Roads, Mexico, France, England, Fleet. N. A. No. 1736. HTA.

Boyer, Howard S., Student Officer, 935 W. State St., Trenton, N. J.

Boyes, Gordon M., Ensign. N. A. No. 1575.

Boynton, Alvah R., Lieut. (j.g.), 130 Oxford St., Cambridge, Mass.

Boynton, Nehemiah, Jr., Ensign, 379 Washington Ave., Brooklyn, N. Y.

Brabson, George Dana, Student Officer, Spring St., Johnson City, Tenn.

Bradbury, James A., Jr., Student Officer, 3495 Broadway, New York City.

Bradfield, J. R., Student Officer, 3907 Gillar Ave., Dallas, Texas. Mass. Inst. of Tech.

Bradford, Smith M., Lieut. (j.g.), Bel Air, Maryland. N. A. No. 506½.

Bradley, Anderville S., Student Officer, Munro Ave., Wynnton, Columbus, Ga.

Bradley, G. Donald, Lieut. (j.g.), 132d and 103d Aves., Edmonton, Alberta, Canada. Mass. Inst. of Tech., Buffalo, Dayton, Ohio.

Bradley, Tudor W., Ensign, 905 Cooper St., Camden, N. J.

Brady, Charles V., Ensign, 3527 Vista Ave., St. Louis, Mo. N. A. No. 1115.

Brady, J. B., Ensign.

Brady, John C., Student Officer.

Brady, Richard M., Ensign, Rapidan, Va. Great Lakes, Ill.; Hampton Roads, Va.

Brainard, M. S., Gunner.

Bramigan, Arthur T., Student Officer, Wayland, Mass.

Brandt, William E., Student Officer, Co. L, 7th Regt., Camp Perry, Great Lakes, Ill.

Brandenstein, Errol W., Ensign. N. A. No. 1190.

Brannan, William Forrest, Ensign, 112 Portland St., Bryan, Ohio. N. A. No. 1959.

Bransome, E. D., Lieutenant, Engineers Club, Philadelphia, Pa. N. A. No. 286.

Branson, Frank L., Ensign, Fairfax, Ala. Mass. Inst. of Tech., Pensacola, Chatham. HTA.

Braun, Christian W., Student Officer, 299 Marshall St., Paterson, N. J.

Breathitt, James, Jr., Student Officer, Hopkinsville, Ky. Mass. Inst. of Tech., Bay Shore. HTA.

Breck, Lewis T., Boatswain, 5547 Waiterman Ave., St. Louis, Mo.

Breen, James W., Gunner.

Breen, Leonard J., Ensign, 152 Graham Ave., Paterson, N. J.

Breese, James L., Jr., Lieut. (j.g.).

Bremier, Fred, Student Officer, University Club, Washington, D. C. Mass. Inst. of Tech. HTA.

Brennan, Edward, Lieut. (j.g.), Southampton, L. I., N. Y.; Bay Shore, N. Y.: Key West, Fla.; Chatham., Mass. HTA.

Brennan, Hubert, Student Officer.

Brennan, John R., Ensign, Harrington Hotel, Washington, D. C.

Brennan, Robert, Ensign, Denison, Texas. Mass. Inst. of Tech., Key West, Miami, Pensacola, Fla. N. A. No. 1668. HTA.

Brenza, Julius C., Student Officer, 923 West Garfield Blvd., Chicago, Ill.

Bressman, A. A., Ensign. N. A. No. 44.

Brett, Donald C., Student Officer, 3400 Walnut St., Philadelphia, Pa.

Brettel, C., Ensign, 131 Nagle Ave., New York City.

Brewer, Edward S., Lieut. (j.g.), 650 Canton Ave. Milton, Mass. Pensacola, Fla.; R. N. A. S. Westgate, Portland; Felixstowe, Eng.; St. Trojan, Arcachon, France. N. A. No. 197. HTA.

Brewer, J. S., Student Officer, 306 S. Monroe St., Baltimore, Md. Pensacola, Fla.

Brewster, Charles H., Lieut. (j.g.), 113 Waverly Place, New York City. Mass. Inst. of Tech., Pensacola, Killingholme, R. A. F.; Catterick, Eng.; Northern Bomb. Group. N. A. No. 326. HTA.

Breyman, Chas. H., Ensign. N. A. No. 700.

Brice, M. D., Ensign.

Brickell, Harry L., Machinist.

Bridge, R. S., Ensign, 229 Van Dyke Ave., Detroit, Mich. Mass. Inst. of Tech., Pensacola, Queenstown, Ire. Rockaway, L. I. N. A. No. 910. HTA.

Bridgeman, Hollis L., Ensign, 471 Broadway, Cambridge, Mass.

Briggs, Clark W., Student Officer.

Briggs, Ferris B., Student Officer, 373 Washington Ave., Brooklyn, N. Y.

Briggs, L. G., Machinist.

Brigham, Wm., Ensign, 2829 Vallejo St., San Francisco, Cal.

Bringham, Lucien M., Ensign.

Brinkmam, Raymond Oliver, Ensign, 41 Woodbine St., Hartford, Conn. Mass. Inst. of Tech., Akron, Ohio; Pensacola, Fla. N. A. No. 2152. LTA.

Britt, Raymond L., Student Officer.

Brittan, Joe M., Student Officer.

Britton, Roswell S., Ensign, Box No. 244, New Bern, N. C. N. A. No. 1953.

Broadfoot, Wm. G., Student Officer, Connelly Springs, N. C.

Brock, Donald C., Ensign, 520 Warwick Rd., Kenilworth, Ill. Dunwoody Inst., Miami, Pensacola. N. A. No. 2337. HTA.

Brockwell, Wm. A., Lieut. (j.g.), 1259 Morse St., N. E., Washington, D. C. N. A. No. 334.

Brokaw, John B., Student Officer, 32 Terrace Court, Tacoma, Wash.

Bronson, Daniel Dorrance, Student Officer, 1301 Fairmont St., N. W., Washington, D. C. Great Lakes, Ill.

Bronson, Hiram S., Jr., Student Officer, 1797 W. First Ave., Columbus, Ohio.

Brooks, Blair M., Student Officer, Hotel Netherland, New York City.

Brooks, D. W., Lieut. (j.g.), Desson, Miss.

Brooks, Garnett T., Student Officer, Royston, Ga. Mass. Inst. of Tech., Miami, Fla. HTA.

Brooks, James L., Student Officer, 1909 Morris Ave., Birmingham, Ala.

Brooks, Walter A., Ensign. N. A. No. 2497.

Brotherhood, John O., Student Officer, 550 First St., Brooklyn, N. Y.

Brown, Allan H., Student Officer, 2123 W. 111th St., Chicago. Mass. Inst. of Tech. HTA.

Brown, Archibald M., Ensign, Stony Brook, L. I., N. Y.

Brown, Carl W., Student Officer, Commercial Hotel, Cresson, Pa.

Brown, Charles O., Student Officer, 1730 Main St., Columbia, S. C. Mass. Inst. of Tech., Wingfoot Lake, Akron, Ohio. LTA.

Brown, Charles Seamans, Student Officer, 726 W. Onondaga St., Syracuse, N. Y. Great Lakes.

Brown, David La Tourette, Ensign, 280 W. End Ave., New York City. Mass. Inst. of Tech., Bay Shore, Pensacola, Brest, Moutchic, Arcachon. HTA.

Brown, E. H., Machinist, P. O. Box 245, Ilion, N. Y.

Brown, Floyd H., Student Officer, Logan, Iowa.

Brown, Geo. W., Student Officer, 595 Riverside Drive, New York City.

Brown, Geo. W., Machinist.

Brown, Herman D., Student Officer, 17 Dresser St., Southbridge, Mass.

Brown, J. N., Ensign.

Brown, John Francis, Lieut. (j.g.), 59 Angell St., Providence, R. I. Mass. Inst. of Tech., Key West. N. A. No. 1489. HTA.

Brown, J. Q., Jr., Ensign, 2100 M St., Sacramento, Cal. Seattle, Wash.; San Diego, Cal., Pensacola, Fla. N. A. No. 1960. HTA.

Brown, Lawrence W., Ensign. N. A. No. 65½.

Brown, Leonard T., Carpenter.

Brown, Milford N., Student Officer, 209 S. State St., Ann Arbor, Mich.

Brown, Stewart W., Student Officer.

Brown, Waldo H., Ensign. N. A. No. 458.

Brown, Wilfred J., Lieut. (j.g.).

Brown, Wm. G., Ensign, Rye Beach, N. H. Mass. Inst. of Tech., Washington, D. C. Aero Engi. Detail, Boston.

Brown, Wm. N., Student Officer, 1208 Eutaw Pl. Baltimore, Md.

BROWNE, H. J., Ensign,. N. A. No. 715.

BROWNING, ROBERT S., Ensign, 1099 Dean St., Brooklyn, N. Y. N. A. No. 1606.

BRUCKHAUSER, WM. K., Lieut. (j.g.), Baldwin, L. I., N. Y. Mass. Inst. of Tech., Pensacola, Moutchic, Fr., Stonehenge, Eng., Killingholme, Eng. N. A. No. 358.

BRUMMITT, L. W., Student Officer, Care of General Motor Corp., Holbrook Ave., and G. T. R. R., Detroit, Mich. Seattle, Wash.; San Diego, Pensacola. HTA.

BRUNELLE, HENRY E., Student Officer.

BRUNER, DONALD B., Student Officer, 1216 22nd St., Rock Island, Ill.

BRUNER, HAROLD MILTON, Student Officer, 1146 Browne Ave., Erie, Pa. Mass. Inst. of Tech. HTA.

BRUNHOUSE, ROBT. S., Student Officer, 1819 Chestnut St., Philadelphia, Pa.

BRUNING, A. J., Student Officer, 1231 W. Jefferson St., Louisville, Ky. Dunwoody Inst., Great Lakes, Miami. HTA.

BRUSSTAR, JAMES S., Student Officer, 758 Lothrop Ave., Detroit, Mich.

BRYANT, R. C., Ensign, 88 Henry St., Binghamton, N. Y. Mass. Inst. of Tech., Pensacola. N. A. No. 339. LTA.

BRYNE, F. J., War. Gun.

BUCHANAN, ARCHIBALD A., Student Officer, 76 Decatur St., Brooklyn, N. Y. Mass. Inst. of Tech., Bensonhurst, Pelham Bay, Key West. HTA.

BUCHANAN, T. S., Ensign.

BUCHANAN, W. W., Machinist, Cornwell, Mass.

BUCK, ELLSWORTH B., Ensign, 60 Marion Ave., Stapleton, S. I., N. Y. Mass. Inst. of Tech., Blue Hill Observatory, Operations, Naval Observatory, Wash.

BUCK, LEONARD J., Lieut. (j.g.), Park St. and Prospect Ave.,Bethlehem, Pa. Mass. Inst. of Tech.,Washington,D. C.

BUCK, WILLIS, Student Officer, 357 Broad St., New London, Conn.

BUCKLEY, WM. A., Boatswain.

BUCKNELL, ELMER J., Ensign.

BUCKSTAFF, JOHN BAY, Ensign, 300 S. 36th St., Philadelphia, Pa.

BUERKIN, JULIUS A., Ensign, 491 Commonwealth Ave., Boston, Mass.

BULKELEY, WARREN, Ensign, 509 Audubon Rd., Brookline, Mass.

BULKLEY, MILTON, Student Officer, 619 Mariposa Ave., Oakland, Cal.

BULL, ALBERT S., Student Officer, Billerica, Mass.

BULLEN, W. G., Ensign.

BULLIS, RICHARD O., Student Officer, 525 S. Westlake Ave., Los Angeles, Cal. Seattle, Wash. HTA.

BULLITT, HUGH K., Student Officer, 1341 3rd Ave., Louisville, Ky. Seattle, Wash. HTA.

BULLOCK, CHARLES A., Student Officer, 1916 16th St., N. W., Washington, D. C.

BULLOCK, JOHN D., Ensign, Fort Atkinson, Wisc. Mass. Inst. of Tech., Miami, Pensacola. N. A. No. 1429. HTA.

BUNKER, ARTHUR H., Ensign, 421 No. Broadway, Yonkers, N. Y.

BUNKER, R. U., Ensign, 615 No. Broadway, Yonkers, N. Y.

BUNT, J. H., Lieut. (j.g.) N. A. No. 1301.

BURCHARD, RUSSELL, Student Officer, Hamilton, N. Y.

BURCHELL, ROBT. L., Student Officer, Erie, Ill.

BURD, THEODORE A., Ensign, 2449 Delaware Ave., Buffalo, N. Y. Mass. Inst. of Tech., Akron, Key West, Fla. N. A. No. 1964. LTA.

BURDEN, WM. D., Student Officer, 7 East 91st St., New York City.

BUREAN, ACHILLE G., Carpenter, 1923 W. Allegheny Ave., Philadelphia, Pa.

BURFORD, EDWARD S., Student Officer, Naval Y. M. C. A., Norfolk, Va.

BURGET, ROBT. V., Student Officer, 1209 E. Wabash Ave., Terre Haute, Ind.

BURGOON, WILLARD T., Student Officer, 1414 Newman Ave., Lakewood, Ohio.

BURKE, FRANK L., Ensign, 13 Brevoort Place, Brooklyn, N. Y.

BURKE, FRANK L., Fnsign. N. A. No. 481.

BURKE, JAMES MICHAEL, Ensign.

BURKE, STANLEY C., Student Officer, Georgetown University, Washington, D. C.

BURKE, THOMAS F., Ensign, 45 W St., N. W., Washington, D. C.

BURKE, THOMAS J., Ensign. N. A. No. 2305.

BURKHART, LORIS E., Ensign.

BURLEIGH, ROY J., Machinist, 107 1st St., N. W., Washington, D. C.

BURN, FARRAR, Ensign.

BURNE, EDWARD R., Ensign.

BURNE, JOHN C., Student Officer, Huntington, L. I., N. Y.

BURNHAM, ADISON C., Ensign, 15 Bracebridge Rd., Newton Center, Mass. N. A. No. 1088.

BURNHAM, DONALD C., Student Officer, Timken Bldg., San Diego, Cal.

BURNHAM, MARSTON, Ensign, 3563 7th St., San Diego, Cal. Mass. Inst. of Tech., Key West, Miami, Pensacola, Coco Solo. N. A. No. 1131. HTA.

BURNHAM, RANDOLPH T., Student Officer, 1505 E. Genesee St., Syracuse, N. Y. Mass. Inst. of Tech., Charleston, S. C., Akron. LTA.

BURNS, A. C., Lieut. (j.g.), 1031 Wall St., Los Angeles, Cal. N. A. No. 610.

BURNS, FREDERICK J., Student Officer.

BURNS, ROBERT W., Ensign, West Carrollton, Ohio, N. A. No. 676.

BURR, SAMUEL H., Student Officer, 99 Monroe St., Brooklyn, N. Y.

BURROWS, LEES J., Ensign, 1013 N. Michigan Ave., Saginaw, Mich. Mass. Inst. of Tech., Bay Shore, L. I.; Pensacola, Fla. N. A. No. 1985. HTA.

BURT, FREDERICK M., Ensign, Westmoreland, Huntington, W. Va.

BURTIS, ERIC F., Ensign.

BURTON, BENJAMIN B., Student Officer, New York City. Mass. Inst. of Tech., Anacostia. HTA.

BURTON, HALBERT G., Student Officer, 3 Walker St., Cambridge, Mass.

BURTON, ROBERT A., JR., Ensign, 1953 Conway Bldg. Chicago, Ill. Mass. Inst. of Tech.

BURWELL, GEO. H., Student Officer, Millwood, Va. Mass. Inst. of Tech. HTA.

BUSH, GEO. ALLEN, Student Officer, 209 Columbia Bldg., Louisville, Ky.

BUSH, GEO. W., Student Officer, 13414 Shaw Ave., E., Cleveland, Ohio.

BUSH, JAMES T., Ensign, University Club, Chicago, Ill. Great Lakes, Hampton Rds., Monchead City, N. C.

BUSHMAN, ROBERT P., Student Officer, 97 Lenox Ave. East Orange, N. J.

BUTCHART, ELLIS J., Ensign, 127 10th St., Duluth, Minn. N. A. No. 307.

BUTLER, H. F., Ensign.

BUTLER, JAMES H., Student Officer, 26 Benefit St., Worcester, Mass.

BUTLER, JOHN JOSEPH, Student Officer, Rear 288 Charles St., Malden, Mass. Mass. Inst. of Tech. HTA.

BUTLER, MARION, Ensign, 1333 15th St., N. W., Washington, D. C. Mass. Inst. of Tech., Pensacola, Moutchic, Fromentine, France. N. A. No. 922. HTA.

BUTRICK, S., Carpenter.

BYERS, JOHN R. B., Student Officer, 935 5th Ave., Coraopolis, Pa. Mass. Inst. of Tech. HTA.

BYERS, WM. L., Student Officer, North Andover, Mass.

BYORK, AMOS, Ensign.

BYRD, EDWARD R., Student Officer, 120 Broadway, New York City.

BYRNE, GILBERT R., Student Officer, 128 S. Hill St., Jackson, Mich. Mass. Inst. of Tech., Akron, Ohio; Rockaway Beach, L. I. LTA.

BYRNE, JOSEPH H., Student Officer, Y. M. C. A., Houston, Texas.

CABER, HORACE C.
Ensign
Stamps, Arkansas. Mass. Inst. of Tech., Bay Shore, Brunswick, Ga., Key West, Pensacola. N. A. No. 2457. HTA.

CALLARD, LYMAN W.
Machinist
140 Circuit Road, Winthrop, Mass. Pauillac, Fr., Eastleigh, Eng., Bay Shore.

CALDWELL, H. W.
Ensign
417 No. Kenilworth Ave., Oak Park, Ill. Mass. Inst. of Tech., S. P. 661, Miami, Pensacola. N. A. No. 1744. HTA.

CAMERON, R. B.
Student Officer
2006 Columbia Road, Washington, D. C. Mass. Inst. of Tech., Bay Shore.

KEY WEST FROM AN HS FLYING BOAT

CAMPBELL, B. J.
Machinist
Mathews Terrace, Rocky River, Ohio. Pensacola, Autangue, Fr., Eastleigh, Eng. HTA.

CAMPBELL, H. R., Jr.
Student Officer
323 N. 8th St., Paterson, N. J. Mass. Inst. of Tech., Miami. HTA.

CAMPBELL, M. JAMES
Ensign
210 W. Iowa Ave., Indianola, Iowa. Mass. Inst. of Tech., Key West, Miami, Pensacola. N.A. No. 2170.

CAMPBELL, W. R.
Ensign
19 Center Hill Ave., Nantasket Beach, Mass. Mass. Inst. of Tech., Pensacola, Portland, U. S. S. *Shur.* LTA

CANTWELL, R. C.
Lieut. (j.g.)
Willmington, N. C. Mass. Inst. of Tech., Pensacola. N. A. No. 341. HTA.

CAREY, W. JAMES
Student Officer
784 Broadway, S. Boston, Mass. Mass. Inst. of Tech., Cambridge; Miami. HTA.

CARLSON, HOMER
Ensign
3027 N. 14th Ave., Omaha, Nebraska. Mass. Inst. of Tech., Bay Shore, Brunswick, Pensacola, Key West. N. A. No. 2336. HTA.

CARPENDER, WM.
Ensign
178 George St., New Brunswick, N. J. Mass. Inst. of Tech., Pensacola, Cape May.

CARPENTER, ALLAN W.
Ensign
1608 Franklin St., Wilmington, Del.

CARPENTER, C. H.
Ensign
640 No. Henry St., Madison, Wisconsin. Dunwoody, Key West, Miami, Pensacola. N. A. No. 2089. HTA.

CARPENTER, PHILIP J.
Ensign
1608 Franklin St., Wilmington, Delaware. Mass. Inst. of Tech., Key West. HTA.

CARR, JOHN EDWIN
Ensign
400 Main St., Porterville, California. Mass. Inst. of Tech., Miami, Pensacola, San Diego. N. A. No. 1506. HTA.

CARRIGAN, E. HARRIS
Student Officer
33 Walnut St., San Francisco, Cal. Mass. Inst. of Tech., San Diego. H. T. A.

CARRINGTON, A. R., Jr.
Student Officer
Parkmont Apts., Lynchburg, Va. Mass. Inst. of Tech., Hampton Roads.

CARROLL. F. W.
Ensign
Lyons, N. Y. Mass. Inst. of Tech., Akron, Rockaway. LTA.

CARROLL, MALCOLM B.
Ensign
316 Bement Ave., Staten Island, N. Y. Mass. Inst. of Tech., Newport, Pelham Bay, Chatham.

CARSON, RUSSELL M.
Ensign
2923 Rutland Ave., Des Moines, Iowa. Mass. Inst. of Tech., Key West, Pensacola. N. A. No. 2356. HTA.

CARTER, PAUL W.
Ensign
Greenwich, N. Y. Mass. Inst. of Tech., Pensacola, Whiddy Island, Ire., Miami, Fleet Air Detachment. N. A. No. 627. HTA.

CARTER, RALPH B., Jr.
Ensign
Haworth, N. J. Mass. Inst. of Tech., Miami. N. A. No. 2415. HTA.

CARTWRIGHT, R. A.
Student Officer
147 Magazine St., Cambridge, Mass. Mass. Inst. of Tech. LTA.

CASEY, JOHN
Student Officer
27 Claremont Ave., Providence, R. I. Mass. Inst. of Tech., Newport, Key West. HTA.

CASSIDY, ROBERT V.
Ensign
48 Flint St., Somerville, Mass. Mass. Inst. of Tech., Pensacola, Queenstown, Ire., Chatham. N. A. No. 1072. HTA.

CASSIDY, WM. P.
Ensign
143 Glendale Park, Rochester, N. Y. Mass. Inst. of Tech., Harvard Radio, Miami, Pensacola. N. A. No. 2624. HTA.

CAUTHEN, CHAS. E.
Ensign
Lynchburg, S. C. Seattle, San Diego, Pensacola. N. A. No. 2373. HTA.

N-9 Gunnery Plane Taking Off

CAVANAGH, G. H.
Ensign
720 Clark St., Evanston, Ill. Great Lakes, Mass. Inst. of Tech., Blue Hill Observatory.

CHAMBERLAIN, F. W.
Ensign
64 Grafton St., Arlington, Mass. Mass. Inst. of Tech., Miami, Pensacola. N. A. No. 2074. HTA.

CHAMBERLAIN, W. M.
Ensign
101 Merrick St., Worcester, Mass. Mass. Inst. of Tech., Key West. HTA.

CHAMBERLIN, J. R.
Ensign
Torresdale, Phila., Pa. Mass. Inst. of Tech., Akron, Pensacola. N. A. No. 2149. LTA.

CHAMBERS, C. F.
Machinist
587 West 177th St., New York City. Columbia University, Eastleigh, Eng., Pensacola.

CHAPIN, ROBERT E.
Ensign
1979 D. St., Lincoln, Nebraska, Seattle, San Diego, Pensacola. N. A. No. 2225. HTA.

CHAPMAN, THOMAS H.
Ensign
208 Lapsley St., Selma, Alabama. Mass. Inst. of Tech., Pensacola, Montauk, Hampton Roads. N. A. No. 249. HTA.

CHAPMAN, THOMAS H
Lieut. (j.g.)
52 R. I. Ave., N. E., Washington, D. C. R. F. C. Toronto; Hamp. Rds., Ft. Worth. Key West, Pensa., Bu. Op. N. A. No. 898.

CHAPPELL, JAY F.
Ensign
622 Fairoaks Ave., Oak Park, Ill. Mass. Inst. of Tech., Key West. N. A. No. 1468. HTA.

CHARLES, THOS. J.
Machinist
238 92nd St., Brooklyn, N. Y. Columbia Univ., Hampton Roads, Brest, Fr., Bay Shore.

CHARPIOT, CHARLES L.
Student Officer
West Unity, Ohio. Seattle, Washington, San Diego. HTA.

CHASE, BURR L.
Ensign
4230 North Main St., Niagara Falls, N. Y. Mass. Inst. of Tech., Pensacola. N. A. No. 2581. HTA.

CHETLAIN, A. LOUIS
Ensign
7414 Sheridan Road, Chicago, Ill. Mass. Inst. of Tech., Miami, Pensacola. N. A. No. 2360. HTA.

CHETLAIN, KENT G.
Ensign
7414 Sheridan Road, Chicago, Ill. Mass. Inst. of Tech., Miami, Pensacola. N. A. No. 2298. HTA.

CHEYNEY, HENRY C.
Student Officer
Green Bay, Wisconsin. Mass. Inst. of Tech., Great Lakes, Miami. HTA.

CHILD, JOHN W.
Student Officer
First St., Willoughby Beach, Va. Dunwoody Inst., Minn. HTA.

CHILSON, C. E.
Ensign
Fargo, N. D. Dunwoody, Great Lakes, New York, Detroit, Miami.

CHILTON, WM E., Jr.
Ensign
1222 Virginia St., Charleston, W. Va. M. I. T., Key West, Pensa., N. Sydney, Miami. N. A. No. 1110. HTA.

CHURCHELL, H. C.
Ensign
116 McLennan Ave., Syracuse, N. Y. Mass. Inst. Tech., Bay Shore, Hampton Roads, Pensacola. HTA.

CHURCHILL, G. K.
Ensign
145 East 35th St., New York City. Mass. Inst. of Tech., Bay Shore, Pensacola. N. A. No. 2208.

CHUTE, JAMES L.
Ensign
63 North St., Saco, Maine. Mass. Inst. of Tech., Key West, Miami, Moutchic, Fr., Malpensa, Italy. N. A. No. 1453. HTA.

CLABAUGH, SAMUEL F.
Student Officer
Tuscaloosa, Ala. Mass. Inst. of Tech. HTA.

CLAFLIN, WILLIAM W.
Student Officer
156 Grant Ave., Newton Center, Mass. Mass. Inst. of Tech. HTA.

(*R*)
CLAPP, KENNETH H.
Lieut. (j.g.)
43 Exchange Place, New York City. Mass. Inst. of Tech., Pensacola, R. A. F., Wales, Killingholme. N. A. No. 229. HTA.

OVER VIRGINIA KEY AT MIAMI

CLARK, C. D.
Ensign
1119 Market St., Sunbury, Pa. Mass. Inst. of Tech., Miami, Pensacola, North Sydney, N. S. N. A. No. 1142. HTA.

CLARK, EDWARD A., Jr.
Student Officer
Pond St., Jamaica Plain, Boston, Mass. Mass. Inst. of Tech. HTA.

CLARK, JOHN C.
Ensign
1154 N. Prairie St., Galesburg, Illinois. Mass. Inst. of Tech., Key West, Pensacola. N. A. No. 2299. HTA.

CLARK, RANSOM B.
Lieut. (j.g.)
202 N. Wood St., Oxford, Ohio. Mass. Inst. of Tech., Bay Shore, Key West, Moutchic, Fr., St. Trojan, Fr. N. A. No. 420. HTA.

CLARKE, A. FIELDER
Ensign
5201 Westminster Place, Pittsburgh, Pa. Mass. Inst. of Tech., Miami, Bay Shore, Pensacola. N. A. No. 2130. HTA.

CLARKE, JOSEPH G.
Ensign
323 Wilson Ave., Cynthiana, Ky. Mass. Inst. of Tech., Miami, Pensacola. N. A. No. 2334. HTA.

CLAUSEN, E. W.
Ensign
202 First National Bank, Atchison, Kansas. Mass. Inst. of Tech., Pensacola. HTA.

CLEMENT, EDWARD J.
Ensign
508 Milton Ave., Syracuse, N. Y. Mass. Inst. of Tech., Bay Shore, Pensacola. N. A. No. 1592. HTA.

CLERY, EDWARD D., Jr.
Student Officer
Plandome, Long Island, N. Y. Seattle, Wash. HTA.

CLIFTON, HENRY C.
Student Officer
3607 McKinley Ave., El Paso, Texas. Seattle, Washington, San Diego. HTA

CLIFTON, JOE A.
Student Officer
3601 McKinley Ave., El Paso, Texas. Univ. of Wash., Seattle, Wash. HTA.

CLINE, J. THADDEUS
Ensign
2401 Durant Ave., Berkeley, California. Mass. Inst. of Tech., Miami, Pensacola, San Diego. N. A. No. 1369. HTA.

COATS, CECIL LYNN
Ensign
4526 Brooklyn Ave., Seattle, Washington. Univ. Wash., Seattle, San Diego, Pensacola. N. A. No. 2262. HTA.

COBB, JAMES O.
Ensign
Winston, Salem, N. C. Mass. Inst. of Tech., Bay Shore, Hampton Roads, Pensacola, Key West. N. A. No. 1605. HTA.

COGAN, GEORGE E.
Student Officer
98 Ave. C, Bayonne, N. J. Mass. Inst. of Tech., Bay Shore. HTA.

COGGESHALL, J., Jr.
Lieut. (j.g.)
9 Autumn St., Boston, Mass. Mass. Inst. of Tech., Hampton Roads, Pensacola, Bu. Operations. N. A. No. 417. HTA.

COHEN, ALVIN F.
Ensign
38 Broad St., Charleston, S. C. Mass. Inst. of Tech., Key West, Pensacola. N. A. No. 2284. HTA.

COILE, WILSON W.
Ensign
Cookeville, Tenn. Mass. Inst. of Tech., Pensa. Moutchic. Avord. Old Sarum, Northern Bomb, Gr., Fr. N. A. No. 362. HTA.

COLBY, ANTHONY D.
Lieut. (j.g.)
Rockville, Mass. Mass. Inst. of Tech., Hampton Roads, Pensacola, Bay Shore. N. A. No. 487. HTA.

COLE, ELWOOD B.
Student Officer
605 Voris St., Peoria, Illinois. Mass. Inst. of Tech., Great Lakes, Key West. HTA.

COLE, HUGH L. M.
Ensign
14 Franklin St, Morristown, N. J. Mass. Inst. of Tech., Miami, Key West, Bay Shore, Brunswick, Ga. N.A. 1020 HTA.

COLEMAN, FREYMAN
Student Officer
Santa Rosa, California. Seattle, Washington; San Diego. HTA.

COLES, WILLIAM M.
Ensign
257 Castro St., San Francisco, California. Mass. Inst. of Tech., Miami, Pensacola, Key West. N. A. No. 1667. HTA.

COLLINS, JEROME J.
Ensign
1602 Pittston Ave., Scranton, Pa. Mass. Inst. of Tech., Key West, Miami, Pensacola. N. A. No. 2025 HTA.

IN THE CLOUDS

COLLINS, JOS. J.
Ensign
163 Salem St., Lawrence, Mass. Mass. Inst. of Tech., Bay Shore, Pennsacola. N. A. No. 1664. HTA.

COLLYER, FRANK F., Jr.
Ensign
Chelsea-on-Hudson, Dutchess Co., N. Y. Mass. Inst. cf Tech., Bay Shore, Pensacola. N. A. No. 1897. HTA.

COLWELL, SAMUEL G.
Ensign
14 Quincy St., Providence, Rhode Island. M. I. T., Pensacola, Moutchic, Le Croisic, Hampton Roads. N. A. No. 932. HTA.

COMBE, WM. H.
Student Officer
673 Carondelet St., Los Angeles, California. Seattle, Washington. San Diego.

COMLY, SAMUEL N.
Student Officer
Port Chester, N. Y. Mass. Inst. of Tech. HTA.

CONDON, EDW. T., Jr.
Lieut. (j.g.)
Morristown, N. J. Curtiss, Buffalo; Bu. of S. E. Wash., I. E. M., Seattle, Washington. HTA.

CONDON, GUY B.
Student Officer
So. Penobscot, Maine. Mass. Inst. of Tech., Bay Shore HTA.

CONE, JAMES HAROLD
Student Officer
Room 328 King St. Station, Seattle, Wash., Seattle LTA.

CONGDON, E. W., Jr.,
Student Officer
267 Ridgewood Ave., Glen Ridge, N. J. Mass. Inst. of Tech., Bay Shore. HTA.

CONGER, K. B., Jr.
Ensign
Irvington-on-Hudson, New York. Mass. Inst. of Tech., Bay Shore, Brunswick, Ga., Miami. N. A. No. 2059. HTA.

CONN, R. DONALD
Ensign
205 Penn St., Point Marion, Pa. Mass. Inst. of Tech., Miami, Key West, Pensacola. N. A. No. 2582 HTA.

CONNELL, BYRON J.
Ensign
Wilkinsburg, Pa. Mass. Inst. of Tech., San Diego, Pensacola, Rockaway. N. A. No. 1715. HTA.

CONNELLY, THOS. J.
Ensign
2722 X St., Sacramento, Cal. Mass. Inst. of Tech., Akron, Pensacola, Hampton Roads, Key West. N. A. No. 1563. LTA.

CONNOLLY, JOHN F.
Student Officer
1748 Larkin St., San Francisco, California. Seattle, Washington. HTA.

CONOLLY, JOSEPH F.
Ensign
61 Somerset St., Rochester, N. Y. Mass. Inst. of Tech., Key West, Miami, Pensacola, Killingholme. N. A. No. 1114. HTA

CONOVER, E. VAN A.
Student Officer
414 Sewall Ave., Asbury Park, N. J. Mass. Inst. of Tech., Cambridge. HTA.

CONSTABLE, HENRY B.
Ensign
2064 East 7th St., Charlotte, N. C. Mass. Inst. of Tech., Pensacola, Hampton Rds., Brest, Pauillac, Moutchic, Fr. N. A. No. 880.

CONWAY, M. A.
Student Officer
369 Mason St., Portland, Oregon. University Wash., Seattle, Key West. HTA.

COOK, THOS. E.
War. Machinist
153 College Ave., Poughkeepsie, N. Y. Columbia Univ., Pensacola.

COOK, T. K.
Ensign
11429 Glenwood Ave., S E., Cleveland, Ohio. Akron, Brest, Fr., Guipavas, Fr. LTA.

CORBETT, JAMES M.
Ensign
35 Central Square, Somerville, Mass. Mass. Inst. of Tech., Miami, Pensacola, Montauk. N. A. No. 997. LTA. HTA.

CORBIN, ROLLAND E.
Ensign
Grand Isle, Vermont. Mass Inst. of Tech., Bay Shore, Pensacola, Key West. N. A. No. 621. LTA. HTA.

CORCORAN, LARRY
Ensign
84 Park St., W. Springfield, Mass. Mass. Inst. of Tech., Key West, Maimi, Pensacola, Bay Shore, Chatham. N. A. No. 426. HTA

CORMACK, WILLIAM S.
Ensign
5 Bigelow Terrace, Newton, Mass. Mass. Inst. of Tech., Pensacola, Rockaway, Paris, Moutchic, Fr. N. A. No. 1089. HTA.

INTERIOR OF AN H-16 FROM THE PILOT'S SEAT

CORNING, DOUGLAS D.
Ensign
58 Hamilton Ave., Lynn, Mass. Mass. Inst. of Tech., Bay Shore, Pensacola. N. A. No. 980. LTA.

CORRY, ARTHUR
Ensign
Quincy, Fla. Mass. Inst. of Tech., Bay Shore, Pensacola, Pauillac, Fr., Moutchic, Fr., L'Aber Vrach, Fr. N. A. No. 739. HTA.

CORYELL, LEWIS S.
Ensign
Osceola, Wisconsin. Dunwoody, Minn., Key West, Pensacola. N. A. No. 2187. HTA.

CORZINE, GEO. WM., Jr.
Student Officer
814 Emporia Ave., Wichita, Kansas. Seattle, Washington. HTA.

COTT, R. S.
Ensign
913 W. Broad St., Columbus, Ohio. Dunwoody, Minn., Miami, Key West, Pensacola. N. A. No. 2592. HTA.

COTTRELL, EDWIN H.
Ensign
36 Watson Ave., East Orange, N. J. Mass. Inst. of Tech., Miami, Key West, Pensacola. N. A. No. 2551. HTA.

COUGHLIN, GEORGE E.
Lieut. (j.g.)
487 8th Ave., New York City. Mass. Inst. of Tech., Miami, Pensacola. N. A. No. 1057. HTA.

COUGHTRY, F.
Student Officer
445 Riverside Drive, New York City. Mass. Inst. of Tech. HTA.

COUNTRYMAN, D. F.
Ensign
213 So. Avon St., St. Paul, Minn. Dunwoody, Miami, Pensacola. N. A. No. 2634. HTA.

CRAIG, RALPH C.
Student Officer
240 Van Dyke Ave., Detroit, Mich. Dunwoody. Inst., Minn. HTA.

CRANE, THOMAS F.
Student Officer
Port Byron, N. Y. Mass. Inst. of Tech. HTA.

CRAWFORD, LEO. C.
Student Officer
719 Central Ave., Greenville, Ohio. Dunwoody, Minn., Miami. HTA.

CRAWFORD, M. D., Jr.
Ensign
3201 Holmes Ave. S. M,inn., Minn. Dunwoody, M. I. T., Pensa., Miami, Pauillac, Montchic, Brest, Bay Sh. N. A. No. 637. HTA.

CREAMER, C. D.
Student Officer
R. F. D. No. 10, Washington H., Ohio. Dunwoody Inst., Minn. HTA.

CRENSHAW, JAMES E.
Student Officer
Care of Texas State School of Mines, El Paso, Tex. Mass. Inst. of Tech., Pensacola. HTA.

CRIPPEN, H. M., Jr.
Student Officer
Ballston Spa, N. Y. Mass. Inst. of Tech., Great Lakes.

CRISP, THEODORE M.
Ensign
66 Broadway, New York City. Mass. Inst. of Tech., Great Lakes, Hampton Roads, HTA.

CRISSEY, ROY J.
Student Officer
3831 Mountain Ave., El Paso, Texas. Seattle, Washington, Great Lakes.

CROCKER, FRANK W.
Ensign
35 Hartwell St., Fitchburg, Mass. Mass. Inst. of Tech., Bay Shore, Brunswick, Ga. N. A. No. 2049. HTA.

CROCKER, JOHN H.
Ensign
210 S. Walnut St., Maroa, Illinois. Mass. Inst. of Tech., Key West, Pensacola. N. A. No. 2239. HTA.

CROMER, PAUL C.
Ensign
R. F. D. No. 1, Clinton, Iowa. Dunwoody, Miami, Key West, Pensacola. N. A. No. 2530. HTA.

CROMWELL, A. C.
Ensign
2 B. Touraine Apts. 31st and Colonial Ave., Norfolk, Virginia. Mass. Inst. of Tech., Bay Shore, Pensacola. N. A. No. 1342.

CRONIN, FRANCIS L.
Ensign
129 Pinkney St., Boston, Mass. Mass. Inst. of Tech., Miami, Pensacola. N. A. No. 2165. HTA.

CRONIN, FREDRICK R.
Student Officer
77 Birchwood St., West Roxbury, Mass. Mass. Inst. of Tech., Pensacola.

N-9 Formation

CROWLEY, HUGH A.
Student Officer
Houston, Texas. Harvard Radio, Mass. Inst. of Tech., Miami, Moutchic, Squadron 214, R. A. F. HTA.

CROXTON, ALBERT M.
Ensign
Arkadelphia, Ark. Mass. Inst. of Tech., Miami, Pensacola, Hampton Roads. N. A. No. 2100.

CRUMB, SIMEON A.
Ensign
82 So. Broad St., Norwich, N. Y. Mass. Inst. of Tech., Miami, Pensacola, Montauk. N. A. No. 1279. HTA.

CRUMPTON, J. R.
Student Officer
Minden, Louisiana. Seattle, Key West. HTA.

CUBBERLEY, H. M.
Student Officer
75 Ashland Ave., East Orange, N. J. Mass. Inst. of Tech. HTA.

CULKIN, W. P.
Student Officer
948 E. Marquette Road, Chicago, Ill. Dunwoody Inst., Minneapolis. HTA.

CUNDALL, ROLAND L.
Ensign
1528 High St., Alameda, California. Seattle, San Diego, Pensacola. N. A. No. 2067. HTA.

CUNNINGHAM. E. A.
Ensign
1214 N. Jefferson St., Mexico, Missouri. Seattle, Miami, Pensacola. N. A. No. 2479. HTA.

CURRIER, L. O.
Student Officer
676 Dennett St., Portsmouth, N. H. Mass. Inst. of Tech. HTA.

CURTIS, GORDON M.
Lieut. (j.g.)
1414 Vermont St., Quincy, Ill. Mass. Inst. of Tech., Miami, Pensacola. N. A. No. 943.

CURTZE, FRED. A.
Ensign
630 Myrtle St., Erie, Penn. Mass. Inst. of Tech., Miami, Pensacola. N. A. No. 1809. HTA.

CUTTHRELL, H. H.
Lieut. (j.g.)
Winston Salem, W. Virginia. Mass. Inst. of Tech., Bay Shore, Miami, Pensacola, Key West. N. A. No. 1590. HTA.

◈ ◈ ◈ ◈ ◈ ◈

Cadle, C. J., Student Officer, Charleston, Ill. Mass. Inst. of Tech., Great Lakes, Ill.; Akron, Ohio; Rockaway Beach, L. I. LTA.

Cadwell, Marion S., Ensign, 212 Lakeview Ave., Jamestown, N. Y. Mass. Inst. of Tech., Key West, Miami, Pensacola, Fla. N. A. No. 1839. HTA.

Cahill, Frank V., Student Officer, 502 Geo. St., New Brunswick, N. J.

Cahill, Geo. A., Jr., Lieut. (j.g.), 147 Milk St., Boston, Mass.

Caldren, Fred G., Student Officer.

Caldwell, Harold B., Student Officer, 130 Summit Ave., Mt. Vernon, N. Y. Mass. Inst. of Tech. HTA.

Caldwell, Lafayette Hardwick, Student Officer, Lookout Mountain, Chattanooga, Tenn. Seattle, Wash. HTA.

Caldwell, Thos. B., Ensign, Carbondale, Ill. Dunwoody Inst., Minn., Key West, Miami, Pensacola. N. A. No. 2131. HTA.

Caldwell, Walter Bruce, Ensign, 601 West 110th St., New York City.

Caldwell, Wm. H., Ensign, 3603 Locust St., Philadelphia, Pa. N. A. No. 1383.

Calhoun, Howell Vincent, Student Officer, 410 Riverside Drive, New York City. Seattle, Wash., New York. HTA.

Callahan, Cornelius J., Ensign, Y. M. C. A., Camden, N. J.

Callahan, Patrick J., Lieut. (j.g.), 123 Cushing Ave., Dorchester, Mass. Mass. Inst. of Tech., Pensacola, Moutchic, Ile Tudy, France. N. A. No. 331. HTA.

Callard, Chas. G., Student Officer, 110 Dyer St., Lansing, Mich.

Callaway, Steven W., Ensign, 1600 Harmon Place, Minn., Minn. N. A. No. 2138.

Callender, John M., Jr., Student Officer, 526 Polk Blvd., Des Moines, Iowa.

Callery, Wm., Ensign, 4875 Ellsworth Ave., Pittsburgh, Pa. Mass. Inst. of Tech., Pensacola, Miami, Moutchic, France: Northern B. G., Campagne, France: Malpensa, Italy. N. A., No. 615. HTA.

Callihan, Roy M., Ensign.

Camp, James L., Jr., Student Officer, 2039 New Hampshire Ave., N. W., Washington, D. C.

Camp, Samuel T., Student Officer, Balboa Park, San Diego, Cal.

Campazzi, E. J., Ensign, 15 Prospect Place, New York City. Mass. Inst. of Tech., Key West, Fla. HTA.

Campbell, David P., Ensign, Douglas Place, Dudley Ave., Louisville, Ky. Mass. Inst. of Tech., Key West, Hampton Roads. N. A. No. 1543. LTA.

Campbell, G. C., Ensign.

Campbell, Hugh Gordon, Ensign, Care of Sigma Phi Place, Geneva, N. Y.

Campbell, Jesse Lee, Student Officer, 1000 Md. St., Columbia, Mo.

Campbell, John R., Student Officer, 343 High St., Mazda Club, Newark, N. J.

Campbell, Parker T., Student Officer, 2160 Scottwood Ave., Toledo, Ohio.

Campbell, Wm., Carpenter.

Canby, John W., Ensign, Hackensack, N. J. N. A. No. 1968.

Canfield, F. D., Ensign, Y. M. C. A., Des Moines, Iowa.

Canfield, Wrenn M., Student Officer, 210 Capital City Bank Bldg., Des Moines, Iowa. Mass. Inst. of Tech., Boston. LTA.

Cannon, A. H., Machinist, 135 Maple St., Gardiner, Me.

Cannon, Geo. C. N. A. No. 903.

Cannon, Harry J., Student Officer, 642 Ohio Bldg., Toledo, Ohio.

Cannon, John J., Student Officer, 515 Tenth St., Brooklyn, N. Y.

Cantwell, Wm. H., Lieut. (j.g.), 729 Prospect Ave., Buffalo, N. Y. Mass. Inst. of Tech., Pensacola, Moutchic. N. A. No. 284. HTA.

Canty, Geo. R., Lieut. (j.g.), 1 Highland St., Boston, Mass. Pauillac, France; Eastleigh, Eng., Northern B. Group.

Capser, Leo W., Ensign.

CARDER, EARLE W., Ensign, 89 Kirtland St., Lynn, Mass. N. A. No. 2433.

CARHART, LEWIS H., Student Officer, 212 Ponce de Leon Ave., Atlanta, Ga.

CARLE, PAUL, Ensign, 1730 La Loma, Berkeley, Cal. Mass. Inst. of Tech., Bay Shore, L. I.. Pensacola. N. A. No. 1327.

CARLETON, W. E., Boatswain. N. A. No. 2094.

CARLSON, H. F., Lieut. (j.g.), Sanford, Fla. N. A. No. 529.

CARLSON, JOHN EDWIN, Student Officer, 91 Bishopsgate Road, Newton Center, Mass. Mass. Inst. of Tech. HTA.

CARLSON, RALPH ANDREW, Student Officer, 49 Norman St., E. Orange, N. J.

CARLUCCI, F. J., Ensign, 29 Evelyn Place, Bronx, New York City.

CARMAN, ALLAN, Student Officer, 85 Hobart Ave., Summit, N. J.

CARMICHAEL, RALPH A., Student Officer, 29 15th St., Washington, D. C.

CARNES, SAMUEL J., Ensign, 123 W. 8th St., Cambridge, Ohio.

CARNEY, C. C., Student Officer, 1526 Lafayette St., Denver, Colo.

CARNOCHAN, G. M., Ensign, New City, Rockland Co., N. Y. Mass. Inst. of Tech., Miami. HTA.

CARPENTER, GRANT H., Lieut. (j.g.), La Porte, Penn. Akron, Pensacola, Hampton Roads, Paimboeuf, Guipavas, Bay Shore, Rockaway. N. A. No. 543. LTA.

CARPENTER, F. S., Ensign, 3 Brigham St., Watertown, Mass. Mass. Inst. of Tech., Pensacola, Moutchic, France, Killingholme, Eng. N. A. No. 897. HTA.

CARRERE, ROBT. M., Student Officer, 137 E. 73rd St., New York City.

CARROLL, CHESTER D., Student Officer, 2 Congress St., Worcester, Mass.

CARROLL, FRANK G., Student Officer, 303 W. 102nd St., New York City.

CARROLL, JAMES EDWARD, Student Officer, 7 Parcell St., Elmhurst, N. Y.

CARROLL, JOHN D., Lieut. (j.g.), Boulevard Apt., Baltimore, Md.

CARSCALLEN, J. D., Ensign, 512 W. End Ave., New York City.

CARSON, A. F., Ensign, 33 Grand St., Oneonta, N. Y., N. A. No. 2418.

CARSON, ALEXANDER F., Ensign, 33 Grand St., Oneonta, N. Y. Mass. Inst. of Tech., Miami, Key West, Pensacola, Fla. N. A. No. 2418. HTA.

CARSON, CLIFFORD C., Ensign, Barstow, Texas. Mass. Inst. of Tech., Buffalo, Washington, Akron. LTA.

CARSON, JOHN L., JR., Student Officer, 844 West Delevan Ave., Buffalo, N. Y. Mass. Inst. of Tech. HTA.

CARSON, L. F., Ensign, 203 S. Court St., Montgomery, Ala., N. A. No. 766.

CARTER, DICKSON H., Student Officer, 401 N. Baylen St., Pensacola, Fla.

CARTER, HERBERT B., Student Officer, 121 King St., St. Augustine, Fla.

CARTER, J. E., Machinist, 340 Halton St., Galesburg, Ill.

CARTER, JAMES ROSE, Student Officer, High Plain Rd., Andover, Mass.

CARTER, JOHN A., JR., Ensign, 1268 Marion St., Denver, Colo. Seattle, Wash., San Diego, Pensacola. N. A. No. 2374. HTA.

CARTWRIGHT, SIDNEY K., Student Officer.

CARY, JOHN, Student Officer, 931 Cass Ave., S. E., Grand Rapids, Mich. Mass. Inst. of Tech. HTA.

CARY, JOHN I., Student Officer, 7315 South Shore Drive, Chicago, Ill.

CASE, WM. W., Ensign, 55 Hanson Place, Y. M. C. A., Brooklyn, N. Y.

CASHION, AVERY TED, Student Officer.

CASHIN, EMMET J., Ensign, 60 Piedmont St., San Francisco, Cal. Mass. Inst. of Tech., Bay Shore, Pensacola, Fla., Rockaway Beach, N. Y. N. A. No. 1438. HTA.

CASON, HARRY T., Student Officer, 450 Prince Ave., Athens, Ga. Mass. Inst. of Tech., Miami, Fla. HTA.

CASSADY, JOHN M., Student Officer.

CASSALLE, CLINTON B., Warrant Machinist, 208 Union Ave., Peekskill, N. Y. Columbia University, Great Lakes, Ill.

CASSIDY, JAMES T., Student Officer, 1339 E. 93rd St., Cleveland, Ohio.

CASWELL, CHESTER F., Student Officer, 664 Pleasant St., Worcester, Mass.

CATE, S. R., Ensign, 892 Watertown St., West Newton, Mass.

CATES, FREDERICK S., Student Officer, 224 N. 11th St., Richmond, Ind.

CATES, SAMUEL C., Ensign, East Vassalboro, Me. Mass. Inst. of Tech., Key West, Pensacola. HTA.

CATTON, W. ROBERT, Ensign, Benzonia, Mich. Mass. Inst. of Tech., Akron, Newport, Pensacola, Hampton Roads. N. A. No. 1210 LTA.

CAUGHEY, ANDREW F., Ensign, 1118 S. University Ave., Ann Arbor, Mich. Miami, Aircraft Fact. Philadelphia, Pa. HTA.

CABENAUGH, JOHN A., Student Officer, 4834 Sheridan Road, Chicago, Ill.

CECIL, J. M., Student Officer, Monroe Terrace Apts., Richmond, Va. Seattle, Wash. HTA.

CHADWICK, J. C., Lieut. (j.g.), 116 S. 49th St., Omaha, Neb.

CHADWICK, NOEL, Lieut. (j.g.), 360 Marlboro St., Boston, Mass. Akron, Ohio, Key West, Montauk, Cape May. N. A. No. 107. LTA.

CHAFFEE, E. L., Student Officer, Boise, Idaho. R. R. No 1. Seattle, San Diego, Cal. HTA.

CHALMERS, EDWIN L., Ensign, 125 Burk Ave., Wildwood, N. J.

CHAMBERS, WALTER A., Student Officer, 166 Park Ave., Atlanta, Ga.

CHAMBERS, EDWARD G., Student Officer, Frankford, Mich.

CHAMBERS, LESTER R., Student Officer, Gould Hall, University Heights, N. Y.

CHAMBERS, WILLARD W., Student Officer, Cameron, Tex.

CHAMBLIN, WALTER W., JR., Student Officer, Care of *The Dayton Journal*, Dayton, Ohio.

CHANDLER, ARTHUR L., Student Officer, 219 Washington St., Leominster, Mass. Mass. Inst. of Tech.

CHANDLER, FITZ-MAC, Ensign, Berkeley, Cal. Stanford University.

CHANDLER, LUMAN W., Machinist, 1310 Taylor St., San Francisco, Cal., Columbia University, Pauillac, Autanges, Fr., Eastleigh, Eng.

CHAPIN, EDW. D., Ensign.

CHAPIN, ROBERT M., Student Officer, Psi U. House, Middleton, Conn.

CHAPLIN, DUNCAN D., JR., Ensign, Ridgewood, N. J., Moutchic, Fr., Bolsena, Porto Corsini, It. N. A. No. 1458.

CHAPMAN, EDWARD T., Student Officer, R. F. D. 3, Excelsior, Minn.

CHAPMAN, JOS. G., Student Officer, 308 Laurel Ave., Olean, N. Y.

CHAPMAN, ROBT. H., Ensign, Care of J. E. Sirrine, Engineer, Greenville, S. C. Mass. Inst. of Tech., Keyport, Detroit, Chelsea, Mich.

CHAPMAN, ROBT. F., Ensign, 3603 Broadway, New York City. N. A. No. 659.

CHAPMAN, W. R., Ensign, 166 Bergen Ave., Ridgefield Park, N. J. N. A. No. 638.

CHALRES, PERRY L., Student Officer, Seattle, Wash.

CHASE, ALBERT W., Ensign.

CHASE, A. PRENTICE, Student Officer, 29 Otis St., Norwich, Conn. Mass. Inst. of Tech., Key West.

CHASE, F. F., Ensign, 611 S. Hobart Blvd., Los Angeles, Cal. N. A. No. 1329.

CHASE, H. GUY, Student Officer, 1312 Rhode Island Ave., N. W., Washington, D. C. Dunwoody, Minn., Mass. Inst. of Tech. HTA.

CHASE, RANDALL, Student Officer, 902 Oak Ave., Sanford, Fla. Mass. Inst. of Tech., Akron, Ohio. LTA.

CHASE, RODNEY, Ensign, 42 Church St., Waterbury, Conn. N. A. No. 2232.

CHASE, WHEELER F., Ensign, 611 S. Hobart Blvd., Los Angeles, Cal.

CHASE, WM. B., Student Officer.

CHATFIELD, CHARLES H., Ensign, 509 Willow St., Waterbury, Conn.

CHEESMAN, W. L., Lieut. (j.g.), Care of Cheesman Elliott, 100 William St., New York City.

CHENEY, E. C., Ensign, 2517 Lincoln St., Evanston, Ill.

CHENEY, PHILIP L., Ensign, 535 Beacon St., Boston, Mass. Mass. Inst. of Tech., Miami, Pensacola, Hampton Roads. N. A. No. 2064. HTA.

CHEVES, LANGDON McCORD, Ensign, 47 South Battery, Charleston, S. C. Seattle, San Diego, Pensacola, N. A. No 2311. HTA.

CHEYNEY, HENRY C., JR., Student Officer, Green Bay, Wisconsin. Mass. Inst. of Tech., Great Lakes, Miami. HTA.

CHILD, T. E., Ensign.

CHILDS, W. G., Student Officer.

CHILDERS, JAMES S., Student Officer, 1224 N. 30th St., Birmingham, Ala. Mass. Inst. of Tech., Key West, Fla. HTA.

CHIPMAN, U. G., Lieut. (j.g.).

CHISLING, ELLIOTT L., Student Officer, 1646 East 8th St., Brooklyn, N. Y. Mass. Inst. of Tech., Bay Shore. HTA.

CHOURRE, EMILE, Ensign, 2115 Alameda Ave., Alameda, Cal. Mass. Inst. of Tech., Key West, Miami, San Diego, Pensacola, Coco Solo. HTA.

CHRISTMAN, RAYMOND BURKE, Student Officer, Ortonville, Minn. Mass. Inst. of Tech. HTA.

CHRIST, LEONE L., Student Officer.

CHRISTENSEN, CLARENCE A., Student Officer, 732 Shepard Ave., Milwaukee, Wis.

CHRISTENSON, HARRY, Lieut. (j.g.)

CHRISTENSON, R., Machinist. N. A. No. 1885.

CHRISTIE, ROBT., Student Officer, 105 Orange Road, Montclair, N. J. Mass. Inst. of Tech. HTA.

CHRISTMAN, FRANKLIN B., Lieut. (j.g.), Care of Ivy Club, Princeton, N. J. N. A. No. 631.

CHRYSLER, C. D., Student Officer, Lake Park, Iowa. Mass. Inst. of Tech. HTA.

CHURCH, GEO., Student Officer, Gt. Barrington, Mass. Mass. Inst. of Tech., Akron, Ohio. LTA.

CHURCHILL, GEO. K., Ensign, Little Silver, P. O., N. J. N. A. No. 2208.

CHURCHILL, P. W., Student Officer, Yreka, Cal.

CHURCHILL, WARREN N., Lieut. (j.g.), 1618 River St., Burlington, Iowa. Mass. Inst. of Tech.

CISSEL, JOHN F., Student Officer, 895 West End Ave., New York City.

CLANCY, WM. C., Ensign, Hotel Shoreham, Wash., D. C.

CLARK, A. S., Ensign, Alexandria Bay, N. Y.

CLARK, ALBERT J., Ensign, Towson, Md.

CLARK, ALFRED M., Ensign, 21 Liberty St., New York City.

CLARK, ALLAN K., Student Officer, 513 West Market St., Akron, Ohio.

CLARK, C. S., JR., Ensign, 1550 Washtenaw St., Ann Arbor, Mich.

CLARK, C. S., Student Officer, Phi Kappa Psi House, Easton, Pa.

CLARK, E. M., Ensign.

CLARK, FRANKLIN S., Ensign, N. Amherst, Mass. Akron, Rockaway Beach, Queenstown, Ire., Roehampton, Eng., Brest, Fr., Halifax, N. S. LTA.

CLARK, JAS. E., Student Officer, 50 Avery Ave., Detroit, Mich. Mass. Inst. of Tech. HTA.

CLARK, JOHN C., Ensign, 912 E. Washington St., Ann Arbor, Mich.

CLARK, JOHN W., Student Officer, Care of Telluride Motor Co., Provo, Utah, Seattle, Wash. HTA.

CLARK, LEICESTER C., Student Officer, 827 Broad St., Meriden, Conn. Mass. Inst. of Tech. HTA.

CLARK, SANFORD S., Student Officer, 13 Front St., Schenectady, N. Y.

CLARK, THOS. A., Carpenter.

CLARK, WALTER L., Student Officer, 105 North Street, Ware, Mass. Mass. Inst. of Tech., Miami, Fla. HTA.

CLARK, WENDELL H., Ensign, 716 Lake Ave., Wilmette, Ill. Mass. Inst. of Tech., Key West, Miami, Pensacola. N. A. No. 1785. HTA.

CLARKSON, LAWRENCE W., Student Officer, 41 Lying St., Newburyport, Mass.

CLARKSON, WM. FLOYD, Lieut. (j.g.), 1303 Shady Ave., Pittsburgh, Pa. Toronto University, Bay Shore, Pensacola, San Diego.

CLAYTON, HENRY C., Ensign. N. A. No. 360.

CLEARY, FRANCIS M., Student Officer, 3529 Locust St. Philadelphia, Pa.

CLEARY, JOS. R., Machinist, 88 Ash St., Nashua, N. H.

CLEMANS, R. M., Student Officer, 77 16th St., Wheeling, West Va. Seattle, Wash. HTA.

CLEMENS, THOS. B., Ensign, 1970 La Salle Ave., Los Angeles, Cal. N. A. No. 1292.

CLEMENT, JAMES K., Ensign, Wayland, Mass. Mass. Inst. of Tech., Hampton Roads, Chatham, Mass. Communication Officer.

CLEMENTS, WARREN, Ensign, 8 Washington Court, Richmond, Ind. Great Lakes, Eastleigh, Eng. HTA.

CLENDANIEL, GEO. W., Ensign, Kennedyville, Md. Mass. Inst. of Tech., Key West, Pensacola, Hampton Roads. N. A. No. 2142. HTA.

CLEVELAND, JULIAN E. G., Student Officer, 4208 8th Ave., N. E., Seattle, Wash.

CLINE, J. C., Ensign, 1563 Elbur Ave., Cleveland, Ohio. N. A. No. 1832.

CLINE, JOHN W., JR., Student Officer, 447 B St., Santa Rosa, Cal.

CLOSE, EUGENE F., Lieut. (j.g.), 330 Perry St., Sandusky, Ohio.

CLUTE, HOWARD H., Student Officer, 470 W. Water St., Elmira, N. Y.

COATES, J. W., Ensign.

CLYDE, L. EARNEST, Student Officer, 509 E. Franklin St., Richmond, Va.

CLUTHE, WM. A., Student Officer.

COATES, ROBERT M., Student Officer, 30 Vanderbilt Hall, Yale College, New Haven, Conn.

COATSWORTH, CALEB, J., Lieut. (j.g.), 580 W. Ferry St., Buffalo, N. Y. No. 1005.

COBB, AMOS H., Student Officer, Penfield Road, Brighton, N. Y.

COBB, GEO. W., Ensign, Huntington, L. I., N. Y. Bay Shore, L. I.; Miami, Fla. N. A. No. 438. HTA.

COBB, RICHARD E., Student Officer, 17 Magnolia St., Arlington, Mass. Mass. Inst. of Tech., U. S. S. *Preston*, U. S. S. *Carola*, U. S. S. *Melang*. HTA.

CODDING, J. ALBERT, Ensign, 3909 Spruce St., Philadelphia, Pa.

CODDINGTON, D. H., Lieut. (j.g.), 106 E. 85th St., New York City. N. A. No. 137.

COE, PHILIP K., Student Officer, 26 Hawthorne Ave., Akron, Ohio. Mass. Inst. of Tech., Wingfoot Lake, Ohio. LTA.

COE, SEYMOUR, Student Officer, 106 William St., East Orange, N. J.

COFFEY, CLAUDE R., Machinist, 15 Fairlawn St., Everett, Mass.

COFFEY, EDWARD H., JR., Student Officer, 9 Lamartins Terrace, Yonkers, N. Y. Mass. Inst. of Tech., Akron, Pensacola. LTA.

COFFIN, LEE K., Student Officer, Melrose, Mass. Miami, Fla.; Brest, France.

COFFIN, ROY R., Student Officer, 507 Hansberry St., Germantown, Pa.

COFFMAN, JOHN B., Student Officer.

COGGESHALL, HARRISON H., Student Officer, 2224 Mass. Ave., Cambridge, Mass.

COKER, WALLACE E., Ensign.

COLE, FRANCIS G., Student Officer, 1900 8th St., N. W., Washington, D. C.

COLE, HAROLD A., Lieut. (j.g.), 191 Maple St., Watertown, Mass. N. A. No. 454.

COLE, HENRY P., Student Officer, 511 Cleveland St., Raleigh, N. C.

COLEGROVE, W. H., Ensign, Box 211, Ridgway, Pa. Mass. Inst. of Tech., Key West, Miami, Pensacola. N. A. No. 2109. HTA.

COLEMAN, CLAUDE, Student Officer, Olympic House, East Lansing, Mich., Dunwoody Inst., Minn.

COLEMAN, CORNELIUS, Ensign, 48 Randolph Hall, Cambridge, Mass.

COLEMAN, HAROLD T., Ensign, 18 Church St., Wellesley, Mass. Mass. Inst. of Tech., Rockaway Beach, Akron. LTA.

COLEMAN, RICHARD L., Ensign, Java, Va. Mass. Inst. of Tech., Bay Shore, L. I.; Pensacola, Fla. N. A. No. 1817. HTA.

COLEMAN, W. L., Machinist.

COLEMAN, WM. C., Student Officer, 5830 Prytania St., New Orleans, La.

COLETTI, PHILIP E., Student Officer, 135 W. Tremont Ave., Bronx, N. Y., N. Y.

COLLIER, NEILL R., Student Officer, 115 New York Ave., N. W., Washington, D. C.

COLLINS, DUDLEIGH C., Ensign, 12 W. 44th St., New York City. Great Lakes, Pensacola, Fla. HTA.

COLLINS, EARL P., Student Officer, 973 Mass. Ave., Cambridge, Mass.

Collins, John, Ensign, 538 W. 114th St., New York City. N. A. No. 1664.

Collins, Orville W., Student Officer, 405 Main St., Henderson, Ky.

Collins, Porter D., Ensign, University Club, Akron. Mass. Inst of Tech., Wingfoot Lake, Akron, Ohio; Pensacola, Fla. N. A. No. 1995. LTA.

Collins, R. E., Student Officer, 2725 Hanover Circle, Birmingham, Ala. Mass. Inst. of Tech.. Miami. HTA.

Colston, T. M., Ensign, San Diego.

Colt, Roswell C., Student Officer, Hope St., Bristol, R. I. Mass. Inst of Tech., Newport, R. I. HTA

Colwell, Harry E., Jr., Student Officer.

Comey, Robt T., Student Officer, 2708 Berkshire Road, Cleveland, Ohio.

Compo, Geo. L., Lieut. (j.g.), Dahlgren, Va.

Compton, R. Parker, Ensign, 5564 Delmar Ave., St. Louis, Mo.

Coniff, E. J., Lieut. (j.g.), 100 Lincoln St., New Britain, Conn.

Conley, D. L., Ensign, Anacostia. N. A. No. 1166.

Conley, Edward M., Jr., Student Officer.

Conley, M. M., Ensign, Madera, Cal. N. A No. 1812.

Connell, Edward M., Ensign, 9 Carleton Ave., Bradford, Mass. Mass. Inst. of Tech., Miami, Pensacola. N. A. No 1926. HTA.

Connelly, Milton E., Ensign, 5646 Michigan Ave., Chicago, Ill. N. A. No. 2038.

Conner, Earl H., Ensign.

Conner, Jos. W., Lieut. (j.g.), Pelham Apt., N. 13th St., Richmond, Ind.

Conners, Wm. J., Jr., Lieut. (j.g.), 250 Main St., Buffalo, N. Y. N. A. No. 517.

Connor, Wm. D., Student Officer, 40 3rd St., Marshfield, Wis.

Conover, Elmer G., Student Officer, 259 S. Main St., Akron, Ohio.

Conover, Howard Wm., Student Officer, Fairmount Hotel, Jersey City, N. J.

Conrad, John D., Student Officer, Hamilton, Mo.

Constantine, A. R., Lieut. (j.g.), Great Lakes.

Contant, Cornelius B., Student Officer, 810 Hudson St., Hoboken, N. J.

Conway, Milton K., Student Officer, 721 Quebec Place, N. W., Washington, D. C.

Conway, Frank. Lieut. (j.g.), 4338 W. Monroe St., Chicago, Ill. Akron, Ohio; Rockaway, Rockampton. Wexford, Queenstown, Paimboeuf, Berehaven. LTA.

Cook, M. R., Machinist

Cook Ralph C., Student Officer. 204 Grand Central Place, Inwood, Long Island, N. Y. Mass. Inst. of Tech., Bay Shore. HTA.

Cook, Robt.. Student Officer, 11429 Glenwood Ave., Cleveland, Ohio.

Cooley, Harold D., Student Officer, Grand Jury Bldg., Nashville, N. C. Mass. Inst. of Tech. HTA.

Cooley, Richard L., Lieut. (j.g.), 34 Prescott St., Newtonville, Mass. N. A. No. 1036.

Coon, Lloyd Frank, Student Officer, 719 Wells Fargo Bldg., San Francisco, Cal.

Coon, Stanley, Ensign, 616 Denham Bldg., Denver, Colo.

Cooney, E. W., Ensign, 40 W. 127th St., New York City.

Cooper, Andrew A., Lieut. (j g.), Rome, Ga. Mass. Inst. of Tech., Pensacola, Fla. N. A. No. 678. HTA.

Cooper, Philip, Student Officer, Amite, La. Seattle, Wash. HTA.

Copeland, Phillips, Student Officer, Care of Rev. Theo Copeland, Pinebluff, Ark.

Corbett, John Dennen. Student Officer, Washington & Lee Univ., S. A. E. House, Lexington, Va.

Corboy, Leo. J., Student Officer.

Corey, James, Student Officer, 23 French St., Pawtucket, R. I.

Corey, Russell B., Lieut. (j.g.). Villa Tranquillity, Far Rockaway, N. Y. N. A. No. 553.

Cornell, Alfred B., Ensign, 420 W. 130th St., New York City.

Corner, Wm. Watson, Student Officer, 5235 17th Ave, N. E., Seattle, Wash.

Cornet, H. L., Jr., Student Officer, 4550 Pershing St., St. Louis, Mo. Mass. Inst. of Tech., Miami, Pensacola. HTA.

Cornish, Donald O.. Machinist. 58 Prescott St., Newtonville, Mass.

Corson, E. T., Ensign, 420 Ocean Ave., Ocean City. N. J. N. A. No. 1417.

Corson, Frederic W., Student Officer, 63 Elm Road. Newtonville, Mass.

Cossitt, Harry R., Ensign, 116 7th Ave., La Grange, Ill. Mass. Inst. of Tech., Key West, Miami, Pensacola. N. A. No. 1686. HTA.

Cotter, Harold J., Ensign, 728 S. Fourth St., Springfield, Ill.

Cottingham, W. S., Ensign, Lake Shore Blvd., Cleveland, Ohio. N. A. No. 1757.

Couch, Flournoy B., Student Officer, Tahlequah, Okla.

Couls, Sidney W., Student Officer, 449 St. Clair Ave., Detroit, Mich.

Coulter, Douglas, Student Officer, Aigburth Park, Towson, Md. Seattle, Wash. HTA.

Courtney, Ernest H., Student Officer, 109 Fifth Ave., Saginaw, Mich.

Cowell, Charles C., Ensign, 164 Beck Ave., Akron. Ohio. Mass. Inst. of Tech., Key West, Miami, Pensacola, Fla.; Cape May, N. J. N. A. No. 1344. HTA.

Cowie, Thos. J., Student Officer, 212 S. Queen St., Martinsburg, W. Va.

Cox, Alex F., Student Officer, 1912 Speedway, Austin. Tex.

Cozens, W. E., Boatswain.

Craft, Merritt S., Student Officer, 704 Jefferson Bank Bldg., Birmingham, Ala. Mass. Inst. of Tech. HTA.

Crafts, Lewis H., Ensign, 20 Anderson Place, Buffalo, N. Y. Mass. Inst. of Tech., Key West, Miami, Pensacola. N. A. No. 1666. HTA.

Crandall, Addison B., Machinist, 116 Stewart Ave., Ithaca, N. Y.

Crandall, C. H., Machinist.

Crandall, Leonard J., Student Officer, 205 E. St., Warren, Pa.

Crane, Joshua, Jr., Lieut. (j.g.), Westwood, Mass. Squantum, Ft. Worth, Hampton Roads, Killingholme. N. A. No. 296. HTA.

Craswell, G. E., Ensign, 1766 Topping Ave., Bronx. N. Y. N. A. No. 1457.

Crawford, Albert M., Ensign, 812 Conn. Ave., N. W., Washington, D. C.

Crawford, Bryce, Jr., Student Officer, 1912 Lothrop St., Omaha, Neb.

Crawford, Frederick C., Student Officer, University Club, Cleveland, Ohio. Mass. Inst. of Tech., Dunwoody Institute. HTA.

Crawford, Robt. B. P., Student Officer.

Crawford, Theo. J., Machinist.

Crawford, W. D., Student Officer, Columbia. S. C. Seattle, Wash. HTA.

Crees, Robt. R., Student Officer, 317 29th St., San Francisco, Cal.

Creighton, Bert H., Ensign, 404 Second St., Pitcairn. Pa. Mass. Inst. of Tech., Pensacola and Miami, Fla. N. A. No. 1016. HTA.

Crinkley, Andrew, Ensign.

Criswell, John R., Ensign, 4535 Forest Ave.. Norwood, Ohio. Mass. Inst. of Tech., Akron, Rockaway Beach. LTA.

Crittenden, Rogers, Student Officer, 711 Manheim Road, Kansas City, Mo. Mass. Inst. of Tech., Key West. HTA.

Crocker, H. J., Student Officer, 2301 Laguna St., San Francisco, Cal. Mass. Inst. of Tech. HTA.

Crom, J. F., Machinist.

Crompton, C., Jr., Lieut. (j.g.), 74 Williams St., Worcester, Mass.

Crone, Edward Arthur, Student Officer.

Crosby, Gould Morgan, Ensign, Sea View, Mass. Mass. Inst. of Tech., Key West, Miami, Pensacola, North Sidney. N A. No. 958. HTA.

Cross, C. M., Ensign, Corcoran, Cal. N. A. No. 1855.

Cross, Chester C., Student Officer, 1818 23d Ave., Seattle, Wash.

Cross, Gorham L., Student Officer, 340 Genesee St. Utica, N. Y. Mass. Inst. of Tech., Bay Shore, L. I. HTA.

Crow, H. S., Student Officer, 317 Clinton St., Jackson, Mich.

Crownover, Lowell G., Student Officer, Benedict, Neb.

Crump, Raymond F., Ensign, 345 Litchfield Road, Akron, Ohio.

Crumpton, Thos. U., Student Officer, Maplesville, Ala. Dunwoody Inst., Minn., Miami. HTA.

Cruzen, Randolph, Student Officer, 305 Center St., Paxton, Ill.

Culbertson, Albert L., Ensign, 300 E. Vine St., Mt. Vernon, Ohio. N. A. No. 1464.

Culbertson, Francis B., Student Officer, 25 Irvington St., Boston, Mass.

Culbertson, Wm. S., Student Officer, 1448 St. James Court, Louisville, Ky.

Culkin, Wm. A., Ensign, 2328 Woodland Ave., Duluth, Minn. Mass. Inst. of Tech., Miami, Pensacola, Rockaway. N. A. No. 1421. HTA.

Cullinan, Craig F., Ensign, Fidelity Trust Co., Houston, Texas. Mass. Inst. of Tech. HTA.

Cullity, Edwin F., Ensign, University of Pennsylvania, Philadelphia, Pa. N. A. No. 1418.

Cullom, Smith, Student Officer, Miami, Fla. Mass. Inst. of Tech. HTA.

Cumberland, Wm. E., Student Officer, 1418 35th St., N. W., Washington, D. C.

Cummings, Wm. H., Student Officer, 715 Clifton Ave., Newark, N. J.

Cundell, Henry G., Student Officer, 95 Park Ave., Paterson, N. J. Mass. Inst. of Tech., Bay Shore, Long Island. HTA.

Cunningham, Benj. A., Student Officer, 116 Saratoga Ave., Yonkers, N. Y.

Cunnington, A. B., Jr., Student Officer, 564 E. Nash St., Akron, Ohio. Mass. Inst. of Tech. LTA.

Cupples, R. T., Machinist. N. A. No. 2095.

Curdts, Wm., Student Officer, 911 Colonial Ave, Norfolk, Va. Mass. Inst. of Tech. HTA.

Curie, E. H., Ensign.

Curley, Dorris D., Student Officer, 466 Belvedere St., San Francisco, Cal.

Curran, Stanley T., Lieut. (j.g.), Cragsmoor, N. Y. N. A. No. 287.

Currey, Robt. S., Student Officer, Dixon, Cal.

Curris, Archibald, M. L., Student Officer, R. F. D. No. 3, Fayettville, N. C.

Curry, Francis J., Student Officer, 109 Chestnut St., Darby, Philadelphia, Pa.

Curry, Gerald G., Ensign, 6 Craigie Circle, Cambridge, Mass.

Curtice, Aubrey, Student Officer, Delta Upsilon House, Stanford University, Cal.

Curtin, Jos. Wm., Student Officer, 412 S. Wells St., Chicago, Ill.

Curtis, LeGrand W., Student Officer, Red Hook, New York. Mass. Inst. of Tech. HTA.

Curtis, Paul W., Ensign. N. A. No. 1284.

Curtiss, Chas. P., Ensign.

Cushing, Howard W., Ensign, N. A. No. 1058.

Cushman, Alvan A., Ensign.

Cushman, Raymond J., Ensign, Bay Shore, L. I. N. A. No. 1415.

Cutler, John F., Ensign, 2620 Bancroft Way, Berkeley, Cal. N. A. No. 1665.

Cutler, Richard H., Student Officer, 108 Elmwood Road, Roland Park, Md.

Cutting, Robt. Hill, Ensign, Oak Knoll, Winchester, Mass. N. A. No. 2041.

Showing Bomb Rack and Release Mechanism

DALE, JOS. S., Jr.
Ensign
643 Lafayette Ave., Mt. Vernon, N. Y. Mass. Inst. of Tech., Miami, Columbia Univ., Packard Plant, Detroit.

DALENBERG, JOHN R.
Ensign
R. R. No. 1, Holland, Michigan. Dunwoody, Miami, Pensacola. N. A. No. 2411. HTA.

DALL, CURTIS B.
Ensign
Princeton Club, New York City. Mass. Inst. of Tech., Howden, Royal Air Force, Guipavas, Paimboeuf. LTA.

DALRYMPLE, F., Jr.
Lieut. (j.g.)
Beauchamp Place, New Rochelle, N. Y. Bay Shore, Miami. N. A. No. 429. HTA.

An Italian Kite Balloon

DALY, LEWIS A.
Ensign
627 S. 6½ St., Monmouth, Illinois. Dunwoody, Minneapolis, Miami, Pensacola. N. A. No. 2365. HTA.

DANIEL, JOHN M.
Ensign
3000 Q. St., N. W., Washington, D. C. Mass. Inst. of Tech., Pensacola. Pauillac, Moutchic, Ile Tudy. N. A. No. 744. HTA.

DANLY, PHILO H.
Machinist
5141 Iowa St., Chicago, Ill. Columbia University, Pelham Bay, Rockaway Beach.

DAUGHTERS, C. G.
Student Officer
Van Wert, Ohio. Mass. Inst. of Tech. HTA.

DAUM, RAYMOND J.
Ensign
139 E. 59th P'.,Los Angeles, California. Mass. Inst. of Tech., Great Lakes, Rockaway, Pensacola, San Diego, *U. S. S. Huntington.*

DAVIDSON, JOHN S.
Ensign
321 West 87th St., New York City. M. I. T., Key West, Miami. Moutchic, Campaigne, N. B. G., B. E. F. N. A. No. 1450.

DAVIDSON, ROBERT B.
Ensign
1525 Adams Ave., Scranton, Pa. Mass. Inst. of Tech., Miami, Pensacola. N. A. No. 2370. HTA.

DAVIS, COURTLAND H.
Student Officer
223 North Columbus, St., Alexandria, Va. Dunwoody, Minn. HTA.

DAVIS, DWIGHT S.
Ensign
Woburn, Mass. Mass. Inst. of Tech., Cambridge. Miami, Pensacola. N. A. No. 1931. HTA.

DAVIS, GEORGE E. W.
Ensign
2627 Hearst Ave., Berkeley, Cal. San Diego, Pensacola. N. A. No. 2005.

DAVIS, HAROLD R.
Lieut. (j.g.)
The Connecticut, Washington, D. C. M. I. T., Pensa., Hamp. Rds., Ft. Worth, Killingholme, Anacostia. N. A. No. 280. HTA.

DAVIS, JOHN LORD
Student Officer
284 W. College St., Oberlin, Ohio. Mass. Inst. of Tech., Key West. HTA.

DAVIS, ROBERT J.
Lieut. (j.g.)
301 Upper Mountain Ave., Upper Montclair, N. J. Mass. Inst. of Tech., Pensacola, Key West. N. A. No. 807. HTA.

DAVIS, THOMAS E.
Ensign
208 Twelfth St., N. W., Canton, Ohio. Mass. Inst. of Tech., Bay Shore, Pensacola, Hampton Roads. N. A. No. 1193½. HTA.

DAVISON. RUSSELL L.
Ensign
5038 Walnut St., Philadelphia, Penn. Mass. Inst. of Tech., Cambridge, Pensacola. N. A. No. 1003.

DAVISSON, CYRUS G.
Ensign
1350 Carroll St., Brooklyn, N. Y. Mass Inst. of Tech., Akron, Pensacola, Newport, New London, N. A. No 1564. LTA.

DAVY, W. MYRON
Lieut. (j.g.)
M. I. T., Cambridge, Mass. Geological Dept. Mass. Inst. of Tech. HTA.

DAWSON, HAROLD K.
Student Officer
51 Edward Ave., Pittsfield, Mass. Mass. Inst. of Tech., Cambridge, Key West. HTA.

DEANE, ANDREW
Ensign
853 Hancock St., Wollaston, Mass. Mass. Inst. of Tech., Key West,Pensacola. N. A. No. 2183. HTA.

DEERING, EDWARD M.
Student Officer
Hamilton Ave., Yonkers, N. Y. Mass. Inst. of Tech. HTA.

DE LA VERGNE, J. H.
Student Officer
5931 St. Charles Ave., New Orleans, La. Seattle, Washington. HTA.

DELAHANTY, T. W.
Lieut. (j.g.)
407 W. 55th St., New York City, Rockaway Beach. LTA.

DELL, EDWARD H.
Student Officer
314 Sutphin Ave., Middletown, Ohio. Mass. Inst. of Tech. HTA.

DE LONG, C. H.
Student Officer
Fithina, Illinois. Dunwoody. HTA.

RESULTS OF HEAD-ON COLLISION IN AIR, GUNNERY ISLAND, PENSACOLA

DEMAREST, K. ELMER
Ensign
55 Gifford Ave., Jersey City, N. J. Mass. Inst. of Tech., Bay Shore, Pensacola. N. A. No. 1971.

DEMILT, MILTON
Carpenter
Pittsburg Ave., Cape May, N. J. L'Aber-Vrach, Fr., Le Croisic, Fr., Bay Shore, N. Y., Cape May, Pauillac, Fr.

DEMONET, G. F.
Ensign
395 Park Place, Brooklyn, N. Y. Whitestone, Mass. Inst. of Tech., Miami, Pensacola. N. A. No. 1024 HTA.

DEMPSEY, PLINN D.
Student Officer
25 Queensbury St., Boston, Mass. Mass. Inst. of Tech., Key West. HTA.

DENISTON, NOBLE G.
Ensign
Sardinia, Indiana. Mass. Inst. of Tech., Great Lakes, Akron, Pensacola. N. A. No. 1728. LTA.

DENNIS, JOHN W.
Ensign
Grundy, Virginia. Mass. Inst. of Tech., Pensacola, Akron, Rockaway, Hampton Roads, LTA.

DENT, ELBERT, Jr.
Ensign
308 West Springfield Ave., Chestnut Hill, Pa. M. I. T., Pensacola, Bolsena, Moutchic, Ile Tudy, Bay Shore. N. A. No. 315. HTA.

DENTON, W. M.
Student Officer
604 Linwood Ave., Evansville, Ind. Mass. Inst. of Tech., Akron. LTA.

DES ROCHERS, GEO. E.
Ensign
157 Montezuma St., Houghton, Mich. Great Lakes, Pensacola.

DETTLING, GEORGE H.
Ensign
1826 Sherman St., Grand Rapids, Mich. Mass. Inst. of Tech., Buffalo, East Greenwich, Great Lakes, Boston, New York. HTA.

DEVENEAU, W. F.
Student Officer
Lee, Illinois. Mass. Inst. of Tech., Cambridge, Key West. HTA.

DEVINEY, AL E.
Ensign
306 W. 19th St., Austin, Texas. Mass. Inst. of Tech., Key West, Miami, Pensacola. N. A. No. 1743. HTA.

DIAL, MORSE G.
Ensign
416 8th St., So. Fargo, N. D. Mass. Inst. of Tech., Key West, Miami, Pensacola. N. A. No. 1389. HTA.

DICKEY, FRED C.
Ensign
131 Newbury St., Boston, Mass. Mass. Inst. of Tech., Key West, Miami. N. A. No. 1530. HTA.

DICKEY, LINDSAY K.
Ensign
3037 So. Vermont Ave., Los Angeles, Cal. Mass. Inst. of Tech., Bay Shore, Pensacola. HTA.

DICKSON, ALBERT C.
Student Officer
2309 Boulevard, Wilmington, Delaware. Mass. Inst. of Tech., Key West. HTA.

DICKSON, CHARLES K.
Ensign
110 Llewellyn Rd., Montclair, N. J. Mass. Inst. of Tech., Bay Shore, Pensacola, Rockaway Beach. N. A. No. 1336. HTA.

DIEHL, HARRY L.
Student Officer
5509 Indiana Ave., Chicago, Ill. Great Lakes. HTA.

DILLON, THEODORE F.
Ensign
903 South 49th St., Phila., Penn. Mass. Inst. of Tech., Key West, Miami, Moutchic, Treguier, Fr. N. A. No. 1636.

DILTS, ALEXANDER R.
Ensign
P. O. Box 215, Hanover, Mass. Mass. Inst. of Tech., Akron, Goodyear Field, Pensacola. N. A. No. 2155 LTA.

DIXON, JOHN P.
Student Officer
735 Bucknum St., Casper, Wyoming. Seattle, Key West. HTA.

DODD, JOHN ALFRED
Student Officer
22 Lawn Ave., Middletown, Connecticut. Mass. Inst. of Tech. HTA.

DODDS, VINCENT G.
Student Officer
39 Rowley St., Gouverneur, N. Y. Mass. Inst. of Tech., Key West. HTA.

DODGE, HARRIS T.
Ensign
2706 Travis St., Houston, Texas. Mass. Inst. of Tech., Cambridge, Key West, Pensacola. N. A. No. 1857. HTA.

THE POINT ST. MATHIEU, FRANCE
Taken from a Plane on the Way to Sea at 700 Feet

DODGE, LESLIE P.
Student Officer
132 Middlesex Road, Chestnut Hill, Mass. Mass. Inst. of Tech., Miami. HTA.

DOHRMAN, FRANK S.
Lieut. (j.g.)
539 North Fourth St., Steubenville, Ohio. Utica, New Haven, Great Lakes.

DOLBEE, GEORGE H.
Ensign
1301 R. I. St., Lawrence, Kansas. Mass. Inst. of Tech., Key West, Pensacola. N. A. No. 2243. HTA.

DOLECEK, EDWARD E.
Lieut. (j.g.)
Wilson, Kansas. Mass. Inst. of Tech., Pensacola, Miami, Brest, Fr., Queenstown, Ire., Hampton Roads N. A. No. 742. HTA.

DONNELLY, DORWIN J.
Ensign
5720 Fifth Ave., Pittsburgh, Pa. Mass. Inst. of Tech., Miami, Pensacola. N. A. No. 1643. HTA.

DONOVAN, JAMES A.
Ensign
16 Summit Ave., Lawrence, Mass. Mass. Inst. of Tech., Pensacola.

DOUGHERTY, F. F.
Ensign
University Club, 546 Delaware Ave., Buffalo, N. Y. Mass. Inst. of Tech., Buffalo.

DOUGHERTY, W. V.
Ensign
1204 No. Market St., Wichita, Kansas. Mass. Inst. of Tech., Key West, Miami, Pensacola. N. A. No. 1901. HTA.

DOUGLAS, ARTHUR L.
Student Officer
Crestline, Kansas. Mass. Inst. of Tech., Miami. HTA.

DOW, EDWARD P.
Student Officer
615 So. 5th St., Grand Forks, N. D. Seattle, U. S. S. *Commodore*, Chicago. HTA.

DOW, LOUIS FENNER
Student Officer
226 Pearl St., Burlington, Vermont. Mass. Inst. of Tech., Cambridge. HTA.

DOWNS, PHILIP W.
Ensign
2433 Pinkney St., Omaha, Nebraska. Mass. Inst. of Tech., Pensacola. N. A. No. 1160.

DOYLE, JESSE IRWIN
Ensign
430 West Hortter St., Pelham, Philadelphia, Pa. Mass. Inst. of Tech., Miami, Pensacola. N. A. No. 1833. HTA.

DREIFUS, M. D.
Student Officer
1415 Pine St., New Orleans, La. Mass. Inst. of Tech. HTA.

DREYFUSS, ARTHUR J.
Student Officer
421 Atlanta Ave., San Antonio, Texas. Seattle, Wash. HTA.

DRISCOLL, ARTHUR D.
Ensign
65 Ferry St., Everett, Mass. M. I. T., Rockaway, Hampton Roads, Akron, Pensacola. N. A. No. 2520. LTA.

DRUMM, GUY
Ensign
Sparkill, New York. M. I. T., Phila., Cape May, Akron, Rockaway, Brest, Bay Sh., Miami, Pensacola. N. A. No. 2651. HTA.

DRURY, P. A., Jr.
Ensign
2400 16th St., Washington, D. C. Mass. Inst. of Tech., Akron, Pensacola. N. A. No. 2643. LTA.

DRY, MORRIS E.
Ensign
Mexico, Missouri. Mass. Inst. of Tech., Key West, Pensacola. N. A. No. 1834. HTA.

DU BOIS, JOHN E.
Ensign
Wichita, Kansas. Mass. Inst. of Tech., Bay Shore, Pensacola. N. A. No. 2198. HTA.

DUCHEMIN, N. M.
Lieut. (j.g.)
Springdale Terrace, St. John's, N. F. Akron, Queenstown. Rochampton, London. Pauillac, Royan, Castletown, Bay Sh. LTA.

DUDLEY, DONALD S.
Ensign
370 Linwood Ave., Buffalo, N. Y. Mass. Inst. of Tech., Miami, Pensacola. N. A. No. 1059. HTA.

DUDLEY, HENRY L., Jr.
Student Officer
Park Hill, Yonkers, N. Y. Mass. Inst. of Tech. HTA.

DUFFETT, WAYNE
Lieut. (j.g.)
1134 Lake Ave., Rochester, N. Y. Bay Shore, Mass. Inst. of Tech., Pensacola. Porto., Corsina, Italy. N. A. No 327. HTA.

(C) Comm. Inf. Bu.

ITALIAN SEAPLANE AT PORTO CORSINI
Real Piloting Is Required to Navigate This 70-Foot Channel

DUFFY, HERBERT S.
Student Officer
416 South Ohio Ave., Columbus, Ohio. Univ. Wash., Seattle, Miami. HTA.

DUFFY, MAURICE F.
Student Officer
118 So. Parkside Ave., Chicago, Ill. Dunwoody, Miami. HTA.

DUKE, RUSSELL E.
Student Officer
445 Groveland Ave., Dayton, Ohio. Mass. Inst. of Tech. LTA.

DUNCAN, EDWARD M
Ensign
524 McDonough St., Brooklyn, N. Y. New York City, Navy Hqtrs., London, N. Bomb. Gr., Autangue, Fr.

DUNCAN, GILBERT W.
Student Officer
1176 Murray Hill Ave., Pittsburgh, Penn. Mass. Inst. of Tech. HTA.

DUNHAM, CHESTER A.
Ensign
58 Sawyer Ave., Boston, Mass. Mass. Inst. of Tech., Hampton Roads, Montauk.

DUNKELBERG, R. C.
Student Officer
2401 Fairfield Ave., Fort Wayne, Indiana. Mass. Inst. of Tech,. Bay Shore. HTA.

DUNLAP, HARRY W., Jr.
Ensign
5533 Beverly Place., Pittsburgh, Pa. Mass. Inst. of Tech., Miami, Pensacola. N. A. No. 1161. HTA.

DUNNELL, R. H.
Student Officer
2400 Aldrich Ave. So., Minneapolis Minn. Seattle Wash., Dunwoody Inst., Minn. HTA.

DUNSIETH, G., Jr.
Lieut. (j.g.)
East Cottage, Ellwood City Pa. Mass. Inst. of Tech., U. S. S *Arizona*, Key West, Miami, Pensacola. N. A. No. 971. HTA.

DUPUY, ALBERT E.
Ensign
Montrose, Colorado. Mass. Inst. of Tech., San Diego, Pensacola. HTA.

DURFEE, THOMAS
Ensign
156 George St., Providence, R. I. Mass. Inst. of Tech., Cambridge,HamptonRoads, Pensacola, Chatham. N. A. No. 415. HTA.

DUSHANE, C. B., Jr.
Lieut. (j.g.)
Mt. Washington, Baltimore Co., Md. M. I. T., Pensa., Moutchic, Milan, N. B. G., St. Inglevert, Hamp. Rds. N. A. No. 400. HTA.

DUTTON, DANIEL F.
Ensign
1115 Kenwood Ave., Houston, Texas. Mass. Inst. of Tech., San Diego, Pensacola. N. A. No. 1889. HTA.

DUTTON, TOM W.
Student Officer
Prairieville, La. Mass. Inst. of Tech. HTA.

DWYER, DALTON
Student Officer
3800 Broadway, New York City. Mass. Inst. of Tech., Bay Shore, Brunswick, Ga., Key West. HTA.

DWYER, MARTIN J.
Ensign
920 W. Graydon Ave., Norfolk, Va. Pensa., M. I. T., Queenstown, Whiddy Island, Hampton Roads. N. A. No. 999. HTA.

◈ ◈ ◈ ◈ ◈

DABROHUA, CASTRO M., Student Officer, 1619 R St., Washington, D. C.

DAHN, JOHN HENRY, JR., Student Officer, 131 Joralamen St., Brooklyn, N. Y.

DAIN, JAMES W., Student Officer, Smithville, Tex.

DALEN, H. JOHN, Ensign, 389 6th St., San Pedro, Cal.

◈ ◈ ◈ ◈ ◈

DALEY, FREDERICK M., Ensign, Hamilton, Mass. Mass. Inst. of Tech., Key West, Miami, Pensacola. N. A. No. 1945. HTA.

DALLETT, MORRIS, Student Officer, Westtown, Pa.

DALTON, THOS. A., Student Officer, 33 N. Laurel St., Hazelton, Pa.

DALY, CLARENCE J., Student Officer, 1425 Williams St., Denver, Colo.

DALY, LE GRAND, Student Officer, 1008 Grand View Ave., Los Angeles, Cal. Seattle, Wash.

DARBY, A. M., Ensign, 909 Land Title Bldg., Philadelphia, Pa.

DARLING, ERLE G., Student Officer, 213 W. Kilborn St., Lansing, Mich.

DARLING, GEO. A., Student Officer, 106 Shaw St., New London, Conn.

DARLING, WALTER C., Ensign, 824 Main St., Coshocton, Ohio.

DAVIDSON, BEALE B., Student Officer, 56 Charles Gate East, Boston, Mass.

Davidson, Donald L., Student Officer, Clifton Ave., Athenia, N. J.

Davidson, John H., Ensign, 1825 F St., N. W., Washington, D. C. N. A. No. 278.

Davidson, L. E., Student Officer, Savannah, Mo. Seattle, Wash. LTA.

Davidson, Lester, Ensign, 1019 Charles St., St. Joseph, Mo.

Davidson, W. H., Ensign, 381 South St., Broadway, Yonkers, N. Y.

Davies, Jefferson W., Student Officer, 202 15th St., Racine, Wis.

Davies, Orville, Ensign, 5202 Magnolia Ave., Chicago, Ill. N. A. No. 1827.

Davis, Benj. H., Student Officer, 1950 E. 90th St., Cleveland, Ohio.

Davis, Edmund J., Student Officer, 2291 Broadway, Beaumont, Tex.

Davis, Edward A., Student Officer, 46 Eye St., N. W., Washington, D. C.

Davis, F. A., Boatswain.

Davis, F. Hamilton, Lieut. (j.g.), 49 Wall St., New York City.

Davis, Frank S. B., Student Officer, Cropseyville, N. Y.

Davis, Frederick D., Ensign, 645 N. Hopart Blvd., Los Angeles, Cal. Mass. Inst. of Tech., Miami, Pensacola, San Diego. N. A. No. 1651. HTA.

Davis, Granville E., Ensign, Grand View, Texas Mass. Inst. of Tech., Pensacola, Fla.; Montauk, L. I. N. A. No. 807.

Davis, Joe C., Student Officer, 798 Washington Ave., Memphis, Tenn.

Davis, Roy E., Ensign, Care of The Pal Cafe, Strawn, Texas. Mass. Inst. of Tech., Miami, Pensacola. N. A. No. 2178. HTA.

Davis, Sydney, Ensign, 1700 Austin Ave., Waco, Tex.

Davis, T. P., Ensign, Four Oaks, N. C. Mass. Inst. of Tech., Key West, Miami, Pensacola, Coco Solo. N. A. No. 1136. HTA.

Davis, Winsor R., Lieut. (j.g.), 244 W. 76th St., New York City.

Davison, F. T., Lieut. (j.g.), 690 Park Ave., N. Y. Palm Beach, Huntington. HTA.

Davison, Lester, Ensign, 1019 Charles St., St. Joseph, Mo. Dunwoody, Minn., Miami, Pensacola. HTA.

Davison, Wm. Walter, Ensign

Davison, William W., Ensign, 1837 Cherokee Ave., Hollywood, Cal. Seattle, San Diego, Pensacola. HTA.

Davisson, Oscar F., Jr., Student Officer, 307 Central Ave., Dayton, Ohio.

Davitt, John A., Student Officer, 314 Page St., San Francisco, Cal.

Davy, James B., Student Officer, 241 Oxford St., Rochester, N. Y. Mass. Inst. of Tech.

Dawson, Herbert H., Ensign, Care of Columbia Club, Indianapolis, Ind.

Day, Cecil E., Student Officer, 227 E. Capitol St., Washington, D. C.

Dayton, Wm. B., Student Officer, 2222 Maine St., Quincy, Ill.

Dean, Joseph L., Lieut. (j.g.), Opelika, Alabama. Mass Inst. of Tech., Pensacola, Moutchic, Avord, N. B. G. Bolsena, Scuola. N. A. No. 363. HTA.

De Bardeleben, Chas. F., Jr., Student Officer, 17 Idlewild Park, Birmingham, Ala. Mass. Inst. of Tech., Miami, HTA.

De Bardeleben, Prince, Student Officer, 17 Idlewild Park, Birmingham, Ala. Mass. Inst. of Tech., Pelham Bay. LTA.

DeBussy, Wales L., Ensign, 134 State St., Meriden, Conn. Mass. Inst. of Tech., Key West, Fla., Pensacola, Fla. N. A. No. 2386. HTA.

Decker, Harold J., Student Officer, 411 East 7th Ave., Denver, Colo. Seattle, Wash., San Diego, Cal. HTA.

Decker, James L., Student Officer, Le Roy, N. Y. Mass. Inst. of Tech., Bay Shore, L. I. HTA.

DeClark, F. F., Lieut. (j.g.).

DeFord, Geo. W., Student Officer, Staplehurst, Neb.

Deitzer, Raymond O., Machinist.

Delano, M. P., Lieutenant, 308 Prince St., West Newton, Mass. N. A. No. 104.

Delany, Theo. Wm., Student Officer, Georgetown College, Washington, D. C.

Delling, Torvald, Ensign, 1225 Hawthorne Ave., Apt. D., Minneapolis, Minn. N. A. No. 1304.

Dement, Cyrus, Student Officer, Smyrna, Tenn. Mass. Inst. of Tech., HTA.

Dempsey, Russell A., Ensign, 1107 Elmwood Ave., Ft. Wayne, Indiana. Mass. Inst. of Tech., Newport, Miami, Pensacola, Hampton Roads. HTA.

Dempster, Ryland N., Ensign, 1414 Harlam Ave., Baltimore, Md.

Denault, Eliot W., Student Officer, Pittsfield, Mass.

Denman, Gilbert M., Student Officer, 109 West French Place, San Antonio, Tex.

Denning, Matthew J., Ensign, 2011 Oakford St., Philadelphia, Pa.

Dennis, John Murdoch, Lieut. (j.g.), 1226 St. Paul St., Baltimore, Md.

Dent, Thos. A., Lieut. (j.g.), 101 Park Ave., New York City. Mass. Inst. of Tech., Miami, Pensacola. N. A. No. 2427. HTA.

De Sibour, H. L. J., Student Officer, 1603 K St., Washington, D. C., Great Lakes, Ill.

DeSonier, Lawrence Adelbert, Ensign. N. A. No. 767.

Deuchler, Gustave H., Student Officer, 624 E. Green St., Champaign, Ill.

Develin, James A., Jr., Ensign, 6052 Overbrook Ave., Philadelphia, Pa. Mass. Inst. of Tech., Bay Shore, L. I., Pensacola, Fla. N. A. No. 1904. HTA.

Devine, James J., Ensign, 61 Centre St., Bridgewater; Mass. Mass. Inst. of Tech., Miami, Pensacola. N. A. No. 2372. HTA.

Devine, Patrick Francis, Machinist.

Devine, Robt. E., Student Officer, 2115 W. Tioga St., Philadelphia, Pa.

De Voe, Raymond F., Student Officer, 109 West 83rd St., New York City.

Dewey, A. B., Lieut. (j.g.). 920 Lincoln Parkway, Chicago, Ill.

DeWitt, Clyde F., Student Officer, 841 Judson Ave., Evanston, Ill. Mass. Inst. of Tech. HTA.

Dexter, Sidney B., Student Officer, 48 West 55th St., New York City.

Deyo, Howard N., Student Officer, 250 Riverside Drive, New York City. Dunwoody Inst., Minn. HTA.

Diamond, Clark G., Ensign, 319 West Ferry St., Buffalo, N. Y. Mass. Inst. of Tech., Akron, Ohio, Rockaway Beach. LTA.

Dibble, Jasper C., Student Officer, Valley Stream, N. Y. Mass. Inst. of Tech. HTA.

Dickey, W. C., Ensign.

Dickson, Donald W., Student Officer, 44 Holder Hall, Provinceton, N. J.

Dickson, Frank, Student Officer, Pittsburgh, Athletic Association, Pittsburgh, Pa. Mass. Inst. of Tech., Chicago Municipal Pier.

Diehl, Walter S., Ensign, Jonesboro, Tenn. Mass. Inst. of Tech., Pensacola, Bu. C. & R., Washington, D. C. HTA.

Diemer, R. D., Ensign, Ten Hills, Baltimore Co., Md.

Diemer, Robt. W., Student Officer, 78 East Penn St., Germantown, Philadelphia, Pa.

Diemer, Robt. P., Ensign, Washington, D. C., Pensacola, Mass. Inst. of Tech., Akron, Rockaway, Halifax.

Dietrich, A. F., Lieut. (j.g.). N. A. No. 115.

Dietrich, Arthur M., Jr., Student Officer, 69 Ingraham Place, Newark, N. J.

Dietrich, Fred C., Ensign, Rio Vista, Cal., and Elks Club, Oakland, Cal. Mass. Inst. of Tech., Miami, Fla., Pensacola, Fla. N. A. No. 2553. HTA.

Dilkes Jos. H., Student Officer, 221 Locust St., Philadelphia, Pa.

Dill, Henry H., Student Officer, Albion Hotel, Baltimore, Md.

Dillon, Edward, Ensign, 31 Clinton St., Newark, N. J. N. A. No. 2439.

Dimit, William R., Ensign, 1323 Summer St., Grinnell, Iowa. Seattle, Wash.; San Diego, Cal.; Pensacola, Fla. N. A. No. 2177.

Dimmick, E. W., Ensign, 828 South 7th St., Terre Haute, Ind. Mass. Inst. of Tech., Key West, Fla. N. A. No. 2611. HTA.

Dinel, Edward P., Student Officer, 1 West 93rd St., New York City.

Dinkins, John H., Student Officer, 7225 Hollywood Blvd., Los Angeles, Cal. Seattle, San Diego, Cal. HTA.

Dixon, Brewer, Student Officer, 165 South St., Talladega, Ala.

DIXON, J. M., Machinist.

DOAK, HUBERT A., Student Officer, Greenville, Tenn Dunwoody Inst. HTA.

DOAN, J. L., Ensign, 229 Queen St., Philadelphia, Pa.

DODD, J. M., Ensign, 27 W. 73rd St., New York City. N. A. No. 739.

DODGE, JAMES WM., Student Officer, Contoocook, N. H.

DODGE, ROY H., Ensign, 1200 E. 65th St., Seattle, Wash. Great Lakes, Camp Saufley, Pensacola.

DODSON, W. C., Ensign, P. O. Box 19, Charlotte, N. C. Mass. Inst. of Tech., Key West, Miami, Pensacola, Coco Solo, Panama. N. A. No. 1138. HTA.

DOGGETT, LESLIE EARL, Machinist, Independence, Kans.

DOHERTY, EMMETT E., Student Officer, 333 University Ave., Missoula, Mont.. N. A. No. 430.

DOLLARD, OAKLEY J., Lieut. (j.g.), Bayport, L. I., N. Y. No. 378.

DOMINICK, EVERETT, Ensign, 37 East 57th St.,New York City.

DONAHUE, FRANK T., Ensign, 13 Bartlett St., Roxbury, Mass. N. A. No. 478.

DONAHUE, JAMES M., Student Officer, 121 Merrifield St., Worcester, Mass. Mass. Inst. of Tech. HTA.

DONALDSON, BRYAN WESLEY, Ensign, H. K. McCann Co., 61 Broadway, New York City. No. 1168.

DONALDSON, JOHN W., Ensign, 16 Wall St., New York City. Mass. Inst. of Tech., Pensacola, Cape May, Bay Shore. N. A. No. 1493. HTA.

DONAVAN, WM. E., Student Officer, 255 Park Place, Decatur, Ill.

DONELSON, WARREN W., Ensign, Huntingdon, Pa.

DONOVAN, HENRY L., Student Officer, 592 E. Third St., S. Boston, Mass.

DONOVAN, WALTER V., Student Officer, 1334 Pacific St., Brooklyn, N. Y.

DONNELLY, FRED'K S., Student Officer, 341 Bellevue Ave., Trenton, New Jersey. Mass. Inst. of Tech., Bay Shore, L. I. HTA.

DORGAN, ALBERT WM., Ensign, 2012 Madison Ave., Toledo, Ohio. Mass. Inst. of Tech., Miami, Pensacola, Coco Solo, Panama. N. A. 1642. HTA.

DORLON, ELIAS G., Student Officer, 15 Sheldon Ave., Troy, N. Y.

DORMAN, RODERICK AITKEN, Student Officer, 30 West 70th St., New York City.

DORNER, FRANK A., JR., Gunner.

DORWIN, OSCAR J., Student Officer, Minocqua, Wis.

DOSS, GILLMAN H., Student Officer, 100 East Main St., Hartselle, Ala. Mass. Inst. of Tech., Miami. HTA.

DOSS, PAUL C., Ensign, Philo, Ill. Mass. Inst. of Tech., Key West, Pensacola. N. A. No. 2007.

DOSTER, T. W., Ensign, 1 East Hanover Circle, Birmingham, Ala. Mass. Inst. of Tech., Key West, Miami, Pensacola. HTA.

DOTTS, WALTER M., Student Officer, 249 Monterey Ave., Pelham, N. Y.

DOUDS, JOHN PATRICK, Ensign, 1928 Emerson St., Denver, Colo. N. A. No. 1981.

DOUGHERTY, D. R., Ensign, 4500 Ellis Ave., Chicago, Ill. Mass. Inst. of Tech., Key West, Miami, Pensacola. N. A No. 115. HTA.

DOUGHERTY, EUGENE, Ensign, 5334 Geraldine Ave., St. Louis, Mo.

DOUGHERTY, G. FRANK, Student Officer, 1462 East 27th St., Brooklyn, N. Y. Mass. Inst. of Tech. HTA.

DOUGHERTY, NELSON, Lieut. (j.g.), 555 Park Ave., New York, N. Y. Columbia University, Pensacola, Fla.

DOUGLAS, GILBERT W., Lieut. (j.g.), Hotel Margaret, Brooklyn, N. Y. Bay Shore, Key West, Akron, Rockaway. N. A. No. 105½. LTA.

DOUSSEAU, RAYMOND A., Student Officer, Electric House Wesleyan Univ., Middletown, Conn.

DOWD, JOHN J., Ensign.

DOWELL, BENJAMIN B., Lieut. (j.g.), 3162 Mt. Pleasant St., N. W., Washington, D. C. Pensacola, Fla.; Cape May, N. J. N. A. No. 330. HTA.

DOWELL, CLEO L., Student Officer, 1905 Procter St., Port Arthur, Tex. Mass. Inst. of Tech., Miami. HTA.

DOWNING, EDGAR E., Student Officer, P. O. Box 767, Montgomery, Ala.

DOWNS, MOREY H., Lieut. (j.g.).

DOWRICK, JAMES P., Student Officer, 1625 First St., Washington, D. C.

DOYLE, LOUIS JOHN, Ensign, Yale Club, 44th St. and Vanderbilt Ave., New York City.

DOYLE, P., Gunner.

DRAKE, PAUL SHIRLEY, Ensign.

DREHER, HARRY W., Machinist.

DRENNEN, DONALD, Student Officer, Care of Birmingham Motor Co., Birmingham, Ala.

DRESSER, HENRY OWEN, Student Officer, Manhattan, Kans., Seattle, Wash. LTA.

DRIVER, BERRY O., Student Officer, Roanoke, Ala.

DRUMMOND, THOS. JOS., Mach., 27 Oak Ave., West Roxbury, Mass.

DRUMMOND, T. KENNETH, Student Officer, 214 West 71st St., New York City. Great Lakes, Princeton Naval Unit. HTA.

DRURY, WALTER E., Student Officer, 951 S St., Roslindale, Mass.

DUCKWORTH, H., Ensign. N. A. No. 2251.

DUDDLESTON, JOHN W., Student Officer, 5 Linden St., Cambridge, Mass.

DUFFIELD, GEORGE, Student Officer, 480 Woodward Ave., Detroit, Mich.

DUHRSSEN, ALFRED, Student Officer, 42 Beck Hall. Cambridge, Mass.

DUKE, JOHN, JR., Ensign, 11 Seymour St., N. Worcester, Mass. N. A. No. 1727.

DULIN, E. S., Student Officer, 43 Westmoreland Place, Los Angeles, Cal. Seattle, Wash. LTA.

DUMAS, GARDNER D., Ensign, 376 Andover St., Lowell, Mass. Pensacola, Fla., Great Lakes, Ill. N. A. No. 193. HTA.

DUNBAR, ERROLL, Student Officer, 1832 Biltmore St., N. W., Washington, D. C.

DUNCAN, C. C., Ensign, Unadille, Ga.

DUNCAN, JAMES W., Student Officer, Room 210, Southern Bldg., Washington, D. C.

DUNKLEE, F. E., Gunner.

DUNLAP, RICHARD W., Ensign, Danville, Kentucky. Northern Bombing Group, France.

DUNLOP, J. M., Ensign, Petersburg, Va. Ellerslie Farm.

DUNN, EDWARD K., Student Officer, 30 E. Preston St., Baltimore, Md. Great Lakes, Princeton.

DUNN, LEWIS B., Student Officer, 314 S. Broad St., Hillsboro, Ill. Dunwoody Inst., Miami. HTA.

DUNN, W. H., Ensign, Weston, Mass.

DUNSEITH, C. R., JR., Lieut. (j.g.), Ellwood City, Pa. N. A. No. 971.

DURANT, WALTER LER., Ensign, 310 Sixth Ave., Spokane, Wash. Mass. Inst. of Tech., Bay Shore, Hampton Roads, Pensacola, San Diego. N A. No. 1195. HTA.

DURKEE, JOHN B., Ensign.

DU TEAU, ALFRED A., Student Officer, 1106 S. 20th St., Lincoln, Neb.

DUVALL, EDWIN M., Ensign, 1117 N. Nevada Ave., Colo. Springs, Colo.

DWIGHT, JOHN W., JR., Student Officer, 17th and H Sts., Washington, D. C.

DWIGHT, MAITLAND, Ensign.

DYER, JAMES EDWARD, Ensign.

DYSART, L. T., Ensign, Melissa, Tex. Mass. Inst. of Tech., Hampton Rds., Va.; Miami, Pensacola, Fla. N. A. No. 2328.

EADES, ROSCOE
Ensign
Palmyra, Illinois. Mass. Inst. of Tech., Charleston, Pensacola, Akron, Rockaway Beach. LTA.

EAGER, AUVILLE
Student Officer
213 Fidelity Bldg., Baltimore, Md. Mass. Inst. of Tech. HTA.

EARNEST, CLYDE T.
Ensign
3112 Floyd Ave., Richmond, Virginia. Mass. Inst. of Tech., Key West. N. A. No. 1482. HTA.

EASTMAN, G. P.
Ensign
48 Highland Ave., Orange, N. J. Mass. Inst. of Tech., Akron, Pensacola, U. S. S. Wacondah, Chatham. N. A. No. 1579. LTA.

A GROUP OF OFFICERS AT TREGUIER, FRANCE

EASTMAN, PHILIP Y.
Ensign
48 Highland Ave., Orange, N. J. Mass. Inst. of Tech., Key West, Miami, Pensacola, Cape May. N. A. No. 1280. HTA.

EBERHARD, W. C.
Ensign
138 Poplar St., Roslindale, Boston, Mass. Mass. Inst. of Tech., Buffalo, Burgess Co., Marblehead, Mass. NAF, Philadelphia.

EBERHARDT, E. C.
Ensign
63 Ridgeview Drive, Indianapolis, Indiana. Mass. Inst. of Tech., Miami, Pensacola, Hampton Roads. N. A. No. 1588. HTA.

ECKERSON, GEO. D.
Ensign
65 Central Park West, New York City. Bay Shore, Key West, Miami. N. A. No. 506. HTA.

EDWARDS, CHESTER S.
Machinist
718 Clinton Ave., Newark, N. J. Pensacola, Hampton Roads, Akron. LTA.

EDWARDS, O. M., Jr.
Ensign
705 Walnut Ave., Syracuse, New York. Mass. Inst. of Tech., Miami, Pensacola. N. A. No. 1587. HTA.

EDWARDS, THOMAS R.
Student Officer
4209 Illinois Ave., N. W. Wash., D. C. Mass. Inst. of Tech., Miami. HTA.

EHLBERT, HENRY L.
Student Officer
1806 Avenue I, Birmingham, Alabama. Mass Inst. of Tech, Key West. HTA.

EHRHART, E. O.
Ensign
351 West 29th St., New York City. Mass. Inst. of Tech., Miami, Pensacola. N. A. No. 2498. HTA.

ELDER, WILLIAM F.
Ensign
2420 Ashby Ave., Berkeley, California. Mass. Inst. of Tech., Miami, Pensacola. N. A. No. 1972. HTA.

ELLIS, ERL HUBERT
Ensign
624 A. C. Foster Bldg., Denver, Colorado. Mass. Inst. of Tech., Miami, Pensacola. N. A. No. 2040. HTA.

ELWARD, ALLEN H.
Ensign
10 Durrell St., Methuen, Mass. Mass. Inst. of Tech., Akron, Rockaway, Halifax, Nova Scotia, Pensacola Hampton Roads. LTA.

EMANUEL, VICTOR
Student Officer
St. Urban Apts. 2 W. 89th St., New York City. Mass. Inst. of Tech., Miami. HTA.

EMERSON R.
Lieut. (j.g.)
Austin, Texas. Washington, D. C. Most foreign sta. Armistice Commission to Germany. N. A. No. 622. It. Dir. Pilot 122. LTA.

EMERY, FRANCIS J.
Lieut. (j.g.)
71 Cedar St., Roxbury, Mass. Mass. Inst. of Tech., Pensacola, Philadelphia. HTA.

EMISON, J. W.
Student Officer
618 Reichman St., Houston, Texas. Seattle, Washington. HTA.

EMRICH, RUSSELL L.
Ensign
415 King Ave., Columbus, Ohio. Mass. Inst. of Tech., Pensacola, Rockaway, Miami. N. A. No. 1407. HTA.

ENGLEMAN, FINIS E.
Ensign
Dunnegan, Mo. Mass. Inst. of Tech., Key West, Miami, Pensacola, Bay Shore. N. A. No. 2195 HTA.

ENGLISH, JAMES G.
Ensign
R. No. 2, Box 41, Greeley, Colo. Mass. Inst. of Tech., Miami. N. A. No. 1529. HTA.

ENO, ARTHUR R.
Student Officer
3219 9th St., Congress Hgts., Washington, D. C. Mass. Inst. of Tech. HTA.

ENOS, GEORGE
Lieut. (j.g.)
Newport, R. I. Pensacola, Moutchic, Fr., L'Aber Vrach, Fr.,Hampton Roads. N. A. No. 61. HTA.

ERDMAN, A. W., Jr.
Ensign
Prospect Ave., & Albany Rd., Hartford, Conn. Mass. Inst. of Tech., Akron, Pensacola, Chatham. N. A. No. 1562. LTA.

ERICKSON, ALFRED
Carpenter
Naval Air Station, Hampton Roads, Va. Annapolis, Guantanamo Bay, Cuba, Pensacola. LTA.

ERICKSON, JOHN K.
Student Officer
Fulda, Minn. Mass. Inst. of Tech., Pensacola. HTA.

H-12 ON THE STEP

ERICSSON, E. SIGURD
Student Officer
38 Beaconsfield Road, Worcester, Mass. Mass. Inst. of Tech. HTA.

ERNI, CHESTER P.
Ensign
807 East Spring St., New Albany, Indiana. Mass. Inst. of Tech., Miami.

ESSICK, WM. R.
Student Officer
Eureka, Kansas. Seattle. Washington. HTA.

ESTERLY, PAUL H.
Ensign
936 N. 4th St., Reading, Penn. Mass. Inst. of Tech., Akron, Rockaway. LTA.

ESTES, WALKER S.
Lieut. (j.g.)
419 Moffet Ave., Joplin, Mo. Columbia Univ., Pauillac, Fr., Arcachon, Gironde, Fr.

EVANS, GUY WESLEY
Student Officer
138 Jefferson Ave., Washington, Pa. Mass. Inst. of Tech., Nantucket, Newport, Key West. HTA.

EVANS, RALPH P.
Lieut. (j.g.)
South Hampton, N. H. Mass. Inst. of Tech., Bay Shore, Key West, Cape May. N. A. No. 411. HTA.

EVANS, SPRINGER F.
Ensign
R. R. No. 3, Twin Falls, Idaho. Seattle, San Diego, Pensacola N. A. No. 1881

EVINS, J. G., Jr.
Student Officer
Capital City Club, Atlanta, Ga. Mass. Inst. of Tech., Rockaway. HTA.

EWELL, WM. P.
Student Officer
Cambridge, Md. Mass. Inst. of Tech. HTA.

EYRE, ROY S.
Ensign
Highland, Howard Co., Md. Mass. Inst. of Tech., Miami, Pensacola. N. A. No. 2300. HTA.

◈ ◈ ◈ ◈ ◈ ◈

EADS, AUBREU L., Student Officer, 44 West 10th St., New York City.

EAGLESFIELD, WM., Student Officer, 3124 Mt. Pleasant St., N. W., Washington, D. C.

EAKIN, JOHN C., Student Officer, 1905 Battery St., Little Rock, Ark.

EAMES, J. C., Ensign.

EARLE, CLARENCE E., Student Officer, Chase, Md.

EASTERLY, M. H., Lieut. (j.g.).

EASTWOOD, J. L., Lieut. (j.g.). N. A. No. 405.

EASTMAN, WM. H., Ensign, 30 Vernon St., Newport, R. I.

EASTON, G., Ensign, 124 West Eighty-sixth St., New York City.

EASTON, WILLIAM, Ensign, Loudonville, Albany Co., N. Y. Mass. Inst. of Tech., Key West, Cape May, Pensacola. N. A. No. 463. HTA.

EATON, ALBION K., Lieut. (j.g.), 16 Oxford St., Cambridge, Mass.

EATON, CARLETON W., Ensign, Orono, Maine.

EATON, JOSEPH A., Lieut. (j.g.), 123 Packard Ave., Tufts College, Mass. Mass. Inst. of Tech., Pensacola, Cattewater, Eng., Felixstowe, Eng., The Hague, Holland, Rockaway, Dahlgren, Va. N. A. No. 184. HTA.

EATON, REA L., Student Officer, Eaton, Colo. Seattle, Wash., Miami, Fla. HTA.

EBELING, P. H., Student Officer, 327 Dwyer Ave., San Antonio, Tex. Seattle, Wash., Key West, Fla. HTA.

EBERSOLE, WM. G., Ensign, 167 Exeter Terrace, Buffalo, N. Y.

ECKELMAN, C. F., Student Officer, Lincoln, Kans. Seattle, Wash. HTA.

EDDT, E. B., Machinist.

EDDY, ROBERT LEWIS, Student Officer, Willard Hotel, Washington, D. C.

EDGERTON, GURDON, IRVING, Ensign, 41 Hawthorn St., Cambridge, Mass. Mass. Inst. of Tech., Pensacola, Fla. N. A. No. 2450. HTA.

EDMONDS, REGINALD W., Ensign, 86 Hewlett St., Roslindale, Mass. Mass. Inst. of Tech., Miami, Fla. HTA.

EDMONDSON, JOHN S., Student Officer, 1875 S. Parkway, Memphis, Tenn.

EDMUNDSON, WILFORD A., Lieut. (j.g.).

EDWARDS, C. H., Machinist, 334 41st St., Brooklyn, N. Y.

EDWARDS, EDWARD MITCHELL, Ensign, 2117 Locust St., Philadelphia, Pa. Mass. Inst. of Tech., Instructor. LTA.

EDWARDS, RICHARD E., Student Officer, 123 W. Main St., Peru, Indiana. Great Lakes, Ill.

EDWARDS, ROBERT B., Student Officer, 1126 South 34th St., Omaha, Neb.

EDWARDS, THOMAS E., Ensign, Care of U. S. Dept. of Labor, El Paso, Tex.

EDWARDS, WILLIAM S., Jr., Student Officer, 213 S. 21st St., Birmingham, Ala.

EHRHART, WILBUR W., Student Officer, 4301 Grant Blvd., Pittsburgh, Pa.

EHRMANNTRAUT, WM. R., Lieut. (j.g.), 1340 Perry Place, Washington, D. C.

EITEL, EDMUND H., Ensign, Highland Park, Ill. Columbia University, Chatham, U. S. N., Gas Engine Sch., Great Lakes.

EIDMANN, FRANK LEWIS, Lieut. (j.g.), 65 Fairfield Ave., Holyoke, Mass. Columbia University, Packard, Detroit.

ELDRED, ANDREW J., Student Officer, 1736 G St., Washington, D. C.

ELDRIDGE, CARLETON G., Ensign, 1332 Mass. Ave., Washington, D. C.

ELDRIDGE, ELTON M., Student Officer.

ELLER, HERBERT T., Student Officer, Euclid Ave. at 90th St., Cleveland. Dunwoody Inst., San Diego. HTA.

ELLICOTT, WM. H., Ensign, 1731 20th St., N. W., Washington, D. C. N. A. No. 1420.

ELLINGTON, K. R., Lieut. (j.g.), Clayton, N. C. N. A. No. 1009.

ELLIOTT, HAROLD ABRAHAM, Ensign, 76 Chope Place, Detroit, Mich. N. A. No. 760.

ELLIOTT, HENRY S., Student Officer, 241 Jefferson St., Henderson, Ky.

ELLIOTT, NIXON C., Ensign, 616 Denham Bldg., Denver, Colo. Mass. Inst. of Tech., Great Lakes, Pensacola, Washington. HTA.

ELLIOTT, REYNOLDS F., Student Officer, Evans City, Pa.

ELLIOTT, ROSCOE C., Student Officer, 37 Lowden Ave., West Somerville, Mass.

ELLIOTT, WM. B., JR., Student Officer, 256 W. Dudley Ave., Westfield, N. J.

ELLIS, JOHNSTONE D., Lieut. (j.g.), 1031 W. Erie Ave., Lorain, Ohio. N. A. No. 701.

ELMORE, LYNWOOD K., Student Officer, Burnside, Conn. Mass. Inst. of Tech. LTA.

ELSAS, NORMAN E., Ensign, Ponce De Leon Apts., Atlanta, Ga. Mass. Inst. of Tech., Key West, Miami, Pensacola. N. A. No. 1687. HTA.

ELVIDGE, EARLE C., Student Officer, Hotel Seguoia, Redwood City, Cal.

ELY, MAHLON L., Ensign, Hutchinson, Kans. Mass. Inst. of Tech., Newport, Bay Shore, Pensacola, Washington, New York. HTA.

EMERSON, ARTHUR J., Ensign, 16 Addington Road, Brookline, Mass. Mass. Inst. of Tech., Key West, Miami, Pensacola, Norfolk, Anacostia. N. A. No. 1163.

EMERSON, EDWARD F., Student Officer, 31 Hovey St., Newton, Mass.

EMERY, CHARLES G., Student Officer, 1400 Hillcrest Ave., Pasadena, Cal.

EMERY, JOHN J., Ensign, 170 Woodmere Ave., Detroit, Mich. N. A. No. 1769.

EMERY, JOHN J., Ensign, 5 East 68th St., New York, N. Y. Mass. Inst. of Tech., Bay Shore, Pensacola. HTA.

EMMERT, ALLAN R., Ensign, 513 South Queen St., Martinsburg, W. Va.

EMORY, FREDERICK INGERSOLL, Student Officer, 19 Willard Road, Brookline, Mass.

ENDERS, JOHN F., Lieut. (j.g.), 17 Highland St., Hartford, Conn. N. A. No. 891.

ENDICOTT, JOHN, Ensign, 386 Longwood Ave., Boston, Mass.

ENGEL, WILLIAM P., Student Officer.

ENGLISH, FRANK K., Ensign, 186 Edwards St., New Haven, Conn. Mass. Inst. of Tech., Miami, Pensacola. N. A. No. 2619. LTA.

EPES, BRANCH P., Ensign, 2016 R St., N. W., Washington, D. C. Mass. Inst. of Tech., Miami, Pensacola. N. A. No. 1713. HTA.

ERDMAN, CHARLES E., Ensign, 246 Bryant St., Buffalo, N. Y. N. A. No. 2159.

ERDMAN, CHAS. R., JR., Student Officer, 20 Library Pl., Princeton, N. J. Mass. Inst. of Tech., Bay Shore, Brunswick. HTA.

ERWIN, JOHN C., Student Officer, 210 West 11th St., Charlotte, N. C.

ESQUIROL, Joseph Alfred, Student Officer, 25 Crooke Ave., Brooklyn, N. Y. Dunwoody, Minneapolis, Minn. HTA.

ESTABROOK, FRED T., Lieut. (j.g.), Odessa, New York. Mass. Inst. of Tech., Bay Shore, N. Y.; Pensacola, Fla. N. A. No. 572. HTA.

ESTABROOK, H. C., Ensign.

EVANS, A. W., Ensign. N. A. No. 695.

EVANS, FREDERICK, Lieut. (j.g.).

EVANS, G. E., Ensign. N. A. No. 166.

EVANS, ROBERT B., Student Officer, 3434 Washington Blvd., Indianapolis, Ind.

EWAN, CHARLES M., Ensign, Covington, Ky. N. A. No. 1988.

EWART, IRVING D., Ensign, 542 W. 112th St., New York City. Columbia Univ., Great Lakes, Ill. HTA.

I'm Scared of It All

I'm scared of it all, God's truth so I am:
It's too big and brutal for me.
My nerve's on the raw and I don't give a damn
For all the sixteens that I see.
I'm lost in the cockpit; the wings are too wide;
The bubble goes slopping about;
Oh I want to go back to the N–9's again—
I wish to hell I was out.

I'd rather go back to my Old Gyrene,
To the F–boats that ride on the foam,
Or even to Saufley with chaos supreme,
Than to have them carry me home.
My brain is packed full of mysterious gloom,
My eyeballs are glazed and aglare;
This sixteen is deadfalled with danger and doom,
It never was meant for the air.

I watch the wan faces under the dash;
All kinds of queer antics I see,
And each one of them is expecting to crash,
And none has a kind thought for me;
Just jaded and panting like fogs in a pack,
Each one contemplating his fate.
Oh, God, but I'm lonesome—I wish I was back
On the beach before it's too late.

My knees knock together; I'm full of unrest;
I cringe—I'm so weak and so small;
I can't get my bearings, I'm crushed and oppressed
With the haste and the waste of it all.
The turns and the spirals—one motor is cut,
And fear in the faces I see.
We've come down for a landing—successfully, but—
It's all blooming torture to me.

I feel its all wrong but I can't tell you why—
The bumps are doing their very best,
Still N–9's and ones are all hogging the sky—
I wish I was back at Key West!
I'm scared of it all; from afar I can hear
The trumpet of Gabriel's call.
We're nothing but men with a little veneer;
Terra firma is best after all.

FAGER, GEORGE E.
Student Officer
Murphysboro, Illinois. Seattle, Washington. HTA.

FAIRLAMB, R. C., Jr.
Ensign
4936 Walnut St., Philadelphia, Pa. Mass. Inst. of Tech., Miami, Pensacola. N. A. No. 1933. HTA.

FAKE, FRANK C.
Ensign
100 Fairview Ave., Piedmont, Cal. Mass. Inst. of Tech., Key West, Miami. N. A. No. 1528.

FALGE, ROBERT N.
Ensign
Care of Goodyear Co., Akron, Ohio. Mass. Inst. of Tech., Bay Shore, Pensacola. N. A. No. 2091 HTA.

FALOON, DALTON B.
Student Officer
125 Du Bois Ave., Du Bois, Penn. Mass. Inst. of Tech., Miami, Pensacola. HTA.

FALVEY, WALLACE J.
Lieut. (j.g.)
71 Strathmore Rd., Brookline, Mass. Mass. Inst. of Tech., Pensacola, Anacostia. N. A. No. 1002. HTA.

FANCHER, PHILIP D.
Ensign
Montevallo, Ala. Mass. Inst. of Tech., Miami, Pensacola. N. A. No. 2514. HTA.

FARMER, EARLAND M.
Ensign
South Dartmouth, Mass. Mass. Inst. of Tech., Key West, Miami, Pensacola. N. A. No. 1219. HTA.

FARNHAM, JAMES P.
Lieut. (j.g.)
57 West 57th St., New York City. Bay Shore, Miami. N. A. No. 500. HTA.

FARRELL, FRANK P.
Ensign
Medford, Oregon. Mass. Inst. of Tech., U. S. S. *Marblehead*, Bay Shore, Key West. N. A. No. 2044. HTA.

FARRER, JOHN A., Jr.
Student Officer
28 Hurlbut St., Cambridge, Mass. Mass. Inst. of Tech. HTA.

FARRIS, ROBERT
Machinist
1105 W. Maple St., Alva, Okla. Pensacola. Le Croisic, Fr., U. S. S. *North Carolina*, Hampton Roads. HTA.

FAY, CHARLES L.
Lieut. (j.g.)
394 South 1st Ave., Mt. Vernon, N. Y. Mass. Inst. of Tech., Miami. N. A. No. 614.

FEHER, A. J.
Ensign
811 Kenmore Pl., Brooklyn, N. Y. Pensacola, Bay Shore, Brunswick, Key West. HTA.

FELDMANN, W. H.
Student Officer
2320 W. Lanvale St., Baltimore, Md. Mass. Inst. of Tech., Key West, Pensacola. HTA.

FELIX, KENNETH A.
Student Officer
204 Tennyson Ave., Pittsburgh, Pa. Mass. Inst. of Tech., Miami. HTA.

FELLOWS, RICHARD C.
Ensign
1437 Arnold Ave., N. W. Canton, Ohio. Mass. Inst. of Tech., Miami, Pensacola. N. A. No. 2477. HTA.

FELTMAN, GEORGE R.
Student Officer
Ansonia, Ohio. Mass. Inst. of Tech. HTA.

FERGUSON, JAMES G.
Ensign
Amsterdam, N. Y. Mass. Inst. of Tech., Akron, Rockaway. N. A. No. 1053. LTA.

FERGUSON, R. D.
Ensign
700 So. 16th St., Lincoln, Nebr. Pensacola, Mass. Inst. of Tech., Miami. N. A. No. 2024. HTA.

(C) *Underwood & Underwood, N. Y.*

MAN-OF-WAR AT ANCHOR IN NEW YORK HARBOR

FERGUSON, R. F.
Student Officer
Carnegie, Oklahoma. Mass. Inst. of Tech., Akron, Key West, Pensacola. LTA.

FERRY, EARL E.
Ensign
84 Elizabeth St., Pittsfield, Mass. Mass. Inst. of Tech., Hampton Roads, Pensacola. N. A. No. 2387. HTA.

FICKINGER, R. B.
Ensign
908 6th St., N. W. Canton, Ohio. Mass. Inst. of Tech., Pensacola, Boston, Anacostia, Washington. N. A. No. 1200. HTA.

FIEDLER, E. C.
Ensign
215 N. Ave., Cranford, N. J. Pensacola, Newport News, Hampton Roads, N. A. No. 616. LTA.

FILLEY, LOUIS J.
Ensign
1421 Wayne Ave., So. Pasadena, Cal. Mass. Inst. of Tech., Key West, Miami, Pensacola, San Diego. N. A. No. 1337. HTA.

FINCH, FOSTER D.
Ensign
Spring Hope, N. C. Mass. Inst. of Tech., Key West, Pensacola. N. A. No. 2277. HTA.

FINGER, ARMIN W.
Student Officer
177 34th St., Milwaukee, Wis. Mass. Inst. of Tech., Cambridge, Pelham Bay. HTA.

FINKLER, ALBERT T.
Ensign
485 Wyoming Place, Milwaukee, Wis. Mass. Inst. of Tech., Key West, Miami, Pensacola, Hampton Roads. N. A. No. 2127. HTA.

FINLEY, JOHN T.
Student Officer
1928 Eye St., Washington, D. C. Seattle, Washington. HTA.

FISHER, CARL A.
Ensign
1206 West Second South St., Salt Lake City. Mass. Inst. of Tech., Bay Shore, Pensacola, Hampton Roads. N. A. No. 998. HTA.

FISHER, J. FRED
Ensign
1908 Louisiana Ave., St. Louis, Mo. Mass. Inst. of Tech., Key West, Miami. N. A. No. 475. HTA.

FISHER, PAUL D.
Machinist
99 Huron St., Brooklyn, N. Y. Columbia Univ., Pauillac, Fr., U. S. Marines. HTA.

FISHER, PORTER G.
Student Officer
33 Penhurst Park, Buffalo, N. Y. Mass. Inst. of Tech. HTA.

FISKE, ROGER B.
Ensign
Topsfield, Mass. Mass. Inst. of Tech., Miami, Pensacola. N. A. No. 2098. HTA.

FITZGERALD, GERALD
Ensign
Ticonderoga, N. Y. Mass. Inst. of Tech., Newport, R. I., Key West, Pensacola. N. A. No. 2410. HTA.

FITZGERALD, JAMES N.
Student Officer
214 N. Seventh St., Newark, N. J. Mass. Inst. of Tech., Bay Shore. HTA.

FITZPATRICK, T. J.
Student Officer
808 Corinthian Ave., Philadelphia, Pa. Dunwoody, Mass. Inst. of Tech. HTA.

FLANIGAN, FRANK J.
Lieut. (j.g.)
235 Harvard Ave., Allston, Mass. Curtiss Aeroplane, Buffalo, Bay Shore.

FLECK, A. L.
Student Officer
929 Quindaro Blvd., Kansas City, Kansas. Mass. Inst. of Tech., Akron, Rockaway, New York. LTA.

FLECK, HAROLD J.
Ensign
304 N. E. 4th St., Newton, Iowa. Dunwoody, Miami, Key West, Pensacola. N. A. No. 2324. HTA.

FLECKENSTEIN, J. G.
Student Officer
610 Bates St., Grand Rapids, Michigan. Seattle, Washington. HTA.

FLEITMANN, W. M., Jr.
Lieut. (j.g.)
114 East 84th St., New York City. Mass. Inst. of Tech., Bay Shore, Pensacola. N. A. No. 950. HTA.

FLEMING, CHAS. Jr.
Ensign
Mansion House, Milford, Mass. Mass. Inst. of Tech., Akron, Pensacola. N. A. No. 2658. LTA.

FLEMING, JAMES D.
Student Officer
454 Seventh St., San Bernardino, California. Seattle, Washington. HTA.

(C) Underwood & Underwood, N. Y.

AERIAL VIEW OF BREST, FRANCE
Showing U. S. Naval Air Station

FLETCHER, FRANK B.
Student Officer
905 E. Missouri St., El Paso, Texas. Mass. Inst. of Tech., Key West, Miami, Pensacola. HTA.

FLETCHER, W. D.
Ensign
Heuvelton, N. Y. Mass. Inst. of Tech., Miami, Pensacola. N. A. No.1716. HTA.

FLICKINGER, C. P.
Ensign
502 N. Grove Ave., Oak Park, Ill. Mass. Inst. of Tech., Bay Shore, Brunswick, Key West, Pansacola. N. A. No. 2312. HTA.

FLYNN, CHARLES E.
Ensign
12 Smith Road, Cliftondale, Mass. Mass. Inst. of Tech., Key West, Miami, Pensacola. N. A. No. 1784. HTA.

FLYNN, FRED T.
Ensign
92 Buckingham St., Hartford, Conn. Mass. Inst. of Tech., Key West, Miami, Pensacola. N. A. No. 2192. HTA.

FLYNN, MAURICE B.
Lieut. (j.g.)
16 Vinton Rd., Madison, N. J. Mass. Inst. of Tech., Miami, Pensacola. N. A. No. 1961. HTA.

FLYNN, W. HUGO
Student Officer
740 N. Burlington Ave., Hastings, Nebraska. Seattle, Washington. HTA.

FOLEY, THOS. P.
Student Officer
Adams Ave. and N. E. Boulevard, Frankford, Pa. Mass. Inst. of Tech. HTA.

FOLWELL, RALPH T.
Student Officer
111 Bethlehem Pike, Chestnut Hill, Penn. Mass. Inst. of Tech. HTA.

FONDEVILLE, E. L.
Student Officer
141 Park Ave., East Orange, N. J. Mass. Inst. of Tech., Cambridge, Goodyear Flying Field, Akron. LTA.

FORBES, WILL
Student Officer
Waterloo, Iowa. Mass. Inst. of Tech., Great Lakes. HTA.

FORGAN, J. B., Jr.
Ensign
38 S. Dearborn St., Chicago, Ill. Mass. Inst. of Tech., Bay Shore, Pensacola. N. A. No. 1780. LTA.

FORKNER, JOE R.
Ensign
4214 14th Ave., N. E., Seattle, Wash. Mass. Inst. of Tech., Key West. N. A. No. 1479. HTA.

FORREST, RONALD C.
Student Officer
712 N. 49th St., Seattle, Wash. Seattle. HTA.

FORSTER, GEORGE F.
Student Officer
111 Rogers Ave., Macon, Ga. Seattle, Washington. HTA.

FOSTER, JAMES R.
Student Officer
152 West 58th St., New York City. Mass. Inst. of Tech., Bay Shore. HTA.

FOW, FRANKLIN RILE
Student Officer
541 Argyle Road, Brooklyn, N. Y. Dunwoody Inst., Minn. HTA.

FOWLER, LEROY A.
Ensign
Bozeman, Montana. Mass. Inst. of Tech., San Diego, Pensacola. N. A. No. 2039. HTA.

FOX, AUSTIN
Student Officer
426 South Oak Park Ave., Oak Park, Illinois. Seattle, Washington. HTA.

FOX, JAMES M.
Student Officer
542 West 112 St., New York City. Mass. Inst. of Tech. HTA.

FOX, NORMAN J.
Student Officer
1502 Indiana Ave., La Porte, Indiana. Seattle, Great Lakes. HTA.

FRANCISCO, CYRUS P.
Ensign
69 Halsey St., Newark, N. J. Mass. Inst. of Tech., Akron, Pensacola. LTA.

FRANZ, CRISS WESTON
Ensign
Restmere, Tallmadge, Ohio, Summit County. Mass. Inst. of Tech., Akron, Miami, Pensacola. N. A. No. 2158. LTA.

FRAWLEY, PAUL B.
Student Officer
150 W. 47th St., New York City. Mass. Inst. of Tech., Bay Shore. HTA.

(C) *Comm. Pub. Inf.*

A BUSY DAY AT KEY WEST

FREELAND, J. M.
Student Officer.
3525 Harrison Blvd., Kansas City, Mo. Mass. Inst. of Tech., Akron, Pensacola. LTA.

FREEMAN, EDMUND L.
Ensign
Cameron, Mo. Mass. Inst. of Tech., Akron, Pensacola. N. A. No. 2157. LTA.

FRIEND, R. D.
Ensign
1646 Mass. St., Lawrence, Kansas. Mass. Inst. of Tech., San Diego, Pensacola. N. A. No. 1767. HTA.

FROASS, PAUL E.
Ensign
203 Main St., Oneida, N. Y. Mass. Inst. of Tech., Pensacola, Queenstown, Wexford, Hamp. Rds., Rockaway. N. A. No. 751.

FROST, EDWARD M.
Student Officer
1407 Harrison St., Lynchburg, Virginia. Mass. Inst. of Tech., Boston, Bay Shore. HTA.

FRYE, EDGAR P.
Ensign
R. F. D. No. 3, Wilton, N. H. Great Lakes, U. S. S. Kansas, Miami, Dayton.

FUHR, HARRY E.
Lieut. (j.g.)
41 Fourth Place, Brooklyn, N. Y. Rockaway, Pensa., Pallice, Paris, Brest, London, Queenstown, Castletown, B. Sh., Wash. LTA.

FULLAWAY, W. M.
Student Officer
2955 Pacific St., Omaha, Nebraska. Seattle, San Diego. HTA.

FULLER, WM. A.
Ensign
1200 Lake Shore Drive, Chicago, Ill. Mass. Inst. of Tech., Key West. N. A. No. 1430.

◈ ◈ ◈ ◈ ◈

FAGAN, P. F., Ensign.

FAGEROS, EDWARD D., Ensign., 2614 Polk St., N. W., Minn., Minn. N. A., No. 750.

FAHY, CHARLES, Lieut. (j.g.), 410 Fifth St., N. W., Washington, D. C. Mass. Inst. of Tech., Pensacola, Ft. Worth, Killingholme, Stonehenge., R. A. F., Fr., Nor. Bomb. Gr. N. A. No. 301. HTA.

FALES, HERBERT G., Ensign, 145 Highland St., West Newton, Mass. Mass. Inst. of Tech., Hammondsport, N. Y., Buffalo, N. Y.

FALLON, C. G., Ensign, 31 Borroughs St., Jamaica Plain, Mass.

FARLEY, ADRIAN M., Student Officer, Harbor Road, Southport, Conn.

FARLEY, Eliot, Ensign, Dedham, Mass. Mass. Inst. of Tech., Pensacola. HTA.

FARLEY, W. SCOTT, Ensign, Opelika, Ala. Great Lakes, Ill.

FARMER, CHAS. RALPH, Ensign, Santa Rosa, Cal. N. A. No. 216.

FARNHAM, WILLARD E., Ensign.

FARNSWORTH, GROVER C., Ensign, 2710 Ontario Road, Washington, D. C.

FARRELL, HENRY E., JR., Student Officer, 918 Security Bldg., St. Louis, Mo.

FARRELL, RAYMOND, Student Officer, Palo Alto, Cal. Mass. Inst. of Tech., Akron. LTA.

FARRELLY, RICHARD L., Ensign, Harrison, N. Y. N. A. No. 887.

FARTHING, WM. J., Lieut. (j.g.), No. 3 Montrose Apt., Houston, Tex. Bu. of Ordnance, Washington, D. C.

FARWELL, J. V., 3rd, Lieut. (j.g.), West Palm Beach, Fla.

FAULDS, JOHN L., Student Officer, 588 Walnut St., New Orleans, La.

FAVORITE, GEORGE UPTON, Ensign, Devon, Pa. Mass. Inst. of Tech., Key West. HTA.

FAWCETT, CHARLES H., Ensign, 411 West 63rd St., Kansas City, Mo.

FAY, J. A., Ensign, 1371 Columbia Road, Washington, D. C. Mass. Inst. of Tech., San Diego, Pensacola. N. A. No. 1241. HTA.

FAY, ROBERT R., Ensign. N. A. No. 1734.

FEAMAN, PHILLIP B., Student Officer, 108 Birchwood Ave., Louisville, Ky.

FEBIEGR, WM. S., Student Officer, 480 Randolph Ave., Milton, Mass. Great Lakes, Ill.

FELLOWS, EARLE H., Ensign, 322 Carrinta St., Rutherford, N. J. Rockaway Beach, L. I., Coco Solo, C. Z.

FELLOWS, HERBERT A., Student Officer. Room 275 Patent Office, Washington, D. C.

FELTON, WM. S., Ensign, 357 Essex St., Salem, Mass.

FENISTON, NOBLE C., Ensign, Box 51, Sardinia, Ind.

FENTRESS, HERBERT S., Student Officer, 1801 Willoughby St., Norfolk, Va., Dunwoody, Minn. HTA.

FEREBEE, SAMUEL W., JR., Student Officer, Newbern, N. C.

FERGUSON, GUY H., Ensign, 480 Pine St., San Francisco, Cal. N. A. No. 1083.

FERGUSON, WILBERT H., Student Officer, 2639 E. 29th St., Kansas City, Mo.

FERGUSON, WILLARD E., Ensign, 61 East 80th St., New York City.

FERRIS, DAKIN DENNETT, Ensign.

FERRIS, JOHN M., Student Officer, 76 Young Ave., Pelham, N. Y.

FESSENDEN, JOHN H., JR., Student Officer, 3402 Nebraska Ave., Tampa, Fla.

FESSLER, JAMES ANDREW, Student Officer, 812 Kercheval Ave., Detroit, Mich.

FEUCHTWANGER, A. J., Ensign, Mastic, Mass.

FIELD, HUGH T., Ensign, Calvert, Tex. Seattle, Key West, Pensacola. N. A. No. 2378. HTA.

FIELDS, J. C., War. Gun.

FILLEBROWN, HOWARD MERRELL, Ensign, 24 Vincent St., Binghamton, N. Y. Mass. Inst. of Tech., Miami, Pensacola, Fla. HTA.

FINCH, VOLNEY C., Ensign, Pacific King Co., Tacoma, Wash. Mass. Inst. of Tech., Pensacola, Miami, Moutchic, Calais, Nor. Bom. Gr., Dunkirk, Hampton Rds. N. A. No. 2353. LTA.

FINCKE, DONALD M., Ensign, 655 Academy St., Astoria, L. I., N. Y. Mass. Inst. of Tech., Akron, Pelham Bay, Brest, Guipavas, Fr. LTA.

FINLEY, ADIN W., Student Officer, 1018 Commercial St., Emporia, Kans.

FINNEGAN, JAMES JOSEPH, Lieut. (j.g.), 527 Fifth Ave., New York, N. Y. New Port News, Va. Washington, D. C., St. Ingleyert, Fr., Hampton Roads, Va., Northern Bombing Group. HTA.

FINNEY, FRANK B., War. Gun.

FINNEY, WILLIAM L., Ensign, 541 W. Jackson Blvd., Chicago, Ill. N. A., No. 2252.

FISH, ALBERT S., Ensign, 212 Linden St., Akron, O.

FISHBACK, GEORGE BENJAMIN, Ensign, Paris, Ky. N. A. No. 1967.

FISHER, EVAN T., Student Officer, Redland, Cal.

FISHER, H. S., Ensign, 2787 Boulevard, Jersey City, N. J.

FISHER, O. W., JR., Ensign, Bellingham, Wash. Care of Fisher Flouring Mills Co., Mass. Inst. of Tech., Keyport, N. J., College Pt., L. I., Elizabeth, N. J.; Seattle, Wash.

FITCH, H. H., Ensign.

FITZGERALD, WYATT E., Carpenter.

FITZGIBBON, WM., Ensign, 371 West 123rd St., New York City. N. A. No. 2338.

FITZ, EDWARD C., Student Officer, 18 Tremont St., Boston, Mass. Great Lakes, Ill.

FITZPATRICK, ELMER J., Student Officer, Radcliff, Ohio.

FITZPATRICK, JOSEPH P., Lieut. (j.g.), 507 110 St., New York City.

FITZPATRICK, PAUL E., Student Officer, 2037 Seneca St., Buffalo, N. Y. Mass. Inst. of Tech. HTA.

FITZSIMONS, JOS. G., Student Officer, 8 Bromley Rd., Charlotte, N. C. Mass. Inst. of Tech., Akron, Pensacola. LTA.

FITZPATRICK, WALTER C., Boatswain.

FLANDERS, SAMUEL J., Student Officer, 929 Quindaro Blvd., Kansas City, Mo.

FLANIGAN, CHAS. W., Student Officer, 1314 Massachusetts Ave., N. W., Washington, D. C.

FLANIGAN, HORACE C., Ensign, Quaker Ridge, New Rochelle, N. Y.

FLEIDNER, CARLYLE S., Ensign, 2913 Michigan Ave., Chicago, Ill.

FLEMING, FOREST E., Student Officer, Stanford University, Cal.

FLEMING, HARVEY C., Ensign, 4846 Kimbark Ave., Chicago, Ill. Mass. Inst. of Tech., Miami, Pensacola. N. A. No. 1882. HTA.

FLEMING, HERBERT PAUL, Ensign, 11 E. Wyoming Ave., Melrose, Mass. Mass. Inst. of Tech., Miami, Pensacola, Fla. N. A. No. 2191. HTA.

FLETCHER, HAROLD HILL, Ensign, 1572 Massachusetts Ave., Cambridge, Mass.

FLETCHER, MILAN P., Student Officer, 418 Peach St., Erie, Pa.

FLETCHER, RALPH ANDREW, Lieut. (j.g.), Westford, Mass. Mass. Inst. of Tech., Ordnance, Seattle, Wash.

FLEURY, EDWARD H., Student Officer, 119 E. 19th St., Care of B. P. Neff, New York City.

FLINT, E. L., Student Officer, Tonica, Ill. Mass. Inst. of Tech., Key West. HTA.

FLINT, GEO. C., Lieut. (j.g.), 842 Gunderson Ave., Oak Park, Ill. Great Lakes. HTA.

FLINT, WM. H., Ensign, 7 Thompson Ave., Larchmont, N. Y.

FLOOD, GEO. W., War. Machinist, 515 W. 111th St., New York City. Columbia University, Packard, Key West, Fla.

FLOOD, J. C., Ensign, N. A. No. 921.

FLOOD, THOMAS B., Ensign, P. O. Box 1105, Tonopah, Nev. Mass. Inst. of Tech., Akron, Key West. N. A. No. 1965. LTA.

FLOOD, WALTER C., Ensign, 918 S. Negley Ave., Pittsburgh, Pa.

FLOYD, GORDON PIERCE, Ensign, 157 Vassar St., Cambridge, Mass. Mass. Inst. of Tech., Key West, Miami, Pensacola. N. A. No. 1615. HTA.

FLOYD, WM. M., JR., Student Officer, 8 Tower Place, Yonkers, N. Y.

FLYNN, JOHN B., Student Officer, Illinois Athletic Club, Chicago, Ill.

FOLEY, ARTHUR C., Student Officer, 236 Summit Ave., St. Paul, Minn.

FORBES, D. P., Lieut. (j.g.), 241 N. Main St., Rockford, Ill.

FORBES, TALBOT, Student Officer, 610 W. 116th St., New York City.

FORD, BURDETTE E., Student Officer, 5498 Cornell Ave., Chicago, Ill.

FORD, NEVIL, Lieut. (j.g.), Care of State St. Trust Co., Boston, Mass. Mass. Inst. of Tech., Operations, Washington, D. C.

FORD, NEWELL A., Student Officer, Western Springs, Ill.

FORD, WM. V., Student Officer, 931 4th St., Boston, Mass.

FORDE, THOMAS H., Ensign, 661 South 2nd East, Salt Lake City, Utah. Seattle, Pensacola, San Diego. N. A. No. 2070. HTA.

FORGAN, DONALD M., Ensign, The Highlands Apt., Washington, D. C.

FORRESTAL, JAMES V., Lieut. (j.g.), 28 Nassau St., New York City. N. A. No. 154.

FORSTER, HENRY, Lieut. (j.g.), 65 White St., Milton, Mass. Dunkirk and St. Inglevert, France. N. A. No. 1075.

FORSTER, L. MARQUAD, Ensign, 6251 McPherson Ave., St. Louis, Mo.

FORTNA, D. E., Ensign, R. F. D. No. 5, Richmond, Va. N. A. No. 1703.

FOSS, FRANK K., Lieut. (j.g.), 4625 Lake Park Ave., Chicago, Ill. Mass. Inst. of Tech., Key West, Miami, Pensacola. N. A. No. 959. HTA.

FOSTER, JAMES G., Student Officer, Union Springs, Ala.

FOSTER, JOHN C., Tuscaloosa, Ala. N. A. No. 142.

FOSTER, JOHN M., Student Officer, 1220 Hinman Ave., Evanston, Ill.

FOSTER, RAYMOND A., Ensign.

FOSTER, ROBT. M., Student Officer, Central Y. M. C. A., Buffalo, N. Y.

FOSTER, ROBERT P. Student Officer, 67 N. 11th St. Newark, N. J.

FOSTER, STERLING J., JR., Student Officer, 1313 Niazuma St., Birmingham, Ala.

FOUST, CHESTER A., Ensign, 1401 Gregory St., Chicago, Ill.

FOWELL, FRED M., War. Machinist.

FOWLE, WILSON F., Ensign, Box 853 Williamson, Mass. N. A., No. 1702.

FOWLER, WENDELL C., Student Officer, 3623 S. Presa St., San Antonio, Tex.

FOY, BYRON C., Ensign.

FOX, E. T., Ensign, 237 Madison Ave., New York City.

FOX, GEO. W., Ensign, 1914 Lincoln Ave., St. Paul, Minn. Dunwoody, Mass. Inst. of Tech., Chatham, Miami, Pensacola. N. A. No. 2279. HTA.

FOX, SAMUEL M., Lieut. (j.g.), Torresdale, Phila., Penn. Mass. Inst. of Tech., Buffalo, Bu. C. & R., Washington.

FOX, THOS. L., War Gunner.

FOY, BYRON C., Ensign.

FRANCIS, C. C., Ensign.

FRANK, INGRAM NATHAN, Student Officer, 2233 Larkin St., San Francisco, Cal.

FRANKE, ALLEN, Student Officer, 6106 Kimbark Ave., Chicago, Ill.

FRANKLIN, LAFAYETTE, Ensign, 351 Lafayette St., Denver, Colo. Seattle, Wash. HTA.

FRANSWORTH, GROVER C., Ensign.

FRANTZ, ROBT. N., Ensign, Smiley Hall, Claremont, Cal.

FRANZHEIM, W. A., Ensign, Wheeling, W. Va. Mass. Inst. of Tech., Akron, Ohio; Pensacola, Fla.; Chatham, Mass. N. A. No. 1197. LTA.

FRASER, ALBERT A., 228 Raymond Ave., South Orange, N. J. N. A. No. 961.

FRASER, DANIEL W., Ensign.

FRASER, GILBERT R., Student Officer, 182 Juniper St., Atlanta, Ga.

FRAZER, J. W., War. Machinist.

FREED, LORING, Student Officer, 605 Locust St., Knoxville, Tenn. Akron, Ohio, Mass. Inst. of Tech. LTA.

FREEMAN, EDWARD E., Ensign.

FREEMAN, HARLEY L., Student Officer, 7609 Wade Park Ave., Cleveland, Ohio. Mass. Inst. of Tech. LTA.

FREEMAN, S. A., Lieut. (j.g.), 2 Fayette Park, Cambridge, Mass. Mass. Inst. of Tech., Hampton Roads, Pensacola, Rockaway. N. A. No. 1091. HTA.

FREDERICK, STANTON W., Ensign, 3641 Locust St., Philadelphia, Pa.

FRENCH, S., War. Boatswain.

FRENCH, CLARENCE B., Ensign, 49 Pleasant St., Waltham, Mass. Mass. Inst. of Tech., Bay Shore, N. Y.; Pensacola, Fla. N. A. No. 1920. HTA.

FRENCH, J. BEDFORD, Lieut. (j.g.), 315 S. 41st St., Philadelphia. Pa. Mass. Inst. of Tech., Bay Shore, Pensacola, Cape May.

FREUDENHEIM, LEON, Ensign, 9 Marshall Road, Yonkers, N. Y. Mass. Inst. of Tech., Pensacola, Bu. Operations, Bu. Con. & Repair, Rockaway.

FREY, ROBT. J., Student Officer, 117 Pendleton St., New Haven, Conn.

FRITTS, J. W., Student Officer, Hughson, Cal. Seattle, Wash. HTA.

FRITZE, J. R., Student Officer, 802 Bigelow St., Peoria, Ill.

FRIZZELL, PAUL J., Ensign, 3566 13th St., N. W., Washington, D. C. Mass. Inst. of Tech., Miami, Pensacola. N. A. No. 2388. HTA.

FROTHINGHAM, PHILIP B., Ensign.

FROTHINGHAM, SAMUEL, JR., Ensign, Overlee, Lenox, Mass. Mass. Inst. of Tech., Key West, Miami, Pensacola. N. A. No. 1152. HTA.

FRYE, HARVEY E., Student Officer, 121 F St., S. W., Ardmore, Okla.

FULLER, ERNEST J., Lieut. (j.g.), Crescent Athletic Club, Brooklyn, N. Y.

FULLER, JOHN E., Ensign, 25 Bickerstaff St., Boston, Mass.

FULLER, R. N., Student Officer, 332 Park St., S. Akron, Ohio.

FULLER, ROBT. L., Ensign, 2605 Durant Ave., Berkeley, Cal.

FUNNELL, C. L., Ensign, 316 Woodworth Ave., Yonkers, N. Y. Mass. Inst. of Tech., Keyport, N. J.; Whitestone, L. I.

GAFFNEY, B. F.
Ensign
Lake City, Michigan. Dunwoody Inst., Minn., Miami, Key West, Pensacola. N. A. No. 2523. HTA.

GAGE, FRED H.
Lieut. (j.g.)
16 Byron St., Haverhill, Mass. Pensacola, San Diego. N. A. No. 265. HTA.

GAINES, CHARLES H.
Student Officer
Gallatin, Tenn. Mass. Inst. of Tech., Pensacola. HTA.

GAINES, LUDWELL E.
Ensign
Fayettesville, W. Va. Mass. Inst. of Tech., Cambridge. HTA.

GALLAGHER, D. C.
Student Officer
O'Neill, Nebraska. Mass. Inst. of Tech., Cambridge, Curtiss, Buffalo, N. Y. LTA.

GALLOUPE, C. A.
Lieut. (j.g.)
212 Ocean St., Lynn, Mass. Squantum, Hampton Rds., Pensacola, Killingholme, Eng., Chatham. N. A. No. 423.

GAMBLE, JOHN G.
Ensign
E. Call St., Tallahassee, Fla. Seattle, San Diego, Pensacola. N. A. No. 2463. HTA.

GAMBLE, ROBERT H.
Lieut. (j.g.)
850 Park Ave., New York City. Mass. Inst. of Tech., Key West, Office Chief Naval Operations. N. A. No. 468. HTA.

GAMMON, F. ROYAL
Ensign
3 West Hill Place, Boston, Mass. Mass. Inst. of Tech., Aghada, Ire., Killingholme, Eng.

GANS, HILARY W.
Ensign
Beaumont, Govans, Md. Mass. Inst. of Tech., Bay Shore, Pensacola. N. A. No. 2006. HTA.

GARDNER, EARL A.
Lieut. (j.g.)
917 N. Union St., Fostoria, Ohio. Akron, Brest, Finistere, France.

GARDNER, GIBSON
Lieut. (j.g.)
74 Lincoln Parkway, Buffalo, N. Y. M. I. T., Hamp. Rds., Pensa., Moutchic, Pauillac, Brest, Treguier, Bay Sh. N. A. No. 344.

GARDNER, GUY N.
Ensign
2315 Albion St., Denver, Colo. Mass. Inst. of Tech., Akron, Pensacola. N. A. No. 1561. LTA.

GARDNER, R. E.
Ensign
1021 Robinson St., Oroville, Calif. M. I. T., Key West, Miami, Pensa., London, Washington, S. Diego. N. A. No. 1116.

GARLOCK, FRED L.
Ensign
Maxwell, Iowa. Seattle, San Diego, Pensacola. N. A., No. 2278. HTA.

GARMON, GEORGE R.
Ensign
76 19th St., Lowell, Mass. Mass. Inst. of Tech., Bay Shore, Pensacola. N. A. No. 2078. HTA.

GARNER, DWIGHT A.
Student Officer
3433 Bryant Ave. So., Minneapolis, Minn. Mass. Inst. of Tech., Miami. HTA.

GARRISON, J., Jr.
Lieut. (j.g.)
1223 Westover Ave., Norfolk, Va. Mass. Inst. of Tech., Pensacola, Moutchic, Fr., Killingholme, Eng. N. A. No. 261. HTA.

GARVER, I. L.
Ensign
40 E. 40th St., New York City, Mass. Inst. of Tech., Key West, Pensacola. N. A. No. 2030. HTA.

GARVIN, J. F.
Student Officer
4334 Evans Ave., St. Louis, Mo. Mass. Inst. of Tech., Akron, Pensacola. LTA.

Result of a Premature Bomb Explosion in Mid-air

GATELY, LEWIS B.
Student Officer
Care of W. S. Johnson, Mamaroneck, N. Y. Mass. Inst. of Tech. HTA.

GATY, THEODORE E.
Ensign
50 Morris Ave., Morristown, N. J. Mass. Inst. of Tech., Pensacola, Miami, Moutchic, Fr., N. A. No. 679.

GEDDY, GEO. B.
Student Officer
Scottland Road, Williamsburg, Virginia. Mass. Inst. of Tech., Hampton Roads, Charleston, Miami. HTA.

GEPPERT, JOHN WM.
Ensign
Collins Rd., Kirkwood, Missouri. Mass. Inst. of Tech., Miami, Pensacola. HTA.

GERE, HOWARD M.
Student Officer
305 Erie St., Syracuse, N. Y. Mass. Inst. of Tech., Miami. HTA.

GERMER, EDWARD, Jr.
Ensign
402 West 6 St., Erie, Penn. Mass. Inst. of Tech., Pensacola, Rockaway. N. A. No. 642. HTA.

GERRY, FRANK H.
Ensign
63 Hobart St., Danvers, Mass. Mass. Inst. of Tech., Bay Shore, Pensacola. N. A. No. 1810. HTA.

GETZ, CHARLES L.
Student Officer
1111 West Lanvale St., Baltimore, Md. Mass. Inst. of Tech. HTA.

GEYER, CLARENCE H.
Ensign
32 Euclid Ave., Buffalo, N. Y. M. I. T, Pensa., R. F. C., S. A. G., Ft. Worth, Hamp. Rds., Killingholme. N. A. No. 254. HTA.

GIBBS, FRANK H.
Ensign
Warrenton, N. C. Mass. Inst. of Tech., Miami, Pensacola, Rockaway Beach. N. A. No. 1361. HTA.

GIBBS, LAUREN W.
Ensign
301 B St., Salt Lake City, Utah. Mass. Inst. of Tech., Akron, Rockaway, Pensacola. N. A. No. 158. LTA., HTA.

GIBBS, WALTER
Ensign
14 Thetford Ave., Dorchester, Mass. Mass. Inst. of Tech., Newport, U. S. S. *Mass.* Akron, Rockaway Beach. LTA.

GIBSON, H. F.
Ensign
1814 17th St., Boulder, Colo. Mass. Inst. of Tech., Miami, Pensacola. N. A. No. 156. HTA.

GILL, LESTER N.
Student Officer
Garden Grove, Iowa. Dunwoody Inst., Minn., Miami. HTA.

GILLAM, C. R.
Student Officer
121 E. Maple Ave., Langhorne, Penn. Mass. Inst. of Tech., Bay Shore. HTA.

GILLEN, FREDERICK J.
Student Officer
16 Prospect St., Lawrence, Mass. Mass. Inst. of Tech. HTA.

GILMAN, JOSEPH T.
Ensign
315 Charles River Road, Cambridge, Mass. Seattle, San Diego, Pensacola. N. A. No. 2200. HTA.

GILMORE, LEON M.
Ensign
Wills Point, Texas. Seattle, Washington, San Diego. HTA.

GILPIN, KENNETH N.
Ensign
Boyce, Virginia. Mass. Inst. of Tech., Miami, N. Bomb. Gr., Calais, Fr., Moutchic, Fr. HTA.

GIVEN, FREDERICK H.
Ensign
59 West St., Cortland, Maine. Bay Shore, Boston, Squantum, Hampton Rds., Pensacola. N. A. No. 752. HTA.

GLENN, GEORGE M.
Ensign
Port Matilda, Pa. Seattle, San Diego, Pensacola. N. A. No. 2361. HTA.

GOEBEL, WILLIAM H.
Ensign
575 76th St., Brooklyn, N. Y., Mass. Inst. of Tech., Buffalo, College Point, Morehead City, Smithfield. N. A. No. 1619.

GOEDECKE, OSCAR A.
Student Officer
91 N. 18th St., East Orange, N. J. Mass. Inst. of Tech. HTA.

GOEPPERT, K. T.
Ensign
2134 Goun St., San Francisco, Cal. Mass. Inst. of Tech., Miami, Pensacola. N. A. No. 1589. HTA.

U. S. Naval Air Station at Gujon, France

GOETZ, A. O., Jr.
Student Officer
160 W. Charles Place, Atlantic City, N. J. Dunwoody Inst., Minn. HTA.

GOING, HENRI R.
Ensign
Union, S. C. Mass. Inst. of Tech., Charleston, Miami, Pensacola. N. A. No. 1568. HTA.

GOLD, JOHN D.
Student Officer
Care of Y. M. C. A., Youngstown, Ohio. Mass. Inst. of Tech. HTA.

GOLDMAN, LOUIS J.
Lieut. (j.g.)
2-16 W. 33rd St., New York City. Pauillac, Gironde, Fr. HTA.

GOLDSMITH, HENRY F.
Ensign
2308 N. Broad St., Philadelphia, Pa. Mass. Inst. of Tech., Keyport, New York, College Point, New Haven. HTA.

GOLDSMITH, N. L.
Ensign
1478 St. James Court, Louisville, Ky. Mass. Inst. of Tech., Miami, Pensacola, Hampton Rds. N. A. No. 2102. HTA.

GOOD, EUGENE A.
Ensign
170 Webster St., Tiffin, Ohio. Mass. Inst. of Tech., Cambridge, Key West, Pensacola. N. A. No. 2237. HTA.

GOODRICH, ALBERT H.
Ensign
2033 Aubert Ave., Chicago, Illinois. Mass. Inst. of Tech., Great Lakes, Pensacola. HTA.

GOODRICH, GRANT
Ensign
522 Deming Pl., Chicago, Ill. Mass. Inst. of Tech., Key West. N. A. No. 1487. HTA.

GOODRICH, MARCUS A.
Ensign
Austin Nat'l Bank, Austin, Texas. Dunwoody, Miami. Key West, Pensacola, N. A. No. 2637. HTA.

GOODSPEED, F. S.
Ensign
344 W. 72nd St., New York City. Mass. Inst. of Tech., Bay Shore, Brunswick, Ga., Key West, Pensacola. N. A., No. 2351. HTA.

GOODSPEED, MORTON
Lieut. (j.g.)
279 Newbury St., Boston Mass. Mass. Inst. of Tech. Pensacola. N. A. No. 640

GORDON, FRANK C.
Ensign
46 Way Ave., Corona, N. Y. Mass. Inst. of Tech., Miami, Pensacola. N. A. No. 2290. HTA.

GORDON, WILMOT G.,
Lieut. (j.g.)
Corona, Long Island, N. Y. Bay Shore, Key West, Miami, N. A. No. 512. HTA.

GORDY, J. E.
Machinist
18 New St. Francis St., Mobile, Ala. Pauillac, La Pallice, Fr., Pensacola.

GORMAN, JOHN P.
Ensign
608 Bellevue Ave., Syracuse, N. Y. Mass. Inst. of Tech., Miami, Pensacola N. A. No. 2583. HTA.

GORMLEY, JOHN V.
Ensign
19 Wyckoff St., Brooklyn, N. Y. Mass. Inst. of Tech., Bay Shore, Pensacola. N. A. No. 1439. HTA.

GOSS, CLARK C.
Ensign
109 E. 11th St., Harper, Kansas. Mass. Inst. of Tech., Miami, Pensacola. N. A. No. 2465. HTA.

GOSS, PIERRE B.
Student Officer
Sheridan, Placer Co., California, Seattle, San Diego. HTA.

GOULD, CHARLES B.
Ensign
1412 Des Moines St., Des Moines, Iowa, Dunwoody Inst., Minn., Miami, Key West, Pensacola. N. A. No. 2652.

GOULLET, ALFRED T.
Student Officer
191 So. 7th St., Newark, N. J. Mass. Inst. of Tech., Pensacola, Key West. HTA.

GOVER, ROBB.
Lieut. (j.g.)
600 N. Carrollton Ave., Baltimore, Md. M. I. T., Pensacola, Miami, Queenstown, Lough Foyle, Norfolk. N. A. No. 713. HTA.

GRADER, G. W., Jr.
Ensign
11 Highland Terrace, Marblehead, Mass. Mass. Inst. of Tech., Norfolk, Pensacola, Morehead City. N. A. No. 1887. HTA.

GRAFFIS, JOS. M.
Ensign
815 Lafayette Parkway, Chicago, Ill., Moutchic, Fr., Lake Bolsena, Italy, Porto Corsini, It. N. A. No. 1503. HTA.

(C) Underwood & Underwood, N. Y.

Italian Mother Ship "Europa" at Valona
Showing Four Seaplanes Hanging from Davits

GRAHAM, ALAN H.,
Ensign
23 S. Maple Ave., East Orange, N. J. Mass. Inst. of Tech., Bay Shore, Pensacola, Rockaway. N. A. No. 1048. HTA.

GRANDIN, ELLIOT C.
Student Officer
Tidioute, Pa. Mass. Inst. of Tech., Miami. HTA.

GRAVES, FORREST L.
Student Officer
Del. Water Gap, Penn. Mass. Inst. of Tech. HTA.

GRAY, ALFRED S.
Ensign
519 Congress St., Portland, Me. Mass. Inst. of Tech. Akron, Hampton Roads, North Sydney, N. S., Rockaway Beach. LTA.

GRAY, GILSON B., Jr.
Ensign
Stronghaven, Aberdeen, Miss. Mass. Inst. of Tech., Key West. N. A. No. 2022. HTA.

GRAY, HAROLD E.
Ensign
799 Monadnock Bldg., San Francisco, Cal Mass. Inst. of Tech., Keyport, New York.

GREEFF, CHARLES A.
Ensign
Quoque, Long Island, N. Y. Mass. Inst. of Tech., Akron, Rockaway. LTA.

GREEN, RAY F.
Ensign
508 Crocker Bldg., San Francisco. M. I. T., San Pedro, San Diego, Akron, Pensacola, Hampton Rds. N. A. No. 1559. LTA.

GREENE, JAMES H.
Ensign
385 Quail St., Albany, N. Y. Mass. Inst. of Tech., Akron, Rockaway, Hampton Roads, Key West. LTA.

GREENE, JOHN H. D.
Student Officer
4050 Greenview Ave., Chicago, Ill. Dunwoody Inst., Minn., Miami. HTA.

GREENE, W. C., Jr.
Lieut. (j.g.)
198 Clifford St., Providence, R. I.

GREENWOOD, F. M.
Student Officer.
Muir, Michigan. Mass. Inst. of Tech., Akron. LTA.

GREER, C. W., Jr.
Student Officer
3220 Pillsbury Ave., S. Minn., Minn. Dunwoody, Miami. HTA.

GRIER, HARRY P., Jr.
Ensign
Statesville, N. C. Mass. Inst. of Tech., Miami, Key West, Pensacola. N. A. No. 2555. HTA.

GRIFFIN, P. V. R.
Lieut. (j.g.)
1127 Forest Ave., Evanston, Illinois. Mass. Inst. of Tech., Rockaway, Akron. N. Sydney, Nova Scotia. LTA.

GRIFFIN, ROBERT H.
Ensign
28 Cottage St., Leominster, Mass. M. I. T., Buffalo, Paris, Pauillac, Moutchic, London, Felixstowe, Killingholme, Grain.

GRIFFITH, F. A.
Student Officer
41 Cuyler St., Palmyra, N. Y. Mass. Inst. of Tech., Akron. LTA.

GRISWOLD, M. P.
Ensign
469 Durkee Ave., Kenosha, Wisconsin. Mass. Inst. of Tech., Miami, Pensacola. N. A. No. 1811. HTA.

GRISWOLD, RETTIG A.
Lieut. (j.g.)
105 West Third St., Peru, Ind. Toronto, Hampton Rds., Ft. Worth, Killingholme, Bolsena, Rockaway. N. A. No. 248. HTA.

GROENE, C. H.
Ensign
604 Locust St., Coshocton, Ohio. Mass. Inst. of Tech., Miami, Pensacola. N. A. No. 2118. HTA.

GROOM, HARRY B.
Ensign
7 Monterey Place, Mobile, Ala. Mass. Inst. of Tech., Akron, Rockaway, Chicago, Great Lakes.

GROSECLOSE, H. F.
Ensign
Pulaski, Virginia. Mass. Institute of Tech., Miami, Pensacola. N. A. No. 2141. HTA.

GROSECLOSE, W. P.
Student Officer
Ceres, Virginia. Mass. Inst. of Tech. HTA.

GRUBBS, HARRY L.
Student Officer
28 Britten Ave., Elmhurst, L. I. Mass. Inst. of Tech. LTA.

Try This for a Weak Stomach

GRUMMAN, LEROY R.
Ensign
Huntington, L. I., N. Y. Mass. Inst. of Tech., Miami. Pensacola, N. A. F. Phila. N. A. No. 1216. HTA.

GRUNDELL, JOSEPH J.
Ensign
3055 Madison Ave., Fresno, California. Seattle, San Diego, Pensacola. N. A. No. 2201. HTA.

GUILD, HERBERT H.
Ensign
1032 Western Ave., Topeka, Kansas. Mass. Inst. of Tech., Bay Shore, Pensacola. N. A. No. 1217. HTA.

GUILLOW, P. K.
Ensign
27 Salem St., Wakefield, Mass. Mass. Inst. of Tech., Key West, Miami, Pensacola. N. A. No. 2235. HTA.

GUINN, T. D. *Ensign* 115 Hurt St., Atlanta, Ga. Mass. Inst. of Tech.,Miami, Pensacola. Morehead City, Hampton Rds. N. A. No. 1912. HTA.	GUNTHER, GORDON *Ensign* 1 Parkland Place, St. Louis, Mo. Dunwoody, Miami, Key West, Pensacola. N. A. No. 2609. HTA.	GWILLIAM, R. C. *Ensign* 2540 Eccles Ave., Ogden, Utah. Seattle, Miami, San Diego, Pensacola. N. A. No. 2426.	GWIN, W. B. *Ensign* Roland Apts., Washington, D. C. Mass. Inst. of Tech., Pensacola, Anacostia. N. A. No. 1010. HTA.

◈ ◈ ◈ ◈ ◈ ◈

GABEL, CUTHBERT C., Student Officer, 216 First St., Belvidere, Ill. Mass. Inst. of Tech. LTA.

GABELINE, C. A., Ensign, 715 N. 5th St., Burlington, Iowa. Mass. Inst. of Tech., Key West, Miami, Pensacola. N. A. No. 2202. HTA.

GADSDEN, PHILIP H., Lieut. (j.g.), 64 Hasell St., Charleston, S. C. N. A. No. 233.

GAETNER, WALTER C. F., Student Officer, 46 Spring Park Ave., Jamaica Plains, Mass.

GALLAGHER, GEO. DOMINIC, Ensign, 133 Lafayette Ave., Buffalo, N. Y.

GALLAGHER, V. L., Ensign, 309 Hartman Bldg., Columbus, Ohio.

GALLIVAN, T. J., Ensign, 65 Hollis St., Framingham, Mass. N. A. No. 1512.

GARDINER, CHARLES M., Ensign, 141 Bucknam St., Everett, Mass. Mass. Inst. of Tech., Pensacola, Coco Solo, C. Z., Chatham. N. A. No. 1831. HTA.

GARDINER, JAMES S., Ensign, Clinton, Md. Mass. Inst. of Tech., Miami, Pensacola. N. A. No. 1622.

GARDNER, ALFRED, Lieut. (j.g.), 46 Cedar St., New York City. N. A. No. 1093.

GARDNER, A. HOWARD, Ensign, 317 Wheeler St., Ft. Worth, Tex. Mass. Inst. of Tech., Miami, Pensacola. N. A. No. 1096. HTA.

GARDNER, HENRY L., Ensign. N. A. No. 2404.

GARDNER, ROBERT ROYER, Student Officer, 456 Prospect Ave., Buffalo, N. Y. Mass. Inst. of Tech. HTA.

GARDNER, W. H., Lieut. (j.g.), Mastic, L. I., N. Y. N. A. No. 343.

GARDNER, WALTER R., Student Officer, 54 Stinson Ave., Providence, R. I.

GARGAN, THOMAS V., Student Officer, 241 East 175th St., New York City. Mass. Inst. of Tech. HTA.

GARLINGTON, JULIUS P., Ensign, Cedartown, Ga. Mass. Inst. of Tech., Miami, Fla.; Pensacola, Fla. N. A. No. 1326. HTA.

GARNETT, WM. T., Ensign, 1834 St. Andrews Pl., Los Angeles, Cal. N. A. No. 1663.

GARRETT, WM. M., Student Officer, 1027 Proctor St., Port Arthur, Tex.

GARRISON, CLIFFORD R., Student Officer, 8 Brentmoor Park, St. Louis, Mo.

GARTNER, WALTER C. F., Ensign, 46 Spring Rd., Jamaica Plains, Mass. N. A. No. 8498.

GARVER, D. B., Student Officer, 334 W. Beaver Ave., State College, Pa. Mass. Inst. of Tech. HTA.

GARVEY, E. T., Ensign. N. A. No. 660.

GARY, JOHN, Student Officer, 154 Ralston Ave. So., Orange, N. J.

GASKINS, PALEMON H., Ensign, Winecoff Hotel, Atlanta, Ga.

GASTON, FREDERICK K., JR., Student Officer, Greenwich, Conn.

GASTON, JOHN M., Ensign, 300 S. 36th St., Philadelphia, Pa. N. A. No. 2231.

GASTON, WILLIAM, Lieut. (j.g.), 97 Bay State Rd., Boston, Mass. Squantum, Hampton Rds., Ft. Worth, Eng.; N. Bomb. Squ., St. Nylevert, Milan, RAF, Sq. 214. N. A. No. 294. HTA.

GATCHET, F. L., War. Machinist, 2814 E. Olive St., Seattle, Wash. San Diego, Columbia University, Eastleigh, Eng.

GATENS, N. R., Ensign.

GATES, CAROL WELLER, Ensign, 36 Groton St., Forest Hills, L. I., N. Y. N. A. No. 1500.

GATES, GARRETT DWIGHT, Student Officer, Oakhurst Clinton, Iowa.

GAUTHIER, CHARLES B., Ensign, 1285 S. Lincoln St., Denver, Colo.

GAVER, WM. U., Student Officer, Mt. Airy, Md.

GAVETT, ROBERT M., Ensign, 318 W. Front St., Plainfield, N. S. Mass. Inst. of Tech., Bay Shore, Pensacola, Hampton Rds. HTA.

GAVIN, ARTHUR, Ensign. N. A. No. 1242.

GAVIN, THOMAS AUSTIN, Student Officer, 411 Oliver St., Whiting, Ind.

GEAHART, A. F., War. Machinist.

GEARY, JOHN WHITE, JR., Lieut. (j.g.), Chestnut Hill, Pa. Newport News and Hampton Rds., Va. N. A. No. 134. HTA.

GABHART, ARTHUR I., Student Officer, 2112 G. St., N. W., Washington, D. C.

GEDDES, HOMER R., Lieut. (j.g.), Lowellville, Ohio, Akron, Ohio; Pensacola, Florida. N. A. No. 552. LTA.

GEDDES, WM. J., Ensign, 1809 E. 18th Ave., Denver, Colo. Mass. Inst. of Tech., Bay Shore, L. I.; Pensacola, Fla. N. A. No. 1621. LTA.

GEE, L. GAYON, Ensign, 4352 Drexel Ave., Chicago, Ill.

GEFFENEY, WM. L., Student Officer, 1701 33rd Ave., Oakland, Cal.

GEHRIS, JOHN B., Student Officer, Melrose Park, Pa. Mass. Inst. of Tech. HTA.

GEIGER, DAVIS E., Student Officer, 115 E. Bath Ave., Ashland, Ky. Mass. Inst. of Tech., Bay Shore, L. I.; Brunswick, Ga.; Key West, Fla. HTA.

GEORGE, HERBERT, Boatswain.

GEORGE, WALTER N., Student Officer, 706 S. Florence St., Springfield, Mo.

GEORGI, CARL H., Student Officer, Grand View, Nyack, N. Y.

GERBER, FRITZ K. E., Ensign, 102 Beach St., Stapleton, L. I., N. Y.

GERHARD, LESTER G., Student Officer, 415 N. Third St., Lehighton, Pa.

GERKE, CARL H., Student Officer, 319 Davlan Apts., Indianapolis, Ind.

GERRN, J. H., War. Boatswain.

GEST, J. H., Ensign. N. A. No. 2128.

GHEEN, JOSEPH W., Ensign, 332 Buttles Ave., Columbus, Ohio.

GIAL, GEO. WM., JR., Ensign, 58 Clarendon Pl., Buffalo, N. Y.

GIBBS, EARLE ED., War. Machinist, 819 Ashland Ave., Wilmette, Ill.

GIBLIN, EDWIN J., Ensign, 17 Mount Vernon St., Dorchester, Mass.

GIBLIN, JEROME EDWIN, Ensign, 1009 New Hampshire Ave., Washington, D. C.

Gibson, Harold F., Lieut. (j.g.), 80 Broadway, New York City, Canada, Bay Shore, Pensacola, Mass. Inst. of Tech. N. A. No. 156. HTA.

Gibson, J. E., War. Machinist.

Gibson, John R., Lieut. (j.g.).

Gifford, John Van Trees, Ensign, 714 S. New Hampshire, Ave., Los Angeles, Cal., Mass. Inst. of Tech., Miami, Pensacola, San Diego. N. A. No. 1616. HTA.

Gilbert, Elon J., Student Officer, Yakima, Washington. Seattle, Washington. HTA.

Gilbert, Harwood J., War. Machinist, 822 S. Michigan Ave., Saginaw, Mich. Columbia University, Packard, Detroit; Eastleigh, Eng.; St. Inglevert, France.

Gildehaus, E. R., Ensign, 1210 Park Ave., Richmond, Va. Mass. Inst. of Tech., Akron, Ohio; Hampton Rds., Va. LTA.

Gilder, Geo., Ensign, 24 Gramercy Park, New York City. Mass. Inst. of Tech., Hampton Rds., Bay Shore, Key West, Brunswick, Miami. N. A. No. 460. HTA.

Giles, Bynum H., Ensign, 1120 Hickory St., Texarkana, Arkansas. Mass. Inst. of Tech., Key West, Fla. N. A. No. 1772. HTA.

Giles, Geo Stewart, Ensign.

Gill, Walter M., Student Officer, 1508 New Hampshire St., Lawrence, Kans.

Gillan, Monroe P., Student Officer, 203 S. 61st St., Birmingham, Ala.

Gillespie, Emerson, Student Officer, Lower Salem, Ohio.

Gillespie, P. E., Ensign, Port Deposit, Md. N. A. No. 2288.

Gillette, Willis C., Ensign, 84 Adams St., Rochester, N. Y. Mass. Inst. of Tech., Akron, Ohio, Rockaway Beach, L. I., N. Y. LTA.

Gillies, F. M., Ensign, 7311 Oglesby Ave., Chicago, Ill. Mass. Inst. of Tech., Key West, Miami, Pensacola, Anacostia. HTA.

Gillies, William R., Student Officer, 114 Cedar Hill Ave., Nyack, N. Y.

Gillman, Louis W., War. Gun.

Gilloghly, Max W., Student Officer, 7211 Union Ave., Chicago, Ill.

Gillon, James L., Ensign, Warren, R. I., N. A. No. 416.

Gillon, James R., Student Officer, 13 Oxford St., Taunton, Mass.

Gilman, Charles, Student Officer, 35 West 73rd St., New York City. Mass. Inst. of Tech.

Gilman, Lewis W., War. Gun.

Gilmore, John D., Student Officer, Warthen, Ga. Mass. Inst. of Tech.

Gilmore, W. S., Care Guy Wallon Union Central Bldg., Cincinnati, O. N. A. No. 1504.

Gilmur, Charles Edward, Student Officer, 4061 Latons Ave., Seattle, Wash.

Ginn, Wm. H., Ensign, 2867 N. Palethorp St., Philadelphia, Pa. N. A., No. 2306.

Giridlian, J. N., Ensign, 8720 Forthill Blvd., Oakland, Cal. Mass. Inst. of Tech., Miami, Pensacola, Great Lakes, Columbia Univ., Hampton Rds.

Gittings, Homer Thompson, Student Officer, McCork, Nebr. Mass. Inst. of Tech. HTA.

Glasheen, Wm. S., Student Officer, 36 Constitution St., Providence, R. I.

Gleason, Harold L., Ensign, 8 Peacevale Rd., Dorchester, Mass.

Gleckler, Victor, Ensign, LaGrange, Tex. Mass. Inst. of Tech., Akron, Ohio; Pensacola, Fla. N. A. No. 2475. LTA.

Glenn, Benjamin D., Student Officer, 220 Wainman St., Greensboro, N. C.

Glomstad, Arthur E., Student Officer, 1264 55th St., Brooklyn, N. Y.

Glosheen, Arthur M., Student Officer, Austin Construction Co., Indian Head, Md.

Goble, Geo. Robert, Student Officer, 145 W. Hancock St., Detroit, Mich.

Godbe, Norman F., Ensign, 340 S. Fifth St., East Salt Lake City, Utah.

Goebel, Wm. John, Ensign, 2505 Russell St., Berkeley, Cal.

Goggines, J. L., Ensign.

Golay, A. A., War. Machinist.

Golder, Benj. M., Ensign, 2011 N. 33d St., Philadelphia, Pa.

Gooch, DeWitt R., Student Officer, Bellflower, Ill. Seattle, Wash.; Chicago, Ill. HTA.

Goodell, Edwin B., Jr., Ensign, 63 Park St., Montclair N. J.

Goodfellow, Arthur N., Lieut. (j.g.), 5131 Morris St., Germantown, Philadelphia, Pa. Pauillac, France.

Gooding, Arthur F., Student Officer, 411 6th Ave., S. W., Rochester, Minn. Dunwoody Inst., Minn.

Goodnow, Charles H., Ensign, Kennebunk, Maine. N. A. No. 1118.

Goodrich, Frederick P., Student Officer, 3 West 47th St., New York City.

Goodspeed, H. L., Lieut. (j.g.), 568 Madison Ave., Grand Rapids, Mich. Mass. Inst. of Tech., R. N. H. S. Cranwell, Lincolnshire, Eng.; R. A. F. Howden, Lowthorpe, Eng.; Paimboeuf, France. N. A. No. 669. LTA.

Goodspeed, Norrison, Student Officer, 279 Newbury St., Boston, Mass.

Goodwin, Harry L., Ensign, Deerfield, N. Y. Mass. Inst. of Tech., Buffalo, N. Y., L. W. F., College Pt., L. I. HTA.

Goodyear, Frank H., Lieut. (j.g.), 762 Delaware Ave., Buffalo, N. Y. Pensacola, Fla.; San Diego, Cal. N. A. No. 122.

Gordon, P. M., Student Officer, 409 S. Kenilworth Ave., Oak Park, Ill. Mass. Inst. of Tech., Pensacola. LTA.

Gordon, Frederick V., Ensign, Care of Gordon Electric Co., Parkersburg, W. Va.

Gordon, Walter H., Student Officer, R. F. D. No. 4, Richmond, Va. Mass. Inst. of Tech. HTA.

Gore, Robert E., Student Officer, 2114 Stearns Rd., Cleveland, Ohio.

Gorman, E. J. B., Ensign, S. W. Cor. 1st and Perry Sts., Dayton, O. N. A. No. 2719.

Gorman, Stephen Ambrose, Ensign, 15 Seaton Pl., N. W., Washington, D. C.

Gormley, John V., Ensign, 19 Wyckoff St., Brooklyn, N. Y. N. A. No. 1439.

Gortner, Harry, Ensign, N. A. No. 1502.

Gorton, A. W., Ensign, 2160 Broad St., Pawtucket, R. I. N. A. No. 1410.

Gosdin, W. E., Student Officer, 2300 West 13th St., Little Rock, Ark. Mass. Inst. of Tech., Akron, Ohio. LTA

Gosser, Geo. Wm., Student Officer, 438 S. 4th St. Coshocton, Ohio.

Gotfredson, Henry L., Student Officer, 103 S. Monroe Ave., Green Bay, Wis. Dunwoody Inst., Minn.

Gottlieb, Lewis, Student Officer, 701 Convention St., Baton Rouge, La.

Gouger, Gratz B., Student Officer, 847 E. Cincinnati Ave., San Antonio, Tex.

Gould, Clifford Perkins, Student Officer, Kenebunk Port, Maine.

Gould, Elwyn B., Student Officer, 2333 Albatross St., San Diego, Cal.

Gould, Lyttleton B. P., Lieut. (j.g.), Yale Club, New York City. Mass. Inst. of Tech., Pensacola, Fla. LTA.

Gould, Stevens, Student Officer, 493 Jackson St., Oshkosh, Wis.

Gourley, Russell C., Ensign, Melrose Park, Oak Lane P. O., Philadelphia, Pa. Mass. Inst. of Tech., Miami, Pensacola, Hampton Roads. N. A. No. 1751. HTA.

Gowan, Jos. H., War. Gun.

Gowell, R. M., Ensign, 22 Kendall St., Framingham, Mass. N. A. No. 1847.

Grabener, Eugene G., War. Carpenter.

Grace, R. V., Ensign, 522 5th St., Bismarck, N. D. N. A. No. 749.

Graham, Gordon C., Student Officer, 5839 Magnolia Ave., Chicago, Ill.

Grambs, Paul L., Student Officer, 624 4th St., Bismarck, N. D.

Granger, Merrill L., Student Officer, Des Moines, Iowa. Seattle, Wash. HTA.

Grant, Alden C., Student Officer, R. F. D., Grass Valley, Cal.

Grant, Earl S., Student Officer, Odlin Road, Box 132, R. 2, Bangor, Maine.

Grant, Edwin S., Student Officer, 815 Massachusetts Ave., N. E., Washington, D. C.

Grant. John L., Ensign, 4598 Oakenwald Ave., Chicago, Ill. Mass. Inst. of Tech., Pensacola, Moutchic, Brest. HTA.

Grant, Wm. D., Ensign, 709 Grant Bldg., Atlanta, Ga. Mass. Inst. of Tech., Bay Shore, Pensacola. N. A. No. 1786. HTA.

Gravely, John O. W., Ensign, Rocky Mount, N. Car. Mass. Inst. of Tech., Bay Shore, Pensacola. N. A. No. 2071. HTA.

Graves, Amos M., Ensign.

Graves, F. Mortimer, Ensign, 2304 Madison Sq., Philadelphia, Pa. Mass. Inst. of Tech., Pensacola, Moutchic, Pauillac, Killingholme. N. A. No. 712. HTA.

Graves, Justin D., Lieut. (j.g.), 40 E. 40th St., New York, N. Y. Squantum, Mass.; Hampton Rds.; Campagne, St. Inglevert, France. N. A. No. 234. HTA.

Gray, Grery B., Ensign, 1451 Elizabeth St., Denver, Colo. Mass. Inst. of Tech., Key West, Fla. N. A. No. 1483. HTA.

Gray, Thomas Asbury, Ensign, Bedford, Va. N. A. No. 2462.

Greely, Benjamin M., Ensign, Dorchester, Mass.

Green, Charles L., Student Officer, 504 E. 21st St., Cameron, Tex.

Green, Geo. B. L., Ensign, 120 Chestnut St., Everett, Mass. Mass. Inst. of Tech., Bay Shore, L. I.; Pensacola. Fla. N. A. No. 1218. HTA.

Green, H. D., Ensign.

Green, H. R., Ensign, The Sherman Apts., Washington, D. C.

Green, Joseph H., Ensign, 1740 Bouvier St., Philadelphia, Pa. N. A. No. 756.

Green, N. B., Ensign.

Green, Walter C., Lieut. (j.g.), N. A. No. 624.

Greene, Alfred E., Jr., Ensign.

Greene, Allen C., Student Officer, 83 W. Second Ave., Columbus, O.

Greene, Royal C., Student Officer, 110 N. 9th St., Beatrice, Nebr.

Greenleaf, Eric R., Student Officer, 38 N. Eighth Ave., Bethlehem, Pa.

Greenlee, George W., Student Officer, Beta Theta Pi House, Evanston, Ill.

Greenley, Howard, Lieut. (j.g.), 101 Park Ave., New York City. Hampton Roads, Va.; Operations, Washington, D. C. HTA.

Greenough, C. W., Lieut. (j.g.), 33 Concord Ave., Cambridge, Mass. N. A. No. 192.

Greer, James M., Student Officer, 411 W. 23d St., Austin, Texas.

Gregory, G. N., Ensign.

Gregory, George L., Lieut. (j.g.), 319 Chestnut St., Mount Carmel, Ill.

Gregory, Howard C., Ensign, 430 Connecticut Ave., Bridgeport, Conn. Mass. Inst. of Tech., Pensacola. HTA.

Grier, James Murray, Ensign, 5012 W. 11th St., Philadelphia, Pa.

Grier, Thomas J., Student Officer, 1675 Buckingham Rd., Los Angeles, Cal.

Griffin, Lloyd M., Student Officer, 2342 Montclair St., Los Angeles, Cal.

Griffith, Charles, Student Officer, 1550 Lafayette St., Denver, Colo.

Griffith, Dorsey James, Ensign, 3104 R St., N. W., Washington, D. C. N. A. No. 1963.

Griffith, Ernest S., Student Officer, 1017 West St., Utica, N. Y. Mass. Inst. of Tech. HTA.

Griffith, John L., Student Officer, 1432 Madison St., Denver, Colo.

Griffith, Wm., Ensign, 411 E. 3d St., Anaconda, Mont.

Grimes, Arthur J., Student Officer, 321 Central Ave., Dover, N. H.

Grimm, John C., Student Officer, 436 E. Buchtel Ave., Akron, Ohio.

Grimstad, Orville K., Ensign, Montana Nat'l Bank, Billings, Mont.

Grizzelle, Miles C., Student Officer, Le Roy, Ill.

Groh, Geo. Richard, Ensign.

Grooch, W. S., Ensign, 501 Rio Grande St., El Paso, Tex. Mass. Inst. of Tech., Pensacola, Key West, Rockaway Beach, St. Trojan, France.

Gross, Gorham L., Student Officer, 340 Genesee St., Utica, N. Y.

Grossman, Leslie H., War. Machinist, 204 1st St., Braddock, Pa.

Grosvenor, T. P., Lieut. (j.g.), 51 Prospect St., Providence, R. I. Squantum, Mass.; Hampton Rds.; Fort Worth, Tex.; R. A. F. Hornsea; Killingholme, Eng. N. A. No. 210½. HTA.

Grout, Ralph C., Student Officer, Battleboro, Vt. Mass. Inst. of Tech., Newport, R. I. HTA.

Groves, B. E., Student Officer, 110 12th St., Ann Arbor, Mich. Seattle, Wash. HTA.

Gurley, Dorris D., Ensign, 2605 Durant Ave., Berkeley, Cal. Mass. Inst. of Tech., Miami, Pensacola, Fla. N. A. No. 2028. HTA.

Gurney, G. Harmon, Ensign, 5233 Wissahickon Ave., Queen Lane, Pa. Mass. Inst. of Tech., Key West, Miami, Pensacola, Fla. N. A. No. 2193. HTA.

Gurney, Howard F., Jr., Student Officer, 907 Esplanade, Pelham Manor, New York.

Gutelius, Fred P., Student Officer, Hopewell, N. J.

Guthrie, J. O., Ensign, 5208 Harper Ave., Chicago. Ill. Dunwoody Inst., Miami, Pensacola. HTA.

Gyger, John T., Student Officer, 536 W. 114th St., New York City.

Logging Airplane Spruce

One of many spruce lumber camps established by the Government.

HAAS, BRUNO P.

Ensign

755 Franklin St., Worcester, Mass. Mass. Inst. of Tech., Bay Shore, Pensacola. N. A. No. 1185. HTA.

HACKNEY, WM. L.

Ensign

McGregor, Texas. Mass. Inst. of Tech., Key West. N. A. No. 1773. HTA.

HACKSTADT, NEIL A.

Ensign

1610 Genesee Ave., Saginaw, Mich. M. I. T., Pensacola, Miami, Moutchic, Hampton Roads, Bay Shore, N. A. No. 1285. HTA.

HAERLE, L. H.

Student Officer

1449 N. Penna. St., Indianapolis, Ind. Mass. Inst. of Tech., Key West. HTA.

U. S. Naval Air Station at Arcachon, France

HAGGKVIST, F. E.

Lieut. (j.g.)

31 Rockwell St., Malden, Mass. Mass. Inst. of Tech., Buffalo, Pensacola. HTA.

HAGY, WALTER W.

Ensign

1608 W. Allegheny Ave., Phila., Pa. Mass. Inst. of Tech., Cape May, Miami, Pensacola. N. A. No. 1225. HTA.

HAHN, ARTHUR M.

Ensign

1213 New Jersey Ave., N. W., Washington, D. C. Mass. Inst. of Tech., Pensacola. HTA.

HAIGLER, PAUL F.

Ensign

Orangeburg, S. C., Mass. Inst. of Tech., Miami, Pensacola. N. A. No. 1902. HTA.

HAINES, H. S., Jr.
Ensign
525 Graydon Park, Norfolk, Virginia. Mass. Inst. of Tech., Pensacola.

HAINES, JOHN F.
Student Officer
5609 Greene St., Germantown, Phila., Penn. Mass. Inst. of Tech., Cape May, Gloucester, Philadelphia. HTA.

HALL, C. ARNOLD
Ensign
915 Downer Ave., Utica, N. Y. Mass. Inst. of Tech., Key West, Newport, Chatham, Pensacola. N. A. No. 2489.

HALL, EDWARD B.
Lieut. (j.g.)
Jackson City Club, Jackson, Mich. Bureau Steam Engineering, Wash., D. C.

HALL, KENNETH V.
Ensign
153 Hamilton Place, Fond du Lac. Wisconsin. Mass. Inst. of Tech., Miami, Pensacola. N. A. No. 1718. HTA.

HALL, LEIGH S.
Ensign
Concord, N. H. Mass. Inst. of Tech., Curtiss A. & M. Corp., Buffalo.

HALL, MYRON C.
Ensign
216 Griffith Ave., San Mateo, Cal. Seattle, San Diego, Pensacola. N. A. No. 1922. LTA.

HALLAGAN, STUART D.
Ensign
Newark, New York State. Pauillac, Fr., Eastleigh, Eng., Bay Shore, Washington, D. C.

HALLETT, J. G.
Ensign
57 Elm Road, Newtonville, Mass. Mass. Inst. of Tech., Pensacola, Miami, Pauillac, Moutchic, St. Trojan, Fr. N. A. No. 682. HTA.

HALSEY, F. K.
Student Officer
27 Prince St., Elizabeth, N. J. Mass. Inst. of Tech., Key West. HTA.

HALSTEAD, C. D. R.
Student Officer
162 Hillside Ave., Newark, N. J. Mass. Inst. of Tech., Bay Shore, Brunswick, Ga., Key West. HTA.

HALSTEAD, H. LOUIS
Ensign
1129 Cherry St., Philadelphia, Pa. Mass. Inst. of Tech., Miami, Key West, Pensacola. N. A. No.2591. HTA.

HAMBLEY, GILBERT F.
Student Officer
Salisbury, N. C. Mass. Inst. of Tech., Cambridge. HTA.

HAMBLY, ALVIN S.
Ensign
2620 Benvenue Ave., Berkeley, California. Mass. Inst. of Tech., Key West, Miami, Pensacola. N. A. No. 1584. HTA.

HAMILTON, WM. H.
Ensign
190 Wadsworth Ave., N. Y. Mass. Inst. of Tech., Bay Shore, Pensacola. N. A. No. 1062. HTA.

HAMMER, LLOYD A.
Lieut. (j.g.)
Care of Humble Oil & Refinin Co., Houston, Tex. Mass. Inst. of Tech., Pensacola. N. A. No. 297. HTA.

HAMMER, T. F.

Ensign

119 Elm St., Branford, Conn., Mass. Inst. of Tech., Bu. S. E. (A), Washington, D. C. HTA.

HAMMOND, H. C.

Ensign

1127 Broad St., Grinnell, Iowa. Mass. Inst. of Tech., Key West. N. A. No. 1694. HTA.

HANCHETTE, H. W.

Ensign

200 Oil Operators Bldg., Ft. Worth, Texas. Mass. Inst. of Tech., Bay Shore, Pensacola. N. A. No. 1617.

HANKINS, W. W.

Student Officer.

601 N. 56th Ave., West Duluth, Minn. Dunwoody, Key West. HTA.

WRECKED NC-1 AT ROCKAWAY BEACH, LONG ISLAND

Occurred Before the Start of the Trans-Atlantic Flight

HANSEN, ALBERT A.

Ensign

University Club, Washington, D. C. Mass. Inst. of Tech., Akron, Pensacola. N. A. No. 1869. LTA.

HARDENBURGH, W. G.

Ensign

215 Danforth Ave., Jersey City, N. J. Mass. Inst. of Tech., Key West, Miami, Pensacola, London. N. A. No. 1419. HTA.

HARDIN, EDW. G.

Ensign

1018 West 20th St., Oklahoma City, Okla. Seattle, Miami, Pensacola. N. A. No. 2557. HTA.

HARDING, LESTER M.

Ensign

1015 Park Ave., Collingswood, N. J. Mass. Inst. of Tech., Great Lakes, Miami, Pensacola. N. A. No. 2106. HTA.

HARDING, M. G.
Student Officer
7120 Normal Blvd., Chicago, Ill. Dunwoody Inst., Minn.; Miami. HTA.

HARDING, W. K.
Ensign
West Lebanon, N. H. Mass. Inst. of Tech., Miami, Pensacola, Cape May, N. J. N. A. No. 979. **HTA.**

HARDY. CLARENCE W.
Ensign
Tecumseh, Mich. Mass. Inst. of Tech., Montauk. N. A. No. 1063. HTA.

HARLOW, WILLIS Y.
Ensign
95 Fulton Ave., Hempstead, L. I., N. Y. Mass. Inst. of Tech., Miami, Key West, Pensacola. HTA.

HARPER, CECIL F.
Ensign
Zillah, Yakima Co., Wash. Mass. Inst of Tech., Pensacola, Miami, Key West. N. A. No. 1215. HTA.

HARRELL, ROBT. H.
Ensign
Austin, Texas. Pensacola, Tours, Fr., Fromentine, Fr., Le Croisic, Ile Tudy. HTA.

HARRINGTON, E. D.
Ensign
112 E. Rockwell Ave., Elkhorn, Wis. Seattle, San Diego. HTA.

HARRIS, F. H.
Ensign
7 North St., Brattleboro Vt. Mass. Inst. of Tech. Bay Shore, Hampton Rds. Pensacola. N. A. No. 1890 HTA.

HARRIS, FRED M.
Ensign
East Orange, N. J. Bay Shore, L. I., Miami, Pensacola, N. Bomb., Gr., Fr., N. A. No. 241. HTA.

HARRIS, HAROLD C.
Lieut. (j.g.)
Prospect St., Dedham, Mass. Akron, Rockaway, Roehampton, La Trinite, Brest, Cape May. N. A. No. 1081. LTA.

HARRIS, JOHN W.
Ensign
1404 Tremont St., Galveston, Tex. Mass. Inst. of Tech., Bay Shore, Pensacola. N. A. No. 1149. HTA.

HARRIS, STEPHEN W.
Ensign
86 Pelham Rd., New Rochelle, N. Y. Bay Shore, Miami, Rockaway. N. A. No. 1521. HTA.

HARRIS, WM. S.
Ensign
Cuero, Texas. Mass. Inst. of Tech., Miami, Pensacola, Queenstown, Ire. N. A. No. 1294. HTA.

HARRISON, E. M.
Lieut. (j.g.)
Elm St., Bowling Green, Ky. Mass. Inst. of Tech., Pensacola.

HART, VAN B.
Ensign
McLean, N. Y. Mass. Inst. of Tech., Akron, Pensacola, Hampton Rds. N. A. No. 1560. LTA.

HARTE, EARLE J.
Student Officer
106 Franklin St., Astoria, L. I., N. Y., Mass. Inst. of Tech. HTA.

HARTFORD, N. B., Jr.
Ensign
363 Mystic St., Arlington, Mass. Mass. Inst. of Tech., Akron, Pensacola. N. A. No. 2153. LTA.

HARTSHORNE, R. D.
Ensign
Seabright, N. J. Mass. Inst. of Tech., Miami, Pensacola, North Sydney, Nova Scotia. N. A. No. 1132. HTA.

HARWOOD, TOM P.
Ensign
Saluda, Va. Mass. Inst. of Tech., Miami, Pensacola, N. Sydney, Nova Scotia. N. A. No. 1032. HTA.

HASKELL, ARMORY L.
Lieut. (j.g.)
139 East 61st St., New York City. Mass. Inst. of Tech., Pensacola, San Diego. N. A. No. 180. HTA.

CLERGET MOTORED HONORIO SCOUT
Type Often Carried on Ships

HASKEW, R. K.
Ensign
South Pittsburg, Tenn. Mass. Inst. of Tech., Miami, Pensacola. N. A. No. 1684. HTA.

HASTINGS, W. J.
Ensign
Cor. Hohman & State Sts., Hammond, Ind. Great Lakes, Pensacola. HTA.

HATHAWAY, CHAS., Jr.
Lieut. (j.g.)
530 W. N. Ave., New York City. Mass. Inst. of Tech.

HATTEMER, V. P.
Ensign
108 Pembrake Place, Kew Gardens, L. I. Mass. Inst. Tech., Bay Shore, Pensacola. N. A. No. 1951. HTA.

HATTER, LOUIS H.
Student Officer
Moody, Texas. Seattle, Washington. HTA.

HAWKINS, C. A.
Lieut. (j.g.)
Care of Operations, Navy Dept., Washington, D. C. Pensacola, Moutchic, St. Trojan, Bay Sh., Brunswick, N. A., No. 63. HTA.

HAWKINS, JAMES H.
Lieut. (j.g.)
Grand Rapids, Mich. Mass. Inst. of Tech., Pensacola, Fleet Air Detachment (Sq. Comdr.) N. A. 574. HTA.

HAWKINS, SAM C.
Lieut. (j.g.)
511 California St., El Paso, Tex. Pensacola, Cattewater, Plymouth, Eng., Killingholme, Eng. N. A. No. 228.

HAWKSWORTH, T. T.
Ensign
652 Stanley St., New Britain, Conn. Mass. Inst. of Tech., Akron, Rockaway. LTA.

HAYES, A.
Machinist
Morehead City, N. C. Pensacola, Hampton Rds., Morehead City. N. A. No. 609. HTA.

HAYES, F. SEVERANCE
Ensign
1820 Hammond Ave., Superior, Wis. Dunwoody, Miami, Pensacola. N. A. No. 2483. HTA.

HAYNE, T. B.
Student Officer
Congaree, S. C. Univ. of Washington, Seattle. HTA.

HAYNES, P. L.
Ensign
18th and Acklen Ave., Windsor Apts., Nashville, Tenn. Mass. Inst. of Tech., Miami, Key West, Pensacola. N. A. No. 2608. HTA.

HAYWOOD, A., Jr.
Ensign
42 Prospect Ave., Flushing, N. Y. Mass. Inst. of Tech., Miami, Pensacola. N. A. No. 2185. HTA.

HAZELTON, E. LUCE
Ensign
15 Carroll St., Portland, Me. Mass. Inst. of Tech., Newport, Akron, Brest.

HEALY, WILBERT M.
Ensign
Lisbon, N. H. Mass. Inst. of Tech., Curtiss Plant, Buffalo, N. Y.

HEARD, J. M., Jr.
Ensign
Long & Jefferson Sts., Aberdeen, Miss. Mass. Inst. of Tech., Miami, Pensacola. N. A. No. 2215. HTA.

HEATH, B. D., Jr.
Student Officer
Heathcote, Charlotte, N. C., Seattle, Washington. HTA.

HEATH, CLYDE J.
Student Officer
183 Fifth St. Muskegon, Mich., Seattle, Washington. HTA.

HEDTLER, ROBERT S.
Lieut. (j.g.)
119 Highland St., Chelsea, Mass. Columbia, Chatham, No. Sydney, Miami. HTA.

HEGEMAN, C. H

Student Officer

540 W. 165 St., New York City. Mass. Inst. of Tech., Newport, Miami.

HELM, ARTHUR R.

Ensign

1720 Humboldt Ave., So. Minneapolis, Minn. Dunwoody, Pensacola, Rockaway N. A. No. 1064. HTA.

HEMMENWAY, L. T.

Lieut. (j.g.)

41 Monadnock St., Dorchester, Mass. Bu. of Steam Engineering, Washington, D. C.

HEMPHILL, R. W.

Ensign

962 Hereford Drive, Akron, Ohio. Mass. Inst. of Tech., Miami. N. A. No. 2055. HTA.

Official, U. S. N. A. S.

THE EXECUTIVE MANSION, WASHINGTON, D. C.

HENDERSON, E. F., Jr.

Lieut. (j.g.)

Monadnock, Dublin, N. H M. I. T., Hamp. Rds., Pensacola, Moutchic, Milan, St. Inglvert, N. Bomb. Gr. N. A. No. 398.

HENDERSON, S. T.

Ensign

607 East Ave., Charlotte, N. C. Mass. Inst. of Tech., Key West, Miami, Pensacola, Rockaway. N. A. No. 1040. HTA.

HENRION, PAUL E.

Ensign

250 Bluff, Wichita, Kans. Mass. Inst. of Tech., Miami, Pensacola. N. A. No. 2325. HTA.

HENRY, CHARLES T.

Lieut. (j.g.)

454 East 7th St., Brooklyn, N. Y. Bay Shore, Key West, Miami. N. A. No 1343. HTA.

HENRY, FREDERICK A.
Ensign
5214 A. Schuyler St., Germantown, Phila., Pa. Mass. Inst. of Tech., Miami, Pensacola. N. A. No. 1343. HTA.

HENRY, H. B.
Lieut. (j.g.)
325 Fullerton Parkway, Chicago. Ill. Mass. Inst. of Tech., Miami, Fla. N. A. No. 1600. HTA.

HENRY, WINSTON P.
Ensign
Tulsa, Okla. Great Lakes, Pensacola.

HERO, GEO. A., Jr
Ensign
1213 3rd St,. New Orleans, La. Mass. Inst. of Tech., Miami, Pensacola. N. A. No. 2092. HTA.

HERRING, FRANK W.
Student Officer
1284 Loma Vista Drive, Long Beach, Cal. Mass. Inst. of Tech., San Diego, Key West. HTA.

HERRINGTON, A. S.
Student Officer
509 East Main St., Latrobe, Penn. Mass. Inst. of Tech., Bay Shore. HTA.

HERRON, JOHN C.
Ensign
Telluride, Colorado. Mass. Inst. of Tech., Pensacola, Miami. N. A. No. 1641. HTA.

HESTER, JULIAN B.
Ensign
Care of Bank of Tyron, Tyron, N. C. Mass. Inst. of Tech., Akron, Pensacola. N. A. No. 2086. LTA.

HEWLETT, J. A.
Ensign
Lawrence, Long Island. Mass. Inst. of Tech., U. S. S. *Gold Shell*, Bay Shore, Pensacola, Rockaway, N. A. No. 985. HTA.

HEYM, HAROLD C.
Ensign
123 Collingwood Ave., Detroit, Mich. Mass. Inst. of Tech., Miami, Pensacola. N. A. No. 1915.

HICKEY, STEFANO J.
Student Officer
3013 N. Broad St., Philadelphia, Penn. Mass. Inst. of Tech., Ft. Niagara, Philadelphia. HTA.

(S)

HICKMAN, BENJ. F.
Ensign
209 Adams Ave., Kirkwood, Mo. Mass. Inst. of Tech. HTA.

HICKS, ALBERTSON
Ensign
Roslyn, N. Y. Mass. Inst. of Tech., Coast Patrol.

HICKS, JOHN E.
Ensign
Onarga, Illinois. Dunwoody, Miami, Pensacola. N. A. No. 2653. HTA.

HICKS, PHILIP M.
Ensign
Avondale, Pa. Mass. Inst. of Tech., Pensacola. N. A. No. 2671. HTA.

HICKS, ROBT. H.
Ensign
713 Woodbourne Ave., Govans, Md. Mass. Inst. of Tech. Miami, Pensacola. N. A. No. 1729. HTA.

HICKS, WM. PAUL
Ensign
713 Woodbourne Ave., Govans. Md. Mass. Inst. of Tech., Bay Shore, Pensacola. N. A. No. 1934. HTA.

HIDEN, ROBERT B.
Ensign
Pungoteague, Virginia. Mass. Inst. of Tech., Miami, Pensacola. N. A. No. 2199. HTA.

HIESTAND, JOHN E.
Student Officer
Bainbridge, Pennsylvania, Dunwoody, Inst., Minn. HTA.

HIGGINS, AUSTIN D.
Ensign
North Cohocton, N. Y. Mass. Inst. of Tech., Miami, Pensacola. N. A. No. 1917. HTA.

(C) Comm. Pub. Inf.

LET'S GO!

HILDING, ARTHUR H.
Ensign
1311 Eddy St., Chicago, Ill. Mass. Inst. of Tech., Miami, Pensacola, Hampton Roads, Great Lakes. N. A. No. 2436. HTA.

HILL, HENRY W.
Ensign
415 Oak Grove St., Minneapolis, Minn. Mass. Inst. of Tech., Miami. N. A. No. 1526. HTA.

HILL, VERNON B.
Ensign
605 N. 12st., Waco, Texas. Mass. Inst. of Tech., Akron, Rockaway, Key West. LTA.

HILLBERG, WALTER R.
Lieut. (j.g.)
81 Hillberg Ave., Brockton, Mass. Mass. Inst. of Tech., Hampton Rds., Pensacola, Montauk. N. A. No. 419. HTA.

HIMES, B. T.
Ensign
West Palm Beach, Fla. Mass. Inst. of Tech., Key West, Miami, Pensacola. N. A. No. 1783. HTA.

HINE, CHAS. R.
Student Officer
R. No. 7, Winston-Salem, N. C. Mass. Inst. of Tech., Bay Shore. HTA.

HIPPLE, J. PARKER
Ensign
4931 North 12th St., Philadelphia, Pa. Mass. Inst. of Tech. HTA.

HITCHCOCK, L. B.
Student Officer
Hillside Terace, Belmont, Mass. Mass. Inst. of Tech. HTA.

HIVELY, ROBERT D.
Ensign
507 Boyd Ave., Baton Rouge, La. Mass. Inst. of Tech., Pensacola, Hampton Roads, New London, N. A. No. 1358. HTA.

HOAG, W. D., Jr.
Student Officer
384 Degraw St., Brooklyn, N. Y. Mass. Inst. of Tech. HTA.

HOBBIS, T. ROGERS
Ensign
19 Edgar St., East Orange, N. J. Mass. Inst. of Tech., Miami, Pensacola, Key West. N. A. No. 2513. HTA.

HODGDON, LYMAN A.
Ensign
8 Indiana Ave., Somerville, Mass. Mass. Inst. of Tech., Pensacola, Paris, Queenstown, Lough Foyle. N. A No. 661. HTA.

HODGES, GEO. S.
Lieut. (j.g.)
R. F. D. No. 5. Pontiac, Mich. Mass. Inst. of Tech., Pensacola, Ft. Worth, Killingholme, Eng. N. A. No. 253. HTA.

HODGES, GRAHAM B.
Ensign
1343 Euclid St,. Washington, D. C. Mass Inst. of Tech., Rockaway. LTA.

HODGMAN, FRANK H.
Student Officer
314 E. 17th St., Brooklyn, N. Y. Mass. Inst. of Tech., Charleston, Akron, Rockaway. LTA.

HOFFMAN, ROY H.
Ensign
North Reading, Mass. Mass. Inst. of Tech., Akron, Rockaway. LTA.

HOFFMEISTER, R. B.
Ensign
1080 13th St., Boulder, Colo. Seattle, San Diego, Pensacola. N. A. No. 2432. HTA.

HOLDEN, JACK P.
Ensign
458 Palmerston Blvd., Toronto, Canada. Mass. Inst. of Tech., Pensacola, Cape May. N. A. No. 1020. HTA.

HOLDEN, N. PARKER
Student Officer
669 Second Ave., Detroit, Mich. Mass. Inst. of Tech., Yale Boat House, Pelham Bay, U. S. S. *Pocahontas*, Key West. HTA.

HOLDEN, WILLIAM H.
Ensign
7 James St., Lynn, Mass Mass. Inst. of Tech., Miami, Pensacola. HTA.

HOLDING, WILLIS A.
Student Officer
705 Hillsboro St., Raleigh, N. C. Mass. Inst. of Tech. HTA.

HOLLETT, NORMAN
Student Officer
Westbury, L. I., N. Y. Mass. Inst. of Tech. HTA.

HOLLINGSWORTH, W.
Ensign
500 E. 14th St., No. Portland, Ore. Seattle, San Diego, Pensacola. N. A. No. 2269. HTA.

HOLLOWAY, WM. E., Jr.
Student Officer
403 West 148th St., New York City, Seattle, Washington. HTA.

(C) Underwood & Underwood, N. Y.

CREW OF C-5 STARTING FOR NEWFOUNDLAND, MAY, 1919

HOLMAN, NEWTON D.
Ensign
425 E. St. Vrain St., Colorado Springs, Colo. Mass. Inst. of Tech., Akron, Rockaway Beach, LTA.

HOLTKAMP, F. G.
Student Officer
1299 Belle Ave.. Lakewood, Ohio. Mass. Inst. of Tech., Key West. HTA.

HOLTON, RICHARD A.
Ensign
77 Pacific St., Fitchburg, Mass. M. I. T., Bay Sh., Pensa., Miami, Moutchic, Fromentine, Chatham. N. A. No. 877. HTA.

HONODLE, HENRY S.
Ensign
655 E. Buchtel Ave., Akron, Ohio. Mass. Inst. of Tech., Akron, Rockaway. LTA.

HOOD, C. CARLYLE
Ensign
453 Auburn Ave., Buffalo, N. Y. Univ. Wash., Key West. N. A. No. 1733.

HOOD, HARVEY P., Jr.
Ensign
2 Benton Road, Somerville, Mass. Mass. Inst. of Tech., Miami, Pensacola. N. A. No. 1850. HTA.

HOOVER, JOHN R. C.
Student Officer
Haddam, Kansas. Mass. Inst. of Tech., Miami. HTA.

HOPKINS, EDWARD G.
Student Officer
Wescoesville, Penn. Mass. Inst. of Tech. LTA.

HOPKINS, JOHN A.
Student Officer
40 Cross St., Medford, Mass. Great Lakes, Pensacola. HTA.

HOPKINS, R. G.
Student Officer
1517 Lake Ave., Wilmette, Ill. Mass. Inst. of Tech. HTA.

HOPLER, HAROLD S.
Student Officer
53 E. 4th St., Williamsport, Pa. Mass. Inst. of Tech., Newport, Brooklyn. LTA.

(*M*)
HORSLEY, WM. H.
Student Officer
936 36th Ave., Seattle Wash. Seattle, Key West. HTA.

HOUGH, HENRY J.
Ensign
3036 Dent Pl., N. W., Washington, D. C. M. I. T., Pensa., Miami, Autingues, Campagne, Moutchic. N. A. No. 748. HTA.

HOUSE, MILES F.
Student Officer
416 So. Meldrum St., Ft. Collins, Col. Seattle, San Diego. HTA.

HOUSMAN, ROBERT L.
Ensign
201 East Orman Ave., Pueblo, Colorado. Mass. Inst. of Tech., Akron, Rockaway Beach, L. I. LTA.

HOWARD, ALAN F.
Ensign
20 Lake St., Winchester, Mass. Mass. Inst. of Tech., Miami, Pensacola. N. A. No. 2490. HTA.

HOWARD, VINCENT E.
Ensign
8 Milford St., Binghamton, N. Y. Mass. Inst. of Tech., Miami, Fla., Pensacola. N. A. No. 2540. HTA.

HOYT, FERDINAND A.
Ensign
16 Dutchess Terrace, Beacon, N. Y. Great Lakes, Pensacola.

HUBACHEK, F. B.
Lieut. (j.g.)
2900 Fifth Ave., S. Minneapolis, Minn. Dunwoody, Pensacola. N. A. No. 906.

HUDSON, ALFRED W.
Lieut. (j.g.)
566 Greene Ave , Brooklyn, N. Y. Mass. Inst. of Tech., Pensacola, Chatham. N. A. No. 490. HTA.

HUGER, DANIEL E.

Ensign

1245 Madison Ave., New York City. Avord, Fr., Moutchic, Fr., Porto Corsini, Italy. N. A. No. 1007. HTA.

HUGHES, DAVID M.

Ensign

17 Gramercy Park, New York City. Mass. Inst. of Tech., Pensacola, San Diego.

HUGHES, J. W.

Ensign.

2145 E. Glisan St., Portland, Oregon. Mass. Inst. of Tech., U. S. S. *South Dakota*, Key West, Miami. N. A. No. 1525.

HUISKAMP, GERARD L.

Ensign

801 Grand Ave., Keokuk, Iowa. Mass. Inst. of Tech., Miami, Pensacola, Moutchic, Fr. N. A. No. 1127 HTA.

OFFICIAL COMPLEMENT OF STATION AT PORTO CORSINI, ITALY

December 14, 1918

HUME, KENNETH W.

Ensign

15 Pierrepont St., Brooklyn, N. Y. M. I. T., Key West, Miami, Pensa., Montauk, Norfolk, Hamp. Rds. N. A. No. 1050. HTA.

HUME, THOMAS L., Jr.

Ensign

2113 S. St., N. W., Washington, D. C. Mass. Inst. of Tech., Miami, Key West, Pensacola. N. A. No. 2391. HTA.

HUMPHREY, H. L.

Ensign

643 Eye St., N. E., Washington, D. C. Mass. Inst. of Tech., Key West, Miami, Pensacola, Hampton Rds. N. A. No. 2090. HTA.

HUNDT, LESTER T.

Ensign

330 E. 139th St., New York City. Mass. Inst. of Tech., Bay Shore, Pensacola. N. A. No. 1586. HTA.

HUNSAKER, JAMES W
Student Officer
794 High St., Denver, Colo. Mass. Inst. of Tech., Bay Shore, Pensacola. HTA.

HUNT, STANLEY F.
Ensign
330 Highland St., Worcester, Mass. Mass. Inst. of Tech., Key West, Pensacola. N. A. No. 2467. HTA.

HUNTER, HAROLD F.
Ensign
82 Pinckney St., Boston, Mass. Mass. Inst. of Tech., Miami, Pensacola. N. A. No. 2345. HTA.

HUNTER, KENNETH H.
Ensign
1001 Forest Court, Palo Alto, Cal. Mass. Inst. of Tech., Miami. Pensacola. N. A. No. 1550. HTA.

HUNTER, ROBT. L.
Ensign
5052 Walnut St., Philadelphia, Penn. Mass. Inst. of Tech., Key West, Miami, Pensacola. N. A. No. 1424. HTA.

HUNTINGTON, E. J.
Lieut. (j.g.)
Geddes Road, Ann Arbor, Mich. Mass. Inst. of Tech., Pensacola, Hampton Rds. N. A. No. 2014. HTA.

HURD, NORMAN C.
Ensign
3 Hugh St., Dover, N. H. Mass. Inst. of Tech., Key West, Pensacola. N. A. No. 2393. HTA.

HURLEY. FRANCIS C.
Ensign
55 Sturbridge St., Mattapan, Boston, Mass. Mass. Inst. of Tech., Key West, Pensacola. N. A. No. 2442. HTA.

HUSTED, JOHN G. W.
Ensign
Peekskill-on-Hudson, N. Y. Mass. Inst. of Tech., Bay Shore, Pensacola, Chatham. N. A. No. 970. HTA.

HUTCHEON, FRANK E.
Ensign
195 Elwood Ave., Newark, N. J. M. I. T., Bay Sh., Pensa., Moutchic, Avord, Amesbury, Bolsena, Rockaway. N. A. No. 349. HTA.

HUTCHINGS, G. B., Jr.
Ensign
123 Prospect St., Stamford, Conn. Mass. Inst. of Tech., Miami, Pensacola. N. A. No. 2108. HTA.

HUTCHINSON, H. D.
Ensign
60 Lincoln St., Uniontown, Pa. Mass. Inst. of Tech., Norfolk, U. S. S. P. 439, Miami, Pensacola, New York. N. A. No. 1350.

HUTCHISON, R. C.
Student Officer
Garden City, Kans. Mass. Inst. of Tech., Pelham Bay, Miami. HTA.

HUTTS, MELVIN K.
Ensign
102 E. St. N. W., Miami, Okla. Mass. Inst. of Tech., Key West, Miami, Pensacola. N. A. No. 1924. HTA.

HYDE, FORREST J.
Student Officer
Colonnade Club, University, Va. Mass. Inst. of Tech., Miami. HTA.

HYER, BOYKIN J
Student Officer
211 West Cervantes St., Pensacola. Mass. Inst. of Tech., Pensacola. HTA.

HYLAND, E. M., Jr.
Student Officer
Utica, N. Y. Mass. Inst. of Tech., Charleston, S. C. HTA.

◈ ◈ ◈ ◈ ◈

HAAREN, P. J., Ensign, N. A. No. 496.

HACK, H. M., Student Officer.

HADDEN, HAMILTON, Student Officer, 1207 19th St., Washington, D. C.

HADFIELD, HAROLD F., Ensign, Youle Adams, Mass. N. A. No. 1838.

HADLEY, FRED L., Ensign. N. A., No. 1793.

HADLEY, HENRY S., Ensign, 13468 Clifton Blvd., Cleveland, O. Mass. Inst. of Tech., Miami, Fla. N. A. No. 1527. HTA.

HAFNER, VICTOR L., Student Officer, 34 Appleton St., Boston, Mass.

HAGER, ROBERT N., Ensign, Omaha, Nebr. N. A. No. 2389.

HAGGERTY, A. G., Ensign. N. A. No. 722.

HAGUE, ALFRED, Ensign.

HAHN, F. H., Lieut. (j.g.), 119 East 35th St., New York City. Mass. Inst. of Tech., Pensacola, Fla. N. A. No. 471. HTA.

HAHN, WILLIAM P., Ensign, Leetsdale, Pa. Mass. Inst. of Tech., Akron, Rockaway, Hampton Roads. LTA.

HAHN, WILLIAM R., Lieut. (j.g.), Hotel Iroquois, 49 West 44th St., New York City. Mass. Inst. of Tech., Pensacola, Fla.

HAIGHT, RICHARD A., Student Officer, 312 Times Bldg., New York City. Mass. Inst. of Tech., Boston. HTA.

HAINES, J. ALLEN, Lieut. (j.g.), 754 Prospect St., Winnetka, Ill.

HALBERT, FRANK DUNN, Ensign, Hampton Roads. N. A. No. 2066.

HALDEN, WILLIAM H., Student Officer, 7 James St., Lynn, Mass.

HALE, ANDREW, Ensign, 48 Rhodes Ave., Akron, Ohio. N. A. No. 1864.

HALE, GEORGE E., Ensign, 167 Sand St., Brooklyn, N. Y.

HALE, LUTHER W., Student Officer, 58 West 47th St., New York City.

HALE, J. D., War. Machinist, Benton Harbor, Mich.

HALEY, JAMES E., Student Officer, 1005 West 3rd St., Dixon, Ill.

HALL, ALEXANDER M., Lieut. (j.g.), 1000 Park Ave., New York City.

HALL, CHARLES C., Student Officer, 2204 West Grace St., Richmond, Va.

HALL, COURTNEY R., Student Officer, 41 Bradburn St., Rochester, N. Y. Mass. Inst. of Tech., Newport, R. I., and New London, Conn. HTA.

HALL, EDWIN M., Ensign, N. A. No. 347.

HALL, HANSELL, Student Officer, 712 Third St., Macon, Ga.

HALL, HUBERT M., Student Officer, Bay Minette, Ala.

HALL, JOHN W., Student Officer.

HALL, KELLY R., Student Officer, R. F. D. No. 10, Crawfordsville, Ind.

HALL, LINCOLN N., Ensign, N. A. No. 1585.

HALL, RALPH C., Student Officer, 4600 Maryland Ave., St. Louis, Mo. Mass. Inst. of Tech., Key West, Fla. HTA.

HALL, RAYMOND AVERY, Ensign, Box 38, Cape Charles, Va.

HALL, W. S., Ensign, 17 Elm St., Rochester, N. Y.

HALLETT, RONALD P., Ensign, 63 Middle St., Gloucester, Mass. Mass. Inst. of Tech., Miami, Pensacola, Fla. N. A. No. 1148.

HALLIBURTON, S. S., War. Machinist.

HALLIWELL, R. D., Ensign, 147 Market St., Bethlehem, Pa. Mass. Inst. of Tech., Key West, Pensacola. N. A. No. 2270. HTA.

HALLUM, O. T., Ensign, N. A. No. 1272.

HALSEY, ELDRED A., Student Officer, 58 East 177 St., New York City.

HALSTEAD, J. STERLING, Ensign, 128 East 78th St., New York City, R. F. C., Canada. Camp Rathbone, Camp Borden, Hampton Roads, San Diego, Cal. HTA.

HALSTED, W. TYDER, Ensign, 682 Ocean Ave., Brooklyn, N. Y. Mass. Inst. of Tech., Bay Shore, Pensacola, Fla. N. A. No. 1061.

HAMBLY, HARRY B., Jr., Student Officer, 2620 Benvenue Ave., Berkeley, Cal. Seattle, Wash. HTA.

HAMILL, CURTIS F., Student Officer, 18 Park St., Stoneham, Mass.

HAMILTON, FROMAN, Student Officer, 205 Lytton Ave., Shceuley Farms, Pittsburgh, Pa.

HAMILTON, RAYMOND N., Student Officer, 291 Prospect Ave., Milwaukee, Wis.

HAMMANN, CHAS. HAZELTINE, Ensign, 2540 E. Baltimore St., Baltimore, Md. N. A. No. 1494.

HAMMANN, HARRY C., Student Officer, 217 N. Maple Ave., Martinsburg, W. Va. Dunwoody Inst.

HAMMER, GEORGE D., Ensign, 218 W. DeSota St., Pensacola, Fla. N. A. No. 2470.

HAMMOND, BURTON H., Ensign, Wareham, Mass. N. A. No. 1224.

HAMMOND, EVERETT HAROLD, Student Officer.

HAMMOND, LEONARD A., Student Officer, Warsaw, Ill.

HAMPHILL, RUSSELL, Ensign, Pelham Bay, N.Y.

HANAGAN, THOMAS P., Student Officer, 20 Euclid Ave., Yonkers, N. Y.

HANCE, E. H., Lieut. (j.g.), N. A. No. 941.

HANCHETT, JAMES MALCOLM, Ensign, South Natick, Mass. Columbia Univ., Squantum, Mass.; Hampton Roads, Cape May, N. J.

HAND, G. C., Ensign, 136 Crickett Ave., Ardmore, Pa. N. A. No. 894.

HAND, H. F., Student Officer, Laurence, N. Y.

HANEY, PAUL S., Student Officer, 29 Sixth St., Quakertown, Pa. Mass. Inst. of Tech. HTA.

HANF, HOBART W., Student Officer, 473 Third St., San Bernardine, Cal.

HANFORD, JOHN WILLIAM, Ensign.

HANIFAN, JOHN C., Student Officer, Emmetsburg, Iowa.

HANLEY, JOHN D., Ensign, 89th St. and 10th Ave., N. E., Seattle, Wash. N. A. No. 2147.

HANNA, WALTER S., JR., Student Officer, 173 Woodland Ave., Columbus, Ohio.

HANNAN, EMMETT D., Student Officer, 502 N. 5th St., Paducah, Ky.

HANSEN, C. L., Ensign.

HANSEN, FRED G., Ensign, 1506 Foster Ave., Toledo, Ohio.

HANSEN, J. E., JR., War. Machinist.

HANSON, WM. H., Student Officer, 3401 Pleasant Ave Minneapolis, Minn.

HAPPER, ANDREW P., Student Officer, 316 Dickson Ave., Bon Avon, Pa.

HARDENDORF, F. M., Ensign. N. A. No. 2456.

HARDER, H. G., Ensign, Nelson St., Bayside, L. I. Mass Inst. of Tech., Pensacola. HTA.

HARDER, KEITH C., Student Officer, Wilkesville, O.

HARDER, RALPH WM., Student Officer, 115 S. Emerson Ave., Indianapolis, Ind.

HARDIN, JOSIAH B., Student Officer, 501 Austin St., Waco, Tex.

HARDY, FRANK K., Student Officer, Shawsheen Road, Andover, Mass.

HARDY, RUFUS, JR., Ensign, 1818 Kalorama Rd., Washington, D. C. N. A. No. 1226.

HARGETT, DANIEL G., Student Officer, Elbres Pharmacy, Miami, Fla.

HARKSON, ULYSSES S., Student Officer.

HARLAN, JOSEPH L., Ensign, 1526 Walnut St., Berkeley, Cal. N. A. No. 1416.

HARLOW, JOHN S., JR., Student Officer, 7 Linnaan St., Cambridge, Mass.

HARMON, AUSTIN, Student Officer, 2128 Penobscot Bldg., Detroit, Mich. Mass. Inst. of Tech., Miami. HTA.

HARMON, LAWRENCE E., JR., Student Officer, 623 Deleware Ave., Buffalo, N. Y.

HARNETT, F. B., Student Officer, Burnett, Cal. Seattle, Wash. LTA.

HARRELL, JERRY D., Student Officer, Box 791, Port Arthur, Texas. University of Washington, Seattle. HTA.

Harrell, Samuel R., Student Officer, 119 N. 10th St., Nobelsville, Ind.

Harrigan, J. J., War. Boatswain, N. A. No. 550.

Harrigan, M. J., Lieut. (j.g.), Grosse, Mich.

Harrington, Arthur S., Student Officer, 326 Wyandotte St., S. Bethlehem, Pa.

Harris, Abram W., Jr., Student Officer, 1701 Arch St.. Philadelphia, Pa.

Harris, Andrew Stewart, Student Officer, 54 East 14th St., Atlanta, Ga. Mass. Inst. of Tech., Akron, O.; Pensacola, Fla. LTA.

Harris, Arthur William, Student Officer, 532 Broad St., Providence, R. I.

Harris, Elliot H., Ensign, 33 West 93rd St., New York City.

Harris, George C., Student Officer, Apt. B, No. 1 Dean Apt., Birmingham, Ala.

Harris, Harold B., Student Officer.

Harris, Harry L., Ensign, Apt. 507 Fontanet Courts, Washington, D. C. N. A. No. 1081

Harris, James C., Student Officer, 238 E. Front St., Missoula, Mont.

Harris, Jall Chandler, Student Officer, 54 East 14th St., Atlanta, Ga. Mass. Inst. of Tech. HTA.

Harris, John H., Student Officer, 2200 East 91st St., Georgetown, Tex. Mass. Inst. of Tech., Akron, Pensacola. LTA.

Harris, John McC., Ensign, 2466 Kenilworth Heights, Cleveland, Ohio.

Harris, Leon B., War. Machinist, 3301 Calhoun Blvd., Minneapolis, Minn.

Harris, Samuel C., Student Officer, Care of Y. M. C. A., Wilmington, Del. Mass. Inst. of Tech. HTA.

Harris, W. N., Ensign, 1118 Main St., Danville, Va.

Harris, Walter P., Ensign. N. A. No. 1777.

Harris, Wilson P., Ensign, 1211 Central Ave., Sandusky, Ohio. Mass. Inst. of Tech., Key West, Miami, Pensacola. N. A. No. 1777. HTA.

Harrison, Donald I., Student Officer, 6963 Frankstown Ave., Pittsburgh, Pa.

Harrison, Sumner D., Ensign, 147 So. Munn Ave., East Orange, N. J. Mass. Inst. of Tech., Pensacola, Key West. HTA.

Harrison, William B., Student Officer, R. D. No. 1, Cartersville, Va.

Harshaw, Frank, Ensign, The Studebaker Corp., South Bend, Ind.

Harshberger, Fred A., Student Officer.

Hart, Alfred L., Ensign, 86 Buckingham St., Waterbury, Conn.

Hart, Herschel R., Student Officer, Crescent St., Williamstown, W. Va.

Hart, Lee P., Student Officer, 332 Maryland Ave., N. E., Washington, D. C.

Hart, Leland P., Ensign, 816 L St., S. E., Washington, D. C.

Hartigan, James C., Ensign, 26 Hayes St., Norwich, N. Y.

Harting, John B., Student Officer, 20 E. Johnson St., Germantown, Philadelphia, Pa. Mass. Inst. of Tech. HTA.

Hartley, Francis, Jr., Ensign, 27 Stone Rd., Belmont, Mass. Mass. Inst. of Tech., Pensacola, Moutchic, L Aber Vrache. HTA.

Hartman, Aubrey C. D., Ensign, Beta Theta Pi House, Middleton, Conn. N. A. No. 1859.

Hartman, Leonard C., Ensign, Lincoln, Nebraska. Seattle, Wash., Miami, Pensacola. N. A. No. 2558. HTA.

Harvey, Harold F., Student Officer, Eldon, Mo.

Haskell, Henry Corvill, Student Officer, 72 Federal St., Brunswick, Me. Mass. Inst. of Tech., Miami, Fla. HTA.

Haskell, M., Ensign, 92 Winter St., Portland, Me. N. A. No. 1752.

Haskins, John E., Student Officer, 1026 Title Inc. Bldg., Los Angeles, Cal.

Hassan, Emin, Ensign, 365 E. 21st St., Brooklyn, N. Y. Mass. Inst. of Tech., Miami, Pensacola. N. A. No. 1598. HTA.

Hassell, Thomas F., Student Officer, Billow St., Clifton, Tenn.

Hasselman, C. H ., Ensign, Hampton Rds., Rockaway. N. A. No. 2444.

Hastings, Eugene T., Ensign, 204 3rd Ave., Joliet, Ill. Mass. Inst. of Tech., Pensacola, Miami, Paris, Moutchic. HTA.

Hastings, Herbert R., Student Officer, 530 West End Ave., New York City.

Hatch, Richard W., Student Officer, North Marshfield, Mass.

Hathaway, S. D., Ensign, Care of W. T. Ham & Co., Inc., Southgate Terminals, Norfolk, Va. Mass. Inst. of Tech., Akron, Norfolk, U. S. S. *New Jersey*, Brooklyn. LTA.

Hauber, Carl, Ensign, Springfield, Ohio.

Hauenstein, Clifford E., War. Machinist.

Haun, Joya Canfield, Student Officer, 2261 Shattrick Ave., Berkeley, Cal.

Havel, Frederick, Ensign, 1906 E. 45th St., Seattle, Wash.

Hawkins, A. D., Ensign.

Hawkins, M. I., Ensign.

Hawkins, Ress, Lieut. (j.g.), Easton, Maryland. N. A. No. 223.

Hawkins, Tom W., Student Officer, 629 N. College St., Charlotte, N. C.

Haworth, Richard, Lieut. (j.g.), N. A. No. 706.

Hawthorn, Arlin E., R. F. D. No. 2, Spencer, Ia. Dunwoody, Minn., Miami, Fla.

Hayden, Philip S., Student Officer, 85 S. Prospect St., Burlington, Vt.

Haye, Edward J., Student Officer, 1173 Bellevue Ave., Syracuse, N. Y.

Hayes, Benjamin S., Ensign, 2620 College Ave., Berkeley, Cal.

Hayes, H. E., Ensign.

Hayes, H. H., Jr., Student Officer, 28 Einhorn Road, Winchester, Mass.

Hayes, L. B., Student Officer, Box 239, Route C, San Jose, Cal. Seattle.

Hayes, Benjamin S., Ensign.

Hayes, H., War. Gun.

Hays, Rolfe M., Ensign, 810 S. Third St., Champaigne, Ill.

Hazard, Charles M., Student Officer, 627 Clark St., Milwaukee, Wis.

Hazleton, Everett L., Ensign, 15 Carroll St., Portland, Me. Mass. Inst. of Tech., Akron, Ohio; Brest, Fr.; Newport. LTA.

Hazen, C. B., War Mach., 286 Dean St., Brooklyn, N.Y.

Hazen, E. R., War. Mach.

Hazen, Maynard T., Ensign, 1008 Asylum Ave., Hartford, Conn. Mass. Inst. of Tech., Pensacola, Fla. HTA.

Hazlett, Harry C., Student Officer, Pleasant Valley, Wheeling, W. Va. Great Lakes. HTA.

Heald, Merwyn, Student Officer, 434 N. 17th St., Lincoln, Nebr.

Heald, Pusey Bancroft, Student Officer, 2231 Hurley Ave., Ft. Worth, Tex. Mass. Inst. of Tech., Miami. HTA.

Heap, George R., Student Officer, Care of Y. M. C. A., 1736 G St., N. W., Washington, D. C.

Heard, Drayton, Student Officer, 322 Chestnut Road, Edgeworth, Allegheny Co., Pa. Mass. Inst. of Tech., Great Lakes, Hampton Roads. HTA.

Heaslip, Charles T., Student Officer, 454 Riverside Drive, New York City.

Heath, Marion C., Student Officer, 2096 Suney Rd., Cleveland, Ohio. Great Lakes, Ill. HTA.

Heath, Otis L., Student Officer, 47 Isabella Ave., Newark, N. J., Mass. Inst. of Tech. HTA.

Heath, William T., Student Officer, 76 Soldiers Pl., Buffalo, N. Y.

Heffelfinger, Totton P., Ensign, 312 Chamber of Commerce, Minneapolis, Minn. Dunwoody Inst., San Diego. HTA.

Heffron, John M., Ensign, 361 N. Maple Ave., Greenwich, Conn. Mass. Inst. of Tech., Instructor.

Hegedorn, Walter, Student Officer, 391 Webster Ave., Jersey City, N. J.

Heider, Raymond F., Student Officer, 55 Yale St., Holyoke, Mass.

Heil, Geo L., Student Officer, 1231 Boswell St., Topeka, Kans.

Heil, J. Kenneth, Student Officer, 5735 University Ave., Chicago, Ill. Dunwoody Inst., Miami. HTA.

Heineman, Edward T., Student Officer, 634 Grace St., Chicago, Ill. Mass. Inst of Tech. HTA.

Heits-Menken, J. M., Ensign.

Held, Lothrop Motley, Lieut. (j.g.), 22 East 82nd St., New York. Pensacola, Ft. Worth, Hampton Roads, Bay Shore, Miami, Brunswick.

Helm, George W., Ensign, 1371 4th Ave., Louisville, Ky. N. A. No. 1365.

Henderson, Colin David, Ensign, Lewisburg, W. Va. Seattle, Wash., San Diego, Cal., Pensacola. N. A. No. 2391. HTA.

Henderson, George R., Lieut. (j.g.), 273 Sayles Ave., Pawtucket, R. I., Mass. Inst. of Tech., Pensacola. N. A. No. 909. HTA.

Henderson, J. W., Student Officer, 2439 Massachusetts Ave., Cambridge, Mass.

Henderson, Paul, Ensign. N. A. No. 2441.

Hendrick, Jack M., Student Officer, 207 Marine Bank Bldg., Long Beach, Cal.

Hendrickson, Frank D., Student Officer, 7 Hanover Sq., New York City.

Henry, Chas W., Ensign, The Racquet Club, Philadelphia, Pa. Mass. Inst. of Tech. Pensacola. HTA.

Herrinian, Morris W., Student Officer, 320 N. Franklin Ave., River Forest, Ill. Mass. Inst. of Tech. HTA.

Herbert, James H., Lieut. (j.g.), 304 West 32nd St., New York City. Bay Shore, L. I., Key West, Montauk. N. A. No. 408. HTA.

Hertel, Joseph P., Student Officer, Chilton, Wis.

Hertner, William, War. Gun.

Herzer, F. H., Student Officer, 189 West Church St., Marion, Ohio. Mass. Inst. of Tech. HTA.

Hessey, John R., Student Officer, 1500 Putnam Ave., Brooklyn, N. Y.

Heth, Louis E., Student Officer, 938 Washington Ave., Racine, Wis.

Hetzel, Harry C., Student Officer, 2518 17th St., Washington, D. C.

Heuchel, Harry J., Student Officer, 519 Third St., Brooklyn, N. Y.

Heusel, Phillip, Ensign.

Heusinger, William, Student Officer, 2019 Marine Ave., San Antonio, Texas. Seattle, Wash. HTA.

Hewitt, Lambert, Ensign, 1142 Van Ness Ave., San Francisco, Cal. N. A. No. 1766.

Hewitt, Roscoe S., Student Officer, 820 N. St. Joe Ave., Hastings, Nebr.

Heydt, Edward F., Ensign, 88 Lincoln St., Montclair, N. J. Mass. Inst. of Tech., Bay Shore, Pensacola. N. A. No. 1863.

Heyman, Morris A., Student Officer, 317 Union Ave., S. E., Grand Rapids, Mich.

Hick, Charles M., Lieut. (j.g.), 45 Sibley St., Hammond, Ind.

Hickey, Benjamin J., Ensign, 317 Fordham Rd., New York City. Mass. Inst. of Tech., Pensacola. HTA.

Hickman, Ernest T., Ensign, Lake Wales, Fla. Mass. Inst. of Tech., Buffalo, N. Y.

Hicks, Frederick B., Lieut. (j.g.), Hingham, Mass. Mass. Inst. of Tech., Pensacola, Chatham. N. A. No. 729. HTA.

Higbie, N. Bradley, Jr., Ensign, 4933 Kimbark Ave., Chicago, Ill. Mass. Inst. of Tech., Key West, Miami, Pensacola. N. A. No. 1373. HTA.

Hihn, F. D., Student Officer, Care of Olympic Club, San Francisco, Cal. Seattle, Wash. HTA.

Hilaire, Chas. F., War. Gun.

Hilbish, Wm. Dale, Student Officer, 102 Adolph Ave., Akron, Ohio. Mass. Inst. of Tech., Miami. HTA.

Hildebrand, E. S., Student Officer, 46 Allen Pl., Hartford, Conn. Mass. Inst. of Tech. HTA.

Hildebrandt, B. E., Ensign, 248 Randolph Ave., Peoria, Ill. Mass. Inst. of Tech., Miami, Pensacola. N. A. No. 1325. HTA.

Hildebrandt, Geo. N., Ensign, 248 Randolph Ave., Peoria, Ill. Mass. Inst. of Tech. Key West, Miami, Pensacola. N. A. No. 1710. HTA.

Hill, Albert E., Student Officer, 205 The Alabama Apts., Washington, D. C.

Hill, Alexander B., Jr., Ensign, 2507 Hearst Ave., Berkeley, Cal. N. A. No. 1647.

Hill, Boyd T., Student Officer, 208 West St., Freeport, Ill.

Hill, Charles F., Student Officer, 705 Taylor St., Washington, D. C.

Hill, Geo. A., Lieut. (j.g.), Hudson, Mass. Mass. Inst. of Tech., Miami, Key West. N. A. No. 1481. HTA.

Hill, Hamilton R., Ensign, Westbury, N. Y. Mass. Inst. of Tech., Bay Shore, Pensacola, Brunswick. N. A. No. 1312. HTA.

Hill, James Pearson, Ensign, Smyrna, Delaware. Mass. Inst. of Tech., Miami and Pensacola. N. A. No. 2176. HTA.

Hill, John W., Student Officer, Inex Hotel, 9th and Troost St., Kansas, Mo.

Hill, John W., Ensign, 471 Beechwood Ave., Bridgeport, Conn. N. A. No. 698.

Hill, Mahlon W., Ensign, 23 Holland Rd., Melrose, Mass. Mass. Inst. of Tech., Akron, Ohio; Pensacola, Fla. N. A. No. 2272. LTA.

Hill, Robert A., Ensign, 11 Third Ave., Northampton, Mass. Mass. Inst. of Tech., Key West, Miami, Pensacola, Hampton Rds., Fleet Air Detachment. N. A. No. 1298. HTA.

Hill, W. H., Ensign, 933 N. 11th St., Reading, Pa.

Hillbert, Webb, Ensign, 2311 Grand Ave., New York City. N. A. No. 427.

Hills, Thos. Oliver, Ensign. N. A. No. 1008.

Hillstrom, Roy A., Ensign.

Hillyer, Douglas, Ensign, 2021 Hillyer Pl., Washington, D. C. Mass. Inst. of Tech., Pensacola, Fla.

Himes, Geo. Heckman, Ensign, 1721 Columbia Rd., Washington, D. C. N. A. No. 1913.

Hinds, Horace S., Ensign, 43 Central Ave., Newtonville, Mass. Mass. Inst. of Tech., Miami, Pensacola. N. A. No. 1147. HTA.

Hines, John Willis, Ensign, 17 Gramercy Park, New York City. Mass. Inst. of Tech., Bay Shore, Pensacola, Moutchic-Lananau, Killingholme, Dundee, Chatham. N. A. No. 338. HTA.

Hinkel, Alvin C., Student Officer, 576 Westminster Ave., Elizabeth, N. J.

Hinton, Sebastian, Ensign, 10 S. La Salle St., Chicago, Ill.

Hipke, Lucius W., Student Officer, 3021 Cedar St., Milwaukee, Wis.

Hirsch, Oliver J., Student Officer, 6611 N. Ashland Ave., Chicago, Ill.

Hiscox, David F., Ensign, East Patchogue, Long Island, N. Y. N. A. No. 1253.

Hite, Hugh Maury, Ensign, 42 Arlington St., Cambridge, Mass. Mass. Inst. of Tech., Key West, Miami, Marine Field, Moutchic, Northern Bombing Group. HTA.

Hite, P. E., Ensign, Frankfort, Ky. Mass. Inst. of Tech., Key West, Miami, Pensacola, Eastleigh, Roehampton, Eng. N. A. No. 1150. HTA.

Hoagland, G. F., Ensign, 76 Maple Pl., Keyport, N. J. Mass. Inst. of Tech., Akron, Ohio; Rockaway Beach, N. Y. LTA.

Hoagland, Porter, Lieut. (j.g.), Red Bank, N. J. Mass. Inst. of Tech., Key West, Rockaway. N. A. No. 450. LTA.

Hobbs, Percy M., Student Officer, 1953 E. 82d St., Cleveland, Ohio. Mass. Inst. of Tech., Miami, Key West.

Hockman, Geo. B., Student Officer, R. F. D. No. 7, Hagerstown, Md.

Hodgdon, Paul E., Student Officer, 39 West Broadway, Bangor, Maine.

Hodges, Chas. E., Ensign, 213 Gardner Rd., Brookline, Mass. N. A. No. 397.

Hodges, K. B., Lieut. (j.g.), 522 Pine St., Albany, Ga. Mass. Inst. of Tech., Pensacola, Moutchic, Killingholme N. A. No. 335. HTA.

Hodgkins, Merton O., Student Officer, 185 South Side Ave., Freeport, N. Y.

Hofer, M. A., Lieut. (j.g.), 2374 Grandin Rd., Cincinnati, Ohio. N. A. No. 194.

Hoff, Paul Frank, Student Officer, 615 Cramer St., Milwaukee, Wis.

Hoffman, J. R., Ensign, 228 Central Ave., Los Angeles, Cal. Mass. Inst. of Tech., Curtis, Buffalo; L. W. F., College Point.

Hoffman, R. G., Ensign, 321 Hawthorn Road, Roland Park, Md. Mass. Inst. of Tech., Miami, Pensacola, N. Bomb. Group. N. A. No. 683. HTA.

Hoffer, R. H., Ensign.

Hohenthal, Louis L., Student Officer, 467 Center St., South Manchester, Conn. Mass. Inst. of Tech. HTA.

Hohl, Stewart M., Jr., Student Officer, 627 W. 113th St., New York City.

Hoisington, H. W., Ensign, 51 E. Woodruff Ave., Columbus, Ohio. Mass. Inst. of Tech., Bay Shore, L. I., Pensacola. HTA.

Holden, Geo. F., Student Officer, 248 Post Ave., San Antonio, Tex.

Holding, R. S., Ensign.

HOLGATE, ROBERT B., Ensign, Evanston, Ill. Mass. Inst. of Tech., Akron, Rockaway Beach. LTA.

HOLLAND, JAMES G., Ensign, 334 Hollister Ave., Grand Rapids, Mich. Dunwoody Inst., Miami, Pensacola. HTA.

HOLLIDAY, FREDERICK T., Student Officer, 1 Hillhouse Ave., New Haven, Conn.

HOLLIS, THOMAS, JR., Ensign, New London, N. H. Mass. Inst. of Tech., Key West. HTA.

HOLLOWAY, T. F., Ensign, River Bank, Beverly, N. J. Mass. Inst. of Tech., Pensacola, Bay Shore, Cape May, Moutchic, Fromentine, France. N. A. No. 878. HTA.

HOLMAN, WM. D., Student Officer, Psi Upsilon House, Middleton, Conn.

HOLMQUIST, CARL W., Ensign, 1103 Major St., Woodlawn, Beaver Co., Pa. Mass. Inst. of Tech., Akron, Rockaway, Marginal Parkway. LTA.

HOLST, EMMERT T., Ensign, Elks Club, Seattle, Wash. N. A. No. 1125.

HOLT, ARTHUR R., Ensign, 15 Rice St., Newton Center, Mass.

HOLT, BENJ. DEAN, Ensign, 548 E. Park St., Stockton, Cal. Mass. Inst. of Tech., Miami, Pensacola, San Diego. N. A. No. 1371. HTA.

HOLT, JOHN W., Student Officer, 8 Atwood St., Hartford, Conn.

HOLTBY, EARL D., Student Officer, 175 Edwards St., New Haven, Conn.

HOLTHAM, EARL A., Ensign, 828 12th St., Modesto, Cal. N. A. No. 1185.

HOLTON, J. BARRY, Ensign, 505 W. 13th St., Austin, Tex. Mass. Inst. of Tech., Key West, Fla. N. A. No. 1888. HTA.

HOLZL, ALFRED P., War. Gunner.

HOMER, JOSEPH W., Ensign. N. A. No. 668.

HONDLE, W. C., War. Machinist.

HONEY, FREDERIC D., Student Officer, Gresham, Ore.

HONNEN, EDWARD H., Student Officer, 1423 N. Lejon St., Colorado Springs, Colo.

HOOPES, THOMAS T., Lieut. (j.g.), 124 High St., Newburyport, Mass. Squantum, Mass.; Hampton Rds.; Pensacola, Fla.; Chatham, Mass. N. A. No. 1094. HTA.

HOPKINS, D. W., Ensign, 3435 Cornell Pl., Cincinnati, Ohio. Mass. Inst. of Tech., Pensacola, Great Lakes, Washington, D. C. HTA.

HOPKINS, J. G., JR., Student Officer, Greenwood, Va. Mass. Inst. of Tech. HTA.

HOPPER, GEO. T., Student Officer, P. O. Box 446, Spokane, Wash.

HORN, HERBERT E., Ensign.

HORNER, JOSEPH, JR., Student Officer, Green Bay, Wis. Care of Press Gazette. Mass. Inst. of Tech., Key West, Fla. HTA.

HORNER, WM. W., Lieut. (j.g.), 4907 Carnegie Ave., Cleveland, Ohio. Mass. Inst. of Tech., Akron, Ohio; Rockaway Beach, N. Y.; Brest, France. LTA.

HORRELL, MARTIN L., Ensign, 600 Karpen Bldg., Chicago, Ill.

HORTON, HARRY D., Ensign, Peconie, N. Y. Mass. Inst. of Tech., Miami, Pensacola. N. A. No. 1675. HTA.

HORTON, JEROME L., Student Officer, 2670 Hudson Blvd., Jersey City, N. J.

HOSFORD, HEMPHILL M., Student Officer, Waxahochie, Tex. Mass. Inst. of Tech., Akron, Ohio; Rockaway Beach, L. I. LTA.

HOSKINS, ARTHUR C., Student Officer, 525 Jefferson Ave., Detroit, Mich.

HOUGH, E. B., Ensign.

HOUGH, WARREN R., Student Officer, 410 E. John St., Champaign, Ill.

HOVEY, LEON B., Ensign, 29 Lancaster St., Cambridge. Mass. Inst. of Tech., Pensacola, Fla.

HOWARD, CHARLES SOTHORON, Student Officer, Frederick, Md. Mass. Inst. of Tech., Charleston.

HOWARD, HOWELL H., Student Officer, 205 W. 2d St., Dayton, Ohio.

HOWARD, JOHN COCRANE, Student Officer, Winchester St., Haverhill, Mass.

HOWARD, JOHN G., Ensign, 210 Lexington Ave., Rochester, N. Y. N. A. No. 1949.

HOWDEN, FREDERICK J., Student Officer, 104 Park Ave. E., Savannah, Ga. Seattle, Wash. HTA.

HOWE, DUDLEY ROGERS, Student Officer, 22 Worthington Rd., Brookline, Mass.

HOWE, HAROLD, Lieut. (j.g.), Care of Tioga Cigar Co., Owego, N. Y. Mass. Inst. of Tech., Key West, Pensacola, Miami, Pauillac, Moutchic, Brest. N. A. No. 518. HTA.

HOWERTON, JAMES, Ensign, N. A. No. 1074.

HOWLETT, W. M., Ensign, 23 Irving St., Cambridge, Mass.

HUBBARD, CHARLES E., Lieut. (j.g.), 30 Powel Ave., Newport, R. I. Mass. Inst. of Tech., Moutchic, Pensacola, Fromentine, Fr.; Miami. N. A. No. 350. HTA.

HUBBARD, MILTON LE COMPTE, Student Officer, 118 Academy St., Cambridge, Md. Dunwoody Inst. HTA.

HUBBELL, NELSON E., Ensign, 135 N. Pearl St., Buffalo, N. Y. N. A. No. 2431.

HUBBELL, WM. I., Student Officer, Canal St., Westport, Conn.

HUCK, LOUIS C., Student Officer, 446 Diversey Parkway, Chicago, Ill.

HUDDLESTON, WALTER D., Ensign, 332 W. Broad St., Texarkana, Tex. N. A. No. 766.

HUFFMAN, KENAZ, Ensign, 411 Ernest & Cranmer Bldg., Denver, Colo. Seattle, Wash., D. C. HTA.

HUGHES, CALEB C., JR., Student Officer, 213 14th St., S. E., Washington, D. C.

HUGHES, ERNEST L., Student Officer, 1206 Hinman Ave., Evanston, Ill.

HUGHES, HARRY H., JR., Student Officer, 1001 Pine St., Rolla, Mo.

HUGHES, PAUL A., War. Machinist, 15 Berkeley Pl., Montclair, N. J.

HUKILL, EMORY W., Ensign, Middletown, Del. Mass. Inst. of Tech., Key West, Miami. N. A. No. 1524. HTA.

HULETT, E. C., Ensign, Holly, Mich. Mass. Inst. of Tech., Akron, Pensacola, Montauk and Rockaway. N. A. No. 2085. LTA.

HULL, WM. B., Ensign, 139 Sheldon Ave., Grand Rapids, Mich. N. A. No. 1719.

HULSE, J. H., Ensign. N. A. No. 1288.

HUMBERT, OSCAR L., Student Officer, 828 S. D St., Arkansas City, Kans. Seattle, Washington. HTA.

HUMISTON, WM. T., Student Officer, Vero, Fla., Seattle, Key West. LTA.

HUMMER, RICHARD P., Ensign, 4535 Beacon St., Chicago, Ill. Mass. Inst. of Tech., Miami, Norfolk, Saunders Range, Md.; Pensacola. N. A. No. 1162. HTA.

HUMPHREYS, WM. V., JR., Ensign. N. A. No. 173.

HUMPHREYS, WM. Y., JR., Lieut. (j.g.).

HUNEKE, ROBERT C., War. Boatswain.

HUNNEWELL, C. F., Ensign, 50 Chandler St., W. Somerville, Mass.

HUNT, VINCENT R., Student Officer, Bricelyn, Minn. Dunwoody Inst., Miami. HTA.

HUNTER, BYRON W., Student Officer, Fremont, Nebr. Seattle, Wash. HTA.

HUNTER, CHARLES N., Student Officer, Burlingame, Cal.

HUNTER, DONALD WM., Student Officer, 80 Westminster Ave., Detroit, Mich.

HUNTER, HARRY H., Ensign, 1119 Judson Ave., Evanston, Ill. Mass. Inst. of Tech., Pensacola, Queenstown, Wexford, Ireland. HTA.

HUNTER, ROBERT D., Ensign, 977 Hackensack Plk. Rd., North Bergen, N. J. Mass. Inst. of Tech., Bay Shore, L. I., Pensacola, Fla. N. A. No. 1950.

HUNTER, T. W., Ensign, 57 Eliot St., Detroit, Mich. Mass. Inst. of Tech., Bay Shore, Pensacola, Miami. N. A. No. 1382.

HUNTINGTON, EDWIN JAY, Lieut. (j.g.), Geddes Road, Ann Arbor, Mich. Mass. Inst. of Tech., Pensacola, Hampton Roads. HTA.

HUNTLEY, ROBERT R., War. Carpenter, 303 Electric Bldg., Buffalo, N. Y. Philadelphia Navy Yard; Pauillac, France; Eastleigh, Eng.

HUNTLEY, W. C., Ensign, East Auburn, Cal. Seattle; San Diego, Cal., and Pensacola, Fla. N. A. No. 1899.

HURT, SHERWOOD L., Student Officer, Bartow County, White, Ga.

HUSSEY, JOHN EDWARD, Student Officer, 5811 Cabanne Ave., St. Louis, Mo. Great Lakes Naval Training Station, U. S. Naval Unit, Yale University, New Haven.

HUTCHINGS, JOHN H., Student Officer, 2805 O Ave., Galveston, Tex. Seattle, Wash. HTA.

HUTCHINS, D. J., Lieut. (j.g.), 256 Tyler Ave., Detroit, Mich., Supt. constr. aircraft, New York City.

HUTCHINSON, ARTHUR EDWARD, War. Machinist.

HUTCHINSON, HUBERT, Student Officer, 311 Mt. Prospect

Ave., Newark, N. J. Mass. Inst. of Tech., Miami and Pensacola, Fla. HTA.

HUTCHINSON, JOHN G., Student Officer, 659 Massachusetts Ave., Arlington, Mass.

HUTCHINSON, LESTER B., Ensign. N. A. No. 618.

HUTCHINSON, REGINALD L., Ensign, 1837 Spruce St., Philadelphia, Pa. N. A. No. 1552.

HUTCHISON, LUCIUS LEE, Student Officer, Ashburn, Va. Seattle. HTA.

HYDE, RUSSELL N., Lieut. (j.g.), 22 Devens Rd., Swampscott, Mass. Mass. Inst. of Tech., Pensacola; Dundee, Sct.; Felixstowe, Eng.; Pauillac, Fr.; Key West, Fla. N. A. No. 181.

HYMER, H. G., Student Officer, Lancaster, Wis. Mass. Inst. of Tech., Key West, Fla. HTA.

HYSOM, ROSCOE H., Ensign, 1200 Massachusetts Ave., Cambridge, Mass. Mass. Inst. of Tech., Akron, Ohio; Rockaway Beach, L. I.; Key West, Fla. LTA.

And I Learned About Flying from Her

I've taken my hops where I've found 'em;
  I've looped and I've spun in my time;
I've 'ad my pickin's o' seaplanes,
  An' some o' the lot was prime.
One was an outcast F-boat,
  One was a dizzy N-9,
Oh, the "twelves" and "sixteens" I still see in my dreams,
  And the Gyrenes that ever were mine.

Now I'm not a 'and with F-boats,
  For, takin' 'em all along,
You never can say till you've tried 'em,
  An' then you are like to be wrong.
There is some that you know that you mightn't,
  There is some that you know that you might;
And you'll often get stunts when you're flyin' your bunks,
  That will help you in tea-table flights!

I was a young man at Miami,
  Keen as a boy to begin;
They gave me a rusty ole flivver,
  The first I had ever been in.
Older than me, but my first 'un,—
  More like an alarm clock she were,—
But she slipped in one night when I spiralled too tight.
  An' I learned about flyin' from her.

Then I was transferred to Suiza's,
  (Else I'd be taxi-in' now),
I was proud as a newly-made Ensign,
  And I told 'em I'd show 'em all how.
I soared up over the islands
  And down where the coral keys were,
And I kept out o' harm near the ole turtle farm—
  And I learned about flyin' from her.

Oh, I've taken my hops where I've found 'em,
  And now I'm through with the fun;
The more time you've got in "sixteens,"
  The more you will think of the "one's."
And the end of its sittin' an' thinkin',
  An' dreamin' more flyin' to see;
So be warned by my lot (which I know you will not),
  An' learn about flyin' from me.

IDE, JOHN JAY
Lieut, (j.g.)
1128 Madison Ave., New York City. Bu. Const. and Repair, Washington, D. C.

INGRAHAM, CLARK E.
Ensign
Dolgeville, N. Y. Mass. Inst. of Tech., Bay Shore, Pensacola. N. A. No. 1942. HTA.

IRVINE, JAMES
Ensign
216 Elysian Ave., Pittsburgh, Penn. M. I. T., Bay Shore, Hampton Rds., Pensacola, San Diego. N. A. No. 1338. HTA.

ISEMAN, JOHN W.
Ensign
2015 Linwood Blvd., Kansas City, Mo. Mass. Inst. of Tech., Miami, Pensacola. N. A. No. 2543. HTA.

IVINS, RALPH S.
Student Officer
S. Bellevue Ave., Langhorne, Pa., Dunwoody Inst., Minn. HTA.

IWIG, HOWARD P.
Ensign
313 N. Elmwood Ave., Peoria, Ill. Mass. Inst. of Tech., Key West, Miami, Pensacola. N. A. No. 1393. HTA.

IZANT, EUGENE T.
Lieut. (j.g.)
1753 Eastham Ave., Cleveland. Ohio. Mass. Inst of Tech., Pensacola. N. A. No. 579. HTA.

JACKSON, CHARLES I.
Ensign
121 N. Bellinger St., Herkimer, N. Y. Bay Shore, Pensacola, Hampton Rds, Rockaway Beach, Montauk. LTA.

JACKSON, C. GORDON
Ensign
5425 Bryan St., Dallas, Tex. Mass. Inst. of Tech., New Orleans, Pensacola, Boston, Miami. N. A. No. 2330. HTA.

JACKSON, CONKLIN
Student Officer
West Jefferson, Ohio. Dunwoody, Inst., Minn., Seattle, Washington HTA.

JACKSON, WILLIAM
Lieut. (j.g.)
Winamac, Ind. Mass. Inst. of Tech., Pensacola, Ft. Worth, Tex., Killingholme, Eng. N. A. No. 272. HTA.

JACOBS, MONROE S.
Ensign
27 West 85th St., New York City. Mass. Inst. of Tech., Pensacola. N. A. No. 1830. HTA.

JACOBSEN, E. H.
Ensign
243 Oakland Ave., West New Brighton, Staten Island, New York. Great Lakes, Pensacola.

JACOBSON, LEE R.
Ensign
1848 Page St., San Francisco, Cal. Mass. Inst. of Tech., Akron, Pensacola, Hampton Rds., LTA.

JAMES, CLIFFORD P.
Ensign
140 Broadway c/o Guaranty Trust Co., New York City. Great Lakes. HTA.

JAMES, JOHN K.
Student Officer
2612 Hopkins St., Houston, Texas. Mass. Inst. of Tech., Akron, Rockaway Beach. LTA.

JAMES, RALPH M.
Ensign
5243 Raymond Ave., St. Louis, Mo Mass. Inst. of Tech., Key West, Columbia University. N. A. No. 2021. HTA.

JAMESON, H. BURTON
Ensign
Linden, Mich. Mass. Inst. of Tech., Key West, Miami, Pensacola. N. A. No. 1908. HTA.

JARVIS, CLARENCE B.
Ensign
Oneida, N. Y. Mass. Inst. of Tech., Miami, Pensacola. N. A. No. 2668. HTA.

SPIRALLING AN N-10 ON ITS BACK AT PENSACOLA

JENCKES, STEPHEN H.
Ensign
88 Prospect St., Providence, R. I. M. I. T, Pensa., Miami, Moutchic, Campagne, Malpensa It., Chatham. N. A. No. 684. HTA.

JENKS, WESTON M.
Ensign
90 Tower Rd., Waterbury. Conn. Mass. Inst. of Tech., Newport, Key West, Pensacola. HTA.

JENNINGS, ALLYN R.
Lieut. (j.g.)
1410 South Penn Square, Philadelphia, Pa. Squantum, Hampton Rds., Key West, Cape May, Chatham. N. A. No. 455. HTA.

JENNINGS, JAMES C.
Student Officer
Box 91. Mineral Wells, Tex. Univ. Wash., Seattle. HTA.

JENNINGS, ROBT. E.
Lieut. (j.g.)
328 Main St., Menominee, Mich. Mass. Inst. of Tech., Great Lakes, Key West, Miami, Pensacola. N. A. No. 1709. HTA.

JERMAIN, HERBERT F.
Ensign
316 Huntington Ave., Boston, Mass. Mass. Inst. of Tech., Miami, Pensacola, Charlestown. N. A. No. 2224. HTA.

JEWETT, ORIS F.
Student Officer
105 N. 5th St., Sawtelle, Cal. Seattle, North Island, San Diego. HTA.

JOBES, HAROLD L.
Ensign
21 Bay View Ave., Prince Bay, New York. Mass. Inst. of Tech., Akron, Key West, Pensacola. N. A. No. 1966. LTA.

JOHANSEN, ELMER L.
Lieut. (j.g.)
5 Arthur St., Somerville, Mass. Mass. Inst. of Tech., Pensacola, Lake Bolsena, It., Porto Corsini, Italy. N. A. No. 325. HTA.

JOHNSON, ARCHIE C.
Ensign
Waseca, Minn. Mass. Inst. of Tech., Akron, Rockaway Beach. LTA.

JOHNSON, FRANK M.
Lieut. (j.g.)
1443 Fairmont St., Washington, D. C. Mass. Inst. of Tech., Pensacola, Hampton Roads. N. A. No. 1096. HTA.

JOHNSON, LACEY F.
Student Officer
50 the Boulevard, Pelham, N. Y., Mass. Inst. of Tech., Bay Shore. HTA.

JOHNSON, MILTON O.
Student Officer
708 Fremont Ave., Morris, Ill. Dunwoody, Miami. HTA.

JOHNSON, WARREN F.
Ensign
Cold Spring Harbor, L. I., N. Y. Mass. Inst. of Tech., Miami, Pensacola, Moutchic, Fr. N. A. No. 1111. HTA.

JOHNSON, W. W.
Ensign
314 Main St., Galva, Illinois. Dunwoody, Miami, Key West, Pensacola. HTA.

JOHNSTON, GALE
Student Officer
122 Jackson Place, Mexico, Mo. Dunwoody Inst. Minn. HTA.

JOHNSTON, OSWALD L.
Student Officer
Care Jas. McNaughton, Bronxville, N. Y. Mass. Inst. of Tech., Bay Shore. HTA.

JONES, ARTHUR L.
Ensign
7 St. Michaels Place, Charleston, S. C. Mass. Inst. of Tech., Miami, Pensacola. N. A. No. 1891. HTA.

JONES, MARK Z.
Ensign
121 Court St., Janesville, Wis. Mass. Inst. of Tech., Akron, Pensacola. N. A No. 2631. LTA.

JONES, PAUL LUCAS
Student Officer
2732 Tracy Ave., Kansas City, Mo. Mass. Inst. of Tech. HTA.

JONES, VICTOR H.
Lieut. (j.g.)
533 Byron St., Mankato, Minn. Akron, Cape May, Hampton Roads, Pensacola. N. A. No. 881. LTA.

JONES, WOOLSEY F.
Ensign
2701 Fifth St., Tuscaloosa, Ala. Mass. Inst. of Tech., Pensacola, Miami. N. A. No. 1441. HTA.

JORDAN RAYMOND D.
Ensign
12 Stebbins St., Springfield, Mass. Mass. Inst. of Tech., Key West, Miami, Pensacola, Anacostia. N. A. No. 1409. HTA.

JORDAN, ROBERT
Ensign
315 West 97 St., New York City. Mass. Inst. of Tech., Pensacola, Chatham. N. A. No. 924. HTA.

Another "Nose-In."

JOUBERT, CLEMENT C.
Student Officer
18 Riverside Square, Hyde Park, Mass. Mass. Inst. of Tech. HTA.

JOVA, JOHN A.
Lieut. (j.g.)
Roseton, Orange Co., N. Y. Mass. Inst. of Tech., Pensacola. N. A. No. 429. HTA.

JULIAN, DALVEN
Ensign
607 Fountain St., Mineral Point, Wisconsin. Mass. Inst. of Tech., Great Lakes, Key West, Miami, Pensacola. N. A. No. 1720. HTA.

JULLIFFE, H. W.
Student Officer
136 Marion Ave., Mansfield, Ohio. Mass. Inst. of Tech. HTA.

IBSEN, NORMAN H., Ensign, 607 S. State St., Ann Arbor, Mich. N. A. No. 1469.

IDOL, MILWARD, Student Officer, Robinson, Kans.

IGLEHEART, G. P., Lieut. (j.g.), 10 Nassau St., Princeton, N. J. Cambridge, Buffalo, New York City.

ILES, MALVERN, W., Student Officer, 324 Mississippi Ave., Davenport, Iowa.

INGALLS, D. S., Lieut. (j.g.), 11808 Lake Shore Blvd., Cleveland, Ohio. Palm Beach, Huntington, L. I., Dunkirk, Eastleigh, Eng. N. A. No. 85. HTA.

INGERSOLL, C. D., Ensign, 251 E. Chestnut St., Canton, Ill. Mass. Inst. of Tech., Great Lakes, San Diego, Cal. HTA.

INGHAM, JAMES R., Student Officer, 1088 Delaware Ave., Buffalo, N. Y. Mass. Inst. of Tech., Bay Shore, L. I. HTA.

INNESS, JOS. K., Student Officer, 833 Prospect Place, Brooklyn, N. Y.

IRVINE, EUGENE L., Student Officer, 3811 McKenney Ave., Dallas, Tex.

INGLIS, J., Ensign, Patterson, N. J. N. A. No. 1199.

IRVINE, RUTLEDGE, Ensign, 157 6th Ave., Brooklyn, N. Y. Mass. Inst of Tech., Pensacola, Hampton Roads. N. A. No. 1001. HTA.

IRVING, CLARENCE B., Ensign, 60 Union Ave., Framingham, Mass. N. A. No. 502.

IRVING, LOUIS D., Student Officer, Red Top, Cleveland Park, Washington, D. C.

ISENBERGER, NATHAN P., Student Officer, 1312 Vermont St., Lawrence, Kans.

IZATT, THOMAS F., Student Officer, 1018 Maple Ave., Wilmerding, Pa.

JACKS, NATHANIEL, Student Officer, 4715 Bryan St., Dallas, Tex.

JACKSON, ANDREW J., Student Officer, 162 Willow St., Waterbury, Conn. Mass. Inst. of Tech., Miami. HTA.

JACKSON, C. C., Ensign.

JACKSON, JAMES A., Student Officer, 506 W. 12th St., Dallas, Tex.

JACKSON, JAMES CLARKE, Student Officer, 22 Sanchez St., Ocala, Fla. Dunwoody Inst., Minn. HTA.

JACKSON, JOHN I., Ensign.

JACKSON, PAUL, Student Officer, 57 W. Second Ave., Columbus, Ohio.

JACOBS, ALBERT H., Student Officer, 20 Palm Ave., San Francisco, Cal. Seattle, Wash. HTA.

JACOBS, FRED C., Student Officer, Memphis, Tenn. Mass. Inst. of Tech.

JACOBS, LESLIE P., Lieut. (j.g.), 412 Grand Ave., Laramie, N. Y. N. A. No. 526.

JACOBS, LORING M., Ensign.

JAECKEL, HARRY J., War. Machinist, 549 Gantenbein Ave., Portland, Ore. Columbia University, San Diego, Cal.; Philadelphia; Eastleigh, Eng.; Paris, Fr.

JAMESON, JOHN T., Ensign.

JANSSEN, WEBSTER E., Student Officer, E. 132d and Brown Pl., Bronx, New York City.

JANUARY, JOHN W., Student Officer, Vacaville, Cal.

JAQUES, BURNETT P., Ensign, 302 N. Cherry St., Jefferson, Iowa. Mass. Inst. of Tech., Miami, Pensacola. N. A. No. 1596. HTA.

JACQUES, HERBERT, Ensign, 491 Beacon St., Boston, Mass. Mass. Inst. of Tech., Operations, Washington, D. C.

JARRETT, H. H., Student Officer, Franklin, N. C. Mass. Inst. of Tech., Charleston, S. C. LTA.

JEANNELLE, R. C., Ensign, Peerless Milling Co., Stockton, Cal. Mass. Inst. of Tech., Bay Shore, Pensacola. N. A. No. 1129.

JEFFEREY, MADISON P., Ensign, N. A. No. 643.

JEFFORDO, WALTER M., Ensign, Glen Riddle, Pa. Mass. Inst. of Tech., Hampton Roads. HTA.

JEFFREY, GEORGE A., Student Officer, 2011 East Broad St., New Castle, Ind. Mass. Inst. of Tech., Bay Shore, Pensacola. HTA.

JELLIFF, HOWARD W., Student Officer, 136 Marion Ave., Mansfield, Ohio.

JENKS, LOUIS ORRIN, Student Officer, 1514 Military Road, Port Huron, Mich. Seattle, Wash.; Miami, Fla. HTA.

JENKS, W. M., Ensign, 90 Towers Road, Waterbury, Conn.

JENNINGS, A. G., JR., Ensign, 2 E. 82d St., New York City. Mass. Inst. of Tech., Bay Shore, Pensacola, Pauillac, Moutchic, L'Aber Vrach. N. A. No. 727. HTA.

JENNINGS, M. C., Student Officer, Ellsworth, Ill. Mass. Inst. of Tech., Miami. HTA.

JENNINGS, RICHARD, Student Officer, 2525 17th St., Washington, D. C.

JENSEN, NEINERT C., War. Machinist, 1011 18th Ave., S. Nashville, Tenn., Columbia Univ., Eastleigh, Eng.

JEROLERSON, MORTIMER N., Student Officer, 55 N. 6th St., Newark, N. J.

JESTER, J. C., Student Officer, 3430 Gillespie Ave., Dallas, Tex. Seattle, Wash. HTA.

JEWELL, ROBT. B., Student Officer, 273 S. Ashland Ave., Lexington, Ky.

JOHN, F. W., Ensign, 182 Nepperhan Ave., Yonkers, N. Y. Mass. Inst. of Tech., Bay Shore, Pensacola, Hampton Roads. N. A. No. 2120. HTA.

JOHN, HENRY VAN DYKE, Ensign, 1770 Pacific Ave., San Francisco, Cal. N. A. No. 1434.

JOHN, LAWRENCE B., Student Officer, 825 19th Ave., So. Nashville, Tenn.

JOHNS, HENRY V., Student Officer, 1770 Pacific Ave., San Francisco, Cal.

JOHNS, WATSON L., Ensign, 2952 California St., San Francisco, Cal.

JOHNSON, BERT N., Ensign, Stuben Co., Atlanta, N. Y. N. A. No. 2017.

JOHNSON, C. B., Ensign, 590 Iroquois Ave., Detroit, Mich. Dunwoody Inst., Minn.; Miami, Pensacola, Fla. N. A. No. 2635. HTA.

JOHNSON, CHAS. M., Ensign.

JOHNSON, CLARENCE R., Ensign.

JOHNSON, CRAWFORD, JR., Student Officer, 2935 Pawnee Ave., Birmingham, Ala. Seattle, Wash.; New Orleans. HTA.

JOHNSON, GEO. E., Student Officer, 4272 Whitman Ave., Seattle, Wash. Seattle, Wash., San Diego, Cal. HTA.

JOHNSON, GERALD REID, Ensign, 1914 22nd St., Sacramento, Cal. Seattle Wash. Miami, Pensacola. N. A. No. 2302. HTA.

JOHNSON, HAROLD F., Student Officer, Amherst, Mass.

JOHNSON, J. M., Carpenter.

JOHNSON, JOHN R., Ensign, Greenwich, Conn.

JOHNSON, LINDLEY, JR., Ensign, Rosemont, Pa.

JOHNSON, MALCOLM F., Student Officer, 889 1st Ave., So., Grand Rapids, Wis.

JOHNSON, MEADE M., Student Officer, 430 Ohio Ave., Etowah, Tenn.

JOHNSON, OREN V., Student Officer, 555 N. Church St., Spartanburg, S. C.

JOHNSON, RICHARD N., Student Officer, 78 Dalton Road, Newton Centre, Mass. Great Lakes, Ill.

JOHNSON, ROSCOE E., Student Officer, 202 Mulberry St., Eureka, Kans.

JOHNSON, RUDY M., Ensign, 815 N. 2nd St., Ishpeming, Mich. Mass. Inst. of Tech., Miami, Fla., Pensacola. N. A. No. 2227. HTA.

JOHNSON, S. H., Ensign, 88 Central Park, West, New York City.

JOHNSON, STEPHEN S., Student Officer, 377 Charlton Ave., So. Orange, N. J.

JOHNSON, THOS. CARY, Ensign, 10 Westwood Ave., Richmond, Va. Mass. Inst. of Tech., Akron, Ohio; Rockaway, N. Y. LTA.

JOHNSON, WALTER, Student Officer, 1930 Benedict Ave., Bronx, N. Y.

JOHNSON, WALTER H., Ensign, Claremont, Cal. R. F. D. Box 50. Mass. Inst. of Tech., Bay Shore, Pensacola, Hampton Roads, Anacostia, London, Brest, St. Nazaire, Fr. N. A. No. 1300.

JOHNSON, W. G., War. Machinist.

JOHNSON, WILLARD C., Student Officer, 2863 29th St., N. W., Washington, D. C.

JOHNSTON, CARL H., Student Officer, Boligee, Ala.

JOHNSTON, D. S., Student Officer, 822 9th St., Huntington, W. Va. Mass. Inst. of Tech. HTA.

JOHNSTON, GUNDER Z., War. Gunner.

JOHNSTON, HAROLD C., Ensign.

JOHNSTON, HAROLD K., Student Officer, 293 Woodward Ave., Buffalo, N. Y.

JOHNSTON, HENRY R., Ensign, 75 Prospect Ave., Montclair, N. J. Hampton Roads, Va. Operations Aviation, Washington, D. C.

JOHNSTON, WILLIAM D., Student Officer, Boligee, Ala.

JONAKER, WM. S., Student Officer.

JONES, ALAN P., Student Officer, Ft. Atkinson, Wis. Mass. Inst. of Tech., Key West. HTA.

Jones, Carroll L., Student Officer, 5042 Walnut St., Philadelphia, Pa.

Jones, Chas. Alvin, Ensign, 1927 Oliver Bldg., Pittsburgh, Pa.

Jones, Clifford B., Student Officer, 1339 Ohio St., Lawrence, Kans.

Jones, Decatur, Ensign, 918 Park Ave., Richmond, Va. Ohio, Mass. Inst. of Tech., Akron, Rockaway, L. I. LTA.

Jones, David Gale, Ensign, 236 McKnight Bldg., Minneapolis, Minn. Mass. Inst. of Tech., Blue Hill Observatory, Seattle, Wash. Aerographer.

Jones, Edwin M., Student Officer, Care of The Jones Co., Jackson, Miss.

Jones, Geo. E., Student Officer, 127 B St., S. E., Washington, D. C.

Jones, Henry C., Student Officer, 829 Monadnock Bldg., Chicago, Ill.

Jones, James R., Ensign, 87 Hawthorne Ave., Akron, Ohio. Mass. Inst. of Tech., Akron, Rockaway, L. I., LTA.

Jones, Kelley Day, Ensign, P. O. Box 1233 Tampa, Fla. Mass. Inst. of Tech., Bay Shore, Pensacola, Anacostia, D. C., Hampton Roads, Va. N. A. No. 1872. HTA.

Jones, Max S., Ensign, 7307 Flora Ave., St. Louis, Mo. N. A. No. 373.

Jones, Minor S., Student Officer, 94 Broad St., Charleston, S. C.

Jones, Nicholas R., Student Officer, 150 Broadway, New York, Great Lakes, Miami.

Jones, P. S., Ensign. N. A. No. 685.

Jones, Raymond S., Student Officer, Puritan Apt. 217, Louisville, Ky.

Jones, Rollin T., Student Officer, 117 Greenwood Pl., Buffalo, N. Y.

Jones Roy A., War. Gunner.

Jones, Samuel Manly, Student Officer, 302 Pembroke Ave., Norfolk, Va. Mass. Inst. of Tech. HTA.

Jones, Saunders P., Ensign, 1048 Cherokee Rd., Louisville, Ky.

Jones, Thomas M., 3rd, Lieut. (j.g.), 844 Ridge Ave., Pittsburgh, Pa. Mass. Inst. of Tech., Hampton Roads, Pensacola, Bay Shore. N. A. No. 495. HTA.

Jones, W. R., War. Machinist.

Jones, Wm. H., Student Officer, Bennett Creek, Va.

Jones, Wm. I., Ensign. N. A. No. 2072.

Jordan, Charles R., Student Officer, 2 West 72nd St., New York City.

Joseph, Roland H., Student Officer, 208 N. Oak St., Owatonna, Minn.

Josey, Samuel B., Student Officer, Hazelhurst, Ga.

Judd, David E., Lieut. (j.g.), 10 Pleasant St., Brookline, Mass.

Judson, John W., Ensign, 115 Broadway, New York City. Mass. Inst. of Tech., Pensacola, Miami, Langley Field, Va. N. A. No. 1297. HTA.

Junell, John, Ensign, Minneapolis Club, Minneapolis, Minn. Mass. Inst. of Tech., Pensacola. N. A. No. 2088. HTA.

Junkin, Geo., 4th, Ensign, 1318 Real Estate Trust Bldg., Philadelphia, Pa. N. A. No. 1959.

Maneuvers at Guantanamo Bay

KANT, EDWIN S.
Ensign
1367 Comm. Ave., Boston, Mass. Akron, Roehampton, Brest, La Pallice, Widdy Island, Bantry Bay. LTA.

KEARNEY, DANIEL W.
Ensign
126 E. Church St., Shamokin, Penn. Mass. Inst. of Tech., Miami, Pensacola. N. A. No. 2164. HTA.

KEARNEY, PATRICK E.
Ensign
58 Maple St., Hudson, Mass. Mass. Inst. of Tech., Pensacola. N. A. No. 892. HTA.

KEELER, RICHARD J.
Ensign
3121 Third Ave., So. Minn., Minn. Mass. Inst. of Tech., Bay Shore, Pensacola. N. A. No. 2194. HTA

KEEP C. RUSSELL
Ensign
273 North Oxford St., Hartford, Conn. Mass. Inst. of Tech., Miami. N. A. No. 2056. HTA.

KEHRER, GEO. C.
Student Officer
344 N. Main St., Doylestown, Pa. Mass. Inst. of Tech. HTA.

KEITH, FREDERICK W.
Lieut. (j.g.)
Sarasota, Fla. Bay Shore, Miami. N. A. No. 379. HTA.

KELLEY, WM. D.
Lieut. (j.g.)
1903 McCallie Ave., Chattanooga, Tenn. Akron, Pensacola, Mass. Inst. of Tech. N. A., No. 548. LTA.

KELLY, STEPHEN F.
Ensign
901 Jackson Ave., Bronx, New York City, M. I. T., Newport, Bay Shore, Key West, Miami, Pensacola. N. A. No. 949.

KELSEY, CARLETON
Ensign
Meriden, Conn. Keyport, N. J.

KEMP, THATCHER J.
Student Officer
2115 Hobart Blvd., Los Angeles, Cal. Seattle, Washington. HTA.

KEMPE, A. F.
Student Officer
14 Oakwood Place, Elizabeth, N. J. Mass. Inst. of Tech. HTA.

KEMPTON, FRANK
Ensign
602 Ponce de Leon Ave., Atlanta, Ga. Mass. Inst., of Tech., Akron, Rockaway. LTA.

KENDALL, JOHN W.
Ensign
Meyersdale, Penn. Mass. Inst. of Tech., San Diego, Pensacola. N. A. No. 1792. HTA.

KENNEDY, JOHN W.
Student Officer
1129 Cleveland Ave., Portland, Oregon. Seattle, San Diego. HTA.

KENT, FRANCIS R.
Student Officer
195 Lincoln St., Worcester, Mass. Mass. Inst. of Tech., HTA.

KENT, SEPTEMUS E.
Student Officer
Hope, Ark. Mass Inst. of Tech., Pensacola. HTA.

KERSHAW, G. H.
Ensign
175 N. Greenwood Ave., Kankakee, Ill. Mass. Inst. of Tech., Miami, Key West, Pensacola. N. A. No. 2488. HTA.

KESER, FLOYD B.
Ensign
Fox Chase, Pa. Mass. Inst. of Tech., Akron, Rockaway, Montauk, Pensacola. LTA.

KETCHAM, JOHN B.
Ensign
2 Rector St., New York City. M. I. T., Key West, Pensa., Queenstown, Whiddy Island, Ire. N. A. No. 1229. HTA.

SEA SLED STARTING AFTER A CRASH

KEYES, CHET. A.
Ensign
818 Scarritt Bldg., Kansas City, Mo. Mass. Inst. of Tech., Key West, Fla. HTA.

KEYES, LLOYD B.
Ensign
Auburn, Wash. Miami, Great Lakes, San Diego.

KIMBALL, CURTIS C.
Student Officer
1268 So. 20th St., Lincoln, Neb. Mass. Inst. of Tech., Great Lakes, Miami. HTA.

KINDY, WARD B.
Ensign
Fayette, Ohio. Mass. Inst. of Tech., Great Lakes, Pensacola, Key West. N. A. No. 2211. HTA.

KING, B. FRANK
Student Officer
Forrest City, Ark. Mass. Inst. of Tech., New Orleans, Pensacola, Miami. HTA.

KING, FRANK
Ensign
326 West 107 St., New York City. Hampton Rds., Calais, Anacostia. N. A. No. 245.

KINTZ. LESLIE H.
Ensign
515 Monroe St., Ann Arbor, Mich Mass. Inst. of Tech., Akron, Pensacola. N. A. No. 2617. LTA.

KIRBY, HAROLD L.
Ensign
Havre, Montana. Mass· Inst. of Tech., Miami· Pensacola, Hampton Rds., Anacostia. N. A. No. 1508. HTA.

KIRBY, PAUL J.
Ensign
426 Cumberland St., Harrisburg, Penn. Mass. Inst. of Tech., Newport, Bay Shore, Miami, Pensacola. N. A. No. 2359. HTA.

KIRK, HERBERT S.
Ensign
305 Highland Ave., New Castle, Pa. M. I. T., Miami, Pensacola, Moutchic, Fr., Bay Shore. N. A. No. 1282. HTA.

KIRK, LE GRANDE F.
Ensign
Youngstown, New York, Mass. Inst. of Tech., Key West, Miami, Pensacola. N. A. No. 2097. HTA.

KIRK, ROY E.
Ensign
186 W. Oxford St., Alliance, Ohio. Mass. Inst. of Tech., Miami, Pensacola. N. A. No. 1414. HTA.

KIRKENDALL, F. C.
Student Officer
84 West Union St., Wilkes-Barre, Pa. Mass. Inst. of Tech. HTA.

KITTRIDGE, L. T.
Ensign
Woolwitch, Maine. Pensacola, Mass. Inst. of Tech., Miami, Pensacola. N. A. No. 2662 HTA.

KLAGER, WALTER H.
Ensign
617 So. Main St., Ann Arbor, Mich. Mass. Inst. of Tech., Miami, Pensacola, Bay Shore. N. A. No. 1360. HTA.

KLOOR, LOUIS A., Jr.
Ensign
219 Avenue E., Crowley La. Pensacola, Hampton Roads, Rockaway, Montauk. N. A. No. 2437. LTA.

KNAUER, H. P
Ensign
Route 2, Pottstown, Pa. Mass. Inst. of Tech., Pensacola, Moutchic, Fr., Killingholme, Eng. N. A. No 726. HTA.

KNIGHT, JOHN A., Jr.
Ensign
931 West 4th St., Williamsport, Pa., Mass. Inst. of Tech., Key West, Miami, Pensacola. N. A. No. 1229.

KOBLEGARD, H. H.
Student Officer
218 East Main, Clarksburg, W. Va. Mass. Inst. of Tech., Bay Shore, L. I., Brunswick, Ga. HTA.

KOCH, HENRY F.
Student Officer
869 Amboy Ave., Perth Amboy, N. J. Mass. Inst. of Tech. HTA.

KOENIG, HERBERT A.
Student Officer
453 McDonough St., Brooklyn, N. Y. Mass. Inst. of Tech., Akron, Rockaway. LTA.

KOENIGER, KARL W.
Student Officer
Kingsport, Tenn. Seattle, Washington. HTA.

KOHLER, WALTER W.
Ensign
337 N. Main St., Old Forge, Pa. Mass. Inst. of Tech., Miami, Pensacola. N. A. No. 1436. HTA.

KOLPIEN, ALTON L.
Ensign
763 Park Ave., Dunkirk, N. Y. M. I. T., Key West, Miami, Pensacola, Bay Shore, Queesntown. N. A. No. 1141. HTA.

TAKING OUT THE DIRIGIBLE AT PAIMBOEUF, FRANCE, TO GIVE ASSISTANT SECRETARY OF THE NAVY ROOSEVELT A RIDE

KONIGSMARK, V. L.
Ensign
Cedar Rapids, Iowa. Mass. Inst. of Tech., Great Lakes, Miami, Pensacola. HTA.

KORFF, HARRY O.
Student Officer
1720 W. Lafayette Ave., Baltimore, Md. Mass. Inst. of Tech., League Island, Navy Yard, Philadelphia, Pa. HTA.

KOTHE, WILLIAM C.
Student Officer
75 Washington Ave., Grantwood, N. J. Mass. Inst. of Tech., Key West, HTA.

KRAMER, C. H.
Student Officer
430 E. Ninth St., Alton, Ill. Mass. Inst. of Tech., Miami. HTA.

KRAMER, IVAN L.
Student Officer
566 Prospect Place, Brooklyn, N. Y. Mass. Inst. of Tech., Akron. LTA.

KREBS, W. W.
Ensign
509 Napoleon St., Johnstown, Pa. Mass. Inst. of Tech., Akron, Hampton Roads. LTA.

KROUSE, S. HARVEY
Ensign
306 Chestnut St., Philadelphia, Penn. Mass. Inst. of Tech., Pensacola, Chatham. N. A. No. 960. HTA.

KRUMM, HARRY W.
Ensign
3000 Arunah Ave., Baltimore, Md. M. I. T., Bay Sh., Key West, Moutchic, Malpensa, N. B. G. N. A. No. 380. HTA.

KUNKEL, CHARLES F.
Lieut. (j.g.)
New Cumberland, Pa. M. I. T., Pensacola, Ft. Worth, Hampton Roads, Killingholme, Eng. N. A. No. 273. HTA.

KURTZWARTH, E. L.
Student Officer
152 King Ave., Detroit, Mich. Great Lakes, Dunwoody, Mass. Inst. of Tech.

◈ ◈ ◈ ◈ ◈ ◈

Kaftan, A. G., War. Gunner.

Kahle, George F., War. Boatswain.

Kahlert, Wm. G., Student Officer, 194 E. Robis St., St. Paul, Minn.

Kahn, Jerome Vemann, Student Officer, 3975 Beechwood Ave., Rose Hill, Cincinnati, O. Mass. Inst. of Tech., LaFayette Escadrille, France. HTA.

Kaiser, Karl H., Ensign, 18 Haviland St., Suite 5, Boston, Mass.

Kaiser, Richard W., Student Officer, Bonnie Crest, New Rochelle, N. Y.

Kamm, Walker W., Student Officer, No. 7 Russian Hill Place, San Francisco, Cal.; Seattle, Wash. LTA.

Kane, Richmond K., Student Officer, Glacier Park Hotel, Glacier Nat'l Park, Mont.

Kane, Robert R., Student Officer, Gate City, Va. Dunwoody Inst. HTA.

Kanke, Bernard, Student Officer, 675 Frederick Ave., Detroit, Mich.

Kastner, A., War. Gunner.

Katourette, Livingston B., Student Officer, 334 Central Bldg., Seattle, Wash.

Kauffman, Allen, Ensign.

Kauffmann, Samuel H., Student Officer, 6 North Dod St., Princeton, N. J.

Kauth, Elliott, Ensign.

Kavana, Luke J., Student Officer, 304 S. Ashland Ave., LaGrange, Ill.

Kavanaugh, L. T., Jr., Student Officer, 60 South Grant St., Memphis, Tenn.

Kaye, Lewis G., Ensign, 44 Campbell Hall, Princeton, N. J. N. A. No. 1228.

Kazanjian, H., Jr., Ensign, New Rochelle, N. Y. N. A. No. 2188.

Keddie, Edward A., Ensign, 804 Center St., Boston, Mass. N. A. No. 747.

Keefe, Owen F., Student Officer, 14 Irving Park, Watertown, Mass.

Keefe, Thomas J., Student Officer, Chester Club, Chester, Pa. Mass. Inst. of Tech. HTA.

Keeler, Harry F., Student Officer, 414 Pratt St., Longmont, Colo.

Keene, Campbell, Ensign, 169 State St., Augusta, Me. Mass. Inst. of Tech., Pensacola, Key West, Miami, Hampton Roads, Fleet Air Detachment. N. A. No. 1423. HTA.

Keenan, Lewis Champlin, Ensign, 1718 Ave. F, Galveston, Tex. N. A. No. 2371.

Keith, Geo K., Ensign, Box 6, Grafton, Mass.

Kellar, John W., Ensign, Lee, Mass. Mass. Inst. of Tech., Akron, Ohio, Pensacola, N. A. No. 2148. LTA.

Kelley, Frank R., Student Officer, 1932 Waldick Ave., Columbus, O.

Kelley, Oliver M., Ensign, 822 N. Fulton Ave., Baltimore, Md.

Kellock, Albro Latimer, Student Officer, Cambridge, Mass.

Kellogg, John P., Ensign, 212 Stone St, Watertown, N. Y. Mass. Inst. of Tech., Key West, Pensacola, N. A. No. 1984. HTA.

Kelly, Daniel F., Ensign.

Kelly, Errol E., Student Officer, 1200 Port St., New Orleans, La.; Seattle, Wash. HTA.

Kelly, Francis J., Student Officer. 11204 Edbrooke Ave., Chicago, Ill.

Kelly, Henry F., Student Officer. 93 Sawyer Ave., Dorchester, Mass.

Kelly, Herbert Charles, Ensign, Union Bldg., San Diego, Cal. Seattle, San Diego, Pensacola. N. A. No. 2458. HTA.

Kelly, Norman W., Lieut. (j.g.).

Kelly, W. R., War Machinist, 132 Cottage Ave., Fall River, Mass.

Kelly, Wm. Arthur, Student Officer, Main St., Bethesda, O. Mass. Inst. of Tech., Akron O.; Rockaway, L. I. LTA.

Kelly, William H., Student Officer, 305 Sorin Hall, Notre Dame, Ind.

Kelsey, Robert P., Ensign, 77 Montvale Road, Newton Center, Mass.

Kelso, Albert D., Student Officer, 2 Holyoke St., Cambridge, Mass.

Kemp, Herndon, Ensign, 905 Magaffin Ave., El Paso, Tex. Mass. Inst. of Tech., Miami, Pensacola, N. A. No. 2363. HTA.

Kendall, Charles H., Ensign, 146 Court St., Brockton, Mass.

Kendall, Everett A., Student Officer.

Kendig, Chas. Hope, Ensign, 2647 Dwight Way, Berkeley, Cal. N. A. No. 1854.

Kenderick, Charles M., Student Officer, 1241 Euclid St., Washington, D. C.

KENDRICK, JOSEPH, Student Officer, 19 Vinson St., Dorchester, Mass.

KENEN, LEONARD CHARLES, Lieut. (j.g.), 712 17th St., N. W., Washington, D. C.

KENNEDY, GEO. L., War Boatswain.

KENNEDY, H. H., Ensign, 4950 Greenwood Ave., Chicago Ill.

KENNEDY, S. C., Lieut. (j.g.) 1432 Victoria St., Honolulu, T. H. Mass. Inst. of Tech., Pensacola, Washington, Killingholme, Eng. N. A. No. 302. HTA.

KENNY, CHRISTOPHER J., Lieut. (j.g.).

KENT, DONALD W., Lieut. (j.g.), 30 Allen Lane, Philadelphia, Pa., Bureau of Steam Engineering, Washington.

KENT, ROLAND W., Ensign., 3106 Emerson Ave., Minneapolis, Minn., Dunwoody Inst., Columbia University.

KERB, LEROY H., Student Officer, 596 Clinton Ave., Newark, N. J.

KERBAUGH, MALCOLM D., Student Officer, Bryn Mawr, Pa. Mass. Inst. of Tech., Miami, Fla. HTA.

KERMAN, JOSEPH F., Student Officer, 448 Willow St., Waterbury, Conn.

KERNS, LELAND CLARE, Student Officer, Baldwin, Kas.; Seattle, Wash. HTA.

KERR, JOHN M., Student Officer, 1336 Massachusetts Ave., N. W., Washington, D. C.

KERR, R. H., Ensign, N. A. No. 178.

KERR, RICHARD CALDWELL, Ensign, 2617 Durant Ave., Berkeley, Cal. Mass. Inst. of Tech., Miami, Pensacola. N. A. No. 1754. HTA.

KERR, STEPHEN L., Ensign, Whitehouse Hotel, Salt Lake City, Utah. N. A. No. 1341.

KERSCHEUSTEINER, M. J., Student Officer, 612 Grant St., Ft. Atkinson, Wis. Great Lakes, Ill.; Pensacola, Fla.

KESSING, Ensign.

KESTERSON, HARRY J., Student Officer, 2205 Reed St., Ft. Wayne, Ind.

KETCHAM, HOWARD S., Student Officer, 239 Harvey St., Germantown, Philadelphia, Pa.

KEYES, KENNETH B., Lieut. (j.g.), Rowley, Mass. Mass. Inst. of Tech., Pensacola, Felixstowe, Lough Foyle, Brest, Treguier, Coco Solo. N. A. No. 182. HTA.

KEYSER, CLARENCE N., Lieut. (j.g.).

KIEFER, GEORGE CRONEY, Ensign, 329 Willow St., New Haven, Conn., Great Lakes. HTA.

KILBURN, HENRY T., Student Officer, 537 West 121st St., New York City. Mass. Inst. of Tech., Bay Shore, L. I. HTA.

KILBURN, JOHN R., Ensign, 646 Maryland Ave., Pittsburgh, Pa.

KILMER, O. P., Lieut. (j.g.). N. A. No. 70.

KIMBALL, DONALD B., Student Officer, 1619 Monroe St., Washington, D. C.

KIMBALL, GEORGE A., Student Officer, 4932 Colfax Ave., So. Minneapolis, Minn.; Seattle, Wash. HTA.

KIMBERLY, STUART, Ensign, Redlands, Cal. N. A. No. 1499.

KIMBROUGH, WILLIAM E., Student Officer, 1008 Elm St., Birmingham, Ala.

KIMMEL, STANLEY P., Student Officer, R. F. D. No. 5, Box 366a, Los Angeles, Cal.

KIMMEL, WALTER L., Student Officer, Cherokee, Kan.

KINCHLEY, H. A., Ensign, Sherman Hotel, 71st St. & Broadway, New York City. Mass. Inst. of Tech., Pensacola, Fla. N. A. No. 1051.

KINDALL, NOLON M., Lieut. (j.g.) N. A. No. 370.

KING, CHARLES CURTIS, Ensign, 62–70 West Iowa Ave., Memphis, Tenn. Mass. Inst. of Tech., Pensacola, Fla. HTA.

KING, DAVID E., Student Officer, 1011 Thirteenth St., Wilmette, Ill. Dunwoody Inst., Minn., Miami, Fla. HTA.

KING, EDWARD MACDONALD, Student Officer, 905 Watchung Ave., Plainfield, N. J. Mass. Inst. of Tech. HTA.

KING, FREDERICK E., Lieut. (j.g.), Kew Gardens, Long Island, N. Y. Bay Shore, Miami, Moutchic, LeCroisic, Hampton Roads. HTA.

KING, FRANCIS R., Student Officer, 73 Murray St., Newark, N. J.

KING, GEO. S., Lieut. (j.g.), 194 Rugby Road, Brooklyn. N. Y. Mass. Inst. of Tech., Akron, Key West, Bu. of C. & R., Washington, D. C., Cape May, Rockaway, Montauk. N. A. No. 1408. LTA.

KING, H. W., Ensign, Covina, Cal. N. A. No. 863.

KING, MACLELLAN E., Student Officer, 712 Waveland Ave., Chicago, Ill.; Dunwoody Inst., Minn. HTA.

KING, WARREN G., Ensign, 2573 Stratford Road, Cleveland, O.

KING, WILLIAM C., Ensign. 416 E. San Bernardino Ave., Covina, Cal. Mass. Inst. of Tech., Miami, Pensacola. N. A. No. 2016. HTA.

KINGSBURY, S. M., Ensign, 33 Norwood Ave., Newton Center, Mass. Mass. Inst. of Tech., Key West, Miami, Pensacola. N. A. No. 1824. HTA.

KIRKLAND, WILLIAM ALEXANDER, Student Officer, 1410 Clay Ave., Houston, Tex. Mass. Inst. of Tech. HTA.

KISKADDON, JOHN M., Student Officer, Tiffin, O.

KISSEL, WILLIAM T., Ensign, 14 Wall St., New York City.

KITCHIN, HOWARD W., War. Gun.

KITTINGER, L. T., Ensign, 403 Terry Ave., Seattle, Wash.

KJOS, H., War Machinist, Kenyon, Minn.

KLOSSNER, WINFRED W., Ensign. N. A. No. 1578.

KNAPP, JOSEPH F., Lieut. (j.g.), 247 Fifth Ave., New York City. Mass. Inst. of Tech., Pensacola, Fla. N. A. No. 638.

KNEASS, GEO. B., Ensign, 418 So. 15th. St., Philadelphia, Pa. Mass. Inst. of Tech., Miami, Pensacola. N. A. No. 1577. HTA.

KNIGHT, DEWEY, Student Officer, Nasvhille, Ga. Dunwoody Inst., Minn. HTA.

KNIGHT, D. B., Ensign, 28 Cambridge Place, Brooklyn, N. Y. N. A. No. 1299.

KNIGHT, GEOFFREY, Student Officer, Fanwood, N. J.

KNIPP, HOWARD FRANKLIN, Ensign, Howard Park, Md. N. A. No. 2052.

KNOERZER, LEO P., Student Officer, 46 Elizabeth St., Hammond, Md. Mass. Inst. of Tech., Great Lakes. HTA.

KNOLLENBERG, BERNHARD H., Student Officer, University Club, Honolulu, T. H.

KNOWLE, CLARENCE, Student Officer, 25 Springdale Road, Atlanta, Ga.

KOBBE, FREDERICK WM., Lieut. (j.g.), 103 East 86th St., New York, Hampton Roads, Va. Communication Officer.

KOECHL, OTTO R., Student Officer, 47 Montgomery Place, Brooklyn, N. Y., Great Lakes, Ill. HTA.

KOGER, E. B., Ensign, 1413 Massachusetts Ave., Washington, D. C. N. A. No. 649.

KOHLER, GERALD E., Student Officer, 104 East Green St., Champaign, Ill.

KONZE, JOHN E., Student Officer, 3419 Beech Ave., Baltimore, Md.

KOON, HENRY F., JR., Student Officer, Amboy Ave., Perth Amboy, N. J.

KOSACK, FRANCIS, Ensign.

KOUNTZE, HAROLD, Ensign, Col. Nat'l. Bank, Denver, Colo.

KRAFT, R. R., Student Officer, 212 Marion St., Oak Park, Ill. Mass. Inst. of Tech., Key West, Fla. HTA.

KRATZ, REGINALD P., Student Officer, 5066 East E St., Ontario, Cal. Personnel Office, Washington, D. C., Akron, Ohio.

KRAUSE, F. ARTHUR, Student Officer, 2307 University St., St. Louis, Mo. Mass. Inst. of Tech. HTA.

KREBS, ALLEN J., JR., Student Officer, Murphts Hotel, Richmond, Va.

KRIEDER, AARON S., JR., Student Officer, 51 N. 3rd St. Philadelphia, Pa. Mass. Inst. of Tech.

KRUEGER, E. A., War. Machinist, 2726 W. 16th St., Chicago, Ill.

KRUEGER, HAROLD H., Student Officer, 1950 Kenwood Parkway, Minneapolis, Minn.

KRUEGER, HARRY H., Student Officer, Utah Power & Light Co., Salt Lake City, Utah.

KRUG, CHARLES STEINWAY, Ensign, 200 West 71st St., New York City. Mass. Inst. of Tech., U. S. N. Torpedo Station, Key West, Miami, Pensacola, Marine Field, London. N. A. No. 1283. HTA.

KRUMRINE, C. S., Student Officer, 5037 Larchwood Ave., Philadelphia, Pa. Mass Inst. of Tech.

KRUPNICK, ALVIN J., Student Officer, 6113 North Broadway, St. Louis, Mo.

KRUSE, ALBERT, Ensign, 2212 Gilpin Ave., Wilmington, Del. Mass. Inst. of Tech., Key West, Pensacola. N. A. No. 2394.

KUEHNLE, CARL F., JR.

KUHN, JEROME H., Student Officer, Burlingham, Cal.

LAFERTY, EDGAR B.
Ensign
Nantasket Beach, Mass. M. I. T., Pensacola, Key West, Paris, Moutchic, L'Aber Vrach, Fr. N. A. No. 635. HTA.

LAGERQUIST, CARL S.
Machinist
701 Elwood Ave., N. Minneapolis, Minn. Columbia University, Cape May, N. J.

LAHMAN, PERCY E.
Student Officer
427 Buchanan St., Topeka, Kansas. Mass. Inst. of Tech., Great Lakes. HTA.

LAIRD, FRED LESLIE
Ensign
7 Clarendon Ave., Montpelier, Vermont. Mass. Inst. of Tech., Key West, Pensacola, N. A. No. 2314. HTA.

LAIRD, JOHN A.
Lieut. (j.g.)
243 Park Ave., East Orange, N. J. Mass. Inst. of Tech., Great Lakes, Washington, D. C., Key West. N. A. No. 1505. HTA.

LAIRD, JOHN EVANS
Ensign
Freehold, N. J. Mass. Inst. of Tech., Bay Shore, Pensacola, N. A. No. 1404. HTA.

LAMBETH, CHAS. E.
Ensign
Charlotte, N. C., Mass. Inst. of Tech., Rockaway Beach, Coco Sola. LTA.

LANCTO, J. WILLIAM.
Lieut. (j.g.)
24 Baker St., Lynn, Mass. Pensacola, Calshot, Eng., New Haven, Eng., Felixstowe, Eng., Queenstown, Ire. N. A. No. 221. HTA.

LANE, EDWARD W.
Ensign
363 75th St., Brooklyn, N. Y. Mass. Inst. of Tech., Key West, Miami, Pensacola. N. A. No. 2184. HTA.

LANE, MINOT E.
Ensign
60 Delaware Ave., Detroit, Mich. Seattle, San Diego, Pensacola. N. A. No. 2204. HTA.

LANE, WILLIAM B., Jr.
Ensign
1646 N. New Jersey St., Indianapolis, Ind. Mass. Inst. of Tech., Key West, Miami, Pensacola. N. A. No. 1159. HTA.

LANG, FRED P.
Lieut. (j.g.)
310 Ridge St., Newark, N. J. M. I. T., Bay Sh., Key West, Moutchic, Clermont, L'Aber Vrach. N. A. No. 422. HTA.

LANG, WALTER B.
Ensign
Rutledge, Del. Co., Pa. Mass. Inst. of Tech., Key West, Pensacola. N. A. No. 2308. HTA.

LANGLEY, WAYNE L.
Ensign
Durham, N. H. Mass. Inst. of Tech., Hampton Rds., Pensacola, Rockaway Beach. HTA.

LANKFORD, M.
Ensign
918 Graydon Ave., Norfolk, Va. Great Lakes, Mass. Inst. of Tech., Blue Hill, Boston. HTA.

LANPHER, HENRY C.
Ensign
43 Wildwood Terrace, Glen Ridge, N. J. Mass. Inst. of Tech., Bay Shore, Pensacola, Norfolk. N. A. No. 1264. HTA.

LARKIN, HAROLD P.
Ensign
Wilmington, Cal. Seattle, Key West, Pensacola. N. A. No. 1941. HTA.

LASHER, HERBERT
Ensign
Tivoli, N. Y. Tours, St. Raphael, Moutchic, Dunkerque, Fr. N. A. No. 763. HTA.

LATIMER, GEORGE T.
Student Officer
111 Pinckney St., Chester, S. C. Mass. Inst. of Tech., Pensacola. HTA.

LAUBENHEIM, C. P.
Student Officer
Volney Hotel, 410 Riverside Ave., Spokane, Wash. Seattle, Wash., San Diego, Cal. HTA.

THE FLYING FISH
Decorated for Regatta at Miami, February, 1919

LAUN, ALBERT C.
Student Officer
St. James, Missouri. Mass. Inst. of Tech., Key West. HTA.

LAVERTY, LEW F.
Ensign
Univ. Mich., Ann Arbor, Mich. Mass. Inst. of Tech., Great Lakes, Miami, Pensacola. N. A. No. 1378. HTA.

LAWLER, FRANK P.
Ensign
990 Geary St., San Francisco, Cal. Mass. Inst. of Tech., Miami. HTA.

LAWLER, LEO T.
Ensign
Coudersport, Penn. Mass. Inst. of Tech., Miami, Pensacola. N. A. No. 1954. HTA.

LAWLER, RICHARD H.
Ensign
345 E. 43 St., Chicago, Ill. Mass. Inst. of Tech., Great Lakes, Miami, Key West, Pensacola. N. A. No. 2559. HTA.

LAWLER, S. W., Jr.
Student Officer
Ft. Myers, Fla. Mass. Inst. of Tech., Cambridge. HTA.

LAWRENCE, H. J., Jr.
Lieut. (j.g.)
Merion Cricket Club, Haverford, Penn. Operations, Washington, D. C. HTA.

LAWRENCE, W. B., Jr.
Ensign
30 Rural Ave., Medford, Mass. Mass. Inst. of Tech., Key West, Miami, Pensacola, Hampton Roads. N. A. No. 1576. HTA.

LAWSON, EDWIN M.
Ensign
99 Cambridge St., Winchester, Mass. Mass. Inst. of Tech., Pensacola. HTA.

LAWTON, JOHN S.
Student Officer
Evans Mills, N. Y. Mass. Inst. of Tech., Cambridge, Mass. HTA.

LAYCOCK, CHAS. H.
Student Officer
Wilkesbarre, Pa. Mass. Inst. of Tech., Key West. HTA.

LEA, C. RUSSELL
Student Officer
White Plains, N. Y. Mass. Inst. of Tech., Cambridge HTA.

LEAK, VIRGIL T.
Ensign
Coconut Grove, Fla. Mass. Inst. of Tech., Hampton Roads, Pensacola, Miami, Moutchic, Fr., St. Trojan, Fr. N. A. No. 383.

LEARNED, N. J.
Lieut. (j.g.)
215 E. Church St., Elmira, N. Y. M. I. T., RNAS., Cranwell, Eng., Roehampton, RAF. Capel, Eng., Cape May, N. A. No. 673.

LEDERER, H. A., Jr.
Student Officer
1921 Eutaw Place, Baltimore, Md. Mass. Inst. of Tech., Cambridge. HTA.

LEEDS, GERALD E.
Ensign
68 Main St., Waterville, Me. School of Aerial Photography, Miami, Pensacola, Rockaway Beach.

LEEMING, JOHN, Jr.
Ensign
771 York St., Denver, Colo. Mass. Inst. of Tech., Miami, Fla. N. A. No. 1523. HTA.

LEFFEN, STANFORD
Ensign
421 Sergeant Ave., Joplin, Mo. Mass. Inst. of Tech., Bay Shore, L. I., Pensacola, Fla. N. A. No. 1853. HTA.

LEGGATT, H. B.
Ensign
640 Broadway, Lowell, Mass. Mass. Inst. of Tech., Miami, Pensacola, Hampton Rds. N. A. No. 1895. HTA.

LEHMAN, T. V.
Student Officer
1173 East 114 St., Cleveland, Ohio. Mass. Inst. of Tech., Cambridge. HTA.

LEIDIG, DONALD M.
Ensign
1730 La Loma Ave., Berkeley, Cal. Mass. Inst. of Tech., Miami, Pensacola. N. A. No. 1822. HTA.

LEISENRING, WM. J.
Lieut. (j.g.)
1856 Mintwood Place, Washington, D. C. Mass. Inst. of Tech., Bay Shore, Key West, Cape May. N. A. No. 451. HTA.

LESLIE, CONRAD C.
Ensign
1411 N. 16th St., Philadelphia, Pa. Mass. Inst. of Tech., Key West, Miami, Pensacola, Fla. N. A. No. 1662. HTA.

LESLIE, ARNETT W.
Ensign
2124 Fremont Ave., So. Minneapolis, Minn. Mass. Inst. of Tech., Great Lakes, Pensacola, Washington, D. C.

U. S. S. Seattle Picking up Wrecked R-6 in the Gulf of Mexico

LEVERICH, L. P.
Ensign
440 E. 19th St., Brooklyn, N. Y. Mass. Inst. of Tech., Miami, Key West, Pensacola. N. A. No. 2522. HTA.

LEWIS, E. DENCH
Ensign
308 Waverly Ave., Syracuse, N. Y. Mass. Inst. of Tech., Key West, Pensacola, Miami. N. A. No. 1265.

LEWIS, GEORGE H.
Student Officer
314 Kent Road, Cynwyd, Pa. Mass. Inst. of Tech., Miami, Key West. HTA.

LEWIS, HAMILTON A.
Ensign
Hastings, Mich. Pensacola, Fla.

LEWIS, PAUL SAXTON
Student Officer
55 East Mitchell St., Atlanta, Ga. Mass. Inst. of Tech. HTA.

LEWIS, P. F.
Ensign
754 Hackett Ave., Milwaukee, Wisconsin. Mass. Inst. of Tech., Pensacola, Rockaway, Akron. N. A. No. 1474. LTA.

(G)
LEWIS, RALPH R.
Lieut. (j.g.)
3302 North 16th St., Philadelphia, Pa. M. I. T., Pensacola, St. Inglevert, Moutchic, Killingholme. N. A. No. 252.

LEWIS, R. R., Jr.
Ensign
Frederick, Md. Mass. Inst. of Tech., Key West, Miami, Pensacola. N. A. No. 1948. HTA.

LIBBY, LEWIE E.
Ensign
637 Central Ave., East Orange, N. J. Mass. Inst. of Tech., Miami, Pensacola. N. A. No. 2208. HTA.

LIDE, B. M., Jr.
Student Officer
6102 Washington Ave., St. Louis, Mo. Mass. Inst. of Tech., Cambridge, Miami, Fla. HTA.

LILE, CHARLES T.
Ensign
First National Bank, Jackson, Tenn. Mass. Inst. of Tech., Miami, Pensacola, Wash., D. C., Morehead City. N. A. No. 1828. HTA.

LINDERMAN, G. B.
Ensign
River Bank, Beverly, N. J. Mass. Inst. of Tech., Key West, Miami, Pensacola. N. A. No. 1799. HTA.

LINE, CLARENCE S.
Student Officer
Westtown, N. Y. Mass. Inst. of Tech., Cambridge, Akron, Ohio. LTA.

LINSERT, ERNEST E.
Student Officer
124 Goden St., Belmont, Mass. Mass. Inst. of Tech., Cambridge. LTA.

LITTLE, GEORGE W.
Ensign
Wadesboro, N. C. Mass. Inst. of Tech., Key West. HTA.

LITTLE, JAMES A.
Ensign
Bramwell, W. Va. Mass. Inst. of Tech., Pensacola, Miami, Moutchic, Fr., Fromentine, Fr. N. A. No. 734. HTA.

LLOYD, F. C.
Ensign
Menominee, Mich. Columbia University. New York, Detroit

LOGAN, DANIEL N.
Ensign
21 Bates St., Washington, D. C. Mass. Inst. of Tech., Miami, Key West, Pensacola. N. A. No. 2585. HTA.

LOHRKE, O. E., Jr.
Ensign
101 Prospect St., East Orange, N. J. M. I. T., Pensa., Moutchic, Bosc. Dns. RAF., N. B. G. N. A. No. 348. HTA.

LOMBARD, RALPH D.
Ensign
76 Magnolia Terrace, Springfield, Mass. Mass. Inst. of Tech., Akron, Pensacola. N. A. No. 2659. LTA.

LONG, GEO. R.
Ensign
28 N. Head St., Carthage, Ill. Mass. Inst. of Tech., Miami, Pensacola, North Sydney, Nova Scotia. N. A. No. 1123. HTA.

LONG, LESLIE A.
Student Officer
127 W. High St., London, Ohio. Dunwoody Inst, Minn., Seattle, Great Lakes.

LOOKER, WALTER J.
Student Officer
1604 So. Delaware Ave., Mason City, Iowa. Great Lakes, Illinois. HTA.

LOTSPEICH, RALPH E.
Ensign
507 Toluca Ave., Alliance, Nebraska. Mass. Inst. of Tech., Miami, Pensacola. N. A. No. 2223. HTA.

ALL READY TO LET GO
Assistant Secretary of the Navy Roosevelt in the Car

LOTT, JOHN M.
Ensign
20 Mackay Place, Brooklyn, N. Y. Mass. Inst. of Tech., Key West, Miami, Pensacola. N. A. No. 1187. HTA.

LOUGHRIDGE, ED. W.
Ensign
17 North Mulberry St., Mansfield, Ohio. Mass. Inst. of Tech., Akron, Pensacola, Cape May. N. A. No. 1151. LTA.

LOVE, J. L.
Student Officer
Somerset, Ohio. Seattle, Washington. HTA.

LOVITT, JOHN V.
Student Officer
1311 So. 52nd St., W. Philadelphia, Pa. Mass. Inst. of Tech., Cambridge. HTA.

LOWMAN, A. M.
Ensign
614 Euclid Ave., Elmira, N. Y. Mass. Inst. of Tech., Akron, Hampton Roads, U. S. S. *Nevada*. LTA.

LOY NOLAN H.
Ensign,
Ligonier Ind. Mass. Inst., of Tech., Cambridge, Miami. N. A. No. 1520. HTA.

LUCCOCK, EMORY W.
Ensign
1245 Beall Ave., Wooster, Ohio. Mass. Inst. of Tech., Miami, Fla. N. A. No. 2051. HTA.

LUDLUM, THEO. T.
Ensign
1040 Northampton St., Holyoke, Mass. Mass. Inst. of Tech., Miami, Pensacola. N. A. No. 1722. HTA.

LUNDGREN, WM. E.
Ensign
901 St. Mark's Ave., Brooklyn, N. Y. Mass. Inst. of Tech., Miami, Pensacola. N. A. No. 2429. HTA.

LUSH, HAROLD I.
Ensign
3705 Texas St., San Diego, Cal. Mass. Inst. of Tech., Akron, Rockaway, Pelham Bay. LTA.

LUTZ, HOBART F.
Ensign
1218 Tenn. St., Lawrence, Kansas. Mass. Inst. of Tech., Miami, Pensacola. N. A. No. 2254. HTA.

LYNCH, JOHN PAUL
Student Officer
11 Woodbine St., Boston, Mass. Mass. Inst. of Tech., Cambridge. HTA.

LYNCH, JOSEPH B.
Lieut. (j.g.)
74 Garfield St., Cambridge, Mass. M. I. T., Key West, Miami, N. A. No. 1519. HTA.

LYNN, DAVID E.
Ensign
915 Mahoning Ave., Youngstown, Ohio. Mass. Inst. of Tech., Pensacola, Hampton Roads. N. A. No. 969.

LYON, MONTAGUE, Jr.
Student Officer
5865 Cates Ave., St. Louis, Mo. Dunwoody Inst., Minn., Miami, Fla. HTA.

LYON, NORMAN M.
Ensign
3842 Reading Rd., Cincinnati, Ohio. Mass. Inst. of Tech., Akron, Pensacola, Hampton Roads. LTA.

LYON, ROBERT F.
Ensign.
2410 Clarendon Rd., Brooklyn, N. Y. Bay Shore, Key West, Miami, Moutchic Hampton Rds. N. A. No. 507. HTA.

◈ ◈ ◈ ◈ ◈

LAFLEICHE, PIERRE, Ensign, Sheridan, Wyo. Seattle, Wash.; San Diego, Pensacola. N. A. No. 2310. HTA.

LAINE, HARRY N., Ensign, 913 East Third St., Los Angeles. Mass. Inst. of Tech., Pensacola, Hampton Roads. HTA.

LAING, FRED M., 707 S. Park Ave., Saginaw, Mich. Mass. Inst. of Tech., Pensacola, Fla.

◈ ◈ ◈ ◈ ◈

LAIRD, CECIL W., Lieut. (j.g.), 1202 Westover Ave., Norfolk, Va. N. A. No. 973.

LAIRD, J. R., DUNHAM, Ensign, 54 New Main St., Haverstraw, N. Y. Rockaway, Pensacola, Hampton Rds. LTA.

LAKE, ALBERT C., Ensign, Hamstead, N. H. N. A. No. 746.

LAKE, R. V., Ensign, 2032 Park Road, N. W., Washington, D. C.

LALLY, FRANCIS S., Student Officer, 53 Olney St., Dorchester, Mass.

LAMB, FRANK, Ensign, 2130 26th St., Sacramento, Cal. N. A. No. 1674.

LAMBERTON, LEWIS M., Student Officer, 1327 Liberty St., Franklin, Pa.

LAMBERTY, JOHN J., Ensign, 331 W. Wilson Ave., Glendale, Cal.

LAMKEY, FREDERICK M., War. Machinist.

LAMPERTI, FRANCISCO A., Student Officer, 8 Court St.. Stapleton St., New York.

LAMPLEY, IRA T., Student Officer, Eufaula, Ala.

LANDER, A. A., Ensign. N. A. No. 1936.

LANDES, WARWICK B., Student Officer, Box 713 Beaumont, Tex.

LANDON, GEORGE, Student Officer, 3812 N. Kedvale Ave., Chicago, Ill.

LANDON, H. R., Ensign, 19 East 53rd St., New York City.

LANDREGAN, WM. E., Ensign, 59 Plaza Drive, Berkeley, Cal. N. A. No. 1708.

LANE, DANIEL D., Student Officer, 5717 Blackstone Ave., Chicago, Ill.

LANE, FRANKLIN K., JR., Lieut. (j.g.), 1866 Wyoming Ave., Washington, D. C.

LANE, OLIVER F., Ensign.

LANG, ROBERT M., Student Officer, 47 W. North Ave., Atlanta, Ga.

LANGDON, JOHN, Student Officer, 719 5th Ave., New York City. Mass. Inst. of Tech., Dunwoody Inst., Minn. HTA.

LANGE, K. L., Lieut. (j.g.). N. A. No. 548.

LANGFORD, R., War. Machinist.

LANGLEY, LESTER L., Student Officer, Madbury Road, Durham, N. H. Mass. Inst. of Tech. HTA.

LASSING, ROBERT B., Student Officer, St. Petersburg, Fla. Mass. Inst. of Tech. HTA.

LATIMER, HOMER H., Student Officer, Idlewild and Webster Sts., Dayton, O.

LATTA, CHAS., War. Machinist, 610 E. Pike St., Seattle, Wash.

LATTIMORE, HALBERT S., Student Officer, 2277 Lipscomb St., Fort Worth, Tex., Seattle, Washington; San Diego. HTA.

LAUGHLIN, DONALD S., Student Officer, 136 Park St., Portland, Me. Mass. Inst. of Tech., Miami. HTA.

LAURENCE, E. G. G., Lieut. (j.g.), 856 Locust St., Cincinnati, O. Mass. Inst. of Tech., Buffalo.

LAURENCE, MORTIMER, Ensign.

LAVERENTS, A., Ensign.

LA VIE, RICHARD E., Ensign, Spring Lake, New Jersey, Mass. Inst. of Tech., Key West, Miami, Pensacola, Montauk, Hampton Roads. N. A. No. 1052. HTA.

LAWLER, R. H., Ensign, 345 E. 43rd St., Chicago, Ill. Mass. Inst. of Tech., Great Lakes, Miami, Key West, Pensacola. HTA.

LAWRENCE, GEO. F., JR., Lieut. (j.g.), 142 East 40th St., New York City.

LAWRENCE, J. B., Ensign, 666 Lincoln Ave., St. Paul, Minn. N. A. No. 580.

LAWRENCE, J. W., Ensign, 1455 North Highland Ave., Pittsburgh, Pa. Great Lakes, Pensacola.

LAWRENCE, MALCOLM R., Student Officer, 27 Montgomery Pl., Brooklyn, N. Y.

LAWRENCE, R. T., Ensign, 52 Kipp Ave., Rutherford, N. J. N. A. No. 1671.

LAWRENCE, WALTER H., Student Officer, Cameron, Tex. Seattle, Washington. HTA.

LAWSON, EDWIN M., Ensign, 99 Cambridge St., Winchester, Mass.

LAWSON, JOEL S., Ensign.

LAYTON, DAVID, Student Officer, Oyster Bay, Long Island, N. Y.

LEACH, PAUL R., Student Officer, 1507 N. Meridian St., Indianapolis, Ind.

LEARNED, HAROLD G., Ensign, 53 Washington St., Meriden, Conn. Mass. Inst. of Tech., Buffalo, College Point, N. Y.

LEARY NELVILLE, Lieut. (j.g.), 235 E. German St., Baltimore, Md.

LEAVENWORTH, EDGAR C., Ensign, Box 55, Cambridge, Mass.

LEE, CLARENCE J., War. Machinist, 183 Hunterdon St., Newark, N. J. Columbia Univ., Philadelphia, Detroit, Pauillac, St. Trojan.

LEE, HORACE J., Ensign, Catholic University, Washington, D. C.

LEE, LAWRENCE W., Ensign, Detroit Athletic Club, Detroit, Mich. Washington, D. C., Fond du Lac, Wisc. N. A. No. 291. HTA.

LEE, LEWIS H., Lieut. (j.g.), 5043 Washington Ave., St. Louis, Mo. Mass. Inst. of Tech., Pensacola, Killingholme. N. A. No. 291. HTA.

LEE, R. D., Student Officer, 2215 Main St., Dallas, Tex. Mass. Inst. of Tech., Akron, Ohio. LTA.

LEE, T. B., Ensign, 821 West 178th St., New York City. N. A. No. 697.

LEE, WALTER A., Ensign, Melvern Tex. N. A. No. 2145.

LEEK, WM. A., Student Officer, 72 Seaman Ave., New York, N. Y.

LEFKOWITZ, DAVID, Student Officer, 687 Preble Ave., Pittsburgh, Pa.

LEGRAND, LEON, Student Officer, Colonial Ave., Hotel Jamaica, L. I., N. Y.

LEHAN, R. A., Ensign, Taunton, Mass. N. A. No. 277.

LEHMAN, FRANKLIN S., Student Officer, Gettysburg, Ohio.

LEHR, HENRY S., Ensign, Y. M. C. A., Wilmington, Del. N. A. No. 2395.

LEHRKE, O. E., Ensign, 101 Prospect Ave., East Orange, N. J. N. A. No. 348.

LEISENRING, E. B., Lieut. (j.g.) N. A. No. 364.

LEISTNER, AUGUST, Ensign, 707 Press, Binghamton, N. Y. N. A. No. 2304.

LELAND, A. F., Student Officer, 141 Archer Ave., Mt. Vernon, N. J. Mass. Inst. of Tech.

LEMANSKI, JOHN A., Ensign.

LENNOX, EDWARD H., Student Officer, Psi Upsilon House, 4532 18th Ave., N. E., Seattle, Wash.

LEONARD, A. B., Lieut. (j.g.), 2811 St. Paul St., Baltimore, Md. Mass. Inst. of Tech., Hampton Roads, Washington, London, Eng., Paris, Moutchic, Paimboeuf, Key West, Fla.

LEONARD, HARRY E., Student Officer, 108 Carnegie Ave., East Orange, N. J.

LEONHARD, E. R., Ensign.

LEONHARD, GEORGE J., JR., Student Officer, 324 Bakemer St., Marshfield, Wis.

LEONHARD, JOHN T., Student Officer, 310 Paulison Ave., Passaic, N. J. Mass. Inst. of Tech. HTA.

LEPPLA, W. J., Student Officer, 1559 Marion St., Denver, Colo.

LESLIE, GAYON G., Ensign, 4352 Drexel Blvd., Chicago, Ill.

LESLIE, JOHN L., Ensign, 306 South 17th St., Allentown, Pa. Mass. Inst. of Tech., Seattle, Wash.

LESTER, ROBERT R., Lieut. (j.g.), 3400 Campbell St., Kansas City, Mo. Mass. Inst. of Tech., Key West, Fla. N. A. No. 1473.

LETZKUS, ELMER ANTON, Ensign. N. A. No. 1634.

LEWIS, H. P., Ensign, 233 1st Park Ave., Springfield, Mass. N. A. No. 493. N. A. No. 1737.

LEWIS, HARLEY B., Leiut. (j.g.).

LEWIS, ISAAC C., Student Officer, 189 E. Main St., Meriden, Conn.

LEWIS, JAMES K., Student Officer, 12 S. 13th St., Minneapolis, Minn.

LEWIS, JOHN A., JR., Student Officer, 1133 8th Ave., Columbus, Ga.

LEWIS, LUDWIG C., Student Officer, 2127 Spruce St., Philadelphia, Pa. Mass. Inst. of Tech. HTA.

LEWIS, ROBT. F., Lieut. (j.g.), 164 Atlantic Ave., Swampscott, Mass. N. A. No. 1474.

LIBBY, PHILIP ALLAN, Ensign, 109 Main St., Gorham, Me. Mass. Inst. of Tech., Miami, Key West, Bay Shore, Pensacola. N. A. No. 2443. HTA.

LIEHR, HARRY, Student Officer, 411 North Noble St., Indianapolis, Ind. Mass. Inst. of Tech., Cambridge. HTA.

LIFFEN, STANFORD, Ensign, 421 Sergeant Ave., Joplin, Me. Mass. Inst. of Tech., Bayshore, Pensacola. HTA.

LIGHT, GEORGE E., Student Officer, 234 King St., Stratford, Conn. Mass. Inst. of Tech. HTA.

LIGHTNER, FRED E., War. Boatswain.

LILE, JOHN A., Student Officer.

LINDAUER, ALBERT J., Student Officer, 5722 Michigan Ave., Chicago, Ill.

LINDEMER, GEORGE F., Student Officer, 715 E. Laurel St., Syracuse, N. Y.

LINDER, JOHN, JR., Student Officer, York St., Canton, Mass. Mass. Inst. of Tech., Pensacola. HTA.

LINDESMITH, O. R., Student Officer.

LINGARD, E., Ensign, 27 W. 44th St., New York City. N. A. No. 540.

LINDSAY, DONALD E., Ensign, 4520 Spruce St., Philadelphia, Pa.

LINDSAY, JEAN C., Ensign. N. A. No. 1848.

LINDSEY, WILLIS C., Student Officer, Washington, Ga.

LIPPMAN, ALBERT F., JR., Lieut. (j.g.), 1056 Webster Ave., Chicago, Ill.

LIPPMAN, HARRY, War. Boatswain.

LIST, DANIEL C., Student Officer, 1844 Columbia Rd., Washington, D. C.

LITCHFIELD, ALLYNE C., Ensign, 200 Bay State Rd., Boston, Mass.

LITTLE, CHAS. K., Ensign.

LITTLE, HENRY, JR., Student Officer, 493 Commonwealth Ave., Boston, Mass.

LITTLE, JOHN C., Ensign.

LITTLETON, C. H. S., JR., Ensign, 555 South Grand Ave., Pasadena, Cal. Mass. Inst. of Tech., Akron, Pensacola, and Chatham, Mass. N. A. No. 1555. LTA.

LIVINGSTON, J. L., Ensign.

LIVINGSTON, RICHARD, Ensign, 540 W. James St., Lancaster, Pa. Mass. Inst. of Tech., Miami, Pensacola. N. A. No. 2206. HTA.

LIVINGSTONE, S. R., Lieut. (j.g.), 40 Eliot St., Detroit, Mich. Washington, D. C. LTA.

LLOYD, EDWARD S., Student Officer, 5620 Cates Ave., St. Louis, Mo.

LLOYD, H. W., War. Mach., 106 Saratoga Ave., Yonkers, N. Y.

LLOYD, J. HUBERT B., Student Officer, 221 Clayton St., San Francisco, Cal. Univ. of Washington, Seattle. HTA.

LLOYD, WALTER P., Student Officer, 1422 Mass. Ave., Washington, D. C.

LOCKE, JOHN L., Student Officer, 1705 13th South, Seattle, Wash. Seattle, San Diego, Cal. HTA.

LOCKMAN, D. E., Ensign.

LOCKWOOD, J. E., Ensign, 38 W. Johnson St., Germantown, Phila., Pa. N. A. No. 1230.

LOER, WILLIAM P., Ensign, 528 S. 14th St., Newcastle, Ind. Mass. Inst. of Tech., Miami, and Pensacola. N. A. No. 1636. HTA.

LOGAN, W. V., Ensign, 1790 Broadway, New York. Great Lakes, Ill.; Pensacola, Fla. HTA.

LOHMAN, FREDERICK W., Student Officer, 158 East Market St., Akron, Ohio.

LOKKER, CLARENCE A., Student Officer, 100 E. 9th St., Holland, Mich. Dunwoody Inst., Minn. HTA.

LONG, CARL HERMAN, Student Officer, 444 Morris Ave., Elizabeth, N. J.

LONG, HERBERT J., Student Officer, 209 E. Jefferson St., Waverly, Iowa.

LONG, MATT RANSOM, Student Officer, Roxboro, N. Car. Mass. Inst. of Tech. HTA.

LONG, PAUL W., Student Officer, 1435 Sixth Ave., Huntington, W. Va.

LOOMIS, RALPH L., Ensign, Bedford, Mass. French Aviation Schools, Dunkirk, Eastleigh. N. A. No. 578. HTA.

LORD, WALTER V., Student Officer, 1033 Avon Place, South Pasadena, Cal.

LORDLY, L. C., Ensign, 308 W. 32d St., New York City.

LORRIMER, ROBT. E., Ensign, 71 West Boston Blvd., Detroit, Mich. Mass. Inst. of Tech., Key West and Miami. N. A. No. 1522. HTA.

LOSE, RALPH D., Ensign, 1217 Oakdale Drive, Ft. Wayne, Ind. Mass. Inst. of Tech., Miami, Pensacola. N. A. No. 1721. HTA.

LOUD, EDWARD C., Ensign.

LOVE, ALFRED H., Student Officer, 764 Putnam Ave., Brooklyn, N. Y. Mass. Inst. of Tech. HTA.

LOVE, W. C., Student Officer, Fremont, Ohio.

LOVELACE, L. M., Ensign.

LOVERING, THOMAS S., Student Officer, 1464 Summit Ave., St. Paul, Minn.

LOVERING, W. K., Student Officer, 66 First Ave., Salt Lake City, Utah. Seattle. HTA.

LOW, GILES J., Student Officer, 193 Sterling Place, Brooklyn, N. Y.

LOWE, H. B., Student Officer, 705 St. Clair Ave., Cleveland, Ohio. Mass. Inst. of Tech. HTA.

LOWE, WILLIAM B., Student Officer, 1526 Bolton St., Baltimore, Md.

LUDINGTON, D. T., Ensign, Clovelly, Ardmore, Pa. N. A. No. 2162.

LUDINGTON, H. J., Ensign, Holley, New York. Mass. Inst. of Tech., Key West, Miami, Moutchic, Camp Malpensa, Northern Bombing Squadron, Italy. N. A. No. 1455. HTA.

LUDLOW, GEO. H., Lieut. (j.g.), 1203 Forest Ave., Evanston, Ill. Mass. Inst. of Tech., Pensacola, Lake Bolsena, Porto Corsini, Venice, Bay Shore. N. A. No. 342. HTA.

LUFKIN, C. F., Lieut. (j.g.), Care of E. C. Lufkin, Texas Co., N. Y. N. A. No. 129.

LUKENS, JAMES W., Ensign, Crum Lynne, Pa. N. A. No. 2326.

LUMPKIN, R. A., Ensign, 101 Wabash, Ave., Mattoon, Ill. Mass. Inst. of Tech., Akron, Pensacola. N. A. No. 1865. LTA.

LUNDIN, ERICK E., Student Officer, 2806 No. Francisco Ave., Chicago, Ill.

LUNT, DUDLEY C., Ensign, 135 Brackett St., Portland, Me. Mass. Inst. of Tech., Akron and Hampton Roads. U. S. S. Arizona. LTA.

LYLE, WESLEY B., Ensign, Idaho Falls, Idaho. Mass Inst. of Tech., Miami and Pensacola. N. A. No. 1986. HTA.

LYLES, BERRY S., Student Officer, 912 Palmetto Bldg,. Columbia, S. C.

LYMAN, CARL, Student Officer, 217 East Capitol St., Washington, D. C.

LYMAN, W. CLARK, Ensign, 118 N. Fourth St., Easton, Pa. Mass. Inst. of Tech., Miami and Pensacola. N. A. No. 2135. HTA.

LYNCH, CECIL J., Student Officer, Lokota, N. D.

LYNCH, HAROLD VINCENT, Student Officer, 622 Wesley Avenue, Ocean City, N. J. Mass. Inst. of Tech. HTA.

LYNCH, JOHN, Student Officer, 3325 Pecos St., Denver, Colo.

LYNCH, JOHN H., Student Officer, 25 Logan St., Lawrence, Mass.

LYNCH, KENNETH R., Ensign, 1236 Sherman St., Alameda, Cal. Mass. Inst. of Tech., Miami, Pensacola. N. A. No. 2023. HTA.

LYON, I. W., Ensign, Larchmont, N. Y. No. 1155.

LYON, ROBERT G., Ensign, 10 E. 58th St., New York, N. Y. Mass. Inst. of Tech., Miami, Pensacola, Norfolk. N. A. No. 1860.

LYON, ROSSMORE D., Lieut. (j.g.), South Road, Poughkeepsie, N. Y. Mass. Inst. of Tech., Key West, Pensacola-Bay Shore. N. A. No. 968. HTA.

LYON, STUART G., Student Officer, 80 Jewett Ave., Buffalo, N. Y.

LYONS, JOHN A., Student Officer, 51 Putnam St., Somerville, Mass.

HANGARS AT AKRON

McBRIDE, GEO. W.
Student Officer
East Ave., Brighton Sta., Rochester, N. Y. Mass. Inst. of Tech., Key West. HTA.

McBROOM, EARL H.
Ensign
703 8th St., Laramie, Wyo. Mass. Inst. of Tech., Miami, Pensacola. N. A. No. 2069. HTA.

McCAHAN, DAVID
Ensign
214 Second St., Huntingdon, Penn. Mass. Inst. of Tech., Miami, Pensacola. N. A. No. 2476. HTA.

McCANDLESS, DAVID
Ensign
4740 Bayard St., Pittsburgh, Pa. Mass. Inst. of Tech., Miami, Pensacola. N. A. No. 1661. HTA.

(C) Underwood & Underwood, N. Y.

ZEPPELIN OUT ON PATROL THE FIRST FEW DAYS OF THE WAR

McCELVEY, GEO. EDW.
Ensign
Temple, Tex. Mass. Inst. of Tech., Key West, Pensacola. N. A. No. 2247. HTA.

McCLELLAND, G. H.
Ensign
1470 Arthur Ave., Lakewood, Ohio. Mass. Inst. of Tech., Pensacola, Miami. HTA.

McCLELLAND, R. L.
Student Officer
Western Springs, Ill. Dunwoody, Miami. HTA.

McCORMICK, A. H.
Ensign
631 Rush St., Chicago, Ill. Mass. Inst. of Tech., Pensacola, Queenstown, Wexford, Ire. N. A. No. 895. HTA.

McCORMICK, C. E.
Student Officer
RFD No. 2 Shepherdsville, Ky. Mass. Inst. of Tech. HTA.

McCORMICK, D. W.
Student Officer
220 E. Exchange St., Owosso, Mich. Mass. Inst. of Tech. LTA.

McCOWN, THOS. C.
Ensign
Richmond, Ky. Mass. Inst. of Tech., Miami, Pensacola, Hampton Roads. N. A. No. 1270. HTA.

McCOY, FRANK
Boatswain
25 S. Pine St., Indianapolis, Ind. Pensacola, Camp Saufly, Pensacola.

McCREA, D. P.
Ensign
618 Story St., Boone, Iowa. Dunwoody, Miami, Pensacola. N. A. No. 2596. HTA.

McCREERY, G. W.
Student Officer
Fall River, Mass. Mass. Inst. of Tech. HTA.

McDANIEL, RUEL R.
Ensign
Slocum, Tex. Mass. Inst. of Tech., Bay Shore, Miami, Key West, Pensacola. N. A. No. 2434. HTA.

McDONALD, W. C. F.
Ensign
536 W. Jefferson St., Ft. Wayne, Ind. Mass. Inst. of Tech., Key West, Pensacola. N. A. No. 1427. HTA.

McDOWELL, C. R.
Ensign
Buckhorn, Ky. Mass. Inst. of Tech., Pensacola, Key West. HTA.

McDOWELL, J. IRVING
Student Officer
166 Eastwood Ave., Providence, R. I. Newport, Mass. Inst. of Tech., Bay Shore. HTA.

McDOWELL, RICHARD
Ensign
619 West 175th St., New York City. Mass. Inst. of Tech., Bay Shore, Brunswick, Ga., Miami. N. A. No. 2060. HTA.

McEVOY, J. H., Jr.
Student Officer
202 McGowen Ave., Houston, Tex. Univ. of Wash. Seattle, Wash. HTA.

McFERREN, WM.
Student Officer
Hoopeston, Ill. Mass. Inst. of Tech., Akron, Pensacola. LTA.

McGILL, MAX P.
Ensign
Central City, Nebraska. Mass. Inst. of Tech., Pensacola, Miami. N. A. No. 1146. HTA.

McGINTY, W. B.
Ensign
Lowell, Okla. Mass. Inst. of Tech., Key West, Pensacola. N. A. No. 1724. HTA.

McGOVERN, M. J.
Ensign
1535 Penn. St., Denver, Colo. Seattle, San Diego. HTA.

McGREGOR, STUART M.
Ensign
Coleman, Tex. Mass. Inst. of Tech., Miami, Pensacola. N. A. No. 2500. HTA.

McGUIRE, JOS. F.
Ensign
512 Beveridge St., Carbondale, Ill. Mass. Inst. of Tech., Akron, Rockaway. LTA.

McINTOSH, WM. C.
Ensign
115 South Davis St., Santa Rosa, Cal. Mass. Inst. of Tech., Key West, Miami, Pensacola. N. A. No. 1357. HTA.

McINTYRE, HARRY M.
Ensign
174 Bowdoin St., Springfield, Mass. Akron, Castletown, Ire., Plymouth, Eng. LTA.

(C) *Comm. Pub. Inf.*

SHAM BATTLE AT KEY WEST

McKAIG. ALVIN W.
Lieut. (j.g.)
411 9th St., Ocean City, N. J. Mass. Inst. of Tech., Miami, Pensacola, Anacostia, Washington, D. C. N. A. No. 1999. HTA.

McKAY, EARLE D.
Ensign
3109 Park Ave., Minneapolis, Minn. Dunwoody, San Diego, Pensacola. N. A. No. 2268. HTA.

McKENNA, VIRGIL V.
Ensign
Westbury, L. I. Mass. Inst. of Tech., Bay Shore, Pensacola, Philadelphia. N. A. No. 1126. HTA.

McKENZIE, K. C.
Student Officer
1414 Watchung Ave., Plainfield, N. J. Mass. Inst. of Tech., Bay Shore. HTA.

McKENZIE, W. C.
Ensign
Bannockburn, S. C. Mass. Inst. of Tech., Key West, Miami, Pensacola, Hampton Roads. N. A. No. 1263. HTA.

McKIM, HORTON A.
Ensign
Box 512, Tonopah, Nev. Mass. Inst. of Tech., Key West, Miami, Pensacola. N. A. No. 1556. HTA.

McKINNEY, W. P.
Ensign
4 Temple Court Apt., Knoxville, Tenn., M.I.T., Miami. Moutchic, Campaing", N. B. G., Malpensa. N. A. No 1454. HTA.

McKINNON, RALPH T.
Ensign
516 W. 12th St., Sioux Falls, S. D. Seattle, San Diego, Pensacola. N. A. No. 2267. HTA.

McKNIGHT, H. W.
Ensign
218 S. Third St., Fulton, N. Y. Mass. Inst. of Tech., Miami, Pensacola. N. A. No. 2455. HTA.

McKONE, CARL S.
Student Officer
15 Center Place, Dubuque, Iowa. Mass. Inst. of Tech., Miami. HTA.

McKOWN, RICHARD E.
Ensign
Boothbay Harbor, Maine. Mass. Inst. of Tech., Miami, Pensacola. HTA.

McLAUGHLIN, GUY
Lieut. (j.g.)
Lynchburg, Virginia. Pensacola, San Diego. N. A. No. 90. HTA.

McLELLAN, C. A.
Ensign
42 Massasoit St., Mattapan, Boston, Mass. Mass. Inst. of Tech., Hampton Roads, Pensacola, Bay Shore, N. A. 492. HTA.

McMAHON, A. W.
Ensign
112½ Whitney Avenue, Hampden, Conn. Mass. Inst. of Tech., Miami, Pensacola, Key West. N. A. No. 2289. HTA.

McMASTER, JOHN D.
Ensign
39 Bentley Ave., Jersey City, N. J. Miami, New York. HTA.

McMURRAIN, S. B.
Ensign
Cusseta, Ga. Cazaux, Fr. Moutchic, Fr., Pensacola. N. A. No. 2663. HTA.

McMURRAY, JOHN W.
Ensign
645 Clackamas St., Portland, Ore. Mass. Inst. of Tech., San Diego, Pensacola. N. A. No. 1432. HTA.

McNALLY, LEO A.
Lieut. (j.g.)
2666 N. Main St., Fall River, Mass. Akron, Rockaway, Queenstown, Castletownbere, Ire., Pauillac, Fr. HTA.

McNAMARA, CHAS. G.
Student Officer
10 Lake St., Hammondsport, N. Y. Mass. Inst. of Tech., Boston, Miami. HTA.

McPHERSON, L. H.
Ensign
Martell, Cal. Mass. Inst. of Tech., Key West, Miami, Pensacola. N. A. No. 2036. HTA.

McTERNAN, E. K.
Ensign
1315 East 127th St., Brooklyn, N. Y. Mass. Inst. of Tech., Bay Shore, Hampton Roads, Pensacola. N. A No. 1699. HTA.

MACCALMAN, D. J.
Ensign
Lakemont, N. Y. M. I. T., Key West, Miami, Pensacola, Coco Solo, Washington, Akron. N. A. No. 1747. LTA., HTA.

MACCHANDLER, FITZ
Ensign
55 Jersey St., San Francisco, Cal. Seattle, Wash., Key West, Miami, Pensacola. N. A. No. 2139. HTA.

MACDONALD, A. G.
Lieut. (j.g.)
41 Liberty St., Barre, Vermont. M. I. T., Pensa., Ft. Worth, Killingholme, Dundee. N. A. No. 275. HTA.

THE REMAINS OF A CRASH ON THE HOIST

MACDONALD, GEO. R.
Ensign
17 Copen St., Dorchester, Mass. Mass. Inst. of Tech., Bay Shore, Pensacola, Hampton Roads. N. A. No. 1791. HTA.

MACDONALD, G. G.
Ensign
665A 39th St., Oakland, Cal. Mass. Inst. of Tech., Akron, Hampton Roads, Pensacola. N. A. No. 2478. LTA.

MACK, JULIAN J.
Ensign
168 W. Thompkins St., Galesburg, Ill., Dunwoody, Miami, Key West, Pensacola. N. A. No. 2561. HTA.

MACKENZIE, H. L.
Student Officer
Hopkinton, Mass. Mass. Inst. of Tech. HTA.

MACKIE, JULIAN J.
Ensign
2537 Hearst Ave., Berkeley, Cal. Mass. Inst. of Tech., Key West, Miami, Pensacola. N. A. No. 1374. HTA.

MACMEEKIN, D. W.
Student Officer
302 So. 28th St., Lincoln, Neb. Dunwoody, Miami, Key West.

MACNEIL, CHAS.
Ensign
RFD. No. 162, Menlo Park, Cal. Seattle, San Diego, Pensacola. N. A. No. 2327. HTA.

MACY, E. DWIGHT
Ensign
Lynnville, Jasper Co., Iowa. Mass. Inst. of Tech., Key West. N. A. No. 1693. HTA.

MADIGAN, JOHN W.
Ensign
15 Clark's Hill Ave., Stamford, Conn. Mass. Inst. of Tech., Bay Shore, Pensacola, London, Eng. N. A. No. 1259. HTA.

MAGEE, WM. A., Jr.
Ensign
5 Montgomery St., San Francisco, Cal. Mass. Inst. of Tech., San Pedro, San Diego, Pensacola. N. A. No. 1399. HTA.

MAGENNIS, FRANK T.
Ensign
79 Atlas St., Akron, Ohio. Mass. Inst. of Tech., Akron, Pensacola, Coco Solo. LTA.

MAGUIRE, J. RUSSELL
Student Officer
188 Hobart St., Meriden, Conn. Mass. Inst. of Tech., Pensacola. HTA.

MAGUIRE, LEO J., Jr.
Student Officer
3105 S. Figueroa St., Los Angeles, Cal. M. I. T., Miami, Cape May, Pelham, New London. HTA.

MAHONEY, JOHN J., Jr.
Ensign
2654 Washington St., Roxbury, Mass. Mass. Inst. of Tech., Miami, Key West, Pensacola. N. A. No. 2634. HTA.

MAINA, WM. V.
Student Officer
6711 Parnell Ave., Chicago, Ill. Dunwoody, Minn., Great Lakes, Seattle. HTA.

MALCOMSON, GEO. W.
Ensign
116 La Salle, Boulevard, Detroit, Mich. Mass. Inst. of Tech., Key West, Miami, Pensacola. N. A. No. 2031. HTA.

MALLORY, N. W.
Ensign
718 Cherry St., Santa Rosa, Cal. Seattle, San Diego, Cal., Pensacola. N. A. No. 2084. HTA.

MANCHESTER, H. L.
Ensign
133 North Main St., Attleboro, Mass. Mass. Inst. of Tech., Miami, Pensacola. N. A. No. 2137. HTA.

MANN, WILLIAM
Ensign
455 Fort Washington Ave., New York City. School of Aerial Photography, Miami, Navy Yard, Phila., Anacostia.

MANN, YULEE W.
Lieut. (j.g.)
Pensacola, Fla. Mass. Inst. of Tech., Washington, D. C.

MARBURY, LEONARD
Ensign
1208 15th St., Washington, D. C. M. I. T, Hamp. Rds., Key West, Miami, Pensa., Moorehead City, Anacostia. N. A. No. 1232. HTA.

MARIS, ARTHUR S.
Ensign
99 W. Lacrosse Ave., Lansdowne, Penn. Seattle, San Diego, Pensacola. N.A. No. 2318. HTA.

MARKLE, GEO. B., Jr.
Ensign
Hazleton, Pa. Mass. Inst. of Tech. (Instructor), U. of Wash., Seattle (Instructor).

MARKS, ROBERT W
Student Officer
Medina Road, Akron, Ohio. Mass. Inst. of Tech., Cambridge. LTA.

CHRISTMAS MORNING AT MIAMI BEACH, FLORIDA
Visiting Blimp from Key West

MARKTHALER, A. F.
Ensign
222 Rahway Ave., Elizabeth, N. J. Mass. Inst. of Tech., Key West, Miami, Pensacola. N. A. No. 1973. HTA.

MARLEY, JOHN S.
Machinist
33 East 53rd St.. Country Club Dist., Kansas City, Missouri. Columbia Univ., Great Lakes.

MARONEY, HUGH W.
Ensign
502 West St., Stillwater, Okla. Dunwoody, Miami, Key West, Pensacola. N. A. No. 2525. HTA.

MARRINELLI, VICTOR F.
Ensign
216 Maryland Ave., N. E., Washington, D. C. Mass. Inst. of Tech., Miami, Pensacola, Key West. N. A. No. 1223. HTA.

MARSCHAT, R. A.
Ensign
Ashley Falls, Mass. Mass. Inst. of Tech., Pelham Bay, Chatham, Pensacola. N. A. No. 1027. LTA.

MARSH, LUCIEN A.
Student Officer
400 Post St., San Francisco. Cal. Univ. of Wash., Seattle, Wash.

MARSHALL, HARRY L.
Student Officer
5921 Kenmore Ave., Chicago, Ill. Mass. Inst. of Tech., Miami. HTA.

MARSHALL, IRVING D.
Ensign
71 Summer St., Everett, Mass. Mass. Inst. of Tech., S. P. Petrel, Miami, Pensacola. N. A. No. 2417. HTA.

MARSHALL, L. P.
Lieut. (j.g.)
71 Summer St., Everett, Mass. Mass. Inst. of Tech., Bay Shore, Pensacola. N. A. No. 915.

MARSHALL, R. B.
Lieut. (j.g.)
1519 Shady Ave., Pittsburgh, Pa. M. I. T., Montauk, Rockaway, C. May, Hamp. Rds., Akron, Key West. N. A. No. 2605. LTA.

MARTIN, CHAS. H.
Student Officer
920 E. Oak St., New Albany, Ind. Dunwoody, Miami, Key West. HTA.

MARTIN, EDWARD
Lieut. (j.g.)
17 Adriance Ave., Poughkeepsie, N. Y. Mass. Inst. of Tech., Pensacola, Montauk, Hampton Roads. N. A. No. 663. HTA.

(L)

MARTIN, HORACE C.
Ensign
1572 Mass. Ave., Cambridge, Mass. Mass. Inst. of Tech., Key West, Miami, Pensacola. N. A. No. 1144. HTA.

MARTIN, LEROY V., Jr.
Ensign
1010 Tenth St., Miami, Fla. Mass. Inst. of Tech., Miami, Key West, Pensacola. N. A. No. 2562. HTA.

MARTIN, R. M.
Student Officer
212 Alamosa Ave., San Antonio, Tex. Seattle, Wash. HTA.

MARTIN, ROBERT R.
Student Officer
31 Prospect Ave., Larchmont, N. Y. Seattle, Wash. HTA.

MARTIN, M. SCOVELL
Ensign
32 Lincoln St., Glen Ridge, N. J. Mass. Inst. of Tech., Bay Shore, Pensacola, Squadron 6. HTA.

MARTIN, W. H.
Ensign
Laurens, S. C. Mass. Inst. of Tech., Miami, Key West, Pensacola. HTA.

MASON. GEORGE S.
Student Officer
119 Temple St., Fredonia, N. Y. Mass. Inst. of Tech., Miami. HTA.

MATHERS, JOHN L.
Student Officer
122 West Hemlock St., Hazleton, Pa. Mass. Inst. of Tech., Miami. HTA.

MATTERN, LEWIS H.
Student Officer
116 S. Williams St., Dayton, Ohio. Mass. Inst. of Tech., Key West. HTA.

MATTHEWS, ROBERT E.
Student Officer
1240 Union St., Brooklyn, N. Y. Dunwoody, Great Lakes, Washington, D. C. HTA.

MATTHIESSEN, R. P.
Ensign
4545 Drexel Blvd., Chicago, Ill. Bolsna, It., New London, Paris, Rome, It. N. A. No. 757.

MATTOX, W. LECKIE
Ensign
Newnan, Ga. Mass. Inst. of Tech., Key West, Pensacola. N. A. No. 2255. HTA.

AUSTRIAN CHASSE PLANE
Note Peculiar Inter-plane Strut Construction

MAUCK, FRANK W.
Ensign
P. O. Box 156, Princeton, Ind. Mass. Inst. of Tech., Miami, Pensacola. N. A. 1189. HTA.

MAXAM, SYLVESTER R.
Ensign
1760 Euclid St., Washington, D. C. Mass. Inst. of Tech., Miami, Pensacola. N. A. No. 1553. HTA.

MAXION, EMIL E., Jr.
Student Officer
462 Fulton St., Jamaica, N. Y. Miami, Brest, Fr. LTA.

MAXWELL, F. R., Jr.
Lieut. (j.g.)
31 Court St., Dedham. Mass. Mass. Inst. of Tech, Pensacola. N. A. No. 2013. LTA.

MAXWELL, FRED R.
Lieut. (j.g.)
2703 6th St., Tuscaloosa, Ala. Pensacola. N. A. No. 2125.

MAXWELL, L. H., Jr.
Student Officer
2703 6th St., Tuscaloosa, Ala. Mass. Inst. of Tech., HTA.

MAXWELL, R. C.
Student Officer
123 Park Drive, Raleigh, N. C. Mass. Inst. of Tech., Miami. HTA.

MAXWELL, WALLACE
Student Officer
120 Newton St., Seattle, Wash. Univ. Wash., Seattle. HTA.

MAYTHAM, THOMAS E.
Ensign
685 Richmond Ave., Buffalo, N. Y. Mass. Inst. of Tech., Akron, Key West, Rockaway. N. A. No. 1544. LTA.

MEAD, ROGER R.
Ensign
4151 Montview Blvd., Denver, Colo. Seattle, San Diego. HTA.

MEADOR, LEWIS E.
Student Officer
Drury College, Springfield, Mo. Great Lakes. HTA.

MEGARGEE, B. J.
Student Officer
708 Madison Ave., Scranton, Pa. Mass. Inst. of Tech. HTA.

MELCHER, BURTON W.
Ensign
216 West Gilman St., Madison, Wis. Dunwoody Inst., Miami, Pensacola. N. A. No. 2367. HTA.

MELLEN, G. F., Jr.
Student Officer
Kingston Pike, Knoxville, Tenn. Univ. Washington, Seattle. HTA.

MELLON, RICHARD K.
Student Officer
6500 Fifth Ave., Pittsburgh, Pa. Great Lakes. HTA.

MENZIES, JOHN C.
Lieut. (j.g.)
194 Orange Street, New Haven, Conn. Columbia Univ., Pauillac, Eastleigh, Dunkerque, Zeebrugge, N. B. G. HTA.

MERRILL, RUSSEL H.
Lieut. (j.g.)
1310 Pleasant St., Des Moines, Iowa. Mass. Inst. of Tech., Key West, Cape May. N. A. No. 469. HTA.

MERRIMAN, E. A.
Ensign
6936 Stewart Ave., Chicago, Ill. Dunwoody, Miami, Key West, Pensacola. N. A. No. 2529. HTA.

MERRITT, HAROLD J.
Ensign
81 Union St., Canton, Pa. Mass. Inst. of Tech., Key West, Miami, Pensacola. N. A. No. 1029. HTA.

MERRITT, M. P.
Ensign
Middleton, Mass. Mass. Inst. of Tech., Bay Shore, Pensacola, Coco Solo. N. A. No. 1277. HTA.

MERRITT, ROSWELL A.
Ensign
403 Orange St., Macon, Ga. Mass. Inst. of Tech., Key West, Miami, Pensacola. N. A. No. 2012. HTA.

MERSHON, EDW. J.
Ensign
27 Spring St., Brockport, N. Y. Mass. Inst. of Tech., Key West, Miami, Pensacola. N. A. No. 1184. HTA.

MERTZ, M. HAWLEY
Ensign
219 West H. St., Ontario, Cal. Seattle, San Diego, Pensacola. N. A. No. 2396. HTA.

MESERVEY, E. C., Jr.
Ensign
3614 Pennsylvania Ave., Kansas City, Mo. Mass. Inst. of Tech., Key West. N. A. No. 2020. HTA.

OBSERVATION BALLOON, PENSACOLA

MESSMORE, CARMAN
Student Officer
556 Fifth Ave., New York City. Great Lakes. HTA.

METLEN, DAVID W.
Ensign
520 N. Davis St., Helena, Montana. Seattle, San Diego, Pensacola. N. A. 2322.

(N)
MEYER, HUSTED McC.
Student Officer
167 Hazel Ave., Glencoe, Ill. Mass. Inst. of Tech., Great Lakes.

MEYER, WM. H., Jr.
Ensign
Grand Canyon, Ariz. Mass. Inst. of Tech., Key West, Cape May, Rockaway, Pensacola. N. A. No. 464. HTA.

MIDWOOD, G. A., Jr.
Ensign
W. Barrington, R. I. Mass. Inst. of Tech., Bay Shore, Hampton Roads, Pensacola, Miami. N. A. No. 1275. HTA.

MILHAM, ALLAN B.
Student Officer
834 W. Lovell St., Kalamazoo, Mich. Mass. Inst. of Tech., Great Lakes, Bay Shore, Brunswick, Ga., Key West. HTA.

MILLER, EARL H.
Lieut. (j.g.)
1050 23rd St., San Diego, Cal. M. I. T., Akron, Pensa., Hampton Roads, Rockaway, Key West. N. A. No. 2678. LTA.

MILLER, GEO. F.
Ensign
Eaton Rapids, Mich. Mass. Inst. of Tech., Pensacola, Miami. N. A. No. 1517. HTA.

MILLER, E. HOWARD,
Ensign
2719 Church Ave., Brooklyn, N. Y. Mass. Inst. of Tech., Pensacola, Miami, Hampton Roads. N. A. No. 1425. HTA.

MILLER, GEORGE C.
Ensign
P. O. Box 849, Richmond Va. M.I.T., Pens., Pauillac, Moutchic, Bay Sh., Hamp. Rds., Morehead City. N. A. No. 893. LTA.

MILLER, J. B.
Ensign
26 St. Pauls Road, Ardmore, Penn. Mass. Inst. of Tech., Miami, Pensacola. N. A. No. 2655. HTA.

(B)
MILLER, J. JEFFERSON
Ensign
Esplanade Apts., Baltimore, Md. Mass. Inst. of Tech., Miami, Pensacola. N. A. No. 2073.

MILLER, ODVER H.
Student Officer
1739 P St., N. W., Washington, D. C. Mass. Inst. of Tech., Great Lakes, Pensacola, Miami. HTA.

MILLER, R. L.
Student Officer
21 East Market St., Indianapolis, Ind. Dunwoody, Miami. HTA.

MILLER, THOMAS R.
Student Officer
84008 Forest Hill Ave., Richmond, Va. Dunwoody, HTA.

MILLER, VAN ROY
Lieut. (j.g.)
3001 East 6th St., Kansas City, Mo. Pensacola. HTA.

MILLER, WM. THOMAS
Ensign
Lyons, Mich. Mass. Inst. of Tech., Key West, Miami, Hamp. Rds., Morehead City. N A. No. 1231. HTA.

MILLS, M. E.
Ensign
Virginia, Ill. Mass. Inst. of Tech., Great Lakes, Miami, Key West, Pensacola. N. A. No. 2526. HTA.

MILNE, JAMES, Jr.
Student Officer
Stony Creek, Conn. Mass. Inst. of Tech. HTA.

MINER, RALPH W.
Ensign
East Greenwich, Rhode Island. Mass. Inst. of Tech., Miami, Key West, Pensacola. N. A. No. 2568. HTA.

MINER, SPERRY W.
Ensign
246 Park St., New Haven, Conn. Mass. Inst. of Tech., Bay Shore, Pensacola. N. A. No. 1698. HTA.

MITCHEL, ELMER L.
Lieut. (j.g.)
166 Devonshire St., Boston, Mass. Mass. Inst. of Tech. Pensacola.

MITCHELL, HAROLD L.
Ensign
RFD. No. 1, So. Portland, Me. Columbia University, Hampton Roads, Detroit, Anacostia, D. C.

MITCHELL, HUGH A.
Ensign
6 College St., Brunswick, Me. Mass. Inst. of Tech., Akron, Rockaway, Pensacola. LTA.

N-9 Zooming Off

MITCHELL, WM. H.
Ensign
229 Lake Shore Drive, Chicago, Ill. Mass. Inst. of Tech., Miami, Key West, Great Lakes. N. A. No. 1475. HTA.

MIX, DONALD G.
Ensign
1 Kensington Hts., Worcester, Mass. Mass. Inst. of Tech., Miami, Pensacola. N. A. No. 2493. HTA.

MODISETTE, R. M.
Lieut. (j.g.)
Salem, Ohio. Great Lakes, Anacostia, Hampton Rds., Pensacola, Great Lakes. HTA.

MOLLER, JOHN P.
Ensign
4505 Woodland Park Ave. Seattle, Wash. Mass. Inst. of Tech., Seattle, Miami, Pensacola. N. A. No. 2077. HTA.

MONAGHAN, JOHN A.
Ensign
44 Ayers St., Waterbury, Conn. M. I. T., Bay Shore, Key West, Miami, Pensacola, Hampton Rds. N. A. No. 1938. HTA.

MONTEITH, M. E.
Ensign
Belton, Tex. Great Lakes, Pensacola.

MONTGOMERY, A. M.
Ensign
801 West End Ave., New York City. Mass. Inst. of Tech., Bay Shore, Pensacola, Cape May. N. A. No. 1406. HTA.

MONTGOMERY, H. E.
Lieut. (j.g.)
41 Midland Ave., Arlington, N. J. M. I. T., Akron, Cape May, Rockaway, Hampton Rds., Coco Solo, Key West. LTA.

MONTGOMERY, J. K.
Ensign
Marion, S. C. Mass. Inst. of Tech., Pensacola, Miami, Hampton Roads. N. A. No. 665. HTA.

MOODY, JUDD W.
Ensign
Lowell, Ark. Mass. Inst. of Tech., Pensacola, Miami, Autingues, Moutchic, Killingholme, N. A. No. 940. HTA.

MOONEY, W. M.
Ensign
141 Water St., Paterson, N. J. Mass. Inst. of Tech., Bay Shore, Pensacola. N. A., No. 2214. HTA.

MOORE, A. K. P.
Ensign
212 Walnut St., Montclair, N. J. Mass. Inst. of Tech. Inspector of Eng. Material Brooklyn Aeronautic District.

MOORE, F. W.
Student Officer
502 W. 13th St., Austin, Tex. Mass. Inst. of Tech., Miami. HTA.

MOORE, HARRY C.
Ensign
1707 Atlantic Ave., Atlantic City, N. J. Key West., M. I. T., Miami, Pensacola. N. A. No. 2081. HTA.

MOORE, J. BALLARD
Lieut. (j.c.)
Wash. Loan & Trust Bldg., Washington, D. C. Mass. Inst. of Tech., Operations Aviation, Washington, D. C. N. A.

MOORE, WM. B., Jr.
Gunner
3028 Hilligas Ave., Berkeley, Cal. U. S. S. *Winchester*, S. P. 159, Miami, Pensacola, Taliaferro Field, Camp Saufley. HTA.

MOORE, WM. P.
Ensign
5 Fairview Circle, Birmingham, Ala. Seattle, San Diego, Pensacola. N. A. No. 2343. HTA.

MORFORD, JAMES R.
Ensign
528 East 10th St., Wilmington, Delaware, M. I. T., Pensacola, Miami. Moutchic, L'Aber Vrach, Hamp. Rds. N. A. No. 730. HTA.

MORGAN, BOWMAN S.
Machinist
Wilton, N. H. Columbia Univ., Squantum, Norfolk, Detroit.

MORGAN, J. L.
Machinist
5122 Camac St., Phila., Pa. Pauillac, Fr., Trompulete, Fr., Queenstown, Ire. HTA.

MORGAN, JOSEPH A.
Ensign
45 Main St., Lonaconing, Md. Mass. Inst. of Tech., Miami, Pensacola. N. A. No. 2220. HTA.

MORGAN, MILLARD
Student Officer
Bailey, N. C. Mass. Inst. of Tech. HTA.

MORRILL, EDGAR W.
Ensign
4208 Drew Ave., So. Minneapolis, Minn. Dunwoody, Miami, Pensacola. N. A. No. 2238. HTA.

MORRIS, CHAS.
Ensign
Mass. Inst. of Tech., Pensacola, Coco Solo, C. Z.

(C) Comm. Pub. Inf.

BEACH SCENE, KEY WEST

MORRIS, EDWARD K.
Student Officer
South Lee, Mass. Mass. Inst. of Tech. HTA.

MORRISS, P. G. B.
Lieut. (j.g.)
7455 Greenview Ave., Chicago, Ill. Great Lakes.

MORROW, THOMAS I.
Ensign
Brookhaven, L. I., N. Y. Mass. Inst. of Tech., Akron, Pensacola, Paimboeuf, Fr. N. A. No. 695. LTA.

MORSE, ARTHUR L.
Ensign
14 Hersom St., Watertown, Mass. Mass. Inst. of Tech., Miami, Pensacola. N. A. No. 2319. HTA.

MORSE, RICHARD A.
Student Officer
34 Russell Street., Milton, Mass. Mass. Inst. of Tech. **HTA.**

MOSELEY, GEORGE C.
Lieut. (j.g.)
160 Prospect Ave., Highland Park, Ill. F. Lafayette Escadrille, Moutchic, Dunkirk, 243 Fr. Spad. Sq. N. A. No. 566.

MOSLEY, A. J.
Student Officer
2647 Race St., Denver, Colo., Seattle, San Diego. HTA.

MUDGE, WM. F.
Lieut. (j.g.)
7 Wedgemer Ave., Winchester, Mass. R. F. C., Borden, Can., Bay Sh., Pensa., Milan, Calais, Killingholme. N. A. No. 157.

MULLER, CHARLES G.
Ensign
68 W. 56th St., New York City. Mass. Inst. of Tech., Key West, Miami, Pensacola. N. A. No. 2189. HTA.

MUNHALL, ALFRED N.
Ensign
2424 Farmers Bank Bldg., Pittsburgh, Pa. Mass. Inst. of Tech., Bay Shore, Pensacla. N. A. No. 1593. HTA.

MURPHY, C. B.
Student Officer
Hillsboro Hotel, Tampa, Fla. Dunwoody Institute, Minneapolis.

MURPHY, DUDLEY B.
Ensign
Fallen Road, Lexington, Mass. Squantum, Hampton Roads, Killingholme, Eng., East Fortune, Scotland. N. A. No. 201. HTA.

MURPHY, JOHN LEWIS
Ensign
41 Woodward St., South Boston, Mass. M. I. T., Hampton Rds., Pensacola, Fleet Air Detach. N. A. No. 269. HTA.

MURPHY JOHN D.
Ensign
Norwich, Conn. M. I. T., Newport, Key West, Miami, Pensa., Moutchic, Fr., Ile Tudy, Fr., Bay Sh., Rockaway. N. A. No. 1122. HTA

MURPHY, THOMAS H.
Lieut. (j.g.)
9 Conant St., Provincetown, Mass. Pensacola, Killingholme, R. A. F. Fortune, Hampton Rds., Washington. N. A. No. 51.

MURPHY, WM. A.
Ensign
372 Dudley St., Roxbury, Mass. Mass. Inst. of Tech., Key West, Miami, Pensacola, Cape May. N. A. No. 965. HTA.

MURRAY, ARTHUR B.
Student Officer
1110 Nott St., Schenectady, New York. Mass. Inst. of Tech., Miami. **HTA.**

MURRAY, HAROLD J.
Ensign
37 May Ave., Brockton, Mass. Mass. Inst. of Tech., Miami, Pensacola. N. A. No. 2037. HTA.

MURRELL, JESSE L.
Student Officer
Champaign, Ill. Mass. Inst. of Tech., Miami. HTA.

MURTOUGH, JAMES F.
Ensign
Chatsworth, Ill. Dunwoody, Miami, Key West, Pensacola. N. A. No. 2409.

MYERS, GEORGE H.
Student Officer
239 Blaine Ave., Detroit, Mich. Mass. Inst. of Tech., Miami. HTA.

MYERS, STANLEY H.
Ensign
202 N. 25th St., Corvallis, Ore. Univ. Wash., San Diego, Pensacola. N. A. No. 1992.

MYERS, W. BLAGDEN
Ensign
509 E. Lockwood Ave., Webster Groves, Mo. Mass. Inst. of Tech., Akron, Hampton Roads. LTA.

◈ ◈ ◈ ◈ ◈ ◈

McAdoo, Robt. H., Ensign, 1312 16th St., Washington, D. C. N. A. No. 1955.

McAdoo, Walter C., Student Officer, The Kenesaw Apt., 16th and Irving Sts., Washington, D. C. Dunwoody Inst., Minn. HTA.

McAdoo, Wm. G., Jr., Ensign, 1213 16th St., Washington, D. C. No. 236.

McAlexander, O. G., Lieut. (j.g.), 1062 Lamar Ave., Memphis, Tenn. Mass. Inst. of Tech., Pensacola, Fla. N. A. No. 662.

McAllister, Albert T., Student Officer, Seminole Ave., Chestnut Hill, Philadelphia.

McAnaw, Frank L. J., Ensign, Knights of Columbus Bldg., Ft. Sill, Okla.

McAtee, J. J., Lieut. (j.g.), 3361 Mt. Pleasant St., Washington, D. C. Washington, Rockaway, Chatham, Miami, Pensacola, Bay Shore.

McBride, D. F., Student Officer, 2 Oswego St., Utica, N. Y. Mass. Inst. of Tech., Pelham Bay. HTA.

McCahill, Eugene P., Student Officer, Georgetown University, Washington, D. C.

McCall, James L., Student Officer, 6029 Freret St., New Orleans, La.

McCallum, Stephen D., Student Officer, 6042 Kingsbury Blvd., St. Louis, Mo.

McCann, R. H., Ensign, 109 E. Washington Lane, Germantown, Pa. N. A. No. 147.

McCarl, Donald E., Student Officer, 729 N. 12th St., Quincy, Ill.

McCarthy, A. L., War.Mach., 1340 Theriot Ave., Bronx, N. Y. N. A. No. 1145.

McCarthy, Chas. F., Ensign, 4045 E. 19th Ave., Denver, Colo. N. A. No. 1781.

McCarthy, G. H., Ensign.

McCarthy, Jerry R., Student Officer, 70 Park Ave., Detroit, Mich.

McCarthy, L. A., Ensign, 2214 Blaisdell Ave., Minneapolis, Minn. No. 1145.

McCarthy, Wm. V., Student Officer, 56 High St., Springfield, Mass.

McCauley, J. E., Student Officer, 11 Tremont Ave., Somerville, Mass.

McCausland, John W., Ensign, 7330 Princeton Ave., Chicago, Ill.

McChesney, M. N., Lieut. (j.g.). N. A. No. 1069.

McClatchy, John B., Student Officer, Marion, Pa.

McClelland, Douglass, Student Officer, 540 West 113th St., New York City.

McClelland, James E., Student Officer, Springfield, Ky.

McClintock, E. K., Ensign, 1301 Lincoln Ave., Tyrone, Pa. Mass. Inst. of Tech., Akron, Pensacola, Rockaway Beach. N. A. No. 1220. LTA.

McClintock, Jack R., Ensign, 1544 Lyle St., Waco, Tex. N. A. No. 1836.

McClintock, James I., Student Officer, 725 Harrison Ave., Canon City, Colo.

McClung, Harrison T., Student Officer, 703 Grand Ave., St. Paul, Minn.

McClure, John T., Student Officer.

McClure, T. H., Ensign, 34 W. 44th St., New York City. Mass. Inst. of Tech., Akron, Norfolk; Brest, Cambrai, Fr. LTA.

McColm, Donald B., Student Officer, 1270 Bryden Rd., Columbus, Ohio.

McComb, Hugh L., Ensign, Care of Dayton Eng. Lab., Dayton, Ohio.

McConnell, Hugh, Ensign, 8 Bigelow St., Cambridge, Mass.

McConnell, Robt. K., Ensign, 61 Crescent St., Northampton, Mass. N. A. No. 1372.

McConnell, Robt. P., Ensign, Mokelumne Hill, Cal.

McConnel, Samuels Y., Student Officer, 1314 Mass. Ave., Washington, D. C.

McConnell, Stuart, Student Officer, 943 President St., Brooklyn, N. Y. Mass. Inst. of Tech. HTA.

McCormack, James Stanley, Ensign, 58 Beechwood Terrace, Yonkers, N. Y. Mass. Inst. of Tech., Blue Hill Observatory, Norfolk, Va., Committee on Experimental Power. HTA.

McCormack, Robt. J., Ensign, Waterbury, Conn.

McCormick, Chas. B., Student Officer, 306 9th St., N. W., Washington, D. C.

McCormick, Herbert H., Student Officer, 180 Center St., S. Manchester, Conn.

McCormick, J. S. F., Ensign, 827 Washington Road, Pittsburgh, Pa. Mass. Inst. of Tech., Akron, Pensacola. Paimboeuf, Fr.; Cape May, N. J.; Pauillac, Fr. N. A. No. 694. LTA.

McCormick, O. L., Student Officer, Raphine, Va. Dunwoody Inst., Minn. HTA.

McCormick, Walter W., Student Officer, Dupont Fabrikoid Co., Wilmington, Del.

McCosker, Dave, Ensign, The Measuregraph Co., St. Louis, Mo. Mass. Inst. of Tech., Great Lakes.

McCracken, Thos. E., Lieut. (j.g.), 642 Lafayette Ave., Brooklyn, N Y.

McCracken, E. P., Ensign, 135 W. 92d St., New York City.

McCraw, Nelson S., Student Officer, 247 Eagle St., North Adams, Mass. Mass. Inst. of Tech., Dunwoody Inst., Minn. HTA.

McCreary, W. C., Ensign, 704 W. Main St., Marshalltown, Ia.

McCruden, Donald B., Student Officer, 157 E. Main St., Westfield, N. Y.

McCulloch, John W., Ensign. N. A. No. 1637.

McCulloch, Wm. R., Student Officer, 449 Park Ave., N. Y.

McDaniel, Thos. H., Student Officer, Floresville, Tex.

McDaniel, Tom W., Student Officer, 14 W. North Ave., Atlanta, Ga.

McDermott, D. I., War. Machinist, 634 Chelton Ave., Philadelphia, Pa.

McDermott, M. J., Ensign, 547 E. Chelton Ave., Philadelphia, Pa. N. A. No. 702.

McDonald, Harold Rowland, Ensign, 1552 L St., Fresno, Cal. Mass. Inst. of Tech., Wingfoot Lake and Rockaway Beach, L. I.

McDonald, Hayward C., Student Officer, 2624 Haste St., Berkely, Cal.

McDonald, Robt. T., Student Officer 602 Monroe St., Ann Arbor, Mich.

McDonnell, E. C., Lieut. (j.g.).

McDonnell, F. R., Lieut. (j.g.), 1430 Park Ave., Baltimore, Md.

McDonnell, Paul A., Student Officer, 601 Lennox St., Baltimore, Md.

McDowell, C. S., War. Machinist, 322 Market North, Canton, Ohio.

McDowell, Richard, Ensign, 619 W. 175 St., New York City. N. A. No. 2060.

McElligott, Edmund W., Student Officer, 1009 University Ave., S. E., Minneapolis, Minn.

McEndy, J. F., Lieut. (j.g.), 122 E 36th St., New York City. Mass. Inst. of Tech., Key West, Mimai. N. A. No. 1518. HTA.

McEwen, Wm. Robert, Ensign, 51 Maple Ave., Wellsville, N. Y. Mass. Inst. of Tech.; Seattle, Wash.; San Diego, Cal. HTA.

McFarland, Andrew L., Student Officer, Lockwood Basin, E. Boston, Mass.

McFarlin, Chas. Kirk, Lieut. (j.g.), 170 Glenwood Ave., East Orange, N. J. Mass. Inst. of Tech., Queenstown, U. S. Headquarters, London, Eng. HTA.

McFayden, Jos. H., Student Officer, 350 N. 41st Ave., Omaha, Nebr.

McFerren, Donald J., Student Officer, Hoopeston, Ill. Mass. Inst. of Tech., Akron, Pensacola. LTA.

McGee, Raymond I., War. Gunner.

McGinnes, Edgar A., Ensign, Millington, Md. Mass, Inst. of Tech., Akron, Pensacola. LTA.

McGinnis, Thos. Polk, War. Machinist, 602 Allison Ave., Roanoke, Va.

McGoldrick, Wm. J., War. Machinist, 27 Vernon St., Waltham, Mass.

McGrail, Thos. E., War. Machinist, Ashfield, Mass. Pensacola, U. S. S. *North Carolina*, U. S. S. *Seattle*, Hampton Roads, Va.

McGranaghan, Jos. J., Ensign, 73 Park St., Carbondale, Pa. N. A. No. 2487.

McGrath, Francis D., Student Officer, 9 Mapleton St., Brighton, Mass.

McGunigal, Patrick, War. Carp.

McGuinness, Wm. V., Student Officer, Calamus Rd., Winfield, L. I., N. Y.

McGuire, John B., Lieut. (j.g.), 51 Chambers St., N. Y. City. Mass. Inst. of Tech., Bayshore, Pensacola. N. A. No. 925. LTA.

McHugh, M. F., War. Mach., 814 Amsterdam Ave., N. Y. City.

McHugh, Marion L., Student Officer, 1302 W. Douglas, Wichita, Kan. Univ. of Washington, Seattle.

McIllwraith, John N., Student Officer, 210 N. St., Bridgewater, Mass.

McIlree, Vance E., Student Officer, West. Union, Iowa.

McIlvan, Greer, Student Officer, Care of Q. Gilvain, 816 Berger Bldg., Pittsburgh, Pa.

McIntire, Donald E., Ensign, 1731 Columbia Rd., Washington, D. C. N. A. No. 1940.

McIntire, John K., Ensign, 360 West 1st St., Dayton, Ohio. Mass. Inst. of Tech., Miami, Pensacola. N. A. No. 1796.

McKain, Jos. N., Student Officer, 19th St., Miami, Fla.

McKean, E. D., Ensign, N. A. No. 697.

McKee, Jewel Chester, Student Officer, Athens, La. Mass. Inst. of Tech. HTA.

McKee, R. S., War. Mach.

McKee, Robt. B., Student Officer, Bingham School, Asheville, N. C.

McKee, Roy J., Ensign, Wycote Rd., Jenkinstown, Pa.

McKellar, E. F., Ensign, 457 W. Delevan Ave., Buffalo, N. Y. N. A. No. 861.

McKelvy, Lockhart C., Ensign, 5901 Fifth Ave., Pittsburgh, Pa. Mass. Inst. of Tech., Key West, Miami, Pensacola. N. A. No. 1697. HTA.

McKelway, Alexander J., Ensign, 2071 Park Rd., Washington, D. C. N. A. No. 1135.

McKinnon, D. A., Student Officer. Mass. Inst. of Tech. HTA.

McKinnon, T. N., Ensign, 1104 E. 36th St., Minneapolis, Minn.

McLaren, Archibald, Ensign, Setauket, L. I., N. Y.

McLaughlin, C. B., Ensign, 51 Creighton St., Jamaica Plain, Mass.

McLaughlin, Wm., Jr., Student Officer, Hyattsville, Md.

McLean, Raymond, Ensign, 103 W. Lanvale St., Baltimore, Md.

McLean, Robt. Jr., Ensign, 103 W. Lanvale St., Baltimore, Md. Mass. Inst. of Tech., Akron, Ohio; Bayshore, L. I.; Brest, Fr.; Guipavas, France. LTA.

McLellan, Douglas H., Lieut. (j.g.).

McLennon, Clyde H., Lieut. (j.g.).

McLeod, J. L., Lieut. (j.g.), 256 Brookline St., Cambridge, Mass; Pauillac, Bordeaux and Brest, France. HTA.

McMahon, J. Edward, Ensign, 6935 Stony Island Ave., Chicago, Ill. Mass. Inst. of Tech., Pensacola, Fla.; Autingues, Campagne, Moutchic, France. N. A. No. 862. HTA.

McManus, J. D., Ensign, 75 Warren Ave., Marlboro, Mass.

McMaster, Marcenus D., War. Mach., 176 Chestnut St., Rochester, N. Y. Pauillac, Fr; Ile Tudy, Fr.

McMillan, H. G., Ensign, Edgewood, Mt. Hermon, Mass. Mass. Inst. of Tech., Key West, Miami, Pensacola; Rockaway Beach, L. I. N. A. No. 1944. HTA.

McMillen, James A., Student Officer, Care Washington University, St. Louis, Mo. Mass. Inst. of Tech. HTA.

McMurrey, Jim, Jr., Student Officer, Camilla, Tex.; Seattle, Wash.; San Diego, Cal. HTA.

McNabb, Duncan J., Student Officer, Grosse Ile, Mich. Mass. Inst. of Tech., Akron, O.; Pensacola. LTA.

McNally, Edwin M., Lieut. (j.g.), Indianapolis, Ind.

McNear, Cyril, Student Officer.

McNeill, Malcom, R., Lieut. (j.g.), Evanston, Ill., Great Lakes.

McNulty, Harold, Lieut. (j.g.), Naval Air Station, San Diego, Cal. Mass. Inst. of Tech., Key West, Miami, Pensacola; San Diego, Cal. N. A. No. 1653. HTA.

McNulty, John P., Student Officer, Georgetown College, Washington, D. C.

McPeake, Enoch, War. Mach., 306 West 114th St., New York City, Columbia University; Pauillac, Fr.; Eastleigh, Eng.

McPhaul, John J., Ensign, 1223 Irving St., Brookland, D. C. N. A. No. 2065.

McPherson, H. A., Student Officer, 806 Florida Ave., Tampa, Fla. University of Wash., Seattle, Wash. HTA.

McQuick, Chas. J., Student Officer. 819 Lawrence Ave., Chicago, Ill.

McQuiston, Dale S., Student Officer, 404 E. Center St., Paxton, Ill.; Dunwoody Inst. Minn.; Great Lakes. HTA.

McQuiston, Irving M., Lieut. (j.g.), 91 Taylor St., Waltham, Mass. Mass. Inst. of Tech., Bayshore, L. I.; Pensacola, Fla. N. A. No. 905.

McRae, Bruce M., Student Officer, 31 Coligni Ave., New Rochelle, N. Y.

McRae, Donald P., Ensign, 618 Story St., Boone, Iowa.

McRae, Kenneth M., Student Officer.

McShane, C. O., Ensign, South Bethlehem, Pa. Mass. Inst. of Tech., Pensacola, Fla.

McVay, Glen A., Student Officer.

McVay, L. O., Student Officer, Sidney, Ohio. Mass. Inst. of Tech. HTA.

Macauley, D. M., Ensign, North Wilbraham, Mass. N. A. No. 204.

MacCart, Raymond D., Ensign, 23 Pleasant St., Dorchester, Mass.

MacCartney, J. G. M., Student Officer, 1817 13th St., Altoona, Pa. Mass. Inst. of Tech. HTA.

MacCoull, Neil, War. Mach., 537 W. 121st St., New York City.

MacCoy, W. Logan, Ensign, Overbrook, Pa., Great Lakes, Ill.; Pensacola.

MacDonald, Lowell, Student Officer, George Smith Hall, C32 Cambridge, Mass.

MacDougall, Chas. B., Ensign 1420 24th Ave., S. Seattle, Wash.

MacElwee, A. T., Ensign, 36 Sawyer St., Portland, Me.

MacEnery, J. E., Ensign, 259 E. 176 St., New York City. Mass. Inst. of Tech., New York; Charleston, Pensacola, Miami, Key West. HTA.

MacFarlane, James W., Student Officer, S. P., 965 New Castle, Del.

MacGregor, Frederick N., Student Officer, 661 S. Barkesdale St., Memphis, Tenn.

MacIver, J., War. Mach., Pasadena, Cal.

Mack, Harry J., Student Officer, 501 Walker St., St. Johns, Mich. Mass. Inst. of Tech. HTA.

MacKavley, Wallace, Student Officer, 456 Mt. Hope Ave., Rochester, N. Y.

MacKay, Donald C., Student Officer, 7100 Yale Ave., Chicago, Ill.

MacKenzie, Kenneth C., Student Officer, 1414 Watchung Ave., Plainfield, N. J.

MacLean, A. D., Student Officer, 1209 E. Main St., New Albany, Indiana. Mass. Inst. of Tech., Key West, Fla. HTA.

MacLean, L. A., Student Officer, 1032 Bella Vista Ave., Oakland, Cal. Seattle, Wash.; San Diego. HTA.

MacMillan, Donald B., Ensign, Freeport, Me.

MacMillan, Kenneth D., Ensign, Pittston, Pa.

MacMillan, Roy W., War. Boatswain.

MacMurray, Donald M., Student Officer, 2911 Pine Grove Ave., Chicago, Ill.

Macrae, Stephen R., Student Officer, 1828 Columbia Rd., Washington, D. C.

Macurdy, Harold, Student Officer, Marion, Ill. Mass. Inst. of Tech., Miami. HTA.

Macwitty, Frank L., Student Officer, 251 Cleveland Ave., Hasbrouck Heights, N. J.

Madden, Matt J., Student Officer, Morrisplains, N. J. Mass. Inst. of Tech. Newport, R. I.; New Bedford, Mass. HTA.

Madison, H. A., Ensign, 3815 Bates St., Pittsburgh, Pa. N. A. No. 316.

Magee, William L., Student Officer, 115 Broadway, Taunton, Mass.

Maginnes, William D., Ensign, Sharon, Mass. Mass. Inst. of Tech., Miami, Pensacola. N. A. No. 2004. HTA.

Magoun, Frederick H., Ensign, 14 Bailey St., Bath, Maine. Mass. Inst. of Tech., Hampton Roads, Pensacola, Miami. N. A. No. 528. HTA.

Magrumm, Harry A., Student Officer, Joseph, Oregon. Seattle, Wash. HTA.

Maguire, Raymer F., Student Officer, 319 Duval St., Key West, Fla.

Mahoney, Daniel F., Ensign, Georgetown Univ., Washington, D. C. N. A. No. 1348.

Mahoney, James B., Student Officer, 5 Custer St., Lawrence, Mass.

Mahoney, John F., Student Officer, Rawlins, Wyo.

Mahoney, S. P., Ensign, 474 Maple St., Holyoke, Mass.

Maier, Edward H., Student Officer, 502 Y. M. C. A. Bldg., Houston, Tex.

Malette, Geo. A., Student Officer, 1315 25th St., San Diego, Cal.

Mall, Ivor C., Ensign, 721 Fremont St., Manhatten, Kans.

Mallers, Edward Benjamin, Student Officer, 4358 Drexel Blvd., Chicago, Ill.

Mallory, R. H., Student Officer, 107 St. Regis Apts., Omaha, Nebr. Mass. Inst. of Tech., Key West. HTA.

Malone, Franklin, Student Officer, 465 5th St., Brooklyn, New York.

Manierre, Harold L., Student Officer, 1507 Dearborn Parkway, Chicago, Ill.

Manierre, Louis, Student Officer, Room 416, 112 W. Adams St., Chicago, Ill.

Mann, Marion R., Student Officer, Gallatin, Mo. Dunwoody Inst., Minn.; Miami, Fla. HTA.

Manners, John V., Ensign, 276 Orange Road, Montclair, N. J. Mass. Inst. of Tech., Pensacola, Hampton Roads. N. A. No. 293. HTA.

Manning, Edgar T., Ensign, 12 Armory Terrace, Nashua, N. H. Mass. Inst. of Tech., Akron, O.; Pensacola, Fla. N. A. No. 1581. LTA.

Manny, Edmund S., Student Officer, 5041 Westminster Place, St. Louis, Mo. Mass. Inst. of Tech. HTA.

Mansfield, Lewis P., Student Officer, 190 Pine St., Portland, Me. Mass. Inst. of Tech., Bay Shore. HTA.

Mansford, Berkeley, Ensign, 1522 Yesterway, Seattle, Wash. N. A. No. 1431.

Marchant, Alfred W., War. Boatswain.

Marheinake, Ernest C., Ensign.

Marr, John W., Student Officer, R. F. D. No. 4, Lexington, Ky.

Marriner, W. F., Lieut. (j.g.), 1710 East Gadsden St., Pensacola, Fla. Pensacola. N. A. No. 213.

Marsden, George C., Student Officer, 30 Bryant St., Portland, Me.

Marsh, Bryan, Student Officer.

Marshall, Edward C., Ensign, 3231 Beredith Ave., Pleasant Ridge, Cincinnati, Ohio. Mass. Inst. of Tech., Akron, Ohio; Pensacola. N. A. No. 2146. LTA.

Marshall, L. K., Lieut. (j.g.). N. A. No. 384.

Marshall, Marcus M., Ensign, 2404 Broadway, San Diego, Cal. N. A. No. 1367.

Marshall, R. W., Lieut. (j.g.), The Lenox Apt., 13th and Spruce St., Philadelphia, Pa. Akron, Ohio, Rockaway, L. I., Pensacola.

Marshall, Richard M., Ensign.

Marshburn, E. O., Student Officer, Goldsboro, N. C.

Marsters, Charles E., Ensign, P. O. Box 2493 Boston, Mass. Great Lakes, Pensacola, Fla.

Marston, Robert L., Ensign, Rolla, Mo. Mass. Inst. of Tech., San Diego. HTA.

Martin, Bernard D., Student Officer.

Martin, Edward S., Student Officer.

Martin, Grady H., Student Officer.

Martin, Hugh S., Student Officer, 650 N. Kenmore Ave., Los Angeles, Cal.

Martin, Isaac Roy, Student Officer, 177 Weatwood St., Akron, Ohio.

Martin, John M., Student Officer, 521 4th St., S. E., Minnneapolis, Minn. Dunwoody Inst., Miami, Pensacola. HTA.

Martin, Laurence C., Student Officer, 32 Lincoln St., Glen Ridge, N. J. Dunwoody Inst., Minn.

Martin, M. S., Ensign, 32 Lincoln St., Glen Ridge, N. J. N. A. No. 1143.

Martin, Rogers A., Student Officer, 277 East 4th St., Atlanta, Ga.

Martin, W. H., Ensign, Laurens, S. C. Mass. Inst. of Tech., Miami, Key West, Pensacola. HTA.

Martindell, D. C., Student Officer, 105 East 14th St., Hutchinson, Kans. Mass. Inst. of Tech. LTA.

Mason, G. S., Lieut. (j.g.), 121 West Walnut Lane, Germantown, Philadelphia, Pa. Mass. Inst. of Tech., Hampton Roads, Pensacola. HTA.

Massey, L. R., Student Officer, 1844 Kenyon St., Washington, D. C. Great Lakes, Ill.

Matchette, William H., Jr., Student Officer.

Mathes, B. W., Ensign, Plainview, Tex. Mass. Inst. of Tech., Pensacola, Akron. N. A. No. 1755. LTA.

Matheson, R. D., Lieut. (j.g.), 743 College Ave., S. E., Grand Rapids, Mich. N. A. No. 1707.

Mathews, Charles E., Ensign, 175 Thayer St., Providence, R. I.

Mathews, Charles M., Student Officer.

Mathias, Robert D., Student Officer.

Mathiasen, Alfred, Student Officer, Keyport, N. J. Mass. Inst. of Tech., Bay Shore. HTA.

Mathiasen, Otto F., Student Officer, 4427 Howard St., Omaha, Nebr. Seattle, Wash. HTA.

Matson, R. C. H., Student Officer, Sewanee, Tenn. Mass. Inst. of Tech., Miami, Fla. HTA.

Matter, Robert, Lieut. (j.g.), 911 S. Washington St., Marion, Ind. Toronto, Canada, RFC.; Hampton Roads, Pensacola; Killingholme, Eng.; N. Bomb. Gr., Fr. N. A. No. 162. HTA.

Matteson, G. C., Ensign, 20 Winthrop St., Rochester, N. Y. Mass. Inst. of Tech., Pensacola, Calais, Fr.; Milan, It.; Bay Shore, Miami. N. A. No. 573.

Matthews, Donald H., Student Officer, Paliser St., Johnston, Pa.

Matthews, Edgar, Student Officer, 423 Lincoln St., Johnston, Pa. Mass. Inst. of Tech. LTA

Mauck, Earle Lewis, Ensign.

Maughan, Wm. E., Ensign.

Maulbetsch, John F., Student Officer, 221 Washington St., Ann Arbor, Mich.

Maurer, Charles F., Student Officer, 243 S. Main St., Wilkesbarre, Pa.

Mavis, Jack R., Lieut. (j.g.), 3145 Sheridan Road, Chicago, Ill. Pensacola, Bay Shore, Columbia University, Detroit, Packard, Great Lakes. Philadelphia. HTA.

Maxwell, H. W., Jr., Lieut. (j.g.), Glen Cove, L. I., N. Y. Bay Shore, Miami, Moutchic, Gallarete, It., Milan, Joya del Colle, St. Inglevert. LTA.

Maxwell, Robert L., Student Officer, 1905 Guadalupe St., Austin, Tex.

Mayes, Wendell W., Ensign, Grunewald Hotel, New Orleans, La.

Maynard, Charles E., Student Officer, Medina Road, Akron, Ohio.

Maynard, Merlin T., Student Officer, 593 South Sixth St., San Jose, Cal.

Mayo, T. F., Lieut. (j.g.), 1729 Coliseum St., New Orleans, La.

Maze, Montgomery, Lieut. (j.g.), 2650 Broadway, New

York City. Mass. Inst. of Tech., Buffalo, Columbia University, N. Y.

Meacham, Eugene M., Student Officer.

Meachen, H. F., War. Machinist.

Meads, Robt. T., Ensign, 423 S. Stone Ave., La Grange, Ill. Dunwoody, Miami, Pensacola. N. A. No. 2342. HTA.

Meany, Robt. E., Ensign.

Mears, Cecil F., Student Officer, Norfolk, Va. Mass. Inst. of Tech. HTA.

Meath, Geo. M., Student Officer, 208 East 4th St., Olympia, Wash.

Medusky, W. J., War. Gun. Naval Air Station, Rockaway Beach, L. I., Pensacola, Fla.; Rockaway Beach, N. Y. N. A.

Meegan, Joseph A., Student Officer, 260 Commercial St., Portland, Me.

Meehan, J. L., Ensign.

Megahan, Howard D., Student Officer, 602 Whitney Ave., Wilkinsburg, Pa.

Meier, Albert O., Student Officer, 1731 13th Ave., Seattle, Wash. Seattle, Wash. LTA.

Meier, Harry A., Student Officer, 1420 36th Ave., Seattle, Wash.

Mell, Brook, Ensign, 44 West Peachtree St., Atlanta, Ga.

Mellen, Arthur Wm., Jr., Ensign, 2676 Morris Ave., New York City.

Mellen, Romney J., Student Officer, 210 Bennett Ave., Cripple Creek, Colo., Seattle, Wash., Key West, Fla.

Mellenbruch, Dale F., Student Officer, 1344 Kentucky St., Lawrence, Kan.

Mellor, Duncan M., Student Officer, Miller Hall Farm, Norfolk, Mass.

Melville, George S., Ensign.

Melville, Kenneth, Student Officer, 2120 E. 47th St., Seattle, Wash.

Mendenhall, James Howe, Student Officer, 25 Main St., Toughkenamon, Pa. Dunwoody Inst., Minneapolis, Minn. HTA.

Mendoza, David, Lieut. (j.g.), 2419 Michigan Ave., Chicago, Ill. Pensacola, Fla., Hampton, Roads., Brest, Fr., Whiddy Island, Naval Base No. 6. HTA.

Menefee, John Wm., Ensign, Graham, N. C. Mass. Inst. of Tech., Akron, Ohio, Rockaway Beach, L. I. LTA.

Mengal, Clarence, R. Jr., Student Officer, Forest and Main Sts., Evanston, Ill.

Mengele, Frank A., Student Officer, 146 Tremont St., Boston, Mass.

Menzel, F. W., Ensign, 15 Poplar St., Brooklyn, N. Y. N. A. No. 509.

Mercer, George W., Student Officer, 43 Society St., Charleston, S. C.

Meredith, Otis, Student Officer, Beaconsfield Apts., Houston, Texas.

Merkle, Edward B., Student Officer, 1373 E. Broad St., Columbus, Ohio.

Merrifield, Samuel A., Ensign, Williamsville, Vt. Mass. Inst. of Tech, Akron, Ohio. Rockaway, L. I., N. Y. LTA.

Merrill, Chas. L. Lieut. (j.g.), 102 Queensberry St., Boston, Mass.

Merrill, Donald H., Lieut. (j.g.), 1679 Mass. Ave., Cambridge, Mass. N. A. No. 672.

Merrill, N. E., Lieut. (j.g.), Osceola Club, Pensacola, Fla.

Merriman, Lawrence C., Ensign, 2401 Bowditch St., Berkeley, Cal. Seattle, San Diego, Pensacola. N. A. No. 2003. HTA.

Merritt, Roswell A., Ensign, 403 Orange St., Macon, Ga. N. A. No. 2012.

Messinger, Chas S., Ensign, 253 Bushkill St., Easton, Pa. Mass. Inst. of Tech., Bay Shore, Hampton Roads, Pensacola, Moutchic, Cape May. N. A. No. 254. HTA.

Metzger, Norman, Student Officer, 1508 Broadway, Indianapolis, Ind. Mass. Inst. of Tech., Miami. HTA.

Meyers, W. Blagden, Ensign, 226 Spring St., Webster Groves, Mo.

Mezger, Erwin R., Student Officer, 175 Delavan Ave., Newark, N. J. Mass. Inst. of Tech. HTA.

Micheals, G., War Machinist, Marshall, Ill.

Mickey, R. Z., Ensign, 1428 W. 25th St., Cleveland, Ohio.

Middleton, Chas. G., Ensign, Inter. Southern Bldg., Louisville, Ky. Mass. Inst. of Tech., Pensacola, Fla.

Miles, Vernon G., Student Officer, 644 8th St., Port Arthur, Texas. Univ. of Washington, Seattle; Key West. HTA.

Millard, I. W., Student Officer, 764 Transportation Bldg., Chicago, Ill. Mass. Inst. of Tech. HTA.

Miller, A. B., Student Officer, Plainsboro, N. J. Mass. Inst. of Tech. HTA.

Miller, Albert P., Student Officer, 70 Worth St., New York, N. Y.

Miller, Chas. G., Ensign. 68 West 56th St., New York City.

Miller, Cleophas E., Ensign.

Miller, Felix G., Student Officer, 509 Walnut St., Chattanooga, Tenn. Dunwoody Inst., Minn. HTA.

Miller, Franklin G., Student Officer, 700 W. 179 St., New York City.

Miller, H. A., Ensign, 119 Magnolia Ave., Riverside, Cal. Mass. Inst. of Tech., Key West, Miami, Pensacola, Rockaway. N. A. No. 1164, HTA.

Miller, H. H., Student Officer, 108 Grove St., Tonawanda, N. Y. Mass. Inst. of Tech., Great Lakes. HTA.

Miller, J. Bernard, Student Officer, 27 West 44th St., New York City. Mass. Inst. of Tech. HTA.

Miller, J. M., Ensign. N. A. No. 494.

Miller, John W., Ensign, Holmsville, Neb. N. A. No. 1516.

Miller, Raymond Percy, Lieut. (j.g.), Middlesex Ave., Swampscott, Mass. Mass. Inst. of Tech., Aeromarine, Keyport, N. J.; L. W. F., College Point, L. I.; Garden City, L. I.

Miller, Richard B., Ensign, 401 S. 15 St., Independence, Kansas. Mass. Inst. of Tech., Bay Shore, L. I., Pensacola, Fla. N. A. No. 1892. HTA.

Miller, Robt. Stewart, Ensign.

Miller, Vaughn, Ensign, Lookout Mountain, Tenn. Rockaway Beach. LTA.

Miller, Wm., Ensign, 1507 E. Gadsden St., Pensacola, Fla. Pensacola, Palm Beach, Huntington, Bay Shore, Hampton Roads, Milan, Italy, St. Inglevert, France, Eastleigh, Eng. HTA.

Miller, E. H., Ensign, 14 W. Peoria St., Chicago, Ill. Great Lakes, Ill., Hampton Roads, Va.

Millikan, Edward P., Student Officer, 473 Park Ave., River Forest, Ill.

Millinix, Bonnie L., War Boatswain.

Mills, James W., Ensign, St. James Hotel, 6th St. and Penn. Ave., Wash., D. C. N. A. No. 2219.

Milson, Thomas H., Student Officer, 528 E. 29th St., Paterson, N. J.

Minnis, James L., Student Officer, 5284 Westminster Place, St. Louis, Mo.

Minty, Casper C., Student Officer, 205 North 15th St., Fort Dodge, Iowa. Dunwoody Inst., Miami, Pensacola. HTA.

Minty, John E., Student Officer, 208 Webster Ave., Muskegon, Mich. Dunwoody Inst., Minn., Miami and Key West. HTA.

Mirkil, Haxelton, Jr., Ensign, 527 Lafayette Bldg., Philadelphia, Pa.

Mishler, Floyd E., Ensign, 314 E. 9th St., Newton, Kansas. Mass. Inst. of Tech., Key West, Pensacola. N. A. No. 2256. HTA.

MisKovsky, James F., Student Officer, 351 E. College St., Oberlin, O. Mass. Inst. of Tech., Chicago, Cleveland. LTA.

Mitchell, Archie Delwood, Student Officer, Ontario, Cal. Seattle, Wash. HTA.

Mitchell, Charles W., Jr., Ensign, 4001 Greenway, Baltimore, Md. Mass. Inst. of Tech., Pensacola, Miami, Moutchic, Killingholme, Eng., Hampton Roads, Cape May. N. A. No. 664. HTA.

Mitchell, Francis H., Ensign, Clinton Springs Ave., Cincinnati, O. N. A. No. 409.

Mitchell, Frost A., Student Officer, 2057 Glenwood Ave., Toledo, O.

Mitchell, Henry B., Student Officer, 207 Hill St., LaGrange, Ga.

Mitchell, John J., Jr., Ensign, 1550 N. State Parkway, Chicago, Ill. Mass. Inst. of Tech., Great Lakes, Key West, Pensacola. N. A. No. 1909. HTA.

Moeller, Sydney D., Student Officer, 890 W. William St., Decatur, Ill. Mass. Inst. of Tech., Cambridge, Bay Shore. HTA.

Moeser, Wm. F. C., Student Officer, Sedro-Wooley, Washington.

Mohr, Herman F., Student Officer, Apalachicola, Fla. Mass. Inst. of Tech. HTA.

MONROE, GEO. E., Student Officer, 146 E. Pine Ave., Grove City, Pa. Mass. Inst. of Tech., Akron, O. LTA.

MONTAGUE, T. G., Student Officer, 235 Washington Bldg., Madison, Wisc. Dunwoody Inst. Minn., Miami, Fla. HTA.

MONTANYE, HAROLD P., Student Officer, 420 West 20th St., New York City.

MONTEITH, D. W., Lieut. (j.g.), University Club, San Francisco, Cal. Mass. Inst. of Tech., Bu. St. Eng., Washington, D. C.; IEM (aero) Brooklyn, Dist., N. Y.

MONTGOMERY, ALLAN D., Student Officer, 1600 Rio Grande St. Austin, Texas. Mass. Inst. of Tech., Miami. HTA.

MONTGOMERY, G. S., Ensign. N. A. No. 300.

MONTGOMERY, JAMES E., Student Officer, 600 Meabane St., Burlington, N. C.

MONTGOMERY, RALPH S., Student Officer, Main St., Warsaw, N. Y.

MONTGOMERY, W. R., Ensign, 1501 Henry St., Berkeley, Cal. Mass. Inst. of Tech., Key West, Pensacola, Miami. N. A. No. 1324. HTA.

MOON, EDW. HARRIS, Ensign, 2711 Rivermont Ave., Lynchburg, Va.

MOORA, C. SHELTON, Ensign, 148 Claremont Ave., Montclair, N. J. Mass. Inst. of Tech., Akron, Chatham, Rockaway, Pensacola. N. A. No. 1759. LTA.

MOORE, BEN McG., Student Officer, Houston Ave., Macon, Ga.

MOORE, CHAUNCEY C., Student Officer, 309 2nd St., No., Great Falls, Montana.

MOORE, LLOYD ROY, War Boatswain, N. A. No. 206.

MOORE, MAURICE MALCOLM, Lieut. (j.g.), 854 Security Bldg., Minneapolis, Minn. Moutchic-Lacanau, Gironde, Dunkerque, France, Zeebrugge Mole, Belgium HTA.

MOORE, NEIL A., Student Officer, 1511 Washtenaw Ave., Ann Arbor, Mich.

MOORE, ROBERT, JR., Lieut. (j.g.), 403 Hennen Bldg., New Orleans, La. Mass. Inst. of Tech., S. P. 630, Key West, Fla. N. A. No. 1476. HTA.

MOORE, REDINGTON, Student Officer, 305 New St., Eaton, Pa.

MOORE, R. G., Student Officer, 154 Pearson St., Chicago, Ill.

MOORE, ROBERT C., Student Officer, Bingham, Maine. Mass. Inst. of Tech. LTA.

MOORE, THEODORE J., Ensign.

MOORE, THEO. W., Student Officer, 617 Ave. B. Miami, Fla. Mass. Inst. of Tech., Key West, Fla. HTA.

MOORE, THOMAS F., Student Officer, 188 South Elm St., Waterbury, Conn.

MOOREHEAD, TOM V. H., Student Officer, 1523 Maple Ave., Zanesville, Ohio.

MOREHOUSE, RUSSEL, Ensign, 1544 Oneida St., Utica, N. Y. Mass. Inst. of Tech., Akron, Hampton Roads. LTA.

MORAN, JOHN F., Student Officer, 9 Kimball Ave., Lowell, Mass.

MORE, ARTHUR L., Ensign. N. A. No. 2459.

MOREY, J. BENEDICT, Student Officer, 127 Summit Ave., Buffalo, N. Y.

MOREY, JAMES B., Student Officer.

MORGAN, BENJ. F., JR., Student Officer, 409 Berkeley Ave., Norfolk, Va.

MORGAN, DAVID P., JR., Lieut. (j.g.), 115 E 72d St., New York City. Mass. Inst. of Tech., Pensacola, Miami, Field A., N. B. G., Fr. N. A. No. 394. HTA.

MORGAN, FRANCIS J., Student Officer, 1127 Euclid, N.W., Washington, D. C.

MORGAN, G. S., War. Machinist.

MORGAN, JAMES CULVA, Student Officer, 459 Portage Ave., Winnepeg, Canada. Mass. Inst. of Tech., Key West. HTA.

MORGAN, LAWRENCE, Student Officer, 17 Hubard St., Boston, Mass.

MORGAN, LAURENCE W., Ensign, 389 Marlborough St., Boston, Mass. Mass. Inst. of Tech., Pensacola, Fla. HTA.

MORIARTY, JOHN F., Student Officer, 177 Allyn St., Holyoke, Mass.

MORRILL, FRANK W., Ensign.

MORRILL, HAROLD B., Student Officer, 19 Highland Ave., Roxbury, Mass.

MORRIS, HENRY H., Ensign.

MORRIS, LEWIS G., Student Officer, 1015 Park Ave., New York City.

MORRIS, JOHN H., Student Officer, Georgetown College, Washington, D. C.

MORRIS, WYLLYS K., JR., Ensign. N. A. No. 2333.

MORRISETTE, WM. L., Student Officer, 26 Dinwiddie St., Portsmouth, Va.

MORRISON, DAVID G., Ensign, 501 E. State St., Sharon, Pa.

MORRISON, JOHN M., JR., Student Officer, 647 Linwood Ave., Buffalo, N. Y.

MORRISON, OCIE B., Student Officer, 437 Harrison St., Petersburg, Va.

MORRISON, STUART T., Student Officer.

MORROW, THAYER K., Ensign, 4201 Ellis Ave., Chicago, Ill.

MORSE, ALLAN L., Ensign, 128 Pleasant St., Arlington, Mass. Akron, Ohio; Rockaway, L. I.; Queenstown, Ire.; H. M. A. S., Roehampton, Eng.; Castletown, Ire.; La Trinite, Brest, Fr. LTA.

MORSE, CLAUDE S., Student Officer, 49 Elm St., Glen Falls, N. Y.

MORSE, GEO. H., Ensign.

MORSE, GEORGE H., War. Gunner.

MORSE, HAROLD M., Student Officer, Clarks, Nebraska. Mass. Inst. of Tech., Miami. HTA.

MORSE, HENRY G., Student Officer, 80 Glendale St., Dorchester, Mass.

MORSE, MAYLAND H., Student Officer, Anson, Maine. Mass. Inst. of Tech. HTA.

MORSE, ROBERT D., Student Officer, 46 Pleasant St., Marlboro, Mass. Mass. Inst. of Tech. HTA.

MORSE, THOS. R., Lieut. (j.g.), Falmouth, Mass. N. A. No. 366.

MORTIMER, LAURENCE, Ensign.

MORTON, A. N., Ensign, 225 Roberts Ave., Yonkers, N. Y. Mass. Inst. of Tech., Pensacola; Moutchic, Fr.; Hampton Roads. N. A. No. 860. HTA.

MORTON, CLARK, Student Officer, 1214 Grand Ave., Fort Smith, Tex.

MORTON, JOHN W., Ensign, 225 Roberts Ave., Yonkers, N. Y. N. A. No. 1041.

MORTON, LINDLEY C., Student Officer, 801 66th Ave., Oak Lane, Philadelphia, Pa.

MORTON, WALTER F., Student Officer, 73 West 29th St., Bayonne, N. J.

MORY, GEO. H., Ensign, 425 College Ave., Appleton, Wisc. Seattle, Wash.; San Diego, Cal.; Pensacola. N. A. No. 2263. HTA.

MOSELEY, HENRY VINCENT, Lieut. (j.g.), Alexandria, La. Mass. Inst. of Tech., Key West, Miami, Pensacola; Field "B" Northern Bombing Group, Fr. N. A. No. 476. HTA.

MOSELEY, HERBERT F., War. Gunner.

MOSES, JAMES, Ensign, 3841 South Broadway, Los Angeles, Cal.

MOSHER, F. R., Lieut. (j.g.), 1446 Belmont St., Washington, D. C. N. A. No. 258.

MOSS, W. R. M., Lieut. (j.g.), Law Bldg., Norfolk, Va. Mass. Inst. of Tech., Pensacola, Fla. N. A. No. 939. HTA.

MOSSER, B. D., Lieut. (j.g.), 117 Edgewood Road, Ardmore, Pa. Mass. Inst. of Tech., Pensacola, Fla. LTA.

MOSSER, PHILIP D., Ensign, 344 Westervelt Ave., Staten Island, N. Y. Mass. Inst. of Tech., Bay Shore, Pensacola. HTA.

MOTT, C. B., Student Officer, 86 W. Forest Ave., Detroit, Mich. Dunwoody Inst., Minn. HTA.

MOTT, ELLIOT W., Ensign.

MOULTON, EVERTS, Student Officer, 7108 Holywood Blvd., Los Angeles, Cal.

MOULTRIE, L. G., Ensign, 210 East 8th St., Rome, Ga. Mass. Inst. of Tech., Key West, Miami, Pensacola. HTA.

MOUNT, LESLIE C., Lieut. (j.g.).

MOUNT, M. B., Student Officer, Riverview Place, Lynchburg, Va. Mass. Inst. of Tech. HTA.

MOUNTFORT, EDGAR PAGE, Student Officer, 128 Selye Terrace, Rochester, N. Y. Mass. Inst. of Tech. HTA.

MOWBRAY, C. C., War. Mach., Detroit, Mich. Columbia University; Pauillac, Gironde, L'Aber Vrach, Finistere, Fr.; Hampton Roads, Va.

MOYLAN, CHARLES E., Student Officer, Jamesville, Md.

MUDGE, E. T., 2d, Ensign, 1752 Park Ave., Baltimore, Md. Mass. Inst. of Tech., Bay Shore, L. I.; Pensacola, Fla. N. A. No. 966. HTA.

MUDGE, RAYMOND C., Lieut. (j.g.), Ludlow, Vermont. Mass. Inst. of Tech., Pensacola, Fla. N. A. No. 298. HTA.

MUGFORD, FRANK M., War Gunner.

MULFORD, EDWARD M., Student Officer, 214 Marlborough Road, Brooklyn, N. Y.

MULLEN, GEORGE J., Student Officer.

MULLIKEN, EDWARD H., Ensign, Short Beach, Branford, Conn. N. A. No. 1868.

MULLIN, JOHN M., Student Officer, Alpha Delta Phi Club, 136 W. 44th St., New York City. Mass. Inst. of Tech., Pensacola, New York. HTA.

MULLINAX, K., War. Boatswain, 524 15th Ave., W. Seattle, Wash. N. A. No. 557.

MUMMERT, A. J., Lieut. (j.g.), 2808 Locust St., St. Louis, Mo. B. S. E. Design Section, Division Aeronautics, Washington, D. C.

MUNGER, LEONIDAS P., Student Officer, Cotton Ave., Motevalle Rd., Birmingham, Ala.

MUNROE, ROBERT, 3rd, Ensign, 365 Pennsylvania Ave., Oakmont, Pa. N. A. No. 1610.

MUNSON, R. F., Lieut. (j.g.), 511 West Ave., Medina, N. Y.

MURISON, RICHARD V., Ensign, 509 E. Chalmers St., Champaign, Ill.

MURPHY, CLARENCE R., Student Officer, 1030 S. Monroe Ave., Green Bay, Wisc.

MURPHY, DANIEL F., Student Officer, 32 Rodney Dorms. Univ. of Penn., Philadelphia, Pa.

MURPHY, GEORGE, Student Officer, Harbor Beach, Mich.

MURPHY, H. C., Lieut. (j.g.).

MURPHY, J. G., Ensign, 2 Gibson Terrace, Somerville, Mass.

MURPHY, JAS. DOYLE, Ensign, Harrison, N. Y. Mass. Inst. of Tech., Pensacola; Montauk, L. I.; Hampton Roads, Morehead City. HTA.

MURPHY, JAMES M., Student Officer, 500 W. 4th St., Dayton, Ohio.

MURPHY, JOEL H., Student Officer, 500 W. 4th St., Dayton, Ohio.

MURRAY, FRANCIS D., Student Officer, 2 Charter Oak Ave., Hartford, Conn.

MURRAY, FRANK, Student Officer, 166 2d Ave., North and Hillsboro Pike, Nashville, Tenn.

MURRAY, GEORGE D., Lieut. (j.g.).

MURRAY, GEO. S., Lieut. (j.g.).

MURRAY, HARRY, Student Officer, R. F. D., No. 9 Hillsboro Rd., Nashville, Tenn.

MURRAY, NORBERT M., Ensign.

MURRAY, R. L., Ensign, 2115 5th St., Port Arthur, Tex. Mass. Inst. of Tech., Akron, Ohio; Rockaway Beach, N. Y LTA.

MURRAY, WILLIAM R., Student Officer, 464 Wayne St., Jersey City, N. J.

MURRIN, WILLIAM R., Ensign, 404 W. 115 St., New York City. Mass. Inst. of Tech., Pensacola, San Diego. HTA.

MUSK, DAVID A., Lieut. (j.g.), 51 Powell Ave., Newport, R. I. N. A. No. 902.

MUSSER, HOWARD B., Student Officer, 312 E St., N. E., Washington, D. C.

MYERS, EDWIN E., Student Officer, 46 First St., Hinsdale, Ill.

MYERS, EDWIN H., Student Officer, Hockley, Texas.

MYERS, KENNETH D., Student Officer, 750 Ave. C, Bayonne, N. J.

MYERS, STANLEY H., Ensign, 130 Kings Road, Corvallis, Ore. N. A. No. 1992.

LEWIS MACHINE GUNS MOUNTED ON AN H-16.

(C) Underwood & Underwood N. Y.

RESULT OF A FLIGHT IN FOGGY WEATHER.

NANGLE, CHARLES J.
Ensign
42 Richdale Ave., Somerville, Mass. Mass. Inst. of Tech., Miami, Pensacola. N. A. No. 2122. HTA.

NAUMER, FRED L.
Ensign
Altamont, Ill. Mass. Inst. of Tech., Akron, Pensacola. N. A. No. 2440. LTA.

NEALE, RAYMOND M.
Ensign
1001 24th St. Parkersburg, W. Va. M. I. T., Pensa., Miami, Moutchic, L'Aber Vrach, Bay Sh., Hampton Rds. N. A. No. 687. HTA.

NEILEY, STEPHEN B.
Student Officer
5 Walcott Rd., Winchester, Mass. Great Lakes. HTA.

HS-1 in Flight

NELSON, IRA R.
Student Officer
169 Irvington Ave., So. Orange, N. J. Mass. Inst. of Tech., Key West. HTA.

NELSON, JOHN E.
Ensign
Belvidere St., St. Johnsbury, Vt. Mass. Inst. of Tech., Buffalo. HTA.

NETHERCOT, D. G.
Ensign
518 Cherry St., Winnetka, Ill. Mass. Inst. of Tech., San Diego, Pensacola. N. A. No. 1801. HTA.

NEWBERN, PLINY A.
Ensign
429 East 3rd St., Oklahoma City, Okla. Mass. Inst. of Tech., Bay Shore, Pensacola. N. A. No. 1692. HTA.

NEWBERY, EARL H.
Ensign
High St., Bound Brook, N. J. Univ. Wash., San Diego, Pensacola. N. A. No. 2368. HTA.

NEWELL, FRANK C.
Student Officer
36 Beverly Court, Detroit, Mich. Mass. Inst. of Tech., Key West. HTA.

NICHOLS, JOHN G.
Student Officer
Care of Corporation Commission, Raleigh, N. C. Mass. Inst. of Tech., Miami. HTA.

NICKERSON, C. M.
Ensign
Y. M. C. A., Berkeley, Cal. M. I. T., Marblehead, Bay Sh., Norfolk, Pensa., Miami, London. N. A. No. 445. HTA.

NICKOLS, FRANK A.
Ensign
2210 Roslyn Ave., Baltimore, Md. Mass. Inst. of Tech., Miami. HTA.

NICOLSON, ROBERT L.
Student Officer
689 Piedmont Ave., Atlanta, Ga. Mass. Inst. of Tech., Dunwoody. HTA.

NIEHAUS, ROBERT L.
Ensign
33 San Carlos Apts., Madison Ave., Cincinnati, Ohio. M. I. T., Miami, Pensacola, Great Lakes. N. A. No. 1652. HTA.

NIELSEN, L. H.
Ensign
20 First St., Weehawken, N. J. Mass. Inst. of Tech., Elizabeth, Whitestone, L. I.

NOBLE, MARK
Ensign
Williams Dimond & Co., 310 Sansome St., San Francisco, M. I. T., Pensacola, Dunwoody. N. A. No. 907. HTA.

NOBLE, RUSSELL C.
Ensign
691 Forest St., New Haven, Conn. Mass. Inst. of Tech., Miami, Pensacola, Hampton Roads. N. A. No. 1233. HTA.

NOEL, CELEST J.
Ensign
1330 Concord Ave., Detroit, Mich. M. I. T., Bay Shore, Hampton Rds., Great Lakes, Pensacola. N. A. No. 1760. HTA.

NOEL, EDWARD T.
Student Officer
Scottsbluff, Nebr. Dunwoody, Mass. Inst. of Tech., Great Lakes. HTA.

NULL, TELFORD B.
Lieut. (j.g.)
2676 Birch St., Denver, Colo. Akron, Cape May, Hampton Rds., Key West, Garden City. N. A. No. 1260. LTA.

◈ ◈ ◈ ◈ ◈

NADEAU, R. A., Ensign, 708 Mason St., Flint, Mich.

NASH, DOUGLAS E., Lieut. (j.g.), 35 High St., So. Norwalk, Conn. Mass. Inst. of Tech., Pensacola, Key West. HTA.

NASH, J. F., Lieut. (j.g.), 30 Professor's Row, Tufts College, Mass. N. A. No. 556.

◈ ◈ ◈ ◈ ◈

NASON, ROBERT C., Student Officer, 5 Chester St., N. Cambridge, Mass.

NATHAN, A., War Machinist, 725 Riverside Drive, New York City.

NAUGLE, PHILIP D., Ensign.

NEAL, A. W., Ensign, Jacksonville, Fla. N. A. No. 1386.

NEAL, E. F., Student Officer, 927 West Grace St., Richmond, Va. Seattle, Wash. HTA.

NEAL, WM. W., Student Officer, Louisburg, N. C.

NEALE, R. W., Student Officer, 15 Felton St., Cliftondale, Mass.

NEALE, WM. F., Student Officer, 1422 Austin St., Waco, Texas.

NEEL, GUY WEAVER, Ensign, N. A. No. 1384.

NEFF, SAMUEL W., Student Officer, 61 Washington Sq. South, New York City.

NELAN, THOMAS F., Student Officer, Mifflintown, Pa.

NELMS, F. JR., Student Officer, 552 S. 48th St., Philadelphia, Pa.

NELSON, ELMER L., Carpenter, 4918 Ashland Ave., Chicago, Ill.

NELSON, FRANK C., Ensign, Campbell, Cal. Mass. Inst. of Tech., Bay Shore, Pensacola. HTA.

NELSON, HERBERT E., Student Officer, Emmerton, Va.

NELSON, E., Ensign. N. A. No. 927.

NELSON, R. K., War Machinist.

NEUMANN, CARL W., Student Officer, 147 Delaware Ave., Detroit, Mich.

NEWBY, HERMAN R., Lieut. (j.g.).

NEWELL, FRANK G., Student Officer, 45 Chestnut St., Marlboro, Mass.

NEWHOUSE, ROLLY W., Ensign, Stanford University, Cal. N. A. No. 1435.

NEWLIN, JAMES C., JR., Lieut. (j.g.)., Haverford, Pa. Mass. Inst. of Tech., Pensacola, Montchic, Boscombe Downs, Eng., Northern B. G., Eastleigh, Eng. N. A. No. 312. HTA.

NEWSOME, THOMAS W., Ensign, 4930 Swiss Ave., Dallas, Tex. Mass. Inst. of Tech., Pensacola.

NEWSOM, E. E., Student Officer, Mediapolis, Iowa. Mass. Inst. of Tech., Key West, Fla. HTA.

NEWTON, HORACE E., Student Officer.

NEWTON, OSCAR, JR., Ensign, 1325 N. State St., Jackson, Miss. N. A. No. 2045.

NEWTON, PHILLIP SMITH, Student Officer, Townsend Apt., 11th and Oak Sts., Oakland, Cal.

NIBLACK, A. H., Ensign, 229 Lake Shore Drive, Chicago, Ill. Mass. Inst. of Tech. HTA.

NICHOLS, ALAN G., Ensign, 1501-12th St., N. W., Washington, D. C. N. A. No. 1625.

NICHOLS, JAMES T., Student Officer.

NICHOLS, JOHN M., Student Officer, 157 Washington St., Hempstead, L. I., N. Y.

NICHOLSON, A. W., Ensign, Upland Rd., Cambridge, Ohio. N. A. No. 1547.

NICHOLSON, CARL B., Student Officer.

NICHOLSON, RALPH W., Student Officer, 423 S. Eighth St., Richmond, Ind.

NICKLAS, FELIX P., Student Officer, 547 Hart St., Brooklyn, N. Y.

NICKOLS, I. F., Ensign, Savannah, Mo. Mass. Inst. of Tech., Key West, Miami, Pensacola. HTA.

NIKLASON, CLARENCE R., Student Officer, 2 Avon St., Cambridge, Mass.

NIEDRINGHAUS, PAUL E., Student Officer, 718 S. Linden Ave., Pittsburgh, Pa.

NIGHTINGALE, GORDON T., Student Officer, Moosup, Conn. Mass. Inst. of Tech.

NIGHTINGALE, WINTHROP E., Ensign, Station 'A' Athol, Mass. Mass. Inst. of Tech., Bay Shore, L. I., Pensacola, Fla. N. A. No. 1914. HTA.

NISBET, JAMES A., Lieut. (j.g.), 1055 Vine St., Denver, Colo. Mass. Inst. of Tech., Pensacola, Moutchic, France; Stonehenge, Eng.; Milan and Turin, Italy; Northern B. G. N. A. No. 18. HTA.

NIXON, JESSE M., Student Officer.

NOBLE, CURTISS G., Ensign, 154 Highland Ave., Buffalo, N. Y. Mass. Inst. of Tech., Bay Shore, Hampton Roads, Pensacola, Fla. N. A. No. 1629.

NOBLE, LELAND F., Ensign, Mannsville, N. Y. Mass. Inst. of Tech., Miami, Pensacola, Key West. N. A. No. 2104. HTA.

NOEL, AUGUSTE L., Ensign, 18 Washington Sq., North, New York City. Mass. Inst. Tech., Great Lakes, Hampton Roads, Va. HTA.

NOLAN, JOHN F., Ensign, 2481 Valentine Ave., Fordham, New York City. Mass. Inst. of Tech., Akron, O., and Rockaway Beach, New York. LTA.

NOLAN, M. D., Ensign, 616 Cheyenne Ave., Alliance, Neb. Mass. Inst. of Tech, Key West, Miami, Pensacola, Fla. N. A. No. 1794.

NOLAND, J. L., Ensign.

NOLEN, MARTIN C., Student Officer, 29 Ransome St., Muskegon, Mich.

NORDGREN, ADOLPH G., Student Officer, 412 So. Front St., Mankato, Minn.

NORDHOUSE, STERLING M., Ensign, 120 Broadway, New York City. Mass. Inst. of Tech., Bay Shore, Pensacola. N. A. No. 188. HTA.

NORMENT, ROBERT T., Student Officer, McDonogh, Md.

NORRIS, A. F., Ensign, 24 Princeton St., Worcester, Mass.

NORRIS, BEVERLY A., Student Officer, 15 W. 74th St., New York City.

NORRIS, RALPH H., Lieut. (j.g.), Chelsea, Mass. Mass. Inst. of Tech., Pembroke, Wales, Mullion, Eng., Paimboeuf, France, Montauk, Rockaway. N. A. No. 671. LTA.

NORRIS, SAMUEL R., Ensign, Chapel Hill, N. C. N. A. No. 2099.

NORTH, GUSS A., Student Officer, Federal Bldg., Des Moines, Iowa.

NORTHROP, AUBREY J., Student Officer, 457 Westcott St., Syracuse, N. Y.

NORTON, ARTHUR W., Student Officer, 400 Charles River Road, Cambridge, Mass.

NORVILLE, G. O., Lieut. (j.g.), 35 Mt. Morius Park, New York City.

NOSWORTHY, F. L. E., Student Officer, Hampton, Conn. Mass. Inst. of Tech., Pensacola.

NOTLEY, HARRY E., Ensign.

NOTTINGHAM, WM., Student Officer, 929 Ackerman Ave., Syracuse, N. Y.

NOURSE, RALPH F., Ensign.

NOWELL, JOHN M., JR., Student Officer, 495 Spring St., Atlanta, Ga.

NOYES, HARRY E., Student Officer, 58 Morton St., Newton Centre, Mass. Mass. Inst. of Tech. HTA.

NUCKOLLS, JAMES T., Student Officer, 1504-4th Ave., Columbus, Ga.

NUCKOLS, IRA FREDERIC, Ensign, Savannah, Mo. N. A. No. 1803

NUDD, THOMAS L., Ensign, Dixon, Cal. N. A. No. 1346.

NULL, TELFORD B., Lieut. (j.g.), 1361 Bellaire St., Denver, Colo. N. A. No. 1260.

NUNAMAKER, L. G., Student Officer, Aurora, Nebr. Mass. Inst. of Tech. HTA.

NUNNEKER, CHAS. L., Student Officer, 1722 Baymiller St., Cincinnati, Ohio. Mass. Inst. of Tech. HTA.

NUTT, MILBURN E., Student Officer, Care of First National Bank, Granbury, Tex. Mass. Inst. of Tech., Miami, Fla. HTA.

Owing to the small size of the personnel cuts it was impossible to run copyright or credit lines beneath each photograph. Symbols were therefore assigned each photographer and placed under all such cuts. A key to these symbols follows.—Editor.

Δ Harris & Ewing.
(*B*) Bachrach.
(*E*) Edmonston.
(*F*) F. A. Swaine.
(*G*) Elias Goldensky.
(*K*) "Kazanjian."
(*L*) Marshall Studio.
(*M*) James & Merrihew.
(*N*) Eugene Hutchinson.
(*O*) J. M. Elliott, Phila.
(*R*) Ira L. Hill.
(*S*) "Strauss Portrait."
(*T*) Townsend.
(*U*) Underwood & Underwood.
(*W*) "Sid Whiting Portrait."
(*X*) Hixon-Connelly Studio.

OAKLEY, GEO. T.
Ensign
932 Riverside Ave., Trenton, N. J. Mass. Inst. of Tech., Bay Shore, Pensacola. N. A. No. 1638.

O'BRIEN, HERBERT S.
Student Officer
240 No. Cass St., Wabash, Ind. Mass. Inst. of Tech. HTA.

O'CONNELL, DENNIS F.
Student Officer
158 Adams St., Dorchester, Mass. Mass. Inst. of Tech. HTA.

O'CONNOR, FERGUS A.
Student Officer
5048 Ridge Ave., St. Louis, Mo., Seattle, Wash. HTA.

ODLAND, THEO.
Student Officer
Erskine, Minn. Seattle, San Diego. HTA.

OETINGER, H. W.
Ensign
Warminster, Bucks Co., Pa. Mass. Inst. of Tech., Key West, Pensacola, Miami. N. A. No. 1437. HTA.

OKELL, JACK
Ensign
98 Monte Vista Ave., Oakland, Cal. Mass. Inst. of Tech., San Diego, Pensacola. N. A. No. 1388

OLMSTED, GARDNER
Ensign
2415 Telegraph Ave., Oakland, Cal. Mass. Inst. of Tech., San Diego, Pensacola, Rockaway. N. A. No. 1335. HTA.

OLMSTEAD, H. G.
Student Officer
Adrian, Mich. Mass. Inst. of Tech., Newport, Miami. HTA.

OLSON, CARL G.
Ensign
690 Lawrence St., Appleton, Wis. Mass. Inst. of Tech., Pensacola, Miami. N. A. No. 1829. HTA.

OLSON, EDWARD M.
Ensign
3725 Byron St., Chicago, Ill. Mass. Inst. of Tech., Miami, Key West, Pensacola. N. A. No. 2486. HTA.

OLSON, ROBERT W.
Student Officer
Amboy, Minn., Dunwoody Inst., Minn., Miami. HTA.

OMARAH, C. B.
Ensign
Eureka, Ill. Mass. Inst. of Tech., Akron, Rockaway Beach. LTA.

O'NEILL, D. EDWIN
Ensign
123 W. 70th St., New York City. Mass. Inst. of Tech., Bay Shore, Pensacola, Pauillac, Moutchic, Fromentin. N. A. No. 876. HTA.

ORAM, ROBERT C.
Ensign
648 South 2nd East St., Salt Lake City, Utah. Mass. Inst. of Tech., Miami, Pensacola, Rockaway Beach. N. A. No. 1080.

ORDWAY, RICHARD S.
Ensign
RFD. No. 1, Manchester, N. H. M. I. T., Moutchic, Avord, Fr., Old Sarum, Eng., No. Bomb. Gro. N. A. No. 368. HTA.

ORR, FRANK WYLIE
Lieut. (j.g.)
203 North Brevard St., Charlotte, N. C. Mass. Inst. of Tech., Gunnery Inst.

ORTON, JAMES W.
Student Officer
3337 Garfield Ave., Kansas City, Mo. Mass. Inst. of Tech., Miami. HTA.

OSBURN, C. W.
Ensign
151 W. Pike St., Clarksburg, W. Va. Mass. Inst. of Tech., Bay Shore, Pensacola, Miami. N. A. No. 1742. HTA.

OSGOOD, FORREST C.
Lieut. (j.g.)
12 Woodland St., Arlington, Mass. Mass. Inst. of Tech., Newport, Pensacola. N. A. No. 530. HTA.

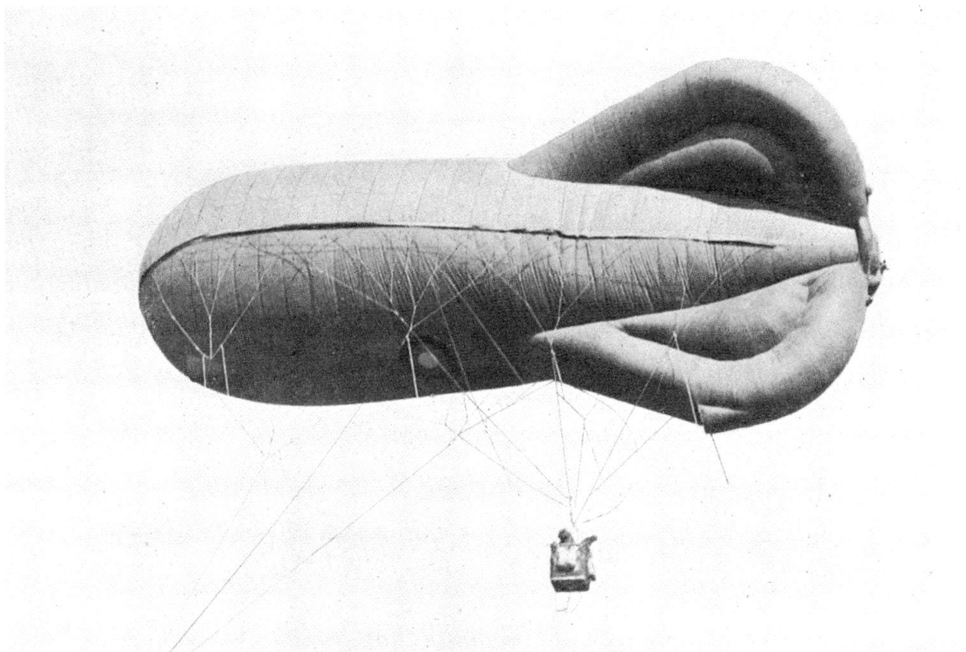

Where the Dashing Heavier-than-Air Pilots Get Seasick

OSGOOD, F. GEORGE
Lieut. (j.g.)
18 Harvard St., Laconia, N. H. Mass. Inst. of Tech., Curtiss Co., Burgess Co. Marblehead, Bu. C. & R. Wash., D. C. LTA.

OSTENBERG, ZENO
Lieut. (j.g.)
R. R. No. 15, Box 75, Los Gatos, Cal. Mass. Inst. of Tech., Pensacola, San Diego. HTA.

OTTAWAY, F. H.
Ensign
Lyons, N. Y. Mass. Inst. of Tech., Bay Shore, Pensacola. N. A. No. 1817. HTA.

OTTERBACK, PHILIP G.
Ensign
3529 13th St., N. W., Washington, D. C. Mass. Inst. of Tech., Akron, Rockaway, Key West. LTA.

OWEN, KNIGHT B.
Lieut. (j.g.)
Vineyard, Haven, Mass. Mass. Inst. of Tech., Pensacola, Moutchic, Fr., Killingholme, Eng. HTA.

OWENS, S. W.
Ensign
213 East Grace St., Richmond, Va. Mass. Inst. of Tech., Miami, Pensacola, Rockaway Beach. N. A. No. 1315. HTA.

◈ ◈ ◈ ◈ ◈ ◈

OAKES, F. WARREN, JR., Lieut. (j.g.), 677 Emerson St., Denver, Colo. Mass. Inst. of Tech., Key West, Fla.; C. N. O. Washington, D. C. N. A. No. 466. HTA.

OBERRENDER, WILLARD H., Student Officer, 482 Summit Ave., South Orange, N. J. Mass. Inst. of Tech.

O'BRIEN, A. W., Ensign, 37 Girard St., N. E., Washington, D. C. N. A. No. 656.

O'BRIEN, HENRY C., Student Officer, 10 Howland St., Cambridge, Mass.

O'BRIEN, HENRY N., Student Officer, 410 W. Sandusky St., Findlay, Ohio.

O'BRIEN, JAMES, Ensign. N. A. No. 764.

O'BRIEN, LAWRENCE T., Ensign.

O'BRIEN, PAUL, Student Officer.

O'BRIEN, WM. VAN R., Student Officer, 1214 N. Calvert St., Baltimore, Md.

OBRIKAT, EDWARD R., Student Officer, 3232 3d St., San Diego, Cal.

O'BRYAN, L. T., Ensign, Springfield, Ky. Mass. Inst. of Tech., Pensacola, Miami. HTA.

O'CALLAGHAN, THOS. E., Student Officer, 1005 W. 10th St., Erie, Pa.

O'CONNELL, DANIEL J., Ensign, 89 Bryant Ave., Milton, Mass. N. A. No. 1245.

O'CONNELL, HAROLD P., Student Officer, 1147 W. 55th St., Chicago, Ill. Mass. Inst. of Tech., Key West. HTA.

O'CONNELL, LELAND D., Student Officer, 393 W. 40th St., Los Angeles, Cal.

O'CONNER, CORNELIUS J., Ensign, N. A. No. 1117.

O'DAY, DANIEL H., Ensign.

O'DONNELL, PAUL F., Student Officer, 400 S. 15th St., Philadelphia, Pa.

OELKERS, A. H., Ensign, San Marcos, Tex. Great Lakes, Ill. LTA.

O'GERMAN, RICHARD J., Student Officer, 3529 Locust St., Philadelphia, Pa.

OGIER, WALTER W., JR., Student Officer.

O'GORMAN, C. J., Ensign, 472 Main St., S. Manchester, Conn.

O'HARRA, ROSWELL B., Student Officer, Carthage, Ill. Dunwoody Institute, Minn.

O'KEEFE, ROBT. R., Student Officer, 29 St. Rose St., Jamaica Plains, Mass.

O'KEEFE, WALTER F., Student Officer, 124 E. Fourth St., Bethlehem, Pa.

OLIVER, JOHN E., Student Officer.

O'LOUGHLIN, LEO T., Boatswain, Brookville, Va. N. A. No. 1321.

OLSEN, CARL G., Ensign, 676 Lawrence St., Appleton, Wis. Mass. Inst. of Tech., Pensacola, Miami. HTA.

OLSEN, HARRY, Ensign, 321 Fulton St., Palo Alto, Cal.

O'MALLEY, PAUL C., Student Officer, Postmaster, N. Y.

O'NEIL, CHAS. R., Student Officer, 10 Central Ave., Flushing, L. I.

O'NEIL, C. F., Ensign, 370 W. Market St., Akron, Ohio. Mass. Inst. of Tech., Akron, Pensacola. N. A. No. 2438. LTA.

O'NEILL, FRANK THOMAS, Student Officer, 541 Tenth Ave., San Francisco, Cal. Mass. Inst. of Tech. HTA.

O'NEILL, NEIL, JR., 750 Bay St., San Francisco, Cal. N. A. No. 1351.

O'NEOL, AUGUSTIN F., Student Officer, 777 Ardmore Ave., Akron, Ohio.

OPPENHEIMER, R. J., Student Officer, 419 Sumner Ave., Springfield, Mass. Mass. Inst. of Tech. HTA.

ORAM, JOHN F., Lieut. (j.g.).

ORAND, JAMES B., Student Officer, 2208 Sangar Ave., Waco, Texas.

ORMSBY, THOMAS F., War. Machinist.

ORR, JAMES O., Student Officer, Woukon, Iowa. Dunwoody, Seattle, Wash. HTA.

ORR, MARSHALL S., Student Officer, Smilry Hall, Claremont, Cal.

ORR, R. C., Ensign, 209 S. LaSalle St., Chicago, Ill. Mass. Inst. of Tech., Pensacola.

ORME, CHARLES D., Ensign.

ORTNER, HOWARD B., Student Officer.

OSBORN, CHARLES A., Student Officer, 1502 Columbia Road, Washington, D. C.

OSBORNE, EDMUND B., Student Officer, Stone Bridge Road, Montclair, N. J. Mass. Inst. of Tech.

OSBORNE, GEO. E., Student Officer.

OSGOOD, WM. P., Ensign, 627 Lake St., Madison, Wis. N. A. No. 2414.

OSTIN, OSCAR L., Ensign, 641 Post St., San Francisco, Cal. N. A. No. 2163.

OSTRIDGE, C. L., Lieut. (j.g.), 198 Summer St., Watertown, Mass. N. A. No. 231.

O'SULLIVAN, H. C., Ensign.

OSWALD, CARL L., Ensign, 17 Rock Creek Church Road, Washington, D. C.

OTT, G., Ensign. N. A. No. 133.

OWEN, GEORGE T., Lieut. (j.g.), 1203 Harvard St., N. W., Washington, D. C. Mass. Inst. of Tech., Pensacola, Queenstown., Aghada, Whiddy Island; Hampton Roads, Va. N. A. No. 274. HTA.

OWENS, JAMES M., JR., Lieut. (j.g.), Box 268, Palm Beach, Fla.

OWENS, THEO., Lieut.(j.g.), College Club, Seattle, Wash.; Pensacola, Fla.; Hampton Roads, Va. HTA.

OXLEY, JOHN H., Ensign, Denver Athletic Club, Denver, Colo. Mass. Inst. of Tech., Pensacola, Wash., New York. N. A. No. 709.

OYEN, A. SCIPIO, Ensign, 1107 Mer. Exch. Bldg., San Francisco, Cal.

PACKARD, ED. B.
Lieut. (j.g.)
12 Marion Rd., Watertown, Mass. Akron, Cape May, Rockaway. N. A. No. 882. LTA.

PACKARD, WARREN
Ensign
612 N. Mahoning Ave., Warren, Ohio. Mass. Inst. of Tech., Buffalo, 3rd Naval Dist. Navy Yard, N. Y.

PACKARD, WM. G.
Ensign
Alpha Delta Phi Club, 136 West 44th St., New York City. Mass. Inst. of Tech., Bay Shore, Pensacola. N. A. No. 1548. HTA.

PAGE, H. M.
Ensign
Keota, Iowa. Mass Inst. of Tech., Pensacola, Operations, Navy Dept HTA,

Silk Parachute in Wind
Showing Shape When Open and Size Relative to Man

PAGE, PHILIP SUMNER
Student Officer
158 Saint Paul St., Brookline, Mass. Mass. Inst. of Tech., Keyport, Elizabeth.

PAILING, STERLING M.
Student Officer
120 North 40th St., Apt. No. 1, Browne, Omaha, Nebr. Mass. Inst. of Tech. LTA.

PAINE, BRYSON
Ensign
Cooper Carlton Hotel, Chicago, Ill. Mass. Inst. of Tech., Key West. N. A. No. 1472. HTA.

PAINTER, ALDEN L.
Ensign
1027 Western Ave., N. S. Pittsburgh, Pa. Mass. Inst. of Tech., Pensacola. HTA.

PALMER, C. A.
Ensign
85 Ann St., Arkon, Ohio. Mass. Inst. of Tech., Akron, Pensacola. N. A. No. 1978. LTA.

PALMER, C. D.
Ensign
Pensacola, Hampton Rds., U. S. S. *Texas*. Anacostia. N. A. No. 116. HTA.

PARET, JOHN W.
Ensign
Quitman, Miss. Mass. Inst. of Tech., Akron, Pensacola. N. A. No. 2156. LTA.

PARKER, ALTON N.
Ensign
Crystal Springs, Miss. Mass. Inst. of Tech., Key West, Pensacola. N. A. No 2132. HTA.

PARKER, KENNETH S.
Ensign
Parker Pen. Co., Janesville, Wis. Mass. Inst. of Tech., Miami, Pensacola. N. A. No. 1042.

PARKER, PARK G.
Ensign
166 N. Mountain Ave., Montclair, N. J. Mass. Inst. of Tech., Bay Shore, Pensacola, Coco Solo, C. Z. N. A. No. 1121. HTA.

PARKS, BENJAMIN S.
Ensign
2712 Halldale Ave., Los Angeles, Cal. Mass. Inst. of Tech., Akron, Rockaway Beach, L. I., N. Y. LTA.

PARKS, RICHARD C.
Student Officer
Timonium, Md. Dunwoody Inst., Minn. HTA.

PARSLEY, CLYDE L.
Ensign
Blackstone Hotel, Omaha, Nebr. Mass. Inst. of Tech., Miami, Pensacola, Chatham. N. A. No. 1989. HTA.

PARSLOW, CHARLES E.
Ensign
913 W. Bishop St., Santa Ana, Cal. Mass. Inst. of Tech., Key West, Miami, Pensacola, Hampton Rds. N. A. No. 1776. HTA.

PARSONS, EBEN
Ensign
48 Humphrey St., Swampscott, Mass. Mass. Inst. of Tech., Blue Hill Observatory, Brunswick, Ga.

PARSONS, LEWIS M.
Ensign
4037 Spruce St., Philadelphia, Pa. Mass. Inst. of Tech., Bay Shore, Hampton Roads, Pensacola. N. A. No. 1157. HTA.

PARTRIDGE, MORRIS
Ensign
Partridge Inn, Augusta, Ga. Pensacola, Mass. Inst. of Tech., Key West. N. A. No. 2491. HTA.

PARTRIDGE, W. H., Jr.
Ensign
Brook St., Wellesley, Mass. Akron, Pensa., Rockaway, Queenstown, R. N. A. S., Roehampton, La Pallice, Brest. LTA.

PATTERSON, W. H.
Student Officer
Devon, Chester Co., Pa. Mass. Inst. of Tech. HTA.

PATTERSON, W. K.
Ensign
208 S. 13th St., Harrisburg, Pa. M. I. T., Key West, Miami, Pensacola, Hampton Rds., Moutchic, N. A. No. 1286. HTA.

PATTISON, WM. H.
Student Officer
1852 Monroe St., N. W., Washington, D. C. Mass. Inst. of Tech., Newport News, Hampton Roads. HTA.

PATTON, JAMES B., Jr.
Ensign
Bon Air, Va. Mass. Inst. of Tech., Miami, Pensacola. N. A. No. 1331. HTA.

PAUL, F. C.
Student Officer
Watertown, Fla. Great Lakes, Pensacola. LTA.

PAXSON, DAVID W.
Ensign
4318 Chestnut St., Philadelphia, Pa. Mass. Inst. of Tech., Akron, Rockaway Beach. LTA.

LIEUTENANT BRONSON LEAVING EXPERIMENTAL CATAPULT IN F BOAT

PEARCE, J. STEELE
Student Officer
23 East Tulpehocken St., Germantown, Philadelphia, Pa. Dunwoody Inst. Minn., Minn. HTA.

PEARSON, FRANCIS H.
Student Officer
66 N. Clay St., Hinsdale, Ill. Mass. Inst. of Tech. HTA.

PEASLEE, ALFRED T.
Ensign
1590 Locust St., Dubuque, Iowa. Mass. Inst. of Tech., Key West, Miami, Pensacola. N. A. No. 1646. HTA.

PECK, F. C.
Ensign
586 Fifth Ave., New York City. Mass. Inst. of Tech., Pensacola, San Diego. N. A. No. 735. HTA.

PECK, L. S.
Lieut. (j.g.)
Sewickley, Pa. Hampton Rds., Moutchic, Fr., Ile Tudy, Fr. N. A. No. 172. LTA.

PEDDLE, J. B.
Student Officer
D'Arlington Apts., Pittsburgh, Pa. Mass. Inst. of Tech., Bay Shore. HTA.

PENDLETON, W. E.
Student Officer
3 Dessau Place, Macon, Ga. Dunwoody, Great Lakes. HTA.

PENNEY, T. C.
Ensign
2501 Girard Ave., So. Minneapolis, Minn. Dunwoody, Miami, Key West, Pensacola. N. A. No. 2397. HTA.

PENNINGTON, S. C., Jr.
Ensign
Paradise Ave., Cantonsville, Md. Mass. Inst. of Tech., Key West, Miami. N. A. No. 1470. HTA.

PERKINS, ERNEST F.
Student Officer
153 E. Emerson St., Melrose, Mass. Mass. Inst. of Tech., Miami. HTA.

PERKINS, M. F.
Student Officer
111 N. Tennessee St., McKinney, Tex. Seattle, Wash. HTA.

PERRIN, JOHN
Lieut. (j.g.)
132 Fisher Ave., Brookline, Mass. Pensacola, Yarmouth. Felixstowe, Lough Foyle, Bay Shore. N. A. No. 202.

PERRY, H. W., Jr.
Student Officer.
18 S. 20th St., Birmingham, Ala. Mass. Inst. of Tech. HTA.

PERRY, R. A.
Ensign
6945 Stewart Ave.,Chicago, Ill. Dunwoody Inst., Miami, Key West, Pensacola. HTA.

PERRY, WARREN M.
Ensign
64 Princeton Ave., Youngstown, Ohio. Mass. Inst. of Tech., Key West, Miami, Moutchic, Campagne. N. A. No. 1456. HTA.

PERRY, WILLIAM M.
Student Officer
4953 Fountain Ave., St. Louis, Mo. Mass. Inst. of Tech. HTA.

PERSONS, ROBERT W.
Student Officer
Marshall, Minn. Mass. Inst. of Tech. HTA.

PETERMANN, F. P.
Lieut. (j.g.)
300 Tamarack St., Laurium, Mich. Dunwoody, Pensacola. N. A. No. 904. HTA.

PETERSEN, EDW. S.
Ensign
726 Drexel Ave., San Antonio (Bexar Co.), Tex. Staff U. S. N. A. Hdqtrs., Paris, Fr., Brest, Fr.

PETERSON, E. ERNEST
Ensign
408 Bellevue Ave., N. Seattle, Wash. Mass. Inst. of Tech., Miami, Pensacola. N. A. No. 1723. HTA.

PETTERSON, S. H.
Ensign
Princeton, Minn. Minneapolis, Miami, Pensacola. HTA.

PETERSON, WM. LOUIS
Lieut. (j.g.)
105 Barry St., Boston, Mass. Mass. Inst. of Tech., R. A. F., Killingholme, Eng., Whiddy Island, Ire. N. A. No. 185. HTA.

PETTIT, ARTHUR E.
Ensign
Stuttgart, Ark. Seattle, San Diego, Pensacola. N. A. No. 2257. HTA.

PHELAN, JAMES
Ensign
43 Bassett St., Lynn, Mass. Pensacola, Norfolk, Killingholme, Eng. N. A. No. 220. HTA.

Dirigible Leaving Hangars at Paimboeuf, France

PHELPS, LABAN P.
Ensign
1317 S. 4th Ave., Louisville, Ky. Mass. Inst. of Tech. Hampton Roads, Key West, Pensacola. N. A. No. 2424. HTA.

PHELPS, WILLIAM S.
Ensign
1121 Vallejo St., San Francisco, Cal. Mass. Inst. of Tech., Key West, Miami, Pensacola. N. A. No. 1762. HTA.

PHILBROOK, W. M.
Ensign
730 Orange Ave., Coronado, Cal. Mass. Inst. of Tech., Bay Shore, Pensacola. N. A. No. 1851. HTA.

PHILLIPS, ELLIOT S.
Ensign
156 E. 79th St., New York City. Mass. Inst. of Tech. Bay Shore, Pensacola, Rockaway. N. A. No. 1680. HTA.

PIERCE, ALLEN F.
Ensign
136 N. Euclid Ave., Westfield, N. J. Mass. Inst. of Tech., Bay Shore, Pensacola, Hampton Rds. HTA.

PIERCE, HAROLD W.
Ensign
224 Adams St., Milton, Mass. Mass. Inst. of Tech., Naval Operations Aviation Division. HTA.

PIERCE, THOMAS D.
Ensign
Langdon, N. D. Mass. Inst. of Tech., Key West, Miami, Pensacola, Hampton Roads. N. A. No. 2079. HTA.

PIERREPONT, S. L.
Ensign
Ridgefield, Conn. Mass. Inst. of Tech., Hampton Roads. HTA.

PINKLEY, GEORGE D.
Ensign
Gibson City, Ill. Mass. Inst. of Tech., Miami, Pensacola. N. A. No. 2321. HTA.

PITTELKOW, A. G.
Student Officer
513 Chalmers Ave., Detroit, Mich. Great Lakes, Pensacola.

PITTMAN, GEORGE H.
Ensign
4932 Worth St., Dallas, Tex. Mass. Inst. of Tech., Key West, Pensacola. N A. No. 2180. HTA.

PLACE, PALMER B.
Student Officer
Newmarket, N. H. Mass. Inst. of Tech. HTA.

(*B*)

PLACE, RUSSELL P.
Ensign
198 St. Paul St., Brookline, Mass. Mass. Inst. of Tech., Pensacola, Eastleigh, Moutchic, Ile Tudy. N. A. No. 686. HTA.

PLANK, EARL F.
Ensign
American Flying Club, 11 East 38th St., New York City. Mass. Inst. of Tech., Miami, Key West, Pensacola. N. A. No. 2638.

PLATT, FRANK C.
Ensign
420 South Elgin St., Tulsa, Okla. Mass. Inst. of Tech., Miami, Pensacola. N. A. No. 2565. HTA.

PLATT, LOUIS J.
Lieut. (j.g.)
30 Church St., New York City. Rockaway. Bu. Steam Engineering, Wash., D. C. LTA.

PLATT, R. L.
Ensign
1127 Grand Ave., Carthage, Mo. Mass. Inst. of Tech., Miami, Pensacola, N. A. No. 1648.

PLUESS, MARTIN D.
Ensign
Ansonia, Ohio. U. of Wash., San Diego, Pensacola. N. A. No. 2303. HTA.

POINDEXTER, CARY A.
Ensign
212 N. 7th St., Temple, Tex. Seattle, Wash., San Diego, Pensacola. N. A. No. 2524. HTA.

POLLARD, JAMES J., Jr.
Ensign
121 Liberty Road, West Somerville, Mass. Mass. Inst. of Tech., Miami, Pensacola. N. A. No. 2226. HTA.

POLLOCK, DUDLEY M.
Student Officer
11623 Euclid Ave., Cleveland, Ohio. University of Washington. HTA.

POOR, ALFRED E.
Ensign
35 East 69th St., New York City. Mass. Inst. of Tech. Key West. HTA.

POPE, JOHN W.
Student Officer
Starkville, Miss. Mass. Inst. of Tech. HTA.

PORE, W. M. H.
Ensign
1016 Foster St., Evanston, Ill. Dunwoody Inst. Minn., Miami, Pensacola. HTA.

SOPWITH MACHINE CONVERTED FOR WATER WORK BY ADDING PONTOONS

PORIKOS, GEORGE S.
Student Officer
Box 38, Des Moines, Iowa Seattle, San Diego. HTA.

PORTER, W. LEROY.
Ensign
St. Ignace, Mich. Mass. Inst. of Tech., Key West, Pensacola, Miami. N. A. No. 1379. HTA.

POST, C. F.
Ensign
5858 Bartlett St., Pittsburgh, Pa. Mass. Inst. of Tech., Cape May, Key West, Miami. N. A. No. 1514. HTA.

POST, GEORGE B.
Lieut. (j.g.)
292 Riverside Drive, New York City. Mass. Inst. of Tech., Bay Shore, Pensacola. N. A. No. 1198. HTA.

POST, L. ABBETT
Ensign
Sound Beach, Conn. Mass. Inst. of Tech., Bay Shore, Brunswick, Ga., Miami. N. A. No. 2046. **HTA.**

POST, THEO. H.
Ensign
Topeka, Kans. Mass. Inst. of Tech., Miami, Pensacola, Hampton Roads, N. A. No. 2105. HTA.

POSTEN, WILLIAM C.
Student Officer
44 Prospect Ave., Atlantic Highlands, N. J. Mass. Inst. of Tech. HTA.

POSTLE, W. E.
Ensign
248 South 17th St., Columbus, Ohio. Mass. Inst. of Tech., Akron, Rockaway, Halifax. LTA.

POTTER, JULIAN W.
Ensign
1257 State St., Bowling Green, Ky. Mass. Inst. of Tech. Pensacola.

POTTINGER, C. A.
Ensign
Fort Atkison, Wis. Mass. Inst. of Tech., Key West, Miami, Pensacola. N. A. No. 1381. HTA.

POTTINGER, EARL H.
Ensign
Fort Atkinson, Wis. Mass. Inst. of Tech., Pensacola, Miami, Autingues, Moutchic. N. A. No. 946. HTA.

POTTS, J. F.
Ensign
1958 East 71 St., Cleveland, Ohio. Great Lakes, Pensacola.

POWERS, H. M.
Lieut. (j.g.)
Hollis, N. H. Mass. Inst of Tech., Pensacola, Ft. Worth, Hampton Rds., Killingholme, Anacostia. N. A. No. 304. HTA.

POWERS, MARSHALL
Student Officer
143 Ridgewood Ave., Glen Ridge, N. J. Mass. Inst. of Tech., Miami. HTA.

POWERS, RALPH A.
Ensign
287 Kent St., Brookline, Mass. Mass. Inst. of Tech., Pensacola, Washington D. C. N. A. No. 259. HTA.

POYNTZ, PEARCE C.
Lieut. (j.g.)
346 Meyran Ave., Pittsburgh, Pa. M. I. T., Key West, Miami, Moutchic, Fr., L'Aber Vrach, Fr N. A. No. 1449. HTA.

PREIL, ALVIN O.
Lieut. (j.g.)
18th and Good Hope Road, Anacostia, Washington, D. C. Mass. Inst. of Tech., Hampton Rds., Pensacola. N. A. No. 538. HTA.

PRESCOTT, FRANK W.
Lieut. (j.g.)
319 Washington St., Dorchester, Mass. Mass. Inst. of Tech., Hampton Rds., Washington, D. C., Pensacola. HTA.

PRETTYMAN, LEE
Lieut. (j.g.)
Cambridge, Md. Mass. Inst. of Tech., Hampton Roads., Pensacola. N. A. No. 1039. HTA.

PRICE, CHARLES C.
Lieut. (j.g.)
1824 Euclid Ave., Cleveland, Ohio. Columbia Univ., Chatham, Mass., Bu. St. Eng. Washington, D. C. HTA.

PRICE, H. STANLEY
Ensign
Bay Shore Blvd., Tampa, Fla. Mass. Inst. of Tech., Miami, Pensacola. N. A. No. 1746. HTA

PRICE, L. P.
Student Officer
5837 Ocean View Drive, Oakland, Cal. Seattle, San Diego, Pensacola.

PRINCE, HUGH W.
Student Officer
112 W. Pope St., Dunn, N. C. Mass. Inst. of Tech., Miami. HTA.

PRYIBIL, PAUL
Ensign
New York A. C., Central Park So., New York City. Mass. Inst. of Tech., Pensacola, Hampton Roads. N. A. No. 731. HTA.

PULITZER, JOSEPH
Ensign
Clayton, Mo. Great Lakes, Hampton Roads.

PURINGTON, C. A.
Ensign
Warren Ave., Plymouth, Mass. Mass. Inst. of Tech., Miami, Pensacola. N. A. No. 1297. HTA.

◈ ◈ ◈ ◈ ◈ ◈

PACE, ASHLEY D., Student Officer.

PACE, WILLIAM G., JR., Woodberry Forest, Va.

PACKARD, EDWARD B., Lieut. (j.g.)., 12 Marion Road, Watertown, Mass. Akron, Cape May, Rockaway. LTA.

PACKARD, LAURENS A., Student Officer, 453 LaGrange St., S. Haven, Mich.

PACKER, ROSCOE W., Student Officer, R. F. D. No. 3, Marshalltown, Iowa. Univ. of Washington, Seattle.

PADDLEFORD, GLENN D., Student Officer, 519 Houston St., Manhattan, Kans.

PAGE, DONALD L., Student Officer, King Edward Apts., Melwood St., Pittsburgh, Pa.

PAGE, KILBY A., Student Officer, 415 W. Davis St., Burlington, N. C. Mass. Inst. of Tech., Bay Shore, L. I.; Brunswick, Ga.; Key West, Fla. HTA.

PAIGE, EDGAR R., Student Officer.

PAINE, STEPHEN, Ensign, 409 Commonwealth Ave., Boston, Mass. Mass. Inst. of Tech., Key West, Fla' N. A. No. 1465. HTA.

PALMEDO, ROLAND, Ensign, The Edgemere, East Orange, N. J. Pensacola; Dover, Portland, Eng.; Op., Washington, Hampton Roads, Va.

PALMER, CHARLES B., Student Officer, 293 Goundry St., N. Tonowanda, New York. Mass. Inst. of Tech. HTA.

PALMER, RICHARD R., Ensign. N. A. No. 1862.

PALMER, T. R., Ensign, 313 Wyoming St., El Paso, Tex. Pensacola; Moutchic, Clermont, Ferrand, L'Aber Vrach, St. Trojan, San Diego. N. A. No. 395. HTA.

PANCOST, MAURICE H., Ensign, R. F. D. No. 6, Lansing, Mich.

PANN, E. H., Ensign, Stanford University, Cal. N. A. No. 1987.

PARDEE, CLARENCE G., Lieut. (j.g.), P. O. Box 231, Hampton Roads, Va.

PARENT, J. H., Ensign. N. A. No. 1303.

PARKE, RICHARD C., Student Officer, Timonium, Md.

PARKER, AUSTIN, Lieut. (j.g.), New York City. Aviation Corps, French Army, Porto Corsini, Venice (241st Squadron, Italian Navy). N. A. No. 1030. HTA.

PARKER, ERLON H., Ensign, Farmington, Me. Tours, San Raphiel, Issoudon, Moutchic, Dunkirk, Fr.; Bolsena, Italy; Scotland; Rockaway Beach. N. A. No. 758. HTA.

PARKER, KNOWLTON, Student Officer, Robinson, Kans.

PARKER, PARK G., Ensign, 166 N. Mt. Ave., Montclair, N. J. N. A. No. 1121.

PARKER, RAYMOND H., Student Officer, Bluehill, Me.

PARKINSON, GEO D., Ensign, 623 1st Ave., Salt Lake City, Utah.

PARKS, REATH WM., Student Officer, 1484 East 108 St., Cleveland, Ohio. Mass. Inst. of Tech. HTA.

PARLETT, RAYMOND C., Ensign, 1509 E. Biddle St., Baltimore, Md. Mass. Inst. of Tech., Packard, Detroit, Mich.

PARONS, R. M., Ensign, Amagansett, L. I.

PARRELL, STEPHEN A., Lieut. (j.g.).

PARSLOW, WM. K., Student Officer, Wesleyan Univ., Middleton, Conn.

PARSONS, JAMES H., Student Officer, 511 Spruce Ave., Kansas City, Mo.

PARVIN, J. L., Lieut. (j.g.), Prosper, Tex. N. A. No. 691.

PASHLEY, WM. P., Student Officer, 132 St. James Place, Brooklyn, N. Y. Great Lakes. HTA.

PASS, R. H., Ensign, S. Avery Ave., Syracuse, N. Y. Mass. Inst. of Tech., Key West, Miami, Pensacola. N. A. No. 1390. HTA.

PATRICK, HARRY, Student Officer, 4943 Blackstone Ave., Chicago, Ill.

PATTERSON, J. D., Ensign, 1039 Magazine St., New Orleans, La.

PATTERSON, Z. H., Ensign, 24 Fountain Place, Poughkeepsie, N. Y. Mass. Inst. of Tech., Bay Shore; Pensacola, Fla.; Rockaway Beach, L. I. N. A. No. 324.

PATTILLO, T. B., Ensign, Terrell, Texas. Mass. Inst. of Tech., Bay Shore, Pensacola, Fla. N. A. No. 1409. HTA.

PATTON, HARRY C., Student Officer, Mill City, Oregon.

PATTON, JOS L., War. Machinist, Bon Air, Va.

PATTON, LAWRENCE H., Student Officer, 80 Rhodes Ave., Akron, Ohio.

PAUKEN, C. H., Lieut. (j.g.), 228 Mt. Hope Place, New York City. Mass. Inst. of Tech., Hammondsport, Gloucester.

PAUL, ARTHUR, Lieut. (j.g.), Chestnut Hill, Philadelphia, Pa. Mass. Inst. of Tech., Pensacola, Hampton Roads, Bay Shore; Brunswick, Ga.; Miami, Fla. N. A. No. 340. HTA.

PAUL, E. R., Ensign, 2412 Piedmont Ave., Berkeley, Cal. N. A. No. 1925.

PAUL, JOHN GILE, Lieut. (j.g.), Watertown, Fla. Mass. Inst. of Tech., Akron, Hampton Roads, U. S. Fleet, (U. S. S. *Shawmut*), Key West. LTA.

PAULSEN, C. H., Ensign, 228 Mt. Hope Pl., New York City.

PAYNE, C. H., Ensign, 201 Weatherfield Ave., Hartford, Conn. N. A. No. 483.

PAYNE, CLYDE S., Ensign, 1350 Jones St., San Francisco, Cal.

PAYNE, ROBERT I., Student Officer.

PAYSON, S. E., Lieut. (j.g.), Loma Portal, San Diego, Cal. N. A. No. 432.

PEABODY, JULIAN, Lieut. (j.g.), Westbury, N. Y. Intelligence Officer, Washington, Moutchic, Paimboeuf, Guipavas.

PEACHY, HENRY KYD DOUGLAS, Ensign, The Decatur Apts., Washington, D. C. Naval Observatory, Washington, D. C.; Aeronautical Accessory Dept., New York City.

PEACOCK, EDWARD L., Ensign, 50 King Ave., Detroit, Mich. Mass. Inst. of Tech., Miami, Pensacola. N. A. No. 1546. HTA.

PEAKES, G. L., Student Officer, General Bakelite Co., Perth Amboy, N. J. Mass. Inst. of Tech. HTA.

PEALE, WM. B., Student Officer, 40 E. 62 St., New York City.

PEARSON, MAURY C., Student Officer, Care of Central Nat'l Bank, Spartanburg, S. C.

PEARSON, P. C., Ensign, Greenwich, Conn. Mass. Inst. of Tech., Miami, Pensacola. N. A. No. 1368. HTA.

PEASE, MAXFIELD, Ensign, 15 Queensberry St., Boston, Mass. Mass. Inst. of Tech., Buffalo, Washington, New York. HTA.

PECK, FREMONT G., Student Officer, 381 Clinton Ave., Brooklyn, N. Y.

PECK, SCOT E., Ensign. N. A. No. 916.

PEDERSON, JOHN E., Ensign.

PEDOTT, SIDNEY, Ensign, 4339 Boulevard, Chicago, Ill. N. A. No. 2294.

PEIFFER, LAWRENCE J., War. Gunner.

PELTON, PAUL C., Student Officer, 125 Pearl St., Rutland, Vt. Mass. Inst. of Tech., Miami, Fla. HTA.

PELTZ, GORDON M., Lieut. (j.g.), 123 Ithaca St., Elmhurst, L. I., N. Y. Mass. Inst. of Tech., Great Lakes Training Station. HTA.

PEMBERTON, HENRY R., Student Officer, 1008 Clinton St., Philadelphia, Pa.

PEMBERTON, WM. L., Ensign, 30 West 44th St., New York City. Mass. Inst. of Tech., Akron, Ohio; Pensacola, Fla. N. A. No. 1364. LTA.

PENDLETON, M. E., Ensign, 247 Rodes Ave., Lexington, Ky.

PENGUE, A. F., Carpenter, 148 Orchard St., Bridgeport, Conn.

PENN, ALBERT W., Ensign, 3112 West Ave., Austin, Tex. Mass. Inst. of Tech., Miami, Fla.; Pensacola. Fla. HTA.

PENNIMAN, C. F., Lieut. (j.g.), Care of R. H. Johnson, 1816 Park Ave., Richmond, Va. N. A. No. 2350.

PENNOCK, E. R., Ensign, 1111 Seventh Ave., Altoona, Pa.

PENRODE, GLENN FRANK, War. Machinist, 42 Woodward Terrace, Detroit, Mich.

PENTZ, R. H., Student Officer, Du Bois, Pa. Mass. Inst. of Tech., Miami. HTA.

PERKINS, ARNOLD M., Ensign, 310 N. Vienna, Ruston, La. N. A. No. 2309.

PERKINS, C. B., Student Officer, 760 Milwaukee St., Denver, Colo. Seattle, Wash.; San Diego. HTA.

PERLMAN, JESSE B., Ensign.

PERIN, OLIVER W., Student Officer, 5368 Hamilton Ave., Cincinnati, Ohio.

PERRIN, G. M., Student Officer, 42 Capen St., Stoughton, Mass. Mass. Inst. of Tech. HTA.

PERRON, H. V., Ensign. N. A. No. 357.

PERRY, P. R., Student Officer, 2515 Columbia Rd., N. W., Washington, D. C.

PERRY R. D., Ensign, 2426 Virginia St., Berkeley, Calif. Mass. Inst. Tech., Bay Shore, Pensacola, Miami, Miami Marine Field, San Diego. HTA.

PERRY, VOLNEY B., Student Officer, Cambridge, Mass.

PERRY, WARREN B., Student Officer, Brattleboro, Vt.

PERRY, WILLIAM M., Student Officer, 4953 Fountain Ave., St. Louis, Mo.

PETERMANN, M. V., JR., Student Officer, Franklin Grove, Illinois. Dunwoody Inst., Minn.; Miami. HTA.

PETERS, E. B., Ensign, 1222 Irving St., Washington, D. C.

PETERS, HARLOW J., Student Officer, 62 West 51st. St., New York City, N. Y. Mass. Inst. of Tech. HTA.

PETERS, KARL A., Student Officer, 310 N. Warren Ave., Big Rapids, Mich. Mass. Inst. of Tech., Miami, Fla. HTA.

PETERS, REED G., Ensign, 4822 Cass St., Omaha, Nebr.

PETERS, THOMAS B., Student Officer, Chandler Hotel, Fort Worth, Tex.

PETERSEN, H. P., War. Machinist, 257 W. Grand St., Elizabeth, N. J. Eastleigh, Eng.

PETERSON, EMMETT J., Student Officer.

PETERSON, F. SOMERS, Lieut. (j.g.), Belvedere, Marin County, Cal. San Diego, Pensacola, Key West. N. A. No. 2236. HTA.

PETERSON, JOEL B., Student Officer, 11132 S. Hoyne Ave., Morgan Park, Ill.

PETERSON, LEROY, Student Officer, 69 West 11th St., New York City. Mass. Inst. of Tech. HTA.

PETERSON, WM. H., Student Officer, 2719 Wheeling St., El Paso, Tex.

PETREE, JAY RALPH, Ensign, Oregon, Mo. Seattle, Wash.; Miami, Pensacola, Fla. N. A. No. 2460. HTA.

PETRING, G. K., Student Officer, Nebraska City, Nebr. Mass. Inst. of Tech. HTA.

PETTYJOHN, C. R., Ensign, 700 Federal St., Lynchburg, Va. Mass. Inst. of Tech., Akron, O.; Rockaway Beach. LTA.

PFEIFFER, LAWRENCE J., War. Gunner.

PHARIS, CHAS, S., Student Officer, 1750 W. Genesee St., Syracuse, N. Y. Mass. Inst. of Tech., Bay Shore, N. Y.

PHEIFFER, ARTHUR E., Ensign, 4 Hadwen Lane, Worcester, Mass. N. A. No. 1193.

PHELPS, DUDLEY W., Student Officer, 1757 K St., N. W., Wash., D. C.

PHELPS, WM. C., Student Officer.

PHILBIN, GERALD G., Ensign, 63 W. 52 St., New York City. Mass. Inst. of Tech., Key West, Miami, Fla., Rockaway Beach, Moutchic, Conyagne, Malpensa. HTA.

PHILLIPS, ARTHUR WM., Student Officer, 29 E. State St., Albion, N. Y.

PHILLIPS, HENRY A., Student Officer.

PHILLIPS, PAUL M., Student Officer, 1218 Washington St., Wilmington, Del.

PHINNEY, JAMES H., War. Gunner.

PIAGET, EUGENE A., Student Officer, Llewellyn Park, West Orange, N. J.

PICCIRILLI, P. J., Lieut. (j.g.).

PICKARD, CLARENCE, Student Officer, 410 E. 4th St., Indianola, Iowa.

PICKARD, WILLARD C., Student Officer, 410 E. Fourth Ave., Indianola, Iowa.

PICKERING, LELAND L., Student Officer, R. F. D. No. 4, Fullerton, Cal.

PICKETT, HAROLD C., Student Officer, 24 Andover St., Georgetown, Mass. Mass. Inst. of Tech., Key West. HTA.

PIEL, W., Ensign, 150 Riverside Drive, New York City.

PIERCE, ALLIN H., Student Officer.

PIERCE, FRANCIS B., Student Officer, 2225 Sedgwick Ave., New York City.

PIERCE, HAROLD W., Ensign, 224 Adams St., Milton, Mass. Mass. Inst. of Tech., Naval Operations Aviation Division. HTA.

PIERCE, JAMES L., Student Officer, Blessing, Tex. Seattle, Wash. HTA.

PIERCE, WILLIAM BROWN, Student Officer, 5114 Harper Ave., Chicago, Ill. Great Lakes. HTA.

PIERS, EBER F., Lieut. (j.g.), 2730 Harrison Ave., Ogden, Utah. Mass. Inst. of Tech., San Diego, Cal.; Pensacola, Fla.; Navy Dept., Washington, D. C. LTA.

PIERSON, LISLE AVERY, Ensign, 441 Greenwich Ave., New Haven, Conn. Columbia Univ., Detroit, Great Lakes.

PIGEON, FRANK B., Student Officer, 174 Lexington St., East Boston, Mass.

PIGON, C. H., Ensign, 36 Wallace St., Somerville, Mass. Mass. Inst. of Tech., Miami, Pensacola, Fla. N. A. No. 1611. HTA.

PIKE, C. M., Ensign, Lubec, Maine. N. A. No. 293.

PILLARS, HERBERT O., Student Officer, 308 Muscatine Ave., Iowa City, Iowa.

PINE, CHARLES A., Student Officer, 44 W. Sydney Ave., Mount Vernon, N. Y.

PINKHAM, GEO. F., Ensign.

PINKNEY, HAROLD M., Student Officer, 247 Ida St., Alegan, Mich.

PIPER, H. C., Ensign, 321 Clifton Ave., Minneapolis, Minn. Mass. Inst. of Tech., Miami. N. A. No. 1515. HTA.

PIPER, ROBERT L., JR., Ensign, Tyrone, Pa. R. N. A. S. Cranwell, Eng.; R. A. F. Capel, Eng.; Paimboeuf, France, and Cape May. N. A. No. 667. LTA.

PIPER, WALTER S., Student Officer, 469 Fourth Ave., L. I. City, N. Y.

PIPP, WALTER C., Student Officer, Care American League Base Ball Club, New York City.

PITTS, J. L., War. Machinist.

PITTS, W. S., Lieut. (j.g.), 116 Grove St., Montgomery, Ala. N. A. No. 470.

PITZER, L. J., War. Machinist, Waukegan, Ill.

PIXLER, L. C., Ensign.

PLASTER, MAX L., Student Officer.

PLATT, WILLIAM, Ensign, 135 E. 66th St., New York City. Mass. Inst. of Tech., Hampton Roads, Pensacola, Anacostia; Moutchic, Brest, France. N. A. No. 489. HTA.

PLUMB, WALTER FITZGERALD, Ensign, 32 Pleasant St., S. E., Grand Rapids, Mich. Mass. Inst. of Tech., Key West, Miami, Pensacola. N. A. No. 1842. HTA.

PLUMB, WALTER G., Ensign, 2123 Cal. St., Washington, D. C.

POLK, EARLE V., Student Officer.

POLK, E. F., Student Officer, Bolivar, Tenn. Mass. Inst. of Tech., Akron, O., Rockaway Beach. LTA.

POLLARD, PATRICK M.

POLLARD, R. V., Ensign, 1016 River St., Hyde Park, Mass. Mass. Inst. of Tech., Squantum, Akron, Rockaway, Brest, Bay Shore, USS. Arkansas, Pensacola. HTA.

POND, CORNELIUS V., Student Officer, 515 W. King St., Owosso, Mich.

POPE, ARTHUR W., JR., Ensign, 428 Charles River Road, Cambridge, Mass.

POPE, LOVERNE A., Lieut. (j.g.), Care of J. H. Pope R. D. No. 1, Hastings, Nebr. RAF, Cranwell, Eng., Howden, Lowthorpe, Yorkshire, Eng., Kingsnorth, Kent, Eng. N. A. No. 1032. LTA.

POPE, WM. H., Student Officer, 163 E. College St., Oberlin, Ohio.

PORCHER, FRANCIS D., Student Officer, 105 Gainsboro, Boston, Mass.

PORTER, FREDERIC H., Student Officer, General Delivery, San Diego, Cal.

PORTER, JOHN, JR., Ensign, Fessenden School, West Newton, Mass. Mass. Inst. of Tech.

PORTER, JAMES M., JR., Ensign, 53 North 3d St., Easton, Pa. Mass. Inst. of Tech., Pensacola, Fla., Miami (Marine Field); Northern Bombing Group, France. N. A. No. 655. HTA.

PORTER, THURMAN H., Student Officer, 1111 4th St., S. E., Minneapolis, Minn.

POTTER, T. W., Ensign, Westchester, N. Y.

POTTER, WM. F., Ensign, 2501 Girard Ave., S. Minneapolis, Minn.

POUND, H. W., Ensign, 1016 E. Center St., Warsaw, Ind.; Dunwoody, Miami, Key West, Pensacola. HTA.

POUNDS, ARTHUR K., War. Boatswain.

POUNDS, LEWIS C., Student Officer, 317 E. 17th St., Brooklyn, N. Y. Mass. Inst. of Tech., Miami. HTA.

POWE, W. C., Ensign, Newton, Miss. N. A. No. 986.

POWEL, BENJAMIN R., Student Officer, P. O. Box 242, Montgomery, Ala.

POWELL, RALPH C., Student Officer, Allendale Farm, Media, Pa.

POWELL, ROBERT JAMES, Ensign, 326 W. 72d St., New York City. Mass. Inst. of Tech., Buffalo, Washington, New York.

POWERS, A. H., Ensign, 611½ Main St., Fort Worth, Tex., Seattle, Washington; San Diego, Cal., Pensacola, Fla. N. A. No. 2291. HTA.

POWERS, EDWARD W., Ensign, 274 Westwood St., Youngstown, Ohio.

POWERS, GEORGE E., Student Officer, 181 Somerset Ave., Taunton, Mass.

POWERS, T. G., Ensign.

PRATT, HENRY Z., War. Machinist, 400 W. 145th St., New York City. N. A. No. 426.

PRATT, JAMES M., Lieut. (j.g.), 371 Central Park West, New York City. Mass. Inst. of Tech., Chatham, Newport, R. I.

PRATT, PHILIP R., Ensign, 2015 Columbia Rd., Washington, D. C. Mass. Inst. of Tech., Pensacola, Hampton Roads, Langley Field. N. A. No. 418. HTA.

PREBLE, FRED C., Student Officer, 218 E. 12th St., Hutchinson, Kans.

PRESTON, CLIFFORD H., Ensign, 50 Washington Sq., East, New York City.

PRESTON, E. M., Student Officer, 515 W. Franklin St., Richmond, Va. Seattle, Washington. HTA.

PRESTON, RALPH A. D.. Ensign. N. A. No. 619.

PRESTON, RANDALL J., Student Officer, 1604 Hyeworth Bldg., Chicago, Ill.

PRICE, ROBERT M., Ensign, 219 N. Laurel St., Hazelton, Pa. Key West, Pensacola. HTA.

PRIDDIE, TAZEWELL PATTON, Student Officer, Waco, Tex., First State Bank & Trust Co. Seattle, Washington. HTA.

PRIDE, ALFRED M., Ensign, 150 Hudson St., Sommerville, Mass. N. A. No. 1119.

PRIEN, WALTER F., Lieut. (j.g.), 63 Nicholson St., Rochester, N. Y. Mass. Inst. of Tech., Washington, London, Dunkerque, Le Croisic, Northern Bombing Group. HTA.

PRINCE, EARL S., Student Officer, Salt Lake City.

PRINDLE, KIRK H., Ensign, Spirit Lake, Idaho. Mass. Inst. of Tech., San Diego, Cal.; Pensacola, Fla. N. A. No. 1804. HTA.

PRITCHARD, A. D., Student Officer, 1515 W. Monroe St., Chicago, Ill.

PRITCHARTT, WM. H., Student Officer, 545 E. Buchtel Ave., Akron, Ohio.

PROCTOR, C. C., Ensign, Dearborn, Mich. N. A. No. 977.

PROCTOR, PAUL MILTON, Ensign, 4021 Main St., Kansas City, Mo. Mass. Inst. of Tech., Key West, Pensacola, N. A. No. 2317. HTA.

PROCTOR, RALPH W., Student Officer, 138 Elm St., North Cambridge, Mass.

PROSAER, JAMES C., Student Officer, 8505 Decker Ave., Cleveland, Ohio.

PROVOST, EUSEBE, Lieut. (j.g.), 16 9th Ave., Haverhill, Mass. Mass. Inst. of Tech., Ile Tudy, Porto Corsini, Italy. N. A. No. 323.

PRUDHOM, HAROLD C., Ensign, 305 Union Sta. Plaza, Kansas City, Mo.

PULITZER, H., Lieut. (j.g.), 7 E. 73d St., New York. N. A. No. 410.

PULSIFER, G. H., Ensign, 20 Birch Hill Road, Newtonville, Mass. Mass. Inst. of Tech. HTA.

PUNNETT, T. R., Ensign, 44 W. 10th St., New York City. Mass. Inst. of Tech., Cranwell, Eng.; Roehampton, Eng.; Paimboeuf, France.

PURCELL, EDWARD W., Student Officer, 1406 Delafield Place, Washington, D. C.

PURDHEN, HAROLD E., Student Officer, 1177 Norten Ave., Los Angeles, Cal.

PURDY, CLAIR J., Ensign, 8 Lansing St., Auburn, N. Y. N. A. No. 1655.

PURDY, HERBERT McL., Ensign, N. A. No. 654.

PURSELL, GEORGE F., Ensign.

MAIN BUILDING, M. I. T.

QUIGLEY, F. R.
Ensign
558 Lexington Ave., New York City. Seattle, San Diego, Pensacola. N. A. No. 2448. HTA.

(*E*)
QUINN, DAVID H.
Ensign
568 Newbury St., Boston, Mass. Mass. Inst. of Tech., Miami, Pensacola. N. A. No. 2403. HTA.

RALPH, THOMAS G.
Ensign
54 Hawthorne Ave., Crafton, Pa. Mass. Inst. of Tech., Bay Shore, Pensacola, Sydney, N. S., Hampton Roads. HTA.

RAMEY, ARTHUR G.
Ensign
311 E. Washington St., Charlestown, W. Va. Mass. Inst. of Tech.

RAMSEY, B. M.
Ensign
348 13th Ave., Newark, N. J. Mass. Inst. of Tech., Pensacola, Halifax. N. A. No. 1077. HTA.

RANKIN, HENRY
Student Officer
Gastonia, N. C. Mass. Inst. of Tech., Miami. HTA.

RATHFON, L. PAUL
Student Officer
The Rosemont, Hutchinson, Kansas. Mass. Inst. of Tech., Miami. HTA.

RAUH, STANLEY E.
Student Officer
328 Central Ave., Dayton, Ohio. Mass. Inst. of Tech., Bay Shore. HTA.

RAYMER, PAUL H.
Ensign
Beaver, Pa. Mass. Inst. of Tech., Miami, Pensacola, Queenstown, Wexford, Ire. N. A. No. 1252. HTA.

REA, THATCHER W.
Ensign
367 Longfellow Ave., Detroit, Mich. Mass. Inst. of Tech., Bay Shore, Pensacola, Hampton Roads. N. A. No. 710. HTA.

REAMS, PAUL E.
Ensign
738 Kirkman St., Lake Charles, La. Mass. Inst. of Tech., Key West, Pensacola. N. A. No. 2612 HTA.

REBER, EARL E.
Boatswain
1231 Lewis St., San Diego, Cal. Mass. Inst. of Tech., Pensacola, Newport News, Chatham, San Diego. HTA.

REESE, CHAS. E.
Student Officer
249 E. Walnut St., Westfield, N. J. Mass. Inst. of Tech., Miami. HTA.

REICHELDERFER, F. W.
Ensign
Harlan, Ind. M. I. T., N. Sydney, Miami, Pensa., U.S.S. *Shawmut* Lisbon in NC4. Trans-Atlantic Flight N. A. No. 2422. HTA.

REMSBURG, JOHN H.
Ensign
Middletown, Md. Mass. Inst. of Tech., Key West, Pensacola. N. A. No. 1923. HTA.

RENISON, WILLIAM J.
Ensign
59 Tonawanda St., Dorchester Dist., Boston, Mass. Great Lakes, Pensacola.

RENN, HARRY J.
Student Officer
College St., Oxford, N. C. Mass. Inst. of Tech. HTA.

RENNIE, ROSWELL M.
Lieut. (j.g.)
2129 Third St., Santa Monica, Cal. Mass. Inst. of Tech., Buffalo. HTA.

RENO, L. M.
Ensign
123 W. Madison St., Chicago, Ill. La Fayette F. C., Flanders, Montdidier, Chateau-Thierry, Moutchic, Corsini, Fr., War Cross. N. A. No. 1352. HTA.

RENTZ, THOS. H.
Ensign
205 Puritan Ave., Forest Hills, L. I., N. Y. Mass. Inst. of Tech., Miami, Pensacola. N. A. No. 2567. HTA.

START OF THANKSGIVING DAY RACE, MIAMI, 1918

REX, EDMUND S.
Ensign
9 Brook St., Pawtucket, R. I., Mass. Inst. of Tech., Bay Shore, Pensacola. N. A. No. 1928. HTA.

REYCROFT, HARLAN L.
Ensign
234 Pleasant St., Arlington, Mass. Mass. Inst. of Tech., Miami, Pensacola. N. A. No. 1745. HTA.

REYERSON, PAUL
Student Officer
Dawson, Minn., Dunwoody Inst. Minn., Miami. HTA.

REYNOLDS, H. E.
Student Officer
782 Main St., East., Rochester, N. Y. Mass. Inst. of Tech. HTA.

REYNOLDS, MORRIS W.
Ensign
728 Second Ave., Westmont, Johnstown, Penn. Mass. Inst. of Tech., Bay Shore, Pensacola. N. A. No. 1391. HTA.

RHODES, C. R.
Ensign
Golden Lake Farm, Wilson, Ark. Mass. Inst. of Tech., Pensacola, Hampton Rds, Morehead City. N. A. No. 711. HTA.

RHODES, RUSSEL R.
Ensign
248 E. Sixth St., Peru, Ind. Mass. Inst. of Tech., Miami, Pensacola, N. Sydney, N. S. N. A. No. 1134 HTA.

RICE, HAROLD E.
Ensign
1139 David Whitney Bldg., Detroit, Mich. Mass. Inst. of Tech., Key West, Miami, Pensacola. N. A. No. 1712. HTA.

RICH, EDMUND G.
Ensign
Maquoketa, Iowa. Dunwoody, Great Lakes, Miami, Pensacola. N. A. No. 2586. HTA.

RICHARDS, C. E., Jr.
Ensign
584 East Broad St., Columbus, Ohio. Mass. Inst. of Tech., Buffalo, Washington, Brooklyn, Garden City.

RICHARDSON, BAYLE
Ensign
3742 Regent Ave., Norwood, Ohio. Mass. Inst. of Tech., Key West, Pensacola, Miami. N. A. No. 1192. HTA.

RICHARDSON, C. S.
Ensign
550 Belmont Ave., Chicago, Ill. Mass. Inst. of Tech., Miami Pensacola, Great Lakes, Seattle. N. A. No. 1108. HTA.

RICHARDSON, G. R.
Ensign
404 St. George St., Farmville, Va. Mass. Inst. of Tech., U. S. S. *Utah.* Key West, Pensacola. N. A. No. 2315. HTA.

RICHMOND, ISIDOR
Ensign
69 Everard St., Beachmont, Mass. Mass. Inst. of Tech., Pensacola, Chatham. N. A. No. 918. HTA.

RICHTER, JOSEPH F.
Ensign
2123 No. Clark St., Chicago, Ill. Harvard Radio, Great Lakes, Miami. HTA.

RIDER, FRANK J., Jr.
Student Officer
Hartford, Conn. Mass. Inst. of Tech., Pensacola. HTA.

RIDGAWAY, THOS. N.
Ensign.
2108 N. Charles St., Baltimore, Md. Mass. Inst. of Tech., Miami, Pensacola, Anacostia, D. C. N. A. No. 1318.

RIDGWAY, EDWIN M.
Machinist
1717 17th St., N. W., Washington, D. C. Col. Univ., North. Bomb. Gr., St. Inglevert, Fr.

RIGGINS, LEONARD
Ensign
1010 S. Fla. Ave., Lakeland. Mass. Inst. of Tech., Miami, Pensacola. N. A. No. 1323. HTA.

ROBBINS, FRED T.
Ensign
1412 So. Main St., Rochester, Ind. Mass. Inst. of Tech., Key West, Miami, Pensacola, Killingholme, Eng. N. A. No. 1124.

ROBBINS, MARVIN R.

Student Officer

324 Torboro St., Rocky Mount, N. C. Mass. Inst. of Tech., Miami. HTA.

ROBBINS, R. P.

Ensign

Titusville, Fla. Mass. Inst. of Tech., Miami, Key West, Pensacola. N. A. No. 2569. HTA.

ROBERTS, F. F.

Ensign

908 Jennings Ave., Fort Worth, Tex. Mass. Inst. of Tech., Pensacola, Miami. N. A. No. 2419. HTA.

ROBERTS, JOHN C., Jr.

Ensign

Clayton, Mo. Mass. Inst. of Tech., Miami, Pensacola, Coco Solo. N. A. No. 1287. HTA.

German Chasse Plane at Pola Surrounded by Italian Mechanics, after the Armistice

ROBERTSON, CECIL M.

Student Officer

Deputy Clerk of the Courts, Norfolk, Va. Dunwoody, Minneapolis. HTA.

ROBERTSON, JOHN E.

Student Officer

110 Old Orchard Ave., Webster Groves, Mo. Mass. Inst of Tech. LTA.

ROBERTSON, W. H.

Lieut. (j.g.)

56 Wellesley Pk., Dorchester, Mass. Mass. Inst. of Tech., Boston, Buffalo. HTA.

ROBINSON, A. P.

Lieut. (j.g.)

Haverford, Pa. Mass. Inst. of Tech., Pensacola. N. A. No. 1102. HTA.

ROBINSON, EDWIN O.
Ensign
2925 Gould St., Dallas, Texas. Mass. Inst. of Tech., Miami, Key West, Pensacola. N. A. No. 2597. HTA.

ROBINSON, GLEN E.
Ensign
542 Pipestone St., Benton Harbor, Mich. Mass. Inst. of Tech., San Diego, Pensacola, Chatham. N. A. No. 1255. HTA.

ROBINSON, J. S.
Ensign
King William, Va. Shore. Inst. of Tech., Bay Mass. Key West, Hampton Rds., Pensacola. N. A. No. 462, HTA.

RODGERS, OLIVER
Student Officer
6500 Fifth Ave., Great Lakes, Ill. Great Lakes.

ROE, G. T.
Lieut. (j.g.)
19 Wharf St., Boston, Mass. M. I. T., Pensa., Yarmouth, Lough Foyle, Queenstown, Bay Shore, Key West. N. A. No. 211.

ROE, HARVEY E.
Ensign
Weston, Ohio. Mass. Inst. of Tech., Key West, Miami, Pensacola, Hampton Rds. N. A. No. 1430. HTA.

ROEDELL, CLARENCE
Ensign
Minneapolis, Minn. Dunwoody, Mass. Inst. of Tech., Pensacola. N. A. No. 927. HTA.

ROGERS, DONALD J.
Student Officer
1614 Girard Ave., No-Minneapolis, Minn. Dunwoody, Miami. LTA.

ROGERS, GEORGE E.
Ensign
1 Jersey St., Dedham, Mass. Mass. Inst. of Tech., Bay Shore, Pensacola. N. A. No. 1178. HTA.

ROGERS, RUSSELL F.
Student Officer
419 Baltimore St,. Muskogee, Oklahoma. Mass. Inst. of Tech., Akron, Rockaway Beach. LTA.

ROHWER, FRANK W.
Ensign
Boulder, Colo. Mass. Inst. of Tech., Key West, Miami, Pensacola, Hampton Rds., Morehead City. N. A. No. 1262. HTA.

ROLAND, P. W.
Lieut, (j.g.)
1046 Morris Ave., New York City. Mass. Inst. of Tech., Key West, Pensacola. N. A. No. 2501.

ROLLINS, J. T.
Student Officer
College Station, Texas. Univ. of Wash., Seattle, San Diego. HTA.

ROOD, ROLLIN T.
Ensign
6 Charter Oak St., So. Manchester, Conn. Mass. Ist. of Tech., Miam , Key, West, Pensacola. N. A. 2402. HTA.

ROSENBERGER. F. A.
Ensign
1862 Ontario St., Toledo, Ohio. M.I.T., Pensa , Montauk, Lough Foyle, Queenstown, Whiddy Is., Bay Sh. N. A. No. 1507. HTA.

ROSENTHAL, MORRIS
Student Officer
26 West 90th St., New York City, Seattle, Wash. HTA.

ROSS, CHARLES E.
Ensign
86 Fayette St., Watertown, Mass. Mass. Inst. of Tech., Miami, Pensacola. N. A. No. 1852. HTA.

ROTERING, VICTOR F.
Ensign
122 W. Grant St., Minneapolis, Minn. Dunwoody. Pensacola, Moutchic, Ile Tudy, Fr. N. A. No. 737. HTA.

ROTH, E. HOWARD H.
Student Officer
102 Oakland Place, Buffalo, N. Y. Mass. Inst. of Tech., HTA.

ROTH, HERMAN L.
Ensign
428 3rd Ave., Westmont, Johnstown, Pa. Mass. Inst. of Tech., Miami, Pensacola, Coco Solo. N. A. No. 1113. HTA.

LOOKING TOWARDS THE TAIL IN AN H-16

ROTHEIM, ROBERT
Lieut. (j.g.)
1765 Broadway, New York City. Columbia, Rockaway, Detroit, League Island.

ROTHROCK, A. A.
Student Officer
Thomasville, N. C. Mass. Inst. of Tech., Miami. HTA.

ROTHSCHILD, R. C.
Ensign
150 W. 87th St., New York City. Mass. Inst. of Tech., Akron, Rockaway. LTA.

ROUDEBUSH, JAMES F.
Ensign
Newtonsville, Ohio. Mass. Inst. of Tech., Akron, Rockaway. LTA.

ROULEAU, LOUIS J.
Lieut. (j.g.)
1222 Quincy St., N. E. Washington, D. C. Mass. Inst. of Tech., Key West, Chatham. N. A. No. 453. HTA

ROULET, ALFRED L.
Ensign
665 Farmington Ave., Hartford, Conn. Mass. Inst. of Tech., Bay Shore, Pensacola. N. A. No. 1173. HTA.

ROUNDS, EDWARD W.
Lieut. (j.g.)
248 Gray St., Arlington, Mass. Mass. Inst. of Tech., Hampton Rds., Pensacola. Rockaway. N. A. No. 1290. HTA.

ROURKE, GRATTAN L.
Student Officer
Lisbon, N. D. Mass. Inst. of Tech., Bay Shore, Brunswick. HTA.

ROUSE, DETOR V.
Student Officer
Dover, Fla. Mass. Inst. of Tech. HTA.

ROWE, HARRY A.
Student Officer
Hampton, Va. Mass. Inst. of Tech. HTA.

ROWE, R. M.
Ensign
82 Hancock St., Brooklyn, N. Y. Mass. Inst. of Tech., Great Lakes, Pensacola. N. A. No. 2430. HTA.

ROWEN, HAROLD J.
Lieut. (j.g.)
44 Rockview St., Jamaica Plain, Mass. Mass. Inst. of Tech., Pensacola, Moutchic, Fr., Ile Tudy, Fr., Key West. HTA.

RUDESILL, CARL J.
Student Officer
Charlotte, Mich. Seattle, Miami. HTA.

RUDLOFF, JOHN A.
Student Officer
54 Myrtle Ave., Montclair. N. J. Mass. Inst. of Tech. HTA.

RUDY, PAUL P.
Ensign
1652 Otis Bldg., Chicago, Ill. Mass. Inst. of Tech., Miami, Key West, Pensacola. N. A. No. 2420. HTA.

RUKEYSER, W. A.
Ensign
4 West 43rd St., New York City. Mass. Inst. of Tech., Pensacola, Miami, Key West. LTA.

RUMILL, GEORGE ED.
Lieut. (j.g.)
Indian Point, Me. Mass. Inst. of Tech., Pensacola, Killingholme, Eng., Key West. N. A. No. 217. HTA.

RUMPELT, MORTIMER
Ensign
15 West 38th St., New York City. Bay Shore, Key West, Miami. N. A. No. 542. HTA.

RUTLEDGE, HENRY B.
Ensign
1922 Willow Ave., Minneapolis, Minn. Dunwoody, Montauk, Pelham Bay, Brest, Fr.

RYAN, EDMUND J.
Ensign
1595 Beacon St., Brookline, Mass. Mass. Inst. of Tech., Miami, Pensacola. N. A. No. 2451. HTA.

RYAN, EDWIN S.
Ensign
31 Douglas Ave., Freeport, Ill. Mass. Inst. of Tech., Miami, Key West, Pensacola. N. A. No. 2482. HTA.

RYAN, HAROLD L.
Lieut. (j.g.)
181 Lexington St., Waverly, Mass. Mass. Inst. of Tech., Hampton Rds., Pensacola, Moutchic, Croisic, Fr., N. A. No. 404.

(*W*)
RYAN, O'NEILL, Jr.
Student Officer
29 Windermere Place, St. Louis, Mo., Seattle, Washington. HTA.

Quakenbush, Perry J., Student Officer, 169 Kearney Ave., Perth Amboy, N. J. Mass. Inst. of Tech. HTA.

Quarrier, H. D., Student Officer, Woodsdale, Wheeling, W. Va. Mass. Inst. of Tech. HTA.

Quick, Francis E., Student Officer, 186 Pleasant St., Newton Centre, Mass. Mass. Inst. of Tech., Key West, Fla. HTA.

Quick, Lansing M., Student Officer, 207 Woodworth Ave., Yonkers, N. Y. Mass. Inst. of Tech., Bay Shore. HTA.

Quilhot, Harold J., Ensign, Johnstown, N. Y. Mass. Inst. of Tech., Key West, Pensacola. N. A. No. 2398. HTA.

Quilty, Samuel E., Student Officer, 603 Pujo St., Lake Charles, La.

Quinlan, Herbert E., Student Officer, 1878 E. 84th St., Cleveland, O.

Quinlan, Ralph E., Student Officer, 329 Powe'l St., Henderson, Ky.

Quinn, Francis W., Ensign, 5464 Northumberland St., Pittsburgh, Pa. Mass. Inst. of Tech., Norfolk, Va.; Akron, Ohio; Boston, Mass.; Rockaway Beach, L. I. LTA.

Quinn, J. J., 102 N. 4th Cavell St., Duluth, Minn. N. A. No. 623.

Quittner, Geo., Student Officer, 828 E. Parkway, Brooklyn, N. Y.

Quxick, Lensing M., Student Officer, 207 Woodworth Ave., Yonkers, N. Y.

Quxillian, Whitcomb W., Student Officer, 81 Culbertson St., Atlanta, Ga.

Rae, John H., Student Officer, 571 Park Ave., Rochester, N. Y.

Rafferty, James A., Student Officer, 327 W. 46th St., New York City.

Raffo, D. O., Ensign, Atlanta, Ga.

Raiterm, Clinton R., Student Officer, Alexandria, Minn.

Ramsey, D. W. C. N. A. No. 45.

Randle, Hanson F., Student Officer, 4339 Drexel Blvd., Chicago, Ill. Great Lakes.

Randolph, Donald W., Student Officer, 9th and Washington Sts., Wilmington, Del.

Ransom, Julius C., Student Officer, 64 Little Hall, Princeton, N. J.

Ransome, Charles C., Student Officer, 120 E. 31st St., New York City.

Rapp, Frank A., Student Officer, 352 W. Elm St., Brockton, Mass.

Rasche, Robert C., Ensign, 417 Olney Road, Norfolk, Va.

Raseman, Richard J., Student Officer, 491 E. Grand Blvd., Detroit, Mich.

Rathbun, Harry R., Student Officer, Glen Ellyn, Ill. Dunwoody Inst., Minn., Miami. HTA.

Rattikn, William J., Student Officer, Anson, Tex.

Raven, A. A., Student Officer.

Rawley, Weldon N., Student Officer, Churchville, Va.

Ray, G. W., Jr, Student Officer, 92 Pinckney St., Boston, Mass.; Seattle. LTA.

Ray, William L., Student Officer, 1600 E. La Rue St., Pensacola, Fla.

Read, Duncan H., Lieut. (j.g.), Hill Crest, Penchase N. Y., R. F. C. Toronto, Camp Borden, Bay Shore, Miami, Pensacola. Mass. Inst. of Tech. HTA.

Read, George R., Ensign, 55 Dearborn St., Manchester, N. H.

Read, Robert E., Lieut. (j.g.), Trinity House, Watertown, N. Y. N. A. No. 564.

Read, Russell Bartow, Lieut. (j.g.), 4 E. 62nd St., New York City.

Read, William A., Jr., Ensign, 28 Nassau St., New York City. Mass. Inst. of Tech., Pensacola, Ft. Worth, Washington, D. C. N. A. No. 1366. HTA.

Reagan, R. J., Student Officer, 439 State Road, Cynwyd, Pa.

Reardon, John L., Student Officer.

Reavia, John W., Student Officer, 2943 Macomb St., Washington, D. C.

Redmond, Geraldyn L., Student Officer, Tivoli, N. Y. Mass. Inst. of Tech., Bay Shore, N. Y. HTA.

Reed, Edward Goodwin, Student Officer, University Club, 3813 Euclid Ave., Cleveland, Ohio.

Reed, Harry A., Switow Bldg., Jeffersonville, Ind.

Reed, Jacob, Lieut. (j.g.), 150 Elm St., Worcester, Mass. Squantum, San Diego. HTA.

Reed, Lawrence A., Student Officer, 1437 N. Jeff St., Springfield, Mo.

Reed, Lawrence Neill, Student Officer, Heber Springs, Ark. Seattle, Wash.; San Diego. HTA.

Reed, Leonard W., Student Officer, 2150 Drake Park Ave., Des Moines, Iowa.

Reed, Royden E., Lieut. (j.g.), 55 Dearborn St., Manchester, N. H.

Reed, Rush H., Lieut. (j.g.).

Reed, William D., Student Officer, Holland, Texas.

Reeder, J. R., Ensign, 641 Park Way, Monessen, Pa.

Reemelin, Clarence B., 3061 Cleinview Ave., Cincinnati, Ohio.

Reeves, Owen T., Student Officer, 266 Randolph Ave., Peoria, Ill. Mass. Inst. of Tech., Key West, Fla. HTA.

Rehman, Norman, Student Officer, 135 Renner Ave., Newark, N. J.

Reich, Frederick C., Student Officer, 457 Fourth Ave., Long Island City, N. Y.

Reich, William F., Jr., Ensign, 11-18 St., Elmhurst, Long Island, N. Y. Mass. Inst. of Tech., Key West.

Reid, Geoffrey L., Student Officer, 111 Main St., N. Andover, Mass.

Reid, Howard C., Student Officer, 110 Morningside Drive, New York City. Mass. Inst. of Tech., Miami. HTA.

Reid, William S., Student Officer, Due West, S. C.

Reider, Francis D., Student Officer, 1003 N. Huron St., Ann Arbor, Mich.

Reifert, Jack H., Student Officer, 134 Lincoln Ave., Syracuse, N. Y. Mass. Inst. of Tech., Pelham Bay, U. S. S. C. 245. HTA.

Reilly, Joseph C., Student Officer, 218 E. Price St., Philadelphia, Pa.

Reinhardt, C. G., Ensign, 103 Rochelle Ave., Philadelphia, Pa.

Remey, John T., Lieut. (j.g.), 1527 New Hampshire Ave., Washington, D. C. N. A. No. 187.

REMMERS, JOHN J., Student Officer, 1149 N. Raymond St., Pasadena, Cal.

RENTSCHLER, PETER E., Student Officer, 917 Campbell Ave., Hamilton, Ohio. Dunwoody Inst., Minn. HTA.

RENWICK, ERLE B., Student Officer, 3 Brinsley St., Grove Hall, Boston, Mass.

RENWICK, J. G., Lieut. (j.g.), Princeton, N. J. N. A. No. 901.

RENZ, EDWARD F., Student Officer, 349 Garfield Ave., Syracuse, N. Y. Mass. Inst. of Tech., Akron, Ohio. LTA.

REPKO, J. S., War. Machinist, Queens Road, Queens, Long Island, N. Y.

REQUA, LAWRENCE K., Ensign, 321 Mountain Ave., Piedmont, Cal. Mass. Inst. of Tech., Key West, Pensacola. N. A. No. 1861. HTA.

REUSCHEL, J. E., War. Gunner, Maryland Hotel, San Diego, Cal. Miami, Pensacola, Harvard, San Diego. N. A. No. 1347. HTA.

REVELLE, HARRY H., Student Officer, 506 Lahoma Ave., Norman, Okla.

REX, WALTER EDWIN, Ensign, 8836 Crefeld St., Chestnut Hill, Philadelphia, Pa. Mass. Inst. of Tech., Pensacola, Fla. N. A. No. 1837. HTA.

REYBURN, FRANCIS C., Student Officer, 4529 Lindell Ave., St. Louis, Mo.

REYCROFT, WENDELL G., Ensign, 234 Pleasant St., Arlington, Mass. Mass. Inst. of Tech., Key West, Miami, Marine Field, Moutchic, N. Bomb. Gr. N. A. No. 1446. HTA.

REYMOND, DALTON S., Student Officer, 442 N. Blvd. Baton Rouge, La.

REYNOLDS, HARRY V., Ensign, 248 S. Flower St., Los Angeles, Cal.

REYNOLDS, SAMUEL W., Ensign, 714 10th St., Oakland, Cal. Mass. Inst. of Tech., Miami, Pensacola. HTA.

RHOADES, DEE J., Ensign, 704 Locust St., Big Rapids, Mich. Seattle, Wash., San Diego.

RHODES, AUGUSTUS L., Student Officer, The Alameda, San Jose, Cal.

RHODES, BRAXTON, 251 E. Gregory St., Pensacola, Fla.

RHODES, FRED B., Ensign, 3006 Albermarle St., Washington, D. C.

RHODES, WASHINGTON I., Student Officer, Toms Brook, Shenadoah Co., Va.

RICE, ALBERT F., Lieut. (j.g.), 16 Hamilton Terrace, New York City. Mass. Inst. of Tech., Pensacola, Fla. N. A. No. 433.

RICE, CHAS. B., Student Officer, 1225 Jarvis Ave., Chicago, Ill.

RICE, CLARENCE E., Student Officer, Hayes Center, Nebr.

RICE, FREDERICK W., JR., Student Officer, 16 Elko St., Brighton, Mass. Mass. Inst. of Tech. HTA.

RICE, J. PERCIVAL, Student Officer, 2510 Rio Grande St., Austin, Texas. Mass. Inst. of Tech., Akron, Rockaway. LTA.

RICE, NEIL W., Ensign, South Hamilton, Mass. Mass. Inst. of Tech.

RICE, STANLEY B., Student Officer, 4142 Parkside Ave., Philadelphia, Pa.

RICE, WILLIAM E., Student Officer, Famous Bldg., Perry, Okla.

RICH, J. J., Student Officer, 27 W. 61st St., New York City.

RICHARD, G. L., Knoxville, Tenn. N. A. No. 497.

RICHARDS, H. DONALD, Ensign, 353 Church St., Royersford, Pa. Mass. Inst. of Tech., Akron, Pensacola. LTA.

RICHARDS, LEON K., Student Officer, Britt, Iowa.

RICHARDS, LORENZO M., Student Officer, Buckingtonham Apts., Salt Lake City, Utah.

RICHARDS, THOMAS G., Ensign, 619 S. B. B. St., Los Angeles, Cal. N. A. No. 2246.

RICHARDS, W. V., Lieut. (j.g.), Fishers, Ind.

RICHARDSON, DAVID W., Student Officer, 28 E 8th St., New York, N. Y.

RICHARDSON, GEO. W., Ensign, 250 W. 82nd St., New York City.

RICHARDSON, GEO. W., JR., Student Officer, 138 E. 79th St., New York City.

RICHARDSON, JAMES M., Student Officer, 627 Lake St., Madison, Wis.

RICHARDSON, JOHN, Student Officer, 204 Trust Bldg., Rockford, Ill. Mass. Inst. of Tech., Miami, Fla. HTA.

RICHARDSON, LAWRENCE, Ensign, 45 Weissinger Gaulvert Apts., Louisville, Ky. Mass. Inst. of Tech., New York, Rockaway.

RICHARDSON, LEON C., Student Officer, 308 Eddy St., Ithaca, N. Y.

RICHARDSON, OMAR BURT, Student Officer, 525 S. Central Ave., Glendale, Cal. San Diego, Columbia, Mass. Inst. of Tech.

RICHARDSON, W. LANDSTREET, Lieut. (j.g.), 228 Lincoln Place, Brooklyn, N. Y. N. A. No. 582.

RICHARDSON, W. A., JR., Student Officer, 34 Chestnut Drive, Hastings-on-Hudson, New York. Mass. Inst. of Tech., Miami. HTA.

RICHDALE, JAY W., Ensign, 7015 Blair Road, Washington, D. C.

RICHMOND, EDWARD G., Lieut. (j.g.), 74 E. Main St., Fredonia, N. Y. Mass. Inst. of Tech., Akron, Rockaway. N. A. No. 914. LTA.

RICHTER, LOUIS A., War. Carpenter.

RICKARD, GUY, Ensign, Schoharie, N. Y. Mass. Inst. of Tech., Bay Shore, Pensacola, Miami, Curtis Field. HTA

RICKER, ELLERY T., Student Officer, 471 Broadway, Cambridge, Mass.

RIDALL, EDMUND W., Ensign, 518 N. Highland Ave., Pittsburgh, Pa. Mass. Inst. of Tech., Key West, Miami, Pensacola, San Diego. N. A. No. 1174. HTA.

RIDDLEBERGER, CHARLES WM., War. Machinist, 15 W. 63rd St., New York City.

RIESENBERGER, FRANK R., Student Officer, 546 Union Place, Weehawken, N. J. Mass. Inst. of Tech., Key West. HTA.

RIGAN, FELIX R., Student Officer, Hayes Store, Glouchester Co., W. Va.

RIGDON, THORNTON F., Ensign, 163 Billcourt West, Lexington, Ky. Mass. Inst. of Tech., Bay Shore, Brunswick, Key West, Pensacola. HTA.

RILEY, CHARLES WILLIAM, Student Officer, Burnside, Conn. Mass. Inst. of Tech., Key West. HTA.

RILEY, FRANCIS X., Student Officer, W. 231st St., Spuyten Duyvil, New York City. Mass. Inst. of Tech., Rockaway, N. Y. LTA.

RILEY, GEORGE J., Student Officer, 5124 Warnock St., Philadelphia, Pa.

RILEY, IVERS W., Student Officer, 821 6th St., Minneapolis, Minn.

RILEY, RUSSELL F., Student Officer, 55 Josephine Ave., Somerville, Mass.

RIPLEY, WILLIAM R., Ensign, Tacoma, Wash.

RISELAY, EDMUND G., Student Officer, 587 Breckenridge St., Buffalo, N. Y. Mass. Inst. of Tech. HTA.

RITTENHOUSE, DAVID, Ensign, 2208 W. 21st St., Minneapolis, Minn. Dunwoody, Key West, Miami, Pensacola, Pacific Fleet, Langley Field. HTA.

ROAN, WILLIAM E., Ensign, Ford Motor Co., New Orleans, La. N. A. No. 1488.

ROARK, EUGENE W., Student Officer, 139 W. Gilman St., Madison, Wis.

ROBBINS, JOE, Student Officer, Owosso, Mich. Dunwoody Inst., Minn., Miami, Key West. HTA.

ROBERSON, ROBERT E., War. Carpenter.

ROBERSON, T. LLOYD, Student Officer, 5410 Lake Park Ave., Chicago, Ill. Mass. Inst. of Tech. HTA.

ROBERTS, ARTHUR E., Student Officer, 26 S. High St., Jackson, O.

ROBERTS, H. F., Student Officer, 17 Dellinger Ave., Batavia, N. Y. Mass. Inst. of Tech. HTA.

ROBERTS, RALPH S., Student Officer, 1843 Idlewood Ave., East Cleveland, O., Univ. of Washington, Seattle.

ROBERTS, ROLAND W., Student Officer.

ROBERTS, THOMAS T., Ensign, 919 W. William St., Decatur, Ill. N. A. No. 385.

ROBERTS, TOBIAS L., Student Officer, 48 Mt. Desert St., Bar Harbor, Me.

ROBERTS, WALTER F., Student Officer, O'Neill, Nebr.

ROBERTSON, FRED L., Student Officer, 15 Arlington St., Chicopee Falls, Mass. Mass. Inst. of Tech., Miami. HTA

ROBERTSON, GEORGE M., Student Officer, 38 College Ave., New Brunswick, N. J.

ROBERTSON, GUY R., Student Officer.

ROBERTSON, HULING, P., JR., Student Officer, 404 N. 9th St., Temple, Tex.

ROBERTSON, THOMAS J., Ensign, Yale Station, New Haven, Conn. N. A. No. 1845.

ROBERTSON, W. V. M., JR., Ensign, 2026 First Ave., Birmingham, Ala. Mass. Inst. of Tech., Operations, Washington, D. C., Miami, Pensacola. N. A. No. 2423. HTA.

ROBESON, FRANK K., Student Officer, 133 W. University Ave., Champaign, Ill.

ROBINS, JOHN Q., JR., Ensign, Tupelo, Miss. N. A. No. 1930.

ROBINSON, A. J., Ensign, 190 Summer St., Malden, Mass.

ROBINSON, CHARLES S., War. Machinist, 317 E. 51st St., New York, N. Y.

ROBINSON, G. B., Student Officer, Mt. Gilead, O. Dunwoody Inst., Minn.

ROBINSON, H. A., Ensign, 101 Court St., Westfield, Mass.

ROBINSON, HARRY L., Student Officer, 850 S. Sante Fe, Salina, Kans.

ROBINSON, LEE C., Student Officer, 1309 Washtenaw Ave., Ann Arbor, Mich.

ROBINSON, LYNN B., Student Officer.

ROBINSON, RUSSELL R., Student Officer, 6353 Greene St., Philadelphia, Pa.

ROBINSON, SAMUEL, Student Officer, 2014 G St., Washington, D. C.

ROBINSON, STANLEY L., Student Officer, Agricultural College, Miss. Mass. Inst. of Tech., Miami. HTA.

ROBINSON, WALTER STEVENS, JR., Student Officer, 149 Mili St., Springfield, Mass. Mass. Inst. of Tech. LTA.

ROBINSON, WM. B., Ensign, 715 E. Buchtel Ave., Akron, O. N. A. No. 2264.

ROBINSON, WM. D., Student Officer, The Cloister, 1 Hillhouse Ave., New Haven, Conn.

ROCHE, F. J., 20 Ellsworth Ave., Cambridge, Mass.

ROCKEFELLER, WILLIAM O., Lieut. (j g.), Greenwich, Conn. Huntington, Bay Shore, Pensacola, New London, Miami, Killingholme, Eng. HTA.

ROCKEY, STUART S., Ensign, Pipestone, Minn. N. A. No. 1802.

ROCKWELL, CHAS. H., JR., Ensign, 4467 Woodlawn Ave., Chicago, Ill.

ROCKWELL, DONALD E., Ensign, 106 Professors Row, Tufts College, Mass. Mass. Inst. of Tech., Miami, Pensacola. N. A. No. 2218. HTA.

ROCKWOOD, ROBERT E., Lieut. (j.g.).

RODEGERDTS, CHRIS A., 956 Height St., San Francisco, Cal.

RODEN, GEORGE ROBERT, JR., Student Officer, 332 Greenwood Ave., Wyncote, Pa. Mass. Inst. of Tech., Philadelphia, Pa. HTA.

RODEN, HENRY W., Ensign, 4118 Live Oak St., Dallas, Texas. N. A. No. 1513.

RODENBAUGH, ELMER S., 130 Irving St., San Francisco, Cal. N. A. No. 1309.

RODER, WALTER L., Ensign, Newark, N. J. N. A. No. 441.

RODES, CLIFTON, Ensign, 2037 Douglas Blvd., Louisville, Ky.

RODGERS, OLIVER, Student Officer, Care of Mellon Nat'l Bank, Pittsburgh, Pa.

RODGERS, WM. B., Ensign. N. A. No. 2160.

ROE, HARVEY E., Ensign, Weston, Ohio. N. A. No. 1430.

ROGERS, CARL W., Student Officer, 36 Parks St., Newton, Mass.

ROGERS, CHAS. A., War. Gun.

ROGERS, GARDNER S., Ensign, 81 S. Fitzhugh St., Rochester, N. Y. Mass. Inst. of Tech., Philadelphia.

ROGERS, HENRY L., Ensign, Ocilla, Ga. Mass. Inst. of Tech., Pensacola, Fla.

ROGERS, JOEL TOWNSLEY, Lieut. (j.g.), Florence Court, Washington, D. C. Mass. Inst. of Tech., Hampton Roads, Pensacola, Miami, Rockaway. HTA.

ROGERS, JOHN F., Student Officer, 66 Cannon St., Poughkeepsie, N. Y.

ROGERS, NATHANIEL S., Student Officer, Auburn, Wash.

ROGERS, RUFUS I., Ensign, 87 Genessee St., Baldwinsville, N. Y. N. A. No. 1177.

ROGERS, SAMPSON, JR., Student Officer, Oak Park, Ill.

ROGERS, WILLIAM A., Ensign, Sound View Ave., Little Neck, L. I., N. Y. Mass. Inst. of Tech., Pensacola, Hampton Roads, Moutchic, Finistere, Morehead City. N. A. No. 634.

ROHRBACH, WILLIAM H., Blacksburg, Va. N. A. No. 1800.

ROHRER, HENRY AUGUSTUS, Student Officer, 45 East Orange St., Lancaster, Pa. Great Lakes, Ill.

ROLLEFRON, K. E., Student Officer, 919 Beekways St., Superior, Wis. Dunwoody Inst., Minn.

ROLLINS, W., Lieut. (j.g.), Brush Hill Lane, Hyde Park, Mass.

ROMNEY, GEORGE O., Ensign, Billings, Mont.

ROMNEY, WILFORD W., Student Officer, 167 E St., Salt Lake City, Utah.

RONALDSON, G. M., Ensign, 448 Pike St., Baton Rouge, La. Mass. Inst. of Tech., Miami. N. A. No. 1535. HTA.

ROONEY, EDWARD F., Student Officer, 201 North Columbus St., Alexandria, Va.

ROONEY, JAMES I., Student Officer, 163 Kent St., Brookline, Mass.

ROOSEVELT, JOHN K., Lieut. (j.g.), 30 Pine St., New York City.

ROOT, BURDETT B., Student Officer, P. O. Box 1023, Colorado Springs, Colo.

ROOT, WARREN J., Student Officer, 434 Sec. For. Savings Bank, Cleveland, Ohio.

RORICK, M. H., Student Officer, 2263 Collingwood Ave., Toledo, Ohio. Mass. Inst. of Tech., Key West, Fla. HTA.

ROSBOROUGH, JAMES G., JR., 7300 Mariette Ave., Maplewood, Mo.

ROSE, A. S., Ensign, Mineral Pt., Wis. N. A. No. 1758.

ROSE, AUSTIN T., Student Officer, 625 North Henry St., Madison, Wis.

ROSE, D. MORTON, JR., Ensign, 803 West Hill St., Knoxville, Tenn. Mass. Inst. of Tech., Pensacola. N. A. No. 262.

ROSE, J. E., Ensign, 39 Draper Terrace, Montclair, N. J. Mass. Inst. of Tech., Pensacola. HTA.

ROSE, JOSEPH H., Student Officer, 425 First Ave, Pittsburgh, Pa.

ROSE, LOUIS, Student Officer, 160 West 87th St., New York City. Mass. Inst. of Tech. HTA.

ROSE, REGINALD W., Student Officer, 176 East Palmer Ave., Detroit, Mich. Dunwoody Inst., Minn.

ROSEBOROUGH, J. C., Lieut. (j.g.), 905 Upson Ave., El Paso, Tex.

ROSS, E. A., Ensign, 1200 Matlock Ave., Pearl Harbor, Honolulu.

ROSS, EDWIN ALBERT, 1865 West 25th St., Los Angeles, Cal.

ROSS, FRANK D., Ensign, 1 Liberty St., New York City.

ROSS, HOWARD L., Student Officer.

ROSS, JOHN W., Ensign. N. A. No. 1534.

ROSS, KENNETH D., Student Officer, N. 1401 Post St., Spokane, Wash.

ROSS, L. W., Ensign.

ROSSITER, RICHMOND, Student Officer.

ROTHENBURG, MERLE E., War. Mach.

ROTHERMEL, ADDISON J., Student Officer, 131 West 93rd St., New York City.

ROTHWELL, JAMES L., Ensign, 513 Herrick St., Elmira, N. Y. Bolsena, Italy; Arcachon, Fr. N. A. No. 1460. HTA.

ROUGHLEY, HUGH W, Ensign.

ROURKE, GRATTAN L., Student Officer, Lisbon, N. D.

ROUSE, HAROLD A., Ensign, 255 West 90th St., New York City.

ROUSSEL, W. D., Student Officer, 422 Gravier St., New Orleans, La.

ROUTH, WILLIAM F., Student Officer, Texas P. & L. Co., Dallas, Tex.

ROWE, CHARLES A., Ensign, Roland Park, Baltimore, Md. Mass. Inst. of Tech., Bay Shore, Key West, Pensacola, Moutchic, St. Inglevert, Fr. N. A. No. 736. HTA.

ROWE, ISAAC S., Ensign, 1709 N. Calvert St., Baltimore, Md.

ROWEN, EDWARD J., War. Mach., Jamaica Plain, Mass. N. A. No. 290.

ROY, REUBEN S., Student Officer, Care of L. S. N. Natchitoches, La.

ROYCE, MILTON P., Ensign, Ithaca, N. Y. R. F. D., No. 5. Mass. Inst. of Tech., Miami, Pensacola. N. A. No. 2464. HTA.

ROYSTER, F. A., Ensign, 303 Colonial Ave., Norfolk, Va. Mass. Inst. of Tech., Pensacola, Fla.

RUBINKAM, H. W., Ensign. N. A. No. 1732.

RUCKER, LYLE W., Student Officer, 1310 June St., Los Angeles, Cal.

RUDY, WALTER D., Student Officer, Mt. Airy, Md.

RUECKERT F., War. Mach., 308 Adams St., Buffalo, N. Y.

RUMPH, FLOYD Ed., War. Mach.

RUNDLE, HENRY M., Student Officer, 305 Aycrigg Ave., Passaic, N. J.

Rush, H. L., Jr., Lieut. (j.g.), 1400 H. St., N. W., Washington, D. C. N. A. No. 390.

Rush, W. L., Student Officer, Shubuta, Miss. Dunwoody Inst., Minn.

Russell, Charles L., Ensign, 3263 Hawthorne Blvd., St. Louis, Mo. Mass. Inst. of Tech., Washington, D. C. HTA.

Russell, James C., Student Officer, 400 Washington St., Camden, Ark.

Russell, Philip Alden, Lieut. (j.g.), Dedham, Mass. Mass. Inst. of Tech., Buffalo, E. Greenwich, R. I. HTA.

Rust, Edgar H., Ensign, 1229 Clarkson St., Denver, Colo. Mass. Inst. of Tech., Bay Shore, Pensacola; Killingholme, Eng. N. A. No. 1291. HTA.

Rust, Lawrence A., Student Officer, Bloomington, Ill. Dunwoody Inst., Miami. HTA.

Ruth, Vincent E., Student Officer, 958 Diversey Parkway, Chicago, Ill.

Rutherford, John M., Lieut. (j.g.), Tuxedo Park, N. Y. Bay Shore, L. I.; Key West, Miami, Washington, D. C. N. A. No. 164. HTA.

Ryan, Edmund J., Ensign, 1595 Beacon St., Brookline, Mass.

Ryan, G. W., War. Mach.

Ryan, James Hilary, Student Officer, 13 Beaver St., Albion, N. Y. Dunwoody Inst., Mass. Inst. of Tech., Great Lakes, Hampton Roads, Pensacola, Bay Shore. HTA.

Ryan, Raymond P., Student Officer, 741 St. Owen Pl., Bronx, New York City.

Ryan, William Miles, Ensign, 2036 Canal St., New Orleans, La. Mass. Inst. of Tech., Key West, Miami, Pensacola. N. A. No. 1958. HTA.

Ryerson, Creighton, Ensign, 515 W. Washington St., Jackson, Mich.

Rylander, Paul N., Ensign, 514 Garrett Bldg., Baltimore, Md.

Creation of Pensacola

When the Lord was designing creation,
And laying out oceans and lands,
With never a moment's laxation,
Not even to spit in His hands—

As anyone will in a hurry
He let things go by now and then,
In all the excitement and worry,
That He should have done over again.

So rather than muss up the outfit,
He saved every blunder and blob,
And laid them away in the corner,
To use at the end of the job.

On the sixth afternoon of the contract—
His time would expire that day—
He boiled out the dregs of creation,
And shoveled the litter away.

He gathered the wreckage and tilling,
The scum and the sewerage and sump,
And He built on the shores of the Gulf Stream
The great International Dump.

He rushed things then in a hurry,
And because of the rush He was in,
He named this place "Pensacola,"
And "Pensacola" it always has been.

Then feeling sarcastic and gloomy,
Because it was Saturday night,
He picked out the nastiest corner,
And named it "San Carlos" for spite.

It is there that they do things backward,
And the sand does not dry between rains,
Where money and high prices are plenty,
And thievery better than brains.

It's the home of the Greek and the slacker
The buzzard and mud-colored crows,
My strongest impression of Pensacola
Got into my head through my nose.

It's the land of the infernal odor
The town of the national smell,
The average American sailor
Would rather be quartered in hell.

So it's back to the north for yours truly—
Though I'm not wishing anyone ill—
Pensacola can hang for all I care,
And really I hope that she will.

Yes, it's back to the north for yours truly,
A sadder but wiser chap,
The Lord played a joke on all mankind
When He put Pensacola on the map.

In all fairness to Pensacola we will have to say that this poem is probably the result of a "morning after" pessimism and does not do justice to the city or its people.—Editor.

SAINSBURY, N. E., Jr.
Lieut. (j.g.)
165 West 83 St., New York City, Hampton Roads. HTA.

SALISBURY, KENNETH
Ensign
201 Main St., S. E. Minneapolis, Minn. Mass., Inst. of Tech., Dunwoody, Pensacola, Miami. N. A. No. 913. HTA.

SALMON, N. M.
Student Officer
Lillington, N. C. Mass. Inst. of Tech. HTA.

SANBORN, C. M.
Ensign
2716 Irving So. Minneapolis, Minn. Dunwoody, Mass. Inst. of Tech., Pensacola, Hampton Roads. N. A. No. 953. HTA.

TUNING UP A MACCHI CHASSE AT PORTO CORSINI, ITALY
Showing the Extreme Narrowness of the Canal, Approximately 70 Feet Wide

SANTLEY, FREDERIC
Student Officer
130 West 44th St., New York City. Mass. Inst. of Tech., Miami. HTA.

SANTOS, ANTHONY S.
Lieut. (j.g.)
20 Gould St., West Roxbury, Mass. M. I. T., Pensacola, Hampton Rd., New York, Boston, Anacostia. N. A. No. 488.

SARGENT, DWIGHT S.
Ensign
417 Union St., New Bedford, Mass. Mass. Inst. of Tech., Key West. N. A. No. 1490. HTA.

SARGENT, JOHN C.
Student Officer
122 Coburn St., Lowell, Mass. Mass. Inst. of Tech., HTA.

SATTERFIELD, D. E., Jr.
Lieut. (j.g.)
834 West Grace St., Richmond, Va. Mass. Inst. of Tech.

SATTERWHITE, R. L.
Ensign
527 Liberty St., Franklin, Pa. Mass. Inst. of Tech., Akron, Hampton Rds., U. S. S. *Arizona.*

SAUNDERS, DAVID G.
Ensign
Emmetsburg, Iowa. Mass. Inst. of Tech., Bay Shore, Pensacola. N. A. No. 1813. HTA.

SAUNDERS, WM. R.
Student Officer
Bedford, Va. Mass. Inst. of Tech., Key West. HTA.

SAVAGE, JASPER V.
Machinist
4527 60th St., Portland, Ore. San Diego, Great Lakes, Columbia Univ. HTA.

SAWYER, LOUIS
Student Officer
Fayetteville, Ark. Univ. of Wash., Seattle, Key West. HTA.

SCANDRETT, R. B., Jr.
Ensign
Engle & Elm Sts., Tenafly, N. J. Mass. Inst. of Tech., Pensacola, Akron.

SCHENCK, JOS. H., 3rd
Ensign
Wynnewood, Penn. Mass. Inst. of Tech., Bay Shore Pensacola. N. A. No. 1740. HTA.

SCHIFF, HERBERT
Lieut. (j.g.)
525 West End Ave., New York City. Mass. Inst. of Tech., Bay Shore, Pensacola, Chatham. N. A. No. 916. HTA.

SCHILLING, WM. C.
Ensign
2850 Gravois Ave., St. Louis, Mo. Pensacola, Columbia Univ., Bay Shore, Great Lakes. HTA.

SCHLUETER, T. L.
Ensign
515 Bellevue Ave., Oakland, Cal. Mass. Inst. of Tech., Miami, Key West, Pensacola. N. A. No. 1392. LTA.

SCHLICHTER, A. B.
Student Officer
Cor. Granby and Main Sts. Hollister, N. C. Dunwoody Inst. Minn., Minn. HTA.

SCHLICHTER, F. P.
Ensign
28 Radford St., Yonkers, N. Y. Mass. Inst. of Tech., Akron, Rockaway, Hampton Roads. LTA.

SCHLOEDER, N. S.
Ensign
3 Eldorado Place, Weehawken, N. J. Mass. Inst. of Tech., Bay Shore, Key West, Miami. N. A. No. 504. HTA.

SCHLUMS, OTTO W.
Ensign
13 Roxbury Terrace, Roxbury, Mass. M. I. T., Pensacola, Moutchic, Brest, Bay Shore, Norfolk. N. A. No. 653. HTA.

SCHMIDT, HELMAN
Carpenter
503 Chesapeake Ave., Eastport, Md. Pensacola, Anacostia, D. C. N. A. No 1026. HTA.

SCHMITT, WALTER E.
Ensign
218 Superior St., Toledo, Ohio. Mass. Inst. of Tech., Bay Shore, Key West, Miami. N. A. No. 1542. HTA.

SCHNABEL, D. C.
Student Officer
Grand Forks, N. D. Mass. Inst. of Tech., Key West. HTA.

SCHOEPPEL, A. F.
Student Officer
Ransom, Kans. Seattle, Wash., Miami. HTA.

SCHULTZ, E. R.
Ensign
2112 Jackson St., Sioux City, Iowa. Seattle, Great Lakes. HTA.

N-9 PICKING ON AN F BOAT AT KEY WEST

SCHWAB, JAMES L.
Ensign
5106 Washington Ave., St. Louis, Mo. Mass. Inst. of Tech., Pensacola, Rockaway, Cape May. N. A. No. 652. HTA.

SCHWARTZ, ED. A.
Student Officer
15 Adriance Ave., Poughkeepsie, N. Y. Mass. Inst. of Tech., Bay Shore. HTA.

SCHWEIZER, R. J.
Ensign
150 East 72nd St., New York City. Mass. Inst. of Tech., Pensacola, Norfolk, Washington. HTA.

SCHWRAR, C. K.
Ensign
335 College Ave., Rock Hill, S. C. M. I. T., Pensacola, Pauillac, Moutchic, Brest, Hampton Roads. N. A. No. 767. HTA.

SCOTT, BAKER P.
Ensign
Bridgetown, Va. Mass. Inst. of Tech., Miami, Key West, Pensacola. N. A. No. 2586. HTA.

SCOTT, FORRESTER H.
Ensign
Stephen Girard Bldg., Philadelphia, Pa. Miami, Hampton Roads, Pensacola. N. A. No. 2273. HTA.

SCOTT, LEE R.
Student Officer
46 West Cayuga St., Oswego, N. Y. Mass. Inst. of Tech., Bay Shore. HTA.

SCOTT, STUART W.
Student Officer
1408 W. Lombard St., Baltimore, Md. Mass. Inst. of Tech., Hampton Roads. HTA.

SCRIVNER, ERVING I.
Ensign
592 Ayrlesford Place, Lexington, Ky. Mass. Inst. of Tech., Miami, Pensacola. HTA.

SEE, PHILIP H.
Lieut. (j.g.)
343 Adelphis St., Brooklyn, N. Y. Mass. Inst. of Tech., Miami. N. A. No. 1541. HTA.

SEFTON, BENJAMIN E.
Carpenter
285 Medford St., Somerville, Mass. Bumkin Is., Gujan Mestras, L'Aver Vrach, Finisterre, Fr.

SELBY, RALPH L.
Ensign
311 Hubbell Bldg., Des Moines, Iowa. Mass. Inst. of Tech., Miami, Pensacola. N. A. No. 1541. HTA.

SELDEN, HAROLD F.
Lieut. (j.g.)
1862 Park Road, Wash., D. C. Newport. Hamp. Rds., Pensa.,Bay Sh., Brunswick, Key West, Miami, Anacostia. N. A. No. 491. HTA.

SHADLE, H. WEBB
Ensign
Pleasantville, Iowa. Mass. Inst. of Tech., Pensacola, Key West, Akron. N. A. No. 2675. LTA.

SHAFER, JACK H.
Ensign
621 St. Andrews Pl., Los Angeles, Cal. Mass. Inst. of Tech., Miami, Pensacola, San Diego. N. A. No. 1627. HTA.

SHAFOR, C. G.
Ensign
1314 Bay View Place, Berkeley, Cal. Mass. Inst. of Tech., San Diego, Pensacola. N. A. No. 1554. HTA.

SHALLOW, E. B., Jr.
Ensign
1090 Dean St., Brooklyn, N. Y. Mass. Inst. of Tech., Bay Shore, Pensacola. N. A. No. 1877. HTA.

SHANNON, JAMES C.
Student Officer
245 Congress St., Bridgeport, Conn. Mass. Inst. of Tech., Bay Shore. HTA.

SHANTS, FRANK L.
Ensign
433 W. Upsal St., Germantown, Philadelphia, Pa. M. I. T., Bay Shore, Pensacola, Brunswick. N. A. No. 1311. HTA.

SHARP, FRANCIS X.
Student Officer
436 9th St., Brooklyn, N. Y. Mass. Inst. of Tech., Miami, Pensacola. HTA.

SHARP, M. A.
Student Officer
Hebron, Neb. Mass. Inst. of Tech., Key West. HTA.

SHAW, G. W.
Lieut. (j.g.)
Caribon, Me. Hampton Roads, RAF. Killingholme, Felixstowe, Queenstown, Wexford, Lough Foyle. N. A. No. 171. HTA.

SHAW, LAUREN L.
Ensign
Shaw Height, Decatur, Ill. Mass. Inst. of Tech., Miami, Pensacola, Great Lakes, Philadelphia. N. A. No. 1659. HTA.

SHEA, FRANK J.
Student Officer
102 First Ave., Irwin. Pa. Mass. Inst. of Tech. HTA.

GALLAUDET SEAPLANE
Showing Propeller Construction Peculiar to This Type of Plane

SHEA, JOHN J.
Ensign
36 Frank St., No. Cambridge, Mass. Mass. Inst. of Tech., Bay Shore, Brunswick, Key West, Pensacola. N. A. No. 2362. HTA.

SHEALY, L. EVANS
Machinist
Little Mountain, S. C. Pensacola. HTA.

SHEEHY, CYRIL, ED.
Ensign
3628 So. 26th, Omaha, Neb. Mass. Inst. of Tech., Great Lakes. HTA.

SHEIDLEY, H. O.
Ensign
3654 Campbell St., Kansas City, Mo. Mass. Inst. of Tech., Key West, Miami, Pensacola. N. A. No. 2171. HTA.

SHEILS, HENRY C.
Ensign
58 Francis St., Roxbury, Mass. Mass. Inst. of Tech., Buffalo, Keyport.

SHELDON, SAMUEL D.
Ensign
2415 Sheridan Ave., So. Minneapolis, Minn. Dunwoody, Mass. Inst. of Tech., Pensacola. N. A. No. 865. HTA.

SHEPHERD, SAM'L R.
Ensign
177 East Main St., Lancaster, N. Y. Mass. Inst. of Tech., Bay Shore, Pensacola. N. A. No. 1814. HTA.

SHEPPARD, L. B.
Ensign
Hanover, Penn. Mass. Inst. of Tech., Bay Shore, Pensacola. N. A. No. 170 . HTA. LTA.

SHERBROOK, W. A.
Student Officer
1405 Beacon St., Brookline, Mass. Mass. Inst. of Tech., Commonwealth Pier. HTA.

SHERMAN, ALDEN W.
Ensign
148 Princeton St., Lowell, Mass. Mass. Inst. of Tech., Miami, Pensacola. N. A. No. 2587. HTA.

SHERRICK, R. G.
Ensign
1937 Tuscarawas St., W. Canton, Ohio. M. I. T., Great Lakes, Charleston, Key West, Pensacola. N. A. No. 2357. HTA.

SHERRILL, CHAS. M.
Ensign
307 E. Laurel St., San Antonio, Tex. Univ. Wash., Seattle, San Diego, Pensacola. N. A. No. 2287. HTA.

SHERWOOD, DAVID W.
Student Officer
Ballston Spa, N. Y. Mass. Inst. of Tech., Miami. HTA.

SHERWOOD, FRANK S.
Ensign
110 East 16 St., New York City. Mass. Inst. of Tech., Key West, Pensacola. N. A. No. 2313. HTA.

SHETRON, JOHN H.
Ensign
118 Victoria Pl., Syracuse, N. Y. M. I. T., Key West Moutchic, No. Bomb. Gr. St., Inglevert, Malpensa, Rockaway. N.A. No. 1448. HTA

SHEWARD, C. M., Jr.
Student Officer
908 Broome St., Wilmington, Del. Mass. Inst. of Tech. HTA.

SHIELDS, EDWARD M.
Lieut. (j.g.)
West Chester, Pa. Mass. Inst. of Tech., Key West, Chatham. N. A. 452.

SHILLING, W. JAMES
Ensign
308 N. Carrollton Ave., Baltimore, Md. Mass. Inst. of Tech., Pensacola, Chatham. N. A. No. 951. HTA.

SHIPP, JOHN V., Jr.
Student Officer
Midway, Ky. Mass. Inst. of Tech., Great Lakes, Philadelphia. LTA.

SHORT, ROBERT W.
Student Officer
214 W. Franklin St., Elkhart, Ind. Mass. Inst. of Tech. HTA.

SHUMAKER, T. FOYE
Student Officer
603 Linden St., Lima, Ohio. Mass. Inst. of Tech., Miami, Camp Hicks, Tex. Killingholme, Eng.

SIBTHORPE, H. K.
Ensign
Point View, Miami, Fla. Newport, Harvard Radio, Miami, Great Lakes, Key West, Pensacola. N. A. No. 2502.

SIGAL, ALBERT ED.
Student Officer
508 E. Cliff St., El Paso, Tex. Seattle, Wash. HTA.

SILL, HAROLD W.
Student Officer
132 Adams St., N. W., Washington, D. C. Dunwoody Inst. Minn. HTA.

PULLING DOWN A KITE BALLOON AT SEA

SIMMONS, VIRGIL
Ensign
801 Knoblock St., Stillwater, Okla. Mass. Inst. of Tech., Miami, Key West, Pensacola. N. A. No. 2503. HTA.

SIMONDS, WALTER
Ensign
727 Harvard St., Rochester, N. Y. Mass. Inst. of Tech., Miami, Pensacola. N. A. No. 2033. HTA.

SINCLAIR, FRAZER V.
Ensign
Brooklyn, N. Y. Roehampton, Cranwell (RAF), Mullion (RAF). N. A. No. 1313. LTA.

SLACK, WM. BEBEE
Ensign
714 W. Fifth St., Taylor, Tex. Seattle, San Diego, Pensacola. N. A. No. 2639. HTA.

SLADE, K. PRENTICE
Ensign
626 Central Ave., Lexington, Ky. Mass. Inst. of Tech., Miami, Pensacola. N. A. No. 1614. LTA.

SLOAN, WM. EYRES, Jr.
Ensign
1250 East Ave., Rochester, N. Y. Mass. Inst. of Tech., Bay Shore, Pensacola, Montauk, Hampton Roads. N. A. No. 1043. HTA.

SMALL, BRAZIER C.
Ensign
Turner, Oregon. Seattle, San Diego, Pensacola. N. A. No. 2265. HTA.

SMALL, BURTON E.
Student Officer
Addison, Me. Mass. Inst. of Tech., Miami. HTA.

SMITH, ALFRED T.
Ensign
Richmond, Va. Mass. Inst. of Tech., Bay Shore, Pensacola, Halifax, North Sydney, N. S., Hampton Rds., N. A. No. 1080. HTA.

SMITH, BASIL B.
Ensign
1224 Montana Ave., Portland, Ore. Mass. Inst. of Tech., Miami, Pensacola. N. A. No. 2323. HTA.

SMITH, BENSON L.
Ensign
821 13th St., San Diego, Cal. M. I. T., San Diego, Pensa., Sidney, Canada., Hampton Rds. N. A. No. 6. HTA.

SMITH, C. W.
Ensign
2421 Harriet Ave., So. Minn., Minn. Dunwoody, Pensa., Great Lakes, Wash., Akron, Rockaway. N. A. No. 1658. LTA.

SMITH, CARLOS B.
Student Officer
104 Prospect Place, Brooklyn, N. Y. Mass. Inst. of Tech., Bay Shore. HTA.

SMITH, C. W.
Ensign
142 Burncoat St., Worcester, Mass. Mass. Inst. of Tech., Miami, Pensacola. N. A. No. 1658. HTA.

SMITH, CLINTON A.
Student Officer
1305 Commonwealth Ave., Boston, Mass. Mass. Inst. of Tech., Miami. HTA.

SMITH, CYRIL R.
Ensign
123 Grand Ave., Akron, Ohio. Mass. Inst. of Tech., Bay Shore, Pensacola. N. A. No. 2136. HTA.

SMITH, F. CAROL
Ensign
620 East Valerio St., Santa Barbara, Cal. Mass. Inst. of Tech., Key West, Miami, Pensacola, Rockaway. N. A. No. 1307. HTA.

SMITH, GLENN I.
Ensign
1958 Berwyn Ave., Chicago. Mass. Inst. of Tech., Pensacola, Miami. N. A. No. 1998. LTA.

SMITH, H. CORNELL
Student Officer
7 Marston Ave., Detroit, Mich. Dunwoody. HTA.

SMITH, HENRY M.
Ensign
4754 Malden St., Chicago, Ill. Dunwoody, Miami, Pensacola. N. A. No. 2400. HTA.

SMITH, HUBERT L.
Ensign
309 No. Main St., Athens, Pa. Mass. Inst. of Tech., Akron, Hampton Rds., U. S. S. *Oklahoma*, Castletown, Ire. LTA.

SMITH, IRA D.
Ensign
222 E. 16th St., Hopkinsville, Ky. Mass. Inst. of Tech., Pensacola, Washington, D. C. HTA.

SMITH, OLIVER H.
Lieut. (j.g.)
908 N. 64 St., Overbrook, Pa. Mass. Inst. of Tech., Pensacola, RAF. Warsash, Eng., Queenstown, Ire.

SMITH, RALPH E.
Ensign
2482 Valentine Ave., New York City. Pensacola, Chatham. N. A. No. 2010. HTA.

ITALIAN SECTION OF HANGARS AT LAKE BOLSENA, ITALY
Showing Macchi Chasse Planes in Water

SMITH, RICHARD W.
Student Officer
Salem, W. Va. Mass. Inst. of Tech., Miami. HTA.

SMITH, RICHARD M.
Ensign
908 Colonial Ave., Norfolk, Va. Mass. Inst. of Tech., Bay Shore, Pensacola, Miami. N. A. No. 1433.

SMITH, SAMUEL A.
Lieut. (j.g.)
47 Academy St., Arlington, Mass. Mass. Inst. of Tech., Hampton Rds., Pensacola, Cape May. N. A. No. 575. HTA.

SMITH, TODD
Ensign
Charlottesville, Va. Mass. Inst. of Tech., Akron, Rockaway Beach. LTA.

SMITH, VAN DOM C.
Ensign
102 Waverly Place, New York City. Mass. Inst. of Tech., Miami, Pensacola. N. A. No. 2034. HTA.

SMITH, WILLARD G.
Machinist
17 Haynes St., Hartford, Conn. Columbia Univ., USS. North Carolina, USS. Stackton, Miami.

SMITH, W. H.
Student Officer
4 Cottage Place, Warren, Pa. Mass. Inst. of Tech. HTA.

SMITH, WILLIAM P.
Ensign
603 Hancock St., Sandusky, Ohio. Mass. Inst. of Tech., Pensacola, Miami, Moutchic, Paris, Brest. N. A. No. 644. HTA.

SNAVELY, RALPH A.
Ensign
725 E. Madison St., Springfield, Mo. Seattle, Wash., San Diego. HTA.

SNOOK, JOHN LLOYD
Ensign
403 Water St., Troy, Ohio. Mass. Inst. of Tech., Key West. HTA.

SNOW, CHARLES H.
Student Officer
512 E. Taylor St., Bloomington, Ill. Dunwoody. HTA.

SOLLEY, ROBERT F.
Student Officer
114 East 60th St., New York City. Great Lakes. LTA.

SOMERS, ANDREW
Ensign
89 Keap St., Brooklyn, N. Y. Mass. Inst. of Tech., Key West, Miami, Pensacola, Moutchic, Fr., Ile Tudy, Fr. HTA.

SOMMERS, JOHN E.
Ensign
Clifton Springs, N. Y. Mass. Inst. of Tech., Miami. N. A. No. 1539. HTA.

SONNABEND, A. M.
Ensign
43 Munroe St., Roxbury, Boston, Mass. Mass. Inst. of Tech., Pensacola, Miami. N. A. No. 1603. HTA.

SONNEBORN, R. G.
Student Officer
2420 Eutaw Place, Baltimore, Md. Mass. Inst. of Tech.

SOUTHER, HUGH S.
Ensign
Cleveland, Ohio. Mass. Inst. of Tech., Miami, Pensacola, Hampton Rds. N. A. No. 1012. HTA.

SOUTHWORTH, A. P.
Ensign
122 Chestnut St., Wakefield, Mass. Mass. Inst. of Tech., Key West, Pensacola. N. A. No. 2542. HTA.

SPARLING, ELLIOTT W.
Ensign
109 10th Ave., W. Ashland, Wis. Dunwoody, Key West, Miami, Pensacola. N. A. No. 1209. HTA.

SPEAKER, TRIS. E.
Student Officer
Hubbard, Tex. Mass. Inst. of Tech. HTA.

(T)
SPEAR, WALLACE E.
Student Officer
Genoa, Neb. Dunwoody, Great Lakes, Miami. HTA.

SPEER, BOYD ALTEN
Student Officer
3645 McRee, St. Louis, Mo. Seattle, San Diego. HTA.

SPENCER, BYRON
Ensign
730 North 22. St. Joseph, Mo. Mass. Inst. of Tech., Key West, Miami, Pensacola. N. A. No. 2011. HTA.

SPRAGUE, E. L.
Ensign
30 West 44th St., New York City. Mass. Inst. of Tech., Key West, Miami, Pensacola. N. A. No. 1209.

N. A.'s Training with the French at Avord-Cher, France
Land Machines Were Used by This Squadron

STACEY, JAMES H.
Ensign
White River Jct., Vermont, Mass. Inst. of Tech., Miami, Pensacola. N. A. No. 1759. HTA.

STACKHOUSE, JOHN M.
Ensign
434 Market St., Bloomsburg, Penn. Mass. Inst. of Tech., Miami, Key West, Pensacola. N. A. No. 2688. HTA.

STALB, A. ROLSTAN
Ensign
Care Loeing Aero Eng. Corp., New York City. Washington, D. C., Hampton Roads. HTA.

STANFORD, M. H.
Student Officer
4406 Cook St., Duluth, Minn. Dunwoody Inst., Minn., Miami.

STANTON, GEO. H.
Ensign
39 N. Fullerton Ave., Montclair, N. J. Mass. Inst. of Tech., Key West. N. A. No. 2018. HTA.

STAPP, C. C.
Student Officer
203 W. Church St., Champaigne, Ill. Dunwoody, Great Lakes. HTA.

STARK, THOMAS E., Jr.
Ensign
Hodgenville, Ky. Mass. Inst. of Tech., Miami, Pensacola. N. A. No. 2320. HTA.

STARKEY, WILMERT
Student Officer
911 Chester Ave., Avalon, Pa. Mass. Inst. of Tech., Key West. HTA.

STARR, LOWELL
Student Officer
152 Deer Hill Avenue, Danbury, Conn. Mass. Inst. of Tech., Bensonhurst; Pelham Bay. HTA.

STAUB, JOHN F.
Lieut. (j.g.)
850 Temple Ave., Knoxville, Tenn. Mass. Inst. of Tech., Pensacola, Ft. Worth, Killingholme, Eng. N. A. No. 263. HTA.

ST. CLAIR, J. R.
Lieut. (j.g.)
1930 E. 4th St., Duluth, Minn. Mass. Inst. of Tech., Miami, Pensacola. N. A. No. 930. HTA.

STEARMAN, LLOYD C.
Student Officer
Harper, Kans. Seattle, Wash.; San Diego. HTA.

STEBBINS, ROBERT P.
Ensign
Covina, Cal. Mass. Inst. of Tech., Akron, Rockaway Beach. LTA.

STEEL, VAN H.
Ensign
2083 Rosedale Ave., Oakland, Cal. Mass. Inst. of Tech., San Diego, Pensacola. N. A. No. 2035. HTA.

STEELE, O. I., Jr.
Ensign
Excelsior Springs, Mo. Mass. Inst. of Tech., Miami, Key West, Pensacola. HTA.

STEEVES, DUDLEY W.
Ensign
Box 54, R. No. 1, Hayward, Cal. Mass. Inst. of Tech., Miami, Pensacola. N. A. No. 1387. HTA.

STEGE, GEORGE H., Jr.
Ensign
34 Monroe Place, Brooklyn, N. Y. Mass. Inst. of Tech., Bay Shore, Pensacola, Rockaway. N. A. No. 1212. HTA.

STEPHENS, A. W.
Ensign
20 Highland Ave., Montclair, N. J. Mass. Inst. of Tech., Pensacola, Hampton Rds. N. A. No. 1630. HTA.

STEPHENS, FRED H.
Ensign
147 Ashmont St., Dorchester Centre, Mass. Mass. Inst. of Tech., Miami. N. A. No. 1537. HTA.

STEPHENS, ROBERT E.
Ensign
University Club, San Diego, Cal. Mass. Inst. of Tech., Miami, Pensacola, San Diego. HTA.

STEPHENSON, F. L.
Ensign
425 N. Center St., Bethlehem, Pa. Mass. Inst. of Tech. HTA.

STEVENS, F. A.
Machinist
Lake Placid, N. Y. Columbia Univ., Great Lakes, Key West.

STEVENS, JAMES W.
Student Officer
Charles and Camden Sts., Baltimore, Md. Seattle, Wash.; Norfolk. HTA.

STEVENSON, M.
Lieut. (j.g.)
Meadow Brook Club, Westbury, L. I., N. Y. Mass. Inst. of Tech., Killingholme, Eng. N. A. No. 499. HTA.

LIFTING OUT A CRASH, U. S. N. A. S., DUNKIRK, FRANCE

STEVENSON, R. B.
Ensign
3237 Michigan Ave., Kansas City, Mo. Mass. Inst. of Tech., Key West, Miami, Pensacola. N. A. No. 2186. HTA.

STEVENSON, V. E.
Ensign
7430 Eberhart Ave., Chicago, Ill. Pensacola, Great Lakes, Miami, U.S.S. *Huntington*, Great Lakes. HTA.

STEWART, CHARLES P.
Ensign
c/o Stewart Boiler Works, Worcester, Mass. Mass. Inst. of Tech., Miami, Pensacola, Moutchic. N. A. No. 1274. HTA.

STEWART, FRANK A.
Signal Officer
Fredonia, Kansas. Mass. Inst. of Tech., Miami, HTA.

STEWART, SIDNEY A.
Ensign
820 N. Highland Ave., Pittsburgh, Pa. Mass. Inst. of Tech., Miami, Pensacola. N. A. No. 2196. HTA.

STILES, HAROLD R.
Ensign
1165 Commonwealth Ave., Boston, Mass. Mass. Inst. of Tech., Pensacola, Hampton Roads. N. A. No. 2511. HTA.

STILES, WM. A.
Ensign
1302 Whitaker St., Birmingham, Ala. Mass. Inst. of Tech., Key West. N. A. No. 1835. HTA.

STILWELL, JAMES G.
Ensign
314 No. Franklin St., Mt. Pleasant, Mich. M. I. T., Great Lakes, Akron, Pensacola, Montauk. N. A. No. 1870. LTA.

STITT, WM. BRITTON
Ensign
1543 St. Nicholas Ave., New York City. Mass. Inst. of Tech., Blue Hill Obs., Miami, Pensacola. N. A. No. 2461. HTA.

STODDARD, THOS. R.
Ensign
Cohassett, Mass. Mass. Inst. of Tech., Boston Navy Yard, Key West, Pensacola. N. A. No. 2599. HTA.

(U)
STOKER, H. C.
Ensign
613 Avery Ave., Syracuse, N. Y. Mass. Inst. of Tech., Miami, Pensacola. N. A. No. 1332. HTA.

STONE, GEO. W.
Lieut. (j.g.)
Potomac, Ill. Pensacola. N. A. No. 111. HTA.

STONE, JAMES B.
Machinist
Meridian, Miss. Pensacola, St. Raphael, Fr., Moutchic, Fr., Pauillac, Fr., Cape May. HTA.

STONEMETZ, P. T.
Ensign
359 Otis St., West Newton, Mass. Mass. Inst. of Tech., Miami, Pensacola. N. A. No. 2029. HTA.

STORRER, ROBERT L.
Ensign
607 W. Main St., Owosso, Mich. Mass. Inst. of Tech., Key West, Miami, Pensacola, Bay Shore, Brunswick. N. A. No. 1308.

STOWELL, D. D.
Ensign
1680 Ashland Ave., St. Paul, Minn. Dunwoody, Key West, Miami, Pensacola. N. A. No. 2174.

STRACHAN, JOHN R.
Ensign
1449 5th Ave., San Francisco, Cal. Mass. Inst. of Tech., San Diego, Pensacola. N. A. No. 1602.

STRAND, AUGUST L.
Ensign
303 Evergreen Apts., Bozeman, Montana. Univ. Wash., San Diego, Pensacola. N. A. No. 1876.

STRATER, C. HELME
Student Officer
Rye, New York. Great Lakes. LTA.

STRAUS, HENRY LOBE
Ensign
4007 Penhurst Ave., Baltimore, Md. Mass. Inst. of Tech., Bay Shore, Pensacola. N. A. No. 2212. HTA.

STRIBLING, H. A. L.
Lieut. (j.g.)
75 Luckie St., Atlanta, Ga. Columbia Univ., Moutchic, Fr., Morehead City, N. C.

STRONG, T. J.
Lieut. (j.g.)
Champaign, Ill. Mass. Inst. of Tech., Bay Shore, Pensacola. N. A. No. 929. HTA.

STUDLEY, BARRETT
Ensign
243 New York Ave., Brooklyn, N. Y. Mass. Inst. of Tech., Bay Shore, Pensacola. HTA.

STUMPF, WM. A.
Lieut. (j.g.)
122 Oak St., Plattsburg, N. Y. Rockaway, Bay Shore, Pensacola, Hampton Rds., Guipavas, Fr., Chatham. LTA.

THE END OF A PERFECT WAR
Tearing Down the HS-1's after the Armistice

STURGIS, ALANSON H.
Lieut. (j.g.)
120 Boylston St., Boston, Mass. Mass. Inst. of Tech., Pensacola. N. A. No. 2015. HTA.

SULLIVAN, ANDREW J.
Ensign
4211 Vincennes Ave., Chicago, Ill. Dunwoody, Miami, Key West, Pensacola. N. A. No. 2647. HTA.

SULZBACHER, C. A.
Student Officer
219 Abingdon Rd., Kew Gardens, L. I., N. Y. Dunwoody, Minneapolis.

SUTHERLAND, G. A.
Ensign
6061 Pershing Ave., St. Louis, Mo. Lake Bolsena, It., Paris, Brest. N. A. No. 2000.

(E)

SWEENEY, FRANCIS J.
Student Officer
550 Metropolitan Ave., Brooklyn, N. Y. Mass. Inst. of Tech., Pelham Bay, Miami. HTA.

SWEETLAND, G.
Ensign
12 Fairlawn St., Everett, Mass. Mass. Inst. of Tech., Akron, Rockaway, Hampton Roads.

SWENNING, KARL A.
Ensign
5 Park St., Brookline, Mass. Mass. Inst. of Tech., Miami, Pensacola. N. A. No. 2173. HTA.

SWIFT, CLIFFORD G., Jr.
Ensign
Temple, Tex. Seattle, San Diego, Pensacola. N. A. No. 2197. HTA.

(E)

SWIFT, WM. E.
Ensign
Lake Forest, Ill. Mass. Inst. of Tech., Great Lakes, Miami, Pensacola. N. A. No. 2329. HTA.

SWINEFORD, OSCAR, Jr.
Ensign
1302 Grove Ave., Richmond, Va. Mass. Inst. of Tech., Pensacola, Miami, Hampton Rds., Berkeley, N. A. No. 1536. HTA.

SYMES, J. P.
Student Officer
2218 Roosevelt Ave., Berkeley, Cal. Mass. Inst. of Tech., San Diego, Pensacola, N. A. No. 1779. HTA.

SYMINGTON, THOS. R.
Ensign
220 Ridgewood Road, Roland Park, Baltimore, Md. Mass. Inst. of Tech., Key West, Pensacola. N. A. No. 1846. HTA.

◈ ◈ ◈ ◈ ◈ ◈

Sabin, Glenn C., Ensign.

Sadenwater, H., Lieut. (j.g.).

Sadowsky, Jack Phelps, Student Officer, 535 W. End Ave., New York City. Mass. Inst. of Tech.

St. Clair, Harry L., Student Officer, Saltville, Va.

St. Clair, J. R., Lieut. (j.g.), 1930 E. 4th St., Duluth, Minn. N. A. No. 930.

Salsman, J., War. Boatswain. N. A. No. 52½.

Sams, Bruce, J., Ensign, 235 Gordon East, Savannah, Ga.

Sams, Lewis P., Ensign, 146 Juniper St., Atlanta, Ga. N. A. No. 1359.

Samstag, H. R., Student Officer, 307 W. 81st St., New York City. Mass. Inst. of Tech. HTA.

Sanderson, Earl J., Student Officer, 32 State St., Seneca Falls, N. Y.

Sanford, Herbert B., Ensign, 758 Waverly St., Palo Alto, Cal.

Sangmaster, Norman I., Student Officer.

Santos, Fileto D., Ensign. N. A. No. 1056.

Sargent, Fitzwilliam, Lieut. (j.g.)., Haverford, Pa. Mass. Inst. of Tech., Akron, O. N. A. No. 643. LTA.

Sargent, Howard C., Lieut. (j.g.), 49 Oliver St., Malden Mass. Mass. Inst. of Tech., Pensacola, Moutchic, St. Trojan, Chatham. N. A. No. 372. HTA.

Saul, John M., Student Officer, 934 New York Ave., N. W., Washington, D. C. Mass. Inst. of Tech. HTA.

Saunders, Don E., Student Officer, Colerain, N. Car. Mass. Inst. of Tech., Key West. HTA.

Saunders, Eugene D., Student Officer, 2925 Coliseum St., New Orleans, La. Dunwoody and Seattle.

Saunders, K. R., Ensign, 1703 Park Ave., Richmond Va. Mass. Inst. of Tech., Pensacola, Miami. N. A. No. 1014. HTA.

Saunders, Maurice, Jr., Student Officer, D. K. E. House, Hanover, N. H. Great Lakes. LTA.

Saunders, William T., Jr., Student Officer, Yale Club, 44th St., New York, N. Y.

Saurer, Louis W., Student Officer, 15 S. Main St., Mainsburg, Ohio.

Savage, Arno Charles, Student Officer, 35 Maple St., Bangor, Me. Mass. Inst. of Tech., Miami. HTA.

Savelle, Mark A., War. Machinist, Mobile, Ala. U. S. S. *Huntington*, San Diego, Pensacola.

Sawyer, Damian C., Ensign. N. A. No. 2399.

Sawyer, Gene F., Student Officer, 1423 East 86th St., Cleveland, Ohio. Mass. Inst. of Tech., Key West. HTA.

Sawyer, Lester B., Student Officer, 2015 G St., N. W., Washington, D. C.

Sawyer, Ralph H., Ensign, 24 Clinton St., Framingham, Mass.

Saxby, J. Bert, Ensign, Santa Barbara, Cal. N. A. No. 2076.

Saxton, Ray D., Student Officer.

Sayles, Philip S., Student Officer, New Bedford, Mass. Mass. Inst. of Tech , Newport, R. I., Bay Shore. HTA.

Sayles, R. W., Ensign, 16 East St., Adams, Mass. N. A. No. 1462.

Saylor, William S., Student Officer.

Sayre, Caryl H., Ensign, 868 Carroll St., Brooklyn, N. Y. Mass. Inst. of Tech., Pensacola, Moutchic, Avord, Old Sarum, Eng., Campaigne, St. Inglevert. N. A. No. 367.

Scarborough, H. C., Ensign, Plattsmouth, Neb. Mass. Inst. of Tech., Akron, Rockaway. LTA.

Scarlett, Ed. G., Ensign, 37 Lake Ave., Lynn, Mass. Mass. Inst. of Tech., Key West, Miami, Pensacola. N. A. No. 1211. HTA.

Scattergood, George B., Ensign, 114 W. Philelena St., Germantown, Philadelphia, Pa. Mass. Inst. of Tech., Akron, Rockaway. LTA.

Schenck, I. P., Ensign. N. A. No. 1402.

Schermerhorn, H., Lieut. (j.g.), 166 Oakleigh Road, Newton, Mass. N. A. No. 208.

Schermerhorn, James, Jr., Student Officer, Detroit Times, Detroit, Mich. Mass. Inst. of Tech.

Schilichter, Fred P., Ensign, 28 Radford St., Yonkers, N. Y.

Schiller, Morgan B., Ensign, 5308 Ellsworth Ave., Pittsburgh, Pa. Mass. Inst. of Tech., Pensacola, Seattle.

SCHIMMEL, VERNON G., Ensign, 205 Colonial Bldg., Winchester, Ky. N. A. No. 2026.

SCHIVERY, A. K., Student Officer, Woodland, Pa.

SCHLOSS, MONROE H., Student Officer, 2314 Eutaw Place, Baltimore, Md.

SCHMID, HERBERT W., Ensign, 100 Elmgrove Ave., Providence, R. I. Mass. Inst. of Tech., Bay Shore, Pensacola, Hampton Roads. HTA.

SCHMIN, JOHN H., Ensign, 19 Vera Place, Montclair, N. J. Mass. Inst. of Tech., Key West, Miami, Pensacola. N. A. No. 1612. HTA.

SCHMIDT, KARL, Student Officer, Santa Barbara, Cal.

SCHMIDTT, PAUL M., Student Officer, Plantsville. Conn.

SCHNEBERGER, GEORGE F., Student Officer, Arlington Heights, Ill. Dunwoody Inst., Minn.

SCHNEIDER, ELMER L., Student Officer.

SCHOEMBS, EDGAR O., Student Officer.

SCHOFIELD, EDWIN R., Student Officer, 227 S. 41st St., Philadelphia, Pa. Mass. Inst. of Tech. HTA.

SCHOFIELD, ROGER S., Student Officer, 49 Monument Road, Philadelphia, Pa. Mass. Inst. of Tech., Bay Shore, L. I. HTA.

SCHOLZ, JACKSON V., Ensign, 5867 Nina Place, St. Louis, Mo.

SCHOONMAKER, E., Ensign. N. A. No. 388.

SCHORTMANN, EDWARD C., Student Officer, 227 Laban St., Providence, R. I.

SCHOUTON, HENRY W., Lieut. (j.g.), 26 East Ave., Rochester, N. Y. Naval Observatory, Washington, D. C., Philadelphia.

SCHRADER, JOSEPH H., Student Officer, 396 S. Maryland St., Brooklyn, N. Y. Mass. Inst. of Tech., Akron, Rockaway. LTA.

SCHROEDER, ARTHUR F., Student Officer, 59 S. Water St., Milwaukee, Wis.

SCHROEDER, JOHN E., Ensign, 572 Newberry Blvd., Milwaukee, Wis. Dunwoody Inst., Minn., Key West, Pensacola. N. A. No. 1900. HTA.

SCHULTHEIS, FREDERICK O., Ensign.

SCHULZE, RALPH H., Student Officer, 702 S. 3rd St., Waco, Texas. Seattle. HTA.

SCHUMACHER, EDWIN F., Student Officer, 29 N. D St., Irvington, N. Y.

SCHUR, MEINRAD A., Ensign, 535 Greenwood Ave., Portland, Oregon. Pensacola, Dunwoody, Hampton Roads, San Diego. HTA.

SCHUSS, WM., War. Gun.

SCHUYLER, HENDER C., Student Officer, 5255 Enright Ave., St. Louis, Mo. Mass. Inst. of Tech., U. S. Naval Air Station, Miami. HTA.

SCHWABE, JOHN C., JR., Ensign, 12 College Ave., Columbia, Mo. Akron, O., Pensacola, Rockaway, Morehead City, Key West. N. A. No. 1109. LTA.

SCHWARTZ, F. B., Ensign, 151 Central Park West, New York.

SCHWARZ, L. L., War. Gun.

SCOTT, EVERETT B., Ensign, 2003 7th Ave., Kearney, Nebr. Mass. Inst. of Tech., San Diego, Pensacola, Miami. N. A. No. 1657.

SCOTT, EVERETT L., Student Officer, 942 16th St., Boulder, Colo.

SCOTT, FRANCIS W., Student Officer, 1374 Peachtree St., Atlanta, Ga.

SCOTT, GEORGE DRAKE, Lieut. (j.g.), 31 Westmoreland Place, St. Louis, Mo. Mass. Inst. of Tech., Bay Shore. L. I., Key West, Brunswick, Miami. N. A. No. 465.

SCOTT, JOHN HIATT, Student Officer, 4338 Oakenwald Ave., Chicago, Ill.

SCOTT, S. G., Student Officer, 309 South New St., Champaign, Ill. Mass. Inst. of Tech. HTA.

SCOTT, WILLIAM B., JR., Ensign, 145 Juniper St., Atlanta, Ga. N. A. No. 1140.

SCOUTT, WILL JERROLD, Student Officer, 23rd St., 7th Ave., Kearney, Nebr. Mass. Inst. of Tech. HTA.

SCRANTON, SERENO S., Student Officer, 839 Edgewood Ave., Trenton, N. J. Mass. Inst. of Tech., Newport, R. I. HTA.

SCUDDER, NORMAN C., Student Officer, 25 Fountain St., West Newton, Mass.

SCULLY, F. P., Lieut. (j.g.), 5 Dexter Park, Cambridge, Mass.

SCURRY, TOM, Student Officer, 1903 Bennett Ave., Dallas, Tex. Mass. Inst. of Tech., Key West, Miami, Pensacola. HTA.

SEARS, WILLIAM, Student Officer, 30 W. 44th St., New York City.

SEATON, DONALD L., Student Officer, 485 Benton St., Santa Rosa, Cal. Univ. of Washington, Seattle.

SEBOLD, CHASE E., War. Mach.

SEEHOF, JEROME F., Ensign, 1407 Jarvis Ave., Chicago, Ill. Mass. Inst. of Tech., Key West, Miami, Pensacola, Montauk. N. A. No. 1322.

SEEMAN, WILLIAM, Student Officer, 264 Riverside Drive, New York City. Mass. Inst. of Tech., Bay Shore, L. I., Pensacola. LTA.

SEIBELS, H. C., Lieut. (j.g.), 211 N. Medford St., Birmingham, Ala. Annapolis, Washington, Pensacola. HTA.

SELIG, ALBERT S., Student Officer, 418 Washington St., Atlanta, Ga. Mass. Inst. of Tech., Miami. HTA.

SELVAGE, EUGENE S., Ensign, 2522 Ridge Road, Berkeley Cal.

SEWELL, A. T., Ensign. N. A. No. 2117.

SEYMOUR, FREDERICK D., Student Officer, 55 Prospect St., East Orange, N. J. Mass. Inst. of Tech., Bay Shore. HTA.

SEYMOUR, H. J., Ensign, Lima, Ohio. Mass. Inst. of Tech., Akron, Hampton Rds., Key West. LTA.

SHACKFORD, ROBERT S., Student Officer, 1045 Beacon St., Brookline, Mass. Mass. Inst. of Tech. HTA.

SHACKNO, JULIEN S., Student Officer, 800 Argyle Road, Brooklyn, N. Y.

SHANDS, RICHARD E., Student Officer, 901 16th St., N. W., Washington, D. C. Mass. Inst. of Tech., Key West. HTA.

SHANK, WILLIAM C., Ensign, Globe Bldg., Pittsburg, Kans. Great Lakes, Pensacola.

SHANLY, JOHN SEXTON, Student Officer, Court Hotel, 555 Bush St., San Francisco, Cal.

SHANNON, WM., Student Officer, 646 76th St., Brooklyn, N. Y.

SHARP, MALCOLM P., Ensign, 659 Mendota Court, Maclisa, Wis. Mass. Inst. of Tech., Miami. N. A. No. 1540. HTA.

SHAVER, ROY W., Student Officer, Care of Metz Mfg Co., Waltham, Mass.

SHAVER, W. A., War. Mach., 111 East Carter Ave., Ashland, Ky.

SHAW, CLIFTON R., Student Officer, Route No. 5, Weather Ford, Tex.

SHAW, LAWRENCE I., Student Officer, Osceola, Nebr.

SHAW, WILLIAM L., Ensign, 2300 McKinney Ave., Dallas, Tex. N. A. No. 1624.

SHEA, EDWARD L., Lieut. (j.g.), 90 Palm St., Nashua, N. H. Royal Flying Corps, Toronto, Hampton Rds., San Diego. N. A. No. 153. HTA.

SHEA, GERALD P., Student Officer, 213 Temple St., Syracuse, N. Y.

SHEHAN, J. M., Lieut. (j.g.). N. A. No. 484.

SHEHAN, WALTER H., Student Officer, 73 Sherman Ave., New Haven, Conn.

SHELDON, KENNETH H., Ensign, The Cloister Club, New Haven, Conn. N. A. No. 2096.

SHELDON, RALPH M., Student Officer, 1879 Ninth Ave., Watervliet, N. Y. Mass. Inst. of Tech., Buffalo, Akron. LTA.

SHELTON, CLARENCE M., Ensign. N. A. No. 2143.

SHELTON, LEONARD W., Student Officer, 497 S. El Molino Ave., Pasadena, Cal. Seattle, Wash. HTA.

SHEPARD, H. B., Lieut. (j.g.), East Derry, N. H. Ordnance, experimental aircraft machine guns and cannon. HTA.

SHEPARD, WILLIAM WALLACE, Student Officer, Auburn, Cal. Seattle, Wash., Key West. HTA.

SHEPHERD, LELAND H., Student Officer, 165 Arlington Ave., Providence, R. I.

SHEPHERD, THOMAS L., Student Officer, 312 N. Chestnut St., Plattsville, Wis.

SHEPPARD, E. W., Lieut. (j.g.).

SHEPPARD, W. H., Ensign, 225 Broadway Market Bldg., Detroit, Mich. N. A. No. 625.

SHERBURNE, G. H., War. Mach., Mystic, Conn.

SHERIDAN, EDWARD J., Student Officer, 147 W. Muskegon Ave., Muskegon, Mich.

SHERIDAN, THOMAS H., Lieut. (j.g.), 1405 Dearborn St., Chicago, Ill. Great Lakes, Pensacola, Washington, D. C.

SHERMAN, H. R., JR., Student Officer, 24 Union St., Montclair, N. J. Great Lakes, Ill. HTA.

SHERMAN, S. F., War. Mach.

SHIELDS, JOHN F., Student Officer, New Rochelle, N. Y. Mass. Inst. of Tech. HTA.

SHIELDS, LOUIS G., Student Officer, 3rd and Maple Sts., Great Neck, N. Y.

Shields, Paul V., Student Officer, Manhasset, L. I., New York.

Shields, William L., War. Gun.

Shirk, Chafee Wright, Student Officer, Main St., Brookville, Ind.

Shirk, Elbert W., Lieut. (j.g.), Richmond, Ind.

Shirley, Elser C., Student Officer, 150 Wilder Ave., Los Gatos, Cal.

Shoemaker, Allan W., Student Officer, 225 East Commerce St., Bridgeton, N. J.

Shoemaker, William, Jr., Student Officer, 112 S. 54th St., Philadelphia, Pa.

Shone, G. C., Ensign, 356 Kingsley Ave., Palo Alto, Cal. N. A. No. 1305.

Shore, Harold F., Ensign, Chillicothe, Mo. Seattle, Wash., San Diego, Pensacola. N. A. No. 2167. HTA.

Shorney, Gordon D., Student Officer, 304 S. Euclid Ave., Oak Park, Ill. Dunwoody, Miami. HTA.

Showalter, W. H., Ensign., Merced, Calif. Mass. Inst. of Tech., Akron, Rockaway. LTA.

Shumaker, Grover C., Student Officer, 324 Main St., Tupelo, Miss.

Shuman, Delwin L., Ensign, 2801 Benvenue Ave., Berkeley, Cal. Mass. Inst. of Tech., Key West, Miami, Pensacola. N. A. No. 1394. HTA.

Shumway, Paul E., Lieut. (j.g.), 43 Grove St., Greenfield, Mass. Mass. Inst. of Tech., Pensacola, Ft. Worth, Hampton Rds.; Killingholme, Eng.; Cape May. HTA.

Sibley, Dean S., Ensign, Newport, N. H. Mass. Inst. of Tech., Curtis Aero Corp. under Bur. of Steam Eng.

Sidlo, Charles T., Ensign, 722 Humboldt St., Denver, Colo.

Sidway, Ralph H., Student Officer, 539 Delaware Ave., Buffalo, N. Y. Great Lakes, Pensacola.

Siedler, Howard D., Student Officer, 36 Oakland Ave., Bloomfield, N. J.

Siegbert, Henry, Student Officer, Hotel San Remo, 74th St., and C. P. West, New York City.

Sievert, Leo Ellsworth, Student Officer, 400 N. Monterey St., Alhambra, Cal.

Simard, C. T., Ensign, 2318 Glen Ave., Berkeley, Cal. N. A. No. 1604.

Simmons, Franklin C., Student Officer, 160 Bellevue Ave., Upper Montclair, N. J.

Simmons, John G., Student Officer, 16 Knickerbocker Road, Englewood, N. J. Mass. Inst. of Tech. HTA.

Simmons, Julian D., Student Officer, 35 West 58th St., New York City.

Simon, Edgar K., Student Officer, Edgemore Club, Edgemore, L. I., N. Y.

Simpson, Colin Campbell, War. Mach.

Simpson, John D., Student Officer, 105 East 15th St., New York City.

Simson, Jess Ray, Ensign. N. A. No. 1191.

Sinclair, Arthur H., Ensign, 3170 17th St., N. W., Washington, D. C. N. A. No. 725.

Singe, Clarence, Student Officer, 465 West End Ave., New York City.

Sittenham, F. W., Lieut. (j.g.), 29 W. 14th St., New York City.

Siulis, Wilbur T., Student Officer, 251 W. 129th St., New York City.

Skelton, Leonard W., Student Officer, 497 So. El Molino Ave., Pasadena, Cal. Seattle. HTA.

Skewes, T., War. Gun.

Skinner, Edmund B.

Skirm, Joseph G., Lieut. (j.g.), 17 Maple St., Princeton, N. J

Skyles, W. F., War. Mach. N. A. No. 613.

Slattery, Alfred M., Student Officer, 137 Savin Hill Ave., Boston, Mass.

Slayter, Richard Eugene, Student Officer, 4417 Gaston Ave., Dallas, Tex. Mass. Inst. of Tech., Key West. HTA.

Sloan, Julian R., Ensign, 20 William St., New York City. Mass. Inst. of Tech., Akron, Hampton Roads, U. S. S. *Rhode Island*, *Arkansas*, Grand Fleet; Berehaven, Ireland. LTA.

Sloan, Vernon G., Ensign, Arlington Heights, Mass. Mass. Inst. of Tech. Garden City, L. I.

Sloane, Douglas, Lieut. (j.g.), 328 Cabot St., Newtonville, Mass. Mass. Inst. of Tech., Miami. HTA.

Sloman, Frank H., Ensign, 185 Dolores St., San Francisco, Cal.

Small, R. B., War. Mach., 1102 West 5th St., Marion, Ind.

Smart, Jackson W., Student Officer, 702 S. University St., Ann Arbor, Mich.

Smart, Roy L., Student Officer, Clayton, Ala.

Smith, Albert V., Student Officer, 32 Oakland St., Winthrop, Mass.

Smith, Alvin W., Jr., Lieut. (j.g.), Care of Dr. Hahne, 414 Grafton Apt., Dayton, Ohio. Mass. Inst. of Tech., Pensacola; Moutchic, Le Croisic, Ferrand, Fr.; Porto Corsini, Italy; Miami, Hampton Roads. N. A. No. 356. HTA.

Smith, Andrew M., Ensign, 1304 Hay Ave., Hollywood, Cal. Seattle, San Diego, Pensacola, Hampton Roads. N. A. No. 2119. HTA.

Smith, C. W., Ensign, 2421 Harriet Ave., S. Minneapolis, Minn. N. A. No. 1658.

Smith, Carl D., Student Officer, 65 Fairfield Ave., Holyoke, Mass.

Smith, Charles R. W., Ensign, 321 Hawthorne Rd., Roland Park, Md. N. A. No. 1878.

Smith, Chester C., Ensign, 3002 Charlotte St., Kansas City, Mo.

Smith, Donald J., Ensign, Sheldon, Ind.

Smith, E. Traver, Lieut. (j.g.), 225 E. Main St., Patchogue, N. Y. Buffalo, R. F. C., Gosport, Turnberry, Ayr, R. A. F., Sq. 213, Dunkirk, Fr. HTA.

Smith, Earl B., Ensign. N. A. No. 365.

Smith, Ellsworth E., Student Officer, Menands, N. Y.

Smith, Elwyn L., Ensign, Syracuse, N. Y. N. A. No. 964.

Smith, Everett, Jr., Ensign, 27 Wall St., New York City.

Smith, Francis P., Jr., Ensign, Mamaroneck, N. Y. N. A. No. 723.

Smith, Frank S., Lieut. (j.g.), Hallettsville, Tex.

Smith, Fred G.

Smith, G. E., Ensign, Box 215, Oklahoma City, Okla. Mass. Inst. of Tech., Akron, Rockaway Beach. LTA.

Smith, Gordon, Ensign. N. A. No. 933.

Smith, Hampton S., Student Officer.

Smith, Harold A., Student Officer, 114 13th Ave., Columbus, Ohio.

Smith, Harry C., Student Officer, 147 Franklin St., Marietta, O.

Smith, Herbert L., Student Officer, 3037, S. Vermont Ave., Los Angeles, Cal.

Smith, Hewitt, Student Officer, 901 S. 30th St., Birmingham, Ala.

Smith, Hugh C., Student Officer, 7 Maraton Ave., Detroit, Mich.

Smith, J. D., Student Officer, Sheldon, Ind.

Smith, James M., Student Officer, 411½ Walnut St. Harrisburg, Pa.

Smith, John E., Student Officer, 357 Ave. C., Bayonne. N. J.

Smith, John P., Ensign, 1340 S. Grant St., Denver, Colo. N. A. No. 1296.

Smith, John P. P., Student Officer, 1756 P St., N. W., Washington, D. C.

Smith, Le Grand, Student Officer, 113 Horner St., Elmira, N. Y.

Smith, Floyd S., Student Officer, 841 W. 23d St., Los Angeles, Cal.

Smith, Nelson H., Ensign, 52 Summer St., Boston, Mass. N. A. No. 703.

Smith, Olin R., Student Officer, 583 W. Delavan St., Buffalo, N. Y.,

Smith, Peter Paul, War. Machinist, 2624 Boulevard, Jersey City, N. J.

Smith, Philip O., Student Officer, 8 W. Roselawn, Danville, Ill.

Smith, Philip H., Student Officer, Princeton, N. J. Mass. Inst. of Tech. HTA.

Smith, Pomeroy, Student Officer, 1359 Girard St., Washington, D. C.

Smith, R. N., Lieut. (j.g.).

Smith, Ralph A., Student Officer, Auburn, Wash.

Smith, Richard H., Student Officer, 82 Gainsborough St., Boston, Mass.

Smith, Richard M., Ensign, Washougal, Wash., Seattle, San Diego, Pensacola. N. A. No. 2297. HTA.

Smith, Robert Bowen, Student Officer, Box 162 Ridgefield, Wash. Seattle. LTA.

SMITH, ROBERT HOOPER, Student Officer, Homewood Apts., Charles and 30th Sts., Baltimore, Md. Mass. Inst. of Tech. HTA.

SMITH, RUTHVEN K., Student Officer, Callahan, Fla. Mass. Inst. of Tech. HTA.

SMITH, THOMAS B., Ensign, 2029 Pine St., Philadelphia, Pa., Great Lakes, Pensacola.

SMITH, WILLIAM A., Student Officer, 16 11th St., Parkersburg, W. Va., Dunwoody Inst., Minn. LTA.

SMITH, WM. J., Ensign, 900 S. Crockett St., Sherman, Tex. Mass. Inst. of Tech., Miami, Pensacola, Hampton Roads. N. A. No. 2121. HTA.

SMITH, WILLIAM N. H., JR., Student Officer, 434 Halifax St., Raleigh, N. C.

SMITH, W. R. L., JR., Ensign, 202 First Natl. Bank Bldg., Richmond, Va. Mass. Inst of Tech., Bay Shore, Pensacola, Halifax, N. S., North Sydney, N. S., Key West. HTA.

SMITH, YATES B., Student Officer, 248 Seminole Ave., Detroit, Mich.

SNEDDON, C. A., War. Machinist, 272 W. William St., Decatur, Ill.

SNELL, HAROLD V., Ensign.

SNODDY, B. L., Ensign, 16 State St., Schenectady, N. Y. N. A. No. 2472.

SNODGRASS, PAUL W., Student Officer, 513 Prospect Ave., Medina, N. Y.

SNODY, ALLAN P., Lieut. (j.g.), 19 Radford Pl., Yonkers, N. Y. Mass. Inst. of Tech., Bay Shore, Key West, Pensacola. HTA.

SNOW, ALFRED T., Ensign, 417 S. 63rd St., Philadelphia, Pa. Mass. Inst. of Tech., Burgess Co., Marblehead, Mass.

SNOW, WILLIAM T., Ensign, 117 Bay State Road, Boston, Mass. N. A. No. 328.

SNOWDEN, JOHN W., Student Officer, 1025 E. Jersey St., Elizabeth, N. J.

SNYDER, CHAS. A., Student Officer, Wellsboro, Pa. Mass. Inst. of Tech. HTA.

SNYDER, NYRON E., Ensign, Berrien Spgs., Mich. N. A. No. 2504.

SNYDER, W. OVERTON, Ensign, Birdsville, Md.

SOBOTS, F., War. Machinist.

SONERS, GLENN W., Student Officer, 803 S. Lafountaine St., Kokomo, Ind., Dunwoody Inst., Minn.; Miami, Key West. HTA.

SONTE, JAMES B., War. Machinist, Meridian, Miss.

SOPER, GEO. A., JR., Student Officer, 391 West End Ave., New York City.

SOPER, HAROLD C., Ensign. N. A. No. 945.

SORUGGS, S. B., Carpenter.

SOULE, V. A., War. Machinist, 50 Saratoga Ave., Yonkers N. Y.

SOULIS, HAROLD A., Student Officer, 251 W. 129th St., New York City. Mass. Inst. of Tech. HTA.

SOULIS, WILBUR T., Student Officer, 251 W. 129th St., New York City. Mass. Inst. of Tech. HTA.

SOUR, ABRY, War. Boatswain.

SOUTHER, RICHARD G., Ensign, 7089 Waterman Ave., St. Louis, Mo.

SOUTHWELL, FRED B., Student Officer, 1107 12th St., Boulder, Colo.

SOUTHWICK, IVAN A., Student Officer, Garver, Okla. Mass. Inst. of Tech., Akron, Pensacola. LTA.

SOUTHWORTH, THOMAS D., Lieut. (j.g.), Box 1, Springville, Utah. N. A. No. 389.

SPAETH, JOHN N., Student Officer, 214 Thurston Ave., Ithaca, N. Y.

SPAHR, RAYMOND A., Ensign, 223 Chestnut St., Sewickley, Pa. N. A. No. 2087.

SPANGLER, CARLETON D., Student Officer, 308 E. Main St., Edmond, Okla. HTA.

SPAULDING, C. A., Student Officer, Hartford, Mich.; Seattle, Wash. HTA.

SPAULDING, IRAH D., Ensign.

SPEARE, HAROLD H., Ensign.

SPEER, FRANK H., JR., Ensign, 6743 Thomas St., Pittsburgh, Pa. N. A. No. 1471.

SPENCE, BERNARD L., Ensign, 529 Third St., Brooklyn, N. Y. Mass. Inst. of Tech., Key West, Miami, Pensacola. N. A. No. 1613. HTA.

SPENCER, ARTHUR W., Student Officer.

SPENCER, LEON C., Student Officer, North Bennington, Vt.

SPERRY, IRVING L., Student Officer.

SPERRY, ROBERT A., Student Officer, 2107 Adelbert Road, Cleveland, Ohio.

SPIEGAL, RALPH A., Student Officer, 190 14th St., Milwaukee, Wis.

SPIEGELBERG, GEO. A., Student Officer, 36 W. 76th St., New York City.

SPIKES, JOSEPH N., Student Officer, Benjamin, Tex. Mass. Inst. of Tech. LTA.

SPILLANE, JAMES J., Student Officer, 189 River St., East Dedham, Mass.

SPINK, E. S., JR., Ensign, Phoenicia, N. Y. Mass. Inst. of Tech., Bay Shore, Hampton Roads, Pensacola. N. A. No. 1778. HTA.

SPRATT, WILLIAM A., Ensign.

SPRINGALL, CYRUS F., Lieut. (j.g.), 18 Spring St., Malden, Mass. Mass. Inst. of Tech., Buffalo, Elizabeth, New York. N. A. No. 1789. HTA.

SPRINGER, EDWARD F., Ensign, Aspermont, Tex. N. A. No. 2316.

SPRUANCE, HORACE E., Asst. Surgeon.

SPRUNT, J. D., Ensign, 223 N. 3d St., Wilmington, N. C. Mass. Inst. of Tech., Key West, Miami, Pensacola. N. A. No. 1183. LTA.

SPURRIER, DONALD P., Ensign, 325 Oliver St., Whiting, Ind.; Dunwoody Inst., Minn.; Key West, Pensacola, Marblehead City. N. A. No. 2133. HTA.

SQUIBB, CHARLES G., Ensign, 30 Stearns Road, Brookline, Mass. Mass. Inst. of Tech.

STACKPOLE, ROBERT E., Student Officer, 3495 Broadway, New York City.

STACY, H., Lieut. (j.g.).

STAFFORD, LAC. F., Ensign.

STAGG, DWIGHT E., Student Officer, 151 West Ave., Bridgeport, Conn.

STAHL, ERIC C., Ensign, 2255 Parkwood Ave., Mass. Inst. of Tech., Key West, Miami, Pensacola. N. A. No. 2080.

STALEY, WILLIAM M., Student Officer, 692 Irma Ave., Beaumont, Texas.

STALL, RICHARD G., Student Officer, Box 217, Monument Beach, Mass.

STANCILL, LESLIE E., Ensign, 2706 Ontario Road, Washington, D. C. N. A. No. 2258.

STANDING, RUSSELL J., Student Officer, Honeyville, Utah.

STANDISH, MILES W., Student Officer, Rochester, Mich.

STONIFORD, ROBERT H., Ensign, 332 Putman Ave., Brooklyn, N. Y., Mass. Inst. of Tech., Pensacola, Chatham. N. A. No. 967.

STANLEY, CLARANCE, Ensign, Great Barrington, Mass. Mass. Inst. of Tech., Miami, Pensacola. HTA.

STANLEY, GERALD T., Ensign, 4241 Westminster Pl., St. Louis, Mo.

STANLEY, HENRY T., Lieut. (j.g.), 20 Greystone Park, Lynn, Mass. Mass. Inst. of Tech., Pensacola, Cattewater, Newlynn, Felixstowe, St. Trojan, Paulliac, France, Key West.

STANLEY, JOHN, Ensign. N. A. No. 1495.

STANLEY, RICHARD B., Ensign, Lincoln, N. H. N. A. No. 1004.

STANTON, EDWIN M., Ensign, 1831 Harrison Ave., New York City.

STAPLES, JOHN F., Student Officer.

STARK, HOWARD B., Ensign, 2524 Cedar St., Milwaukee, Wis. N. A. No. 2221.

STARK, WALTER R., Student Officer.

STARNES, WILLIAM E., Student Officer.

STARR, FREDERIC H., Ensign, Easton, Md.

STARUS, HENRY L., Ensign, 4007 Penhurst Ave., Baltimore, Md.

ST. CLAIR, HARRY L., Student Officer, 316 First Natl. Bank Bldg., Roanoke, Va. Mass. Inst. of Tech. HTA.

STEARMS, TIMOTHY R., Student Officer, Brunswick, Me.

STEDMAN, W. M., Ensign, 84 Van Winkle St., Dorchester, Mass. N. A. No. 1538.

STEELE, DUNN K., Student Officer, 372 Walnut Ave., Roanoke, Va.

STEELE, FRANCIS B., Student Officer, 32 Ellicott Ave., Batavia, N. Y. Mass. Inst. of Tech., Buffalo.

STEELE, PERCY D., Ensign, McArthur, Ohio. N. A. No. 2366.

STEFANONICH, C. J., Student Officer, 3140 Salmon St., Philadelphia, Pa.

STEFFENS, FREDERICK R., Student Officer, 37 Seaton

Pl., N. W., Washington, D. C. Mass. Inst. of Tech., Key West. HTA.

Stein, Hugo B., Student Officer, 3554 Bogart Ave., Avondale, Cincinnati, Ohio. Dunwoody Inst., Minn.

Steiner, Howard C., Student Officer, 700 Patterson Ave., S. W., Canton, Ohio.

Steller, Warren E., Student Officer, 3333 Archwood Ave., Cleveland, Ohio.

Stenberg, Lyman H., Student Officer, R. F. D. No. 3, Box 324, Puyallup, Wash.

Stengel, Alvin L., Ensign, 408 Jones Ave., Fort Atkinson, Wis.

Stephanowich, Clement J., Ensign.

Stephens, H. T., Ensign, 17 Urban St., Mt. Vernon, N. Y.

Stephens, Stanford H., Student Officer, 295 Beacon St., Boston, Mass.

Stevens, F. H., Ensign, Lake Placid, N. Y.; U. S. Naval Air Sta., Brest. N. A. No. 1977.

Stevens, John L., Student Officer, 314 River St., Valdosta, Ga. Mass. Inst. of Tech., Key West. HTA.

Stevens, Louis G., Student Officer, Care of B. F. Machlan, Takoma Park, Washington, D. C.

Stevens, William D. B., Student Officer.

Stevens, William F., Ensign, 1526 Sherwin Ave., Chicago, Ill.

Stevenson, George William, Ensign, Waverly, Pa. Mass. Inst. of Tech., Miami, Key West, Pensacola. HTA.

Stevenson, Markley, Ensign, 803 Finance Bldg., Philadelphia, Pa. Great Lakes, Washington, D. C.

Stevenson, Paul E., Student Officer, 44 Boylston St., Cambridge, Mass.

Stevenson, W. A., Student Officer, 412 West College St., Rochester, Minn. Mass. Inst. of Tech., Montauk, Miami. HTA.

Stewart, Bernie R., Student Officer, Apt. 512 G St., N. W., Washington, D. C.

Stewart, Geo. S., Student Officer.

Stewart, John C., Ensign, 518 Grove St., Sewickley, Pa. Mass. Inst. of Tech., Bay Shore, Pensacola. N. A. No. 1601. HTA.

Stewart, Ross, Student Officer, 310 Dennis Ave., Houston, Tex.

Stewart, Slayton J., Ensign, 504 N. 4 St., Camden, N. J. Mass. Inst. of Tech., Miami, Key West, Pensacola. N. A. No. 2340. HTA.

Stewart, Vance, Ensign. N. A. No. 1440.

Stickley, Wellington E., Ensign, Woodstock, Va. Mass. Inst. of Tech., Bay Shore, Pensacola, Hampton Roads. N. A. No. 1688. HTA.

Stickney, Joseph B., Student Officer, Care of F. Adams, Pan American Union. Washington, D. C.

Stifel, Arnold G., Ensign, 4944 Lindell Blvd., St. Louis, Mo.

Stillwell, Richard N., Ensign, Quincy, Ill.

Stilphen, M. B., Student Officer, 65 Church St., Swanton, Vt. Mass. Inst. of Tech. HTA.

Stimson, Donald C., Ensign, Eaton Rapids, Mich. Mass. Inst. of Tech., Bay Shore, Pensacola. N. A. No. 1894.

Stimson, Thomas D., Ensign, The Highlands, R. F. D. No. 2, Seattle, Wash. Great Lakes, Pensacola.

Stitt, Edward W., Student Officer, 1708 R. St., Washington D. C.

Stockard, Henry J., Ensign, 316 Bonding St., Raleigh, N. C. Mass. Inst. of Tech., Pensacola, Key West. HTA.

Stocker, Robert M., Lieut. (j.g.), The Brighton, Washington, D. C.

Stockett, John W., Student Officer, 312 4th St., S. E., Washington, D. C. Mass. Inst. of Tech. HTA.

Stockton, Manley, Student Officer, 2823 13th St., N. W., Washington, D. C.

Stockwell, W. F., Ensign. N. A. No. 692.

Stohlman, Edwin L., Student Officer, 328 Dorset Ave., Chevy Chase, D. C.

Stokes, Sylvanus, Jr., Student Officer.

Stolts, Charles L., Student Officer, 226 E. 60th St., Portland, Ore.

Stolts, Wm. E., Student Officer.

Stone, Arthur C., Ensign. 501 Old State Bank Bldg., Evansville, Ind. Mass. Inst. of Tech., Akron, Ohio; Pensacola, Fla. LTA.

Stone, C. L., Jr., Ensign, 22-32nd Ave., San Francisco, Cal. Mass. Inst. of Tech., Miami, Pensacola. HTA.

Stone, Chauncey W., Student Officer, 12 Fifth Ave., New York City.

Stone, G. L., Lieut. (j.g.).

Stoner, Harold E., Student Officer, 125 N. 18th St., Ft. Dodge, Iowa. Seattle, Wash., Miami, Fla. HTA.

Stoppel, Fred H., Lieut. (j.g.).

Stoppelman, E. A., War. Machinist, Route 4, Box 170, Seattle, Wash. Columbia University, N. Y., San Diego, Great Lakes, Ill. HTA.

Stout, Henry L., Lieut. (j.g.).

Stowe, Byron S., War. Machinist, Hemstead, L. I.

Stowe, J. B., War. Machinist.

Stowell, F. M., Student Officer, 1903 Girard Ave., So. Minneapolis, Minn. Mass. Inst. of Tech., Dunwoody, Philadelphia, Coco Solo.

Stratford, Wm. Malcolm, Student Officer, 62 Branard Ave., Houston, Tex. Seattle, San Diego, Cal.; Pensacola, Fla. HTA.

Stratton, Samuel S., Ensign, 7 Lafayette St., Newburyport, Mass. Mass. Inst. of Tech., Akron, Ohio,; Rockaway N. Y. LTA.

Strawn, Harry Omar, Student Officer, Landover, Md. Mass. Inst. of Tech., Bay Shore, L. I., N. Y. HTA.

Strebel, Arthur C., Ensign.

Streng, Geo. W., Student Officer, 98 William St., Pittson, Pa.

Stritmatter, Frank H., Student Officer, 843 Orchard St., Toledo, Ohio.

Strivings, Roscoe S., Student Officer, Castile, N. Y. Mass. Inst. of Tech. HTA.

Strobel, C. E., Ensign, Oakland, Cal. Mass. Inst. of Tech., Key West, Miami,; Pensacola, Fla.; San Diego, Cal. N. A. No. 1645. HTA.

Strohm, W. E., Student Officer, Powell, Wyoming.

Stromer, Bryan Wm., Student Officer, 410 W. 4th St., Hastings, Neb. Mass. Inst. of Tech., Miami. HTA.

Stromeyer, W. H., Ensign, 1008 Trinity Ave., New York City. N. A. No. 917.

Strong, L. S., Student Officer, 2324 Pillsbury Ave., Minneapolis, Minn. Mass. Inst. of Tech., Dunwoody Inst., Minn. HTA.

Strough, Wm. L., Ensign, 93 College Ave., New Brunswick, N. J. Mass. Inst. of Tech., Bay Shore, Hampton Roads, Pensacola, Fla.

Stroock, Bertram A., Student Officer, Newburgh, N. Y. P. O. Box 706. Mass. Inst. of Tech. HTA.

Strotz, Harold C., Ensign, 365 Sheridan Road, Winnetka, Ill. Dunwoody, Miami, Key West, Pensacola. N. A. No. 2485. HTA.

Struble, F. H., Ensign, 916 Montana Ave., Gladstone, Mich. Mass. Inst. of Tech., Akron, Ohio, Pensacola, Fla. LTA.

Stuart, John G., Ensign.

Stuart, Kimberly, Ensign, 406 Wisconsin Ave., Neenah, Wis., Lake Bolsena, It. Moutchic, Fr., Porto Corsini, It. HTA.

Stuart, L. B.

Sturgeon, Andrew, Ensign, 36 Maple St., New Haven, Conn. Mass. Inst. of Tech., Pensacola, Miami, Moutchic, Campagne, Malpensa, Italy. N. A. No. 651. HTA.

Suber, C. A., Student Officer.

Sughrue, John J., Student Officer, 328 Bay State Road, Boston, Mass. Mass. Inst. of Tech. HTA.

Sullivan, Frederick, Student Officer, 3016 11th St., N. W., Washington, D. C.

Sullivan, Giles J., Ensign, 1606 Fairchild St., Manhattan, Kan. N. A. No. 2203.

Sullivan, Harry W., Ensign, 501 8th St., Brooklyn, N. Y. Mass. Inst. of Tech., Bay Shore, Pensacola, San Diego. N. A. No. 889. HTA.

Sullivan, Herbert F., Lieut. (j.g.) 649 Walnut St., Fall River, Mass. N. A. No. 486.

Sullivan, John W., Student Officer, 43 West St., Manchester, N. H. Mass. Inst. of Tech., Key West, Fla. HTA.

Sullivan, Paul R., Ensign, Jamestown, N. Y. N. A. No. 1486.

Sullivan, Timothy E., Student Officer, 718 S. 30th St., Omaha, Neb.

Sullivan, Upton S., Ensign, 1910 Walnut St., Philadelphia, Pa.

Sullivan, Wm. A., Student Officer, 2005 Terrace Place, Nashville, Tenn.

Sullivan, Wm. P., Carpenter.

Sulzberger, Marion B., Lieut. (j.g.), 30 West 70th St., New York City. N. A. No. 628.

Summersby, G. W., Lieut. (j.g.), 125 Prospect St., Lawrence, Mass.

Sunderland, J. E., Student Officer, 508 N. 38th St., Omaha, Neb. Seattle, Wash., San Diego, Cal. HTA.

Sundheim, Geo. M., Student Officer.

Supuy, Albert E., Ensign, Montrose, Colo.

Surber, John M., Ensign, University Club, Akron, Ohio.

Surpernant F., Ensign, Glen Falls, N. Y.

Sutton, Frederick T., Student Officer, Mercantile Bank of the Americas, 44 Pine St., New York City. Mass. Inst. of Tech. HTA.

Sutton, Geo. O., Student Officer, 703 W. Church St., Knoxville, Tenn.

Sutton, Mercer P., Student Officer, 2 Oakdale Road, Roland Park, Md.

Swan, Henry, Ensign, 740 Emerson St., Denver, Colo.

Swan, Horace G., Lieut. (j.g.), 173 Westminster Road, Rochester, N. Y. Mass. Inst. of Tech., Naval Aircraft Factory, Philadelphia. HTA.

Swan, John H., Student Officer, Gardnesville, Nev.

Swanson, Chas. E., Student Officer, 931 Foster Ave., Chicago, Ill.

Swanson, Emil, Lieut. (j.g.).

Swanson, Oscar W., Student Officer, 1475 Minnehaha St., St. Paul, Minn.

Swanton, Edward R., Student Officer, National Bank of Commerce, Rochester. N. Y. Mass. Inst. of Tech., Miami, Fla. HTA.

Sweeney, B. O., Student Officer, 2034 Columbia Road, Washington, D. C.

Sweeney, P. A., Ensign, Wayside, Okla.

Sweeney, John F., Jr., Ensign, 654 Maryland Ave., Pittsburgh, Pa. Mass. Inst. of Tech., Key West, Miami, Pensacola. HTA.

Sweeney, J. M., Ensign, 664 Higgins Ave., Paris, Ky. Mass. Inst. of Tech., Great Lakes, Akron, Hampton Roads, *Pennsylvania*, *Arkansas*. N. A. No. 1910. LTA.

Sweet, Carlyle W., Ensign, N. A. No. 1320.

Sweetser, Geo. T., Ensign, 26 Gramercy Park, New York City.

Swenson, S. R., Ensign.

Swett, Gilbert N., Ensign, 7 Bacon St., Winchester, Mass. Mass. Inst. of Tech., Hampton Roads, Pensacola, Moutchic, Detached duty in Italy, Northern Bombing Group. HTA.

Swett, Wm. O., Student Officer, 10560 Longwood Drive, Chicago, Ill. Dunwoody, Miami, Key West. HTA.

Swigert, Wm. G., Student Officer, 1085 Thurman St., Portland, Ore.

Swinton, J. R., War. Machinist, 229 Johnson Ave., Trinidad, Colo.

Swinton, R. H., Ensign, 20 Sullivan Ave., Port Jervis, N. Y. Mass. Inst. of Tech., Miami, Pensacola. N. A. No. 2505. HTA.

Swope, Leslie M., Student Officer, 2505 Park Ave., Richmond, Va. Dunwoody Inst., Minn. HTA.

Swope, Jos. A., Student Officer, 317 Bundy Ave., Newcastle, Ind.

Symmes, Chandler W., Student Officer, 230 Main St., Winchester, Mass. Mass. Inst. of Tech. HTA.

Symons, Dan B., Ensign, 324 Fifth St., Elyria, Ohio.

A Three-Point Landing

TAFT, PHILLIP E.
Machinist
Box 417, Hampton, Va., Columbia Univ., Pensacola, Yorktown, Newport News, Hampton Rds., Anacostia, Rockaway, Miami.

TAINTOR, CHARLES W.
Ensign
124 Brattle St., Cambridge, Mass. Mass. Inst. of Tech., Miami, Pensacola. N. A. No. 2027. HTA.

TALBOT, ANDREW B.
Lieut. (j.g.)
San Rafael, Cal. Akron, Paimboeuf, Fr., Operations, Washington. N. A. No. 98. LTA.

TALBOT, ROBERT A.
Lieut. (j.g.)
270 Buckminster Rd., Brookline, Mass. Mass. Inst. of Tech., Pensacola. N. A. No. 456. HTA.

TALCOTT, C. H.
Ensign
192 Prospect St., Torrington, Conn. Mass. Inst. of Tech., Key West, Miami, Pensacola. N. A. No. 1299. HTA.

TALIAFERRO, A. P., Jr.
Ensign
440 Riverside Drive, New York City. Moutchic, (Fr.), Lake Bolsena, It., Porto Corsini, It. N. A. No. 1497. HTA.

TANGREN, A. E.
Machinist
1960 Cheremoya Ave., Hollywood, Cal. San Diego, Annapolis, Guantanamo, Pensacola, U. S. S. *Huntington*, Montauk. HTA.

TAYLOR, JAMES B., Jr
Lieut. (j.g.)
471 Park Ave., New York City. Bay Shore, Miami, Bu. Operations, Washington, D. C., Hampton Rds. N. A. No. 437.

TAYLOR, JAMES S.
Ensign
1012 Euclid Ave., Berkeley, Cal. Mass. Inst. of Tech. HTA.

TAYLOR, RAYMOND S.
Ensign
411-412 H. W. Hellman Bldg., Los Angeles, Cal. Mass. Inst. of Tech., Akron, Key West. N. A. No. 1395. LTA.

TEAGUE, A. DAWSON
Ensign
1201 Lamar Bldg., Augusta, Ga. Mass. Inst. of Tech., Miami, Pensacola. N. A. No. 1875. HTA.

TEETS, JOHN N.
Ensign
Box 453, Newton, Ill. Mass. Inst. of Tech., San Diego, Great Lakes, Pensacola, Anacostia, Seattle, Wash.

TEMPLE, WILLIAM G.
Ensign
928 Detroit St., Denver, Colo. Mass. Inst. of Tech., Akron, Rockaway, N. Y. LTA.

TEMPLETON, J. S.
Ensign
Walnut, Bureau Co., Illinois. Great Lakes, Pensacola.

TERHUNE, EDW. A., Jr.
Ensign
54 Mellen St., Dorchester, Mass. M. I. T., Key West, Miami, Moutchic, Calais, Malpensa, It. N. A. No. 1444. HTA.

TERHUNE, HOWARD H.
Ensign
54 Mellen St., Dorchester, Mass. Mass. Inst. of Tech., Pensacola. HTA.

TERRY, JESSE L.
Ensign
P. O. Box 1649, Tulsa, Okla. Seattle, Great Lakes, Hampton Roads.

TEULON, PARKER
Lieut. (j.g.)
30 Webs er St., W. Newton, Mass. M. I. T., Pensa., Yarmouth. Felixstowe, Lough Foyle. Queenstown, Bay Sh. Key West. N. A. No. 212. HTA

TEWKSBURY, H. H.
Ensign
14 Landseer St., West Roxbury, Mass. M. I. T., Pensacola, Miami, Calais, Milan, Killingholme. N. A. No. 584. HTA.

THACKRAY, GEO. E., Jr.
Ensign
126 Fayette St., Westmont, Johnstown, Pa. M. I. T., Pensacola, Miami, North Bomb. Sq., L'Aber Vrach. N. A. No. 688. HTA.

On the Way Back to Camp Saufley after a Week End at Pensacola.

THOMAS DE LOS,
Ensign
119 9th Ave., S. E., Roanoke, Va. Mass. Inst. of Tech., Key West, Pensacola, Hampton Rds., Miami. N. A. No. 1023.

THOMAS, DUNCAN G.
Lieut. (j.g.)
1146 Wyoming Ave., Kingston, Pa. Mass. Inst. of Tech., Cape May, Pensacola. N. A. No. 884. HTA.

THOMAS, WILLIAM S.
Student Officer
Orchard Hill, Roanoke, Va. Seattle, Washington. HTA.

THOMPSON, ABBOTT B.
Student Officer
Melrose, Conn. Mass. Inst. of Tech. HTA.

THOMPSON, A. E.
Student Officer
Greer Apts., New Castle, Pa. Mass. Inst. of Tech., Akron. LTA.

THOMPSON, CLIVE I.
Student Officer
Day Ave., Suffield, Conn Mass. Inst. of Tech., Miami. HTA.

THOMPSON, E. L., Jr.
Ensign
Prospect St., Dover, N. J. Mass. Inst. of Tech., Bay Shore, Pensacola. N. A. No. 1182.

THOMPSON, OWEN
Student Officer
1657 31st St., N. W., Washington, D. C. Mass. Inst. of Tech. HTA.

THORPE, LESLIE
Lieut. (j.g.)
703 Genesee St., Rochester, N. Y. Mass. Inst. of Tech., Pensacola. N. A. No. 1103. LTA.

THORPE, RAYMOND G.
Ensign
100 Stadium Place, Syracuse, N. Y. Mass. Inst. of Tech., Key West, Miami, Pensacola. N. A. No. 1919. HTA.

THROCKMORTON, G. P.
Student Officer
140 West Jersey St., Elizabeth, N. J. Mass. Inst. of Tech. HTA.

TILLETT, HENRY A., Jr.
Ensign
540 Butternut St., Abilene, Tex. Mass. Inst. of Tech., Key West, Pensacola. N. A. No. 2259. HTA.

TILTON, THOMAS A.
Ensign
86 Dalton Rd., Newton Center, Mass. Mass. Inst. of Tech., Key West, Miami, Pensacola. N. A. No. 2168. HTA.

TILTON, WARNER B.
Ensign
Raymond, N. H. Mass. Inst. of Tech., Miami. N. A. No. 2054. HTA.

(*X*)
TIMANUS, C. S.
Student Officer
3118 Karnes Blvd., Kansas City, Mo. Mass. Inst. of Tech., Hingham. HTA.

TINGEY, HAROLD C.
Ensign
11 Sheridan St., Haverhill, Mass. Mass. Inst. of Tech., Miami, Pensacola. N. A. No. 2339. HTA.

TINGLEY, H. V. S.
Student Officer
23 Union St., Bristol, R. I. Mass. Inst. of Tech., Miami. HTA.

TINSLEY, TIMOTHY W.
Ensign
Jackson, Tenn. Mass. Inst. of Tech., Key West. N. A. No. 2019. HTA.

TIPTON, JOSEPH S.
Student Officer
Pulaski, Va. Mass. Inst. of Tech., Key West. HTA.

TIPTON, M. C.
Ensign
614 Twelfth St., E. Las Vegas, New Mexico. Goat Island, Mass. Inst. of Tech., Great Lakes, Miami. HTA.

TISCHLER, ANTON W.
Student Officer
511 Fortune Ave., Cincinnati, Ohio. Dunwoody, Univ. of Wash.

TITUS, HARRY L., Jr.
Ensign
800 Orange Ave., Coronado, Cal. Mass. Inst. of Tech., Miami, Pensacola, San Diego. N. A. No. 1819. HTA.

TOWNSHEND, BAILEY
Ensign
45 W. 35th St., New York City. Mass. Inst. of Tech., Bay Shore, Brunswick, Miami, Pensacola. N. A. No. 2576. HTA.

TRABUCCO, J. EUGENE
Ensign
San Rafael, Cal. Akron, Mass. Inst. of Tech., Rockaway, Montauk.

At Miami Beach.
Who Has Been Stationed at Miami That Does Not Remember These Sunday Mornings?

TRABUE, WM. A.
Student Officer
102 E. Mistletoe Ave., San Antonio, Tex. Mass. Inst. of Tech., Akron. LTA.

TRACY, FREDERICK L.
Ensign
1730 Capouse Ave., Scranton, Pa. Mass. Inst. of Tech., Pensacola, Hampton Rds. N. A. No. 724. HTA.

TRAIL, OSCAR
Lieut. (j.g.)
Easton, Md. Mass. Inst. of Tech., Pensacola, Moutchic, Fr.; L'Aber Vrach, Fr. N. A. No. 375. HTA.

TRANT, EDGAR
Student Officer
204 Court St., Portsmouth, Va. Mass. Inst. of Tech., Miami. HTA.

TRASK, CHARLES H.
Ensign
18 King St., Rochester, N. H. U. S. S. *Paulding*, U. S. S. *Virginia*, Pensacola., U. S. S. *Teal.*

TRAVER, C. H.
Ensign
Red Hook, N. Y. Mass. Inst. of Tech., Bay Shore, Pensacola. N. A. No. 1180. HTA.

TREMBLAY, L. A.
Ensign
541 Pine St., Manchester, N. H. Mass. Inst. of Tech., Miami, Pensacola. N. A. No. 1849. HTA.

TREMELIN, M. D.
Ensign
282 West Broad St , Cuyahoga Falls, Ohio. Mass. Inst. of Tech., Akron, Pensacola. N. A. No. 2276. LTA.

TRETHAWAY, R. C.
Ensign
120 George Ave., Parsons, Pa. M. I. T., Key West, Miami, Pensacola, Montauk, Hampton Roads. N. A. No. 1068. HTA.

TRIMBLE, A. KING
Student Officer
Massachusetts Ave., Cambridge, Mass. Mass. Inst. of Tech., Miami. HTA.

TRIMBLE, RUFUS J.
Student Officer
Care of Rufus W. Weeks, 346 Broadway, New York City. Seattle. LTA.

TRIPPE, J. TERRY
Ensign
163 East 78th St., New York City. M. I. T., Bay Shore, Hampton Roads, Miami, Pensacola. N. A. No. 1806. HTA.

TROSS, LUDWIG C.
Ensign
516 Franklin St., Johnstown, Pa. Mass. Inst. of Tech., Miami, Pensacola. N. A. No. 1983. HTA.

TROXEL, LYNN
Ensign
28 Clay St., Tiffin, Ohio. Mass. Inst. of Tech., Akron, Pensacola. N. A. No. 1363. LTA.

TRUBEY, CYRIL C.
Student Officer
P. O. Box 76, North Chelmsford, Mass. Mass. Inst. of Tech. HTA.

TRUMAN, JOHN R.
War. Boatswain
820 N. 2d St., Phoenix, Ariz. Huntington, Bay Shore, Key West, San Diego. N. A. No. 1696. HTA.

TUCKER, FRANK T.
Student Officer
324 Windsor Place, Milwaukee, Wis. Mass. Inst. of Tech. LTA.

TUCKER, GORDON
Ensign
3953 Harriet Ave., Minneapolis, Minn. Dunwoody, M. I. T., Miami, Pensacola, Coco Solo, C. Z. N. A. No. 1333. HTA.

TUPPER, VIRGIL B.
Student Officer
179 E. 2d St., Corning, N. Y. Mass. Inst. of Tech. HTA.

TURNER, GROVER B.
Lieut. (j.g.)
Fulda, Minn. Mass. Inst. of Tech., Key West, Miami, Pensacola, N. A. No. 1025.

TURNER, WILLIAM H.
Lieut. (j.g.)
260 Fairmount Ave., Hyde Park, Mass. Mass. Inst. of Tech., Pittsburgh, Pa., Detroit, Mich.

TUTTLE, A. DARWIN
Ensign
10th St., Colusa, Cal. Mass. Inst. of Tech., San Diego, Pensacola. N. A. No. 1599. HTA.

TUTTLE, CHAS. W.
Ensign
10th St., Colusa, Colusa Co., Cal. Mass. Inst. of Tech., San Diego, Pensacola. N. A. No. 1181. HTA.

TUTTLE, THOMAS W.
Ensign
25 Brookdale Ave., Verona, New Jersey. Mass. Inst. of Tech., Miami, Pensacola. N. A. No. 1957. HTA.

(C) *Photo. by A. E. Wells.*

E-1 AT PENSACOLA.

TWEED, JOHN H.
Lieut. (j.g.)
Box 421, Madison, Conn. Mass. Inst. of Tech., Pensacola, Coco Solo, C. Z. N. A. No. 257. LTA.

TYLER, EDWARD J.
Student Officer
Enosburg Falls, Vermont. Mass. Inst. of Tech., Key West. HTA.

TYNER, GERALD K.
Ensign
194 Park Ave., Orange, N. J. Mass. Inst. of Tech., Miami, Pensacola, Great Lakes, N. A. No. 1246. HTA.

UNGER, JOHN S.
Student Officer
43 Chestnut St., Boyertown, Pa. Univ. of Wash., Seattle, Wash.

UNGER, WILLIAM S.
Ensign
122 South 5th St., Duquesne, Pa. Mass. Inst. of Tech., Miami, Pensacola. N. A. No. 1319. HTA.

UPTON, VIRGIL M.
Ensign
4532 18th Ave., N. E. Seattle, Wash. Mass. Inst. of Tech., Miami, Pensacola. N. A. No. 2508. HTA.

URNER, GORDON
Ensign
Martine Ave., Fanwood, N. J. Mass. Inst. of Tech., Key West. N. A. No. 1492. HTA.

UTT, ARTHUR H.
Student Officer
1104 So. 2nd St., Springfield, Ill. Mass. Inst. of Tech., Key West. HTA.

◈ ◈ ◈ ◈ ◈ ◈

Taber, Leslie R., Ensign, 18 Park Place, Auburn, N. Y. N. A. No. 620.

Taber, Philip, Ensign, 321 W. 12th St., Tulsa, Okla. Mass. Inst. of Tech., Miami, Pensacola. N. A. No. 1695. HTA.

Tague, Wm. H., Student Officer, Portsmouth, Ia.

Talbot, John C., Jr., Student Officer, 603 W. 140 St., New York City.

Talbot, P., Ensign. N. A. No. 71.

Talks, Chas. P., Student Officer, 1309 Park Road, Washington, D. C.

Tallman, F. G., Jr., Ensign.

Tallman, Thos. A., Ensign, 629½ Maryland Ave., S. W., Washington, D. C.

Talmage, R. A., War. Gunner.

Tanner, J. W., Ensign, 2315 Nueces St., Austin, Texas. N. A. No. 2150.

Tardif, Paul J., Student Officer.

Taussig, Francis B., Student Officer, 191 Park Ave., Yonkers, New York City.

Tavenner, Geo. T., Ensign, Stoddart Apt. 4, 2900 Q St., N. W., Washington, D. C. Pauilliac, France and Eastleigh, Eng.

Taylor, A. G., Ensign. N. A. No. 2375.

Taylor, Austin B., Ensign, 2313 Broadway, Little Rock, Ark. N. A. No. 1717.

Taylor, C., Ensign, LeRoy St., Newburgh, N. Y. N. A. No. 1067.

Taylor, C. J., Lieut. (j.g.), 4 S. Maple Ave., East Orange, N. J

Taylor, Chas. E., Jr., Student Officer, 2312 Broadway, Little Rock, Ark.

Taylor, H. L., War. Machinist.

Taylor, Harold C., Student Officer, 171 Ridgewood Ave., Glen Ridge, N. J.

Taylor, Heinrich C., Student Officer, Bloomfield, Ia.

Taylor, James Irwin, Student Officer, 7 N. Queen St., York, Pa. Mass. Inst. of Tech., Akron, Rockaway Beach, L. I. LTA.

Taylor, R. S., Ensign, 103 E. 86th St., New York City. N. A. No. 1395.

Taylor, Roscoe L., Ensign, 559 Monroe St., Rochester, N. Y. N. A. No. 1370.

Taylor, William D., Ensign, Bloomsburg, Pa. Mass. Inst. of Tech., Pensacola, Bay Shore, Brunswick, Pa. N. A. No. 955. HTA.

Tead, Phillips, Student Officer, 407 Boulevard, Atlantic, Mass. Mass. Inst. of Tech,. Key West, Fla. HTA.

Teasley, John R., Student Officer, Canton, Ga.

Tebbe, Cyril H., Ensign, Care Lanier Hotel, San Antonio, Texas.

Temple, Benj. F., Ensign. Mass. Inst. of Tech., Miami, Pensacola. HTA.

Temple, Frank E., Ensign.

Tenney, Thorvald F. H., Student Officer, 172 Main St., Branford, Conn. Mass. Inst. of Tech. HTA.

Teroller, Dark R., Student Officer.

Terrell, Wm. A., Student Officer, Frederick Hall, Va.

Terry, Charles C., Jr., Student Officer, 905 W. Colfax Ave., South Bend, Ind. Mass. Inst. of Tech., Miami, Fla. HTA.

Terry, Whitelaw J., Student Officer, 5231 Westminster Place, St. Louis, Mo. Mass. Inst. of Tech. LTA.

Thackers, Alex M., Jr., Lieut. (j.g.).

Tharp, Carey E., Student Officer, 101 E 21st St., Austin, Texas.

Theard, Albert L., Ensign.

Therrien, Z. W., Student Officer, 120 Park St., Portland, Me. Mass. Inst. of Tech., Key West, Fla. HTA.

Thibadeau, W. L., Lieut. (j.g.), 208 Peoples Bldg., Charleston, S. C.

Thomas, Benjamin Hilton, Ensign, 410 E. Thomas St., Rocky Mount, North Carolina. Mass. Inst. of Tech., Miami, Key West, Pensacola. HTA.

Thomas, Berkely A., Student Officer, Florence Apts., Scranton, Pa.

Thomas, Charles Neil, Ensign, 2478 Lake View Ave., Chicago, Ill., Great Lakes, Pensacola, Fla.

Thomas, Charles S., Student Officer, 2422 S. Western Ave., Los Angeles, Cal.

Thomas, Howard H., Student Officer.

Thomas, John V., War. Machinist, 77 Durham Ave., Buffalo, N. Y.

Thomas, Kenneth A., War. Boatswain, Grandview, Washington, R. F. D. No. 2, Box 50, Pensacola, Fla.

Thomas, Lyman H., Ensign, 4654 Dodge St., Omaha, Nebr. Mass. Inst. of Tech., Miami, Fla. N. A. No. 2057. HTA.

Thomas, Morris L., Ensign, 25 Windermere Place, St. Louis, Mo.

Thomas, R. D., Lieut. (j.g.), Bx. 111 Central Ave., Weston, Mass. N. A. No. 207.

Thomas, R. P., Ensign, 60 James St., Dorranceton, Wilkes-Barre, Pa. Mass. Inst. of Tech., Pensacola, Fla.; Rockaway Beach, L. I., N. Y. N. A. No. 626. HTA.

Thomas, Robert K., Student Officer, 1427 Greenleaf Ave., Chicago, Ill.

Thomas, Robert W., Ensign, 470 Lyell Ave., Rochester, N. Y. Mass. Inst. of Tech., Miami, Key West, Pensacola. HTA.

Thomas, Thornton H., Student Officer, Nederland, Colo.

Thomas, Wm. Stephenson, Student Officer, Orchard Hill, Roanoke, Va.

Thomason, Benjamin W., Student Officer.

Thompson, Coy R., Student Officer, 327 W. 22nd St., New York City.

Thompson, E. C., 112 S. 30th St., Louisville, Ky.

Thompson, Edward A., Student Officer, 1620 Tyler St., Topeka, Kans.

Thompson. Frederic De. L., Ensign, Bx. 286, Sound Beach, Conn. N. A. No. 2506.

Thompson, G. L. Lieut. (j.g.), Racquet Club, Philadelphia, Pa. Communication Officer Naval Air Station, Rockaway Beach, L. I., N. Y.

Thompson, Guy W., Student Officer, 1303 E. 41st St., Seattle, Washington. San Diego, Cal. HTA.

Thompson, J. S., Ensign, The Cloister Club, New Haven, Conn. N. A. No. 650.

Thompson, Lawson B., Student Officer.

Thompson, Silvert W., Student Officer.

Thompson, W. D., Jr., Lieut. (j.g.), 319 Pine St., Concord, N. H. N. A. No. 382.

Thoms, Charles Davis, Student Officer, 1099 East Ave., Rochester, N. Y. Mass. Inst. of Tech., Cambridge, Mass. LTA.

Thorburn, Harry H., Lieut. (j.g.), Care of Miss Pearl E. Thorburn, Athol, Mass.. Mass. Inst. of Tech., Pensacola, Hampton Roads, Morehead City (Commanding Officer). N. A. No. 399.

Thornton, Douglas A., Student Officer, Gering, Nebr. Seattle, Washington. HTA.

Thornton, S. D., War. Machinist.

Thrall, W. A., Ensign.

Thralls, Warren H., Student Officer, 520 N. Washington, Ave., Wellington, Kans.

Thurlow, Paul E., Student Officer, 9 Stratford St., Melrose, Mass.

Thurman, E. C., War. Machinist, U. S. N.

Tichener, Byron H., Student Officer, 215 W. Walnut St., Princeton, Ind.

Tighe, Edmund J., Student Officer, 34 E. North St., Buffalo, N. Y.

Tilburne, Albert R., Lieut. (j.g.), 915 Queen St., Cape May, N. J. Moutchic, Fr., Felixstowe, Eng., Brest, Fr., Porto Corsini, It., Cape May. LTA.

Tileston, Edward M., Ensign, 2132 Cherokee Parkway, Louisville, Ky. Mass. Inst. of Tech., Miami, Pensacola, Cape May. N. A. No. 2001. HTA.

Tillotson, R. F., Ensign, Dime Savings Bank, Detroit, Mich. N. A. No. 2260.

Tillson, Ernest F., Ensign, 341 Court St., Plymouth, Mass. Mass. Inst. of Tech., Miami, Pensacola, Fla. N. A. No. 1911. HTA.

Tilton, J. H., Jr., Lieut. (j.g.), The Ontario, Washington, D. C.

Timmerman, G. F., War. Machinist.

Timothy, Hugh Wm., Student Officer, 573 E. 22nd St., Brooklyn, N. Y.

Tinges, Chas. Howard, Ensign, 1305 Linden Ave., Baltimore, Md. Mass. Inst. of Tech., Key West, Miami, Pensacola, Fla. N. A. No. 1044. HTA.

Tinker, Herbert D., Ensign, Wolfeboro, N. H. Mass. Inst. of Tech., Bay Shore, L. I., Brunswick, Ga., Key West, Pensacola, Fla. N. A. No. 2401. HTA.

Tipton, Harold R., Student Officer, Logan, Ohio.

Tison, Alexander, Jr., Student Officer, 15 William St., New York City.

Titcomb, Wm. S., Ensign, Kennebunk, Me. Mass. Inst. of Tech., Bay Shore, L. I., Pensacola. N. A. No. 1422.

Tobey, Edward S., Student Officer, 105 W. 55th St., New York City.

Tobias, Hugh Kelso, Student Officer, 273 3rd St., Albany, N. Y. Mass. Inst. of Tech., Miami. HTA.

Tobin, G. J., Ensign, 380 DeWolf Place, Hackensack, N. J. N. A. No. 1268.

Todd, A. B., Jr., War. Machinist, 71 1st St., San Francisco, Cal.

Todd, E. H., Lieut. (j.g.), 3925 Ibis St., San Diego, Cal., San Diego, Columbia University, St. Ingelvert, France; Rome, Italy.

Toivonen, Roivo A., War. Carpenter.

Toll, Oliver, Ensign, Care of Prof. Toll, Amherst, Mass.

Tolman, Chester A., Student Officer.

Tolmie, T. W., War. Machinist, 308 S. Jama St., Manchester, Ia.

Tomassene, John Warren, Student Officer, 2657 Highland Ave., Cincinnati, O. Mass. Inst. of Tech.

Tomlinson, Edward H., Student Officer, 247 Orchard St., Elizabeth, N. J. Mass. Inst. of Tech., Bay Shore. HTA.

Tomlinson, Gilbert E., Ensign, 1906 N. 32nd St., Philadelphia. Pa. Mass. Inst. of Tech., Key West, Pensacola, Fla. N. A. No. 2042. HTA.

TouVelle, Guy T., Student Officer, 802 First Nat'l. Bank Bldg., Lincoln, Nebr.

Towle, Max G., Student Officer, 1328 N. 26th St., Lincoln, Nebr.

Towler, J. Barber, Student Officer, 212 Newbern Ave., Raleigh, N. C. Mass. Inst. of Tech. HTA.

Townsend, Charles Howard, Ensign, 71 Cleveland St., Orange, N. J. Mass. Inst. of Tech., Pensacola, Miami, Moutchic. N. A. No. 740. HTA.

Townsley, W. W., Ensign, 420 E. College St., Oberlin, Ohio. N. A. No. 320.

Tracy, Wm. H., Student Officer, 1927 Cleneay Ave., Norwood, Ohio.

Traintor, Chas. W., Ensign, 124 Brattle St., Cambridge, Mass.

Tramel, J. H., Student Officer, South Shore, Country Club, Chicago, Ill. Mass. Inst. of Tech. HTA.

Treadwell, L. H., Student Officer, Arcadia, Florida. Mass. Inst. of Tech. HTA.

Tree, Ronald L., Ensign, 138 N. La Salle St., Chicago, Ill. N. A. No. 285.

Trefts, Harry H., Ensign, Newman, Cal. Mass. Inst. of Tech., San Diego, Pensacola. N. A. No. 1843. HTA.

Treuhaft, Wm. C., Student Officer, 3765 Cleveland, Ohio.

Tribkin, I. B., Ensign. N. A. No. 376.

Trimble, Robert M., Jr., Student Officer, 7180 Brighton Road, Ben Avon, Pa.

Tritschler, Ernest R., Student Officer, 12 Bell Place, Woodhaven, L. I., N. Y.

Troutman, Ned, Lieut. (j.g.), Shreve, Ohio. Mass. Inst. of Tech., Hampton Roads, Va., Pensacola, Fla. HTA.

Trowbridge, Alexander B., Student Officer, 1 W. 64th St., New York City.

Trowbridge, John H., Ensign, Main St., Chatham, N. J. N. A. No. 2209.

Troy, Manderville, Ensign.

True, Herbert W., Student Officer, Tech. Chambers, 8 Irvington St., Boston, Mass.

Trygve, Tolnas, Student Officer, 521 4th St., N. W., Washington, D. C.

Tucker, Claude, War. Boatswain, U. S. N.

Tucker, Harold S., Student Officer, 1908 W. Tioga St., Philadelphia, Pa.

Turnbull, Archibald J., Student Officer, 5002 20th St., N. E., Seattle, Wash.

Turner, Arthur E., Ensign, Junction City, Ore.

Turner, Geo. H., Ensign.

Turner, R. S., Ensign, Billerica, Mass. N. A. No. 2123.

Tuttle, Albert E., Lieut. (j.g.) 350 Charles River Road, Cambridge, Mass.

Tutwiler, Robert E., Student Officer, 274 Edgewood Place, River Forest, Ill., Seattle, Washington. HTA.

Tweedell, Wm. T., Jr., Student Officer, 9 E. View St., Edg. Sta., Pawtucket, R. I. Mass. Inst. of Tech., Miami. HTA.

Twining, C. S., Jr., Ensign, 850 Park Ave., New York City. Mass. Inst. of Tech. HTA.

Twitchell, P. E., Ensign, 153 S. Oxford St., Brooklyn, N. Y. Mass. Inst. of Tech. LTA.

Twomey, E. F., Ensign, 66 Rockaway St., Lynn, Mass. Mass. Inst. of Tech., Buffalo, Bu. C. & R., Washington, Sup. Con. Aircraft, New York City.

Tygert, E. A., Ensign, 1529 Green St., Philadelphia, Pa.

Tyler, Raymond F., Lieut. (j.g.), Middlebury, Conn.

Tyler, W. A., Ensign, 80 Pierrepont St., Brooklyn, N. Y.

Tylor, J. Ellwood, Student Officer, Easton, Md.

Tym, Norris F., Ensign, 642 Bee Bldg., Omaha, Nebr.

Tyndall, C. W., Ensign, New York City, Pensacola. Mass. Inst. of Tech., Akron, Hampton Roads. N. A. No. 987. HTA and LTA.

Uhri, W. C., Jr., Ensign, 2163 S. Grand Ave., St. Louis, Mo. Mass. Inst. of Tech., Pensacola, Akron, Hampton Roads. LTA.

Ulery, U. J., Jr., Student Officer, 139 Caryl Ave., Yonkers, N. Y. Mass. Inst. of Tech., Miami, Key West. HTA.

Ulrich, Carl T., Student Officer, 120 Broadway, New York City.

Urmy, H. S., Student Officer, 290 Mt. Prospect Ave., Newark, N. J. Mass. Inst. of Tech., Key West, Fla. HTA.

VALENTE, JOHN
Student Officer
English Dept., University of Pittsburgh. Mass. Inst. of Tech. HTA.

VALENTINE, S., Jr.
Ensign
62 Eighth Ave., Brooklyn, N. Y. Mass. Inst. of Tech., Bay Shore, Pensacola. N. A. No. 1600.

VAN ARNAM, MELO E.
Ensign
602 10th St., So. Fargo, N. D. Univ. of Wash., San Diego, Pensacola. N. A. No. 2407. HTA.

VAN ATTA, R. C.
Ensign
449 Park Ave., Waverly, N. Y. Mass. Inst. of Tech., Bay Shore, Great Lakes.

VAN AUKEN, FRANK H.
Ensign
Glen Ridge, N. J. Mass. Inst. of Tech., Bay Shore, Pensacola. N. A. No. 1573. HTA.

VAN BERGEN, G. L.
Ensign
Brandon Hall, 1501 Beacon St., Brookline, Mass. Mass. Inst. of Tech., Key West, Pensacola. N. A. No. 2625. HTA.

VANCE, H. C.
Ensign
615 Washington Ave., Greenville, Ohio. Seattle, San Diego, Pensacola. N. A. No. 2364. HTA.

VAN CLEVE, C. G.
Ensign
162 Nassau St., Princeton, N. J. Mass. Inst. of Tech., Miami, Pensacola, Hampton Roads. N. A. No. 2082. HTA.

VAN DEREN, F. P.
Ensign
3832 Brighton Ave., Oakland, Cal. Mass. Inst. of Tech., Pensacola, Moutchic, Fr. N. A. No. 693. HTA.

VAN DE WATER, L.
Ensign
19 Broad St., Pittsfield, Mass. Mass. Inst. of Tech., Akron, Rockaway. LTA.

VANDIVER, C. W.
Student Officer
106 Cherokee St., Rome, Ga. Mass. Inst. of Tech., Bay Shore. HTA.

VAN DUSEN, F. CLAIR
Ensign
Southold, L. I., N. Y. Mass. Inst. of Tech., Pensacola, Chatham. N. A. No. 937. HTA.

VAN EMDEN, A. L.
Lieut. (j.g.)
46 Lindsey St., Dorchester, Mass. Akron, Rockaway, Queensown, Roehampton, Castletown, Pallice, Brest, B. Sh. LTA.

VAN EVERA, EDWARD
Ensign
Marquette, Mich. Mass. Inst. of Tech., Miami, Pensacola. N. A. No. 2499. HTA.

VAN HOUTEN, E. L.
Lieut. (j.g.)
535 Boylston Ave., North, Seattle, Wash. Pensacola, Moutchic, Gironde, Fr., N. A. No. 269.

VANN, DAN M.
Ensign
Howardsville, Md. Mass. Inst. of Tech., Akron, Pensacola. N. A. No. 2666. LTA.

VAN TUYL, W. H.
Lieut. (j.g.)
Park Ave., Wantagh, L. I. N. Y. Mass. Inst. of Tech., Bay Shore, Pensacola. N. A. No. 983. HTA.

VAUGHAN, C. L., Jr.
Lieut. (j.g.)
407 Brook St., Providence, R. I. Mass. Inst. of Tech., Newport, Blue Hill Observatory, Queenstown, Wexford.

VENNEMAN, H. S.
Student Officer
235 Parker Ave., Buffalo, N. Y. Mass. Inst. of Tech., Bay Shore. HTA.

VERNER, E. M.
Ensign
605 Hulton Rd., Oakmont, Pa. Mass. Inst. of Tech , Key, Pensacola. N. A. No. 1841. HTA.

A SUNDAY MORNING HOP AT MIAMI.

VIGEANT, NAPOLEON
Ensign
48 Riverside St., Lowell, Mass. Mass. Inst. of Tech., Akron, Rockaway Beach. LTA.

VILMAR, FREDERICK
Student Officer
18 Theresa Place, Staten Island, New York. Dunwoody, Mass. Inst. of Tech. HTA.

VOGELGESANG, C. E.
Student Officer
R. F. D. No. 4, Massilon, Ohio. Dunwoody, Mass. Inst. of Tech. HTA.

VOGELL, C. G.
Lieut. (j.g.)
2040 Seventh Ave., New York City. Mass. Inst. of Tech., Bay Shore, Pensacola. N. A. No. 1631.

VOLCKENING, LLOYD I.
Ensign
392 Clinton Ave., Brooklyn, N. Y. Mass. Inst. of Tech., Newport, Akron, Pensacola. N. A. No. 1582. LTA.

VON MAUR, JAMES W.
Ensign
1800 East River St., Davenport, Iowa. Mass. Inst. of Tech., Pensacola, Miami, N. A. No. 1015. HTA.

VOORHEES, EDW. K.
Ensign
Evanston, Ill. Dunwoody, Miami, Pensacola. N. A. No. 2577. HTA.

VOSS, EUGENE L.
Ensign
128 Walnut St., Denison, Iowa. Dunwoody, Miami, Pensacola. N. A. No. 2544. HTA.

VAIL, DONALD B., Ensign, 174 Upper Boulevard, Ridgewood, N. J. Mass. Inst. of Tech., Miami, Pensacola. N. A. No. 1019. HTA.

VAIL, MALCOLM D., Ensign, 437 Lincoln Ave., Highland Park, Ill.

VALDES, V. F., Lieut. (j.g.), 3337 Walnut St., Philadelphia, Pa. N. A. No. 256.

VANAKEN, HARRY H., Student Officer, 117 St. Johns Place., Brooklyn, N. Y.

VANCE, C. D., Ensign, 1727 11th Ave., South Birmingham, Ala. Mass. Inst. of Tech., Miami, Pensacola. N. A. No. 2217. HTA.

VAN CLIEF, COURTLANDT, Lieut. (j.g.), 215 Manor Road, W. Brighton, Sta. Island, N. Y. Moutchic-Lacanau, Pauillac, France. HTA.

VANCOURT, K., Ensign, 428 Nuber Ave., Mount Vernon, N. Y. Mass. Inst. of Tech., Langley Field, Miami, Fla., Killingholme, Eng., Hampton Roads, Va.

VAN DAM, L., Ensign, 20 Berkly Road, Merion Sta., Pa.

VANDECARR, NORMAN A., Student Officer, 11 Amherst St., Rochester, N. Y.

VANDERBUILT, CHESTER W., Student Officer, 545 Valley St., Orange, N. J.

VANDERBILT, W. S., JR., Lieut. (j.g.).

VAN DEWATER, D. G. V., Ensign, 177 High St., Passiac, N. J. N. A. No. 1818.

VAN DUSEN, E. T., Student Officer, 129 N. Hill St., Pasadena, Cal.

VAN FLEET, W. C., JR., Ensign, 2020 Pacific Ave., San Francisco, Cal. French Army, U. S. N. A. S., Dunkirk, Fr., U. S. S. *Texas*, Croix de Guerre with Palm. N. A. No. 1731. LTA.

VAN GUY, MALCOLM, Student Officer, 1109 M St., Washington, D. C.

VAN HULSTEYN, J. M. C., Ensign, Baltimore, Md.

VAN NESS, JOHN W., Student Officer.

VAN PELT, WM. D., JR., Student Officer, 864 Riverside Drive, New York City.

VAN RAALE, ARTHUR, Student Officer.

VANSCHAACK, HENRY C., Student Officer, Hotel Washington, Washington, D. C.

VANVALKENBURG, WM., Student Officer, 319 Trust Co. of Ga. Bldg., Atlanta, Ga.

VANVOORHIS, NOBLE, Student Officer, 104 Richelieu, New Castle, Pa.

VARINI, F., Ensign.

VAUGHAN, HINES F., Ensign, 116 W. Henry St., Spartanburg, S. C. Seattle, Washington, San Diego, Cal., Pensacola, Fla. N. A. No. 2346. HTA.

VEHSLAGE, FRANK C., Student Officer, 61 Shanley Ave., Newark, N. J.

VERNOR, JOHN W., Student Officer, 201 Flat Iron Bldg., Fort Worth, Texas.

VERSTINE, F. P., Student Officer, 173 Main St., Brookville, Pa. Mass. Inst. of Tech., Bay Shore, L. I., HTA.

VIALL, L. S., Ensign, 84 Clinton Ave., S. Rochester, N. Y. N. A. No. 2285.

VILAS, LOGAN ARCHIBALD, Lieut. (j.g.), 279 E. Central St., Highland Park, Ill.

VINCENT, FRED W., JR., Student Officer, 698 Canyon Road, Portland, Ore. Mass. Inst. of Tech. LTA.

VINING, MERRITT A., Lieut. (j.g.), 69 Paterson St., Brunswick, N. J.

VISCO, PETER B., War. Machinist, 1060 Acushnet Ave., New Bedford, Mass.

VOGEL, HUGO, C. R., Student Officer, 395 Lake Drive, Milwaukee, Wisc.

VOLLMER, ALBERT M., Student Officer, 3789 Daley Ave., San Diego, Cal. Mass. Inst. of Tech. HTA.

VOLPE, A. M., War. Carpenter, U.S.N.

VORIS, BRYANT B., Student Officer, Waterloo, Ill.

VOSS, R. E., Ensign, St. James, Minn. Mass. Inst. of Tech., Key West, Pensacola. N. A. No. 2275. HTA.

VROOMAN, F. E., Ensign, 3641 Wyandotte St., Kansas City, Mo. N. A. No. 1618.

VROOMAN, JOHN E., Student Officer, 3936 S. Benton St., Kansas City, Mo.

WADE, FRANK E.
Ensign
434 Birch St., Richmond Hill, New York City. Mass. Inst. of Tech., Pensacola. N. A. No. 1000. HTA.

WADLEIGH, PAUL F.
Lieut. (j.g.)
12 West Baltimore St., Lynn, Mass. Mass. Inst. of Tech., Pensacola, Hampton Roads., Bay Shore. N. A. No. 401. HTA.

WAGENET, JOHN D.
Student Officer
2428 E. 23rd St., Oakland, Cal. Seattle, Washington. HTA.

WAGGONER, H. E.
Ensign
1502 Mohawk St., Los Angeles, Cal. Mass. Inst. of Tech. Bay Shore, San Diego, Pensacola. N. A. No. 1595. HTA.

WAITING FOR A CLIENT, DUNKIRK, FRANCE.

WAGNER, PAUL
Ensign
Care of Bank of Italy, Market St. Branch, San Francisco, Cal. Seattle, San Diego, Pensacola. N. A. No. 1947. LTA.

WAIT, EDGAR F.
En sign
442 Franklin St., Johnstown, Pa. Mass. Inst. of Tech., Miami, Pensacola, Bay Shore. N. A. No. 935. HTA.

WAITE, LEON J.
Ensign
Berlin, N. Y. Mass. Inst. of Tech., Miami, Key West, Pensacola. N. A. No. 2484. HTA.

WAITE, MARSHALL W.
Student Officer
28 East 52nd St., New York City. Mass. Inst. of Tech.

WALKER, ERNEST E.
Ensign
Paoli, Indiana. Great Lakes, Mass. Inst. of Tech., Blue Hill Observatory. HTA.

WALLER, PHILIP R.
Student Officer
2934½ Fuhrman Ave., Seattle, Wash. Seattle.

WALLER, ROLAND E.
Ensign
112 W. Newell Ave., Rutherford, N. J. Mass. Inst. of Tech., Miami, Bay Shore, Pensacola. N. A. No. 1403. HTA.

WALSH, ARTHUR E.
Student Officer
766 Ostrom Ave., Syracuse, N. Y. Mass. Inst. of Tech., Bay Shore, Brunswick, Key West. HTA.

WALSH, FREDERICK I.
Student Officer
2430 Rucker Ave., Everett, Washington. Mass. Inst. of Tech., Bay Shore. HTA.

WARBASSE, C. N.
Ensign
131 Seventy-sixth St., Brooklyn, N. Y. Mass. Inst. of Tech., Bay Shore, Pensacola. N. A. No. 2169. HTA.

WARBURG, JAMES P.
Lieut. (j.g.)
983 Charles River Road, Cambridge, Mass. Newport News, Hampton Roads, Washington, Bureau of Nav. HTA.

WARBURTON, WM.
Lieut. (j.g.)
122 East 76th St., New York City, RFC., B. Sh., Calshot, Newhaven, Amien, Campagne, N. B. G. N. A. No. 163.

WARNER, HERBERT R.
Ensign
Plymouth, Mich. Mass. Inst. of Tech., Pensacola, Miami, No. Bomb. Gr., Fr., Moutchic, Fr. N. A. No. 732. HTA.

WARNER, J. LAIRD.
Ensign
Ten Sleep, Wyo. Mass. Inst. of Tech., Akron, Pensacola. N. A. No. 2648. LTA.

WARNER, PAUL CHAS.
Lieut. (j.g.)
35 Lockwood Ave., New Rochelle, New York. Mass. Inst. of Tech., Key West. Pensacola. N. A. No. 2620. HTA.

WARREN, ALDRED K.
Lieut. (j.g.)
12 Summer St., Salem, Mass. Mass. Inst. of Tech., Pensacola, San Diego. N. A. No. 183. HTA.

WASS, WARREN H.
Ensign
32 E. Islay St., Santa Barbara, Cal. Mass. Inst. of Tech., Key West, Miami, Pensacola. N. A. No. 1396. HTA.

WASSELL, HERBERT L.
Student Officer
Little Rock, Ark. Mass. Inst. of Tech., Bay Shore. HTA.

WATERMAN, FRANCIS
Ensign
2001 Allston Way, Berkeley, Cal. Mass. Inst. of Tech., Key West, Miami, Pensacola. N. A. No. 1821. HTA.

WATERS, ROBERT S.
Ensign
Southmont, Johnstown, Pa. Mass. Inst. of Tech., Moutchic, Pensacola, Treguier. N. A. No. 921. HTA.

WATERWORTH, WM.
Ensign
8808 Meridian Ave., Cleveland, Ohio. Great Lakes, Pensacola. HTA.

WATKINS, GEO. L.
Ensign
1606 Beeck St., Birmingham, Ala. Mass. Inst. of Tech., Pensacola. HT.A

WATSON, PAUL
Lieut. (j.g.)
Beacon, N. Y. Mass. Inst. of Tech., Bay Shore, Pensacola, Moutchic, Fr., Fromentine, Fr. N. A. No. 359.

WATTS, GILBERT S.
Student Officer
215 E. Foster Ave., State College, Pa. Mass. Inst. of Tech. HTA.

(C) Photo by A. E. Wells.

MORNING INSPECTION AT PENSACOLA.

WEATHERHEAD, C. H.
Lieut. (j.g.)
183 E. Gay St., Columbus, Ohio. Mass. Inst. of Tech., Pensacola, Fort Worth, Killingholme, Eng. N. A. No. 305. HTA.

WEBBER, HAROLD
Ensign
3341 N. 17th St., Philadelphia, Penn. Mass. Inst. of Tech., Miami, Pensacola. N. A. No. 1247. HTA.

WEBSTER, MORTON S.
Ensign
Lawrence, L. I., N. Y. Mass. Inst. of Tech., Miami, Pensacola, Hampton Rds. N. A. No. 1413. HTA.

WEDDELL, REID
Ensign
Atlanta, Ga. Mass. Inst. of Tech., Miami, Pensacola. HTA.

WEGENER, FRANCIS A.
Ensign
610 West 116th St., New York City. Columbia Univ., Pauillac, Fr. HTA.

WEIR, HORACE M.
Student Officer
2142 Ashland Ave., Indianapolis, Ind. Mass. Inst. of Tech., Great Lakes, Miami. HTA.

WEISS. HAROLD T.
Ensign
Edgehill Road, Euclid Heights, Cleveland, Ohio. Mass. Inst. of Tech., Akron, Rockaway Beach, Hampton Roads. LTA.

WELLBAUM, R. O.
Student Officer
728 River St., Dayton, Ohio. Mass. Inst. of Tech. LTA.

WELLS, OLIVER S.
Ensign
1329 N. Central, Oklahoma City, Okla. Seattle, San Diego, Pensacola. N. A. No. 2347. HTA.

WENDLER, PAUL B.
Ensign
711 Salem Ave., Dayton, Ohio. Mass. Inst. of Tech., Miami, Pensacola. N. A. No. 2344. HTA.

WENTWORTH, R. S.
Ensign
Strafford, Pa. Mass. Inst. of Tech., Brooklyn Aero. Dist., Bu. St. Eng.

WENTZ, WILLARD W.
Ensign
127 Aycrigg Ave., Passaic, N. J. Mass. Inst. of Tech., Bay Shore, Pensacola, Miami. N. A. No. 1401. LTA.

WESSON, HARRY B.
Student Officer
111 So. Mountain Ave., Montclair, N. J. Mass. Inst. of Tech., Pensacola.

WEST, HOWARD E.
Lieut. (j.g.)
Brighton, Mass. Mass. Inst. of Tech., Hampton Rds., Pensacola, Moutchic, Fromentine. N. A. No. 402. HTA.

WEST, JOHN DORMAN
Ensign
11 Mountain Ave., Maplewood, N. J. M. I. T., Bay Shore, Pensacola, Moutchic, Arcachon. N. A. No. 888. HTA.

WESTERFIELD, A. L.
Ensign
Hotel Gibbons, Dayton, O. Mass. Inst. of Tech., Miami, Pensacola. N. A. No. 1644. HTA.

WESTERFIELD, JASON
Ensign
Orange, N. J. Great Lakes, Pensacola.

WESTON, CARLYLE D.
Ensign
2201 Aldrich Ave., S. Minn., Minn. Mass. Inst. of Tech., Pensacola, Chatham. N. A. No. 928. HTA.

WETHERILL, WM. C.
Lieut. (j.g.)
Chestnut Hill, Phila., Pa. Mass. Inst. of Tech., Buffalo, Elizabeth, New York, Westervelt Board.

WETTACH, ROBERT H.
Ensign
2831 Espy Ave., Pittsburgh, Pa. Mass. Inst. of Tech., Pensacola, Pauillac, Moutchic, Ile Tudy, Fr. N. A. No. 733. HTA.

WHEELER, ARTHUR G.
Lieut. (j.g.)
Stow, Mass. Mass. Inst. of Tech., Pensacola, Moutchic, Fromentine, Fr. N. A. No. 361. HTA.

WHEELER, STUART S.
Ensign
202 Garfield Ave., Endicott, N. Y. Mass. Inst. of Tech., Key West, Miami, Pensacola. N. A. No. 1921. HTA.

WHITCHER, RUSSEL K.
Student Officer
306 W. Mason St., Jackson, Mich. Seattle, Key West. HTA.

WHITCOMB, H. D.
Lieut. (j.g.)
3001 East 7th St., Kansas City, Mo. Mass. Inst. of Tech., Pensacola, Comdr. Squ. V. HTA.

REMAINS OF A CRASH AT HAMPTON ROADS.

WHITE, DALE T.
Lieut. (j.g.)
432 Earl Court, Elyria, Ohio. Akron, Rockaway, Queenstown, Roehampton. Castletown, Gujan, B. Sh, N. A. No. 972. LTA.

WHITE, FRANK K.
Student Officer
1110 Columbia Rd., N. W., Washington, D. C. Great Lakes. HTA.

WHITE, RICHARD D.
Lieut. (j.g.)
Snow Hill, Md. Mass. Inst. of Tech., Hampton Rds., U. S. S. *Bulgaria*, U. S. S. *Flihawk*, Key West, Miami, Pensacola. N. A. No. 972.

WHITE, RUSSELL, H
Ensign
3329 East Madison St., Seattle, Wash. Mass. Inst. of Tech., Seattle. Miami, Pensacola. N. A. No. 972. HTA.

WHITE, THOS. G.
Student Officer
2081 Maine St., Quincy, Ill. Dunwoody, Miami, Key West. HTA.

WHITEHOUSE, R. T., Jr.
Ensign
108 Vaughan St., Portland, Me. Mass. Inst. of Tech., Hampton Rds., Pensacola, Moutchic, Fr., Le Croisic, Fr. N. A. No. 391. HTA.

WHITESCARVER, W. F.
Student Officer
234 Broad St., Georgetown, S. C. Mass. Inst. of Tech. HTA.

WHITING, EDMUND A.
Ensign
76 Gates Ave., Montclair, N. J. Mass. Inst. of Tech., Buffalo, Keyport.

WHITING, IRVING H.
Student Officer
2975 Corydon Road, Cleveland, Ohio. Seattle, San Diego. HTA.

WHITMAN, R. L.
Lieut. (j.g.)
150 East 72nd St., New York City. Mass. Inst. of Tech., Great Lakes. HTA.

WHITMORE, F. R.
Ensign
143 So. Barkley St., Waterloo, Iowa. Columbia Univ., Bay Shore, Great Lakes, Pensacola. HTA.

WHITNEY, PAUL LeB.
Ensign
Elmcourt, Medina Road, Akron, Ohio. M. I. T., Hampton Rds., Brest, Fr., Key West, N. A. No. 2601. LTA.

WHITNEY, RICHARD T,
Lieut. (j.g.)
219 Hope St., Providence, R. I. Mass. Inst. of Tech., Hampton Roads, Pensacola, Moutchic, L'Aber Vrach. N. A. No. 393.

WHITTED, JAMES A.
Lieut. (j.g.)
200 West Ga Rua St., Pensacola, Fla. Pensacola. N. A. No. 179. HTA.

WHYEL, THOS. M.
Ensign
183 E. Fayette St., Uniontown, Pa. Mass. Inst. of Tech., Key West, Pensacola. N. A. No. 1700.

WHYTE, DAVID R.
Ensign
930 Queen St., East Toronto, Canada. Bay Shore, Key West, Miami, Pensacola, Hampton Rds. N. A. No. 2161. LTA.

WHYTE, RUSSELL I.
Student Officer
2503 14th St., N. W., Wash., D. C. Mass. Inst. of Tech. HTA.

WICKER, J. C.
Ensign
Blackford, Va. Mass. Inst. of Tech., Norfolk, Pensacola, Moutchic, Brest, Brooklyn. N. A. No. 689. HTA.

WICKWIRE, A. M., Jr.
Student Officer
149 Highland Ave., Westfield, N. J. Mass. Inst. of Tech., Bay Shore. HTA.

WIEBUSCH, E. G. L., Jr.
Ensign
207 North 7th St., Waco, Texas. Seattle, San Diego, Pensacola. N. A. No. 2510. HTA.

WIGELY, ROBERT G.
Ensign
Albuquerque, New Mexico. Mass. Inst. of Tech., San Diego, Miami, Key West. N. A. No. 2058. HTA.

WIGGLESWORTH, A. G.
Ensign
426 Central Ave., Wilmette, Ill. Mass. Inst. of Tech., Key West, N. A. No. 1466. HTA.

WIGGLESWORTH, F.
Lieut. (j.g.)
2 West Hill Place, Boston, Mass. Mass. Inst. of Tech.

WILBUR, ROBT. A., Jr.
Ensign
606 W. Clinton St., Elmira, N. Y. Mass. Inst. of Tech., Miami, Pensacola. N. A. No. 2283. HTA.

JUST ENTERING THE WATER FOR THE FIRST U. S. N. FLIGHT IN IRELAND.

WILKES, JOE L.
Student Officer
5010 Gaston Ave., Dallas, Tex. Seattle, Washington; Miami. HTA.

WILKINSON, H. N.
Machinist
Whiteville, Tenn. Pensacola, Le Croisic, Fr.

WILKINSON, N. LEE
Ensign
3403 Campbell St., Kansas City, Mo. Mass. Inst. of Tech., Miami, Pensacola. N. A. No. 2179. HTA.

WILLARD, EDWARD A.
Student Officer
13 Clinton St., Hartford, Conn. Dunwoody Inst., Minn. HTA.

WILLCOX, HAROLD M.
Lieut. (j.g.)
2011 Pine St., Philadelphia, Pa. Mass. Inst. of Tech., Pensacola, London, Killingholme, Eng., N. A. No. 222. HTA.

WILLIAMS, A. J., Jr.
Ensign
373 East 207th St., Bronx, New York City. Mass. Inst. of Tech., Bay Shore, Pensacola. N. A. No. 1820. HTA.

WILLIAMS, A. S.
Lieut. (j.g.)
Chapin, S. C. Akron. Montauk, Key West. N. A. No. 114. HTA.

WILLIAMS, CLANCEY L.
Ensign
254 Elm St., Oberlin, Ohio. Mass. Inst. of Tech., Hampton Roads, Pensacola, Miami, Moutchic, Paris. N. A. No. 570. HTA.

WILLIAMS, FRANK C.
Student Officer
284 Prospect Pl., Brooklyn, N. Y. Mass. Inst. of Tech., Bay Shore, Brunswick, Key West. HTA.

WILLIAMS, J. A.
Ensign
157 Slarm Ave., Buffalo, N. Y. Mass. Inst. of Tech., Bay Shore, Pensacola, New London. N. A. No. 1820.

WILLIAMS, J. W., Jr.
Ensign
931 22nd St., San Diego, Cal. Seattle, San Diego. N. A. No. 2083. HTA.

WILLIAMS, JOHN McM.
Student Officer
254 Elm St., Oberlin, Ohio. Mass. Inst. of Tech., Key West. HTA.

WILLIAMS, ROBERT M.
Student Officer
1600 Arch St., Little Rock, Ark. Mass. Inst. of Tech., Bay Shore. HTA.

WILLIAMS, STANLEY B.
Printer
1401 Main St., Pine Bluff, Ark. Miami, Hampton Roads.

WILLIAMS, VICTOR J.
Student Officer
Bolivar, New York. Mass. Inst. of Tech

WILLIAMSON, F. V.
Ensign
112 So. Portland Ave., Brooklyn, N. Y. Mass. Inst. of Tech., Miami, Pensacola. N. A. No. 1354. HTA.

WILLING, ARTHUR
Ensign
Box 349, Morehead City, N. C. M. I. T., Pensa., Miami, Calais, Killingholme, Hamp. Rds. Morehead. N. A. No. 385. HTA.

WILMETH, JAMES L., Jr.
Student Officer
300 Takoma Ave., Takoma Park, Wash., D. C. Dunwoody, Minneapolis. HTA

WILSON, ALFRED C.
Ensign
1006 N. Calvert St., Baltimore, Md. Mass. Inst. of Tech., Pensacola, Coronada Beach. N. A. No. 1633.

WILSON, A. F.
Ensign
Hollister, San Benito Co., Cal. Mass. Inst. of Tech., Key West, Miami, Pensacola. N. A. No. 1306.

WILSON, E. F.
Lieut. (j.g.)
51 Main St., Thomaston, Me. Mass. Inst. of Tech., Pensacola. N. A. No. 2471. HTA.

WILSON, RUSSEL E.
Ensign
General Del. Bosworth, Mo. Mass. Inst. of Tech., Miami, Pensacola. N. A. No. 2245. HTA.

WILSON, W. HENRY
Ensign
186 State St., Perth Amboy, N. J. Mass. Inst. of Tech., Buffalo, Elizabeth, Garden City. N. A. No. 1018. HTA.

WIMMER, EDWARD L.
Machinist
7120 Emerald Ave., Chicago, Ill. Columbia Univ., Great Lakes, Rockaway Beach. HTA.

THE START OF A DAY'S FLYING.

WININGS, W. C.
Ensign
1655 N. Alabama St., Indianapolis, Ind. Mass. Inst. of Tech., Akron, Rockaway Beach. LTA.

WISE, K. S. N.
Ensign
Moutchic, Lake Bolsena, Porto Corsini. HTA.

WISSMAN, LEO B.
Student Officer
554 East Thirteenth St., Cincinnati, Ohio. Miami.

WITTE, EDWARD B.
Ensign
1294 Fillmore Ave., Buffalo, N. Y. M. I. T., Key West, Miami, Moutchic, Outang, Malpensa. N. A. No. 1447. HTA.

WOLF, JAMES EDWIN
Ensign
17 St. Lukes Place, New York City. Mass. Inst. of Tech., Great Lakes, Bay Shore, Brunswick, Charleston. N. A. No. 2107. HTA.

WOLFE, ALEX McW.
Ensign
1931 St. Paul St., Baltimore, Md. Mass. Inst. of Tech.. Pensacola, Moutchic, Bay Shore. N. A. No. 899. HTA.

WOLFER, J. F.
Ensign
170 E. King St. Lancaster, Pa. M. I. T., Pensacola, Miami, Hampton Rds Langley Field, U. S. S. *Arizona.* N. A. No. 1214. HTA.

WOLFF, ALFRED
Ensign
607 Milwaukee Ave., Janesville, Wis. Mass. Inst. of Tech., Great Lakes, Pensacola, Hampton Rds. N. A. No. 645. HTA.

WOMER, P. B.
Ensign
139 W. Green St., Hazleton, Pa. Mass. Inst. of Tech., Pensacola, Akron, Rockaway Beach. N. A. No. 2667. LTA.

WONDERS, MAX E.
Student Officer
3512 Lincoln Blvd., Omaha, Nebr. Mass. Inst. of Tech., Key West. HTA.

WOOD, ALFRED M.
Student Officer
Wildie, Ky. Dunwoody Inst., Miami, Key West.

WOOD, CEDRIC W.
Student Officer
86 Dorchester Rd., Buffalo, N. Y. Mass. Inst. of Tech., Bay Shore. HTA.

WOOD, D. G.
Ensign
Birdwood, Va. M. I. T., Hampton Roads, Pensa., Queenstown, Whiddy Island, Wash., Miami. N. A. No. 1250. HTA.

WOOD, LEON FORREST
Ensign
De Golia, Pa. Mass. Inst. of Tech., Buffalo, Akron. LTA.

WOOD, W. PERRY
Ensign
515 Shatto Place, Los Angeles, Cal. Mass. Inst. of Tech., Key West, Miami, Pensacola, Coco Solo, C. Z N. A. No. 1130. HTA.

WOODS, JOHN H.
Ensign
17834 Lake Ave., Lakewood, Ohio. Mass. Inst. of Tech., Bay Shore, Pensacola. N. A. No. 1213.

WOODS, WM. R., Jr.
Ensign
Becket, Mont. Mass. Inst. of Tech., Key West, Miami, Pensacola. N. A. No. 1597. HTA.

WOODY, WARREN V.
Ensign
Barnard, Kan. Seattle, Wash., Miami, Pensacola. HTA.

WOOLSEY, WILLIAM E.
Ensign
Formoso, Kan. Mass. Inst. of Tech., Pensacola, Chatham. N. A. No. 934. HTA.

WORLEY, FRED M.
Student Officer
1416 W. 6th St., Topeka, Kans., Seattle, Miami. HTA.

WORTH, IRVING H.
Student Officer
61 East 95th St., New York City. Mass. Inst. of Tech. LTA.

WRIGHT, ROBERT F.
Ensign
338 Kingsway Ave., Winnipeg, Canada. Dunwoody, San Diego, Pensacola. N. A. No. 2266. HTA.

WRIGHT, WEBSTER M.
Lieut. (j.g.)
Bivouac Place, Fort Thomas, Ky. M. I. T., Moutchic, Fr., Brest, Fr., L'Aber Vrach, Pensacola. N. A. No. 322. HTA.

WYLIE, HAROLD H.
Ensign
Bowesmont, N. D. Seattle, Univ. Wash., San Diego, Pensacola. N. A. No. 1918. HTA.

◈ ◈ ◈ ◈ ◈ ◈

Wachter, Ferdinand, Ensign. Mass. Inst. of Tech., Miami, Pensacola. HTA.

Wackman, Lee Daniel, Student Officer, Albert Lea, Minn. Seattle, Wash. HTA.

Waddell, Reid, Student Officer, Room 456 Elec. & Gas Bldg., Atlanta, Ga.

Wadsworth, Horace E., Student Officer, New Ocean House, Swampscott, Mass.

Wagenseil, Edgar White, Lieut. (j.g.), 5788 E. Circle Ave., Chicago, Ill.

Waggener, C. E., Ensign, 414 Beatty St., Columbus, Ind.

Wagner, Arthur C., Ensign, 1541 Cleveland Place, Denver, Col. N. A. No. 1626.

Wagner, T. H., Ensign.

Wagner, Thos. H., Jr., Ensign. N. A. No. 1461.

Waldon, Russell E., Ensign, 427 Seward Ave., Detroit, Mich. N. A. No. 2144.

Wales, L. A., Ensign, Care of A. B. Leach & Co., 62 Cedar St., New York City.

Walker, Donald, Ensign, 85 Washington St., East Orange, N. J. N. A. No. 2048.

Walker, H. W., Ensign, 1233 Munsey Bldg., Washington, D. C.

Walker, James Carl, Ensign.

Walker, Jos. R., Student Officer, 158 Summer St., Boston, Mass.

Walker, Leslie A., Lieut. (j.g.), 1449 Pike Road, Ensley, Birmingham, Ala. Mass. Inst. of Tech., Pensacola, Fla. N. A. No. 718. HTA.

Walker, Leon B., Student Officer, 1 Hillhouse Ave., New Haven, Conn.

Walker, O. P., Ensign, 1313 E. Boulevard St., El Paso, Tex. N. A. No. 2116.

Walker, W. J., Lieut. (j.g.), N. A. No. 1167.

Wallace, Clayton M., Student Officer, 8 Lake St., Wolfeboro, N. H. Mass. Inst. of Tech. HTA.

Wallace, G. H., War. Machinist, 6203 Palatine Ave., Seattle, Wash. Puget Sound Navy Yard, San Diego Air Station.

Wallace, Luther T., Student Officer, 806 Marguette Bldg., Detroit, Mich.

Wallace, Ray Beach, Ensign, 530 N. Central Ave., Austin, Chicago, Ill. Mass. Inst. of Tech., Cape May, Miami, Pensacola, Norfolk. HTA.

Wallick, L. D., Ensign, Hotel Deshler, Columbus, Ohio.

Walling, E. S., Lieut. (j.g.).

Wallingford, J. K., Ensign, 107 N. Miller St., Cynthiana, Ky. N. A. No. 1705.

Walsh, Cline J., Student Officer, 1058 Second Ave., Detroit, Mich.

Walsh, Edward J., Student Officer, 313 Southbrook Courts, Washington, D. C. Univ. of Washington, Seattle. HTA.

Walsh, Garnar V., Student Officer, 122 Willoughby Ave., Brooklyn, N. Y.

Walsh, Jos. R., Student Officer, 3 E. 128th St., New York City.

Walter, Edwin H., Ensign, 806 West St., Wilmington, Del. N. A. No. 2124.

Walter, Otto F., Student Officer, Columbus, Neb. Mass. Inst. of Tech. HTA.

Walters, C. W., Ensign, Casselton, N. D.

Ward, Alfred, War. Machinist.

Ward, Harrison F., Student Officer.

Ward, Jasper I., War. Gunner.

Ward, Max F., Student Officer.

Ward, Thomas Wm., Student Officer, Sharon, Pa.

Wardwell, Charles Ed., Ensign. N. A. No. 759.

Ware, Henry M., Student Officer, 2 Magnolia Court, Greensboro, N. C. Mass. Inst. of Tech. HTA.

Ware, Robt. Hughes, Student Officer, Country Club. Brookline, Mass. Mass. Inst. of Tech. HTA.

Warford, Henry W., Student Officer, Genesee, N. Y.

Warner, Edward A., Student Officer, Republic Bldg., Kansas City, Mo. Seattle, Wash., Miami, Fla. HTA.

Warner, H., Student Officer, Grafton Hotel, Washington, D. C. Mass. Inst. of Tech. LTA.

Warren, R. A., Student Officer, 32 Weston St., Waltham, Mass.

Warren, R. Bates, Ensign, 1341 Columbia Road, Washington, D. C. Mass. Inst. of Tech., Miami, Pensacola, Cape May. N. A. No. 1314. HTA.

Warren, Walter K., Student Officer, 8401-17th Ave., Brooklyn, N. Y.

Washburn, Frederick A., Student Officer.

Washburn, J. R., War. Boatswain, 705 13th Ave., Milwaukee, Wis. Pensacola, Squantum, Mass., San Diego, Cal., North Island. HTA.

Waters, Harris M., Ensign, Alexandria, Va. N. A. No. 1990.

Waters, Opal Selby, Ensign, 2647 Durant Ave., Berkeley, Cal. Mass. Inst. of Tech., Miami, Fla., Pensacola, Fla. N. A. No. 1594. HTA.

Watkins, J. L., Student Officer, 412 W. Clinton St., Elmira, N. Y. Mass. Inst. of Tech., Akron. LTA.

Watkins, Ronald G., Student Officer, 1641 Lucile Ave., Los Angeles, Cal. Mass. Inst. of Tech., Miami, San Diego. HTA.

Watson, Edw. B., Student Officer, 487 Adams St., Milton, Mass.

Watson, J. W., Ensign, 38 W. Loo St., Frostburg, Maryland. N. A. No. 1962.

Watson, L. Savage, Ensign, Mamaroneck, N. Y.

Watson, R. M., Student Officer, North Bend, Neb. Seattle, Wash., Key West, Fla. HTA.

Watt, Geo. Y., Ensign.

Watters, Louis H., Student Officer, 106 Ocean View Ave., Santa Cruz, Cal. Mass. Inst. of Tech., Akron, Ohio. LTA.

Watts, Curtis C., Ensign, Hansel Hall Apts., Windsor Hills, Baltimore, Md. Mass. Inst. of Tech., Akron, Ohio, Pensacola, Fla. LTA.

Watts, Wm. B., Ensign, 413 First Ave., Rome, Ga. Mass. Inst. of Tech., Bay Shore, L. I., Pensacola, Fla. N. A. No. 1340. HTA.

Waugh, R. S., Ensign.

WEAVER, R. B., Ensign, 620 Columbus Ave., Boston, Mass.

WEBBER, RALPH B., Student Officer, 1195 Beacon St., Brookline, Mass. Mass. Inst. of Tech. HTA.

WEBER, CHARLES M., Ensign, 1117 Trust & Sav. Bldg., Los Angeles, Cal.

WEBSTER, FRED N., Ensign, 7730 E. Lake Terrace, Chicago, Ill.

WEED, GEO. W., Student Officer, 1912 Avenue H., Brooklyn, N. Y. Dunwoody Inst., Minn. HTA.

WEEKS, W. L., Ensign, Carmen St., Patchogue, N. Y. N. A. No. 2261.

WEEMS, CHAS. L., Ensign, 1651 York St., Quincy, Ill. N. A. No. 1172.

WEGNER, FRITZ W., Ensign, Frankfort, N. Y.

WEIL, EDWARD A., Student Officer, 4202 Parkside Ave., Philadelphia, Pa.

WEINBERG, HARRY W., War Boatswain.

WEINIG, C. A., Student Officer, 604 Linwood Ave., Buffalo, N. Y. Mass. Inst. of Tech. HTA.

WEIS, CHARLES W., JR., Ensign, 430 Oxford St., Rochester, N. Y. N. A. No. 611.

WEIS, ERWIN T., Student Officer, 2482 Glenwood Ave., Toledo, Ohio. Mass. Inst. of Tech. HTA.

WELBOAN, LEE C., Student Officer, 34 N. 23rd St., New York City.

WELCH, E. P., Ensign, Gloucester, Mass. N. A. No. 997.

WELCH, LEO. D., Student Officer, 169 Clinton St., Brooklyn, N. Y.

WELCH, RICHARD E., Student Officer, 25 Barton St., Newburyport, Mass.

WELD, FRANK E., Ensign.

WELD, L., Lieut. (j.g.), 82 Brever St., New York City. N. A. No. 219.

WELLER, MICHAEL, Student Officer, 2002 H St., N. W., Washington, D. C.

WELLES, C. R., Student Officer, Stratford, Conn. Mass. Inst. of Tech. HTA.

WELLES, RUSSELL, Ensign, 71 Town St., Norwich, Conn. Mass. Inst. of Tech., Miami, Pensacola. N. A. No. 1186.

WELLS, CHANDLER, Lieut. (j.g.), 490 Linwood Ave., Buffalo, N. Y. Packard Motor Co.

WELLS, R. H., Ensign, 104 Charles River Road, Cambridge, Mass.

WELLS, THOMAS M., Student Officer, 314 Orange St., Wilmington, N. C.

WELSH, MADISON F., Lieut. (j.g.), 404 Elderado St., Decatur, Ill. Mass. Inst. of Tech., Hampton Roads, Pensacola, Fla., Rockaway Beach. N. A. No. 414.

WELTY, HENRY HARRISON, Student Officer, 1242 Western Ave., Topeka, Kansas. Mass. Inst. of Tech., Miami, Fla. HTA.

WELTY, LEONARD A., War. Boatswain, Franklin, Delaware County, N. Y., Pensacola, Fla., Killingholme, Eng.; Bay Shore, L. I.; Miami, Fla.; Anacostia, D. C.; Hampton Roads, Rockaway, L. I.; U. S. S., *North Carolina*, U. S. S. *Seattle*, U. S. S. *Shawmut*. HTA.

WELZANT, GEO. P., Ensign, 721 S. Broadway, Baltimore, Md. Mass. Inst. of Tech., Akron, Pensacola. N. A. No. 1994. LTA.

WENNER, FRANK H., Ensign, 110 Addington Place, Utica, N. Y. Mass. Inst. of Tech., Miami, Pensacola. HTA.

WENZ, E. A., Ensign.

WERXELMAN, D. J., JR., Ensign, 3529 Locust St., Philadelphia, Pa. N. A. No. 2332.

WESLEY, HAROLD H., Ensign, Terra Ceia, N. C.

WESSELLS, WALTER B., Ensign, 315 Dolphin St., Baltimore, Md. Mass. Inst. of Tech., Miami, Pensacola, Fla. N. A. No. 1844. HTA.

WEST, JAMES W., Student Officer, 35 W. 15th St., Atlanta, Ga.

WEST, W. M., Lieut. (j.g.), 56 Nightingale St., Dorchester, Mass. N. A. No. 220½.

WESTON, C. F., Ensign, Royal St., Medford, Mass.

WETHERBY, JOHN K., JR., Student Officer, 1519 Spruce Place, Minn., Minn.

WHALEN, EDMUND A., JR., Student Officer, 153 Clifton Place, Brooklyn, N. Y.

WHALES, T. C., War. Boatswain.

WHATLEY, WM. J., Student Officer, 2248 Arlington Ave., Birmingham, Ala.

WHEELAN, WM. L., Student Officer, 834 Carlton Ave., Plainfield, N. J.

WHEELER, HENRY C., Student Officer.

WHEELER, J. L., Ensign, 524 Riverside Drive, N. Y. City. N. A. No. 2008.

WHEELER, JOHN E., Student Officer.

WHEELER, OSCAR G., Lieut. (j.g.), 8 Greylock Road, Allston, Mass. Pensacola, Washington, D. C. N. A. No. 237. HTA.

WHEELER, R. A., Ensign, Orchard Park, N. Y.

WHELTLE, ALBERT FRANCIS, Student Officer, 105 E. West St., Baltimore, Md. Mass. Inst. of Tech. HTA.

WHELAN, T. J., Ensign, 95 Cottage St., Lynn, Mass. N. A. No. 2062.

WHERRY, KENNETH S., Student Officer, 3433 Carnegie Ave., Cleveland, Ohio.

WHIDDEN, WM. B., Ensign, 39 Sterling St., West Newton, Mass. Mass. Inst. of Tech., Bay Shore, L. I., Pensacola, Fla. N. A. No. 1815. HTA.

WHIGHAM, WM., JR., Ensign, 5815 Fifth Ave., Pittsburgh, Pa. Mass. Inst. of Tech., Bay Shore, L. I., Pensacola, Fla. HTA.

WHIPPLE, RUSSELL A., Student Officer, 1335 Smith St., Providence, R. I.

WHITAKER, E. L., Ensign.

WHITAKER, H. D., Ensign, 3133 Menlo Ave., Hyde Park, Cincinnati, Ohio. N. A. No. 1445.

WHITAKER, L. J., Ensign.

WHITAKER, R. A., Ensign, 1116 Main St., Baton Rouge, La. N. A. No. 1946.

WHITCOMB, FRANKLIN L., Student Officer.

WHITCOMB, K. F., Ensign, 1123 Asbury Ave., Evanston, Ill. Mass. Inst. of Tech., Rockaway, L. I.; Hampton Roads, Va.; Akron, O.; Pensacola, Fla. N. A. No. 2430. LTA.

WHITCOMB, ROLLIN L., Student Officer, 2436 Girard Ave., So. Minneapolis, Minn.

WHITE, C. W., Ensign, Hertford, N. C. N. A. No. 1706.

WHITE, EDW. I., Student Officer, 615 Blackstone Ave., Fresno, Cal.

WHITE, ERSKINE N., Student Officer, 1125 Madison Ave., New York City. Great Lakes, Ill.

WHITE, JOS. H., Student Officer, 5610 Dorchester Ave., Chicago, Ill.

WHITE, L. G., Lieut. (j.g.), 203 Court St., Portsmouth, Va.

WHITE, RAYMOND M., Ensign, Great Western Sugar Co., Billings, Mont. Mass. Inst. of Tech., Miami, Fla., Pensacola, Fla. N. A. No. 1551. HTA.

WHITE, RUSSELL H., Ensign, 3329 East Madison St., Seattle, Wash. Mass. Inst. of Tech., Univ. of Wash., Pensacola.

WHITE, SIBLEY L., Ensign, 128 E St., S. E., Washington, D. C. N. A. No. 1764.

WHITE, WALTER, Ensign. N. A. No. 1496.

WHITE, WM. M., JR., Student Officer, Mexico, Tex.

WHITEHEAD, CHARLES P., Student Officer.

WHITEHEAD, JOHN T., Student Officer, 1322 E. Marquette Road, Chicago, Ill.

WHITEHEAD, V. L., JR., Ensign, 2 Mechanic St., Buffalo, N. Y. Mass. Inst. of Tech., Miami, Pensacola. N. A. No. 2425. HTA.

WHITEHURST, BEN. W., Ensign, The Earlington, 16th St., Washington, D. C. Mass. Inst. of Tech., Washington. HTA.

WHITELAW, GEO. P., Student Officer, 5291 Westminster Place, St. Louis, Mo. Mass. Inst. of Tech. LTA.

WHITEMAN, Z. H., JR., Ensign, 106 E. 4th St., Williamsport, Pa. Mass. Inst. of Tech., Key West, Miami, Pensacola, Fla., Hampton Roads, Va., Cape May, N. J. N. A. No. 1654. HTA.

WHITING, BRAINARD S., Student Officer.

WHITING, ROBERT B., Ensign, Station B., Winsted, Conn. Great Lakes, Ill., Pensacola, Fla. LTA.

WHITNEY, J. R., Ensign, Sewickley, Pa. N. A. No. 1084.

WHITNEY, KING, Ensign, Geneva, N. Y. Akron, R. N. A. S., Roehampton, Eng.; Queenstown, Ire.; Brest, France; La Trinite, France. LTA.

WHITTAKER, JAMES E., Student Officer, 5 Trumbull Square, Worcester, Mass.

WHITTLE, GEO. V., Lieut. (j.g.), Crestwood, Town of Eastchester, N. Y. Akron, Ohio, Washington, D. C., Hampton Roads. LTA.

WICK, HENRY C., JR., Student Officer, 13124 Euclid Ave., Cleveland, Ohio.

WICKES, BRADFORD, Student Officer, 105 E. 53rd St., New York City.

WICKET, J. CALDWELL, Ensign, Richmond, Va. Mass.

sInt. of Tech., Norfolk, Pensacola, Miami, Moutchic. HTA.

WICKHAM, REX H., Student Officer.

WICKMAN, WILBUR F., Ensign, 117 E. 8th St., Concordia, Kansas. Mass. Inst. of Tech., Pensacola, Fla.; Cape May, N. J.; Akron, Ohio. N. A. No. 1557. LTA.

WICKS, JOHN H., Machinist, Bay Shore, L. I., New York. Pensacola, Bay Shore, Brunswick. HTA.

WIDENER, SETH G., Student Officer, Chili Station, N. Y.

WIDMER, W. R., Ensign, 429 W. 117th St., New York City. N. A. No. 1201.

WIDMER, W. E., Ensign, 508 S. Main St., Centerville, Iowa. Mass. Inst. of Tech., Key West, Miami, Fla., Hampton Roads, Va., Pensacola, Fla. HTA.

WIGMAN, WALTER W., Ensign, N. A. No. 1775.

WILBAR, WADSWORTH, Ensign. 155 Cohannet St., Taunton, Mass. N. A. No. 896.

WILCOX, ROBT. B., Ensign, Elks Club, Amsterdam, N. Y. Mass. Inst. of Tech., Key West, Miami, Pensacola, Queenstown, Ireland; Wexford, Ireland. N. A. No. 1251. HTA.

WILD, MARCELLUS F., Ensign, 143 Spg. St., Rochester, N. Y. N. A. No. 1405.

WILD, ROBT. S., Student Officer, 3641 Locust St., Philadelphia, Pa.

WILDER, EMORY H., Lieut. (j.g.), 1622 Forest Place, Evanston, Ill. Mass. Inst. of Tech., Great Lakes, Key West, Port Sewal, Miami, Pensacola. N. A. No. LTA.

WILDER, HERBERT F., War. Machinist.

WILEY, JAMES DUNCAN, Student Officer, 1548 Beacon St., Waban, Mass. Mass. Inst. of Tech., Hampton Roads, Va., Pensacola, Fla., New York, Boston. HTA.

WILEY, N. CHESTER, Student Officer, 10 Crocker St., Somerville, Mass. Mass. Inst. of Tech. LTA.

WILKINS, CLEON, Student Officer, Spanish Fork, Utah.

WILKINS, E. B., Ensign, 3771 Clay St., San Francisco, Cal. N. A. No. 1765.

WILKINSON, WM., War. Gunner.

WILLETT, JOSEPH J., JR., Student Officer, 1325 Ave. F., Anniston, Ala.

WILLIAM, ARTHUR S., Lieut. (j.g.), Chapin, S. C. N. A. No. 114.

WILLIAM, C. D., Lieut. (j.g.), 32 Stinson St., Detroit, Mich.

WILLIAMS, A. J., Ensign, 373 E. 207th St., New York City.

WILLIAMS, CHAS., Student Officer, 365 W. Clinton St., Elmira, N. Y.

WILLIAMS, C. E., War. Gunner.

WILLIAMS, ERNEST N., Student Officer.

WILLIAMS, EUGENE A.,Student Officer, 309 Massachusetts Ave., N. W., Washington, D. C.

WILLIAMS, IRA JASON, Student Officer, 1122 Fairmont St., Washington, D. C.

WILLIAMS, J. G., Student Officer, 712 Candler Bldg., Atlanta, Ga., Seattle, Washin ton. HTA.

WILLIAMS, JOHN WARREN, Student Officer, 136 Edgewood St., Hartford, Conn.

WILLIAMS, LANGDON T., Student Officer, 223 Woodland Ave., Columbus, Ohio. Dunwoody Institute, Minn.

WILLIAMS, MARCUS E., Ensign.

WILLIAMS, RICHARD T., Ensign, 394 Elmwood Ave., Buffalo, N. Y. Mass. Inst. of Tech., Miami, Pensacola, Key West. HTA.

WILLIAMS, SIDNEY D., Student Officer, 209 State St., Harrisburg, Pa. Mass. Inst. of Tech., Miami, Florida. HTA.

WILLIAMS, STAUNTON, Student Officer, 990 Prospect Ave., Hartford, Conn. Mass. Inst. of Tech. HTA.

WILLIAMS, VERNON M., Ensign. N. A. No. 2210.

WILLIAMS, WM. K., Student Officer, 160 Wilson Ave., Columbus, Ohio.

WILLIAMSON, ARTHUR DOUGLASS, Student Officer, 6 Division St., Ilion, N. Y. Mass. Inst. of Tech. HTA.

WILLIAMSON, R. L., Ensign. N. A. No. 629.

WILLINGHAM, JUDSON, Student Officer, 703 Piedmont Ave., Atlanta, Ga.

WILLIS, P. CONNALLY, Student Officer, 925 N. 16th St., Waco, Texas. Seattle, Washington, San Diego, Cal. HTA.

WILLS, BERT W., Ensign. N. A. No. 1739.

WILSON, A. G., War. Boatswain, 136 W. 90th St., New York City. N. A. No. 1463.

WILSON, C. M., War. Machinist, 3961 Ashland Ave., St. Louis, Mo., Columbia University, Great Lakes, Ill.; Philadelphia, Pa.; Pauillac, Dunkirk ,Paimboeuf, France.

WILSON, CHARLES C., Student Officer, 213 Webster Ave., Muskegon, Mich.

WILSON, D., Lieut. (j.g.), 63 Hancock St., Lexington, Mass. Mass. Inst. of Tech., Pensacola and aboard U. S. S. *Shawmut*.

WILSON, EVERETT ROWLAND, Ensign. High Park, Grand View Drive, Peoria, Ill. Mass. Inst. of Tech., Bay Shore, L. I., Pensacola, Hampton Roads. HTA.

WILSON, FRANK M., Student Officer, 5533 Sierra Vista St., Los Angeles. Cal.

WILSON, JAMES H., Student Officer, 332 McKinley Ave., Salem, Ohio. Mass. Inst. of Tech., Miami. HTA.

WILSON, JULIUS L., Ensign, 416 W. 122nd St., New York City. Mass. Inst. of Tech., Key West, Pensacola. N. A. No. 1795. HTA.

WILSON, LINCOLN S., Lieut. (j.g.), R. F. D. No. 61, Norwalk, Conn. Mass. Inst. of Tech., Bay Shore, Hampton Roads, Pensacola. N. A. No. 1171.

WILSON, LESLIE E., Student Officer, U. S. Naval Hospital, Fort Lyon, Colo.

WILSON, MILTON A., Student Officer, 1 State St., Wethersfield, Conn.

WILSON, SAMUEL J., Student Officer.

WILSON, W. H., Ensign, Tallahassee, Fla. N. A. No. 1018.

WILSON, W. HENRY, Ensign, 186 State St., Perth Amboy, N. J.

WILSON, WALTER G., Ensign, 34 15th St., Lowell, Mass. N. A. No. 1045.

WILSON, WM. S., Ensign, 1239 Girard St., N. W., Washington, D. C.

WINANTS, F. H., Ensign, 15 W. Madison St., Baltimore, Md.

WINDSOR, JOHN J., Student Officer, 119 Don Gaspar Ave., Mass. Inst. of Tech., U. S. S. *Minnesota*, San Francisco. HTA.

WING, HERBERT C., Lieut. (j.g.), 231 W. 10th Ave., Columbus, Ohio, Akron, Rockaway Queenstown, Ireland; Wexford, Ireland; R. N. A. S. Roehampton, Eng., La Trinite, Brest, France.

WINN, FRED M., Student Officer, 629 W. 10th St., Oklahoma City, Okla. Seattle, Washington. HTA.

WINSLOW, BURNSIDE, Ensign, 145 Cold Spring St., New Haven, Conn., Great Lakes, Pensacola.

WINSLOW, ROBERT C., Student Officer, Union Trust Co., Indianapolis, Ind. Mass. Inst. of Tech., Key West, Pensacola, Fla. HTA.

WINSTON, JAMES W., Student Officer, Duarte, Cal.

WINTERHALTER, WILLIAM CHARLES, Ensign, 75 Lin vood Ave., Crafton, Pa. Mass. Inst. of Tech., Miami, Fla. N. A. No. 2050. HTA.

WINTERSTEEN, JOHN, Ensign, 2220 Delancey St., Philadelphia, Pa. Mass. Inst. of Tech., Key West. N. A. No. 1478. HTA.

WIPPERMAN, WALTER K., Student Officer, Loan & Trust Co., Logansport, Ind.

WISEMAN, C. J., Student Officer, 2224 Fulton St., San Francisco, Cal.

WITHERILL, LISTON L., Student Officer, 100 Walnut St., Syracuse, N. Y.

WOLF, E. L., Lieut. (j.g.), 1931 St. Paul St., Baltimore, Md.

WOLFE, J., Lieut. (j.g.), Brooskide Farm, Ossining, N. Y.

WOLFILN, GEO. L., Ensign, 1705 Walnut St., Berkeley, Cal., Seattle, Washington; San Diego, Cal., Pensacola, Fla. N. A. No. 2244. HTA.

WOOD, ARTHUR R., War Carpenter, U. S. N.

WOOD, FREDERICK S., Student Officer, 7600 Euclid Ave., Cleveland, Ohio.

WOOD, G. L., Ensign. N. A. No. 1937.

WOOD, HENRY L., Ensign, Huntington, L. I., N. Y. Mass. Inst. of Tech., Instructor.

WOOD, QUINTAN, Ensign, Logan, La. Seattle, Washington, Key West, Pensacola, Fla. N. A. No. 2307. HTA.

WOOD, R. C., Ensign. N. A. No. 1397.

WOOD, R. W., Ensign, Ivy Depot, Albermarle Co., Va. N. A. No. 2009.

WOOD, R. WARNER, Ensign, 56 Warren Ave., East, Detroit, Mich. Mass. Inst. of Tech., Key West, Miami, Pensacola. HTA.

WOOD, ROY W., Student Officer, 4206 Fairview Road, P. H., Little Rock, Ark.

WOOD, THOMAS W., Student Officer, La Fayette, Ala.

WOODHOUSE, HARTLAND, Student Officer, 549 W. End Ave., New York City.

WOODLIEF, HAROLD BOY, Student Officer, Ottawa, Kan.

Woodruff, Bruce F., Ensign, Hopkinsville, Ky. Mass. Inst. of Tech., Key West, Pensacola. N. A. No. 1873. HTA.

Woodruff, C. C., Jr., Ensign, 525 University Ave., Ithaca, N. Y. N. A. No. 1139.

Woodruff, T., Ensign, 130 Atlantic St., Bridgetown, N. J.

Woods, T. F., Ensign, 314 State St., Albany, N. Y.

Woods, William R., Student Officer, 1444 Lafayette St., Denver, Colo.

Woodside, L. R., Ensign, 24 E. Madison St., Baltimore, Md.

Wooley, George T., Lieut. (j.g.).

Woolsey, T. J., Ensign, 350 Post St., San Francisco, Cal. N. A. No. 1334.

Worden, Leslie J., Student Officer.

Worley, Fred M., Student Officer, 1416 W. 6th St., Topeka, Kans. Seattle, Miami. HTA.

Worth, L. K., Ensign, 728 W. Colorado Ave., Colorado Springs, Colo. N. A. No. 2075.

Wray, James R. L., Ensign, 2218 Locust St., Philadelphia, Pa. Mass. Inst. of Tech., Bay Shore, Pensacola, Moutchic, Fromentine. N. A. No. 936. HTA.

Wrenn, Canfield M., Student Officer, 210 Capital Bk. Bldg., Des Moines, Iowa. Mass. Inst. of Tech. LTA.

Wright, Allyn Lee, Ensign, Columbus, Wisc.

Wright, Edward P., Lieut. (j.g.), 225 Taylor Ave., Detroit, Mich. Mass. Inst. of Tech., Bay Shore, Pensacola. N. A. No. 954. HTA.

Wright, F. H., Ensign, Liberty, Ky. N. A. No. 148.

Wright, Francis M., Student Officer, 911 W. Green St., Urbana, Ill.

Wright, James N., Ensign, 345 Gilpin St., Denver. Colo., Great Lakes, Pensacola.

Wright, Kenneth M., Student Officer, Rolla, Mo.

Wright, Marc S., Ensign, 669 Washington St., Brookline, Mass. Mass. Inst. of Tech., San Diego, Cal., Pensacola, Fla. N. A. No. 1782.

Wright, Ralph E., Student Officer, R. F. D. No. 5, Celina, Ohio.

Wright, Richard S., Student Officer, 657 Asbury St., San Jose, Cal. Seattle, Washington. HTA.

Wright, Theodore Paul, Lieut. (j.g.), 22 Lafayette St., Hempstead, L. I., N. Y. Mass. Inst. of Tech., Buffalo, Garden City, N. Y. HTA.

Wright, W. F., Ensign, 864 W. Market St., Lima, Ohio. N. A. No. 1558.

Wyant, Lynton D., Student Officer.

Wyman, Edward E., Ensign, 403 Lancaster Ave., Haverford, Pa. Mass. Inst. of Tech., Buffalo, Elizabeth.

◈ ◈ ◈ ◈ ◈ ◈

To the men who were qualified early in the history of Naval Aviation, the list given below will be of particular interest as it shows the order in which the first 250 men were designated as Naval Aviators. Up to the present time the Navy has trained and so designated over 2,700 naval fliers.

No.	Name
1.	Ellyson, T. G.
2.	Rogers, J.
3.	Towers, J. H.
4.	Herbster, D. D.
5.	Cunningham, A. A..
6.	Smith, B. L.
7.	Chevalier, G. deC.
8.	Bellinger, P. N. L.
9.	Billingsley, W. D.
10.	Murray, J. N.
11.	Mustin, H. C.
12.	McIlvaine, W. M.
13.	Richarhson, H. C.
16.	Whiting, K.
17.	Maxfield, L. H.
18.	McDonnell, E. O
19.	Capehart, W.
20.	Spencer, E. W.
21.	Bartlett, H. T.
22.	Murray, G.
23.	Corry, W. M.
24.	Read, A. C.
25.	Johnson, E. F.
26.	Evans, F. J.
27.	Paunack, R. R.
28.	Scofield, H. W.
29.	Childs, W. G.
30.	Dicman, G. C.
31.	Young, R. T.
32.	Gillespie, G. S.
33.	Mitscher, M. A.
34.	Strickland, G. B.
35.	Montfort, J. O. C.
36.	Cabaniss, R. W.
37.	Chase, N. B.
38.	Stone, E. F.
39.	McKitterick, E. H.
40.	Leighton, B. G.
41.	Griffin, V. C.
42.	Cecil, H. B. R.
43.	Sugden, C. E.
44.	Bressman, A. A.
45.	Ramsey, D. W. C
46.	Hull, G. T.
47.	Peyton, P. J.
48.	Kirkpatrick, R. D
49.	Geiger, R. S.
50.	Bonner, W. D.
51.	Murphy, T. H.
52.	Mason, C. P.
52½.	Salsman, J.
53.	Simpson, Jr., F.
54.	Donahue, R.
55.	Brewster, D. L. S.
55½.	Sunderman, J. T.
56.	Barin, L. T.
57.	Parker, S. V
58.	Masek, W.
59.	Coffin, E. A
60.	Eaton, P. P.
61.	Enos, G.
62.	Varini, F.
63.	Hawkins, C. A.
64.	Ruttan. C. E.
65.	Gates, A. L.
65½.	Brown, L. W.
66.	Lovett, R. A.
67.	Ames, A. W.
68.	Gould, E. C. B.
70.	Kilmer, O. P.
71.	Talbot, P.
72.	Davison, H. P.
73.	Vorys, J. M.
74.	McLeish, K.
75.	Beach, C. F.
76.	Farwell, J. V.
78.	Read, R. B.
79.	Brush, G. M.
80.	James, O. B.
81.	Rockefeller, W. A.
82.	McIlwaine, A. G.
84.	Ireland, R. L.
85.	Ingalls, D. S.
86.	Walker, S. S.
87.	Smith, K. R.
88.	Lynch, F. R. V.
89	Lawrence, G. F.
89½.	Merrill, N. E.
90.	McLaughlin, G.
91.	McGrary, F. R.
92.	Coombe, R. G.
93.	Landon, H. H.
94.	Culbert, E. P.
95.	Feher, A.
95a.	Fitz Simon, R.
95b.	Pichon, C. F.
95c.	Zar. M. A.
96.	Coil, E. W.
96½.	Chamberlin, E. G.
97.	Strader, R. M. N.
98.	Talbot, A. B
99.	Whitehouse, W. B.
100.	Crompton, G.
101.	Hamlen, W. L.
102.	Little, C. G.
103.	Brewer, A. D.
104.	Delano, M. P.
105.	Lansdowne, Z.
106.	Bell, G. W.
107.	Chadwick, N.
108.	Ditman, A. J.
109.	Donnelly, T.
110.	Carter, R. C.
111.	Stone, G. W.
110½.	Allen, G. L.
112.	Atwater, W. B.
113.	Fallon, N.
114.	Williams, A. S.
115.	Dietrich, A. F.
116.	Palmer, C. D.
117.	Murray, C. D.
118.	Taylor, M.
119.	Townshend, R. S.
120.	Walton, W. W.
121.	Depew, G. G.
122.	Goodyear, F.
123.	Hutchins, Hurd.
124.	Schieffelin, J. J.
125.	Rodman, T. C.
126.	Smith, E. T.
127.	Otis, T. S.
128.	Hawkins, A. W.
129.	Lufkin, C.
130.	Potter, S.
131.	Fuller, P. S.
132.	Gernea, E. de
133.	Ott, G. A.
134.	Geary, J. W.
134½.	Wetheral, R. W.
135.	Hinton, W.
136.	Willcox, W.
137.	Lee, B. L.
138.	Stone, E. A.
139.	Fuller, C. F.
141.	Stocker, R. M.
142.	Foster, J. C.
143.	Allen, F. S.
144	Amory, F. I.
145.	Read, D. H.
146.	Goldthwaite, D. R.
147.	McCann, R. H.
148.	Wright, A. H.
149.	Swift, H.
150.	Butler, S. M.
151.	Gordon, H. B.
152.	Zunino, F. A.
153.	Shea, E. L.
154.	Forrestall, J. V.
155.	Brackenridge, G.
156.	Gibson, H. F.
157.	Mudge, W.
158.	Clarkson, W.
159.	McCoid, P. H.
160.	Halstead, A. H.
161.	Randolph, R. D.
162.	Matter, R.
163.	Warburton, W. J.
163½.	Peterson, H. A.
164.	Rutherford, J. M.
165.	Laughlin, G. M.
166.	Evans, G. B.
167.	Johnson, A. R.
168.	McCulloch, D. H.
169.	Pierce, T. J. H.
171.	Shaw, G. W.
172.	Peck, L. S.
173.	Humphreys, W. V.
174.	Berger, F. G. B.
175.	Boyd, T. P.
175½.	Alexander, W. H.
176.	White, B. C.
177.	Coddington, D. H.
178.	Kerr, R. H.
179.	Whitted, J. A.
180.	Haskell, A.
181.	Hyde, R. N.
182.	Keyes, K. R.
183.	Warren, A. K.
184.	Eaton, J. A.
185.	Peterson, W. L.
186.	Stanley, H. T.
187.	Remey, J. T.
188.	Palmedo, R.
189.	Forbes, D. P.
190.	Allen, F. G.
191.	Baker, C. S.
192.	Greenough, C. W.
193.	Ames, C. B.
194.	Hofer, M. A.
195.	Ives, P. F.
197.	Brewer, E. S.
198.	Dumas, G. D.
199.	McNamara, J. F.
200.	Rowen, H. J.
201.	Compo, G. L.
202.	Perrin, J.
203.	Hutchinson, L. B.
204.	MacCaulay, D. M.
205.	Lochman, D. E.
206.	Moore, L. R.
207.	Thomas, R. D.
208.	Clements, J. R.
209.	Schermerhorn, H.
210.	Murphey, D. B.
210½.	Grosvenor, T. P.
211.	Roe, G. T.
212.	Tuelon, H. P.
213.	Marriner, W. T.
214.	Pumpelly, H. A.
215.	Biggers, R. L.
216.	Farmer, C. R.
217.	Greenfield, E. R.
219.	Weld, L. M.
220.	Phelan, J.
221.	Lancto, G. W.
222.	Wilcox, H. M.
223.	Hawkins, R.
224.	Wenz, E. A.
225.	Alvord, D. B.
226.	Baum, J. E.
227.	Smith, F. S.
228.	Hawkins, S. C.
229.	Clapp, K. H.
230.	Dowell, B. B.
231.	Ostridge, C. L.
232.	Bergin, T. M.
233.	Gadsden, P. H.
234.	Graves, L. D.
235.	Connelly, L. W.
236.	McAdoo, Jr., W. G.
237.	Wheeler, O. G.
238.	Benjamin, H. R.
239.	Souther, A. F.
240.	Roberts, Jr., C. H.
241.	Harris F. M.
242.	Naylor, H. R.
243.	Voorhees, D. A.
244.	Maxfield, H. W.
245.	King, F. E.
246.	Lamar, L. E.
247.	Bancroft, Jr., F. W.
248.	Griswold, R. A.
249.	Chapman, T. H.
250.	Frothingham, P. B.

YANCEY, WILLIAM B.
Student Officer
Liberty, Mo. Mass. Inst. of Tech., Miami, Key West. HTA.

YAWGER, FOSTER C.
Ensign
78 Linden St., Rochester, N. Y. Mass. Inst. of Tech., Key West, Miami, Pensacola. N. A. No. 2172. HTA.

YEOMANS, SIMPSON
Lieut. (j.g.)
3530 Gladstone Blvd., Kansas City, Mo. Mass. Inst. of Tech., Pensacola. N. A. No. 902. HTA.

YERXA, THOMAS E.
Ensign
Redlands, Cal. Mass. Inst. of Tech., Pensacola, Akron. N. A. No. 1580. HTA., LTA.

THE END OF A FIVE HOURS' PATROL.

YOUNG, A. C., Jr.
Ensign
220 Shafer St., Richmond, Va. Mass. Inst. of Tech., Instructor in Meteorology and Theory of Ballooning. LTA.

YOUNG, FRANKLIN
Ensign
Ozona, Fla. Dunkirk, Key West, Moutchic Bolsena, Pensacola, U. S. S. *Mississippi.* N. A. No. 761. HTA.

YOUNG, HOWARD P.
Ensign
2107 Boulevard, Wilmington, Del. Mass. Inst. of Tech., Key West, Pensacola. N. A. No. 2295. HTA.

YOUNG, KENNETH L.
Lieut. (j.g.)
Hingham, Mass. Mass. Inst. of Tech., Pensacola, Hampton Rds., Morehead City. N. A. No. 515. HTA.

ZEISER, J. S.
Ensign
1113 Union St., Schenectady, N. Y. Mass. Inst. of Tech., Akron, Bay Shore, Pensacola. N. A. No. 1871. LTA.

ZELLER, HUBERT R.
Ensign
Trumbull Ave., Stonington, Conn. Mass. Inst. of Tech., Miami, Key West, Pensacola. N. A. No. 2580. HTA.

ZELLER, JOHN H.
Student Officer
308 W. King St., Shippensburg, Pa. Mass. Inst. of Tech., Miami. HTA.

ZIEGLER, ARTHUR W.
Ensign
556 N. 12th St., E. St. Louis, Ill. Dunwoody, Miami, Key West, Pensacola. N. A. No. 2453. HTA.

ZIESING, RICHARD, Jr.
Lieut. (j.g.)
10610 Magnolia Drive, Cleveland, Ohio. Mass. Inst. of Tech., Akron, Pensacola. N. A. No. 1035. LTA.

◈ ◈ ◈ ◈ ◈

YATES, C. O., JR., Student Officer, 1204 Walnut St., Almedo, Cal.

YAVENNER, GEO. T., Ensign, Rm. 704 Cent. Y. M. C. A., Cleveland, Ohio.

YERINGTON, JOHN G., Student Officer, Watervlit, Mich.

YOST, WM. A., Student Officer.

YOUNG, ARTHUR, Student Officer, Care of Franklin & Marshall Academy, Lancaster, Pa.

YOUNG, J. H., Ensign, 1012 New Hampshire Ave., Washington, D. C.

YOUNG, R. D., Ensign, Galesville, Wisc. London, Eastleigh, Eng., Great Lakes, Ill.

YOUNG, WILLIAM, JR., Student Officer, 245 Stuyvesant Ave., Brooklyn, N. Y. Dunwoody Inst., Minn. HTA.

YOUNGMAN, ARTHUR V., Student Officer, Lloyd Road, Montclair, N. J.

YUNGMAN, A. T., Lieut. (j.g.), 152 W. Hortter St., Philadelphia, Pa.

ZABRISKIE, ALEXANDER C., Lieut. (j.g.), 23 Gramercy Park, New York City. Intelligence office, Lough Foyle, Ireland, H. M. Naval Base, Buncrana, Lough Swilly, Ireland.

ZABRISKIE, GEORGE GRAY, Lieut. (j.g.), 23 Gramercy Park, New York. Mass. Inst. of Tech., Lough Foyle, Ireland, H. M. Naval Base Buncrana, Lough Swilly Ireland.

ZARECOR, MERCER O., Student Officer.

ZIEGER, HAROLD M., Student Officer, 830 Pacific Ave., Long Beach, Cal.

ZELLER, WM. M., JR., Student Officer, 111[illegible] N. Meridian Brazil, Ind.

ZERFOSS, GEO. E., Student Officer, 412 Linden Walk, Lexington, Ky.

ZIMMERMAN, JOHN L., JR., Student Officer, 363 East High St., Springfield, O.

ZOOK, RICHARD M., Student Officer, 141 S. Scoville Ave., Oak Park, Ill.

ZUCKER, ARTHUR A., Student Officer, 60 Broadway, New York City.

ZUGER, J. R., Ensign, Georgetown College, Washington, D. C. N. A. No. 1867.

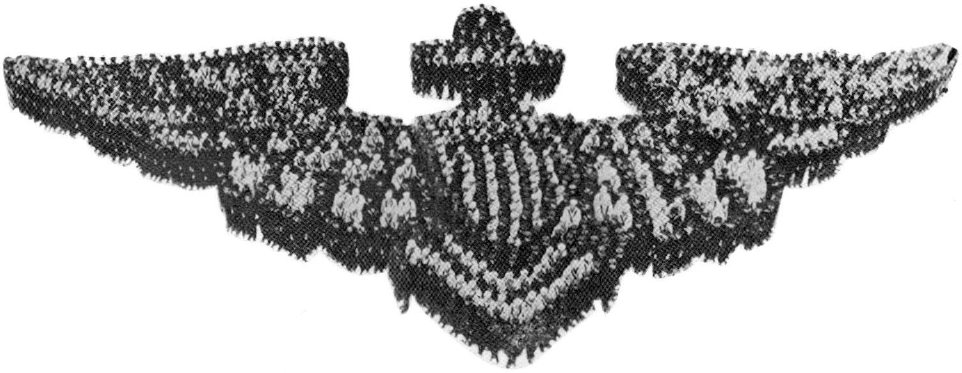

THE END